The Great Depression in America

The Great Depression in America

A CULTURAL ENCYCLOPEDIA
Volume 1: A–M

WILLIAM H. YOUNG
and
NANCY K. YOUNG

GREENWOOD PRESS
Westport, Connecticut • London

Library of Congress Cataloging-in-Publication Data

Young, William H., 1939–
    The Great Depression in America : a cultural encyclopedia / William H.
Young and Nancy K. Young.
        2 v.
    Includes bibliographical references and index.
    ISBN 0-313-33520-6 (set : alk. paper) — ISBN 0-313-33521-4 (v. 1 :
alk. paper) — ISBN 0-313-33522-2 (v. 2 : alk. paper)
    1. Popular culture—United States—History—20th century—
Encyclopedias. 2. United States—Civilization—1918–1945—
Encyclopedias. 3. United States—Intellectual life—20th century—
Encyclopedias. 4. United States—Social life and customs—1918–1945—
Encyclopedias. 5. United States—Biography—Encyclopedias. 6.
Depressions—1929—United States—Encyclopedias. I. Young, Nancy K.,
1940– II. Title.
E169.1.Y595   2007
973.91'003—dc22   2006100693

British Library Cataloguing in Publication Data is available.

Library of Congress Catalog Card Number: 2006100693
ISBN-10: 0-313-33520-6 (set)   ISBN-13: 978-0-313-33520-4 (set)
        0-313-33521-4 (vol. 1)   978-0-313-33521-1 (vol. 1)
        0-313-33522-2 (vol. 2)   978-0-313-33522-8 (vol. 2)

First published in 2007

Greenwood Press, 88 Post Road West, Westport, CT 06881
An imprint of Greenwood Publishing Group, Inc.
www.greenwood.com

Printed in the United States of America

The paper used in this book complies with the
Permanent Paper Standard issued by the National
Information Standards Organization (Z39.48–1984).

10 9 8 7 6 5 4 3 2 1

In memory of Gary Sederholm,
whose spirit inspired us all

Contents

Alphabetical List of Entries

Guide to Related Topics

ART
Advertising
American Gothic
Art Deco
Benton, Thomas Hart
Century of Progress Exposition
　(Chicago World's Fair)
Comic Books
Comic Strips
Design
Disney, Walt
Fashion
Federal Art Project (FAP)
Hopper, Edward
Illustrators
Marsh, Reginald
Photography
Regionalism
Rockwell, Norman
Sculpture
Sheeler, Charles
Social Realism
Streamlining
Wood, Grant
Wyeth, N. C.

ARCHITECTURE
Architecture
Art Deco
Century of Progress Exposition
　(Chicago World's Fair)
Chrysler Building, The
Empire State Building, The
International Style
New York World's Fair
Rockefeller Center
　(Radio City)
Wright, Frank Lloyd

AVIATION
Airships
Aviation
China Clippers
Douglas DC-3
Earhart, Amelia
Lindbergh Kidnapping
Transportation
Travel

COMIC BOOKS & STRIPS
Apple Mary
Big Little Books
Blondie
Comic Books
Comic Strips
Dick Tracy
Flash Gordon
Gumps, The
Hillbillies
Illustrators
Li'l Abner
Little Orphan Annie
Prince Valiant
Serials
Superman
Tarzan
Terry and the Pirates

EXPOSITIONS/FAIRS
Century of Progress Exposition
　(Chicago World's Fair)
Circuses
Fairs & Expositions
New York World's Fair

FADS/GAMES
Contract Bridge

Preface

The 1930s: this fascinating chapter in history will continue to be examined, discussed, and debated for the foreseeable future—and no doubt beyond—just as people have been doing since the decade began. Which leads to this encyclopedia: what it is, how it works, and how to use it.

Throughout the pages that follow, readers will gain a sense of American life during the 1930s, from the onset of the Great Depression to the beginnings of World War II. The focus of this encyclopedia centers on popular culture, those activities, events, institutions, and individuals that constitute the routines of normal, everyday life. Movies, radio programming, popular music, best sellers, entertainers and celebrities—the elements that define popular culture—receive primary attention, as opposed to the more traditional and formal content of elite, or high, culture. Thus swing, a component of popular music, receives more space than does classical music, *Life* magazine more than an academic journal, a diner and fast food more than a gourmet restaurant, *42nd Street* more than "serious" drama, the dancing of Fred Astaire and Ginger Rogers more than avant-garde choreography, and so on. Whenever possible, examples from the vibrant popular culture of the 1930s serve as illustrations of what interested and engaged people during the decade.

For example, under the entry "Crime," the inclusion of popular movies and radio shows, along with pulp magazines and mystery novels, demonstrates how people perceived lawbreaking and criminals at that time. Similarly, the article titled "Gangster Films" reinforces a number of the ideas advanced in "Crime," as do such entries as "Federal Bureau of Investigation," "Lindbergh Kidnapping," and "Mysteries & Hard-Boiled Detectives." In each, a rich sampling from popular culture gives depth to *The Great Depression in America: A Cultural Encyclopedia* and makes it unique in its emphases.

The 200 entries comprising the encyclopedia deal in a variety of ways with the decade and are listed alphabetically, going from "Advertising" and "Airships" through "*Your Hit Parade*" and "Youth." In the case of peoples' names, surnames receive first listing, followed by the given name so that the entry reads "Crosby, Bing," not "Bing Crosby." At the first mention of any individual within an article, every effort has been made to provide birth and death dates.

In the final pages of this encyclopedia, a detailed index will aid readers in locating information about topics or people not found under "Entries." Thus cartoonist Al Capp does not appear as an individual entry, but discussion of him and his influence will be found under "*Li'l Abner*," his famous comic strip. He can be located in the index under his own name. Similarly, the trendsetting 1934 Chrysler Airflow automobile, so stylistically advanced for its time, will not be found under that heading, but instead under "Automobiles" and by name in the index. The index entry for Chrysler will also direct readers to other information about the car.

Each article contains words or phrases in **boldface** that indicate additional related entries. For example, the *Li'l Abner* entry mentions, in the course of its text, Erskine Caldwell, comic strips, *Grand Ole Opry*, hillbillies, the *National Barn Dance*, radio, and religion. Each term is in boldface and can be found under that name in the encyclopedia. At the conclusion of each article, a boldface **See also** suggests other encyclopedia topics, not mentioned in the entry, that may prove helpful in the subject area. In this case, *Li'l Abner* includes cross-references to "Movies," "Newspapers," and "Radio Networks."

Immediately following the "See also" recommendations, a listing called "Selected Readings" gives titles of some useful books, articles, and websites about the entry subject. These minibibliographies provide a starting point for further research but are not exhaustive. An extensive listing of selected resources, found immediately before the index, presents a wealth of additional books, articles, and Web sites covering a myriad of subjects dealing with the Depression era. Many of the citations in this section address relevant topics not discussed directly in any particular entry.

In the text itself, whenever monetary figures appear in their original amounts, their present-day equivalents follow parenthetically. These contemporary numbers represent dollars adjusted for inflation, showing what a product or service purchased in the past would cost today. Because dollars have shifted dramatically over the years, the adjusted values have gone through many changes between the Depression years and the present.

It is the authors' hope that anyone interested in American life and activities during this tumultuous decade will find much that is informative and useful within these pages.

Acknowledgments

Many individuals have contributed, directly and indirectly, to the creation of this encyclopedia. Once again, our sincere thanks to everyone at the Lynchburg College Library. Director Chris Millson-Martula saw that all the library's facilities were available to us, making what could have been an impossible task into something doable. Ariel Myers, the college archivist and the person to see for interlibrary loans, found items that some considered unfindable. Elizabeth Henderson and Linda Carder deftly handled research and Internet questions—and dug out the answers.

Another, larger library also deserves recognition: LOC, the Library of Congress. Jan Grenci and her team—Jeff Bridgers, Maja Keech, and Lewis Wyman—in the Prints and Photographs Division always made us feel welcome and went the extra mile in finding pictures and other illustrative materials in their vast holdings. In the Rare Books Section, curator Clark Evans provided first editions of significant best sellers from the era, including the original dust jackets. In Photographic Services, Sandra Lawson, Shirley Burry, Yusef el-Amin, Jim Higgins, and Erica Kelly guided us through the procedures for obtaining glossies of some of the library's treasures, and they did a fine job shooting them. Sam Perryman, of the Performing Arts Reading Room, likewise gave us guidance about his section's collection.

An evening with Ethan Becker is not to be missed. The son of Marion Rombauer Becker and grandson of Irma Rombauer, creator of *The Joy of Cooking*, he reminisced about growing up among master cooks. Jane Graziani, who works with the national office of the American Automobile Association, gave of her time and knowledge about this important organization during the 1930s. Susan White of King Features Syndicate cheerfully assisted us with obtaining copyright permissions and locating other materials as well.

Nancy Blackwell Marion and others at the Design Group in Lynchburg, Virginia, brought their skills to bear on assembling illustrations. Thanks to their extensive collections of artifacts and memorabilia from the 1930s, Jere Real was able to provide information about Big Little Books, and Bryan Wright found some rare 78-rpm recordings from the era. Tiffany Palmeri helped with information about Coca-Cola advertising, and Al Harris supplied sheet music that captures the period well.

As always, the people at the Greenwood Publishing Group have extended helping hands. Rob Kirkpatrick got things started, and Sarah Colwell, our primary editor, capably took the reins and followed the project through. She proved particularly helpful in working through the maze of illustrations, captions, and permissions.

To all who participated in this project, our hearty thanks. Any errors of commission or sins of omission remain ours and ours alone.

Introduction

Like ripples on a pond, the events of the Great Depression and its aftermath eventually reached all Americans, regardless of wealth, social standing, race, education, or any other variables. Children saw their own parents, especially fathers, out of work and standing in breadlines with scores of other unemployed people, or selling apples on a street corner. Teens looked on as jobs disappeared, idled by forces they barely understood. Adults watched—some with high expectations, others with cynicism, and more than a few with disdain—as the government tried ineffectually to cope with the crisis. Then a flurry of new legislation—a "new deal"—promised relief for all the economic and social woes plaguing the country.

As the 1930s wore on, the Depression did lessen in its severity, but it left in its wake scars and dashed hopes. As the economy improved, people witnessed a new danger, a world tumbling out of control toward another world war. They knew that the United States would eventually be drawn in, an unwilling participant in that growing conflict. Financial security, more promised than real, had briefly seemed within reach, but international politics now threatened everything. The horrors of a new global conflagration replaced many of the uncertainties that had marked the first years of the decade.

For some, the 1930s were the tempering years, for others the anxious years, and still others called them the angry years, the years of protest. By whatever appellation it was known, the decade presented contradictions galore: for a lucky few, those with money and security, the era offered luxuries on a lavish scale. They drove automobiles—Duesenbergs, Cords, Lincolns—unlike any motorized vehicles previously manufactured; they traveled in style, choosing opulent steamships, elegant passenger trains, or even an aerial China Clipper. The world of high fashion rejected the boyish flapper look of the 1920s and embraced a soft, feminine style that caressed the figure, while the average homemaker wore shapeless housedresses and smocks called "Hooverettes."

As individuals warily watched events, the built environment transformed itself. Skyscrapers rose amid a falling economy, and modern designers streamlined everything, from houses to radios to pencil sharpeners. The sinuous curves of polished chrome banisters, the stark whites of modernistic interiors, and the gleaming black Bakelite surfaces of expensive furnishings beckoned those observers, even as banks foreclosed on their dilapidated homes for nonpayment of mortgages. Those sleek statements of modernity suggested a less fractious society, a symbol of hope that somehow in the days to come

Times were hard for many, and people had to make do as best they could during the grim years of the Great Depression. (Courtesy of the Library of Congress)

the economy and its accompanying social issues would be smoothed out and function as they were supposed to.

A wave of European émigrés brought an austere internationalism to architecture, and Frank Lloyd Wright, a survivor of numerous shifts in styles, absorbed and adapted these new trends, creating during the 1930s some of his finest, most memorable structures. For those in the vanguard, ornamentation, a hallmark of earlier eras, became passé, replaced by unadorned curtain walls and ribbon windows. The average citizen, however, preferred an early American, colonial, or period revival house to the modernist dwellings seen in many magazines. Nostalgia for a golden-hued past that never really existed expressed itself in furniture and accessories readily available at department stores and through catalogs; this avoidance of contemporary design involved a subconscious rejection of present problems more than a conscious dislike for the work of artists and craftsmen of the day.

Many of the cultural changes of the 1930s found ready acceptance by the public. Housewives flocked to the new supermarkets that began to replace the older mom-and-pop grocery stores, and travelers certainly preferred the motor hotels—a term quickly shortened to "motels"—to the cramped hotels and ramshackle auto camps that once sufficed for a night on the road. The chain restaurant, another innovative concept, promised better food and ambience than the greasy spoons and diners of the recent past. Getting to these places required an automobile, and even during the Depression, Americans clung to their cars. Throughout the decade, hard-pressed local and state governments found the funds to pave and improve existing roads, as well as construct new ones. By the late 1930s, the first modern, multilane highways began to snake across the landscape, laying the groundwork for the tremendous growth of the suburbs that would characterize the remainder of the twentieth century.

American popular culture, in all its modes and manifestations, offered the well-off, the family on relief, and the young and old a veritable smorgasbord of entertainments and diversions, and the menu kept changing as time marched on. The federal government, traditionally a stranger to cultural trends, even played a role, underwriting the arts through agencies like the Federal Writers' Project, the Federal Music Project, the Federal Theatre Project, and the Federal Art Project. Guidebooks to the states, put together by skilled writers, described the highways and byways, the towns and cities of the nation; plays that boasted low ticket prices and fine actors introduced millions to live theater; and painters created numerous murals in public spaces, giving many their first glimpse of quality art. Unlike any previous era, the 1930s witnessed the rise of a true mass popular culture available to all.

For many, however, time hung heavy in this pretelevision era. Even those with jobs sought diversions to keep their minds off the dark shadows cast by the Depression. Radio, hugely popular throughout the country, allowed listeners to engage in other activities while tuned in to their favorite programs, and that meant an increase in games and hobbies of all kinds. Contract bridge became a fad, as did Monopoly, the classic board game about real estate acquisition. In good weather, and thanks to New Deal programs that greatly increased the number and accessibility of recreational facilities, people flocked to new diamonds to play softball. Extravagant fairs and expositions exhibited their wares throughout the decade, with Chicago's 1933–1934 Century of Progress and New York's 1939–1940 World's Fair setting the standards. Miniature golf enjoyed a brief craze early in the 1930s, and jigsaw puzzles sold in the millions for much of the period. For the really desperate, marathon dancing promised inevitable exhaustion and a cot, some free meals, and maybe a paltry prize for the couple that stayed on their feet the longest.

Thanks to electronic technology, sound movies, recordings, and—in particular—radio, Americans shared images, sounds, and ideas. The newspaper pictures of the airship *Hindenburg* exploding at Lakehurst, New Jersey, competed with breathless radio commentary about the flaming wreckage, and it grew from a tragic event to an icon of modern disasters, a testament to the power of instantaneous communications. The image of the newly inaugurated president Franklin D. Roosevelt, chipper with his cigarette holder up at a jaunty angle, reassured millions that the country would get through the Depression and that FDR would lead the way. In the meantime, Bing Crosby crooned, as did Rudy Vallee and Russ Columbo, and a generation's concept of romantic love would be forever altered. The verbal and visual anarchy of the Marx Brothers, Joe Louis's knockout of Max Schmeling, the blonde bombshell look of Jean Harlow, the comic strip adventures of Dagwood Bumstead and Andy Gump and Little Orphan Annie, the streamlined pizzazz of modern transportation, from the

DC-3 to the Chrysler Airflow—all these and so much more etched themselves into the national psyche, a communal experience that allowed people to make sense of the world around them.

Of all the media, radio ruled. Two giant networks, the National Broadcasting Company (NBC), so big that it split into Red and Blue divisions, and the Columbia Broadcasting System (CBS), a worthy rival, stretched their electronic tentacles into every living room in the country. From late morning to early afternoon, soap operas, such as *Ma Perkins* and *David Harum*, dispensed folksy wisdom and dramatic pathos, giving way later in the day to the serialized exploits of the likes of *Jack Armstrong, the All-American Boy* and *The Tom Mix Ralston Straight Shooters* for kids home from school. The evenings belonged to music with vocalists and bands, comedy with Jack Benny and variety with Fred Allen, and the rat-a-tat-tat of machine guns on *Gang Busters*, a reminder that criminals sometimes lurked in unexpected places, waiting for the unwary. Thwarted romance, serials, domestic comedy, cops and robbers—each and every day the nation tuned in.

Close behind radio in popularity came the movies. Between 60 and 90 million people—almost half the population—went to the movies week in and week out. To satisfy the paying customers' quenchless thirst for thrills and laughter, Hollywood produced hundreds of feature films each year. The fare ranged from the rubber-faced antics of comedian Joe E. Brown to the peerless acting of Greta Garbo and Paul Muni. Gary Cooper, Errol Flynn, and Ronald Coleman displayed quiet heroism in the face of danger, while Cary Grant, Carole Lombard, and Irene Dunne muddled through their share of screwball comedies. Who could forget Shirley Temple dancing with Bill "Bojangles" Robinson or the adolescent innocence of Judy Garland and Mickey Rooney in *Love Finds Andy Hardy*? And on Saturdays, theaters opened their doors early for matinees that gave their youthful audiences two Westerns, with stars such as Gene Autry and Roy Rogers, some shorts and cartoons, plus the latest installment of a wondrous, cliff-hanging serial.

Lots of people had free time, wanted or unwanted, and for some books offered an easy escape. Readers immersed themselves in *Anthony Adverse* and *The Good Earth*, along with a host of other best sellers, page-turners all. *Gone with the Wind*, first as a novel and then as a much-publicized blockbuster movie featuring the sizzling chemistry between Clark Gable and Vivian Leigh, generated an unheard-of amount of excitement. Margaret Mitchell's epic story of life in the Civil War South topped everything and anything the decade produced.

More cerebral, perhaps, were the many mysteries and detective tales that found a receptive public. From the intellectual whodunits of Ellery Queen to the courtroom challenges in Erle Stanley Gardner's Perry Mason series to the shadowy world of hard-boiled private eyes like Sam Spade and Philip Marlowe, stories of crime and detection sold millions of books.

But reading did not stop with novels. Each week the mail carrier delivered a new issue of the *Saturday Evening Post*, *Collier's*, or *Liberty*, tempting readers with a mix of fiction and fact, making the 1930s a heyday for big-circulation magazines. A handy diversion from the everyday world, these weeklies, along with hundreds of more specialized magazines for women, hobbyists, sports fans, children, and just about anyone else, opened doors to knowledge, leisure, and entertainment. If the articles got too dense, *Life* came along at mid-decade to explain the world in pictures, the first magazine given over wholly to photojournalism. And *Newsweek* and *U.S. News and World Report* challenged *Time*'s leadership in the area of condensed news coverage. Despite all these choices, circulations generally stayed strong, another strand of the mass-media fiber that wove together the nation.

Along with magazines, at sunrise and at sunset newsboys delivered the daily newspapers right to the front porch of millions of homes. Most larger cities boasted competing papers, usually morning and evening dailies, and many households subscribed to both. The dailies served as journalistic eyes on the ongoing world, and people felt out of touch without at least one newspaper. Loaded with features, from bridge columns to horoscopes, they also offered comic strips, the part of the paper that most people ranked as their favorite. Everybody read them, from the family humor of *Blondie* to Popeye gulping down a can of spinach. Dick Tracy battled crime with realistic-looking bullets, and Li'l Abner went his merry way in Dogpatch. *Little Orphan Annie* and *Apple Mary* dared to depict the grim Depression, something new for the comics, and through grit and gumption their heroines gave a daily lesson in surmounting all the difficulties life can throw at you.

Providing a sometimes soothing, sometimes raucous, always rhythmic background to this menu of endless choices, American popular music, on record and in jukeboxes, on radio and movie soundtracks, and on bandstands and in theaters, rose to the challenges of the 1930s. Those already well established, such as the Gershwins, Cole Porter, and Jerome Kern, along with a significant number of other songwriters and lyricists, composed so many standards that orchestras and vocalists will never exhaust them. Blues and jazz and even a smattering of folk and country had their adherents, and a new generation of composers sought modernity in the classical idiom. And then, accompanied by a danceable beat that got more pronounced with each passing year, another body of music evolved that produced a legion of ardent fans: swing. Sweet bands and innocuous lyrics dominated at first, but when the powerhouse swing bands rolled into town, they pushed the competition aside. Benny Goodman, Duke Ellington, Artie Shaw, Count Basie, and a hundred others ruled the airwaves, the dance floors, and the recording industry. Swing united the country's musical tastes under a common umbrella, a musical phenomenon that brought people together as never before, further stitching together the tapestry of popular culture.

As these media marvels wove still more connecting threads, a cultural consensus arose, but one that offered, in its synthesis, a simultaneous study in contradictions. In the arts, the Social Realists painted urban loneliness and social injustice, while the Regionalists celebrated the fecundity of the rural heartland and looked to a mythic past. Meanwhile, traditional painters like Edward Hopper and Charles Sheeler, along with illustrator Norman Rockwell and his evocative covers for the *Saturday Evening Post*, belonged to no school and still found a broad, appreciative public.

The decade blurred gangsters with heroes, watched Jesse Owens and Joe Louis with awe, but still staunchly supported strict segregation. Americans built Hoovervilles in the shadows of gleaming skyscrapers. And they either loved or hated Franklin D. Roosevelt and his New Deal's social programs that came into being as a host of "alphabet agencies," such as the CCC, the NRA, the WPA, the FHA, and so many others. The decade brought the presence of the federal government, wanted or not, into everyone's lives.

Despite these paradoxes, the country displayed that optimism peculiar to its citizens. Faced with a wrenching depression, cultural clashes, and a string of other unhappy events, people continued to laugh. Knock-knock jokes, goldfish eating, flagpole sitting,

George Burns and Gracie Allen, the dialect humor of *Amos 'n' Andy*, and the heart-warming comedies of Frank Capra kept a smile on their lips. Plus just about everyone went gaga over five little girls in Canada.

In all, "the best of times, the worst of times"; certainly, in retrospect, the most interesting of times. The subject of almost constant study since that Tuesday in October 1929 when the stock market crashed, signaling the end of one era and the onset of something new and unknown, the 1930s really began before the 1920s had officially expired. Although the Great Depression did not make its weight felt until 1930–1931, the crash makes for convenient, easily remembered dating. A genuine crisis, the impact of the Depression did not lessen until after 1933 and the beginnings of the New Deal, a time when many thought "happy days are here again." But then a 1937–1938 recession and the threat of a new world war came along, and the nation turned inward, isolating itself from the world, a stance it could not maintain. National politics nonetheless caused the decade to run a bit overtime. Most people would say the real outbreak of World War II occurred when the Wehrmacht overran Poland in September 1939, and some would argue even earlier than that, what with events that unfolded in Asia during the mid-1930s. The U.S. entry into this new world war, however, would not occur until December 7, 1941, amid the explosions and destruction at Pearl Harbor. As the last of the Japanese pilots flew back to their carriers, the 1930s once and for all drew to a somber, bloody close.

A

ADVERTISING. During the so-called Roaring Twenties, a nineteenth-century term came into renewed vogue: ballyhoo. It means blatant exaggeration, a way to win attention in any way possible. A fitting term, because advertising in the 1920s tended to pull out all the stops as it clamorously demanded the consumer's notice. A reflection of the era, a time when people saw prosperity as unending and advertising revenues had achieved a record-breaking 1929 total of $3.4 billion, ballyhoo urged more and more consumption. The good times, it seemed, would never end. But of course, they did end with the stock market crash and the onset of the Great Depression. Advertisers faced a new challenge: how to promote products and consumption in straitened times.

With the 1930s, advertisers designed their promotions to show how much people needed goods and services; the older themes of social status, benefits, and pleasure did not entirely disappear, but they received reduced emphasis. Economic pressures meant cutting the bloated ad budgets of preceding years, and most advertising agencies felt the pinch. After a decade of almost uninterrupted growth, managers had to eliminate nonessential jobs, slash salaries, and produce ad copy as cheaply as possible. The public witnessed this change by being exposed to a steadily shrinking number of commercial appeals, at least in print. An exception, however, occurred in the thriving medium of **radio**. As print advertising declined, on-air promotions increased, although even radio stations saw a drop in revenues in 1932, one of the darkest years of the Great Depression.

Unemployment soared in all sectors of American life in the first years of the decade, and with less money to spend, people looked on much advertising with a certain distrust. Claims that might have gone unchallenged in the exuberant 1920s the public now began to question. A series of books with titles like *Your Money's Worth* (1927), *100,000,000 Guinea Pigs* (1933), *Skin Deep* (1934), *Eat Drink and Be Wary* (1935), *The Popular Practice of Fraud* (1935), and *Partners in Plunder* (1935) fueled these fears and sold well. In 1931, a new magazine, *Ballyhoo*, appeared on newsstands. Dedicated to deriding most advertising, *Ballyhoo* did well its first two years. The editors refused all paid ads and instead ran trenchant parodies of the real thing. With the slow economic recovery, the novelty of *Ballyhoo* wore off, and the magazine died a lingering death, ceasing publication in 1939.

Organizations like Consumer's Union and Consumer's Research enjoyed rapid growth and prosperity throughout the decade, their success reflecting public discontent with inflated claims and shoddy products. By the end of the decade, they boasted memberships of 80,000 and 60,000, respectively. The federal government at this time launched several investigations into advertising practices, and from these came the Pure Food, Drug, and Cosmetic Act, passed in 1934. The Federal Trade Commission and the Security and Exchange Commission, along with the U.S. Post Office and the Internal Revenue Service, increased their supervisory and regulatory controls over advertising, another reflection of the general distrust the medium suffered.

Advertisers took heed of the changing times and toned down much of the hoopla that no one had questioned just a few years earlier. And, in order not to upset the public any further, little advertising produced during the Depression reflects the economic problems of the day, at least not directly. Despair and social upheaval receive almost no notice, and most copy glosses over economic realities. Occasionally, ads or radio commercials hint at the need for good personal appearance in order to gain or hold a job, or they might urge sympathy for those less fortunate, but little else. Instead, most Depression-era advertising shows the consumer, comfortable and assured, in the presence of the product being touted.

In a period of uncertainty, these ads nonetheless perform a service by giving information about prices, quality, brands, reputation, and so forth. At the same time, they reassure the public by, paradoxically, saying on the one hand that "prosperity lies right around the corner" and on the other that hard work and sacrifice may be needed to weather any economic storms. To accommodate this two-edged approach, ads often focus less on the product and more on the consumer. The thrust of a promotion might be to buoy sagging spirits and bolster confidence. Throughout the 1930s, this kind of message grew in importance as the certainties of earlier times came into question.

Despite a refusal to acknowledge the crisis directly, advertising nonetheless changed with the decade. The gauzy, optimistic future of years past has been replaced with a more hard-edged depiction of the present, a present, however, minus any Depression. They reflect aspirations, not realities. To make their points, many agencies and clients favored loud, brash messages, but without the ballyhoo of the 1920s. They replaced the graceful **Art Deco** typefaces of the 1920s with a plain block style taken from **newspapers**, losing no opportunity to get the message directly to the consumer. Bold type, harsh black-and-white photographs, and a terse prose style that abandons nuance and subtlety for the hard sell characterize many print ads during the 1930s. Any nostalgia for the more elegant styles of the 1920s gets put aside. More and more ads also include contests and giveaways; this emphasis on promotions came from the success they had on radio employing similar techniques. In all, advertising displays a nervous, tense quality, perhaps echoing the tenor of the times more than readers knew. As the decade progressed, agencies continued to cut costs in every way possible, usually making lush illustrations and imaginative graphics their first victims.

The world portrayed by magazine ads, large and small, almost always exists as a contemporary urban or suburban one. Although over a quarter of the nation's population still resided on farms or in what were considered rural areas in the 1930s, the milieu of advertising had long since been urbanized. Skyscrapers represent the office environment; large factories the manufacturing one; and apartments, houses on a city street, or cozy dwellings in the suburbs of a large metropolis, the residential one.

With this urban imagery, American advertising brought forth a sense of modernity. Many ads integrated innovative ideas in technology, **design**, **architecture**, and the like into the world of style; they made the "new" seem chic—for example, color-coordinated ensembles in such mundane products as plumbing fixtures, **automobiles**, china, and silverware. Elements of contemporary art—expressionism, cubism, abstraction, impressionism—surface with some regularity on the pages of mass-circulation **magazines**. Some attempt to keep words to a minimum, evoking emotional responses by color choices and breaking down shapes to their basic elements. For example, technology might be suggested by deliberately distorted arrangements of motifs, summoning up the new and the novel visually. Although use of modern art remained scattered, when used it functions as a reaction to the illustrative styles of preceding decades.

For many agencies, the Depression seldom offered the luxury of experimenting with new styles. They saw the realistic, folksy paintings of, say, a **Norman Rockwell** as infinitely preferable to any attempts at modernism in advertising, and many firms attempted to retain their **illustrators**. Too often, however, they found such work in less demand, and oils and watercolors became secondary to the print message. Such economic realities brought on an aesthetic and philosophical split in advertising art: a portion of 1930s advertising cannot be distinguished from that of preceding decades, but a significantly larger segment employs a modernistic, abstracted kind of imagery. This dichotomy between old and new continued on into the war years.

To instill their message, advertisers sometimes invoke collective guilt. If consumers do not possess or employ a specific product, they may pay a high price for their neglect. Lapsed insurance policies will force children to drop out of school and go to work; the absence of a particular appliance could lead to social ostracism; failure to practice good hygiene will create a bad first impression. Images of sobbing women and regretful men provide evidence of what will happen when they fail to buy certain products or perform particular acts. This kind of finger-pointing, however, appears in a minority of ads; the majority promises a better life and better days ahead, and thereby reinforces goals and objectives already held by the public.

Regardless of approach, advertisers continued to see their revenues decline, plunging to a low of $1.3 billion in 1933, or about a third of what they had been three years earlier. As income fell off, some agencies changed course, bowing to the belief that simplicity serves as the key to communicating a message. Pioneer market researchers like George Gallup (1901–1984) and A. C. Nielsen (1897–1981) discovered that the majority of Depression audiences desired clear, simple ads. The wordy parables and long testimonials, so beloved of copywriters, begin to disappear, replaced by a format consisting of short, straightforward sentences or headline-like fragments. As the economy improved after 1933, more and more images of gracious living reappear, but the accompanying copy has lost most of its wordiness.

In addition, researchers found that the use of characters and cartoon drawings from **comic strips** appealed to a broad public. People, especially youthful readers inured to the comics, liked speech balloons, a device taken from the popular daily series for impact. Many ads employ cartoon characters (some recognizable, others created exclusively for advertising purposes) that extol such disparate products as breakfast cereals, **desserts**, and beverages; this device proved an effective means of promotion. In fact, the extended Sunday comics in a typical newspaper contained a mix of straight strips and virtually identical advertising messages, and frequently the readers had to determine which was which. By 1937, over 300 newspapers carried comic advertising of one form or another.

Children play atop a soft drink stand advertising various brands. (Courtesy of the Library of Congress)

The following mail-order campaign serves as a good example of successful comic-strip advertising: generations of American boys have dreaded being "97-lb. weaklings," thanks to the classic cartoon ads of one Charles Atlas, holder of the title "The World's Most Perfectly Developed Man." This honor had been bequeathed on Angelo Siciliano (1892–1972) in 1922, a one-time "weakling" who soon thereafter dubbed himself "Charles Atlas."

Starting in the late 1920s, and blossoming during the Depression years, Atlas and his skilled promoters created a business that quietly boomed for the next half century and became in itself an icon of American popular culture. In an unending series of advertisements, usually found in the back pages of **comic books** and cheap **pulp magazines** aimed at male readers, Atlas showed through rather crude cartoons how brawny bullies victimize weak men. Help came in the form of a coupon that would bring a booklet demonstrating how *dynamic tension* (Atlas's secret method of developing muscles and power; today it would be called isometrics) changes one's physique and outlook on life. This was classic come-on, as old as advertising itself, but the comic strip format in time lured over 6 million men into trying the booklet *Dynamic Tension* at $30 (about $244 in contemporary dollars) for 12 lessons on breathing, exercises, diet, and the like.

Even with difficult choices and grim prospects, a number of other advertising formats enjoyed success during the Depression. Outdoor advertising proved to be a growing industry at this time; the 1920s, often called "the golden age of billboards," brought outdoor ads to a new level, and the 1930s continued that exuberance. About 320 agencies deployed outdoor promotions on a nationwide basis in 1932; seven years later over 500 companies had entered the field. Outdoor advertising traditionally aims at a broad middle and lower middle-class audience. Direct and realistic, it conveys its entire message quickly. Whereas magazines turned increasingly to **photography** to display products, billboards clung to the traditional painted and airbrushed illustration.

The Burma-Vita Company, a small, Minnesota-based firm struggling to market a men's brushless shaving cream, launched one of the most unusual ad campaigns in the long history of American outdoor advertising in 1925. The company had tried giving out sample jars, but that approach did little to increase sales. Then, in one of those serendipitous moments, someone hit upon the idea of using scrap pieces of wood to erect small roadside signs that presented a serial message. As cars raced by, the drivers could read, in order, rhyming slogans for Burma-Shave, the brushless cream. Shortly thereafter Burma-Vita ordered professionally done signs, but the messages continued to be simple, lighthearted poems, one sign for each line. By the 1930s, the campaign had moved into high gear and gone national; Burma-Vita even staged yearly contests urging consumers to send in their own verses and the little red Burma-Shave signs could be found alongside virtually every highway in the country.

So it went throughout the decade. Some 200 new verses had been written and posted by 1940, and the campaign continued unabated until 1963. Over 7,000 separate Burma-Shave sets dotted the roadscape by 1938, which translates to more than 40,000 individual signs. The company watched its fortunes grow sharply, and the demise of the campaign signified the loss of a part of Americana known to everyone who ever traveled by car in those bygone days.

Not all advertising involved visual appeals. People might quote, verbatim, ad copy they saw in a magazine, but more likely they could repeat the jingles and slogans they heard on radio, and singing commercials emerged as one of the most popular formats for broadcast advertising. Words and **music** on radio had as much impact as print and pictures in other media. Although radio advertising had its inception in 1922, it did not hit its stride until the 1930s, when agencies began to realize the power of the aural commercial. Radio advertising helped bring about greater homogeneity in national patterns of taste and consumption. Regional barriers fell away as **radio networks** linked the entire nation.

The agency-run "radio department" emerged as one of the most important divisions at broadcast studios. Although the networks had the right to approve programming, big sponsors had grown so influential that such approval symbolized more a formality than a privilege. In addition, various syndicates began to prepackage all manner of shows for both network and independent station consumption. These productions proved attractive to smaller stations that could not afford to put together programming of their own that approached the syndicates' caliber of work.

By advertising nationwide on network radio, manufacturers established unparalleled brand loyalty. For example, by sponsoring *The Chase and Sanborn Hour* over many years (1929–1948), a once little-known coffee rose to become a national leader in sales. Miracle Whip dressing, introduced in 1933, enjoyed significant promotion on the *Kraft Music Hall* (1934–1949). Hosted by the popular **Bing Crosby** (1903–1977) for most of its years on the air, within a decade Miracle Whip had won half the market for sandwich spreads.

Pepsodent, a toothpaste, likewise found a vast audience with its sponsorship of the enormously popular **Amos 'n' Andy** from 1929 until 1939; just before dropping *Amos 'n' Andy*, the company began to underwrite *The Pepsodent Show Starring Bob Hope*, a relationship that would last until the days of **television**. Pepsodent soon became a major player in the competitive field of dental hygiene. Jell-O, Lucky Strikes, Ovaltine, Johnson Wax, Pepsi-Cola, Fitch Shampoo, and a host of other products likewise came to be identified and purchased because of their association with network broadcasting.

Because most radio commercials ran from 30 seconds to a minute, little information could be conveyed about the product, but repetition, music, and sound effects removed any doubt about the brand name. Radio also fostered the illusion of intimacy; the announcer spoke directly to the listener. Print ads may address the consumer, but establishing any relationship, any closeness, with the reader can be problematic when the ad copy remains removed and somewhat distant, no matter how dramatic the visual presentation. With radio the listener gets "to know" the announcer, a fact that broadcasters used to their advantage. Names like Milton Cross (1897–1975; *The Metropolitan Opera* and Texaco), Ed Herlihy (1909–1998; *Kraft Music Hall* and Kraft foods), Westbrook Van Voorhis (1904–1968; **The March of Time** and *Time* magazine), Harry Von Zell (1906–1981; *The Eddie Cantor Show* and Pabst Blue Ribbon beer), Harlow Wilcox (1900–1960; *Fibber McGee and Molly* and Johnson's Wax), and Don Wilson (1900–1982; *The Jack Benny Program* and Lucky Strike cigarettes) emerged as celebrities in their own right, often becoming significant parts of the shows as well as spokesmen for the sponsors' products.

Although radio challenged other media for a share of the advertising dollar, magazines and newspapers continued to carry the bulk of most American commercial messages. The economic ups and downs of the Depression years can be tracked by the relative numbers and types of ads appearing in any particular medium. For example, between 1930 and 1933, advertising pages decline steadily in most major periodicals. That period, of course, corresponds to the depths of the economic crash, and it stands to reason that real and potential advertisers would be watching their budgets closely. With sharply diminished sales, profits would be down, and thus less could be expended on advertising. This drop shows up in the magazines themselves: they contain fewer pages than they did in the late 1920s. And yet the number of features (articles, stories, columns, etc.) remains about the same, which means the loss reflects missing advertisements.

A gradual upturn, documented by increased manufacturing and sales, occurred between 1934 and 1937 and can be seen in most magazines by a growing number of pages, most of which carry advertising. In 1938–1939, a recession hit the nation, and once again fewer pages and advertisements chronicle the new economic woes. Expensive full-page spreads decline, and cheaper partial-page ads increase.

Advertising of the era tends to depict a woman as the typical consumer—a sophisticated, modern woman who makes most of the purchasing choices for her family. A man's home may be his castle, but a woman manages it; men hold down jobs, but women do the shopping and keep themselves informed about products and services—at least in the world pictured by advertisers. Given this milieu, most, but not all, commercial messages direct themselves at women, even if that approach results in rampant stereotyping of both sexes.

For example, liquor ads made a statement about the repeal of **Prohibition** and the propriety of home consumption of **alcoholic beverages**. Various brands of beers and whiskies grace many magazine pages (various restrictions prevented liquor advertising over the air) after 1933 and Repeal. In deference to the mores of the era, however, distilleries targeted men with their messages; the times may have been changing, but liquor companies appear unwilling to cross any gender lines, real or imagined.

Gender aside, the American breakfast serves as an example of advertising's cumulative impact on national taste. Commercially packaged dry cereals appeared in the late nineteenth century, but with limited choices: shredded wheat and corn flakes about summed up what could be found on grocers' shelves. Most people still thought that bacon and eggs, plus other meats and potatoes, constituted the mainstays of the morning meal. Through ceaseless advertising, the public became aware of new cold cereals, such as Wheaties, Grape-Nuts, Pep, and Cheerios. Ovaltine, Postum, and Bovril strove to be accepted as coffee substitutes, and marketers pushed vitamin supplements by the end of the decade. These changes can be tracked on the advertising pages of national magazines.

Beyond breakfasts, in order to pitch their messages at a certain emotional level, a number of American food products, such as Cream of Wheat (hot cereal), Aunt Jemima (pancake mix), and Uncle Ben (rice products), have long used black Americans as part of their labeling. Obvious racial stereotyping, right down to the demeaning use of "Uncle" and "Aunt," draws uncomfortable connections between race and servitude. For example, Rastus, the grinning porter on the Cream of Wheat label, clearly creates an image of master and servant. Throughout the 1930s, print ads showed him serving white children steaming bowls of their favorite hot cereal. Certainly, images like these support much of the racial stereotyping so rampant in the U.S. during the first half of the century.

When these two-dimensional figures spoke in their ads, they employed a minstrel show form of English. The agency writers who created such bits of hackneyed dialect thereby perpetuated destructive images of black Americans. In large-circulation, middle-class magazines, such egregious stereotyping unfortunately proved commonplace during the 1930s. It took but a small step from these degrading advertisements to the embarrassing antics of Eddie Anderson (1905–1977) as Rochester on *The Jack Benny Program* (1932–1958) or the steady stream of dialect jokes on the tremendously popular *Amos 'n' Andy* (1928–1960). This kind of media cross-reinforcement of deeply set cultural racism continued well beyond the 1930s.

Another pernicious side of popular American advertising during the Depression years involved the heavy promotion of smoking. Most magazines, newspapers, and radio stations ran tobacco ads. For men and women alike, at least in the ads, cigarettes signified urbanity, sophistication. As a rule, advertisers picture attractive people smoking, and often celebrities endorse one brand or another. From a gender standpoint, little of an earlier bias against women smoking remained in advertising of the 1930s, although a national survey, done in 1937, found that 95 percent of respondents thought men could smoke openly on the street, whereas only 28 percent thought women should have the same privilege. Those interviewed could find some support for their attitudes: throughout the 1930s, most religious magazines continued to rail against women smoking at all. Tobacco use, thanks in large part to its acceptance in advertising, nevertheless continued its climb among both men and women throughout the decade. Ad agencies viewed smoking as a generational custom, one aimed at the fashionable young, and they stoked their ceaseless campaigns with messages that pushed for increased tobacco consumption.

Lucky Strikes urged smokers to avoid overeating. "When tempted, reach for a Lucky instead!" In women's magazines, their slogan said, "Reach for a Lucky instead of a sweet!" This ploy apparently worked; Lucky Strikes increased their market share throughout the decade. Chesterfields, competitors of Lucky Strikes, mounted a memorable—and successful—campaign of their own that ran illustrations of women happily staring at men smoking and saying, "Blow Some My Way." This imaginative piece of prose first appeared in 1926 and enjoyed a revival in 1931. With a growing proportion of younger women taking up smoking in the 1930s, these advertisements had obviously struck a chord.

Of all the tobacco campaigns, one of the most successful series began in 1933 with the introduction of the Philip Morris brand of cigarettes. The company, looking for a distinctive ad strategy, decided on one that could work both in print and on radio. Simplicity itself, the ad consisted of a bellhop crying out, "Call-l-l for Philip Mor-r-riss-s-s-s!" On radio, the voice belonged to Johnny Roventini (1910–1988), a page at the New Yorker Hotel. In print, the image showed Roventini, spiffy in his black pageboy hat, red jacket, and black pants, calling out to readers. Either way, radio or print, the Philip Morris ad worked well. Almost overnight, Philip Morris gained a sizable market share and America had a new advertising icon.

Advertising does not mirror society. It presents objects and people in situations that may bring recognition on the part of the audience, but it distorts any reflection of the time, and deliberately so. An advertisement presents, in whatever medium, a product or service, and seldom makes any kind of comment about the passing social scene. It may reflect aspirations or visions of "the good life," but it hardly portrays the times with any accuracy. Through the repeated use of familiar motifs and stereotypes, American advertising in the 1930s rose to the difficult challenges of the Depression. It dispensed with the old ballyhoo and told consumers they would survive the crisis and could go on consuming, that hard work and the genius of American capitalism would lead to better times, and that advertising would serve as a guide during the journey.

See also Coffee & Tea; Grocery Stores & Supermarkets; Race Relations & Stereotyping; Serials; Soft Drinks; Toys; Youth

SELECTED READING

Fox, Stephen. *The Mirror Makers: A History of American Advertising and Its Creators*. New York: William Morrow, 1984.

Goodrum, Charles, and Helen Dalrymple. *Advertising in America: The First 200 Years*. New York: Harry N. Abrams, 1990.

Lears, Jackson. *Fables of Abundance: A Cultural History of Advertising in America*. New York: Basic Books, 1994.

Marchand, Roland. *Advertising the American Dream: Making Way for Modernity, 1920–1940*. Los Angeles: University of California Press, 1985.

AIRSHIPS. Nothing captured the American imagination quite as much as the magnificent airships that traversed the skies during the 1920s and early 1930s. Also called dirigibles, zeppelins, and lighter-than-air craft, these sleek, hydrogen-filled behemoths of the air owe much of their existence to Count Ferdinand von Zeppelin (1838–1917) and Dr. Hugo Eckener (1868–1954), two German engineers and visionaries. They pioneered the development of lighter-than-air **travel** and, in the process, made airships a brief but significant element in **aviation** history.

During the 1920s, Germany worked diligently to perfect these unwieldy craft and led the world in overall airship utilization. The *Graf Zeppelin*, a mammoth 775-foot dirigible and pride of the German fleet, circumnavigated the globe in 1929 with Dr. Eckener at the controls. The itinerary included stops at Lakehurst, New Jersey, and Los Angeles, California. As a result of these exploits, the U.S. Post Office in 1930 issued a set of three commemorative airmail stamps, each depicting the *Graf Zeppelin* in flight. Extremely rare and valuable, the stamps came in denominations of 65 cents, $1.30, and $2.60 ($7.88, $15.76, and $31.53 in contemporary dollars). Three years later, to celebrate Chicago's **Century of**

Progress Exposition, the post office printed yet another stamp, this one showing the *Graf Zeppelin* above the ocean, a dirigible hangar on the right, the skyscrapers of Chicago on the left. Available in a 50-cent denomination ($7.79 in contemporary dollars), it became a prize eagerly sought by philatelists.

The U.S. Navy envisioned dirigibles as an effective extension of the fleet and lobbied strongly to get such aircraft included in their budget. In the midst of the Depression, the admirals pushed Congress to approve the construction of the *Akron* (1931) and the *Macon* (1933). The *Akron* generated good publicity for the navy, flying around the country and engaging in maneuvers. It even carried four small biplanes on its huge frame, releasing them while airborne and then "recapturing" them while still aloft. The *Akron*, however, went down in a 1933 storm with the loss of 73 lives, the worst air disaster up until that time. The *Macon* plunged into the ocean in 1935. With these two failures, the U.S. government effectively retreated from any further airship development until World War II.

Two airships fly near the Washington Monument. (Courtesy of the Library of Congress)

Seemingly unfazed by American military problems, the Germans pushed ahead. The *Graf Zeppelin* proved a popular airship, one known to millions. To complement "the Graf," in 1936 Germany constructed a sister ship, the *Hindenburg*, a huge 804-foot-long craft that carried almost 100 passengers and crew. Promoted as the most luxurious dirigible in the skies, Germany entertained hopes that airship travel would become commonplace, linking the United States, South America, and Europe. The *Hindenburg* flew without incident from Germany to Lakehurst and back in May 1936, accomplishing the journey in the record time of just under 65 hours. This feat focused public attention on airships, and it appeared the era of regular, convenient dirigible travel had arrived. Nine more transatlantic flights ensued, usually with a number of celebrities on board, and virtually everyone raved about the smooth, quiet ride.

The future for airship travel looked so rosy that the original plans for New York City's **Empire State Building** (1931) boasted a towering mooring mast for dirigibles. No lighter-than-air craft ever attached there (it would later be adapted as the city's primary **television** antenna), but at the time its placement atop the world's tallest skyscraper seemed an eminently sensible way to attract a futuristic generation of airships. No one foresaw a series of disasters that would dampen enthusiasm for zeppelin travel.

On a return trip to Lakehurst in May 1937, a crowd turned out for the *Hindenburg*'s arrival, as was the custom. Herb Morrison (1905–1989), a reporter for Chicago's WLS, an NBC **radio** news affiliate, stood among the curious as the *Hindenburg* approached the mooring mast. But something went terribly wrong and the great airship burst into flames. Morrison, microphone in hand and wits about him, managed to record the disaster live. As he watched and reported, the anguish and emotions of the unfolding disaster gripped the newscaster. "Oh, the humanity!" he cried out, one of those memorable moments in broadcast history, while 38 people died in the flaming wreckage before him. The debacle closed a fascinating chapter in aviation history; no one wanted anything more to do with military or commercial airships.

Despite these setbacks, the privately owned Goodyear Tire and Rubber Company, long active in dirigible development, continued work with nonrigid airships, or blimps. Goodyear employed nonflammable helium instead of the more explosive hydrogen, and by 1941 their blimps had safely transported several hundred thousand passengers and carried countless **advertising** messages on their exteriors.

Hollywood, always a reflector of trends and styles, brought out several **movies** that featured airships in their stories. Howard Hughes (1905–1976), himself an aviation pioneer, directed *Hell's Angels* in 1930. A special effects–filled picture, it features exciting World War I dogfights; one in particular involves a German zeppelin.

The Lottery Bride (1930) uses a dirigible in a few scenes supposedly taking place in the Arctic, but the camera focuses on Jeanette MacDonald (1903–1965), not the airship, in this tedious romance. MacDonald would later rise to acclaim in a series of filmed **operettas**, and *The Lottery Bride* merely stands as an early role of no particular distinction.

Shortly after the two films above came *Madame Satan* (1930), a bedroom farce of sorts directed by the colorful Cecil B. DeMille (1881–1959). A tale about upper-class high jinks, this curious feature uses a dirigible as the setting for a number of its scenes. DeMille, a master of lavish productions, staged some of this melodrama in what has to be the most surreal, **Art Deco**–drenched passenger compartment ever envisioned for a zeppelin. The special effects staff at Metro-Goldwyn-Mayer had to figure out how to simulate a realistic in-flight disaster, one that would involve lightning and the packed compartment suspended in the air, a scene that culminates with the passengers parachuting back to earth. In typical DeMille fashion, *Madame Satan* serves as a stylish representation of the latest **fads** and **fashions**, and it provides the thrill and spectacle of an aerial calamity. Although by modern standards this movie may be judged only moderately successful in either area, *Madame Satan* can nevertheless be considered a bizarre film, one that clearly demonstrates how Hollywood always remains on the lookout for new gimmicks—in this case, airship travel—couched in contemporary terms to lure in the customers.

The fascination with lighter-than-air craft continued in 1931 with the movie debut of *Dirigible*, another aerial epic, directed by none other than Frank Capra (1897–1965), a man who would become one of the most celebrated film directors of the decade. This early effort concerns polar exploration, and it employs a dirigible to carry people to their destinations. Despite its provocative title, *Dirigible*, like most Capra pictures, addresses human conflicts, not the capabilities of an airship.

In 1934, animal trainer Clyde Beatty (1903–1965) had achieved considerable popularity, and he made several films during the decade that capitalized on that fame. One, *The Lost Jungle* (1934; both as a serial and as a feature), has Beatty playing himself in a bit of hokum that involves, among other things, a dirigible crash. The movie suggests that, by 1934, airships had become a normal way to travel, especially to remote places.

See also Circuses; Serials; Stamp Collecting; Transportation

SELECTED READING

Botting, Douglas. *Dr. Eckener's Dream Machine: The Giant Zeppelin and the Dawn of Air Travel.* New York: Henry Holt [Owl Books], 2001.

Ege, Lennart. *Balloons and Airships.* New York: Macmillan, 1974.

Toland, John. *The Great Dirigibles: Their Triumphs and Disasters.* New York: Dover Publications, 1972.

ALCOHOLIC BEVERAGES. Prohibition, which lasted from 1920 until 1933, made Americans acutely aware of alcohol and drinking. In 1920, the nation had adopted the Eighteenth Amendment to the Constitution, a measure that forbade the manufacture, distribution, and sale of alcoholic beverages. It followed on the heels of the Volstead Act of 1919, which defined intoxicating, or alcoholic, drinks as beer, wine, and liquor ("spirits"), if any contained more than half of a percent (0.5 percent) alcohol by volume. Despite this definition, cocktails—drinks made from one or more alcoholic beverages, along with a mixer, such as soda or tonic water—proved especially popular during the Prohibition years, a period that drew to a close with the repeal of the Eighteenth Amendment in 1933.

Favorite cocktails included such concoctions as Long Island iced tea, a potent drink born during Prohibition that contained several alcoholic beverages, along with a "splash" of Pepsi-Cola or Coca-Cola as the mixer. Despite its name, it contained no iced tea. Many more cocktails achieved popularity during this period, including the old fashioned, the Manhattan, the zombie, the Bacardi, and the martini. President **Franklin D. Roosevelt** (1882–1945) in fact saluted the end of Prohibition by sipping a martini, or so the legend goes. Carrying on that tradition, the mint julep, a drink with origins that predate Prohibition, became the signature offering for the Kentucky Derby in 1938.

Prohibition describes a time when a well-meaning law put **restaurants**, bars, and saloons out of business, ruined an emerging wine industry, and increased the production of **soft drinks**. It probably curtailed the development of haute cuisine because of the lack of fine wines to accompany gourmet dining, spurred the growth of tearooms and cafeterias, and removed an array of alcohol-based products from grocery store shelves. Finally, it created deficits from lost tax revenues, and caused illness and death from the reckless consumption of legal medications with a high alcohol content and from drinking contaminated alcoholic beverages illegally produced, often referred to as "moonshine."

The government deemed the production and sale of moonshine, basically a fermented corn beverage, as illegal both during Prohibition and after Repeal. Much of the government's concern revolved around lost tax revenues, not health. Moonshine rose to prominence as a way to satisfy public demand for banned alcoholic beverages, and its manufacture flourished particularly in rural areas, where access to corn was more convenient and government surveillance less likely.

In the decade prior to the imposition of Prohibition, the per capita consumption of alcohol (beer, wine, and liquor) ranged from a high of 2.60 gallons from during 1906 to 1910 to a low of 1.96 gallons from 1916 to 1919. Prohibition probably reduced the consumption of alcoholic beverages—since the sale of alcohol was technically illegal, no reliable figures exist—but statistics for 1934, the period immediately following Repeal, show per capita consumption standing at 0.97 gallons, rising to 1.20 gallons in 1935. Households could make 200 gallons of nonintoxicating cider or fruit juice per year. But "nonintoxicating" led to loose interpretations of the term, and many citizens became home winemakers; some even took up bootlegging by selling homemade alcoholic beverages illegally. In 1931 the Bayer Company started marketing Alka-Seltzer as a remedy for hangovers, a sure sign some people had consumed too much alcohol.

Urban speakeasies, or illegal drinking establishments, multiplied at this time. The term, dating from the nineteenth century, suggests the use of passwords to gain entry and talking quietly to avoid arousing attention; it often was shortened to "speak" during Prohibition. Many individuals enjoyed frequenting such clubs, places that existed beyond the law and allowed for a display of conspicuous consumption and rebellion; going to a speak became a fashionable thing to do. As the number of speakeasies grew, so did the illegal business of smugglers, bootleggers, and gangsters, the suppliers of these businesses. Moonshine, produced by uncounted stills around the country and readily available, also took on a certain cachet, and its providers charged outrageous prices. Products like "bathtub gin" became an illegal luxury, and many thought it culturally sophisticated to ignore any dry laws. With the end of Prohibition in 1933, many speakeasies continued to operate, but legally, calling themselves bars or cocktail lounges.

The cocktail party, a stylish new means of home entertainment, became emblematic of the 1920s and continued on into the 1930s. At these gatherings, sweet cocktails, or "flips," another name for such drinks, emerged as a preferred beverage during Prohibition days, perhaps because the sweetness disguised the taste of bad, or illegal, alcohol. After repeal, cocktail parties required neither home brew nor the purchase of illegal alcohol, but flips maintained their popularity. To accompany the drinks, the hosts usually would offer an array of "finger **food**," and these various appetizers took their place in recipe pamphlets, cookbooks, and on party serving trays.

As the cocktail party gained in popularity, it became fashionable for women to drink not only at home, but in public. In the country's past, drinking had been a male prerogative. But customs changed with the onset of the twentieth century, especially after World War I. Short stories and novels depicted women consuming alcoholic drinks, and **movies** reinforced the concept visually. Many successful films made drinking, especially by women, a normal part of everyday experience, creating images of expected behavior for those in the audience. To cite just two examples, the enormously popular Greta Garbo (1905–1990), in 1930's *Anna Christie*, uttered her first words in a sound film, whispering, "visky with ginger ale." Jean Harlow (1911–1937), another big star of the day, sipped a cocktail in *Platinum Blonde* (1931) while clad in one of her trademark slinky gowns.

Clearly, fashionable people downplayed any secrecy about the consumption of alcohol. **Fred Astaire** (1899–1987) **and Ginger Rogers** (1911–1995), the consummately elegant dancers who starred in many a 1930s movie, often performed their numbers in stylish and sophisticated nightclubs that encouraged drinking. Tuxedoed waiters brought cocktails in crystal glasses on silver trays; musicians played while people dined and sipped fine wines; and the imagery all combined to suggest that alcohol enhanced any social situation.

Prohibition also affected the sale and consumption of beer, another favorite alcoholic beverage. Around 1880, over two thousand breweries operated in the United States, but fierce competition caused that number to decline. Approximately fourteen hundred breweries produced beer in 1914. With the passage of the Eighteenth Amendment and the implementation of Prohibition, beer production on a national scale came to a halt. Anticipating the restrictions on the sale of alcoholic beverages, some plants already had "near beers" or "cereal beers" on the market. These products achieved immediate popularity; they had some of the taste of beer, but offered a lower alcohol content (less than one half of 1 percent). These beer substitutes could be "spiked" with illegal alcohol to give them a considerable kick. Near-beer labels included Pablo by Pabst, Famo by Schlitz, Vivo by Miller, Lux-O by Strohs, and Bevo by Anheuser-Busch.

Not all breweries resorted to making near beers. Some, in an attempt to remain solvent, pursued secondary lines of business, such as building truck bodies and refrigerated cabinets. Others tried **ice cream** production, or curing and smoking hams and bacon. Still others, in keeping with their past endeavors, produced malt and yeast.

Following the April 1933 repeal of Prohibition, breweries returned to their original business as quickly as possible; 31 had resumed operations by June of that same year and business boomed. The Anheuser-Busch Company, for example, sold 218,073 barrels of beer in 1919, and from April through December 1933 the figure stood at 607,511 barrels. The company, in a gesture of appreciation for the coming of Repeal, inaugurated a tour of New England and the mid-Atlantic region. A bright red beer wagon drawn by six Clydesdale horses made ceremonious deliveries of two cases of complimentary beer to New York's governor Al Smith (1873–1944) and to President Roosevelt. Wagons and horses have long been corporate symbols for the Anheuser-Busch Company, and their appearance in Albany and Washington could not have harmed business.

By 1934, 756 American breweries had resumed producing beer in massive amounts to serve pent-up demand. Most of these breweries remained primarily regional; not until after World War II did national brewing companies become a reality. Although only half as many breweries produced beer in 1940 as had been in business in 1910, actual beer production reached pre-Prohibition levels by the end of the decade. Despite depressions and recessions, Americans always seemed to have enough loose change for a glass of beer during the decade.

The American Can Company and Kreuger Brewing in 1935 introduced the metal beer can, a move that led to increased home consumption. Consumers liked the no-deposit feature of cans (most bottles at this time were returnable and required a deposit), as well as their being nonbreakable, fast-cooling, and stackable.

Prohibition also included wine in its restrictions. Wine had never enjoyed as much popularity as whiskey and beer in the United States, so in the years prior to Prohibition, the facilities for the manufacture of wine and wine-related products had lagged behind those used for whiskey and beer. In 1919, the per capita consumption of wine stood at a miniscule 0.12 gallons, as opposed to 1.08 for beer and 0.76 for liquor (total per capita consumption was 1.96 gallons). Not until the mid-1800s had the cultivation of grapes even become a recognizable industry. Supported primarily by immigrants from cultural traditions that enjoyed wine with meals, most other Americans chose not to serve it, and many looked askance at those who did.

In the years immediately prior to World War I, the American wine industry had exhibited some growth, but the imposition of Prohibition in 1920 effectively stifled it. Before 1920, over one thousand commercial wineries had competed for customers;

following Repeal, slightly more than 150 remained. To survive economically, wine producers applied for and received permits to make wines for medicinal and sacramental purposes. They also converted many of their vineyards to grow more juice grapes. In an ironic twist of fate during the Prohibition years, American grape production actually increased; individuals bought them in large quantities attempting to make home-brewed wines, not nonalcoholic grape juice.

But for the wine industry as a whole, problems continued throughout Prohibition. The costs of maintaining vineyards, along with the loss of domestic sales, especially to restaurants, crippled the industry, and by the time of Repeal, American wine producers faced a long road back to profitability. More than two-thirds of the wine consumed after Repeal came from dessert varieties, like port, sherry, and muscatel. For the industry to grow, table wines, never particularly popular in the United States, had to gain a base of customers. **Eleanor Roosevelt** (1884–1962) helped wine producers, at least symbolically, when she began serving table wines at the White House following Repeal. Throughout the 1930s, however, the comeback proved slow and difficult; it took time to replant fields with the proper grapes and then allow them to grow to maturity.

In retrospect, Prohibition did not curtail the American appetite for alcoholic beverages; those who wanted to drink liquor, beer, or wine usually could find a way, and Repeal made their choices legal in most localities. The end of Prohibition also put thousands of people back to work in breweries and distilleries, with a ripple effect spreading to distributors and truckers, restaurants and lounges, and liquor stores and supermarkets.

See also Advertising; Alcoholics Anonymous; Coffee & Tea; Food; Grocery Stores & Supermarkets

SELECTED READING

Alcohol Statistics. http://www.niaaa.nih.gov/resources
Baron, Stanley [Wade]. *Brewed in America: A History of Beer and Ale in the United States.* New York: Arno Press, 1972.
Krebs, Roland. *Making Friends Is Our Business: 100 Years of Anheuser-Busch.* St. Louis, MO: Anheuser-Busch, 1953.
Mariani, John F. *The Dictionary of American Food and Drink.* New Haven, CT: Ticknor & Fields, 1983.

ALCOHOLICS ANONYMOUS (A.A.). This unique organization, dedicated to fighting the disease of alcoholism, came into being in June 1935. Bill Wilson (1895–1971; known primarily as "Bill W" in keeping with the anonymity theme that helps unite members) and Dr. Robert Smith (or "Dr. Bob," 1879–1950) had met in Akron, Ohio, the previous year. Both men suffered from alcoholism, although at the time of their meeting Bill W enjoyed a tenuous sobriety, whereas Dr. Bob still actively drank. They realized that most people, including members of the medical community, viewed their addiction as an incurable condition, and they sought to discover ways of achieving lasting sobriety. Working together, they developed a program of recovery that showed considerable promise.

The two men, along with a patient in an Akron hospital, created what has come to be known as the first A.A. group, although no formal name existed at the time. Unique because it involved alcoholics working with fellow alcoholics through a series of 12 steps in a nonjudgmental way, the idea slowly spread. Additional groups were organized in other cities, and by the end of the decade the 12-step concept had received national attention. The basic text, and the source of the organization's name, *Alcoholics Anonymous*, also known as the "Big Book," first came out in 1939, and it has remained continuously in print since then. It combines history, philosophy, and the Twelve Steps; each new member of A.A. receives a copy, making it one of the most widely circulated titles in the history of American publishing.

Because alcoholism had long been viewed in America as a moral failing, a social disgrace, the disease received little serious medical attention prior to the founding of Alcoholics Anonymous. In a break with tradition, the Twelve-Step program treated alcoholism as a disease and not a personal failing. Both **Prohibition and Repeal** had made Americans very aware of problem drinking, and the early successes of the pioneering A.A. groups received favorable media publicity. These facts combined to position the fledgling Alcoholics Anonymous at the end of the 1930s as the primary group prepared to deal with alcoholism.

See also Alcoholic Beverages

SELECTED READING
Alcoholics Anonymous. 3rd edition. New York: Alcoholics Anonymous World Services, 1976.
Dr. Bob and the Good Oldtimers. New York: Alcoholics Anonymous World Services, 1980.

AMERICAN GOTHIC. This title identifies a 1930 painting executed by Regionalist **Grant Wood** (1891–1942); it had its first public exhibition at the Art Institute of Chicago that same year. Arguably the most recognizable painting in the annals of American art, it elicited almost instantaneous discussion from the moment of its first unveiling.

A simple composition, *American Gothic* depicts a woman and a man standing before an Iowa farmhouse constructed in the Carpenter Gothic style. Although it did not win first prize in the Art Institute's competition (also known as the American Artists Exposition), the museum nevertheless purchased the picture for its permanent collection, paying $300 (about $3,600 in contemporary dollars) for the portrait. Since then, Wood's painting has become an American icon, an artifact that has taken on meanings larger than itself. After briefly touring the country, it became part of an Art Masterpieces display at Chicago's **Century of Progress Exposition** during 1933–1934; it turned out to be a big hit and quickly entered a select circle, that of popular, well-known American paintings. Countless cartoonists have since parodied the image, and advertisers have employed likenesses of the couple, usually humorously, as a means of pitching every conceivable product and service. In both cases, the re-creators have relied on the audience's familiarity with the painting, although *American Gothic*, in and of itself, may have little or nothing to do with the message being presented.

After struggling for some years as an artist, but with little success, Grant Wood in the summer of 1930 saw a modest farmhouse in the tiny community of Eldon, Iowa. He did a quick painting of it on the spot, and thus created the background for his later masterpiece. Subsequent sketches placed two figures in the composition, with the man clasping a rake. When he had worked out the other details, Wood chose his sister Nan

(1899–1990) and his dentist, Byron H. McKeeby (1867–1950), as the two foreground subjects. In the meantime, the rake evolved into a three-tined pitchfork, or hay fork.

A variation on nineteenth-century photographs of couples posed before their residences, the unsmiling McKeeby looks straight at the viewer, while Nan Wood diverts her gaze slightly off to the right side of the picture. Their "home" looms behind them, precise in its structural details, including a plain gothic window that gives the painting its title. An accomplished technician, Wood gives his work a wealth of detail (the brooch at Nan Wood's collar, McKeeby's gold collar button, a snake plant on the porch, stylized spherical trees, and so on), much of which deepens any interpretation of the work.

Initial public reaction to the painting bordered on outrage, particularly among Midwesterners, those first exposed to the picture. For many, *American Gothic* suggested a satirical attack on traditional American values. Nan Wood's figure represented—or so some interpreted it this way—a prudish, cringing wife, whereas McKeeby's glaring character, pitchfork at the ready, depicted a mean-spirited man, closed to anything new or threatening.

Many art critics also saw satire in the picture, but celebrated it as satire directed at narrow-mindedness and small-town America. Instead of taking offense, they felt the subject matter and its treatment put Wood in league with such admired social commentators as Sinclair Lewis (1885–1951) and H. L. Mencken (1880–1956), themselves caustic observers of American mores. In fact, Wood in 1936 did a set of illustrations for a special edition of Lewis's 1920 *Main Street.*

With time, however, an intriguing reversal occurred: the public began to embrace *American Gothic* as an affirmation of solid American (not just Midwestern) values, and viewers ignored, or overlooked, any satirical implications. The Depression, followed by the looming threat of world war, heightened people's sense that this strong pair of citizens could look adversity in the eye and not be frightened. From figures of artistic ridicule, the couple came to represent positive sensibilities in stressful times.

Many of the art world's critics likewise shifted in their attitudes, stepping away from their previous praise and condemning *American Gothic* as kitsch, a cheap dilution of artistic merit in order to appeal to the mass market. They characterized Wood as a mere illustrator and accused him, along with his fellow Regionalists, of playing to the crowd and ignoring aesthetic excellence. Wood did not help clarify any confusion about the painting with his public comments. He had at first identified the couple as husband and wife, but later retreated, saying they were father and daughter. His early hints at sarcasm about the picture's meaning mellowed into support for the couple, accompanied by praise for their salt-of-the-earth honesty and straightforwardness. Wood capitalized on his newfound fame, posing for publicity photographs attired in bib overalls, a folksy Iowan who came from and represented the Heartland. As the critical and popular winds shifted, Wood set his sails accordingly.

Grant Wood went on to create many other notable paintings, but nothing else he produced ever matched *American Gothic* in popularity. In that single work, he had struck a resonant chord with virtually all Americans, even those who had never seen the original. He spoke obliquely about the work, and many of his subsequent efforts plainly show an attempt to recapture, or replicate, whatever magic *American Gothic* possesses. None, however, achieves that goal, and *American Gothic* continues to be parodied and admired, the very act of parody attesting to its hold on the American imagination.

See also Advertising; Illustrators; Photography; Regionalism

SELECTED READING

Biel, Steven. *American Gothic: A Life of America's Most Famous Painting*. New York: W. W. Norton, 2005.

Corn, Wanda. *Grant Wood: The Regionalist Vision*. New Haven, CT: Yale University Press, 1983.

Dennis, James. *Grant Wood: A Study in American Art and Culture*. Columbia: University of Missouri Press, 1986.

Hoving, Thomas. *American Gothic: The Biography of Grant Wood's American Masterpiece*. New York: Chamberlain Bros., 2005.

AMOS 'N' ANDY. Freeman Gosden (1899–1982) and Charles Correll (1890–1972), two white male performers of many voices, happened into **radio** at just the right time, the mid-1920s when the new medium was still defining itself. The pair created *Amos 'n' Andy*, one of the earliest comedy series, a prototype for the soap opera, and arguably the most popular radio show of all time. It ran from 1928 until 1960, and even attempted a brief foray into **television** from 1951 until 1953.

Gosden, who voiced Amos, and Correll, who did Andy, rank among the first stars of radio, and their radio personas happened to be black Americans. In time, the two created a large cast that included both men and women, and they accomplished it all using only their own vocal talents. In those early days, the two actors frequently posed in full blackface makeup for publicity shots, but made no attempt to hide their identities.

The original concept for *Amos 'n' Andy* started out as *Sam 'n' Henry* on Chicago's WGN in 1926. Freeman and Correll had joined the station in 1925 as a musical variety team, providing patter and some songs. *Sam 'n' Henry* emerged as a "colored comedy," a nightly radio show with roots in the American blackface and minstrel tradition. In the 1920s and 1930s, minstrel shows (white performers made up in blackface dispensing patronizing, stereotypical racial humor and **music**) still retained substantial audiences and regularly played across the country. After just a few broadcasts, *Sam 'n' Henry* had found a large Midwestern listenership, and by 1928 the two performers wanted to expand beyond WGN's signal limits.

The National Broadcasting Company (NBC radio) expressed interest in the program, but WGN refused to cooperate. As a result, Correll and Gosden moved to WMAQ, another Chicago station, but one with network connections. To avoid copyright problems, *Sam 'n' Henry* changed to *Amos 'n' Andy* and the new show made its WMAQ debut in March 1928. The following year, NBC radio picked up their contract as a network offering, a shift that gave *Amos 'n' Andy* national exposure. Placed in a 15-minute nightly time slot at seven o'clock, it became an immediate hit, and its popularity continued, unabated, throughout the 1930s.

Rather than lose potential audiences to home radios, theaters would delay starting films until 7:15 or stop their **movies** and pipe in the nightly broadcasts. Department stores installed speakers so shoppers would not miss an episode. Such loyalty did not go unnoticed; in the 1930s, *Amos 'n' Andy* had only two sponsors: Pepsodent toothpaste (Procter and Gamble) carried the show from 1929 to 1937; Campbell's Soup took it over from 1937 onward. Success rewarded Correll and Gosden well; in 1933, the bleakest year of the Depression, they each earned $50,000 (about $800,000 in contemporary dollars), making them two of the highest paid individuals in the country.

The adventures of Amos, Andy, Kingfish, Lightnin', Calhoun, Sapphire, Madame Queen (whose goal in life focused on marrying Andy), along with the elaborate schemes involving the Mystic Knights of the Sea and the Fresh-Air Taxicab Company, made for a series filled with warm, gentle humor. Those characters might mean little to most people nowadays, but mentioning *Amos 'n' Andy* will evoke a response from anyone familiar with the early years of broadcasting.

The two actors, who did their own scriptwriting, employed a stereotypical "Negro dialect" and delivered their lines exactly as written. Phrases like "I'se regusted," "Hello dere, Sapphire," "Ain't that sumpin!" "Holy mackerel, Andy!" and "Awah, awah, awah" (a lament voiced by Amos when things went wrong—as they often did) became part of national speech, and listeners exchanged summaries of the previous night's episode, usually delivering them in some approximation of the characters' patois. What should have been an issue of racial stereotyping seldom entered any superficial discussions of *Amos 'n' Andy*.

In the period before World War II, overt racism came in many forms, most of which the public blithely overlooked. The movies did not hesitate to caricature nonwhite groups, but they focused especially on black characters. Stores sold—if they carried them at all—**recordings** featuring black artists as "race records." Even cartoons and **comic strips** depicted black figures as degrading stereotypes, and **newspapers** showed no qualms about carrying them. It should therefore come as no surprise, given the times and popular attitudes, that *Amos 'n' Andy* stirred minimal criticism in its early years. A few civil rights organizations attacked the series as racist, but to no avail; the network and the sponsors turned deaf ears to their protests. In the meantime, the show continued to attract a true mass audience that cut across lines of race, age, and gender. For those directly involved with *Amos 'n' Andy*, there seemed little point in arguing with success.

In retrospect, many of the episodes remain genuinely funny. The entanglements of the characters cross racial lines; everybody can identify with them. The scripts present likeable personalities; the plots tell tight stories and avoid meanness or violence. Plus, *Amos 'n' Andy* played on radio, an aural medium. In 1930, at the peak of their popularity, Gosden and Correll made a movie, *Check and Double Check*; the odd title comes from an expression used in the series. Despite the popularity of *Amos 'n' Andy*, the film, after little time in release, did poorly at the box office.

Listening to the radio show—as opposed to seeing the characters in a movie—tempers the more blatant stereotyping. The mind and ear create whatever images they want, a discovery that American radio made during its formative years. Of course, that means it can also erase any hints of racism with relative ease, something that audiences must have done during the nightly broadcasts. For black listeners, and there were many, the show presented the challenge of enjoying the stereotypical humor and, at the same time, finding in it a validation of their experience in America. That both Amos and Andy appear as naive bumpkins allows black listeners to insulate themselves from the characterizations; this dissociation bestows a freedom to laugh without being the butt of the joke. Despite the charges of racism leveled against *Amos 'n' Andy*, it drew a remarkably diverse audience, a testament to its universality.

In late 1928, a short-lived comic strip based on the show debuted; it was syndicated by the *Chicago Daily News*, the owners of WMAQ, the series' NBC radio affiliate station. A **candy** bar also bore the name "Amos 'n' Andy" on its wrapper. Dolls, toy taxis, and other reminders of the series likewise enjoyed brief runs. Nothing, however, lasts forever, especially in the realm of popular culture. After so many years on the radio, *Amos 'n' Andy* began a long, slow decline in the 1940s, and NBC radio finally cancelled the show in 1960. During its 30-odd years on the air, *Amos 'n' Andy* nonetheless attracted one of the largest returning audiences in the history of radio.

See also Race Relations & Stereotyping; Radio Networks; Transportation

SELECTED READING

Ely, Melvin Patrick. *The Adventures of Amos 'n' Andy: The Social History of an American Phenomenon.* Charlottesville: University Press of Virginia, 1991.

Hilmes, Michele. *Radio Voices: American Broadcasting, 1922–1952.* Minneapolis: University of Minnesota Press, 1997.

Nachman, Gerald. *Raised on Radio.* Berkeley: University of California Press, 1998.

APPLE MARY. Throughout the history of **comic strips**, only a few women have achieved success as cartoonists. Martha Orr (1908–2001) must be counted among that select group, and she did it in 1934 by creating a single strip, *Apple Mary*. Unusual in that it dealt directly and realistically with the Great Depression, *Apple Mary* quickly captivated newspaper readers. Orr took the theme of economic hardship and blended it with the melodramatic plot devices of **radio soap operas**, an extremely popular medium at the time. The strip told serialized stories, and Mary proved wise in the ways of solving the problems of the lovelorn. Despite the emphasis on relationships, *Apple Mary* reflected its time, with unemployment and poverty a major part of the strip's visual and story components. Since the 1930s stand as the golden age of newspaper comics, it seems fitting that such a strip would make its debut then.

Orr's creation may have been influenced by *Lady for a Day*, a 1933 film from director Frank Capra (1897–1991), itself an adaptation of a 1929 Damon Runyon (1884–1946) short story titled "Madame la Gimp." The main character in both, a somewhat disreputable older woman who sells apples from a pushcart, goes by the name of Apple Annie. She aspires to greater social acceptance, and story and movie humorously track her progress toward that goal. A sequel, *Lady by Choice*, directed by David Burton (1877–1963), followed *Lady for a Day* in 1934; both **movies** star May Robson (1858–1942) as Apple Annie and achieved box office success. Possible or probable antecedents aside, *Apple Mary* succeeds on its own merits, and it pleased readers until 1939.

In the comic strip, Mary likewise hawks apples from a pushcart in Depression-ridden America, but she accepts her lot and displays little inclination to move up the social ladder. In reality, the apple-selling movement lasted only about a year, and as more and more vendors became disillusioned about easy money, it faded away. But people did not forget the image of someone trying to peddle apples for a nickel on a street corner; it emerged as one of those iconic memories of the Depression. Despite a changing economic climate, Orr kept Mary at her trade far longer than anyone would have expected.

Unlike the glamour girls that decorate the frames of most cartoon series, Mary herself is older, a widow, a bit dowdy, and down on her luck. But hard work and a tough spirit prevail, and she struggles along, meeting a wide collection of characters in the course of her adventures. In time, Martha Orr retired from cartooning and devoted herself to family concerns. Nothing, however, ever really dies in popular culture; it simply metamorphoses into something that will gain a larger audience. And so *Apple Mary* became *Apple Mary and Dennie* in 1939. A new artist, Dale Conner (active 1930s), took on the illustrations, and Allen Saunders (1899–1986) wrote the continuity. Signing themselves "Dale Allen," the two renamed the strip *Mary Worth's Family*, a title that survived from 1940 to 1942, whereupon it evolved into the more familiar *Mary Worth*, the series' present name. These changes meant the kindly white-haired widow would carry on with the soap opera plotting but without the nuisance of the apple cart.

See also Illustrators; Newspapers

SELECTED READING
Goulart, Ron, ed. *The Encyclopedia of American Comics*. New York: Facts on File, 1990.
Horn, Maurice, ed. *100 Years of American Newspaper Comics*. New York: Gramercy Books, 1996.

ARCHITECTURE. It might appear to the casual onlooker that no designing, no building, took place for much of the decade, and any review of the general U.S. economy during the Depression years supports such a generalization. By 1932, manufacturing output had fallen 54 percent from 1929 figures, and the automobile industry saw a drop of 80 percent during that same period. Banks closed, unemployment rose, and breadlines became commonplace in many cities. In the first years of the Depression, housing starts declined by 90 percent. That translates as 84,000 new units in 1933, compared to 937,000 in 1925. In addition, over 1.5 million homes were in default or in the process of foreclosure by 1933. For the architectural profession, these numbers meant that, by 1933, two-thirds of all workers in the building trades had lost their jobs, and 85 percent of all the architects in New York City had joined the jobless ranks. Equally grim information came from other cities and towns.

Contrary to what many believe, however, architecture did not retreat into a moribund state and wait out the Depression. Construction of new buildings, commercial and residential, continued, albeit at a greatly reduced rate, and architects, both employed and unemployed, worked with new and innovative **design** concepts, many of them European, throughout these troubled years. Economic recovery began to manifest itself in the later 1930s, and with it came a small building boom that would continue until the onset of World War II and accompanying material shortages.

Commercial & Public Architecture. Some of the great urban skyscrapers of the twentieth century—the **Chrysler Building**, the **Empire State Building**, **Rockefeller Center**, for example—went up during the 1930s. These commercial enterprises often boasted lavish interior decoration in addition to their striking exteriors. The decade also witnessed the evolution of the **International Style**, an approach to design that incorporated the modernist theories of many architects from around the world, giving added meaning to its name. With the unrest brought on by World War I, the social upheavals in its aftermath, and the clouds of a new world war gathering in Europe, a number of prominent European architects fled to the relative safety of the United States, and their influence hastened the internationalization of American design.

The Viennese architect Rudolf Schindler (1887–1953) served as an early leader in this exodus; he came to the United States in 1914 and began a lucrative practice on the West Coast. In 1923, another Austrian, Richard Neutra (1892–1970), made the journey. Schindler and Neutra eventually created a lucrative partnership in Los Angeles. Relatively unaffected by the Depression—the popular movie industry kept Los Angeles prosperous—the two boasted many commissions and contributed some pioneering work, especially in the area of apartments and private residences, in the International Style throughout the decade.

Eliel Saarinen (1973–1950), a Finnish designer, had likewise left Europe in 1923, settling in the Midwest. The buildings of Michigan's Cranbrook Academy of Art bear his signature. That same year, the Swiss-born William Lescaze (1896–1964) arrived in New York City. In 1929, he joined with George Howe (1886–1955), and from that collaboration came the Philadelphia Savings Fund Society (PSFS) office tower in 1931, generally conceded to be one of the masterpieces of the emerging International Style.

A virtual rush of architects embarked for the United States as totalitarianism rapidly shut down free artistic expression in Europe: Marcel Breuer (1902–1981; Hungarian), Walter Gropius (1883–1969; German), and Mies van der Rohe (1886–1969; German), the most notable; all emigrated in 1937. Collectively, these architects established lasting roots for modern design, and their shared influence, particularly in the postwar years, had enormous impact on the directions American architecture would follow.

Although modernism marked the road to future developments, traditional architecture continued to have a hold in some sectors, especially in the design of public buildings. Thus a classicist like John Russell Pope (1874–1937) could be contracted to create such neoclassic monuments as the National Gallery (Washington, D.C., 1937–1941) and the Jefferson Memorial (Washington, D.C., 1934–1943). Admired as they are by millions of visitors each year, they also represent the last vestiges of tradition and stand as veritable anachronisms amid a sea of change.

Movie Palaces. The Hollywood film industry prospered during the Depression, and millions of Americans went to the **movies** every day. From the time that Samuel "Roxy" Rothafel (1881–1936) first opened his posh Regent Theatre in New York City in 1913, the American movie theater took on the trappings of a palace that reflected in its architectural splendor the success of the medium. These frothy concoctions of applied ornament lured customers throughout the silent-picture era, offering them escapism from humdrum lives with promises of thrills, romance, suspense, and comedy—all in luxurious comfort and opulent surroundings. No matter how trifling the picture, as these theaters proliferated around the country, they encouraged patronage, and "going to the movies" meant more than watching flickering images on a screen.

The advent of sound in 1927 gave the industry pause while it retooled for the new technology, but the atmospheric palaces continued to rise, and the 1930s saw new facades, arcades, lobbies, and garish neon signs, all of it designed to keep the customers coming. The Depression also affected Hollywood's fortunes, but by 1934 attendance and profits commenced an upward swing that would last throughout the remainder of the decade.

Working with imagined replicas of European castles, to the latest in **Art Deco** and Streamline moderne, dozens of architects specialized in theater architecture, with C. Howard Crane (1885–1952), John Eberson (1875–1954), Thomas W. Lamb (1871–1942),

S. Charles Lee (1899–1990), B. Marcus Priteca (1889–1971), and the brothers Cornelius W. and George L. Rapp (1861–1927 and 1878–1942, respectively, often listed as Rapp & Rapp) ranking among the leaders in the field during the 1930s. Not as flamboyant as the sumptuous palaces of the 1920s, one imaginative design after another nevertheless emerged from their drawing boards, ranging from the fanciful Loew's 175th (New York City; 1930, Lamb), to the lavish Art Deco Paramount (Aurora, Illinois; 1931, Rapp & Rapp), to the modest Anaconda (Washoe, Montana; 1936, Priteca) and the modernistic La Reina (Sherman Oaks, California; 1938, Lee); these Depression-era flights of fancy offered moviegoers a make-believe environment, one that blurred fantasy and reality and guaranteed relief from anxieties about the outside world.

Restaurants & Shopping. When traveling a highway at 50 miles an hour, a driver has little time to interpret signs, so the sign must relay its message clearly and forcefully. After much trial and error, mimetic architecture, a new language designed for the roadside, came into being. Mimetic design ("mimetic" means imitative or representative) manifested itself on American thoroughfares through giant hamburgers and hot dogs, towering **ice cream** cones and frosty **soft drinks**, three-dimensional shoes and pocketbooks, rotating furniture and appliances—all part of an ongoing gallery of edible delights and consumer goods presented in a way to capture the eye of the passing motorist.

Although the heyday of the drive-in snack shop and suburban shopping mall still lay in the future, architects and designers had begun to acknowledge the importance of **automobiles** in their planning. Accommodations for parking assumed significance, as did easy access to shops and eateries. Despite the business downturn of the early 1930s, eventual recovery meant more cars on the road and the necessity of increased convenience for the motorized public. In addition, American cities displayed a fondness for horizontal expansion, both commercial and residential. The growth of suburbs meant improved traffic flow, and two-lane roads became three- and four-lane highways. The accompanying architecture had to adapt to a mobile population that relied on automobiles for transport, a realization that commenced in the 1930s.

Gas Stations. A business as ordinary and commonplace as a gas station reflected the trend toward an automotive culture. In the early years of the twentieth century, the concept of the service station barely existed. A dirty garage, with maybe a gas pump at curbside, fulfilled this function. These places repaired vehicles, and they dispensed oil and gasoline, if at all, as a sideline to their regular business. They followed no architectural format and might be housed in any kind of structure, or often as an appendage to a building performing some unrelated function. As the demand for automotive service facilities grew, the greasy repair shops began to be displaced by more savory establishments, and they slowly took on an identity of their own.

Standard house or cottage plans—with important modifications, of course—served as the favored designs for the construction of gas stations during much of the 1920s and into the 1930s. Usually consisting of boxlike structures, not unlike a typical foursquare house, these "new" stations usually featured a canopy that extended out over the pump(s). For example, both the Pure and Phillips oil companies introduced variations on the traditional English cottage in the late 1920s. With their steeply pitched shingle roofs, these stations proved popular among consumers, and almost seven thousand such period structures had gone up, mainly in Midwestern states, by the early 1930s. Their success led to colonial, Georgian, Mission, and even some Oriental-style stations. Others, in the spirit of mimeticism, imitated lighthouses, giant oilcans, icebergs, tee-pees, coffee pots, and windmills—anything to catch the driver's eye.

In 1934, the Texas Oil Company (Texaco) hired Walter Dorwin Teague (1883–1960), a respected designer, to create a more modern gas station. The commission resulted in a classic International Style building, smooth and sleek, complete with white porcelain enamel steel tiles. It boasted no "Early American" wood or stucco that produced an anachronistic identity. Several other designers, working in a similar vein, tackled the lowly gas station during the Depression. Raymond Loewy (1893–1986) created plans for both Shell and Union Oil prototypes, as did Norman Bel Geddes (1893–1958) for Mobilgas. Their designs evoked modernity, although few reached the construction stage and existed mainly on drawing boards and in journals. But from this move toward a more contemporaneous structure emerged the generic station of the later 1930s and 1940s, a flat-roofed box with lubrication bays, plenty of glass, and a fuller range of services, such as clean rest rooms, free maps, and coolers for soft drinks.

Residential Building: Modernism & Tradition. Most discussions about architectural modernism, pro or con, tend to ignore everyday housing. Although some modernistic dwellings were built at this time, especially by architects like Richard Neutra, Rudolf Schindler, and **Frank Lloyd Wright** (1867–1959), much residential building instead looked to the past for its inspiration.

Most homes that might be called modernistic went unseen by the general public. Chicago's 1933 **Century of Progress Exposition** did display 14 contemporary houses, and at least two of them, both designed by George Fred Keck (1895–1980), could be deemed "futuristic." His House of Tomorrow and Crystal House elicited some enthusiasm among fairgoers (over 1 million people visited them), but most of it died out following the close of the exposition in 1934.

The House of Tomorrow stood three stories tall, and each level, set back from the preceding one, featured an exterior that boasted 12 sides. Built on a steel frame and almost completely enclosed in glass, anyone living in it could control exterior light through shades and drapes. A central core provided heating and cooling and proved remarkably efficient. A built-in hangar for a private airplane gave the dwelling perhaps its most unusual feature; the dream of owning one's own airplane has long occupied a favored spot in the thinking of many futurists (and even more **science fiction** writers), and Keck clearly embraced the notion.

The Crystal House, true to its name, employed glass and steel almost exclusively in its construction. An exposed, weblike frame surrounded a glass-encased box that served as the living quarters. Keck made few attempts to give warmth to his exterior design, and it did not meet with any great popular success. Whereas the House of Tomorrow attracted considerable attention, the Crystal House did not, and officials dismantled it at the close of the fair.

One of the most forward-looking American designers of the day, R. Buckminster Fuller (1895–1983), developed what he called the 4D Dwelling Unit, or Dymaxion House, in 1927. A neologism of Fuller's making, "Dymaxion" derived from *dynamic maximum tension* and represented some of his theories about engineering and construction techniques. His prototypes for houses came from approaches to aircraft and automotive manufacturing, and the Dymaxion House employed prefabricated parts that could be assembled into modular units. For Fuller and his dedicated followers, rational design and efficiency predicated everything, and creature comforts and aesthetics lagged behind. He tinkered with his Dymaxion concepts, including a Streamlined automobile, throughout the 1930s, and attempted to have his 4D House displayed at Chicago's Century of Progress Exposition, but he could find no backers. Undeterred, Fuller continued, until his death, to proselytize for his Dymaxion theories, and remained a fascinating—if minor—gadfly on the fringes of ongoing American design.

Prior to Keck's displays at the Chicago exposition, A. Lawrence Kocher (1885–1969) and Albert Frey (1903–1998) had collaborated in 1931 on a concept they called the Aluminaire, a starkly modern structure constructed of aluminum and glass. Far ahead of its time, the Aluminaire borrowed from several avant-garde European architects and employed prefabrication and nontraditional materials that would allow it to be mass-produced cheaply. Unfortunately, the public deemed it cold, mechanical, and noisy, and no developers wanted to risk erecting Aluminaires on any large scale. It did, however, offer some new building ideas, and its innovations, especially the widespread use of aluminum, would find a place in construction following World War II.

A handful of other pioneers of modern residential design worked during the 1930s. Howard Fisher (1903–1979) formed General Houses, Inc., in 1932 to promote prefabrication and offered several basic models. Although he also exhibited at the Century of Progress Exposition, he failed to find buyers for his adventurous designs and General Houses went out of business. Frank Lloyd Wright, still active in the 1930s (and for another 30 years or so thereafter), promoted his concept of the Usonian House, a compact, modern house that could be economically constructed. Like Fisher and the others mentioned above, Wright lacked broad public acceptance for these innovative designs, but he retained a fondness for them and kept building them whenever he could find a client. Over 30 Usonian homes were built between 1936 and 1959, making him one of the most successful of this visionary group of architects.

These futuristic homes could all be mass-produced, just like any other machine-made products, but neither consumers nor the housing industry seemed particularly interested in exploring the subject. The building trades did not, however, ignore all the innovations found in these experimental houses. In an attempt to keep construction prices as low as possible, and to emerge from the depressed building market, manufacturers came up with products like prefabricated door and window units, exterior-grade (i.e., weather-resistant) plywood, along with improved drywall and better glues and caulking.

During the years following World War I, a typical residential street (as well as s commercial strip or corridor) often displayed a hodgepodge of building styles. A bungalow might reside next to a Foursquare next to a Spanish or Tudor or Georgian or Romanesque or Gothic revival next to a Victorian fantasy and so on to the end of the block. Commercial buildings likewise exhibited a proliferation of facades, from neoclassic to Art Deco, with everything in between. As a rule, no attempts were made, as might be the case in a European community, to blend styles, to present a unified front to the passerby. Therein lies the glory and the bane of much American architecture—its noisy insistence that every structure, from the grand to the banal, be individual, a reflection both of the owner and the architect.

Lack of significant technological innovation merely represented part of a larger Depression problem. Most middle-class Americans lacked financial resources during these troubled years and therefore continued living in traditional houses throughout the decade. As a result, the residential landscape consisted of an eclectic mix of older homes, not new ones. Despite the insistence on individualism, that right of choice, American cities and suburbs during the decade (or any other period, for that matter) look remarkably alike, their patchwork constituent parts virtually interchangeable.

Several companies introduced various kinds of wall paneling, and knotty pine became a best seller for those who could afford it and wanted to achieve a colonial look, then a popular decorating trend and a reflection of the fondness for the nation's colonial past. The term "Early American" had achieved some status in the 1920s. It signaled a return to days gone by in residential architecture and decoration, a fashion that continued unabated into the 1930s. By and large, the nation continued to vote for tradition, both in design and construction, as far as personal residences were concerned. Americans have long insisted on their perceived right to choose whatever style they wanted; their homes may differ in size and cost, but each exists as a miniature estate in the eyes of its owners.

The year 1931 saw the formation of the American Institute of Interior Decorators (now the American Society of Interior Decorators), a reflection of a growing interest in applied design. But this group, and others like it, also concerned itself with historical accuracy in the many revival movements gaining interest in the country. Amid a flurry of publicity, colonial Williamsburg opened to the public in 1932, providing added impetus to the aim of accurate preservation. Specialty **magazines** with titles like *Decorator's Digest* (1932) and *Interior Decorator* (1934) found a ready public, and a fad for the authentic "Early American" look ensued.

An open fireplace, surrounded by knotty pine paneling and complemented by a replica spinning wheel and a cobbler's bench serving as a coffee table, became a popular look. Fueled by this widespread acceptance of such antiquities, the number of professional interior decorators swelled in the U.S. during the 1920s and 1930s. Women entered their ranks, with many coming from upper-class backgrounds. Mainstream women's magazines, such as *House and Garden* and *Better Homes and Gardens*, began to feature these newcomers' work and ideas, bringing them to a mass audience. Not to be outdone, large, influential department stores like Wanamaker's, Marshall Field, Macy's, Lord & Taylor, and B. Altman included the latest in Early American decorating trends in their furniture and accessory displays.

This popular movement toward a usable past remained in vogue throughout the decade. For those few who could afford new homes, historical motifs dominated much residential architecture, and the resultant styles gained the name "period revivals." By and large, the favorites involved colonial (especially the "Early American" New England farmhouse look), Tudor (or anything vaguely medieval), and Spanish Revival (or the hacienda look). Large firms like Sears, Roebuck and Montgomery Ward, along with many smaller ones such as Aladdin, Gordon Van-Tine, Lewis, and Sterling, had long offered houses in kit form. They shipped the parts, mostly precut, to the owner's site, and it became the buyer's responsibility to erect it. Tens of thousands of kit houses were bought and built between 1900 and 1940, and many fit into the period revival classification. From Montgomery Ward's "Coventry" (1931; French Provincial), to Lewis's "La Salle (1934; Colonial Bungalow), to Aladdin's "Hamilton" (1937; Tudor), their catalogs featured an endless array of homes boasting period designs. Given the economies of kit construction, they proved popular, but the general downturn in construction of all kinds forced sales even of kits to drop during the Depression.

Quaintness and eclecticism nonetheless emerged as two distinctive traits of the era, regardless of the actual style. People desired something cozy, something harking back to a simpler, more secure, past, a far cry from the plain functionalism of the International Style. In 1933, **Walt Disney** (1901–1966) released a cartoon titled *The Three Little Pigs*. An enduring image from the picture involves the sturdy house that one of the pigs has constructed, in contrast to the flimsy ones built by the other two. Many Americans wished for the same image of security in their period homes; they wanted to be able to sing the cartoon's theme, "Who's Afraid of the Big Bad Wolf?" (1933; music by Frank Churchill [1901–1942], lyrics by Ann Ronell [1906–1993]) and keep the Depression from their door, just as the three pigs did in that prophetic animated feature.

Automobiles & Architecture. Throughout the first decades of the twentieth century, American architects tried different approaches to incorporating the increasingly omnipresent automobile into their home designs. Sometimes an obvious solution presented itself: since cars had replaced the horse-drawn carriages of just a few years earlier, many larger, older homes often utilized their now-empty carriage houses and stables as garages. The designers of new homes took a cue from this past, and many modern homes of the 1920s and 1930 boasted garages, brand-new structures that sheltered Fords and Chevrolets, not horses. Built simultaneously with the house itself, but functioning as an independent structure, the contemporary garage usually stood behind the residence and most of the time could be accessed from the street via a driveway that ran alongside the house.

Alleys, a vestige of eighteenth- and nineteenth-century town planning, survived in many communities with the coming of the horseless carriage. With houses tightly arranged on a block, there existed little room for a driveway running beside the structure, but alleys could bisect a city block, providing access for cars behind the homes. Alleys made the driveway unnecessary, eliminated the aesthetic distractions that garages and drives presented, and allowed the architect to focus on the house itself rather than an appendage for sheltering vehicles. They also permitted a developer to place houses more closely together, thereby making up for the land lost with the construction of an alley.

In 1919, a new comic strip began appearing in the *Chicago Tribune*. Its title, *Gasoline Alley*, contributed a unique phrase to the language. Written and drawn by Frank King (1883–1969), the strip took its name from those very alleys found behind many American houses built on typical city blocks. Here, the characters of the strip—usually males—could gather to talk about their cars, do repairs, and otherwise participate in the automotive culture becoming so pervasive in American life. Immensely successful, *Gasoline Alley* reflected, throughout the 1930s, middle-class American values and cast them in a gently humorous but positive light.

The negative connotations associated with alleys—"back alley," "alley cat," and so on—along with the conspicuous consumption that displayed itself in a desire to "show off" one's new car (or cars—the two-car family came into being during the 1920s) in front of the house, soon brought about a move to eliminate alleys. Architects turned the garage around so it faced the street, and, if possible, put in a driveway beside the house. In the years following World War I city planners gradually dropped the urban alley concept. By the 1930s, most homes had backyards that backed up to similar back-yards, and the garage meanwhile crept closer to the house, sometimes even attaching itself to the main dwelling. Of course, in the building boom that followed World War II, the attached garage, or often a built-on carport, became a distinguishing feature of residential design.

The Second World War brought the construction of most nonessential commercial and residential structures to a halt. The postwar years would witness an unparalleled building boom, and it would be accompanied by significant architectural changes. In retrospect, the 1930s augured many of these changes—a greater acceptance of modern-ism, in particular—but economic realities prevented most from blossoming. The popu-larity of traditional formats reflected the insecurity the nation felt during these difficult years, and the corresponding reluctance to embark on any new, uncharted courses.

See also Aviation; Comic Strips: Grocery Stores & Supermarkets; Motels; New York World's Fair; Streamlining; Transportation; Travel

SELECTED READING
Baeder, John. *Gas, Food, and Lodging*. New York: Abbeville Press, 1982.
Clark, Clifford Edward, Jr. *The American Home: 1800–1960*. Chapel Hill: University of North Carolina Press, 1986.
Jandl, H. Ward. *Yesterday's Houses of Tomorrow: Innovative American Homes, 1850 to 1950*. Washington, DC: Preservation Press, 1991.
Liebs, Chester H. *Main Street to Miracle Mile: American Roadside Architecture*. Baltimore: Johns Hopkins University Press, 1985.
Schweitzer, Robert, and Michael W.R. Davis. *America's Favorite Homes: Mail–Order Catalogues as a Guide to Popular Early 20th-Century Houses*. Detroit: Wayne State University Press, 1990.
Valentine, Maggie. *The Show Starts on the Sidewalk: An Architectural History of the Movie Palace, Starring S. Charles Lee*. New Haven, CT: Yale University Press, 1994.

ART DECO. In 1925, from April until October, Paris served as the site for the Expo-sition des Arts Decoratifs et Industriels Modernes. Over 16 million people viewed the show, an international celebration of new **design** trends, giving legitimacy to many of the latest movements in art and design. On a more popular level, the exhibition brought the concepts of Art Deco—the term derives from the Arts Decoratifs, or "decorative arts," of the title—to people's attention. Already well established in the salons and ateliers of Europe, Art Deco had made only a few inroads into American design following World War I. Officially, the United States sent no exhibits to the sprawling show, although the government, under the direction of then-Secretary of Commerce **Herbert Hoover** (1874–1964), did dispatch a commission of 108 interested individuals who observed the proceedings and took note of the ascendancy of Art Deco.

Any discussion of the term presents seeming contradictions. Ideally, the style boasts of stripping away needless or ostentatious ornamentation, and yet many items deemed "Art Deco" appear drenched in applied decorative elements. Over time, some identifying standards have nonetheless come into place, and Art Deco can be interpreted broadly to include the following generalized characteristics: products that obey basic geometric and rectilinear dictates, including symmetry. In addition, stylized motifs, such as stripes and bars, ziggurats (or zigzags and lightning bolts), chevrons, and fans (or sun rays) mark Art

Deco creations, from large buildings to tiny pieces of jewelry. The style freely employs modern materials (or traditional ones in modern ways), such as terra-cotta, stainless steel, chrome plating, metal tubing, glass blocks, and many plastics, like Vitrolite, Lucite, and Bakelite.

In a belated response to the Paris exposition, the Metropolitan Museum in New York City organized a 1929 show that featured "The Architect and the International Arts." It consisted of eight rooms, each decorated by a different architect and displaying artifacts manufactured by American companies. Expensive and elitist, just like its European counterpart, the exhibition alerted middle-class consumers of new trends in domestic design, trends that included numerous Art Deco elements.

That same year, and then again in 1934, New York's Museum of Modern Art presented shows about "machine art"; similarly, the Brooklyn Museum in 1931 sponsored "Modern Industrial and Decorative Art." The fact that these exhibitions occurred in museums and not at manufacturers' trade shows acknowledged that mass production could not be dismissed in discussions of the decorative arts. In all these presentations, however, the curators attempted to create a blend between a machine aesthetic and the warmth of natural materials and craft. The human element could not be dismissed; comfort had to be combined with utility and economy.

During this period, the United States usually displayed one of two minds in its approach to new cultural trends: deferential or xenophobic. On the deferential side, the consensus among government officials and their advisers revolved around the perception that the nation lacked any coherent approach to modern design, and thus had to look to Europe, "the Old World," for inspiration. This feeling of cultural inferiority had little basis in fact, but had held sway among many people since the late eighteenth century and the founding of the country. With its reluctant rise as a world power, the United States began to shed that cultural reticence, but the transition took time, and not until the first third of the twentieth century—the very period of the Paris exposition—would American decorative arts begin to take their place on the world stage.

In the meantime, a form of cultural xenophobia sometimes manifested itself among American designers and manufacturers. They often dismissed anything remotely "European," arguing that native products possessed an inherent superiority over "foreign" goods and ideas. For example, much of what was exhibited in Paris consisted of carefully handcrafted luxury items made from rare or expensive materials, or both. By and large, that exposition displayed the elegant, the sumptuous, the one-of-a-kind, and often the ostentatious. It appealed to a wealthy clientele that wanted luxury goods, and cost was no barrier.

American firms, on the other hand, substituted machine-made products for handcrafting in order to attract a growing middle class eager to possess the newest of the new but at a modest cost. Xenophobic or not, Americans wanted a commercialization of modernism. Art Deco would finally be embraced in the United States in the later 1920s and on into the 1930s, but with significant changes that separated it from the earlier European versions; what gained a popular American following melded the continental penchant for luxury with the practical concerns of cost and marketability.

The range of Art Deco design is limited only by one's imagination. Thus towering American skyscrapers, such as the **Chrysler Building** (1930) and the **Empire State Building** (1931), are categorized as Art Deco **architecture** because of many decorative elements incorporated into their designs. The same would hold true for many of the great movie palaces of the 1930s, a final outburst of Art Deco architectural flamboyance. Its use in architecture has, however, usually been limited to commercial and government buildings; only on rare occasions can it be found in small residential structures. The economies imposed on new construction during the 1930s hampered the full expression of Art Deco concepts. The grand entryways, a common Art Deco practice, to public and commercial buildings may conceal an otherwise rather pedestrian structure. Shorn of ornament, save for the entries, these buildings in actuality spoke of financial restraint.

Further afield, furnishings, from office suites to kitchen appliances, frequently receive Art Deco touches, as do smaller items like jewelry, cigarette cases, watches, and perfume bottles. Dinnerware, silver, and book bindings likewise attract designers, and unusual materials, such as onyx, or polychrome lacquer and enamels, enhance the products. Again, the range appears limitless.

Too often employed as a blanket term, "Art Deco" can be presented in many guises. There exists "high" Art Deco, as seen in the finely crafted items on display at the Paris show. But mass-produced Art Deco, the decided preference in the United States, tends to freely employ certain motifs (too freely, some critics would say) and gives a comforting illusion of financial security without being terribly expensive. In many ways, the popularity of many cheap Art Deco–inspired knickknacks in the Depression era served as a comforting reaction to the austerity imposed by the financial crisis. The glossy figurines (many of them unabashedly erotic with their sensuous nude women) that could be found in many middle-class homes in the 1930s clearly reflected some of the imagery carried over from countless **movies** that featured Art Deco sets.

Regardless of how its designers and manufacturers presented it, Art Deco fit a fashionable niche for much of the 1930s. It served, both commercially and domestically, as a widely accepted symbol of glamour. More importantly, it heralded the future. When pared down to simple shapes and stripped of superfluous ornamentation, items once identified as "Art Deco" lost that designation and instead fell under more inclusive labels of "Modernism" or "Moderne."

See also Fashion; International Style; Rockefeller Center; Streamlining

SELECTED READING
Arwas, Victor. *Art Deco*. New York: Harry N. Abrams, 1992.
Menten, Theodore. *The Art Deco Style*. New York: Dover Publications, 1972.
Robinson, Cervin, and Rosemarie Haag Bletter. *Skyscraper Style: Art Deco New York*. New York: Oxford University Press, 1975.
Sternau, Susan A. *Art Deco: Flights of Artistic Fancy*. New York: Todtri Book Publishers, 1997.

ASTAIRE, FRED, & GINGER ROGERS. Of all the many dancers in Hollywood **musicals** during the 1930s, the team of Fred Astaire (1899–1987) and Ginger Rogers (1911–1995) proved the most popular and the most enduring. In the nine films in which they appear together, they, more than anyone else, epitomized both style and elegance on the dance floor.

Nebraska-born Astaire came from a stage background; he had costarred in vaudeville with his sister Adele (1897–1981) when both were children; they carried on the partnership in stage musicals that commenced in 1917, eventually making it to Broadway and

Fred Astaire (1899–1987) and Ginger Rogers (1911–1995) in *Shall We Dance* (1937). (Courtesy of Photofest)

several major shows. In 1932, Adele left the team to marry, and Fred began to search for new ventures. He looked to Hollywood and, despite a disappointing screen test, managed to land a contract. His film debut consisted of a bit part in a 1933 Joan Crawford (1904–1977) vehicle called *Dancing Lady*. Astaire, not surprisingly, plays a dancer, and it got him noticed; RKO paired him with Ginger Rogers for second-tier roles in *Flying Down to Rio* (1933), a frothy musical featuring the then-popular Dolores del Rio (1905–1983), the ostensible star of the movie.

While Fred Astaire labored to establish his film credentials, Ginger Rogers had already become a veteran of the silver screen. By the time she first danced with him in *Flying Down to Rio*, she had appeared in 22 **movies** in the 1930s alone, plus two shorts in 1929. Despite making so many pictures in so brief a time, Rogers still had not achieved top-star ranking, but her energetic dancing and singing turns in films like **42nd Street** (1932) and *Gold Diggers of 1933* (1933) had earned her considerable notice. In *Gold Diggers of 1933* she wowed everyone with her rendition of "The Gold Digger's Song (We're in the Money)" by virtue of being scantily clad in large gold coins and inexplicably doing some of the lyrics in pig Latin. When RKO offered her a part in *Flying Down to Rio*, she even received billing over newcomer Astaire who could offer no comparable accomplishments.

Once paired in *Flying Down to Rio*, Rogers and Astaire get to sing and dance "The Carioca," one of the featured numbers in the picture, and they steal the show. The rest of the cast stands aside as their flawless timing and remarkable fluidity introduce a style of cinematic ballroom dancing not seen before. Within a year, the two would be together again, but now in their own musical, stars in their own right.

Eight additional Astaire/Rogers pictures followed *Flying Down to Rio* during the 1930s: *The Gay Divorcee* (1934), *Roberta* (1935), *Top Hat* (1935), *Follow the Fleet* (1936), *Swingtime* (1936), *Shall We Dance?* (1937), *Carefree* (1938), and *The Story of Vernon and Irene Castle* (1939). Each film typifies elegance and poise. With the worst of the Depression waning by 1934, the confident, glossy imagery displayed by Rogers and Astaire replaced the earnestness, the sense of responsibility that characterized so many of the musicals of the earlier 1930s. This self-assuredness carried over into the dancing itself: instead of being regimented and geometric in their choreography, certainly the approach taken in musicals made during the 1930–1933 period, Fred and Ginger dance in a seemingly carefree and fun way, avoiding the synchronized movements associated with a previous generation of musicals. Astaire insisted on doing his own choreography, and he brought a new, never before seen level of sophistication to movie dancing.

Every detail in their movies reveals a cinematic vision of modernity, and all their collaborations have a singular look about them, as well they should. Each exhibits the work of RKO's art director/production designer Van Nest Polglase (1898–1968), one of the best interpreters of the **Art Deco–Streamlining** approach to interior design. Polglase saw to it that the two danced in Hollywood's distinctive interpretation of the big-city nightclub; stark blacks and whites, along with chrome and other polished surfaces, set off Astaire's trademark tuxedoes and Rogers's gowns. Aesthetic escapism at its best, these sequences satisfied audiences hungry for images of good fortune. Instead of the theme about a plucky chorus girl who finally makes good and stars in a hit, the basic plot of so many earlier musicals, the movies with Astaire and Rogers dispense with any **Social Realism** and focus their energies on being stylish and sophisticated. The formula worked; their films ranked among the biggest box office draws of the decade.

After the 1939 release of *The Story of Vernon and Irene Castle*, and not wanting the magic to wear thin, Fred Astaire and Ginger Rogers ceased doing movies together. Both pursued independent careers, Astaire continuing in musicals and **recordings**. Not just a marvelous dancer, he could also sing, and well. Possessed of a somewhat thin, high-pitched voice, he chose his songs carefully and displayed impeccable phrasing. Over time, he would introduce and record more standards than any other male vocalist, and major **songwriters and lyricists** like **Cole Porter** (1891–1964), **George Gershwin** (1898–1937), and **Irving Berlin** (1888–1989) often had him in mind when writing their **music**. In the process, he enjoyed many a hit record.

Ginger Rogers likewise branched out into other areas. In 1940, she won an Academy Award for Best Actress with her role in the nonmusical *Kitty Foyle: The Natural History of a Woman*, a film that showcased her talents as a dramatic performer. She would continue to appear in a variety of films throughout her long career. The two would be reunited one last time in 1949 with *The Barkleys of Broadway*, and they demonstrated that, despite an absence of 10 years, they remained one of the screen's most captivating dancing combinations.

SELECTED READING
Astaire, Fred. *Steps in Time*. New York: Harper & Brothers, 1959.
Croce, Arlene. *The Fred Astaire & Ginger Rogers Book*. New York: Outerbridge & Lazard, 1972.
Delamater, Jerome. *Dance in the Hollywood Musical*. Ann Arbor, MI: UMI Research Press, 1981.

AUTO CAMPS. Long before **motels** offering every imaginable amenity dotted American highways, a crude ancestor called an auto camp served weary travelers. A combination of a small general store and primitive lodging, these accommodations ranged from tent sites to a bare-bones room with a cot or bed. Such camps served basic needs and nothing more, but they provided a cheap place to park off the highway for the night. Some motorists, called "auto gypsies," created their own roadside lodging, often by trespassing on private property, pitching a tent, and usually leaving litter. Official auto camps, established by local governments in the early 1920s, attempted to cope with this problem by designating sites to sleep in the car or put up a tent.

An outgrowth of the popularity of **automobiles**, auto camps in the 1920s and 1930s seldom lacked for customers. Through both decades, many American families, middle-class professionals, and white-collar workers had the desire and the means to utilize their cars for recreation, to be on the road longer than the Sunday afternoon outing. They craved adventure, the sense of leaving home and seeing the country, "roughing it," and enjoying the intimacy of gathering around an evening campfire. Not everyone searched for the romance of the road, of course; the worst days of the Depression saw large numbers of unemployed people drifting, hoping for piecemeal work and a break in their economic situation.

Salesmen and businessmen traveled because their professions demanded it (the idea of a woman traveling alone still raised eyebrows). With the Depression and the growing popularity of the automobile, more and more of these travelers switched from **trains** and took to the highways. Cost and convenience often motivated them to stay at places other than the expensive **hotels** located in the center of town. Auto camp patrons, still enamored of the idea of being away from home, eventually desired a more comfortable setting that provided additional amenities, and in time the auto camp would be replaced by the motel.

Both privately operated and municipal auto camps sometimes euphemistically billed themselves as tourist parks, but originally most tended to be situated in cities, near downtown, in order to generate business for local merchants. The early days of the Depression witnessed an increase in the number of drifters stopping at auto camps, and many municipalities tried to keep out less affluent guests by charging fees. In time, private entrepreneurs took over most of the auto camp trade, seeing it as an attractive business opportunity, especially if located along the increasingly busy highway. Privatization also brought about competition, which in turn led to better facilities, and crude tent sites soon sported raised wooden platforms to keep the occupants dry in rain.

Many auto camps built cabins where tents once stood and offered varied levels of service: a basic cabin (or "cottage," as quaint advertisements sometimes called them) might offer one or two single beds, electricity (a bare bulb hanging by a cord), and access to public bathroom facilities for 50 cents (about $7.50 in contemporary dollars), whereas a deluxe cabin might provide larger beds, brand-name mattresses such as Simmons Beautyrest or Sealy, a chair and a lamp, and a private bathroom with sink, toilet, and tub or shower for $2.00 (about $29.50 in contemporary dollars). Most travelers rented for the night, but some opted for a week's vacation at one spot. Tourists swapped recommendations and would drive extra miles to stay at a particularly well-known facility or find a good deal.

Cottages and services in a typical auto camp. (Courtesy of the Library of Congress)

With a constant push for improved facilities and more auto camps opening, *Popular Mechanics*, a magazine with a large following among do-it-yourselfers, in the 1930s ran articles with instructions on how to build quality tourist cabins. Simple bungalow designs predominated, but log cabins, English Tudor, and colonial designs could also be found. Well-constructed cabins replaced ramshackle ones. Owners promoted such amenities as gasoline, meals, **ice cream**, maybe a pond or lake along with fishing tackle for rent, club houses, dance halls, and laundry rooms. Catchy names like "Kozy Kamp," "Para Dice," "Dew Drop Inn," "U Pop Inn," and "Tumble Inn" served as a popular marketing gimmick.

One of the greatest films of the Depression era, Frank Capra's **It Happened One Night** (1934), provides moviegoers unfamiliar with auto camps an opportunity to become acquainted with this mode of traveling. Filled with contemporary detail, the picture tells the story of a rugged reporter (Clark Gable; 1901–1960), a wealthy heiress (Claudette Colbert; 1903–1996), and how this unlikely couple travels Depression-era America by bus and by car. In one classic scene, they share a run-down auto camp that typifies what could have been found at that time.

As the 1930s progressed, many of the country's auto camps went out of business, replaced by more sophisticated lodging, or they themselves evolved into motor courts, the direct predecessor of the motel. Others became sites for a new kind of traveler, those pulling their own "cabins" (i.e., **trailers**) behind their cars.

See also Advertising; Architecture; Buses; Leisure & Recreation: Magazines; Movies; Screwball Comedies; Travel

SELECTED READING

Belasco, Warren James. *Americans on the Road: From Autocamp to Motel, 1910–1945.* Cambridge, MA: MIT Press, 1979.

Young, William H., with Nancy K. Young. *The 1930s: American Popular Culture through History.* Westport, CT: Greenwood Press, 2002.

AUTOMOBILES. In a survey conducted in the 1920s and repeated in the 1930s, Americans ranked the automobile as their preferred means for **travel**. They even declared ownership of a car to be more important than a home, telephone, electric lighting, or indoor plumbing. Prior to the stock market crash of October 1929, American automobile companies had experienced explosive growth as vehicle designs became standardized and closed bodies greatly improved passenger comfort whatever the weather. With these advances, the automobile, in addition to its use for general **transportation**, errands, or visiting relatives and friends, served as the means for a new kind of recreation, the Sunday drive, a time when the family went "out for a drive," strictly for the pleasure of being in the car. During the worse days of the Depression, families, as much as possible, continued to treat themselves to the joys of this new-found activity.

Improvements in automobile technology during the 1920s led to the manufacture of luxury cars, vehicles that functioned as status symbols, another reason for car ownership. Described as the largest, grandest, most beautiful, and elegant motorized vehicles ever built, luxury cars created a flurry of enthusiastic attention when presented at the Detroit, New York, and Chicago auto shows during the Roaring Twenties. The classic Duesenbergs, Cords, Pierce-Arrows, and Cadillacs contained countless innovations, such as Cord's front wheel drive and retractable headlights, and sold to the rich and famous who could afford a chassis price tag as high as $8,500 ($100,000 to $125,000 in contemporary dollars), plus the cost of a custom-made coach. Publicity for the cars came easily and photographers captured movie stars like Gary Cooper (1901–1961) with his Duesenberg or Ginger Rogers (1911–1995) and Tom Mix (1880–1940) with their Pierce-Arrows. Mix also owned a Cord 812, the car he was driving at breakneck speed when he had a fatal accident on an Arizona highway.

Following the onset of the Great Depression, more and more Americans, especially the noncelebrities, decided against assuming installment debt in order to replace a car that still ran well. Whenever possible, people held on to their automobiles, even if it meant removing the wheels and setting the car on blocks. During the grimmest years of the crisis, the purchase of used cars actually exceeded that of new ones. By mid-decade, 95 percent of all the automobiles sold cost under $750 ($11,000 in contemporary dollars).

Out of 60 American companies manufacturing a significant number of cars in 1930, only 18 remained in production at the end of the decade. Some of the best-known small firms closed—Essex in 1931, Reo and Franklin in 1934, Stutz in 1935, Durant Motors in 1936, and the Hupp Motor Car Company in 1940. Despite their glowing reputations for creating top-of-the-line vehicles, the financial effects of the Depression finally proved to be too much for the manufacturers of luxury cars. Cord and Duesenberg stopped production in 1937, followed by Pierce-Arrow in 1938. Only the term "doozie" remained, meaning something extraordinary or excellent. It possibly derived from the Duesenberg's nickname of "Duesy."

The three largest American automobile manufacturers—Ford, General Motors, and Chrysler—had supplied nearly 75 percent of the cars sold at the beginning of the 1930s; even this trio of giants experienced declining sales until 1933. During this turnaround year, all three shared in a sales increase of almost 500,000 cars over 1932, and by 1939 accounted for 90 percent of automobile sales. As the decade advanced, more and more Americans looked for vehicles that emphasized improved mechanical qualities, and the Big Three responded with synchromesh transmissions that allowed for smooth shifting, automatic chokes, adjustable seats, built-in trunks, defrosters, and hydraulic brakes. A car radio called Motorola first appeared during the late 1920s and played on the obvious connections between "motor" and mobility. It could be purchased from the Galvin Corporation as an extra for around $110 ($1,300 in contemporary dollars). Cadillac included a no-draft ventilation system in its 1933 models; individual front wheel suspension became a feature in 1934; and the first sunroofs and a gearshift on the steering column appeared in 1938.

Walter P. Chrysler (1875–1940), president of the Chrysler Corporation, in a daring move introduced the Airflow model in 1934. A combination of **Art Deco** and Streamlined **design**, it offered a roundly sloping hood, a swept-back windshield, chrome detailing, and headlights that appeared to blend in smoothly with the flow of the chassis. Chrysler counted on **Streamlining**, with its imagery of speed, as a marketing approach for the Airflow. Employing an almost unlimited **advertising** budget for its "car of the future," along with wide brand recognition, a relatively low sticker price, and a large chain of dealerships, the Airflows initially gained wide public attention. But consumer interest soon waned; many felt that beneath the showy exterior lurked an ordinary Chrysler with few real changes. The recession in 1937 further hindered commercial success, causing the company to withdraw its sleek, forward-looking car from production in order to concentrate on more traditional models.

But even with its failure, the Airflow had prepared consumers for the direction that automotive design would follow. During the last years of the decade, other manufacturers experimented with more modern treatments and, through heavy advertising, introduced each year's new model with an emphasis on improvements and sleek looks. Soon the American buyer began to accept the concept of "planned obsolescence"; the changes might consist of little more than cosmetic additions rendered in sheet metal, but the growing consumer market rushed to buy the newest models anyway.

The willingness to own and drive an automobile during the 1930s involved some challenges. Bricks and cobblestones, among the materials used for those city streets that might be described as paved, made for a rough ride no matter what the features of the car. Once on the approximately 500,000 miles of road that crisscrossed the country outside regular city limits, a driver encountered more obstacles and discomforts. Not just the absence of pavement, but narrow two-lane highways with unexpected turns and a lack of bridges created a certain degree of uncertainty. No multilane interstates existed, although an occasional three-lane road, considered quite modern, could be found.

Construction started on two significant roads in 1926—U.S. Route 66, from Chicago, Illinois, to Los Angeles, California, and U.S. Route 40, "the National Road," from Atlantic City, New Jersey, to Oakland, California. For most of the 1930s, however, they remained unpaved, bumpy, and messy during inclement weather. Truck drivers favored Route 66 because of its flat, straight stretches in the Southwest. Identified as the "Mother Road" by John Steinbeck (1902–1968) in his famous novel ***The Grapes of Wrath*** (1939), it served as the major pathway for migrant farmers uprooted by dust storms and soil erosion.

Thanks to President **Franklin D. Roosevelt** (1882–1945) and his **New Deal** programs, such as the **Civilian Conservation Corps** (CCC; 1933–1942) and the Works Progress Administration (WPA; 1935–1943; name changed to Work Projects Administration in 1939), portions of major routes improved and more and more roads got built. During his administration, the number of paved highways doubled, important bridges and tunnels were constructed, and scenic parkways and byways became a part of state and national parks.

Even with all their deficiencies, roads—old, new, under construction—served as a network that connected large population centers, allowing people to venture out in their cars for business and vacation travel, as well as the Sunday afternoon drive. One-half of American families owned a vehicle and gasoline turned out to be one of the few commodities to enjoy steady sales throughout the Depression years. Car ownership stood at over 20 million autos by 1935 and continued to rise steadily as did the number of miles traveled in motor vehicles, increasing from 201 billion in 1933 to 285 billion by 1939.

From the early days of the twentieth century, cities grew and residential building spread from the center of the city to its fringes, creating the American suburb in the process. Mass transportation for getting to and from work and for pleasure saw decreased usage as more families acquired cars. This in turn created the problem of what to do with the vehicle when not in use. The title of a popular comic strip of the era, *Gasoline Alley*, by Frank King (1883–1969), refers to a narrow lane that bisected many residential blocks of the time. People erected garages that fronted this alley, not the street; the conventional driveway beside a house remained a relatively unknown concept in crowded cities. The content of this gentle, good-natured series often focused on the activities of the alley: cars, their repair and performance, and general automotive lore.

During the 1920s and 1930s, *Gasoline Alley* ranked among the most popular newspaper **comic strips**. It found a large, receptive audience in a nation looking for stability. The quiet humor and warmth of its characters served as a welcome antidote to the fear and anxiety felt throughout the nation during the Depression. Nothing much exciting happened in its frames, but the occurrence of the timeless cycle of birth and life, marriage and family, young and old, while suburban, middle-class America tinkered with its cars reassured readers, and it clearly met their expectations.

As automobiles grew in popularity, business owners and city planners recognized a need to address the issue of parking in work and shopping areas. A 1933 survey conducted by the Kroger Grocery and Baking Company revealed that 80 percent of their customers used an automobile for shopping. That year, when the company opened a new store in Cincinnati, Ohio, it built a lot to accommodate 75 cars, the first such parking feature to surround a grocery store. In another innovative move related to the increased number of cars on urban streets, the city fathers of Oklahoma City, Oklahoma, in 1935 installed the first parking meters, the "Park-o-Meter." The devices provided orderly parking on certain streets and also raised income for the municipality. Other communities lost no time in adopting them, and the inescapable parking meter became a part of the American scene.

Once out of the garage and onto the open highway, whether for business, a short family trip, or extended vacation, the scarcity of amenities such as service stations, rest

Given the poor roads and lack of service stations during the 1930s, car repairs often had to be made with the tools at hand. (Courtesy of the Library of Congress)

rooms, lodging, and **restaurants** required careful planning. What with small gas tanks and low mileage per gallon of fuel, the average automobile had a cruising range of about 50 miles and required frequent stops for refilling. The best tires tended to be unreliable. In fact, well-equipped drivers always set forth with a spare or two plus a tire repair kit with glue and patches.

Enterprising merchants, ever mindful of business opportunities, accommodated increased traffic and its uncertainties by erecting **gas stations**, eateries, cabins, cottages, **motels**, and souvenir shops along the roadways. Along with new businesses, the placement of signs at a Texaco gasoline station, a Howard Johnson's Restaurant, or an Alamo Plaza Tourist Court announced the possibility of gas, **food**, and a comfortable night's sleep on a Sealy mattress. These signs turned the highway into a promenade displaying American efficiency and know-how.

Auto camps offered a place for tourists to park their cars and convert them into a quasi tent-cabin for the night. By opening the car doors and attaching an extended cover to the top of the vehicle, the traveler had a protected spot for cooking and eating before spending the night inside the car. **Movies**, a popular form of entertainment, soon could be enjoyed from the convenience of the automobile. The first drive-in theater, located in New Jersey, opened in 1933, followed by others across the country.

The first official organized stock car race took place in 1936 on a part packed sand, part paved, four-mile track in Daytona Beach, Florida. Legend has it that the roots of such racing originated with moonshiners on dusty dirt roads hauling illegal distilled corn whiskey; they raced in an attempt to get away from the police. Through the remaining years of the decade, the popularity of stock car competition grew under the leadership of William France Sr. (1909–1992), with the Daytona race continuing as its biggest event.

Over the years, as more and more Americans considered purchasing a new car, the automobile industry had the opportunity to display its wares at four world's fairs, Chicago in 1933, San Diego in 1935, and San Francisco and New York in 1939. The **Century of Progress Exhibition** in Chicago hosted the "dream cars" exhibit that included Cadillac's introduction of its V-16 limousine. In San Diego, the highly popular Ford Building designed by Walter Dorwin Teague (1883–1960), a famous industrial designer, contained a fountain resembling the Ford V-8 emblem. Teague also designed another successful exhibit for Ford, a winding, half-mile road called the "Road of Tomorrow," for the **New York World's Fair**. General Motors' "Progress on Parade" exhibit in San Francisco allowed crowds of interested visitors to try the new gearshifts and see exactly what happened when they turned the steering wheel with their own hands.

But perhaps the ultimate experience occurred at the New York World's Fair's Futurama exhibit, also sponsored by General Motors. Created by Norman Bel Geddes (1893–1958), another of the era's outstanding industrial designers, Futurama presented a scale model of America in 1960, complete with homes, urban complexes, bridges, dams, surrounding landscapes, and, most important, an advanced highway system that permitted sustained speeds of 100 miles per hour. The exhibit could be viewed from moving chairs with individual loudspeakers; visitors exited the building sporting a small blue and white pin containing the phrase "I Have Seen the Future."

Through both a depression and a recession, many American drivers kept their older cars in running condition. Nevertheless, the decade saw an increase in vehicle ownership. Advertising encouraged everyone to purchase the newest model and, for a brief period, offered consumers the opportunity to flirt with the idea of owning a luxury car. But for most, the realities of the decade left the sensible, reliable family car, be it old or new, as the dominant vehicle on America's roads.

See also Aviation; Buses; Fairs & Expositions; Grocery Stores & Supermarkets; Hotels; Leisure & Recreation; Prohibition & Repeal

SELECTED READING

Automobile Manufacturers Association. *Automobiles of America*. Detroit: Wayne State University Press, 1968.

Coffey, Frank, and Joseph Layden. *America on Wheels: The First 100 Years, 1896–1996*. Los Angeles: General Publishing Group, 1998.

Rae, John B. *The Road and the Car in American Life*. Cambridge, MA: MIT Press, 1971.

Sears, Stephen W. *The American Heritage History of the Automobile in America*. New York: American Heritage, 1977.

AVIATION. From the Wright Brothers' first flight at Kitty Hawk in 1903 to the horrors of the London blitz brought by Luftwaffe bombers in 1940, aviation held the attention of everyone through the first third of the twentieth century. People craned their necks when they heard a plane buzz high in the sky, whereas they ignored the rumble of a truck on a nearby highway. For many, the 1920s and 1930s can be called "the golden age of aviation." Despite the fascination, few Americans ever set foot in an airplane during the 1930s. Deemed unsafe, unnatural, inconvenient, and just too expensive, the development of commercial aviation languished. Not until long after World War II would the airline industry finally begin to draw in large numbers of passengers.

Many forces conspired to block the arrival of aviation as an everyday form of **travel** in the United States. Comfortable, welcoming facilities for passengers proved virtually nonexistent both on the ground and in the air. Only large urban airports boasted terminals equipped to handle crowds, and most airplanes, at least in the early years of the decade, can only be described as noisy and cramped. With these limitations, people viewed flying as something reserved for the adventuresome. **Train** travel offered luxury at modest prices, and **automobiles** and **buses** grew larger and more comfortable at the same time. Planes might fly higher and farther and faster than ever before, but the average citizen remained hesitant about boarding one.

The U.S. Postal Service unexpectedly emerged as an important booster of aviation. As early as 1917, postal authorities had allocated money to start an experimental airmail service, an activity that commenced in 1918. Walter F. Brown (1869–1961), postmaster general in 1929, moved the airmail project forward when he established three primary aerial routes for the country: a northern, central, and southern cross-country pattern. Although this division ostensibly came about to speed up mail service, it also led to the creation of several early airlines, since Brown identified who he wanted to perform this function. In 1931, four small carriers merged to become United Airlines and took on the northern route. Transcontinental & Western Airlines (later Trans World Airlines, or TWA) in 1930 flew the central portion, and for the southern tier several secondary operations joined forces as American Airlines. These moves generated considerable enthusiasm among business people, because most sensed that money stood to be made in the fledgling airline industry.

Other prominent domestic lines at this time included Delta Air Services (it changed to Delta Air Corporation in 1930, and later identified itself by its present-day Delta Air Lines) and Pitcairn Aviation, a small carrier founded in 1926. Pitcairn became known as Eastern Air Transport in 1929, and then took its better-known name of Eastern Air Lines in 1938. On the eve of the Great Depression, 44 airlines operated within the United States. The government's support of United, Transcontinental & Western, and American Airlines through its airmail service contracts made them the country's major carriers throughout the 1930s. In the process, three main hubs for air travel and transport evolved: New York, Chicago, and Los Angeles.

The airmail contracts covered only domestic routes, and some entrepreneurs hungrily eyed foreign markets. As the range that airplanes could fly increased, there remained little reason to limit commercial flight to the continental United States. American businessman Juan Trippe (1899–1981) in 1927 took over a struggling Florida-based carrier and proceeded to win an exclusive contract to carry mail between Key West and Cuba. Within a year, Trippe had landed two more foreign routes—one to Puerto Rico and the other to the Canal Zone, places that had heavy U.S. investments—and in so doing laid the foundation for Pan American World Airways (PAA).

Eager to procure additional routes, Trippe looked farther afield. At that time, Great Britain refused permission for commercial planes to land and refuel in Bermuda or

Newfoundland in order to limit competition with British airlines. Given fuel limitations, aircraft headed toward Europe had to refill their tanks in Newfoundland before
heading out over the sea. The restrictions effectively blocked American carriers from
establishing direct routes from the United States to Europe. Trippe therefore turned his
attention to the Pacific. He ordered several large seaplanes, or flying boats, that carried
sufficient fuel for extended flights. In 1935, PAA made the first transpacific airmail flight
from San Francisco to Manila, refueling in Hawaii, Midway Island, Wake Island, and
Guam. Before long, even longer-range aircraft would shrink the Pacific, and the vision
of opening up markets in Japan, the Philippines, and China held great promise.

Charles Lindbergh's epochal solo transatlantic flight in 1927 had effectively dispelled
the idea that airplanes could not cross great distances. His feat received an outpouring
of media attention, so much that it awakened the public to the growing possibilities of
flight. In the following year applications for pilots' licenses jumped from 1,800 to 5,000.
Although the oceans no longer seemed so vast and general optimism about flight ran
high, the occasional crash and the inevitable death continued to cause most Americans
to question the safety of commercial flying.

In 1929, and still flush from his solo success, Lindbergh agreed to lend the prestige of
his name to the young Transcontinental & Western Airline (TWA), and he and his
wife, Anne Morrow Lindbergh (1906–2001), made a record-breaking flight to Asia, a
flight she captured in her best-selling memoir *North to the Orient* (1935). The "Lone
Eagle" took to the air once again in 1933, working to create a North Atlantic route for
future airliners. His wife continued to chronicle their adventures, and in 1938 *Listen!
The Wind* further evoked their travels.

By any measure, however, passenger air travel during the 1930s cost a good deal of
money, although the airlines strove to keep prices competitive with first-class rail travel.
Those flying on business accounts and a handful of wealthy individuals made up the
bulk of people booking flights. A few went a step further and bought airplanes for private business and pleasure flying. But little changed for the average traveler; the airlines
had to compete for that tiny minority who did fly. In the meantime, both the airlines
and aircraft manufacturers strove to **design** and fly the safest, fastest, and most economical planes possible.

In the early 1930s, Transcontinental & Western Airlines approached the Douglas Aircraft Company about the possibility for an all-metal monoplane capable of carrying up to
12 passengers at a speed of 150 miles her hour. The company's answer, the DC-1, evolved
into the DC-2, and then into the justly famous **Douglas DC-3**. Its manufacture and subsequent success made commercial aviation a profitable business.

The Boeing Company, a direct competitor with Douglas, experimented with building
its own all-metal monoplane; their version, called the Boeing 247, made its debut in
1933. This craft carried 10 passengers and could fly on one engine, if necessary. Not as
large or fast as the rival DC-1, it faced a bleak future. Yet another company, Lockheed
Aircraft, introduced its L-10 Electra in 1934. Small in comparison to the Boeing or
Douglas models, it instead boasted a higher top speed than they, and it enjoyed lower
operating costs. For awhile, the Electra challenged the Douglas line.

In addition to concerns about speed and safety, service emerged as a factor in the competition for passengers. The pilot and copilot often could not assist with the frequent
cases of airsickness or fear, nor had they time to distribute **food** and **soft drinks**. Boeing

Air Transport, later to become part of United Airlines, in 1930 hired eight nurses known as "sky girls" to work as stewardesses in its fleet of airplanes. The idea had been presented to Boeing Air by Ellen Church (1904–1965), a registered nurse, and on May 15, 1930, she became the world's first stewardess, working a flight from San Francisco, California, to Chicago, Illinois. Not until 1933 did other airlines follow suit, but the once-novel idea of an attendant on board did in time catch on as an industry standard.

In those early days, stewardesses worked many jobs. They handled all the baggage, made sure interiors sparkled, and often helped in the fueling of the aircraft. When aloft, they prepared and served beverages and meals, and kept passengers and themselves as comfortable as they could in unheated, unair-conditioned, and unpressurized cabins. Toward the end of the decade, TWA equipped a number of its DC-3s with radios in the passenger cabin. It fell to the stewardess to find stations, keep them in tune, and find new ones as the plane passed out of range of the signal. Individual loudspeakers allowed patrons to listen or not, and also permitted the pilot to speak directly to the cabin, if need be.

In 1929, Bernt Balchen (1899–1973) became the first person to pilot an airplane over the South Pole; he continued to be a popular aviator for years afterward. (Courtesy of the Library of Congress)

While the airlines tried to please a few paying customers, a number of individuals brought additional publicity and color to the aviation industry, and some even occasionally made the headlines. Various prizes, most of them monetary, enticed daring pilots to attempt new feats. Wiley Post (1898–1935), a colorful Texan who wore a signature eye patch, the result of an accident, had spent a considerable portion of his life among pilots and airplanes. In 1931, he raced around the world in the *Winnie Mae*, a single-engine, high-wing Lockheed Vega monoplane that featured detachable landing gear. This device reduced drag and gave the craft increased speed and distance. Post, who made the lengthy journey with copilot Harold Gatty (1903–1957), telegraphed accounts of his journey to a news syndicate, and people lined up at newsstands to read the latest chapter in his flight. Post flew around the world in 8 days, 15 hours, and 51 minutes, a time that eclipsed the 1929 record of 21 days set by the *Graf Zeppelin*, the famous German airship.

Not satisfied, and bitten by fame, Post took off again in 1933, but this time he sat alone in the *Winnie Mae*. Battling fatigue and the elements, although he carried a radio direction finder and had an early autopilot, he beat his own record by over 21 hours, making him both the fastest pilot ever and the first to circumnavigate the globe solo. Two years later, flying an experimental airplane and this time again with a companion, the beloved humorist Will Rogers (1879–1935), Post suffered a crash near Point Barrow, Alaska. A tragedy, and a blow to aviation as well, the accident killed them both.

Despite the loss of Wiley Post, other equally colorful daredevils continued to challenge the skies during the 1930s. Roscoe Turner (1895–1970) won many racing trophies and set a number of records, such as a 1930 transcontinental speed mark, Los Angeles to New York in 15 hours, 37 minutes. Sporting a splendid moustache that flared to waxed spikes, Turner epitomized the image of a dashing aviator. He fashioned his own flying suit, a powder blue affair with exaggerated whipcord breeches, and traveled briefly with a pet lion cub, Gilmore. To the delight of the press, Turner had a custom parachute made for his mascot, and Gilmore usually sat up front in the cockpit.

Turner established much of his fame through aerial racing, a popular spectacle that flourished in the Depression era. Two events in particular garnered public attention, the National Air Races, also known as the Thompson Trophy races (which Turner won three times in the 1930s), and the Bendix Trophy flights (he won this event once). Both carried with them a mix of prestige and considerable danger to the pilots.

In the Thompson Trophy, a closed-course race that had its origins in 1929, small planes, both military and civilian, zoomed around a prearranged pattern that employed tall pylons as markers. The closer and faster a pilot could shave a pylon, the better the elapsed time. Competing for cash and recognition, the pilots pushed themselves and their airplanes to the limit. A number of fliers crashed and died, but such tragedy only whetted the audience's appetite for more.

Initiated in 1931, the Bendix Trophy involved a coast-to-coast cross-country flight. Elapsed time and total distance flown determined the winner. A challenging race, it drew the top aviators of the day, such as Jimmy Doolittle (1896–1992) of the army air corps, Howard Hughes (1905–1976), "Meteor Man" Frank Hawks (1897–1938), and Roscoe Turner.

Hughes, a movie director, inventor, and multimillionaire, designed his own craft for the race. His *Hughes Special* reached the almost unbelievable airspeed of 325 miles per hour in 1935. Two years later he sped across the country from Los Angeles to New York in 7 hours, 28 minutes and 25 seconds. Then in 1938, he set another record by completing a flight around the world in 3 days, 19 hours, and 14 minutes in a Lockheed 14, more than halving Wiley Post's 1933 record.

Aviatrix **Amelia Earhart** (1897–1937), famous as the first woman to fly solo across the Atlantic in 1932, planned a circumnavigation of the globe for 1937. In the last leg of her journey, her plane disappeared over the Pacific. Despite a massive search, no traces were ever discovered, making her disappearance one of most tantalizing mysteries of the 1930s.

Although Amelia Earhart captured the public imagination through much of the decade, other women also set records and garnered occasional headlines. Ruth Nichols (1901–1960), for example, established a new world altitude record for women, 28,743 feet, in 1931. Nichols thereby flew twice as high as an earlier mark of 14,000 feet, made in 1922 by none other than Amelia Earhart. Since at the time Nichols worked for Crescent Aircraft, her job allowed her to spend most of her time in competitions. She repaid the favor by breaking a number of women's speed and distance records. In 1939, Nichols founded Relief Wings, a civilian air ambulance service. The Civil Air Patrol (CAP) absorbed this project when the United States entered the Second World War in 1941.

The colorfulness and derring-do of these pilots spread, not unexpectedly, to the newspaper comic pages. Adventure series like *Barney Baxter in the Air* (1935–1950), drawn by Frank Miller (1898–1949), went for the **youth** market. The series involves an adolescent boy in all sorts of aerial adventures. With the approach of World War II, Barney pushes hard for military preparedness, and *Barney Baxter* became one of the first **comic strips** to suggest the inevitability of war and the importance of being ready.

Ace Drummond (1935–1940) likewise competed for space on the crowded funny pages. Purportedly drawn by Captain Eddie Rickenbacker (1890–1973), a renowned World War I flying ace, Clayton Knight (1891–1969) actually handled the chores of drawing and writing the series. Knight even included a small panel titled *Hall of Fame of the Air* where the exploits of real fliers could be celebrated. Noel Sickles' (1910–1982) *Scorchy Smith* (1930–1961) also did well, as did *Tailspin Tommy* (1928–1942), drawn by Hal Forrest (1892–1959) and written by Glenn Chaffin (1897–1978).

Probably the claim of being the most popular of all the flying strips, however, fell to *Smilin' Jack* (1933–1973), a long-lived mix of humor, romance, and adventure. The creation of Zack Mosley (1906–1993), its mustachioed hero might easily remind readers of Wiley Post or Roscoe Turner. A galaxy of women fliers also wanders in and out of the stories, so Amelia Earhart or Ruth Nichols might come to mind. Awkwardly drawn at best, the strip enthralled its readers with its meticulous attention to mechanical detail. The romance may have come directly from radio **soap operas**, but the airplanes and the exploits came from the headlines.

The comics had their aviation hits, but Hollywood, always alert to the public pulse, also celebrated flight. The 1930s saw the theatrical release of over 25 aviation-oriented commercial films. The decade opened with two World War I dramas, director Howard Hughes's *Hell's Angels* (1930) and Howard Hawks's (1896–1977) *The Dawn Patrol* (also 1930). This latter picture, starring Richard Barthelmess (1895–1963) and Douglas Fairbanks Jr. (1909–2000), proved so successful that the studios remade it in 1938 under the same title. The second version features Errol Flynn (1909–1959), Basil Rathbone (1892–1967), and David Niven (1910–1983), three of the top names in **movies** at the time These pictures indicated the direction the majority of future aviation pictures would take: war stories that allowed for lots of combat footage.

Forgotten titles like *Lucky Devils* (1932), *Sky Devils* (1932), *Airmail* (1932), *Wings in the Dark* (1935), *Devil Dogs of the Air* (1935), and *It's in the Air* (1935) brightened marquees during the early days of the Depression. Mostly potboilers, they did provide an exciting moment or two of flying. But a pair of exceptions also came along: **King Kong** (1933) and *Flying Down to Rio* (1933).

Few might think of *King Kong* as an aviation film, and they would be right. Its mix of horror, fantasy, and special effects makes it one of the memorable movies of the thirties. But the final sequence, with the giant ape perched atop the newly built **Empire State Building**, brushing off attacking army biplanes like annoying gnats, stands as one of those cinematic moments that has become an icon. The most advanced aerial weapons of the day prove virtually impotent against this primeval force. Their flashy acrobatics and speed signify little. Popular culture eagerly embraces technology with one hand, while with the other it regularly displays an accompanying undercurrent of distrust in too much reliance on science.

Ostensibly a musical, *Flying Down to Rio* likewise can hardly be remembered as a picture about the wonders of flying, but it happens to contain one of the great film flight sequences. In this delightful musical, the talents of dancers **Fred Astaire** (1899–1987) **and Ginger Rogers** (1911–1995) receive a cinematic showing for the first time. But even Astaire and Rogers take a backseat to a bevy of chorines as they kick their heels in unison while standing on the wings of a large airplane "flying down" to the famous Brazilian city. A triumph of camera effects, the scene makes absolutely no social or technological comments, but it does display the wonder and fun only movies can provide.

Most of the films for the remainder of the decade returned to more traditional aerial imagery. As the war clouds over Asia and Europe darkened perceptibly, American movies turned to thoughts of preparedness. Exceptions, however, occasionally showed up on theater screens. *Fly-Away Baby* (1937), part of an ongoing Warner Brothers series, chronicles the adventures of reporter Torchy Blane. Ably portrayed by Glenda Farrell (1904–1971), this particular episode has the intrepid newswoman taking to the air in order to catch some killers and get her story. The Torchy Blane movies, based on a pulp magazine series, totaled nine features and ran from 1936 until 1939.

Test Pilot (1938), a shared vehicle for superstars Spencer Tracy (1900–1967) and Clark Gable (1901–1960), portrays fliers (Gable) and mechanics (Tracy) who put experimental aircraft through their paces. The story includes footage about testing the military's then-new B-17 bomber and the importance attached to military superiority. In a similar vein, *Wings of the Navy* (1939) extols the training received by young recruits in the armed forces. By the late 1930s, any thoughts of neutrality were in the process of being conveniently forgotten by Hollywood, and the content of many action films reflects this loss of innocence.

The romance of flight also carried over to radio, especially the late afternoon **serials** aimed at children and adolescents. Typical of this genre would be *The Air Adventures of Jimmie Allen* (1933–1937). Although the broadcasts were limited primarily to the Midwest, the show met with unexpected success. The tale of a boy pilot, it featured a member's club, premiums, and occasionally even sponsored an air show. It enjoyed so many listeners that a largely forgotten movie, *Sky Parade* (1936) came out that featured an actor calling himself "Jimmie Allen" in the lead. *Captain Midnight* (1939–1949), *Jimmie Allen*'s successor, had the distinction of recruiting some 1 million youngsters to join the captain's flight patrol, for which they received membership cards and "secret decoders." Another aviation show, *Skyblazers* (1939–1940), played on Saturday evenings, and featured narration by Roscoe Turner, the famous pilot.

See also Airships; Automobiles; China Clippers; Horror & Fantasy Films; Newspapers; Pulp Magazines; Spectacle & Costume Drama Films; Transportation

SELECTED READING

The American Heritage History of Flight. New York: Simon & Schuster, 1962.

Corn, Joseph J. *The Winged Gospel: America's Romance with Aviation, 1900–1950*. New York: Oxford University Press, 1983.

Hudson, Kenneth. *Air Travel: A Social History*. Totowa, NJ: Rowman & Littlefield, 1972.

Young, William H., with Nancy K. Young. *The 1930s: American Popular Culture through History*. Westport, CT: Greenwood Press, 2002.

B

BASEBALL. The Depression had a serious, negative impact on professional baseball. Most of the major-league clubs, often family-owned, were undercapitalized. The New York Yankees, the Boston Red Sox, the Detroit Tigers, the Cincinnati Reds, and the Chicago Cubs, rich with private funds, stood as the exceptions. With the financial crisis and rising unemployment, many people could no longer afford to attend ball games. For the majority of teams, the strength of the reserve clause, a legally binding restriction that kept players with a team and salaries low, proved about the only thing that allowed baseball to stay afloat in the face of falling attendance throughout the decade. The game did not recover until after 1945 and the end of World War II.

On top of the economic problems facing baseball, the 1930s witnessed a changing of the guard, as older players retired and newer, younger ones stepped to the plate. The game lost its biggest, best-known star when Babe Ruth (1895–1948), "The Sultan of Swat," "The Bambino," quit actively playing in 1935. Ruth, who had first signed with the Red Sox from 1914 until 1919, commenced his glorious tenure with the Yankees in 1920. He remained with New York throughout the twenties and on into the 1930s. Age caught up with him, however, and he returned to Boston—but this time with the Braves—for the 1935 season, his final one. An era had ended, and everyone knew it.

Lou Gehrig (1903–1941), the "Iron Horse" of baseball and a teammate of Ruth's, retired in 1939. They batted back-to-back in the Yankees' feared "murderers' row" lineup—Ruth third, Gehrig fourth—from 1925 to 1934. He also played in 2,130 consecutive games, a remarkable record that remained unbroken for many years. But amyotrophic lateral sclerosis (ALS), a debilitating illness often called Lou Gehrig's disease, stopped him toward the end of the decade. He quit playing after a dismal opening of the 1939 season and died in 1941.

While the 1930s saw the Yankees lose two of their most memorable players, the team also gained a new sensation. In 1936 Joe DiMaggio (1914–1999) joined the house that Ruth built and shortly became known as "the Yankee Clipper" for his prowess both with a bat and as a fielder. Not yet the equal of Ruth or Gehrig during the late 1930s—his best years lay ahead of him—DiMaggio nonetheless appeared a fitting replacement for the two retiring greats.

In the National League, the happy-go-lucky St. Louis Cardinals of the 1930s enlivened games with their antics and won themselves the moniker "the Gas House Gang." The term had originated in the latter part of the nineteenth century after an infamous

An umpire makes a call at the plate during a baseball game. (Courtesy of the Library of Congress)

gang of thugs who congregated in the so-called gas house district of New York City, an area where tanks stored gas for lighting and heating. Hardly vicious, the Cardinals exhibited a rowdy, raucous sense of humor, and it endeared them to fans, serving as just the right antidote for the Depression blues. Led by the Dean brothers, Dizzy (born Jay Hannah Dean, 1910–1974) and Daffy (born Paul Dean, 1913–1981), a winning pitching duo, the team also included a host of other colorful Cardinals who collectively energized the Gas House Gang. The team won pennants in 1930, 1931, and 1934, and brought a sense of fun to baseball when it most needed it.

With racial segregation the rule in the 1930s, black players could not be hired by then-white teams. This injustice meant denying recognition to many fine and deserving players. For example, Satchel Paige (1906?–1982) began pitching in 1924 with the Mobile Tigers, a black semipro aggregation. He soon moved on to various professional teams in the Negro Leagues, compiling an extraordinary set of statistics. In 1933, he had a 31-4 record; he claimed he pitched 64 scoreless innings and had 21 straight wins, but accurate information remains notoriously hard to come by. He had maybe 100 no-hitters, and won over 2,000 games out of some 2,500 pitched. He probably worked for over 250 different black teams, including the Birmingham Black Barons, the Pittsburgh Crawfords, and the Kansas City Monarchs. He also barnstormed as an individual pitcher.

The record books do show that in 1948 Paige finally realized his dream of playing in the major leagues when he crossed the color bar and joined the Cleveland Indians at about age 42. He later put on a uniform and pitched a couple of innings for the Atlanta Braves to qualify for a pension in 1968, making him the oldest major leaguer in memory. Although much about Paige may be hearsay, he certainly played at his peak in the 1930s and most American baseball fans unfortunately knew nothing about him.

As the decade drew to a close, June 12, 1939, saw the National Baseball Museum and Hall of Fame open its doors in Cooperstown, New York. Legend has it that baseball supposedly began 100 years earlier in Cooperstown. The new museum initially enshrined 13 immortals, and remarkably 11 of them could be present for their inauguration.

Throughout its colorful history, American baseball has been cloaked in layers of imagery and myth. A case in point would involve lights and night play. For traditionalists, baseball has always been a "daylight game," with 3:00 P.M. as the proper starting time. The club owners, anxious to keep costs at an absolute minimum during the 1930s, fought any modernization, any new technology. Economics, however, also brought about some changes of heart. In 1935, the Cincinnati Reds, despite objections, installed lights and watched their attendance soar. Quickly, other teams either followed suit or made plans to change. In another move to boost attendance, 1933 witnessed the first major-league All-Star game. The American League won the contest, which included a home run by Babe Ruth. Staged in conjunction with Chicago's ongoing **Century of Progress Exposition** (1933–1934), its success made it an annual event.

Traditionally, **newspapers** or specialized journals covered baseball for fans, and the *Sporting News* ranked as the premier sports magazine of the 1930s. Founded in 1886, by the Depression era the *News* devoted most of its reporting to baseball and enjoyed a high level of respect. Newspapers emulated the *Sporting News*, thereby popularizing complete box scores and all the endless statistics and in-depth articles about players that have come to characterize baseball reporting. Following a custom initiated in the 1920s, newspapers sent their best sportswriters on the road, accompanying the home team as it played away games.

Both listeners and broadcasters discovered that **radio** could also be an effective way to cover ongoing events. A knowledgeable commentator could bring the game into people's homes. At first, however, owners and leagues opposed such broadcasting, arguing that it would keep away the crowds and thus reduce income, and newspapers and the *Sporting News* likewise tended to deride the practice. In a makeshift agreement, baseball's officialdom allowed two stations per community to broadcast games, but that modest figure soon grew. By 1938, 260 different stations carried live baseball broadcasts and radio had become an important part of promoting the game. By the later 1930s, sports ranked second only to **music** for consumption of radio time.

A generation of electronic reporters came to the fore, breathlessly broadcasting the play-by-play over the family Philco. Among those early sportscasters can be counted a young man named Ronald "Dutch" Reagan (1911–2004), who broadcast Chicago Cubs games for an Iowa station. He would later become an actor and then the fortieth president of the United States.

In actuality, much radio baseball in the 1930s could not be called "live"; it just seemed that way. Broadcasts might be re-created games, narratives done in studios, not at the ballparks. Technical limitations often forced sportscasters to be isolated behind studio microphones, reliant on telephones to bring them details of the unfolding contest. Their job entailed filling empty airtime, creating the illusion of constant action. A sportscaster mastered "chatter," the ability to keep listeners interested, and millions faithfully tuned in to hear descriptions of a runner sliding home or a "long, pop fly to center field . . . he's under it . . . ," and so on for nine innings.

Together, the sportswriters and broadcasters tended to create images of athletes that often exceeded their actual feats. Thus the era witnessed the rise of the sports celebrity and sports hero, or idol. The rigorous training and endless practice were forgotten, replaced by images of instant success and adulation for the lucky few. At the beginning of the decade, Babe Ruth served as the biggest star in major league ball. In 1930, he made $80,000 ($970,000 in contemporary dollars) as a Yankee—more than any other player, more, even, than President **Herbert Hoover** (1874–1964). Ruth epitomized the Horatio Alger story, going from rags to riches and achieving power. But, great as he was, the Sultan of Swat also epitomized something else, a product of publicity, a figure created by mass media and zealous press agents.

Some of the ways publicity created baseball heroes included bubblegum cards, an immensely popular form of recognition. Often, inside the wrapper, coupons good for baseball paraphernalia could be found. Manufacturers put out baseball-shaped radios, and listeners might hear such tunes as "Tigers on Parade" (1935; music and lyrics by J. Fred Lawton [active 1930s] and Will E. Dulmage [active 1930s]) and "I Can't Get to First Base with You" (1936; words and music by Fred Fisher [1875–1942]). Baseball-labeled cigars, along with enameled pins and pendants, proliferated, as did baseball-themed cartoons and games. Players willingly endorsed—for a fee—a variety of products: Wheaties and Grape-Nuts cereals, tobacco items, **soft drinks**, beer, gum, **candy**, and numerous other goods striving to make a profit from baseball.

This attitude carried over into several **movies**, but nothing of great merit. For whatever reason, baseball did not do well at the box office. Comedian Joe E. Brown (1892–1973) stars in *Fireman, Save My Child* (1932), *Elmer the Great* (1933) and *Alibi Ike* (1935); Spencer Tracy (1900–1967) plays on a prison team in 1930s *Up the River*; a mystery titled *Death on the Diamond* (1934) features a young Robert Young (1907–1998); and Rita Hayworth (1918–1973) has a bit part in *Girls Can Play* (1937), but baseball proved difficult for the silver screen during the 1930s.

See also Leisure & Recreation; Magazines; Race Relations & Stereotyping; Softball

SELECTED READING

Burk, Robert F. *Much More Than a Game: Players, Owners, & American Baseball since 1921.* Chapel Hill: University of North Carolina Press, 2001.

Coffin, Tristam Potter. *The Old Ball Game: Baseball in Folklore and Fiction.* New York: Herder and Herder, 1971.

Okrent, Daniel, and Harris Lewine, eds. *The Ultimate Baseball Book.* Boston, MA: Houghton Mifflin, 1979.

Seymour, Harold. *Baseball: The Golden Age.* New York: Oxford University Press, 1971.

White, G. Edward. *Creating the National Pastime: Baseball Transforms Itself, 1903–1955.* Princeton, NJ: Princeton University Press, 1996.

BASIE, COUNT. Born William Basie in Red Bank, New Jersey, in 1904, this piano player, organist, and popular orchestra leader initially studied with his mother and various area musicians. By the mid-1920s, Basie had gained a variety of experiences and knew firsthand about the hardships of working with traveling entertainment groups.

He persevered, however, and his career blossomed in the 1930s. By the time of his death in 1984 he had outlasted most of his contemporaries, remaining until the end in the first rank of successful, respected bandleaders.

In 1927, Basie found himself touring with a vaudeville troupe that received billing as "Gonzelle White's Big Jazz Jamboree." Whatever its merits, the act broke up in Kansas City, Missouri. After a few odd jobs, including playing organ in a theater to accompany silent **movies,** Basie in the summer of 1928 joined bassist Walter Page's (1900–1957) Blue Devils, a popular Kansas City band. The pianist had already heard Page's group, and its style impressed him tremendously, especially its fluid rhythm and dedication to the blues.

Basie left Page in early 1929 and played in some of the innumerable nightclubs that dotted Kansas City, a fact that gave the city a reputation for lawlessness but also made it a mecca for musicians. Basie wanted to become a member of Bennie Moten's (1894–1935) Kansas City Orchestra, a well-known Midwestern group. Since Moten himself played piano, Basie had to sell the leader on his other talents, and he finally got himself hired as an arranger in the summer of 1929. His charts emphasized blues-based tunes and featured an infectious, pulsating rhythm, something that became the trademark of later Basie bands.

Within a short time, Basie's skill with the piano caused Moten to make him the band's primary pianist, a position he would hold for the next four years. At the same time, Moten began systematically hiring members of the Blue Devils, a situation that persisted until Walter Page broke up his own band and joined the aggregation in the early 1930s. A series of personnel changes and financial ups and downs caused Basie to briefly leave Moten in the 1933–1934 period; he formed the Cherry Blossom Orchestra (named after the club in which it played). The nucleus of Basie's future bands could be discovered within the Cherry Blossom Orchestra's ranks, but the group dissolved and Basie returned to a reconstituted Moten ensemble.

Fate intervened when Moten unexpectedly died in 1935, bringing about another reorganization. Basie gathered some of the best players from the band and created an aggregation he called the Barons of Rhythm. The name did not stick, but in the meantime the new band landed a long-term contract with the Reno, a Kansas City nightclub. Thanks to a local **radio** station and a high-powered, experimental one, this new Basie orchestra did late-night broadcasts from the Reno, and John Hammond (1910–1987), a young jazz critic who also doubled as a record company talent scout, caught them, hundreds of miles away, on his car radio. He liked what he heard and immediately decided to find out more about this swinging group.

While Hammond pursued his investigations, an admiring radio announcer bestowed on Basie the royal title of "Count"; he would retain the nickname for the remainder of his long career. In early 1936, Hammond got in touch with Basie and urged him and his band to come east for better exposure. After finishing their run at the Reno, the musicians set out for New York City, stopping first in Chicago. An instant hit with Windy City audiences, they optimistically continued their trek eastward, interrupting it with one-night stands, They finally opened at the Roseland Ballroom to enthusiastic reviews in December 1936.

John Hammond saw his expectations fulfilled when Decca Records, a major label, signed the Basie band to a recording contract. They cut their first sides in early 1937 and thereafter came to be considered a significant part of the growing **swing** scene, not just at the regional level but nationally. The Columbia Broadcasting System (CBS radio) put them on the air, and at the end of the decade Basie and his musicians moved to Columbia Records, another important label for **jazz** and swing artists.

As the band's star rose, Basie attracted some of the best jazz instrumentalists of the day. The rhythm section, considered one of the steadiest in the annals of swing, featured Jo Jones (1911–1985) on drums, Walter Page on bass, Freddie Green (1911–1987) on rhythm guitar, and of course, Basie himself on piano. Its light, airy, but insistent beat kept dancers on the floor and listeners happy. Many of the arranging chores fell to the skillful Eddie Durham (1906–1987). In addition, with the likes of Lester Young (1909–1959; nicknamed "Prez") on tenor saxophone, Dicky Wells (1909–1985) on trombone, and Buck Clayton (1911–1991) on trumpet, along with vocalists Jimmy Rushing (1903–1972), Helen Humes (1913–1981), and Billie Holiday (1915–1959; nicknamed "Lady Day"—the band was full of royalty), the Basie orchestra's lineup made for one of the most jazz-inflected ensembles of the 1930s.

"One O'Clock Jump" (1937; **music** by Count Basie), the band's up-tempo theme, typified its hard-swinging Kansas City style. Since Basie, once a sideman himself, knew all his musicians personally, a friendly atmosphere permeated their performances. Hard-driving, but with a simultaneous air of relaxation, the Count Basie Orchestra personified swing. Boasting the best timekeeping machine in the business, the band easily moved from hit to hit with swing selections like "John's Idea" (1937; music by Eddie Durham; the title refers to John Hammond and what he did for the band), "Every Tub" (1938; music by Count Basie and Eddie Durham), "Jumpin' at the Woodside" (1938; music by Count Basie), and blues like "Sent for You Yesterday" (1938; music and lyrics by Eddie Durham and Jimmy Rushing), and the Basie orchestra quickly climbed to the top in popularity. Unlike many black bands of the day, the Basie aggregation found itself welcome at white venues, and black audiences likewise flocked to the band's performances where they could. Wherever Count Basie played, the welcome mat came out, and people settled back for a session of swinging music.

See also Radio Networks; Race Relations & Stereotyping; Recordings

SELECTED READING
Dance, Stanley. *The World of Count Basie*. New York: Charles Scribner's Sons, 1980.
Simon, George T. *The Big Bands*. New York: Macmillan, 1967.
Yanow, Scott. *Swing*. San Francisco: Miller Freeman Books, 2000.

BASKETBALL. As with **football** during the 1930s, people enjoyed basketball primarily as a collegiate sport. The first big college tournament occurred in 1934 at New York City's Madison Square Garden. More than 16,000 fans attended the event, enough to warrant its continuation. By 1938, the gathering had been christened the National Invitational Tournament (NIT) and had become firmly established in American sports culture.

For professional play, sparse crowds and racial segregation ruled the day. White players could join one of two competing groups, the American Basketball League (ABA), reestablished in 1933 after folding in the 1920s, and the National Basketball League

A coach gives pointers to a boys basketball team. (Courtesy of the Library of Congress)

(NBA), formed in 1937. Black players did not have the luxury of league play; they had to rely on pickup games with other teams. The New York Rens, active in the 1920s and lasting until 1948, typified a black team: they not only had to find games but also had to battle unfair referees, deliberately rough play, and boorish fans. Despite such disadvantages, the Rens played spectacular basketball, rolling over most opponents.

The Harlem Globetrotters, another black team, also rose to prominence during the 1930s. Initially organized and coached by Abe Saperstein (1901–1966) in 1927 as the Savoy Big Five, contractual disagreements led to the creation of a new team bearing the name the New York Globetrotters. Somewhere along the way, New York changed to Harlem. Regardless of what people called them, Saperstein envisioned his players as a conventional basketball team, but they proved so skillful and superior to anyone willing to face them that bookings were hard to come by. In order to keep audiences happy, and to attract more people to their performances, Saperstein added comedy and trick ball handling. He had unknowingly discovered the secret of longevity for his Globetrotters. Playing any teams that would join them on the court, the Harlem Globetrotters continued to demolish virtually all their opponents; at the same time they put on a show that has continued to entertain generations of fans.

Black teams or white, these early professional basketball pioneers traveled to wherever a paying game could be found, sometimes appearing as many as 150 times in a season. Only a few stars emerged during these formative years, and the sport struggled mightily to survive. After lengthy discussions, the two white leagues merged to form the National Basketball Association (NBA) in 1949.

The basketball played in the 1930s usually consisted of slow, defensive tactics, which resulted in far fewer baskets than contemporary fans expect. Scores of 18–14 or 21–15 might be the final tallies for an entire game. In an attempt to speed things up and lure more spectators, the leagues adopted the 10-second rule in 1932, meaning that the ball had to be in play and shots attempted quickly. Even with the new regulation, each time a player scored, the ball would then be returned to center court and the teams reassembled for a new tip-off. Officials abolished that cumbersome rule for the 1937–1938 season, speeding up the game and increasing scores.

Angelo "Hank" Luisetti (1916–2002) of Stanford University emerged as one of the first real stars of basketball, either collegiate or professional. He scored 1,300 points for Stanford between 1936 and 1939, plus he perfected the one-handed jump shot. Until then, players attempted virtually all shots with a two-handed approach. His popularity earned him top billing in a 1938 movie called *Campus Confessions*. Hardly a lurid tale, despite its title, promoters billed it as "a peppy college romance [with] a real basketball game!"

As a final note, most players in the pre–World War II era stood under six feet in height. Anyone over six feet most coaches saw as awkward and uncoordinated, whereas they believed a shorter person possessed greater speed and superior ball-handling abilities. Not until the 1950s would tall players change the entire game of basketball.

See also Movies; Race Relations & Stereotyping

SELECTED READING

Grimsley, Will, ed. *A Century of Sports by the Associated Press Sports Staff*. New York: Associated Press, 1971.

Rader, Benjamin G. *American Sports: From the Age of Folk Games to the Age of Televised Sports*. 3rd ed. Englewood Cliffs, NJ: Prentice-Hall, 1996.

BENTON, THOMAS HART. Born in the rural community of Neosho, Missouri, Thomas Hart Benton (1889–1975) grew to be one of the most influential American artists of the 1930s. Since his father served in the U.S. House of Representatives from 1897 to 1905, young Thomas studied at Washington's Corcoran Gallery of Art. In 1908 and still in his teens, Benton moved to Paris, France, returning to Neosho in 1911. During these years, he met many artists and displayed an interest in a number of modernist movements.

After a short stay in Missouri, Benton traveled to New York City where he continued to associate with avant-garde painters, and some of this exposure appears in his early work. In 1918–1919, he served with the U.S. Navy as a draftsman and began exhibiting in New York galleries. Following World War I, he commenced work on a monumental series of murals he called *American Historical Epic*. It consisted of 10 panels, although he had initially envisioned it with 60. The project did not reach completion until 1926. This realistic, historical mural marked a significant change in his style and ran counter to his early career, when he had presented himself as a European-influenced modernist. A brief flirtation with Marxism in the 1920s also had little impact, but his readings in American history did, and *American Historical Epic* shows that Benton had decided on a thematic direction for his artistic life: a continuing explication of American subjects through painting.

Benton emerged as an artist imbued with feelings about the goodness and strength of everyday people. He became convinced that the common man possessed an inherent energy that could best be presented through art. He often tried to present himself as a "man of the people," deliberately striking anti-intellectual poses that often clashed with the attitudes of his colleagues in the art world.

The completion of *American Historical Epic* urged Benton, along with many other American painters of the era, forward in the creation of public murals. In 1930, he did a series of eight large-scale paintings for the New School for Social Research in New York City. Titled *America Today*, they depict average Americans engaged in a variety of activities, and Benton made no attempt to glamorize his figures or place them in heroic attitudes as had been the fashion.

The Whitney Museum of American Art in New York City had its founding in 1931. In the midst of the Depression, the new institution celebrated American art and artists, and Thomas Hart Benton in 1932 created a five-panel mural for the museum, *The Arts of Life in America*. Today the mural may be found in the New Britain Museum of American Art in Connecticut. Democratic in tone, the panels argue that art should not be restricted to an elite group or hidden in museums. To reinforce this idea, he incorporated popular figures from newspaper **comic strips** and cartoons and did not restrict himself to images taken from "high art."

Benton maintained his interest in murals by undertaking *The Social History of the State of Indiana* in 1933. Intended for display at the Indiana Pavilion at Chicago's **Century of Progress Exposition** (1933–1934), this 22-panel work focused on everyday life. He filled his pictures with common people at ordinary pursuits instead of the more traditional political and military leaders from textbooks.

In light of the attention these various large-scale efforts attracted, in December 1934, *Time* magazine selected Benton for one of its weekly covers. The editors ran a wide-ranging feature on contemporary American art, with special emphasis on **Regionalism**, a movement then gaining adherents across the country. In interviews, Benton took the opportunity to lambaste much of the then-current artistic community and claimed that Regionalism superseded any modernist movements.

Increasingly taken with American history, Benton in 1935 moved permanently to Kansas City, Missouri. The success of his Indiana murals led to a similar set, *The Social History of the State of Missouri*, unveiled in 1936. Once more, his cast of characters consisted of numerous surprises—Huckleberry Finn, Frankie and Johnny from the folk ballad, and Jesse James (1847–1882)—but their inclusion fit well with Benton's populist leanings. At the same time, politicians and business leaders received short shrift from the artist, both in this mural and other works. More often than not, he showed them taking bribes or attempting dishonest deals to fatten their wallets, as in *Preparing the Bill*, executed in 1934.

Never one to avoid public pronouncements about his or others' work, Benton soon served as the self-appointed spokesman for the Regionalist movement. At times, his pleas for greater recognition and acceptance of his staunchly Americanist view of art sank into polemics, a strident voice that lacked diplomacy. He demanded a "manly," representational art, free of the false affectations and European influences he saw in modernism. In

1937, he published *An Artist in America*, a somewhat self-serving defense of his artistic credo, but also a spirited defense of Regionalism. His outspoken approach, although it soon grew tiresome, played well to unsophisticated audiences, particularly those unfamiliar with artistic trends since the turn of the century.

Despite his tendency to pontificate and exaggerate, Benton enjoyed considerable popular acclaim, and his willingness to speak out made him more visible than most of his counterparts. He freely used allegories (*Persephone*, 1938; *Susannah and the Elders*, 1938), along with the tales (*Huck Finn*, 1936) and legends (*The Ballad of the Jealous Lover of Lone Green Valley*, 1934) of heartland America as his inspiration. His writhing, elongated figures, as in *Romance* (1932), with all their serpentine contours, became his trademark, along with unique perspectives, and he formularized these elements into his compositions. Among his contemporaries, Benton clearly stood out as the most colorful, and his visibility helped immeasurably to make people aware of the Regionalist approach to art.

As his fame grew, Benton fashioned a succession of paintings that focused on the land itself. His common people remained in the pictures, but his brush sought out details about crops and various plants and trees (*Butterfly Chaser*, 1932). He painted rich landscapes, as in *Cradling Wheat* (1938) and *Threshing Wheat* (1939), and most involved rural themes, which put him more in step with the other Regionalists. Thomas Hart Benton had not necessarily mellowed, but his emphases evolved with his age. The fecundity of the earth became a theme, and he took care to make it a strong image in his painting, often placing his once-dominant figures more in the background.

Benton remained active until his death in 1975. Murals, historical paintings, and numerous other works continued to come from his studio. As he aged, the exhibitions and the honors bestowed on him never ceased. Perhaps no artist before or since has taken so seriously the myths and legends that help constitute American history.

See also Federal Art Project; Newspapers; Social Realism; Grant Wood

SELECTED READING

Adam, Henry. *Thomas Hart Benton: An American Original*. New York: Alfred A. Knopf, 1989.

Baigell, Matthew. *Thomas Hart Benton*. New York: Harry N. Abrams, 1975.

BERLIN, IRVING. Born Israel Baline in Siberia, Irving Berlin (1888–1989) and his family immigrated to the United States in 1892 and settled in New York City. He quickly familiarized himself with his new country, and first made his mark on the American theatrical scene in 1908. He contributed a long-forgotten song, "She Was a Dear Little Girl," to an equally long-forgotten show, *The Boys and Betty*. It established Berlin as an up-and-coming young composer on both Broadway and Tin Pan Alley. The latter phrase identifies a section of Manhattan's 28th Street between Fifth Avenue and Broadway where **songwriters and lyricists** congregated and interacted with various **music** publishers; it came to mean the popular music business in general.

After the advent of sound **movies** in 1927, Berlin turned to creating themes and interpolated songs for film scores, adding them to his expanding universe of show tunes and individual melodies. Unable to read music—an arranger would transcribe his ideas—Berlin had, by the 1930s, composed hundreds of songs, and he ran his own music publishing house.

During the decade, Berlin contributed the music for several Broadway shows. In 1932, he collaborated with playwright and librettist Moss Hart (1904–1961) to create *Face the Music*, a musical revue. Since the Great Depression had by that time begun to affect large numbers of people, one song stands out: "Let's Have Another Cup o' Coffee." A carefree little tune, it reflected the attitude expressed by many toward the crisis: in tough times, have another cup of coffee and wait things out. It quickly established itself as a Depression hit, suggesting the resiliency of Americans in trying times.

A year later came *As Thousands Cheer*, another collaboration with Moss Hart. The play's structure mimics a daily newspaper, with headlines, such as "Lonely Hearts Column" or "Heat Wave Hits New York," introducing different sections of the revue. The play satirizes real people, such as **Herbert Hoover** (1874–1964), **Franklin D. Roosevelt** (1882–1945), and John D. Rockefeller (1839–1937). A trenchant, topical musical, *As Thousands Cheer* ran for 400 performances, suggesting that sophisticated Broadway audiences could laugh at the difficult times, if only for a few hours in a theater.

Topicality aside, the play featured several musical numbers that have come down to the present as standards, the kind of popular music that transcends time and place and gets to be known for itself. "Easter Parade" a melody Berlin had written back in 1917 and called "Smile and Show Your Dimple" fits this category. Recycled with new lyrics for *As Thousands Cheer*, it enjoyed great popularity and has become a part of American musical history.

In that same play, Ethel Waters (1896–1967) performed a show-stopping "Heat Wave," another of his compositions. A star in her own right, Waters' exuberant rendition gave Berlin one more hit in his growing collection. After the success of *As Thousands Cheer*, the composer turned his sights once more toward Hollywood. Not until 1940 and the opening of *Louisiana Purchase* would he return to Broadway.

Already established on the West Coast, Berlin experienced few problems in 1934 when he commenced writing songs for the movie medium once more. In 1928, he and James Gleason (1882–1959) had worked on a minstrel play titled *Mr. Bones*. Two years later, the show had its movie incarnation as *Mammy* (1930). It stars Al Jolson (1886–1950), then still riding on the publicity generated by his speaking role in *The Jazz Singer* (1927). Berlin's compositions include "Across the Breakfast Table," "Here We Are," and "To My Mammy." His variations on "Mammy" songs, with all their stereotypical images, may make contemporary audiences squirm, but they must be understood in the context of their times. The minstrel tradition died hard in American musical culture.

That same year saw *Puttin' on the Ritz*, another piece he did with James Gleason. This film contains, in the title song, one of Berlin's best-known compositions. Harry Richman (1895–1972), a popular song-and-dance man, sang "Puttin' on the Ritz" in the film and he considered it "his." But when the incomparable Fred Astaire (1899–1987) performed the same song some years later in the movie *Blue Skies* (1946), audiences promptly forgot Richman. "Puttin' on the Ritz" had a new owner, and Astaire has been associated with the number ever since.

In 1931's *Reaching for the Moon*, crooner **Bing Crosby** (1903–1977) gets to sing Berlin's "When the Folks High-Up Do the Mean Low-Down," a sprightly little number that showcases Crosby's ability to handle up-tempo songs. The movie also marks the beginning of the two men's long association. Years later, Crosby, a major star by then, would introduce Berlin's classic "White Christmas" in the film *Holiday Inn* (1942). His version for many years held the distinction of being the biggest-selling single record in history.

Upon his 1934 return to Hollywood from Broadway, Berlin proceeded to amaze everyone in the music business by writing some of the greatest songs of his already illustrious career. He began the cycle with *Top Hat* (1935), the fourth pairing of the immensely popular **Fred Astaire and Ginger Rogers** (1911–1995). Audiences got to hear "Top Hat, White Tie, and Tails," "Cheek to Cheek," "No Strings," "Isn't This a Lovely Day?" and "The Piccolino."

In almost no time at all his music could be heard in *Follow the Fleet* (1936), the fifth Astaire/Rogers vehicle. In this film, Berlin crafted "I'm Putting All My Eggs in One Basket," "Let's Face the Music and Dance," "Let Yourself Go," and "I'd Rather Lead a Band."

Riding on the crest of popularity generated by those two films, Berlin stayed at the top with 1937's *On the Avenue*, a musical featuring Dick Powell (1904–1963) and Alice Faye (1915–1998). Its soundtrack contains two particular gems, "I've Got My Love to Keep Me Warm" and "This Year's Kisses"

Berlin resumed his association with Fred Astaire and Ginger Rogers for the third time with *Carefree* (1938), a picture that gave audiences "Change Partners," "Carefree," "Since They Turned Loch Lomond into Swing," and the humorous "Yam." The composer said Astaire was one of his favorite vocalists, an assertion that bore tribute to Berlin's own skills and Astaire's impeccable taste. *Carefree* marked the last of the Astaire/Rogers films Berlin would score, although two more would be produced without him, *The Story of Vernon and Irene Castle* (1939) and *The Barkleys of Broadway* (1949). Berlin's three contributions to the series have been rated as almost flawless models of the 1930s Hollywood musical.

Alexander's Ragtime Band came out in 1938, and it serves as a pastiche of older Berlin favorites, like "Blue Skies," "Easter Parade," and the title song. Old wine in new bottles, the movie offers nothing new, instead capitalizing on the songwriter's considerable fame. Berlin's final film for the decade, *Second Fiddle* (1939), features Norwegian ice skater Sonja Henie (1912–1969), a popular star of the day. Proving he could adapt to any script's needs, Berlin contributed "Dancing Back to Back" (which might bear comparison to his more famous "Cheek to Cheek") and "When Winter Comes."

The song "God Bless America" (1918) lies outside the composer's Broadway and film music. He wrote this ode to patriotism for a World War I production called *Yip Yip Yaphank*. Deciding it did not fit the play, he kept the tune in a trunk with other scores. It reappeared as the shadows of World War II began to stretch across the nation. In the recorded version sung by **radio** star **Kate Smith** (1907–1986), "God Bless America" became a virtual second national anthem and has retained that honored status down to the present.

One of a handful of composers/songwriters to escape anonymity, Irving Berlin achieved a certain celebrity with the general public. Given his extraordinarily long life, Berlin wrote for most of the twentieth century; he composed over 1,000 songs, hundreds of which went on to become hits, and many of those are now considered standards. He personified Tin Pan Alley, a songwriter who could work in virtually any format.

See also Coffee & Tea; Ice Skating & Hockey; Musicals; Newspapers; Olympic Games; Race Relations & Stereotyping; Stage Productions

SELECTED READING
Bergreen, Lawrence. *As Thousands Cheer: The Life of Irving Berlin.* New York: Viking-Penguin, 1990.
Block, Geoffrey. *Enchanted Evenings: The Broadway Musical from* Show Boat *to Sondheim.* New York: Oxford University Press, 1997.
Zinsser, William. *Easy to Remember: The Great American Songwriters and Their Songs.* Jaffrey, NH: David R. Godine, 2000.

BEST SELLERS (BOOKS). First used in the late nineteenth century, the term "best seller" (dictionaries do not agree on the spelling of this term, allowing *best seller*, *bestseller*, and *best-seller*, with no overwhelming favorite) applies to any new book that sells briskly shortly after its initial appearance. Technically, it should not be used for books that continue to have strong sales long after their first publication, such as the Bible or plays by Shakespeare. Classics, like some of the works of Nathaniel Hawthorne (*The Scarlet Letter*, 1850), Herman Melville (*Moby-Dick*, 1851), or Mark Twain (*Adventures of Huckleberry Finn*, 1884), for example, do not fall under this rubric; their continuing large sales derive from required reading at schools and colleges, as well as interested readers. The term applies to both hardcover and paperbound books, although many lists separate the two. Qualifications aside, the 1930s certainly did not lack for best sellers.

Many question the whole concept of best sellers, couching their argument in terms of quality versus quantity. Those who disparage best sellers say they reward mediocrity and big sales, thus giving a distorted picture of what the public prefers to read. A large percentage of best sellers also can be considered ephemeral; they burst upon the scene, attract momentary attention, and then disappear. But, when a best seller reaches countless people, if only briefly, it may cause some of them, who otherwise might not, to read. Pro or con, best sellers reap huge profits for their publishers and thereby sustain the book industry.

The listings below attempt to give a sense, year by year, of shifting literary tastes in the United States during the 1930s. The selections have been compiled from several sources and present a highly condensed view of reading choices, focusing only on those books that ranked in the top 10 (selling over x-number of copies; the actual figures vary from year to year) for any given year. Since paperback reprints had just begun to make serious inroads on hardcover publishing at the end of the decade, the books listed below should be thought of as hardcover editions. Wherever possible, cinematic adaptations have been noted. Books frequently spur the film industry, and **movies** derived from famous books often lead people back to the written source.

A number of titles that have survived the 1930s and are now considered important for an understanding of the decade will not be found; they failed to sell in sufficient quantities to receive the "best seller" accolade. Their omission points out just how arbitrary such categories can be. For example, the absence of William Faulkner's (1897–1962) *Light in August* (published in 1932), F. Scott Fitzgerald's (1896–1940) *Tender Is the Night* (published in 1933), John O'Hara's (1905–1970) *Appointment in Samarra* (published in

Pearl Buck (1892–1973), author of *The Good Earth* (1931). (Courtesy of the Library of Congress)

1934), John Dos Passos' (1896–1970) complete trilogy *USA* (published in 1937), and Richard Wright's (1908–1960) *Native Son* (published in 1940) hardly lessens their importance. The inclusion of works like *Cimarron* (1930), *Anthony Adverse* (1933 and 1934), and *Green Light* (1935) makes no claim for greatness or longevity, just that they generated sufficient sales to rank first for their respective year (or years) on the best seller lists.

Fiction Best Sellers, 1930–1940.

1930: No. 1: *Cimarron*, Edna Ferber (1885–1968). Adapted for film in 1931; redone in 1960. A sprawling novel about the Oklahoma land rush, its popularity demanded an equally big movie, and Hollywood complied; the filmed version won Best Picture for the 1931 Academy Awards, the first Western to win that honor.

On the other hand, who recalls *Exile*, by Warwick Deeping (1877–1950), the no. 2 book for the year? Deeping had been a yearly visitor to the lists during the later 1920s, but given the ephemeral quality of so many best sellers, he is all but forgotten today.

1931: No. 1: *The Good Earth*, Pearl S. Buck (1892–1973). Adapted for film in 1937. The success, both critical and popular, of *The Good Earth* led to the Nobel Prize in Literature (1938) for Buck, the first American woman so recognized.

The no. 2 book for 1931 was *Shadows on the Rock*, by Willa Cather (1873–1947), another important American author. Perhaps better known for such classics as *My Antonia* (1918) and *Death Comes for the Archbishop* (1927), *Shadows on the Rock* finally brought her the popular and commercial recognition missing in her earlier career.

1932: No. 1: *The Good Earth* (see 1931). American readers clearly liked Buck's tale of a Chinese family, and its escapist setting in what most saw as an "exotic land" provided a welcome escape from the harsh realities of the Depression at home.

Another forgotten title, *The Fountain*, by Charles Morgan (1894–1958) took second place for the year. A study of English attitudes during World War I, it also had a film version in 1934, which, from all reports, proved equally forgettable.

Pearl S. Buck, riding on the success of *The Good Earth*, could claim third place honors with a lesser known novel, *Sons*, the second part of her trilogy about Chinese family life (the final volume, *A House Divided*, came out in 1935 and did not reach the best-seller lists).

1933: No. 1: *Anthony Adverse*, by Hervey Allen (1889–1949). Adapted for film in 1936. A historical novel of lavish proportions (over 1,200 pages), hundreds of characters, a $3.00 cover price—expensive by Depression standards; it would cost roughly $45.00 in contemporary dollars. Price proved secondary, and *Anthony Adverse* swept away the competition. Its phenomenal sales doubtless kept many a struggling bookseller in business during those dark days. A vast coming-of-age tale, its titular hero wanders the world, encountering adventure at every turn, and entranced readers turning its endless pages.

God's Little Acre, a steamy 1933 novel by **Erskine Caldwell** (1903–1987) originally came out in hardcover the same year as *Anthony Adverse*. It enjoyed respectable sales, but nothing spectacular. Not until the 1940s did cheap paperback editions become widely available; at that point, the book (and countless others by a variety of writers) sold in the millions. Today, *God's Little Acre* ranks among the all-time American best sellers—with cumulative sales much greater than those for *Anthony Adverse*—but not until 15 years after its initial publication did those large sales begin. A similar history can be given for a number of titles issued prior to the paperback revolution of the 1940s and thereafter.

Gladys Hasty Carroll's (1904–1999) *As the Earth Turns* came in a distant second for 1933, although it did garner a 1934 film adaptation. A story of life in rural Maine, its bleakness could not hold a candle to the rousing excitement of *Anthony Adverse*.

1934: No. 1: *Anthony Adverse* (see 1933). Continuing its hold on readers everywhere, not until Margaret Mitchell's (1900–1949) **Gone with the Wind** came along in 1936 did another book challenge its unparalleled popularity.

A long-forgotten tale of romance, *Lamb in His Bosom*, by Caroline Miller (1903–1992), enjoyed sufficient sales to place second. Margaret Mitchell claimed *Lamb in His Bosom*, a story of the old South, was her favorite novel.

1935: No. 1: *Green Light*, Lloyd C. Douglas (1877–1951). Adapted for film in 1937. Almost a breather between *Anthony Adverse* and the forthcoming *Gone with the Wind*, Douglas's novel about a physician (a frequent theme in his work) stands as a light read with soap opera qualities in its plotting. His *Magnificent Obsession*, published in 1929, had belatedly made the best seller lists in 1932 (no. 8) and 1933 (no. 4).

Three books destined to be classics—Thomas Wolfe's (1900–1938) *Of Time and the River* (1935) and James Hilton's (1900–1954) *Good-Bye, Mr. Chips* (1934) and his *Lost Horizon* (1933)—placed no. 3, no. 5, and no. 8, respectively, on the 1935 listings. Wolfe, a major American writer by any criterion, seldom appeared on any best-seller charts, so *Of Time and the River* stands as something of an exception. Hilton's *Good-Bye, Mr. Chips* set a record by being adapted for film in 1939 and 1969, plus **television** versions in 1959, 1984, and 2002. His *Lost Horizon* went on to be a Hollywood smash in 1937 (remade in 1973).

1936: No. 1: *Gone with the Wind*, Margaret Mitchell. Adapted for film in 1939. The epitome of historical novels, Mitchell's masterpiece outsold all other fiction for the next two years, with sales in the millions. Like *Anthony Adverse* before it, this equally long (1,000+ pages) work, set in the South before and during the Civil War, encompasses many characters and numerous subplots. Scarlett O'Hara and Rhett Butler have become one of literature's best-known couples.

Although *Gone with the Wind* overshadowed all of the competition, *The Last Puritan*, a cerebral novel by George Santayana (1863–1952), claimed second place.

1937: No. 1: *Gone with the Wind* (see 1936). Continuing as America's favorite best seller, its commercial success prompted an outpouring of historical fiction. *Northwest Passage*, by Kenneth Roberts (1885–1957) took follow-up honors and went to film in 1940. Another historical epic, *Drums along the Mohawk*, by Walter D. Edmunds (1903–1998) came in fifth (it had placed no. 4 in 1936) and played on theater screens in 1939. In the midst of economic woes and a growing threat of war, readers seemed to want to examine their roots and be reassured by what they found.

1938: No. 1: *The Yearling*, Marjorie Kinnan Rawlings (1896–1953). Adapted for film in 1946 and again in 1994 in a television version. Often categorized as a book for young adults, *The Yearling* transcends age categories. The story of a boy growing up in rural Florida, this book struck many readers with its simplicity and warmth. Winner of a Pulitzer prize, it enjoyed the further distinction of coming out in a Scribner Classic edition, with illustrations by **N. C. Wyeth** (1882–1945) just a year after its release.

The Citadel, by A. J. Cronin (1896–1981), had held third place in 1937, and then advanced to second in 1938. This novel about a young Scottish doctor went to film that same year and then three times to television, in 1960, 1983, and 2003. *Northwest Passage* also enjoyed a second year on the lists, this time in fifth position.

1939: No. 1: **The Grapes of Wrath**, John Steinbeck (1902–1968). Adapted for film in 1940. The story of the Dust Bowl and the plight of dispossessed Oklahoma farmers, this novel quickly established itself as an enduring American classic. Its film version proved no less powerful and won several Academy Awards. It was one of the few books to address directly the economic problems faced by rural America during the early 1930s; readers might not be keen to read about such problems, but the strength of Steinbeck's writing and his gifts as a storyteller overrode any such aversions.

Rebecca (1938), a twentieth-century Gothic novel by Daphne du Maurier (1907–1989), had first appeared in 1938's list at no. 4; it continued its popularity in 1939 and advanced to third place. It was adapted for film in 1940 in a splendid version by director Alfred Hitchcock (1899–1980) and won Best Picture at the 1940 Academy Awards; it has had four television versions (1947, 1962, 1979, and 1997). Although it fell to seventh place, *The Yearling* held on for a second year.

1940: No. 1: *How Green Was My Valley*, by Richard Llewellyn Macmillan (1906–1983). Adapted for film in 1941, where it won Best Picture and then to television in 1975. The nostalgia of *How Green Was My Valley*, a story of growing up in Wales, played in sharp contrast to World War II then unfolding in Europe.

Another classic for the era, *For Whom the Bell Tolls*, by Ernest Hemingway (1899–1961), came in at no. 4, one of the few times Hemingway, another major American author, managed to achieve this distinction. A novel of the Spanish Civil War (1936–1939), it addresses the twin themes of war and fascism. *For Whom the Bell Tolls* had its film incarnation in 1943 and a television adaptation in 1965.

Nonfiction Best Sellers, 1930–1940. Since nonfiction seldom attracts the level of popular attention given novels, only the more prominent or noteworthy titles in this broad category are mentioned.

1930: Although it ranked seventh in sales, *The Story of Philosophy*, by Will Durant (1885–1981), has, over the years, established itself as a perennial favorite. A somewhat similar book, *The Outline of History*, by H. G. Wells (1866–1946), came in at no. 8, but has likewise continued to sell well in various editions.

1931: In response to the ongoing craze for **contract bridge**, two titles by Ely Culbertson (1891–1955) entered the year's list: *Culbertson's Summary* at no. 5, and *Contract Bridge Blue Book* at no. 6.

1932: Columnist Drew Pearson (1897–1969) raised some eyebrows with his gossipy *Washington Merry-Go-Round* (also on the 1931 list) and its sequel, *More Merry-Go-Round* (both written with Robert S. Allen [1900–1981]).

1933: For the third year in a row, Ely Culbertson made the list, this time with *Contract Bridge Blue Book of 1933* (no. 8). A sensational exposé, *100,000,000 Guinea*

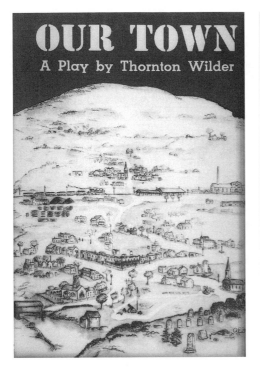

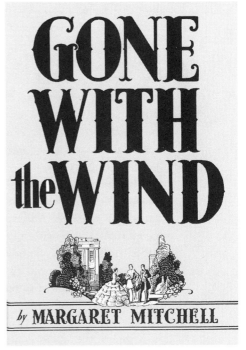

The original first-edition jackets of four of the many best sellers published during the 1930s. (Courtesy of Library of Congress, Rare Books Division)

Pigs, by Arthur Kallett (1902–1972) and Frederick John Schlink (1891–1995), had readers discussing truth in **advertising** and the nation's health; it would remain a best seller for two years.

1934: *Life Begins at Forty*, a simple self-help book by Walter B. Pitkin (1878–1953), enjoyed its second year on the list.

1935: A monumental history of General Robert E. Lee (1807–1870) aroused interest in the Civil War. Written by Douglas Southall Freeman (1886–1953), it signaled a rash of publishing, both nonfiction and fiction, about America's past and history in general.

1936: *Inside Europe*, by journalist John Gunther (1901–1970), the first of several "inside" books by the author, focused attention on the Continent and the many problems that would eventually lead to World War II.

1937: Dale Carnegie (1888–1955) burst upon the literary scene with his *How to Win Friends and Influence People*; this motivational book would be a best seller for the next two years and lead to seminars, classes, and a Dale Carnegie Institute. It has sold in the millions and remained in print ever since its 1937 publication.

1938: Admiral Richard E. Byrd (1888–1957), an aviator and pioneering polar explorer, wrote *Alone*, ninth on the year's list, a harrowing account of his solitary 1934 vigil in Antarctica.

1939: John Gunther returned at no. 3 with *Inside Asia*, a disturbing region given Japan's expansionist policies, and Adolf Hitler (1889–1945) contributed no. 7, *Mein Kampf* [My Battle], a complete translation of the text originally written in 1925–1926 and first issued in the United States as an abridged edition in 1933. Hitler's personal, meandering rant confirmed many of the fears expressed in Gunther's *Inside Europe* just three years earlier.

1940: In the shadow of World War II, Americans enjoyed *I Married Adventure*, by Osa Johnson (1894–1953), wife of explorer Martin Johnson (1884–1937). The couple had made numerous popular films about wild animals and exploration, and this book chronicled their adventures; escapist nonfiction, *I Married Adventure* had absolutely nothing to do with warfare and it reflected the denial about the conflict that many Americans felt. Such an isolationist stance would of course change with Pearl Harbor a year later.

In looking over the best-seller lists, it becomes apparent that the general reader neither wanted nor bought great numbers of books dealing with the Depression. Living through it apparently satisfied any need to examine the crisis. At the same time, books on history, especially an earlier America, did well, suggesting an interest in the past and how other people faced adversity.

As the Depression became less severe, the impending dangers in Europe and Asia did generate interest, especially in nonfiction. But novelists continued to crank out escapism and readers continued to buy their wares. The best-seller compilations in fiction would provide, for the most part, little indication about current events. At the very end of the decade, John Steinbeck's *Grapes of Wrath* proved an exception.

Three of the "great American writers of the 1930s"—John Dos Passos (1896–1970), William Faulkner (1897–1962), F. Scott Fitzgerald (1896–1940)—are conspicuous by their absence, proving, perhaps, that people do not always recognize enduring literature at the time of its publication. On the other hand, three other names in that elite grouping—Thomas Wolfe, John Steinbeck, and Ernest Hemingway—make single appearances on the lists: Wolfe with *Of Time and the River* (1935), Steinbeck with *The Grapes of Wrath* (1939), and Hemingway with *For Whom the Bell Tolls* (1940). If the lists as a whole suggest anything, it would be that Americans continued to read an eclectic range of books throughout the decade and that any indicators of trends or literary shifts seem virtually impossible to ascertain.

See also Aviation; Book Clubs; Food; Illustrators; Soap Operas; Western Films

SELECTED READING
Hackett, Alice Payne. *60 Years of Best Sellers, 1895–1955*. New York: R. R. Bowker Co., 1956.

Korda, Michael. *Making the List: A Cultural History of the American Bestseller, 1900–1999*. New York: Barnes & Noble Books, 2001.

Mott, Frank Luther. *Golden Multitudes: The Story of Best Sellers in the United States*. New York: R. R. Bowker Co., 1947.

Tebbel, John. *A History of Book Publishing in the United States*. Vol. 3, *The Golden Age between Two Wars, 1920–1940*. New York: R. R. Bowker Co., 1978.

BIG LITTLE BOOKS. Before the rise of **comic books** late in the 1930s, two other formats for comic art also tried to capture an audience during the decade: pop-up books and Big Little Books. In 1932, Blue Ribbon Books introduced a line of imaginative publications they called pop-up books. Blue Ribbon wanted to capitalize on the large readership for newspaper comics by using the heroes of the daily strips in their products. Thanks to creative folding, the series consisted of small booklets featuring characters that would pop up from the pages when the volume was laid flat.

The pop-up books enjoyed only modest success, and lack of consumer interest immediately led publishers to other innovations, the clever Big Little Books in particular. This marketing phenomenon also came out in 1932, a product of the Whitman Publishing Company of Racine, Wisconsin. Their introductory title involved the adventures of none other than **Dick Tracy**, a police detective then appearing in the newspaper comics. It measured $3^5/_8$" wide, $4^1/_2$" tall, and $1^1/_2$" thick with cardboard covers, and contained 350 pages. The left-hand page held printed text, and the right-hand page featured a single frame taken from the comic strip. Staffers erased the traditional speech balloons—which often resulted in a butchering of the picture—and instead ran a caption across the bottom. With the exception of the garishly colored covers, everything in this first Big Little Books came in black and white, cost the consumer a dime (about $1.50 in contemporary money), and set the standards that most succeeding volumes would follow.

An overnight sensation, Big Little Books began to be published in great numbers. Cheap to produce, they consisted almost entirely of recycled materials. The paper came from the waste that occurred when regular, full-size publications were trimmed after printing—thus accounting for the tiny page size—and the illustrations consisted of copies taken from already-existing **comic strips**. The books had few editorial costs, with the text adapted from the speech balloons of those same comics. About the only original part of a Big Little Book involved its colorful cover, and the illustration adorning it more often than not consisted of a reproduction, not an original work of art. The cheap paper pages, glued directly to the cardboard covers, provided little durability, and Big Little Books gained a reputation for falling apart after just a few readings.

At only a dime, however, they garnered a lot of readers, and Whitman alone eventually issued over 400 separate titles. Other publishers soon created their own lines. Dell had "cartoon story books" and "fast-action stories," while Engel-Van Wiseman boasted its "five-star library." Fawcett Publications entered the fray with "dime action books." Goldsmith Publishing, looking to other media, had the "radio star series." Lynn Publishing advertised its "Lynn books," and in a confusing play on words, Saalfield Publishing Company introduced "little big books." Another handful of small publishers, at one time or another during the 1930s, also introduced variations on the Big Little Book concept. In 1938, industry leader Whitman changed their product line's name to "Better Little Books" and "Big Big Books" in an attempt to differentiate themselves from their counterparts. Regardless of publisher, print runs for most titles averaged 250,000 to 350,000 copies, and readers usually obtained them in five-and-dimes or chain and variety stores. In time, inflation hit the publishers and most titles went to 15 cents (about $2.15 today) in the latter years of the decade.

Initially, the majority of the Big Little Books consisted of reprints from leading newspaper strips like *Dick Tracy*, **Flash Gordon**, *Buck Rogers*, **Little Orphan Annie**, **The Gumps**, **Tarzan**, and various **Walt Disney** characters. Within a short time, however, they came to include illustrated novels and plays, such as *Moby-Dick*, *Treasure Island*, *A Midsummer Night's Dream*, and many others, along with **radio** favorites, including *The Lone Ranger*, *Gang Busters*, *The Green Hornet*, and *Jack Armstrong*. **Shirley Temple** (b. 1928), Jackie Cooper (b. 1922), Jane Withers (b. 1926), Will Rogers (1879–1935), Tom Mix (1880–1940), and other then-current movie stars enjoyed their own Big Little Books stories, some of which tended toward biography, while others drew inspiration from their films. Even news events served as a source for stories. Admiral Richard E. Byrd's (1888–1957) expedition to Antarctica in 1934 prompted a "Little America" volume. Regardless of subject, children and adolescents soon built "libraries," some quite extensive, of these popular, inexpensive volumes.

With time, the novelty of Big Little Books began to wear off. The popularization of comic books in the late 1930s took many readers away. Similarly priced at a dime, but featuring color throughout and in a magazine format, many of the newer comic books contained new, original adventures, not reprints of newspaper strips. But Big Little Books nonetheless hung on; World War II brought about a brief resurgence (paper shortages, however, shrank them to under 300 pages), and there have been sporadic attempts to repopularize the genre ever since the 1940s.

See also Blondie; Illustrators; Magazines; Movies; Newspapers; Science Fiction; Youth

SELECTED READING
Big Little Books. http://www.biglittlebooks.com
Borden, Bill, and Steve Posner. *The Big Book of Big Little Books*. San Francisco: Chronicle Books, 1997.
Goulart, Ron. *Over 50 Years of American Comic Books*. Lincolnwood, IL: Mallard Press, 1991.
———, ed. *The Encyclopedia of American Comics*. New York: Facts on File, 1990.

BLONDIE. One of the most popular **comic strips** of all time, *Blondie* first began appearing in **newspapers** in 1930. Cartoonist Murat "Chic" Young (1901–1973), like most artists in his profession, struggled for several years to find a winning combination of picture and story. During the 1920s, Young tried several strips, none of which attracted much attention. Finally, in the fall of 1930, he convinced King Features syndicate to take on *Blondie*, what those in the trade called a "girlie strip." In its original format, *Blondie* chronicled the light-hearted adventures of a pretty young woman-Blondie Boopadoop—played out against a backdrop of parties, **fashion**, and general silliness.

For the Roaring Twenties, such an approach might have worked, but Young's timing was bad. With the onset of the Great Depression, the world of 1930 hardly resembled that of preceding years, and newspaper readers showed little interest in the humorous activities of a flapper (or "gold digger," in the language of the 1930s) and her friends. Young realized, given the times, that changes had to be made to *Blondie* if the comic strip stood a chance of surviving.

During her life as a stereotypical party girl, Blondie enjoyed the attentions of numerous suitors. One of her beaux bore the name Dagwood Bumstead, and Young eventually singled him out to be more than a boyfriend. The son of a fabulously wealthy industrialist, Dagwood fell in love with Blondie—but at the risk of losing his family fortune. Because of his parents' resistance to the match, Dagwood went on a 28-day hunger strike in January 1933. Each day, Young would conclude a strip with cliff-hanger endings—"how much longer can Dagwood go on?"—and the ploy won unprecedented reader involvement. Letters poured in, and *Blondie* overnight became a popular favorite. Of course, love conquered all, Dagwood won his battle (but lost his inheritance), and he and Blondie married in February 1933, the depth of the Depression for most Americans.

Young took a chance when he so abruptly changed his strip, but it proved an astute move. The newlyweds began their married life with virtually nothing except hope and humor. As they settled into the normal patterns of middle-class living, Dagwood and Blondie became the favorite cartoon couple for millions of daily newspaper readers, and by decade's end *Blondie* stood as the most popular comic strip in the nation.

Over the years, Young chronicled the Bumsteads' life in loving detail. A host of characters came to populate the strip, and fans looked forward to them all. Dagwood labors faithfully for the irascible Mr. Dithers; Blondie, for the most part a caring and patient wife, cannot resist a sale at Tudbury's, a local department store. Their best friends, Herb and Tootsie Woodley, live next door; Mr. Beasley delivers the mail; they acquire a dog, Daisy; and—most important of all—the Bumsteads become parents in the spring of 1934 with the birth of their first child, Alexander, or "Baby Dumpling." Although the self-imposed censorship that then existed in the comics did not allow Blondie to appear pregnant, readers knew she was expecting, and everyone rejoiced when the Baby Dumpling finally arrived.

This portrait of American normalcy never overtly referred to the Depression or other topical events, and yet the strip detailed American life in the 1930s. Readers saw themselves reflected in the little day-to-day activities of this typical family. Alert to the growing popularity of *Blondie*, King Features allowed its leading strip to be merchandised in a variety of ways. Coloring books, dolls, cards, **jigsaw puzzles**, cosmetics, clothing, and trinkets of every description carried the images of Dagwood and Blondie, and reprints of the strip appeared in **Big Little Books**.

Hollywood joined the craze in 1938 with *Blondie*, and canny studio executives at Columbia Pictures knew the one-word title gave more than enough information to potential audiences. The movie stars Penny Singleton (1908–2003) as Blondie and Arthur Lake (1905–1987) as Dagwood. An immediate success, it led to three more pictures in 1939 (*Blondie Meets the Boss, Blondie Takes a Vacation,* and *Blondie Brings Up Baby*), and then 24 additional *Blondie* pictures between 1940 and 1950. Every one features Singleton and Lake, two actors who built their careers around a comic strip. A bit late in realizing the comic potential of *Blondie,* network **radio** nonetheless finally added a comedy show based on the couple in 1939; it would run until 1950, and Singleton and Lake reprised their movie roles in the series.

One of the enduring images to emerge from *Blondie* involves Dagwood raiding the refrigerator to put together a huge sandwich made from anything he can find. Those episodes even contributed a phrase to the language: Dagwood sandwich. Today's popular "submarine" owes a great deal to Dagwood's inventiveness, and the thick, multi-ingredient sandwich has permanently entered the culture. In the meantime, *Blondie* goes on under new artists, still one of the most popular comic strips in existence.

See also Food; Movies; Radio Networks

SELECTED READING
Goulart, Ron, ed. *The Encyclopedia of American Comics.* New York: Facts on File, 1990.
Horn, Maurice, ed. *100 Years of American Newspaper Comics.* New York: Gramercy Books, 1996.
Young, Dean, and Rick Marschall. *Blondie and Dagwood's America.* New York: Harper & Row, 1981.

BOOK CLUBS. The precise origin of book clubs (i.e., commercial organizations that sell books to members) cannot be traced to an exact place or time. But in the late 1920s, the founding of two major book clubs in the United States revolutionized the way Americans bought books. The country's high literacy rate at the time (90+ percent) assured a high number of potential readers and buyers.

Easy accessibility and low prices had already contributed to the wide distribution and readership of **newspapers, magazines,** and advertisements. Books presented a different story. In addition to economic conditions, educational levels, and amounts of leisure time, locations influenced people's ability to obtain books. Only those who lived near public libraries, bookstores, or some large department stores could readily acquire books from a broad range of titles.

Direct subscription services, available since the 1800s, gave people a way to purchase books, but they provided few choices. Door-to-door agents sold encyclopedias, dictionaries, or sets of books bought on an installment plan. Sets usually consisted of volumes by one author, such as Mark Twain (Samuel Langhorne Clemens, 1835–1910) or a collection of classics, such as Dr. Charles William Eliot's (1834–1926) Five-Foot Shelf, also known as the Harvard Classics.

During the 1920s and 1930s, E. Haldeman-Julius (1889–1951) and his wife Marcet (1887–1941), through mail-order publishing, successfully sold millions of Little Blue Books, cheap, miniature $3^{1}/_{2}$-by-5-inch volumes with semistiff covers. These usually consisted of reprints of literary titles as well as a smattering of self-improvement, amusement, fantasy, horror, and other genres. Harry Scherman (1887–1969), a writer, businessman, and book lover, along with colleagues Robert Haas (active 1910s, 1920s, & 1930s) and Maxwell Sackheim (1890–1982), had experimented in 1916 with the mass distribution of books through mail orders, selling old classics they called the Little Leather Library. Their business quickly fizzled, but Scherman remained convinced that Americans from all walks of life wanted to read good and current literature. That posed the question of how to make the purchase of books easy and affordable, especially at a time of increasing competition from **radio** and **movies** for the use of leisure time.

Scherman found the answer in 1926, when he incorporated the now-famous Book-of-the-Month Club (BOMC), an organization that provided yet another means for selling books on a national scale through the mail. In addition, it boasted some unique features—membership, several titles to select from, bonus books, and an editorial board composed of literary experts who determined the choices. By joining, members committed themselves to the purchase of four books a year from an offering of one new book a month. Bonus books became available after a member purchased a required number of books.

Scherman initially did not send promotional materials directly to potential members; he instead attracted those already buying books as well as new consumers through heavy mass **advertising** in weekly book review sections of newspapers and in magazines such as *Literary Digest* and *Atlantic*. The club's first selection, *Lolly Willowes* (1926), written by Sylvia Townsend Warner (1893–1978), an English writer, went to 4,750 members at a price of $3.00 (about $34.00 in today's dollars) plus postage. For an initial selection, *Lolly Willowes* did not come cheap, but it apparently did well enough to encourage everyone involved in the venture.

During its first year, BOMC featured five authors, including Edna Ferber (1885–1968) with *Showboat* (1926) and Ellen Glasgow (1873–1945) with *The Romantic Comedians* (1926). The approach worked well; membership in BOMC approached 100,000 subscribers by 1928. Holding true to its original commitment to provide variety, to introduce new books as well as some classics, BOMC offered selections by such diverse writers as Willa Cather (1873–1947), Robert Frost (1874–1963), Marjorie Kinnan Rawlings (1896–1953), John Steinbeck (1902–1968), Carl Van Doren (1885–1950), and Thornton Wilder (1897–1975) during the 1930s. Even former president **Herbert Hoover** (1874–1964) contributed a title, *The Challenge to Liberty* (1934); it appeared as a selection that same year. Margaret Mitchell's (1900–1949) best seller **Gone with the Wind** (1936) made the list almost immediately upon publication. Pearl S. Buck (1892–1973) had the honor of the highest number of club appearances during the decade with four books between 1931 and 1939, including *The Good Earth* as her initial offering. At the end of its first full year of operation, BOMC had surpassed $1 million in net sales which, with the exception of the Depression years, steadily grew thereafter.

The Literary Guild, conceived in 1927, just a few months after BOMC, had Samuel W. Craig (active 1920s and 1930s) and Harold K. Guinzburg (active 1920s and 1930s) as its founders. It operated in a manner similar to BOMC by employing subscriptions, monthly offerings decided by a review committee, and a required number of purchases, along with bonus books when members qualified. The club mailed its first selection, *Zola and His Times* (1928), by Matthew Josephson (1899–1978), to 5,732 members. Like its rival Book-of-the-Month Club, the Literary Guild claimed a growing membership. It presented conventional books of various kinds—fiction, biography, **travel**, romance, mystery, and classics—with many of its selections achieving noteworthy reputations.

During the late 1920s, the book club idea spread and many smaller, specialty clubs formed. They tended to be organized in fields such as religion, history, mysteries, and children's books. In 1929, the Literary Guild created the Junior Literary Guild, a children's division. Its success either eliminated or absorbed most of the other children's clubs then in existence. Following the already established adult format, children joined as members and received membership pins and a monthly magazine, *Young Wings*.

Book clubs during the 1930s used the mails to deliver selections to a large number of communities which had no other literary outlets. Initially the book trade business saw the emergence of these clubs, especially BOMC and the Literary Guild, as price-cutting schemes to undermine the livelihood of booksellers. But bookstores continued to operate in the black and eventually cooperated by collecting and processing subscriptions for their erstwhile competitors.

The Depression brought with it troubling times to both publishing and book clubs. Overstocked warehouses, along with a movement by publishers to sell reprints for one dollar (about $14.50 in current dollars) or less, and an accompanying loss of club members, caused considerable concern among book club executives. Many of the smaller clubs went out of business, and even the well-established BOMC and Literary Guild felt the need to introduce a variety of pricing schemes. For example, instead of bonus books, members received discount coupons toward their next purchase. Some groups temporarily dropped the membership requirement; anyone could buy a book through a club. Marketing to public libraries increased and some clubs acquired the member lists and inventories of others. At the same time, the more daring tried new ventures. The Literary Guild launched its own Dollar Book Club, and Robert M. McBride (active 1920s & 1930s) founded the Laugh Club, a group that distributed six books of humor a year at figures below retail price.

Despite the challenges presented by the Depression, the Book-of-the-Month Club and the Literary Guild remained fairly stable and actually flourished in the second half of the decade. By 1935, membership in BOMC had risen by 50 percent, gained significantly again in 1936, and by 1939 exceeded 300,000 subscribers. The Literary Guild enjoyed comparable success, and smaller clubs, usually in special fields, reappeared.

See also Best Sellers; Education; Leisure & Recreation; Mysteries & Hard-Boiled Detectives; Youth

SELECTED READING

Book-of-the-Month Club editors. *The First Forty Years of the Book-of-the-Month Club*. New York: Book-of-the-Month Club, 1966.

Kyvig, David E. *Daily Life in the United States, 1920–1940*. Chicago: Ivan R. Dee, 2004.

Radway, Janice A. *A Feeling for Books: The Book-of-the-Month Club, Literary Taste, and Middle-Class Desire*. Chapel Hill: University of North Carolina Press, 1997.

Tebbel, John. *A History of Book Publishing in the United States*. Vol. 3, *The Golden Age between Two Wars, 1920–1940*. New York: R. R. Bowker Co., 1978.

West, James L. W., III. *American Authors and the Literary Marketplace since 1900*. Philadelphia: University of Pennsylvania Press, 1988.

BOWLING. An ancient sport, bowling strove for recognition and respectability during the early years of the twentieth century. Most communities boasted a bowling alley or two, but unlike today's glossy, totally automated complexes, boys set the pins by hand, crouched in tiny cubbyholes, hoping no stray balls or pins would come crashing into them. Often located in old, run-down buildings, and lacking the niceties so taken for granted today, such as computerized scoring and pleasant eating facilities, the downtown alleys of the 1930s tended to be male enclaves and placed bowling on the shadowy fringes of family recreation and entertainment.

Despite the disreputable connotations some associated with the sport, the American Bowling Congress (ABC), a national federation of small, local groups, had been formed in 1895 in an attempt to bring about national standards for the game. A women's branch, the Women's National Bowling Congress (WNBC), came into being in 1916. As the sport grew, both in numbers and acceptance, it received significant media coverage in the 1930s. **Newspapers** in particular devoted large amounts of space to players' detailed averages and scores. In 1934, New York City served as host to the International Bowling Association's (IBA) annual tournament, a competition that featured the best bowlers from around the world.

Regionally, churches, schools, offices, and industries all sponsored leagues, and this kind of mass participation diminished some of the criticism leveled at the game. Still, not until after World War II and the rise of huge suburban shopping complexes with brightly lit alleys as part of their allure, did bowling receive the respectability it had so long sought.

Although no famous names dominate bowling during the 1930s, Fioretta McCutcheon (1888–1967), or "Mrs. Mac," did her share to advance bowling for women. A latecomer to the game, she had won enough matches by 1930 to be recognized as an outstanding bowler. She toured throughout the decade, and accomplished 10 perfect 300 games during that time. She retired in 1939, whereupon she began to teach in New York City, opening Mrs. McCutcheon's School of Bowling.

Joe Norris (1910–2001), nicknamed "the Boy Wonder of Bowling," also gained some publicity in the 1920s and 1930s, especially as a team player. His groups consistently won tournaments they entered, and Norris received recognition for his superlative style. Throughout the decade, team and league play slowly grew in popularity.

Metro-Goldwyn-Mayer released an unusual bowling film—MGM labeled it an "oddity"—titled *Strikes and Spares* in 1934. Put together by producer-director-writer-actor Pete Smith (1892–1979), the creator of innumerable films about various sports, it consisted of tricks and stunts performed by Andy Varipapa (1891–1984), a noted bowler who had established his name by performing pranks and gag shots around the country.

Several inventors had designs for automatic pin setters, or pinspotters, in the 1930s, but the Depression and World War II delayed their installation. In the period immediately preceding the war, bowling increasingly received favorable publicity in newspapers and **magazines**, and plans had been laid to build newer, nicer bowling centers. But most of those ideas and plans would have to wait until the fighting had ended and the nation returned to a peacetime footing.

See also Comic Strips; Leisure & Recreation; Movies

SELECTED READING

Grinfelds, Vesma, and Bonnie Hultstrand. *Right Down Your Alley: The Complete Book of Bowling.* West Point, NY: Leisure Press, 1985.

Weiskopf, Herman. *The Perfect Game: The World of Bowling.* Englewood Cliffs, NJ: Prentice-Hall [Rutledge Books], 1978.

BOXING. The 1930s witnessed a remarkable interest in boxing, especially in the heavyweight division. A pole apart from any other sport, boxing has always been a bruising, bloody contest. Its marketing would suggest that the audience for this spectacle consisted primarily of red-faced men puffing on cigars, derbies propped on their heads; clearly, its promoters did not make appeals to women, although women could usually be found scattered among the spectators.

Americans have long been of two minds about professional prizefighting: supporters view the sport as a demonstration of the "manly art of self defense," a choreographed dance between two opponents that employs both science and brawn. Those opposed read no poetics into it but instead see it as legalized mayhem, even slaughter. Both sides garnered support for their arguments during the thirties, a time when professional boxing regularly made headlines.

For most Americans, "boxing" translates as heavyweight boxing. The other divisions—featherweight, lightweight, welterweight, middleweight, etc.—mean little and therefore receive only cursory attention. And, in a kind of musical chairs, the heavyweight crown rested uneasily on a whole series of heads until 1937.

The antics began in 1930, when a German boxer named Max Schmeling (1905–2005) gained the heavyweight title after the referee disqualified the reigning champion, the American Jack Sharkey (1902–1994), on a foul. Two years later, Schmeling lost to Sharkey in a 15-round rematch. Sharkey, however, regained his crown only briefly; Primo Carnera (1906–1967) of Italy knocked him out for the title in 1933 and became the second non-American to hold the championship since 1906. But Carnera's reign quickly ended when Max Baer (1909–1959) gave him a frightful drubbing in June 1934.

Throughout his career, Baer enjoyed considerable popularity. Dubbed the "Clown Prince of Boxing" for his antics in and out of the ring, he provided a refreshing change from the dour line of contenders and champions preceding him. World events had by this time also influenced attitudes about fighters, and Baer, who happened to be Jewish, gained a measure of crowd respect by wearing a Star of David on his trunks. This custom began when he fought Schmeling in 1933 in a nonchampionship bout and defeated him, saying that his victory represented a defeat for anti-Semitism, Nazis, and Hitler in particular. But Baer's time in the limelight proved fleeting.

A veteran boxer named James J. Braddock (1905–1974), who had suffered through an up-and-down career, somehow gained a title shot against Baer. Another crowd favorite, Braddock for many represented the hapless working man of the Depression, a fellow buffeted by fate, but one who survives life's hard knocks. A 10 to 1 underdog, Braddock in 1935 pulled off a major upset by defeating Baer in 15 rounds, making him, in the words of famed journalist Damon Runyon (1884–1946), a "Cinderella Man."

In the midst of the heavyweight title passing from hand to hand, two important events took place that would profoundly influence ring history. First, promoters staged a nonchampionship bout in 1936 that involved, once more, Max Schmeling. This time he faced a rising young American boxer named Joe Louis (1914–1981). Schmeling floored Louis and clearly seemed in line to regain the title. But he would be denied the opportunity; through a series of deals and agreements, the very kind of thing that gives boxing a shady reputation, reigning champion Braddock refused to meet Schmeling in the ring. And so the second event saw Joe Louis facing Braddock and getting a shot at the crown. Louis won the 1937 fight, making him the world's new heavyweight champion.

Joe Louis, by now nicknamed "the Brown Bomber," became an immensely popular champion. He reigned, undefeated, from 1937 until his 1949 retirement, defending his title 25 times, more than any other heavyweight champion. In comparison, Baer and Braddock defended their titles only once apiece, and each lost when they did so. From early in his career, Louis seemed invincible; the press dubbed his hapless opponents "Bum of the Month." But of all his victories, none proved sweeter than his defeat of Schmeling in a much-ballyhooed 1938 rematch that also had the championship at stake. Across the United States, people touted the encounter as the "good" Louis versus the "bad" Schmeling.

For both fighters, the bout involved significant national pride and politics, especially for the challenger. Adolf Hitler (1889–1945) had come to power in Germany, and Schmeling's handlers talked of him as the "hope of the Aryan race." The Nazi propaganda machine spewed out reams of racist hate in the days preceding the fight, and it added mightily to the excitement pervading the match, one that incidentally established the power of

A 1936 shot of heavyweight champion Joe Louis (1914–1981), nicknamed the Brown Bomber. (Courtesy of Photofest)

radio as a sports broadcasting medium. More than half the radio owners in the U.S.—over 22 million people—listened in as sportscaster Clem McCarthy (1882–1962) described how Louis pummeled his opponent. For his part, the quiet Louis typified much that was good about America in an era of segregation in most sports, and hopes ran high. Once in the ring, and in front of 70,000 fans, Louis flattened Schmeling just two minutes into the first round. A clear knockout: the referee called the fight and the nation breathed a collective sigh of relief. Louis's decisive victory salvaged American honor, plus it silenced many race-baiters and Nazi sympathizers.

Although few Americans ever attended a prizefight, considerable public interest surrounded the sport during the Depression era. Hollywood found staging and filming a match an easy thing to do, and over two dozen fight **movies** played theaters during the 1930s. The opening of the decade saw *The Big Fight*, starring "that shufflin' laugh-maker, Stepin Fetchit" (1902–1985), a popular black comedian unfortunately forced by race to take on many stereotypical roles. Joe E. Brown (1892–1973) lent his comedic talents to *Hold Everything* (1930), and Wallace Beery (1885–1949) and Jackie Cooper (b. 1922) made the justly famous *The Champ* in 1931. Even comedian Charlie Chaplin (1889–1977) tried his hand at a boxing episode, a hilarious one in his 1931 *City Lights*.

James Cagney (1899–1986) continued his action films with 1932's *Winner Take All*, returned to the ring with *The Irish in Us* (1935), and then made a third boxing picture with *City for Conquest* in 1939.

An emerging Spencer Tracy (1900–1967) plays a bit part in *Society Girl* (1932). That same year saw Douglas Fairbanks, Jr. (1909–2000) in *The Life of Jimmy Dolan*, a feature that also included a young John Wayne (1907–1979) in a small role as a prizefighter. In 1933, real-life boxer Max Baer, living up to his reputation as something of a playboy, shared the lead in *The Prizefighter and the Lady* with Myrna Loy (1905–1993). Baer displays some acting abilities in the picture and would go on to appear in almost 20 additional movies.

Other movies include *Police Call* (1933), which despite its title, stands as a B-grade boxing epic, along with *Kelly the Second* (1936) and *The Kid Comes Back* (1937). Another boxing picture, *Conflict* (1936), based on a Jack London (1876–1916) short story, has the distinction of starring John Wayne in another role as a boxer instead of a cowboy. *Kid Galahad* (1937) headlines an all-star cast—Edward G. Robinson (1893–1973), Bette Davis (1908–1989), Humphrey Bogart (1899–1957)—and proved a box office success. Similarly, *Cain and Mabel* (1936), a pugilistic comedy with Clark Gable (1901–1960) and Marion Davies (1897–1961), and *The Crowd Roars* (1938), with the unlikely casting of romantic lead Robert Taylor (1911–1969) in the role of a fighter, showed that boxing pictures could draw audiences to theaters.

Cartoonist Ham Fisher's (1900–1955) popular comic strip character Joe Palooka receives featured status in *Palooka* (1934), as well as in two shorts, *For the Love of Pete* (1936) and *Taking the Count* (1937). Boxing films with primarily black casts include *Spirit of Youth* (1937), which stars Joe Louis as himself, and *Keep Punching* (1939), featuring light heavyweight Henry Armstrong (1912–1988). Finally, *They Made Me a Criminal* (1939) stars John Garfield (1913–1952), and a screen adaptation of playwright Clifford Odets' (1906–1963) *Golden Boy* (play, 1937; movie, 1939) features William Holden (1918–1981) in a star-making role. Both pictures take a serious look at the fight business, focusing on more than just the knockouts and mayhem in the ring. Boxing may not have been universally liked, but during the 1930s it certainly emerged as a significant component of American popular culture.

See also Comic Strips; Newspapers; Race Relations & Stereotyping; Stage Productions

SELECTED READING

Baker, Aaron. *Contesting Identities: Sports in American Film*. Urbana: University of Illinois Press, 2003.

Romano, Frederick V. *The Boxing Filmography: American Features, 1920–2003*. Jefferson, NC: McFarland & Co., 2004.

Sammons, Jeffrey T. *Beyond the Ring: The Role of Boxing in American Society*. Urbana: University of Illinois Press, 1988.

Sugar, Bert Randolph. *100 Years of Boxing*. New York: Galley Press, 1982.

"BROTHER, CAN YOU SPARE A DIME?". A few people, mainly New Yorkers, first heard "Brother, Can You Spare a Dime?" in a minor and short-lived Broadway revue titled *Americana* (1932; 77 performances). On stage, the relatively unknown Rex Weber (active 1930s) sang the lyrics, written by E. Y. "Yip" Harburg (1896–1981), with **music** by Jay Gorney (1896–1990).

The melody derives from a lullaby Gorney, who came to the United States in 1906, had heard as a child in his native Russia. For his part, Harburg had lost a small appliance business with the onset of the Depression, and turned to music for work. He would later say that he overheard other unemployed citizens, on street corners, asking, "Can you spare a dime?" as he walked to his job. The lyrics thus originated with the straits in which many found themselves, adding a real poignancy to the piece.

Although not many theatergoers saw *Americana*, millions of listeners eventually heard the Gorney/Harburg song via **recordings** and **radio** broadcasts. **Bing Crosby** (1903–1977), an increasingly popular crooner of the day, recorded the tune for Brunswick Records just three weeks following the show's opening in October 1932 (it would close in December 1932). Shortly thereafter, **Rudy Vallee** (1901–1986), at the time better known than Crosby, cut a version for Columbia Records. This rendition includes an unusual spoken introduction by Vallee in which he mentions that "Brother, Can You Spare a Dime?" may sound "a bit out of character" for him, noted as he was for more romantic numbers. The two interpretations vied for listeners and buyers, and both recordings received considerable air play, a fact that greatly enlarged the audience. Entertainer Al Jolson (1888–1950) also sang it in late 1932 on his popular radio show carried by the National Broadcasting Company (NBC radio), exposing still more people to the trenchant lyrics. Together, these three vocalists, almost never associated with lyrics even vaguely social in content, made the intensely topical "Brother, Can You Spare a Dime?" one of the top 20 songs of 1932.

By and large, the American public did not want musical reminders about the Depression, but "Brother, Can You Spare a Dime?" serves as the exception that proves the rule. Despite its grim story of a man—farmer, construction worker, veteran, or everyman—suffering through the crisis, it touched a nerve and became a classic that continues to attract listeners today.

Other **songwriters and lyricists** attempted to allude to the Depression, and a few good numbers have come down from the era. But most of their efforts have ended up as forgotten, curiosity pieces. Tunes like "There's No Depression in Love" (1931; music by Dan Dougherty [1897–1955] and lyrics by Jack Yellen [1892–1991]) and "Are You Makin' Any Money?" (1933; words and music by Herman Hupfield [1894–1951]), went nowhere. Yellen had earlier contributed the lyrics to another song frequently associated with the Depression, "Happy Days Are Here Again." Written in 1929 in collaboration with composer Milton Ager (1893–1979), it had been part of the score for an MGM musical titled *Chasing Rainbows*, released in 1930. Although the picture has since been forgotten (apparently, no complete prints exist anymore), "Happy Days Are Here Again" enjoyed renewed life with **Franklin D. Roosevelt** (1882–1945) and his rise to the presidency with the Democratic Party. The melody became the party's theme song during the 1932 presidential campaign, promising as it did better times ahead. Not truly a Depression-era song, since Ager and Yellen had composed it prior to the market collapse, it nevertheless emerged as a political anthem for the period, and even today loyal Democrats occasionally revive it for election battles.

"Life Is Just a Bowl of Cherries" (1931), written by Ray Henderson (1896–1970) and Lew Brown (1893–1958), also spoke to the era. Audiences first heard it in *The George White Scandals of 1931*, a periodic Broadway revue. The popular Ethel Merman (1908–1984) performed it on stage, and its optimistic lyric played well in those difficult years.

On a less upbeat side—more in keeping with the mood established by "Brother, Can You Spare a Dime?"—would be "Remember My Forgotten Man"; it comes from a Hollywood musical, *Gold Diggers of 1933*, that features music by the songwriting team of Harry Warren (1893–1981) and Al Dubin (1891–1945). The lyrics refer to the "forgotten" veterans of World War I and their attempts to win bonuses promised by the government. That same movie also boasts "The Gold Digger's Song (We're in the Money)," a silly little ditty sung by Ginger Rogers (1911–1995) that sarcastically challenges "old man Depression" and the lack of money most citizens faced. Neither composition, however, achieved hit status and remained simply as parts of the musical score for a popular picture.

Out of the thousands of popular songs written during the early 1930s, only the smallest handful considered the darker dimensions of the economic collapse. Of those, "Brother, Can You Spare a Dime?" stands out from all the others, a powerful indictment of the neglect and confusion spawned by the crash.

See also Fred Astaire and Ginger Rogers; Jazz; Jukeboxes; Movies; Musicals; Political Parties; Radio Networks; Swing

SELECTED READING
Barnet, Richard D., Bruce Nemerov, and Mayo R. Taylor. *The Story Behind the Song: 150 Songs That Chronicle the 20th Century*. Westport, CT: Greenwood Press, 2004.
Hamm, Charles. Liner Notes. "American Song during the Great Depression." *Brother, Can You Spare a Dime?* LP. New World Records, 1977.
Young, William H., and Nancy K. Young. *Music of the Great Depression: American History through Music*. Westport, CT: Greenwood Press, 2005.
Zinsser, William. *Easy to Remember: The Great American Songwriters and Their Songs*. Jaffrey, NH: David R. Godine, 2000.

BUSES. Americans have always treasured their mobility. Most citizens would have preferred to **travel** by personal automobile during the Depression years, but cost and operational expenses prevented many from doing so. Commercial buses, however, provided a cheap alternative mode of **transportation**. The term "bus" derives from "omnibus," meaning, roughly, "for all," and in its original form enjoyed some usage in the horse and buggy era. With the coming of motorized transport, the shortened "bus" came to designate a large motor vehicle designed to carry passengers, usually for a fare and over a scheduled route.

The 1920s and 1930s witnessed the slow demise of streetcars and trolleys, once the mainstays of public transportation. Since buses did not have to follow fixed routes, such as those established by rails or overhead power lines, buses began, gradually, to take their places. Names like ACF (American Car & Foundry), Fageol, Fixible, General Motors, Kenworth, Mack, Reo, White, and Yellow Coach took the lead as manufacturers, and smaller companies appeared and disappeared, often absorbed by larger ones.

In 1926, with intercity bus services proliferating, *Russell's Official National Motor Coach Guide* became a valuable aid for travelers and ticket agents. Published annually, it contained intercity bus schedules for most of the United States and Canada; it grew out of *Russell's Guide*, a detailed book of **train** schedules dating back to the late nineteenth century.

By the mid-1920s, over 6,500 companies provided bus transportation, most of them small operations with only one route. More and more, buses traveled outside the city limits to suburbs and neighboring communities, eating away at previous railroad monopolies. As buses moved in, railroad branch lines shut down, eliminating many local stops. For distances up to about 150 miles, buses eventually proved as popular as rail service. After 1935, however, both buses and railroads had to acknowledge a new competitor: commercial air travel. With the development of economical airliners, routes exceeding 150 miles in length became hotly contested among buses, rail, and air.

One area where buses had virtually no competition involved the transportation of schoolchildren. The school bus grew up in the 1920s and flourished in the 1930s. To cut costs in straitened times, communities closed traditional one-room schools, and buses transported their pupils to consolidated ones. A bit of historic Americana began disappearing as rural districts relied on buses and country life underwent a profound change.

Bus service advanced from short intercity runs to the first truly transcontinental service in 1928 when a bus for the Yelloway line traveled from Los Angeles to New York City in 5 days and 14 hours. In March 1929, the Minnesota-based Hibbing Transportation Company, known then as the Motor Transit Corporation, bought Yelloway and soon changed its name to the Greyhound Corporation. The new company then launched its first nationwide **advertising** campaign, urging cross-country travelers to "take the bus." Its full-page, four-color advertisements ran in national **magazines** such as the *Saturday Evening Post*, but the Depression hit the Greyhound Company hard and its profits turned into losses. In 1932, General Motors assumed some of Greyhound's debts, a move that kept the company on the road and also gave the automaker greater access to the bus business.

In search of elusive profits and riders, the cross-country bus industry tried various innovations to turn red ink into black. For example, Pickwick Stages, and later Greyhound, offered night coaches, or sleeper service. They employed double-decker buses in which the top level provided an observation area and the lower deck contained sleeping berths. The big bands of the thirties, always on the road, found the sleepers to be perfect for their lengthy tours, although the ruts, potholes, and curves of many a dilapidated highway discouraged sleep. The sleepers intrigued other potential passengers, but few became regular users, making the specially equipped buses economic liabilities. By 1934, the sleepers had fairly well vanished.

Meanwhile, buoyed by new routes and increasing numbers of riders, Greyhound introduced the 37-passenger Super Coach, advertising the vehicle as ideal for families, not just individual travelers. Toward the end of the decade, General Motors built 500 elegant cruisers for the company, calling them Silversides because of their distinctive exterior paneling. Raymond Loewy (1893–1986), one of the most celebrated industrial designers of the decade, created the Streamlined motifs and unusual fluted aluminum strips that set these buses off from their competition.

Greyhound had received an important boost in 1933 when it became the official carrier to Chicago's **Century of Progress Exposition**. The **New York World's Fair** repeated the gesture in 1939. In both instances, Greyhound devised special "fair buses." For the New York extravaganza, the company even created a separate subsidiary line, Exposition Greyhound Lines. Each bus measured 45 feet long and 9 feet wide and could transport 160 passengers through the fairgrounds. It proved an ideal advertising ploy; the Streamlined buses introduced millions of Americans to the latest in comfort and convenience of public transportation. That same year, Greyhound organized a large display of their super coaches at San Francisco's ongoing Golden Gate Exposition, thus promoting bus travel on both coasts.

Except for the darkest days of the Depression, the 1930s produced handsome profits for Greyhound lines, and their success helped in creating a transportation first: in 1935, more people rode buses than trains, a trend that had been developing since early in the decade. With ridership up, representatives from several independent motor coach companies in 1936 formed an association to assure continuing profitability. They worked together to enable passengers to transfer freely among association members as their travels took them from one company's territory to another's. This association called itself Trailways and linked 40 motor coach companies. Trailways participants gave Greyhound some organized competition.

The bus industry, particularly Greyhound, received some helpful publicity from the **movies**. One of the biggest hits of the decade, 1934's ***It Happened One Night***, starred the popular Clark Gable (1901–1960) and Claudette Colbert (1903–1996). The comedy tells a story about an on-again, off-again trip from Florida to New York City, and portions of it take place in a Greyhound bus. Cinematographers shot many of the scenes inside a typical coach, giving movie audiences exposure to this form of travel.

Other bus-oriented pictures include *Cross Country Cruise* (1934) and *Fugitive Lovers* (1934); both involve characters taking long bus trips. Visually, the films introduce audiences to the concept of viewing beautiful scenery without the stress of driving. *Cross Country Cruise* enjoyed a long run at the Orpheum Cinema in San Francisco, and for the entire time Greyhound parked a huge sleeper—open for inspection—outside the theater. *Fugitive Lovers*, another comedy, stars Robert Montgomery (1904–1981) traveling cross-country with none other than the zany Three Stooges, a trio of funnymen then breaking into the movies.

The decade's end, however, brought mixed messages concerning the bus industry. Over 1,800 companies operated 12,200 buses, a significant drop from 1931. Much of this decrease resulted from mergers and acquisitions and the closure of smaller companies. Comfort and services had improved and for the first time more people rode buses than they did streetcars and trolleys. This encouraging news had been brought about, not just by consumer choice, but because large corporations like General Motors, Mack Truck, Firestone Tire & Rubber, Phillips Petroleum, and the Standard Oil Company of California bought street railroads in a number of major cities and replaced streetcars with buses. Thus the bus industry had more riders, but somewhat by default, and after World War II it would never compete with the automobile.

See also Automobiles; Aviation; Design; Douglas DC-3; Education; Fairs & Expositions; Screwball Comedies; Streamlining; Swing

SELECTED READING

Jackson, Carlton. *Hounds of the Road: A History of the Greyhound Bus Company*. Bowling Green, OH: Bowling Green University Popular Press, 1984.

Luke, William A. *Bus Industry Chronicle: U.S. and Canadian Experiences*. Spokane, WA: William A. Luke, 2000.

Wood, Donald F. *American Buses*. Osceola, WI: MBI Publishing Co., 1998.

C

CALDWELL, ERSKINE. The once-controversial author of 25 novels, some 150 short stories, and a number of nonfiction books, Erskine Caldwell (1903–1987) was one of the most widely read American writers of the twentieth century, although he had to wait a number of years to reach that position. He wrote his most enduring works during the 1930s, the peak of his creativity. They eventually sold well over 80 million copies, were translated into dozens of languages, and have been adapted for stage and screen.

Born near Moreland, Georgia, a tiny rural town southwest of Atlanta, Caldwell grew up amid poverty, although he himself came from a modest middle-class family. His father, a minister deeply interested in social problems, especially among the poor, took young Erskine with him on visits to communities in the Southeast where he would attempt to lend assistance to the destitute. This exposure to the needy stirred his conscience and influenced his subsequent writing.

In 1925, while a student at the University of Virginia (he never received a college degree), he published an essay on rural Georgia; its acceptance in a literary magazine led him to continue writing. Various pieces, mainly from little presses with small followings, kept him going, and finally caught the eye of F. Scott Fitzgerald (1896–1940), one of the leading authors of the day. Fitzgerald recommended Caldwell to the legendary Maxwell Perkins (1884–1947), his editor at Charles Scribner's Sons and mentor to some of the era's finest writers.

With such high-powered backing, Caldwell bore a heavy responsibility to produce, which he did. In 1931, Scribner's released *American Earth*, a collection of short stories. Following its mainly positive reception, Caldwell rocked the genteel literary establishment with a 1932 novel titled *Tobacco Road*. A forthright tale of abject poverty in the Deep South, it mixed gritty detail with a generous helping of realistic sex and violence, and plunged Caldwell into a controversy about the merits of his fiction, one that would continue throughout the 1930s and beyond. Traditionalists and apologists for the South argued his work should be deemed obscene; some demanded his books be pulled off shelves and that he be censored.

These opinions, however, did not reflect the feelings of all his readers—many saw him as a literary bright light in dreary times. While the arguments raged, playwright Jack Kirkland (1901–1969) staged a version of *Tobacco Road* on Broadway. Its unparalleled box office success would suggest that the Caldwell critics constituted a minority voice.

Erskine Caldwell (1903–1987), author of *Tobacco Road* (1932) and *God's Little Acre* (1933). (Courtesy of the Library of Congress)

The play went on stage in December 1933 and ran for a record 3,182 performances (or seven and a half years). Just as enthusiasm for the play began to wane, Hollywood released a motion picture adaptation in 1941. Directed by John Ford (1894–1973), close on the heels of his 1940 film version of novelist John Steinbeck's (1902–1968) *Grapes of Wrath* (1939), another book and movie about rural poverty, the film capitalized on the previous picture's success.

In 1933, Caldwell followed *Tobacco Road* with—some would say—an even more scandalous book, *God's Little Acre*. The sex (or salaciousness, depending on point of view) exceeded in explicitness anything found in its predecessor. Once again cries for censorship and widespread book bannings followed its release, and a number of critics argued that Caldwell ranked not far above a pornographer. No playwrights rose to take on the challenge of converting the story to some form of acceptable drama. The movie industry, reluctant to violate any tenets of the **Hollywood Production Code** then in effect, held back from filming *God's Little Acre* until 1958, a full quarter-century after its initial publication.

In the meantime, he published more short stories during the mid-1930s, many dealing directly with racism as well as poverty. Caldwell's social conscience grew increasingly agitated in the later years of the decade: he saw a soulless industrialism grinding down workers as the South moved from an agrarian society to one with more emphasis on factories and cheap hourly labor.

Two additional novels, *Journeyman* (1935) and *Trouble in July* (1940), came out during this period but lacked the power and the commercial success of his earlier work. He met photographer Margaret Bourke-White (1904–1971) in 1936. They agreed to collaborate on a book containing Caldwell's text and Bourke-White's photographs, a nonfiction work about conditions in the Depression-era South. Their efforts resulted in *You Have Seen Their Faces* (1937), a blending of Caldwell's observations about the grinding poverty and injustices people suffered during these years and Bourke-White's remarkable black-and-white photographs that provide the visual proof.

Modern Age Books of New York originally published the work, since documentary **photography**, especially under the auspices of the **New Deal**'s Farm Security Administration (FSA), had come into vogue as a means of chronicling current events. *Life* magazine, a new concept in periodicals, featured photojournalism and offered its premier issue on newsstands in the fall of 1936. A stark photo of a Montana dam taken by Margaret Bourke-White appeared on its cover. With Caldwell enjoying considerable fame for his writing and Bourke-White well established as a photographer, the pairing virtually assured brisk sales. Over the course of their enterprise, the two decided to wed, tying the knot in 1939. Devotion to their professions, however, brought the marriage to an end after only three years.

Caldwell continued to publish, but his greatest accomplishments lay behind him. The paperback revolution—the ready availability of virtually any recent book in a cheaper paperbound edition—occurred at about the time of World War II. Although Caldwell's novels and collected short stories had done reasonably well during the 1930s, their sales set no records and he seldom made the **best seller** lists. With the advent of inexpensive paperbacks, coupled with garish, often lurid, covers, books like *Tobacco Road* and *God's Little Acre* took off. Often promising or at least suggesting more than they could deliver, they made publishing history.

The sales of Caldwell's fiction soared, and he made far more money in royalties in the decades following the war than he ever did during the 1930s. This kind of success further distanced many literary critics from him, since they equated huge sales with mediocrity. Not until late in his life did he receive the critical recognition that had been denied him during his most productive years. Today, Erskine Caldwell has sold more titles than almost any other American writers, living or dead.

Despite all the controversy that swirled around him, perhaps no writer of the decade, with the possible exception of John Steinbeck, better captured the suffering of rural Americans during the Great Depression. His naturalistic depictions of the dehumanizing effects of illiteracy and cultural deprivation, coupled with relentless poverty, both financial and spiritual, offended many, perhaps because they carried more truth than those readers were willing to acknowledge.

See also Magazines; Movies; Race Relations & Stereotyping; Stage Productions

SELECTED READING
Cook, Sylvia Jenkins. *Erskine Caldwell and the Fiction of Poverty: The Flesh and the Spirit.* Baton Rouge: Louisiana State University Press, 1991.
Miller, Dan B. *Erskine Caldwell: The Journey from Tobacco Road.* New York: Alfred A. Knopf, 1994.
Mixon, Wayne. *The People's Writer: Erskine Caldwell and the South.* Charlottesville: University of Virginia Press, 1995.

CANDY. Candy ranks among America's favorite **foods**, and during the 1930s, just about everyone could find 5 cents to spend on this special treat or at least a penny for cheaper versions of some brands (about 78 cents and 16 cents in contemporary money). Innovators like the Hollywood Candy Company and the Klein Chocolate Company offered 3-cent bars (about 47 cents today). The national craving for candy seemed insatiable and the industry strove to satisfy everyone's sweet tooth. To attract attention, some Sperry Candy Company bars sported unusual names—Chicken Dinner, Club Sandwich, and Denver Sandwich. These bars contained candy, not chicken or other nonsweets, but supposedly they provided a satisfying and filling meal substitute.

During the 1930s, low sugar prices allowed manufacturers to produce and sell copious quantities of candy and prompted Americans to consume the most sugar per capita in their history. At the same time, the industry welcomed the discovery of a new synthetic coating for candy bars. First used in 1934 by the Hollywood Candy Company on its Zero candy bar, this coating stayed harder in hot weather than traditional milk chocolate coverings and boosted the potential profitability of the candy business.

Despite all these advantages, the industry briefly endured lean times at the beginning of the Depression. To lure customers in those cost-conscious years, the Curtiss Candy Company proclaimed that "Baby Ruth makes a light lunch more invigorating than a heavier meal; a way to make lunches more delightful, and save money, too." The **advertising** worked; candy sales picked up as the decade progressed, convincing confectioners to retain their current products and even to introduce a number of new, sweet concoctions as illustrated in the chart below.

Candy and the 1930s

Year Introduced	Popular Name	Manufacturer
1930	Small versions of Mr. Goodbar, Hershey Milk Chocolate, & Hershey Honey-Almond Milk Chocolate (They were available for a penny apiece from vending machines.)	Hershey Chocolate Company
	Dip; Buy Jiminy (Dip and Buy Jiminy sold well for a few years and were then phased out.)	Curtiss Candy Company
	Zagnut	Clark Candy Company
	Snickers	Mars, Inc.
1931	Tootsie Pops	Sweets Company of America
	Bing Bar	Palmer Candy Company
1932	3 Musketeers	Mars, Inc.
	Heath Bar	Heath Company
	PayDay	Hollywood Candy Company
	Red Hots	Ferrara Pan Candy Company
Circa 1932	Sugar Daddy (Name change for a 1926 candy called Papa Sucker.)	Welch's Candy Company
1933	Kraft Caramels	Kraft Foods
1934	Zero Bar	Hollywood Candy Company
	Dreams (It had the same coconut filling as Mounds but was covered with milk chocolate instead of bittersweet.)	Peter Paul Candies
	Choward's Violet Mints	C. Howard Company
Mid-1930s	Chunky (Named for Silverstein's overweight daughter.)	Philip Silverstein, now Ward-Johnson Division of Terson Company
1935	Sugar Babies	Welch's Candy Company
1936	Mars Bar	Mars, Inc.
	5th Avenue	Luden Candy Company
	Mallo Cup	Boyer Brothers
1937	Dipsy Doodle (Named after a popular 1937 tune.)	Beich Company
	Sky Bar	NECCO Company

Year Introduced	Popular Name	Manufacturer
1938	Crunch	Nestlé
	Krackel	Hershey Chocolate Company
	Peco Brittle Bar	Atkinson Candy
	Rainbow Coconut Bar	Atkinson Candy
	Mint Stick	Atkinson Candy
	Chicken Bone	Atkinson Candy
1939	Giants	Overland Candy Company

Candy bars at times alluded political issues. The Eighteenth Amendment Bar ("with that Pre-War Flavor") from the Marvel Candy Company entered the market in the early 1930s. This chocolate-covered candy with a rum-flavored center presented a tongue-in-cheek statement about Prohibition and the restrictions on the manufacture, sale, or **transportation** of intoxicating liquors. The repeal of the Eighteenth Amendment in 1933 ended sales of this unique sweet.

Candy, of course, comes in shapes other than a bar; jelly beans, for example, have a distinctive ovoid or egg appearance. Experts disagree as to the exact origin of the jelly bean, but many think that the jelly center derives from a Middle Eastern confection known as Turkish delight, a sweet that dates back to biblical times. In an 1861 advertisement, William Schrafft (active nineteenth century), a Boston candy maker who had recently arrived in America, urged people to send jelly beans to soldiers in the Union Army. Schrafft's advertising efforts earned the jelly bean a place among the glass jars of candies on the shelves of general stores, and by the 1930s this type of candy had become enshrined as a part of Easter festivities, a popular tradition that has continued ever since.

Other candy makers made appearances in various popular culture venues across the country. The Paul F. Beich Candy Company had children throughout the Midwest chanting its jingle, "Whiz, best nickel candy bar there iz-z". For the **Century of Progress Exposition** in Chicago (1933–1934), the Beich Candy Company manufactured the Sky Ride Candy Bar. Wrapped in blue, red, and yellow paper, with a drawing of the fair's observation towers and the skyways complete with passenger cars, it sold well during the fair but disappeared soon after the exposition closed.

In the 1930s, a cartoon series, *Nestlé's Nest*, could be found on the comic pages of Sunday **newspapers**, and the accompanying advertisements featured both *Nestlé's* Milk Chocolate and *Nestlé's* Milk Chocolate Bar with Almonds. Candy bars also had connections with **radio**. Along with several other advertisers, Walnettos, individually wrapped chews made of hard caramel containing walnut bits, occasionally sponsored *Uncle Don* (1928–1949), a popular children's program; *Dr. I. Q.* (1939–1950), a quiz show that gave away silver dollars, broadcast under the advertising banner of the Mars Candy Company throughout most of its run. The Williamson Candy Company's **Amos 'n' Andy** candy bar flourished along with the radio series of the same name; it disappeared when the show dropped in popularity.

Some celebrities and sports figures at the height of their fame loaned their names to candy bars and candy advertisements. Immediately prior to the opening of the decade, the A. G. Morse Company offered the Winning Lindy bar in honor of aviator Charles Lindbergh (1902–1974), and in the early 1930s the **Rudy Vallee** (1901–1986) candy bar recognized the popular crooner. The Johnston Company, in advertisements for Valentine's Day candy, had Vallee, "the Vagabond Lover," touting their boxed candy. On the sports side, Bob Feller (b. 1918), a popular and successful Cleveland Indians pitcher, smiled from the wrapper of a candy bar bearing his likeness. Manufactured by the Euclid Candy Company of Brooklyn, New York, it appeared in candy displays from the late 1930s to the early 1940s.

Clarence Crane, a candy maker in Cleveland, Ohio, in 1912 created a mint candy in an attempt to have a summer treat that did not melt. These round mints with a hole gave them an appearance similar to the life preservers used by ships; seeing the connection, Crane called his new candy Crane's Peppermint Life Savers. The name stuck, of course, and capitalizing on the popularity of this candy, in 1935 the familiar five-flavor Life Saver rolls appeared on the market.

A large assortment of candies and candy bars clearly satisfied America's sweet tooth during the 1930s and almost everyone had some loose change to splurge on a purchase of one kind or another. Eighty percent of the candy bars made had a chocolate covering or some form of chocolate inside; clearly, chocolate ranked at the top. Various other ingredients also went into the making of candy such as nuts, peanut butter, crèmes, caramel, and fruit. Admiral Richard E. Byrd (1888–1957), took $2^1/_2$ tons of the New England Confectionery Company's sugary wafers to the South Pole on one of his expeditions during the 1930s. He provided each of his men almost a pound a week of NECCO sweets while in the Antarctic. What better way to acknowledge America's love affair with candy?

See also Comic Strips; Desserts; Fairs & Expositions; Grocery Stores & Supermarkets; Ice Cream; Prohibition & Repeal

SELECTED READING
Broekel, Ray. *The Chocolate Chronicles*. Lombard, IL: Wallace Homestead, 1985.
———. *The Great American Candy Bar Book*. Boston: Houghton Mifflin, 1982.
Candy. http://www.uwm.edu/ano/project4.html
Jelly Beans. http://www.foodreference.com/html/fjellybeans.html
Kimmerle, Beth. *Candy, the Sweet History*. Portland, OR: Collectors Press, 2003.

CARTER FAMILY, THE. Alvin Pleasant Carter (1891–1960), always known as A. P., his wife Sara (1898–1979; born Sara Dougherty), and her cousin Maybelle (1909–1978; born Maybelle Addington) performed, recorded, and sold records under the name of The Carter Family between 1927 and 1943. Certainly not the first family band, the Carters became one of the most influential groups in country **music** history. Their commercial breakthrough occurred in 1927 when they cut several sides in Bristol, Tennessee, for Ralph Peer (1892–1960), a pioneering A&R (artists and repertoire) man. As a result, the trio signed a contract with the Victor Talking Machine Company, manufacturers of Victor records, one of the leading record labels of the day. The Carters no doubt felt fortunate to already have a contract in hand when the

Depression struck, a time when both the industry and many of its artists struggled economically.

A. P. had worked for many years as a fruit tree salesman and as he traveled in remote parts of western Virginia and Tennessee he collected old and unusual Appalachian folk songs. Using this rural music as a basis for the trio's programs, A. P. served as the group's arranger, as well as planning and organizing their engagements. A fiddler, he also strummed a guitar, and occasionally added his bass voice. Sara sang lead with a strong contralto and played banjo, second guitar, and autoharp. Maybelle provided the harmony line and also displayed a mastery of the guitar, banjo, and autoharp. Their utilization of vocal harmony, and Maybelle's revolutionary technique of playing solo lead on guitar instead of just rhythm, brought the most immediate and lasting recognition to the group.

Success came quickly; the threesome had sold over 700,000 records by 1930. The Carter Family's songs of love and loss, desperation and joy, captured the attention of many as the nation entered the darkest days of the Depression. Their most famous songs came from their first seven years of recording, numbers such as "Wabash Cannonball," "My Dixie Darling," "Wildflower," "I'm Thinking Tonight of My Blue Eyes," and their signature piece, "Keep on the Sunny Side."

During the economic turndown, the Carters worked sporadically. Maybelle had married A. P.'s brother Ezra (usually called "Eck," 1898–1975), and both couples stayed busy establishing their homes and raising children. A. P. and Sara eventually separated, but the trio continued to perform and record. In 1932, Peer continued his association with the Carters, and this time they contracted directly with him instead of Victor. Three years later, Peer moved from Victor to the American Recording Company (ARC) and took the Carters with him. In 1936, still under Peer's management, the trio began cutting sides for Decca Records. Most critics agree that their best overall **recordings** followed during the next two years, many of them being rerecordings of their previous Victor hits.

Their fame expanding, the Carter Family in 1938 signed a contract with Dr. John Brinkley's (1885–1941) powerful XERA **radio** station in Ciudad Acuna, Mexico. The Carters settled just across the border in Del Rio, Texas, in order to be close to the station's studios. A. P. and Sara, despite their marital separation, also made the move, along with their daughter Janette (b. 1923), as did Maybelle, accompanied by her children Helen (1927–1998), June (1929–2003), and Anita (1933–1999). They crossed into Mexico each day to perform two shows at the 500,000-watt station that allowed them to broadcast their music over much of the continental United States, the greatest exposure of their career.

Sara remarried in 1939, but the Carter Family continued with XERA for a second year, adding the daughters as a regular feature. After the Mexican government forced the closure of XERA, the Carters went to a much smaller station in Charlotte, North Carolina, for two years. But Sara and her husband had established a home in California and her interest in continuing with the trio waned. In March 1943, the Charlotte contract expired and the original Carter Family disbanded.

Over the course of 16 years, the Carter Family assembled a collection of some 275-plus songs—a mix of ballads, love songs, and gospel and folk music that have provided roots for much traditional American country and bluegrass music. Many country music performers, including such famous ones as Roy Acuff (1903–1992) and **Woody Guthrie**

(1912–1967), had at least one Carter song in their repertoires. When the group broke up, Maybelle continued in the music business with her daughters, performing under the name of Mother Maybelle and the Carter Sisters. Daughter June married a rising country singer named Johnny Cash (1932–2003) in 1968 and emerged as a popular country entertainer under the name June Carter Cash. Rosanne Cash (b. 1956), June's stepdaughter, continues the musical dynasty as do some of the descendents of A. P. and Sara.

See also Grand Ole Opry; *The National Barn Dance*; Religion; Western Films

SELECTED READING
Carter Family. http://www.pbs.org/wgbh/amex/carterfamily/timeline/index.html
Golbey, Brian. *The Carter Family: Wildwood Flower*. CD. Liner notes. AJA 5323, 2000.
Zwonitzer, Mark, with Charles Hirshberg, *Will You Miss Me When I'm Gone? The Carter Family and Their Legacy in American Music*. New York: Simon & Schuster, 2002.

CENTURY OF PROGRESS EXPOSITION (CHICAGO WORLD'S FAIR). Interest in **fairs and expositions** waned during the prosperous 1920s, but the 1930s witnessed an increase in both the number and popularity of this inexpensive means of entertainment. These events encouraged consumerism and provided many communities an opportunity to boost a Depression-ridden economy.

For the decade, Chicago's Century of Progress Exposition (1933–1934) and the **New York World's Fair** (1939–1940) rank as the most important and successful examples of major exhibitions. Sited on 427 acres of parkland along Lake Michigan, and just south of the downtown Loop, the Chicago extravaganza drew a steady stream of paying visitors. Originally scheduled to run only during 1933, its success allowed it to continue for an additional year.

The planners had a twofold intent: to celebrate the centennial of Chicago's 1833 founding and to highlight the scientific and industrial progress of the United States. Organizers rejected government subsidies and instead raised money from concession contracts, issuing of bonds, and selling certificates of membership that allowed the purchaser 10 admissions. The federal government paid for its own pavilion and exhibits, and the theme of technological innovation attracted industrial giants such as General Motors, Ford, Chrysler, and Sears, Roebuck and Company, among many others; these corporate supporters willingly covered their costs, seeing the resultant publicity as money well spent.

Planning for the fair commenced in 1927 with the intention of building temporary structures. The final scaled-down model exemplified economy and consisted of buildings following a functional but decorative **Art Deco** style of **architecture**. Some exhibitors used pylons or towers to provide a distinctive feature. For example, the Electrical Building had two 100-foot pylons framing a water gate through which visitors could arrive by boat from across the lagoon.

The **Travel** and **Transportation** Building, perhaps the most distinctive structure, featured a domed roof suspended 125 feet high by cables attached to 12 steel towers around its exterior perimeter. This provided an interior height of over 100 feet uncluttered by columns or load-bearing walls. Westinghouse and General Electric, lighting designers for

Aerial view of the Century of Progress Exposition, the 1933–1934 Chicago World's Fair. (Courtesy of the Library of Congress)

the fair, used both indirect and colored lighting to enhance the 23 brilliant colors tying the buildings together. People nicknamed the site "Rainbow City."

Postmaster General James A. Farley (1888–1976) officially opened the gates to the exposition on May 27, 1933. Just two days earlier, 1-cent and 3-cent commemorative stamps honoring the fair had been issued and flown to Chicago. October 2, 1933, saw the release of a 50-cent airmail stamp showing the **airship** *Graf Zeppelin* on a flight from Germany, heading toward the beckoning exposition towers of Chicago. Extremely rare, collectors continue to eagerly seek this unusual airmail issue.

True to previous exposition formats, the Century of Progress visitor could walk through gardens or beside pools with fountains and choose from a broad variety of educational and entertainment opportunities—an operating oil refinery, an automobile assembly line, a radio-controlled tractor, an early **television** receiver, a toothpaste tube–packing demonstration, or important scenes from Chicago's history. A five-acre playground called the Enchanted Island functioned as a day-care center, with each child being examined by a doctor upon entrance. The mile-long midway, featuring many amusement park rides, included Frank Buck's wild animal show, *Bring 'em Back Alive*, as well as exhibits from Ripley's *Believe It or Not!*

Dioramas have long been a common feature of fairs, but mechanized ones provided a new wrinkle on an old concept at the Century of Progress. Scenes that received particular attention included moving human figures as a part of a re-creation of an historic event and International Harvester's full-size mechanical cow that chewed its cud, blinked its eyes, mooed, and gave milk.

As a study in contrasts, many flocked to the performance tent of fan dancer Sally Rand (1904–1979), while others gathered at the more formal American art exhibit housed at the nearby Art Institute. Miss Rand, possibly the biggest hit of the fair, danced, apparently nude, behind giant ostrich fans and, as a finale, behind a huge translucent bubble. An unexpected success, she wowed the audience. The American art display included works by Thomas Eakins (1844–1916) and Winslow Homer (1836–1910), as well as James McNeill Whistler's (1834–1903) *Portrait of My Mother* (commonly called *Whistler's Mother*; 1871), and **Grant Wood**'s (1891–1942) *American Gothic* (1930). The popularity of Wood's portrait resulted in its becoming the best-known American painting of all time.

Most states and many ethnic groups celebrated their own days, which added to the festive atmosphere. Additional days also received official sanction. To commemorate the end of Prohibition, the fair provided free beer and sandwiches on November 8, 1933, and called the occasion Personal Responsibility Day. On November 10 people on relief rolls received free admittance. Nearby Comiskey Park, home of the Chicago White Sox, became the site of the first major league All-Star **baseball** game on July 6, 1933.

During the first year, foreign participation consisted of many offerings, such as France presenting the "Streets of Paris," while Belgium built a model village. China, Czechoslovakia, Italy, Japan, Sweden, and Ukraine also erected pavilions, and other countries exhibited in the Hall of Nations located in the Travel and Transportation Building. These successes in attracting fairgoers brought about an increase in foreign exhibitors in 1934.

Special **trains** traveled to Chicago from across the continent and served to introduce the public to the first Streamliners. Once in Chicago the sleek cars and engines of the Union Pacific's City of Salina and the Burlington Line's Pioneer Zephyr became parts of the displays. The Pioneer Zephyr even established a speed record in 1934, reaching Chicago from Denver—a distance of just over 1,000 miles—in 13 hours, or at an average speed of 77.6 mph. Fledging airlines had nothing on the speedy railroads.

Once people arrived at the fair, transportation continued to be a popular attraction. The Sky-Ride, a 1930s version of a monorail, carried visitors 1,850 feet across the fairgrounds in cable cars 200 feet above the ground. Two 628-foot tall twin towers, named **Amos and Andy** after the main characters in the popular **radio** show of the same name, supported the ride. Greyhound had a fleet of 60 modern **buses** ready to transport visitors around the fair. Called World's Fair Greyhounds, they could accommodate 90 people (50 sitting, 40 standing).

The exposition's first season closed on November 12, 1933, then everything reopened on May 26, 1934, with some new attractions. Chrysler sponsored stock car races and Standard Oil Company replaced a film on the oil industry with a free wild animal act. But the most significant addition came with the Ford Motor Company pavilion. The wall of a rotunda within the building, created by Walter Dorwin Teague (1883–1960), well known for his industrial **design** work, showed an automobile assembly procedure. Other exhibits showcased Ford's latest technological innovations. Seventy percent of the daily fair visitors toured the Ford pavilion, making it the most popular exhibit of the year.

Immersed in contemporary surroundings that hinted at a new and exciting future, the fair had to have an impact on the average visitor. The Hall of Science, the largest and most important exhibit building, offered working models of new technological devices that supported the idea of a hopeful future. It made the comic-strip world of the popular *Buck Rogers* not so unbelievable, after all. If nothing else, the fair personified optimism in the face of economic troubles.

But the architecture accomplished even more. A $37 million display of modernity, the fair's sparkling promenades dazzled the eye and helped to popularize architecture based on Art Deco and modernist designs, as well as machine age–based structures in the emerging **International Style** and **Streamlining**. Builders exhibited a number of single-family homes, and the futuristic ones, such as the House of Tomorrow and the Crystal House, gave visitors a hint of domestic architecture to come. In its entirety, the Century of Progress Exposition served as the perfect antidote to the dreariness of the Depression.

The largest such venture up to this time, the Chicago World's Fair ended its two-year run with a surplus of a little over half a million dollars and a final profit of $160,000 (approximately $2.4 million in contemporary dollars), a remarkable feat considering the national economic crisis at the time. When it closed at the end of October 1934, over 39 million people had flocked to see its combination of opulence and tawdriness. Its success encouraged other cities such as Dallas, Texas, San Diego, California, Cleveland, Ohio, and, of course, New York City, to hold large fairs of their own.

See also Automobiles; Aviation; Circuses; Comic Strips; Education; Prohibition & Repeal; Science Fiction; Stamp Collecting

SELECTED READING
Findling, John E., and Kimberly D. Pelle, eds. *Historical Dictionary of World's Fairs and Expositions, 1851–1988.* Westport, CT: Greenwood Press, 1990.
Official Pictures of a Century of Progress Exposition: Photographs by Kaufmann & Fabry Co., Official Photographers. Chicago: Reuben H. Donnelley Corp., 1933.
Rydell, Robert W., John E. Findling, and Kimberly D. Pelle. *Fair America: World's Fairs in the United States.* Washington, DC: Smithsonian Institution Press, 2000.

CHILDREN'S FILMS. Child actors, performers under about 12 years of age, have always been an integral part of the film industry. Children's **movies** made money in the silent era, especially in comedies, and with the advent of sound in 1927, Hollywood saw no reason to tinker with success.

When considering the children's films made during the Depression era, one need look no further than the *Our Gang* comedy shorts, all 220 or them (plus one full-length feature, 1936's *General Spanky*), that ran from 1922 until 1944. Producer Hal Roach (1892–1992), a true motion picture pioneer, got the idea to create the series after watching some kids at play. In 1922, he introduced *Hal Roach's Rascals*, two-reel (roughly 20 minutes long) silent comedies that featured youngsters doing what they do best, playing, getting into mischief, and generally having fun. Roach contended—correctly—that audiences would enjoy their youthful high jinks.

For the next 20 years, new *Rascals* pictures showed at movie houses everywhere. Called *Our Gang* comedies at the time, the series officially became *The Little Rascals* in 1956 when it went to **television** and copyright concerns would not allow the use of the old name. *Our Gang*, originally silent, first utilized sound in 1929. One-reel shorts, the comedies served to flesh out theater billings as owners sought ways to lure in customers. Despite the technical changes, the kids' antics remained the same throughout the decade. George McFarland (1928–1993) took the role of Spanky in 1931 and kept it until 1942. He probably remains the best-remembered Rascal of the day, although Billie Thomas's (1931–1980) Buckwheat and Carl Switzer's (1927–1959) Alfalfa run a close second.

Often overshadowed by splashy, full-length productions with popular stars, *Our Gang* continued on its comfortable way delighting millions as it did so. The series inspired many imitators, such as *Mickey McGuire*, with Mickey Rooney (b. 1920), and *Baby Burlesks*, with **Shirley Temple** (b. 1928), but nothing seemed to equal the original.

Jackie Cooper (b. 1922), one of a number of successful child actors of the day, got his start in the *Our Gang* shorts; he played Jackie from 1929 to 1931. This exposure led to *Skippy* (1931), a full-length feature in which he plays the popular character from Percy Crosby's (1891–1964) long-running comic strip of the same name. Riding a crest of popularity, Cooper costarred with Wallace Beery (1885–1949) in *The Champ* (1931), a sentimental **boxing** picture, and received an Academy Award nomination for Best Actor at

10 years of age, the youngest ever to be so honored. *Treasure Island* (1934) teamed him with Beery again, and he even reprised his Jackie role with the *Our Gang* cast in 1937's *Our Gang Follies of 1938*, a show-within-a-show short that has the group imitating famous adult entertainers. By the following year, however, adolescence had caught up with Cooper, removing him from the roster of child actors, and *That Certain Age* (1938) matched him up with another teenager, Deanna Durbin (b. 1921), in a musical tale of youthful romance. Unlike many of his contemporaries, Cooper went on to a successful career in motion pictures in his adult years.

A number of other youthful players also charmed audiences during the 1930s. The Dublin-born Freddie Bartholomew (b. Frederic Llwellyn, 1924–1992) landed the title role in *David Copperfield* (1935), and his career soared after that. He starred in Frances Hodgson Burnett's (1849–1924) classic *Little Lord Fauntleroy* in 1936, and later won the coveted role of Harvey in a filmed adaptation of Rudyard Kipling's (1895–1936) *Captains Courageous* (1937). A string of other successes followed, including *Kidnapped* (1938), *The Swiss Family Robinson* (1940), and *Tom Brown's School Days* (1940), but by the early 1940s his career had petered out, and he disappeared from the movie scene, another victim of encroaching adulthood.

A similar fate awaited Jane Withers (b. 1926). As a child, she enjoyed major parts in *Ginger* (1935), *Paddy O'Day* (1935), *Can This Be Dixie?* (1936), and a few others. But, like Freddie Bartholomew, she, too, grew up and out of movies during the 1940s. She enjoyed a comeback of sorts with the rise of television, especially in commercials. Many people doubtless remember Jane Withers as "the Lady Plumber" in a series of advertisements for Comet Cleanser.

Fortunately for many young players during the 1930s, films about teens and their concerns mushroomed in popularity and so a number of former child stars stayed busy. Desperate for new faces, the studios constantly searched for a fresh crop of promising child performers, and many hopeful parents groomed their little ones to become movie stars. Despite the Depression, dancing schools flourished as kids tried to master tap and ballroom techniques. By the mid-1930s, the studios faced a glut of would-be, but unemployed, youthful actors, an ironic situation that mirrored the real world beyond the sound stages. Of the thousands of youngsters who tried out for various parts, only a tiny handful ever got on screen, and even fewer achieved any long-term success.

Of course, exceptions exist to everything, and in this case the exception could be found in a truly precocious little girl named Shirley Temple. Without a doubt she emerged as the most popular movie star of the era. Between 1934 and 1939, Shirley Temple took top billing in 13 films, and reigned as the top box-office draw of any age.

After a couple of unremarkable one- and two-reelers made at age five, along with *Baby Burlesks*, she stole the show in *Stand Up and Cheer!* (1934), her first full-length feature. In quick succession, Paramount Pictures cast her in *Little Miss Marker* (1934) and *Now and Forever* (1934). That was all it took; the boom was on. Within two years, her fan mail topped 60,000 letters a month; a huge Shirley Temple industry had moved into high gear, mass-producing an array of records, books, playthings, and clothes popularized in her movies; and her income from endorsements exceeded anything the studio paid her.

Just prior to Shirley Temple's arrival as a star, several other youngsters—mere toddlers—seemed primed to dominate in children's movies. Baby Rose Marie (b. Rose Marie Mazetta, 1923) caused a sensation as a singer at age three, making a name for herself on various **radio** shows. She appeared in her first film, a short titled *Baby Rose Marie the Child Wonder*, in 1929. Several more shorts followed, along with a singing role in the full-length *International House* (1933), but by then she had reached the ripe old age of 10 and Shirley Temple's rising career had begun to blossom, eclipsing all the competition. Baby Rose Marie disappeared for some years, only to reappear on television in the 1950s.

Another "Baby," in this case Baby LeRoy (b. Ronald Le Roy Overacker, 1932–2001), made one of the youngest debuts of all. At age six months, he appeared in *A Bedtime Story* (1933), more of an adult comedy than a children's film. But his performance as an infant impressed Paramount Pictures, and the studio cast him in another three movies in 1933 alone. One of them, *Tillie and Gus*, paired Baby LeRoy with comedian W. C. Fields (1880–1946), a man notorious for his onscreen dislike of children. The two managed to get on, although Baby LeRoy often upstaged the veteran actor.

Another four pictures followed in 1934, including *The Old Fashioned Way* and *It's a Gift*, both of which team Fields and Baby LeRoy again. On screen, the child star makes the comedian's life miserable whenever the two appear together, creating a Hollywood legend about how much Fields detested him. Like most such legends, it contained some elements of truth, but overall it was an exaggeration.

In 1935, Baby LeRoy made *It's a Great Life*; it would be his final film. At age three, his movie days came to an end. If nothing else, his short career reflects the rigors of show business and the fragility of fame. An abortive comeback in 1939 never materialized because of illness. Baby LeRoy, seven years old, no longer fit his screen persona.

In the meantime, cartoons captivated children throughout the decade, climaxing in 1938 with the beautifully drawn **Snow White and the Seven Dwarfs**. An immediate success, it announced the dominance of **Walt Disney** (1901–1966) and his studio technicians in the field of animation.

Not all films for children featured child actors. The strictures of the **Hollywood Production Code** made the content of virtually any film produced during the later Depression years appropriate for young and old. A slew of rousing adventure pictures, such as Errol Flynn's (1909–1959) *Captain Blood* (1935) and *Robin Hood* (1938), any **Western film** with Gene Autry (1907–1998) or Roy Rogers (1911–1998), and slapstick comedies, fantasies, dance-filled **musicals**, heroic biographies, along with cliff-hanging **serials** for Saturday matinees, meant children could select from a wide range of choices, choices that went far beyond those movies made explicitly for the preadolescent set.

Never the equal, at least in box office receipts, of other movie genres, children's films nonetheless had their following, and they always entertained a guaranteed audience. The motion picture industry continued to produce these movies throughout the decade and on into the years to follow. Most of them proved ephemeral at best, but they constituted a small but vital part of Hollywood's overall output.

See also Comic Strips; Judy Garland; Race Relations & Stereotypes; Spectacle & Costume Drama Films; Teenage & Juvenile Delinquency Films; Toys; Youth

SELECTED READING

Cary, Diana Serra. *Hollywood's Children: An Inside Account of the Child Star Era.* Dallas: Southern Methodist University Press, 1997.

Child Stars. http://www.classicmoviekids.com

Zierold, Norman J. *The Child Stars.* New York: Coward-McCann, 1965.

CHINA CLIPPERS. Pan American Airways (PAA) began using flying boats—large seaplanes that take off and land on water—in the late 1920s for flights to Cuba and later to points in South America. By 1931, with the introduction of the Sikorsky S-40 seaplane, the company coined the term Pan American Clipper for its aircraft, an allusion to the speedy American sailing vessels that had plied the seas in the mid-nineteenth century.

Juan Trippe (1899–1981), the founder of PAA, had already established routes in the Caribbean and South America. Charles Lindbergh (1902–1974), famous for his solo flight across the Atlantic Ocean in 1927, served as a technical adviser for the airline; he flew a Sikorsky S-42, a larger version of the S-40, from Miami, Florida, to Buenos Aires, Argentina, in 1934. It accommodated up to 32 passengers and had a 1,200-mile range, not enough to make the Florida-Argentina flight without help from additional fuel tanks.

In the meantime, Trippe turned his attention to the Pacific. He needed flying boats capable of crossing thousands of miles of open sea, and he chose the Martin M-130, which employed a crew of five to eight, and carried 46 passengers. Boasting a range of 3,500 miles, the first M-130 flew a portion of the Pacific on November 22, 1935, and returned on December 6, 1935. It had gone from California to Hawaii with 111,000 letters on board, the first transpacific airmail flight. It was launched with much fanfare, and 25,000 people witnessed its San Francisco departure; 3,000 greeted its arrival at Pearl Harbor, Hawaii.

With its exceptional range, the M-130 allowed PAA in 1936 to take on the challenge of flying from San Francisco to Manila, with prearranged refueling stops at Hawaii, Midway Island, Wake Island, and Guam along the way. Christened the Philippine Clipper and cruising at 150 miles per hour, the trip took one week, stops included, whereas a steamer, sailing direct, would have taken at least 17 days.

With its flights getting closer to mainland Asia, the company renamed its fleet the China Clippers, and in 1937 they commenced passenger travel to Hong Kong, more than 8,500 miles away from the United States. In 1939, PAA purchased three Boeing 314 Flying Boats, the largest yet in its class. Boasting a top speed of 199 miles per hour, the Boeings entered service in 1939 and became the largest civilian aircraft then flying. This glamorous behemoth displayed a modern, Streamlined exterior set off by a distinctive three-fin tail assembly.

The interior, created by industrial designer Norman Bel Geddes (1893–1958), displayed the then-popular Streamlined look. It housed two interior decks, an upper for the crew and a lower for up to 74 passengers, although that number fell to 36 persons if everyone required sleeping accommodations. Luxuriously, but functionally, appointed, these aircraft offered travelers an extravagant experience, with such amenities as staterooms and suites that included seating that converted into beds. A smoking lounge, a self-service pantry, dressing rooms, men's and women's restrooms, and a dining room that served full-course meals in a space wider than that found on a Pullman club car, finished off the Boeing Clippers.

Shortly before the outbreak of World War II, the British relented on their refueling limitations for Bermuda and Newfoundland, which meant Trippe could add a European route to the Clipper's schedule. On May 20, 1939, Pan American Airways inaugurated its first transatlantic mail service. In these huge flying boats, almost one ton of mail could travel to Europe in 29 hours. Passenger service commenced on June 28, 1939, aboard the

A China Clipper afloat, with crew and passengers disembarking. (Courtesy of the Library of Congress)

Yankee Clipper. Atlantic or Pacific, this luxurious means of **transportation** proved expensive. Pacific flights to Hong Kong cost approximately $950 (or some $14,000 in contemporary dollars) for a one-way ticket; Atlantic flights ran about $650 (or $9,500), sharply limiting the number of Americans able to enjoy such a grand experience.

Thanks to Hollywood, however, the public could enjoy, vicariously, the pleasure of a China Clipper flight through a 1936 Warner Brothers production of the same title. Actor Pat O'Brien (1899–1983) plays a character that starts out with a small airline. He experiences financial problems and then joins flying ace Hap Stuart, portrayed by Humphrey Bogart (1899–1957), in piloting flying boats in the Caribbean. Eventually they move to a transpacific route. The film suffers from a formulaic plot but includes footage of China Clippers, and it heightened public interest in commercial aviation.

The great flying boats disappeared after World War II, replaced by more efficient and economical land-based airplanes. For a brief moment in the 1930s, their flights to exotic locales, their fashionable passengers coddled in every way, removed air travel from the humdrum and struck a romantic chord in the hearts of many.

See also Airships; Aviation; Movies; Travel

SELECTED READING
China Clipper. http://www.aviation-history.com/martin/m130.html
————. http://www.pbs.org/kcet/chasingthesun/planes/clipper.html

Clarke, Gerald. "Pan Am's Clippers: The Revolutionary Planes That Transformed 1930s Travel." *Architectural Digest* 61:5 (May 2004): 280–285.

Gandt, Robert L. *China Clipper: The Age of the Great Flying Boats.* Annapolis, MD: Naval Institute Press, 1991.

CHRYSLER BUILDING, THE. In 1930, New York City continued a seemingly non-stop downtown building boom. One skyscraper after another had arisen on Manhattan Island throughout the later 1920s, and each challenged previous records for height, number of stories, available office space, and amenities. Although the Depression would eventually put the brakes on this boom, construction workers still clambered over the steel girders of a number of large, ongoing projects as the new decade began.

In the city's financial district, craftsmen applied the finishing touches to the Bank of Manhattan Trust Building, sometimes referred to as 40 Wall Street. The work of architect H. Craig Severance (1879–1941), with the assistance of Yasuo Matsui (1883–1956), its backers felt confident that the new structure would become the world's tallest building. The title had been long held by Cass Gilbert's (1859–1934) venerable Woolworth Building, built in 1912, which was 792 feet tall with 60 floors.

Severance and his crew knew that a new midtown structure, the Chrysler Building, would be a competitor for the coveted designation, but they felt confident that 40 Wall Street would tower over all others. Toward the end of 1929, they claimed the title, announcing that their almost-finished building measured, when counting a hastily added flagpole, 927 feet. It boasted 71 stories.

But any joy they felt proved short-lived. At Lexington Avenue and 42nd Street, the architect behind the unfinished Chrysler Building had a surprise up his sleeve. William Van Alen (1882–1954) realized his initial **design** for the Chrysler Building would make it about the same height as 40 Wall Street. And so he constructed and cleverly concealed a 185-foot spire, or "vertex," within the skyscraper's crown. To Severance's dismay, Van Alen hoisted his spire in November 1929. As it slowly climbed toward the sky, the Chrysler Building achieved a record-breaking height of 1,048 feet, successfully claiming the title of "world's tallest." In so doing, it even eclipsed the 1889 French Eiffel Tower, which measured 1,024 feet. Van Alen's design claimed the title both for a regular building and for any other kind of man-made structure.

Severance's 40 Wall Street and Van Alen's Chrysler Building received their finishing touches in 1930. Just a few blocks from the new champion, at Fifth Avenue and 35th Street, yet another contender had been taking form. In 1931, less than a year after the race between Severance and Van Alen, the **Empire State Building** would open its doors, an engineering marvel that reached 1,252 feet into the sky, a new record holder, and one that would remain unchallenged for the rest of the decade.

William Van Alen had been a partner with H. Craig Severance from 1914 to 1924. The two architects, however, suffered a falling out and went their separate ways. In 1928, a developer had commissioned Van Alen to design an office structure on the site where the Chrysler Building would eventually arise. Following some financial problems on the part of the original developer, automotive magnate Walter P. Chrysler (1875–1940) acquired the land. He saw potential in Van Alen and kept him on, commissioning the architect to design something more spectacular than what had originally been envisioned. A colorful personality, Chrysler wanted a statement, a building that would reflect both his and his company's success, and he got his wish.

One of the most beloved buildings in a city that boasts a remarkable collection of outstanding skyscrapers, the Chrysler Building employs the then-fashionable decorative motifs of **Art Deco**, but it also possesses an individuality that goes beyond stylistic trends. Van Alen clad the tower in Nirosta (also called Enduro), a chromium and nickel precursor to stainless steel, a material that endlessly shimmers, and then he used the symbols of automotive manufacturing to honor his patron. Shiny Chrysler Motor hubcaps and radiator caps embellish the facades; patriotic eagles modeled after Chrysler hood ornaments serve as nontraditional gargoyles. At night, strategically placed lighting illuminates the entire structure, a beacon of success. In all, it bespeaks an optimism about a modern, technological age, one in which **automobiles** (preferably Chrysler products) will play a major role. The encroaching Great Depression might diminish some of the glitter for awhile, but like most great architecture, the Chrysler Building transcends time. For later generations, the Depression may have become a hazy memory, but Van Alen's masterpiece remains fresh and new.

See also Architecture; International Style; Streamlining

SELECTED READING

Bascomb, Neal. *Higher: A Historic Race to the Sky and the Making of a City.* New York: Doubleday, 2003.

Dupre, Judith. *Skyscrapers.* New York: Black Dog & Leventhal, 1996.

Robinson, Cervin, and Rosemarie Haag Bletter. *Skyscraper Style: Art Deco New York.* New York: Oxford University Press, 1975.

Stravitz, David. *The Chrysler Building: Creating a New York Icon, Day by Day.* Princeton, NJ: Princeton Architectural Press, 2002.

CIRCUSES. The first circus to entertain American audiences opened in Philadelphia, Pennsylvania, in the spring of 1793. Within a few years, companies large and small played the larger cities and took their extravaganzas to the far reaches of the country, traveling by river boat, wagon train, and rail. By the 1920s, a variety of circuses, such as Ringling Bros. and Barnum & Bailey, Sells-Floto, Sparks, Hagenbeck-Wallace, John Robinson, and the Christy Brothers, performed to capacity crowds. The shows consisted of cowboy and equestrian performances, interspersed with animal displays and acts, acrobatic high-wire daredevils and thrills, and juggling acts. Clowns bounced around the sawdust rings with their antics, and sideshows offered the opportunity to see sword-swallowers, fire-eaters, knife-throwers, and various other "freaks."

The onset of the Depression dealt a heavy blow to circuses everywhere. Upkeep and **transportation** were costly and even with tickets only 25 cents (roughly $3.00 in contemporary dollars), attendance dropped drastically. Smaller companies went bankrupt and larger ones had to cut back on the length of the season, as well as the number of shows and performers. The circus parade, once as important as the show under the tent, changed. Instead of marching down Main Street in all their glory, circuses now stole into town in the dead of night without a barker, a band, or colorfully dressed people and animals. On the practical side, this tactic eliminated free entertainment for all those along the way and perhaps added a few to the paying crowd.

Circuses appealed to audiences for several reasons. The **food**, such as sandwiches, **soft drinks**, and **ice cream**, offered almost as much pleasure as the entertainment. Of all the concessions, **candy** perhaps served as the most prominent temptation; many circuses featured a concession wagon devoted just to candy and staffed by a candy butcher. A rash of new 1930s candy bars helped boost sales and increase profits.

Of course, the amazing, breathtaking thrills of the center ring remained the primary attraction. The Hagenbeck-Wallace Circus, owned but not controlled by Ringling Bros., filled this requirement with one of the most popular acts of the time, wild animal trainer Clyde Beatty (1903–1965). In 1928, Beatty set a record by performing with 28 lions and tigers in one cage; he broke that record in 1929 and went on to handle his largest number in 1930—40 jungle-bred lions and tigers of both sexes.

Ringling Bros. had not presented wild animal acts in its shows since 1924, stating expense, danger, and public concerns about cruelty to animals as reasons. Because of Beatty's growing popularity, circus officials made an exception and scheduled him for appearances in "the Greatest Show on Earth" in New York City and Boston, Massachusetts, in 1932.

In a dress rehearsal early that year, a tiger knocked Beatty to the ground and bit him deeply in the thigh. **Radio** and **newspapers** repeatedly ran stories about the incident and Beatty's fight to recover. Six weeks after the attack, his life spared, Beatty left his wheelchair and resumed working with his animals. Audiences welcomed his remarkable return in time for the opening of the 1932 season, with repeat performances planned for 1933 and 1934. By overcoming fear in times of extreme adversity, Beatty immediately became a symbol of hope for the country just as President **Franklin D. Roosevelt** (1882–1945) had exhorted people to do in his 1933 inaugural address when he said, "we have nothing to fear but fear itself."

In addition to circus work, Beatty portrayed himself in the movie *The Big Cage* (1933), based on a book by the same name that he wrote with Edward Anthony (active 1930s). Both the book and the film reveal the dangers and thrills of training wild animals. Throughout the decade, Beatty continued with his circus act and movie career, and he graced the cover of *Time* magazine on March 29, 1937.

Tom Mix (1880–1940), the popular star of countless **Western films**, left Hollywood in 1929 and joined the Sells-Floto Circus as a cowboy celebrity. Universal Studios lured him back to the **movies** in 1932, but 10 films later, he bought a half interest in the Sam. B. Dill Circus. The name changed to the Sam B. Dill Circus and Tom Mix Wild West Show until 1935, when Mix assumed full ownership after Dill died. Under the new title of the Tom Mix Circus, the show ran until 1938, when it closed down, another victim of the times.

Because of the Depression, heavy unemployment occurred across the arts. As did many actors and actresses, circus performers found themselves without work. As part of President Roosevelt's **New Deal**, provisions of the Works Progress Administration (WPA; 1935–1943; name changed to Work Projects Administration in 1939) included assistance for individuals associated with the performing arts. Under the aegis of the WPA, the Federal Theatre Circus Program came into being. It ran from 1935 to 1939, the only government-operated circus in American history. It hired 375 performers a year to give free shows, primarily for hospital patients and the poor.

But not the WPA Circus, not new candy bars, and not breathtaking acts such as Clyde Beatty could pull circuses out of their Depression slump. Labor unrest, expenses, and strikes caused some shows to close during the last years of the decade. Also, Americans, listening to their radios and attending movies, had become more sophisticated in their entertainment requirements. Potential audiences felt that circuses did not live up to the spectacles of the costumes, lighting, and **music** coming from their receivers and Hollywood.

At the height of this challenge, two notable events helped to stabilize one particular circus: Ringling Bros. In 1938, they purchased an eight-year-old disfigured gorilla named Gargantua (1930–1949), better known through an incredible publicity campaign as Gargantua the Great. Facial scars, the result of an accident when young, gave him a nasty sneer. Well over five and a half feet in height, weighing 550 pounds, and possessed of his frightening expression, Gargantua easily filled the bill as "the world's most terrifying living creature" and "the most fiendishly ferocious brute that breathes," descriptions that made almost everyone desirous of seeing him. Warner Brothers immediately recognized similarities between Gargantua and the title ape in their 1933 hit, *King Kong*. The studio rereleased the film, a move that provided a financial boost to Warner Brothers and Gargantua's owners.

That same year, Ringling Bros. featured a show built around Frank Buck (1888–1950), creator of the Dallas Zoo in the 1920s, author of a 1930 best seller, *Bring 'em Back Alive*, and an animal supplier for circuses. Buck had already participated in four movies, so people knew about him. The circus program described his opening act as "Nepal," portraying it "in fantasy, splendor, and exotic opulence the royal welcome to 'Bring 'em Back Alive' Frank Buck by the Maharajah of Nepal and his native court." It worked; business for Ringling boomed for the rest of the decade. Buck, who had exhibited a Jungle Camp at the **Century of Progress Exhibition** in Chicago in 1934, also benefited: following his Ringling Bros. appearance, he repeated the Jungle Camp at the 1939 **New York World's Fair**.

Although the 1930s witnessed the introduction of some significant pieces of circus history, the decade also bade farewell to many shows. Those that survived, such as Ringling Bros., did so with difficulty. The American circus no longer occupied the upper tiers of popular entertainment; it had been replaced by the easy illusions of mass media.

SELECTED READING

Candy. http://www.circushistory.org/Bandwagon/bw-candy.htm

Culhane, John. *The American Circus: An Illustrated History*. New York: Henry Holt, 1990.

WPA Circus Project. *New York Times*, 3 November 1935, "WPA Circus Ready for Uptown Debut," 1 August 1938; "2,500,000 in Year Viewed WPA Plays." *Historic New York Times*. Proquest, Lynchburg College Library, Lynchburg, VA.

CIVILIAN CONSERVATION CORPS (CCC). Inaugurated on March 4, 1933, President **Franklin D. Roosevelt** (1882–1945) almost immediately began numerous social initiatives designed to lessen the effects of the Depression on families and individuals. Within the first 100 days of his administration, the federal government implemented several programs under an umbrella called the **New Deal**. One, the Civilian Conservation Corps (CCC), personally designed by the president, focused on placing groups of 150 to 200 single, unemployed young men in centers, or camps, to improve public land and conserve natural resources. Congress passed the bill on the last day of

March 1933 and Roosevelt signed it five days later. The CCC inducted its first corpsmen within two days of his signature.

To succeed, this program depended on cooperation among several federal agencies. Robert Fechner (1876–1939), the first CCC director until his death, and his deputy, James J. McEntee (active 1930s and 1940s), who served as director from 1939 until the program's end in 1942, ably worked toward this end. The coordination started with the Department of Labor. Through state and local offices, it established quotas, developed effective recruitment posters, and selected and enrolled young men on relief between the ages of 18 and 25. The age requirements changed in 1935, with a new range of 17 to 28.

The U.S. Army played a vital role in establishing the first CCC camps, erecting and equipping barracks, feeding and clothing the men, and maintaining discipline. Whenever possible, officials assigned enrollees to projects within their home state. The bulk of the recruits resided in the East, but many work sites were in the West. The army therefore mobilized the nation's **transportation** system in order to move thousands of men from induction centers to camps. Two other government agencies, the Departments of Agriculture and Interior, had the responsibility for planning, organizing, and supervising the actual work performed.

Despite some controversy, the CCC was an instant success. It distinguished itself as the first federal effort to eliminate racial discrimination; Roosevelt's bill contained an amendment stating "that no discrimination shall be made on account of race, color, or creed." But many Southern states ignored the provision and refused to select blacks. Although officials showed little interest in challenging this violation, blacks gradually succeeded in enrolling throughout the country. By 1937, black enrollees accounted for about 9 percent of the corpsmen, a percentage close to the black population of the United States. Some lived in integrated camps, mostly in New England; others resided in camps for blacks only, mainly in the South.

At the CCC's inception, criticism arose concerning the army's involvement and the military atmosphere found in the camps. Columnists presented the pros and cons of this and other aspects of the program in many news articles. At the same time, local **newspapers** featured announcements about CCC activities, human interest stories about the young men from their communities who had enrolled, and reports on the work and the personnel in nearby camps. In retrospect, the CCC easily emerged as President Roosevelt's most popular initiative.

Within weeks after the signing of the bill that founded the CCC, the organization had inaugurated its own press and published a national weekly, *Happy Days*. The newspaper ran from May 1933 to August 1942. Roosevelt's political theme song, "Happy Days Are Here Again" (1930; **music** by Milton Ager [1893–1979], lyrics by Jack Yellen [1892–1991]), inspired the name. Over the years of its publication, this newspaper recounted the many facets of the CCC story, provided a way for government and CCC officials to report progress and offer observations, educated readers on a number of topics such as how to get a job, gave corpsmen an opportunity to describe their hopes and dreams, experiences and opinions, and even supplied a forum to have their poems printed. *Happy Days* also encouraged the establishment of local newspapers or newsletters at all the camps; eventually more than 5,000 publications circulated among residents with many camps exchanging their various editions.

Shortly after enlistment began in April 1933, recruits found themselves transferred from induction centers to work sites at the rate of almost 9,000 a day. Thus, by July some 300,000 men resided in 1,520 camps. In addition to room, board, healthy outdoor work, and medical services, each man received at least $30 a month (approximately $465 in contemporary dollars), with an average of $25 (about $390) sent home to his family. Some enrollees advanced to leadership positions and received increased compensation. Not only did these financial benefits help the corpsmen and their relatives, the communities close to camps experienced enough increase in business to prevent the failure of many small enterprises. Also, foresters, construction foremen, and supervisors gained employment as instructors with the program, giving an economic boost to their lives. Eventually, camps existed in all the states as well as in Hawaii, Alaska, Puerto Rico, and the Virgin Islands. The CCC peaked in 1935 with 500,000+ men in over 2,500 camps.

Enrollment in the CCC was for a minimum of six months, but it could be renewed for up to two years, an option that many selected. Early in the history of the program, procedural modifications took place. American Indians, many of whom lived in deplorable economic conditions, eventually became eligible and joined. Also, President Roosevelt issued an executive order allowing for the enrollment of veterans of the Spanish-American War and World War I, a step that enlisted older men, another group struggling with the hardships of the Depression.

The addition of a training and **education** component strengthened the benefits of the program, both for the enrollees and the nation. A little over 100,000 illiterate men learned to read and write; 25,223 received eighth-grade diplomas; 5,007 graduated from high school; and 270 earned college degrees. With the CCC's emphasis on schooling and self-improvement, members received training in vocational skills such as typing, first aid, supervision, journalism, forestry, carpentry, masonry, and so on.

In the public mind, the CCC dealt primarily with reforestation, and the corpsmen, referred to as "Roosevelt's Tree Army," did indeed plant about 2 million seedlings. But the program undertook many other tasks as well. The building of facilities in national, state, county, and metropolitan parks set recreational development in the United States ahead by at least a decade. Hiking trails, picnic shelters, swimming pools, fireplaces, restrooms, and camp sites added to the nation's leisure and **travel** possibilities. In 1937, the CCC initiated construction of the Appalachian Trail, a hikers' path that runs for over 2,000 miles from Georgia to Maine. Two popular scenic highways, the Blue Ridge Parkway (1935–1987) and the Natchez Trace Parkway (1937–2005), also had their beginnings with the CCC.

The group's accomplishments were varied: the preservation and restoration of historical sites, the construction of 97,000 miles of fire roads, the building of 41,000 bridges and 3,470 fire towers. Irrigation ditches performed erosion control and ultimately saved more than 20 million acres. The CCC protected natural wildlife habitats, particularly in wetlands. Stream and pond improvements included stocking fish and building over 3 million small dams. When necessary, the CCC participated in fighting natural disasters.

By 1936, America had emerged from the worst of the Depression and looked forward to a degree of renewed prosperity. Roosevelt wanted to cut spending, which brought some uncertainty to various New Deal programs. The CCC continued to be supported financially, but new polices and procedures slowed the enrollment process. Also with war clouds hanging over Europe, many corpsmen resigned either to enlist in the armed forces or take the many new jobs developing in the United States.

By late summer of 1941, the declining number of applicants and increased withdrawals had reduced the Corps to fewer than 200,000 men, a far cry from its peak times. In light of deteriorating world events, Congress had undertaken a review of all federal agencies to identify those essential to a possible war effort. The lawmakers recommended that the Civilian Conservation Corps be abolished, and it ceased to exist on July 1, 1942.

See also "Brother, Can You Spare a Dime?"; Leisure & Recreation; Musicals; Race Relations & Stereotyping

SELECTED READING

Bernstein, Irving. *A Caring Society: The New Deal, the Worker, and the Great Depression.* Boston: Houghton Mifflin, 1985.

Civilian Conservation Corps. http://www.cccalumni.org/history1.html

Cornebise, Alfred Emile. *The CCC Chronicles: Camp Newspapers of the Civilian Conservation Corps, 1933–1942.* Jefferson, NC: McFarland & Co., 2004.

Merrill, Perry H. *Roosevelt's Forest Army: A History of the Civilian Conservation Corps, 1933–1942.* Montpelier, VT: Perry H. Merrill, 1981.

COFFEE & TEA. In the nation's colonial years, high importation and production costs limited the consumption of tea and coffee. But with growth and prosperity, more and more Americans added those beverages to their diets, and tea became the more popular of the two. Events and inventions of the nineteenth and twentieth centuries, however, moved the coffee industry forward and, by the 1930s, coffee had surpassed tea in popularity.

During Prohibition, speakeasies had pushed coffee as a sobering drink for those who consumed too much illegal alcohol. Other establishments suggested coffee as a nonalcoholic alternative to liquor and beer, with the result that coffeehouses and lunch counters proliferated, particularly in larger cities. At this same time, Americans began expressing a preference for simpler meals; a light midday lunch at luncheonettes and soda fountains usually meant a request for soup and a sandwich, along with a cup of coffee or tea. Some people even made do with a breakfast consisting of a quick cup of coffee.

The tea industry capitalized on the growing practice of light meals in public establishments by providing quiet settings called tearooms. In order to please everyone, they also offered coffee. Because of their intimate atmosphere, tearooms enjoyed a special appeal for women and families. Many of these businesses used historic buildings or quaint, refurbished houses as their locations, an approach that peaked in popularity in the 1920s. Tearooms continued into the Depression, but many had to close when economic hardships allowed fewer people to eat out. "Tea parties," small gatherings held in the home in the 1920s and 1930s, provided an easy way for women to visit. Dainty sandwiches and sweets complemented the tea—served piping hot in winter and iced on the porch or veranda in summer.

The national shift from tea to coffee became apparent following World War I. The U.S. per capita consumption of coffee hovered around 10 to 11 pounds in 1918, and by 1923 had risen to 13 pounds, a level maintained throughout the 1930s. A national survey conducted in 1939 indicated that a high percentage of American families—adults and children—drank coffee. By 1941, per capita consumption had risen to 15.9 lbs. Heavy

advertising throughout the 1930s, especially on **radio**, by both American coffee roasters and Latin American coffee plantations, influenced this growth.

Despite the positive outlook, the stock market crash of 1929 dealt a blow to the coffee industry and caused a brief drop in consumption. Small firms went out of business and some old family businesses sold out to corporations both before and after the crash. Chase and Sanborn, founded in 1878, became a part of Standard Brands in 1929, and Maxwell House Coffee, founded in 1892, joined General Foods in 1928. Several other major brands—for example, the Great Atlantic & Pacific Tea Company's (A&P) Eight o'Clock, Red Circle, and Bokar coffees, and rival Jewel Coffee—suffered brief declines in their revenues.

As an illustration, Maxwell House saw profits of nearly $3 million a year on sales of 50 million pounds before the crash. Profits dropped to virtually nothing on sales of only 39 million pounds three years later. In desperation, the managers at General Foods considered several ways to rescue the floundering Maxwell House, ideas that included a cut in the retail price and a smaller advertising budget. With fewer funds for ads, the company made a daring move for the time, applying the entire reduced budget to radio. Prior to the Depression, most major coffee firms had invested primarily in print advertising, especially **newspapers**.

Radio provided coffee advertisers a vital, growing medium. As early as March 1924, A&P had sponsored *The A&P Gypsies*, first on a New York City radio station and then, from 1927 until the fall of 1936, on both the Blue and Red Networks of the National Broadcasting Company (NBC radio). Recognized as one of radio's most distinctive programs, *The A&P Gypsies* featured exotic **music** with a nomadic motif and A&P gained a reputation as one of America's leading chain grocery stores.

A&P also participated in Chicago's **Century of Progress Exposition** (1933–1934) with a 2,000-seat amphitheater featuring the A&P Carnival and numerous other performances. The company sponsored a canopied boardwalk with tea dances and free tea and coffee samples. Throughout the 1930s, A&P continued to employ a combination of print and radio advertising. From October 1935 through 1937, the chain sponsored the long-running (1931–1952) *Kate Smith Hour*, with **Kate Smith** (1907–1986) singing a variety of music three times a week.

Other radio outlets that allowed coffee promotion included *The Maxwell House Show Boat*, a musical variety program that ran on NBC radio from October 1932 until October 1937. For two of those years, 1933–1935, it ranked as the most popular radio show in the country. Realistic sound effects included the surging water from a paddle wheel and the scream of a steam whistle, causing thousands of listeners to believe the production involved a real steamboat; many people would gather in the towns on the banks of the Mississippi the show had scheduled to visit, hoping to get a glimpse of the studio-created showboat. Ever mindful of the importance of advertising, in 1935 Maxwell House, in addition to its radio advertising, offered a new twist by presenting in its print ads little vignettes about its coffee in the form of popular **comic strips**.

Not to be outdone, Chase & Sanborn Coffee sponsored *The Original Amateur Hour* with host Major Edward Bowes (1874–1946) on NBC radio from March 1935 until September 1936 (the show itself ran from 1934 until 1945 with network changes). The *Amateur Hour*, which became something of a national rage during the mid-1930s, traveled from city to city featuring local talent while also focusing attention on Chase &

Sanborn's sponsorship. A skinny baritone by the name of **Frank Sinatra** (1915–1998) got his start on this show in 1935 as part of the Hoboken Four, a winning quartet. Many other famous entertainers likewise saw their careers blossom with Major Bowes, and Chase and Sanborn profited from the show's remarkable popularity.

By the end of 1935, *Major Bowes' Original Amateur Hour* had passed *The Maxwell House Show Boat* to become the top-ranked program on radio. With success and the offer of a higher salary, Major Bowes found a new sponsor, the Chrysler Corporation, in September 1936. Ventriloquist Edgar Bergen (1903–1978) and his dummy Charlie McCarthy took over the *Chase and Sanborn Hour*. The popularity of Bergen and McCarthy forced *The Maxwell House Show Boat* off the air during the last days of 1937. In the midst of all this, the American public had definitely come to link certain brands of coffee with many well-known stars and vice versa.

Decaffeinated coffees—Kaffee-Hag in Germany, Sanka (sans caffeine) in France, and Dekafa, from the U.S. pharmaceutical firm Merck & Company—had first appeared on the market in the early 1900s, but they did not receive heavy promotion until the 1930s. These decaffeinated variations strove to instill the notion that regular, caffeinated coffee could be unhealthy and that their brands offered the same pungent aroma and flavor, but without the caffeine. Despite the advertising campaigns, decaffeinated coffees gained only a small foothold in the overall market.

A new coffee product appeared on grocery shelves in 1938 when Nestlé, a Swiss firm, introduced Nescafé, an improved instant coffee. The first instant brew had been sold around 1910 in a product called Refined Coffee. It consisted of a powder made from dried, condensed coffee particles and required the addition of boiling water, just like Nescafé. But Refined Coffee failed to catch on, whereas Nescafé appealed to a small but growing group of consumers.

Soft drinks also cut into the coffee market during the 1930s. They capitalized on the seasonal aspect of coffee—and sales did drop from winter to summer even with advertisements for iced coffee. In addition, a significant number of people around the nation had switched to Coca-Cola as a breakfast beverage.

Against a backdrop of economic depression and varied competition that included negative advertising, it took technology to advance the coffee business. Many households switched from making coffee with a percolator, first invented in 1829 with an electric version available in the 1930s, to either a drip method or a vacuum coffeemaker. To accommodate these new appliances, many coffees were sold in different grinds for different methods. A&P even guaranteed freshness by allowing the customers to grind the coffee beans at the time of purchase. In 1933, Italy and France introduced the first automatic espresso machines, making way for what would become, in the twenty-first century, an American fad.

Eastern Air Transport (later called Eastern Air Lines), in order to attract passengers, advertised the availability of coffee on its flights, as did rival Pan American Airways. The American Can Company, a producer of vacuum cans used by coffee roasters, in 1936 hired famed photographer Margaret Bourke-White (1904–1971) to travel to Brazil and photograph coffee cultivation and harvesting. With the intent of making coffee attractive to school-age children, American Can included these photographs in free educational packets distributed to over 700,000 students.

The 1939–1940 **New York World's Fair** offered a singular opportunity to the coffee industry: the fair celebrated Coffee Day on August 31, 1939. In response, Standard

Brands hosted the world's longest coffee bar, one that served only Chase & Sanborn. At the same time, an open-air theater offered Edgar Bergen and Charlie McCarthy; the pair entertained guests and plugged Standard Brands coffee.

But not everyone supported coffee's growing popularity. Some health enthusiasts such as John Harvey Kellogg (1852–1943) lectured on the harmful effects of the caffeine in coffee. C. W. Post (1854–1914), a former patient at Kellogg's sanitarium in Battle Creek, Michigan, had begun to manufacture Postum, a grain-based coffee substitute, in 1895. By 1924 sales had declined and, during the 1930s, General Foods employed a cartoon character, "Mr. Coffee Nerves," in hopes of increasing the popularity of Postum. "Mr. Coffee Nerves" tried to disrupt people's lives with caffeine, but always found his efforts thwarted because his victims consumed Postum. General Foods, however, saw their own goals thwarted when Postum sales did not increase.

The Wander Company pushed another health drink, Ovaltine. Made of eggs, barley, and malt extract, it attempted to woo coffee drinkers. From April 1931 to January 1940, Ovaltine sponsored **Little Orphan Annie** on the NBC radio network. It proved a most successful marriage. *Annie*, based on the immensely popular comic strip character created by Harold Gray (1894–1968) in 1924, came to radio as a serial in 1930; it would remain on the air until 1942.

Little Orphan Annie, instantly popular with children, pioneered the distribution of premiums. Listeners could save the labels and seals from containers of Ovaltine and earn decoders, compasses, badges, and shake-up mugs. All that for listening to an exciting serial and drinking lots of Ovaltine. For the nine years Ovaltine sponsored the red-haired heroine, they were flooded with requests for the various premiums that could be had for a handful of labels and maybe a dime (roughly $1.50 in contemporary dollars). Seldom, in advertising, have a product and a fictional character meshed so well. Today, the Ovaltine premiums have become expensive collectibles.

The tea industry struggled to keep pace with the success of the coffee business. Despite the lowered prices of the mass-marketed black teas and the convenience of premeasured tea in bags, by the 1930s national tea consumption had declined. But a new custom of drinking iced tea had developed, a habit that perhaps saved the tea industry in America. With Prohibition, the popularity of iced tea grew as Americans sought alternatives to illegal beer, wine, and liquor. Iced tea recipes began appearing in cookbooks, especially those relating to Southern cooking. Many cooks, however, complained of problems brewing a consistently tasty pitcher without cloudiness. In July 1938, *Good Housekeeping*, a popular, influential magazine, apologized to its readers for not addressing these problems earlier and earnestly reported that their testing indicated that a cold water method tasted best and prevented clouding.

Many tea and coffee drinkers felt that additives enhanced the taste and pleasure of drinking both beverages. From colonial days through the 1930s, sugar served as an important addition to coffee and tea, hot or cold. For coffee, the cheap sweetener made the bitter brew more palatable, and for tea, it masked the somewhat inconsistent flavor of loose tea leaves. During the Depression, the use of sugar in foods and beverages soared simply because of affordability. By the 1940s, over two-thirds of all tea consumed contained sugar.

Few people in the United States added milk or cream to coffee before 1800. By the 1930s, however, the use of either in these beverages had become commonplace, with cream being preferred. Adding a slice of lemon to tea started in the 1800s and became more popular when, in 1869, transcontinental railroads made fresh citrus fruit affordable throughout the country.

The American thirst for coffee, clearly the beverage of choice in the 1930s, had built slowly. The repeal of Prohibition in 1933 and the legal return of **alcoholic beverages** to the marketplace did not measurably hurt coffee sales. Nor did the Depression do great harm. Well advertised and entrenched in the public mind, coffee continued to sell—as a beverage to accompany meals, as a drink for taking a break, as a sobering agent when too much alcohol had been consumed, and as a stimulant when driving. Coffee had become a staple of American life.

For American **songwriters and lyricists**, both coffee and tea found a place in the nation's popular music. Examples would include "You're the Cream in My Coffee," with music by Ray Henderson (1896–1970), and lyrics by Buddy DeSylva (1895–1950) and Lew Brown (1893–1958), which came along in 1928 as part of the Broadway musical *Hold Everything*. The great **Irving Berlin** (1888–1989) penned "Let's Have Another Cup o' Coffee" in the depths of the Depression for the musical *Face the Music* (1932). In 1934, "Coffee in the Morning, Kisses at Night" featured music by Harry Warren (1893–1981) and lyrics by Al Dubin (1891–1945); it delighted audiences in the movie *Moulin Rouge*. The following year, Al Hoffman (1902–1960), Al Goodhart (1905–1955), and Maurice Sigler (1901–1961) combined their talents for "Black Coffee," a musical comment on the associations with coffee and feeling blue.

Tea had its day also. Broadway's *No, No, Nanette* (1925) featured the standard "Tea for Two," with music by Vincent Youmans (1898–1946) and lyrics by Irving Caesar (1895–1996) and Otto Harbach (1873–1963). Sammy Fain's (1902–1989) music and Pierre Norman (1895–1952) and Irving Kahal's (1903–1942) lyrics distinguished "When I Take My Sugar to Tea"; it promptly became a hit after being heard in the **Marx Brothers** film *Monkey Business* (1931). "Tea on the Terrace," a Sam Coslow (1902–1982) effort, played on radios and **jukeboxes** in 1937.

See also Aviation; Education; Food; Grocery Stores & Supermarkets; Magazines; Music; Musicals; Prohibition & Repeal; Radio Networks; Restaurants; Serials

SELECTED READING

Pendergrast, Mark. *Uncommon Grounds: The History of Coffee and How It Transformed the World.* New York: Basic Books, 1999.

Smith, Steven, and Steven L. Wright. *Iced Tea: The Distinctively American Beverage.* The Winthrop Group. http://www.teausa.com/general/icedtea.cfm

Tea. http://www.fda.gov/fdac/features/296_tea.html

COLUMBO, RUSS. Born in Camden, New Jersey, Russ Columbo (b. Ruggerio de Rudolfo Columbo, 1908–1934), along with **Bing Crosby** (1903–1977) and **Rudy Vallee** (1901–1986), formed for the era a triumvirate of leading crooners. Before emerging as a vocalist, Columbo had played violin professionally while still in his teens. A strikingly handsome man, cut in the mold of film idol Rudolf Valentino (1895–1926), Columbo emerged as a minor Hollywood personality in the late 1920s. He landed several uncredited roles in forgotten pictures like *Dynamite* (1929), *The Wonder of Women* (1929), and *Street Girl* (1929). Sometimes his voice can be heard, dubbed over another actor's.

Columbo's good looks, coupled with an ability to write **music** and sing, finally got him noticed, and he won a handful of movie contracts that went beyond uncredited walk-ons. Although nothing memorable resulted, *Broadway through a Keyhole* (1933) and *Wake Up and Dream* (1934), gave him a chance to do some acting. A 20-minute short, *That Goes Double* (1933), allowed him to both act and sing. In addition to playing a dual role, Columbo performs in this picture two of his biggest hits, "Prisoner of Love" (1931; music by Russ Columbo and Clarence Gaskill [1892–1947]; lyrics by Leo Robin [1895–1984]) and "You Call It Madness (but I Call It Love)" (1931; words and music by Russ Columbo and Con Conrad [1891–1938]). Despite the placement of these popular songs, *That Goes Double*, perhaps by virtue of being a short, did little to advance his career in **movies**.

In one of his early uncredited film roles, Columbo appears with Gus Arnheim (1887–1955) and his orchestra in a musical short titled *Gus Arnheim and His Ambassadors* (1928). Columbo served as a vocalist with the band, a group that also happened to have Bing Crosby and the Rhythm Boys as performers. When Crosby took the stage, Columbo obviously listened attentively, and elements of Crosby's early crooning style color his work. Listeners of the day claimed to be unable, at times, to tell them apart on **radio** or **recordings**. Since the two shared a bandstand, Crosby also had to know about Columbo. In fact, Crosby later starred in a full-length feature called *Going Hollywood* (1933). A big-budget production, it costars Marion Davies (1897–1961), with Raoul Walsh (1887–1980) as director. During the course of the film, a singer named Henry Taylor (1907–1969) performs "You Call It Madness (but I Call It Love)" in direct imitation of Columbo's hit recorded version.

Although Columbo spent considerable energy trying to ignite his sputtering film career, it never really burst into flame. His singing, however, attracted considerable attention. Around the beginning of the decade, Columbo befriended composer Con Conrad, a man who envisioned bigger things for the vocalist. Conrad became Columbo's agent and manager, and the two cowrote "You Call It Madness (but I Call It Love)" in 1931. At about the same time, Columbo and composer Clarence Gaskill, along with noted lyricist Leo Robin, had written "Prisoner of Love." Thanks to radio and records, these two songs, along with Conrad's ceaseless efforts to promote his client, catapulted the singer to fame.

On the strength of his music, Columbo enjoyed a stint with the National Broadcasting Company (NBC radio) from 1931 to 1933, the network's attempt to pit him against Crosby, who then appeared on the rival Columbia Broadcasting System (CBS radio) network. Wags promptly dubbed the competing radio shows "the Battle of the Baritones." A contract with RCA Victor recordings also came along that resulted in several more hits, including "Lies" (1931; music by Harry Barris [1905–1962], lyrics by George Springer [active 1930s]) and "Too Beautiful for Words" (1934; words and music by Russ Columbo, Bernie Grossman [1885–1951], and Jack Stern [1896–1985]). People started to tout Columbo as a star crooner, someone who could rival, maybe surpass, anyone then on the scene. But the "Romeo of Radio," "Radio's Revelation," the "Vocal Valentino," as publicity agents would have it, died in a mysterious 1934 shooting incident when only 26 years old. Although his death brought him more fame and notoriety than he had enjoyed in life, the media circus soon pulled up stakes and his name disappeared from the news.

At the time of his demise, Columbo had just finished filming *Wake Up and Dream* (1934). The singer has the lead, and it appeared that his film career had been resuscitated and he might be headed for real movie stardom. But *Wake Up and Dream*—a cheaply made backstage musical—established no box office records despite the furor over his death, and it has quietly disappeared from any discussion of American motion pictures of the 1930s.

Columbo's singing, however, has endured and can still be found in recorded compilations of the decade's music. He projected an erotic quality into his breathy, intimate manner of vocalizing, much more so than did his primary rivals Crosby and Vallee. His legacy consists of just a few outstanding recordings and some mediocre movies; the promise of his life went unfulfilled. For a brief moment, he actually stood shoulder to shoulder with the two best vocalists of the decade. In a final irony, Bing Crosby served as one of the pallbearers at his funeral, a ceremony attended by thousands of mourners.

See also Musicals; Radio Networks; Songwriters & Lyricists

SELECTED READING

Lanza, Joseph, and Dennis Penn. *Russ Columbo and the Crooner Mystique*. Los Angeles: Feral House, 2002.

Pierce, Max. "Russ Columbo: Hollywood's Tragic Crooner." http://www.classicimages.com/1999/April99/Columbo.html

Whitcomb, Ian. "The First Crooners, Volume One: The Twenties." http://www.picklehead.com/ian/ian_txt_first crooners1.html

———. "The First Crooners, Volume Two: 1930–1934." http://www.picklehead.com/ian/ian_txt_first crooners2.html

———. "The First Crooners, Volume Three: 1935–1940." http://www.picklehead.com/ian/ian_txt_first crooners3.html

COMIC BOOKS. The combined success of newspaper **comic strips** and **Big Little Books** in the early 1930s hastened the birth of the modern comic book. During the earlier years of the century, sporadic attempts had been made to reprint popular newspaper comics in booklet form. Although some did well, and a few publishers even printed them in color, there existed no concerted effort within the industry to popularize comic books. One company, Cupples and Leon (or C&L), led the limited field until well into the 1930s, creating collections of such favorites as **Little Orphan Annie**, *Bringing Up Father*, *Joe Palooka*, and **Dick Tracy**. By the standards of the time, their publications tended to be expensive, running from 25 to 75 cents an issue (approximately $3.50 to $10.50 in contemporary dollars). Cupples and Leon withdrew from comic reprints in 1934, an unfortunate move, because comic books were poised to become a successful medium in the years to follow.

The 1933 publication of *Funnies on Parade*, a giveaway that featured several popular cartoon characters then running in daily papers, had further popularized the concept pioneered by Cupples and Leon. A one-shot publication, *Funnies on Parade* led other publishers to consider similar collections, but not necessarily for free.

The following year, 1934, *Famous Funnies* appeared on newsstands. This periodical, generally accepted as the first modern comic book, carried a cover price of a dime (about $1.50 in contemporary dollars) and contained 64 pages, mainly of Sunday newspaper reprints. It did well, and other publishers quickly accepted both the price and the length, thus creating the standards for all comic books in the years ahead.

As word of the success of *Famous Funnies* grew, competition entered this new market. In 1935, Dell Publishing issued *Popular Comics*, another reprint series. Within a couple of years, titles like the *Funnies*, the *Comics*, *Comics on Parade*, *Super Comics*, *King Comics*, *Ace Comics*, *Tip Top Comics*, and *Crackajack Funnies* had joined the fray. Most of these newcomers offered a mix of newspaper reprints and new, original material, and they all contained bright, garish color. A unique, popular art form had been born.

By 1938, the combined sales of comic books reached a staggering 2.5 million yearly copies. To meet this demand, publishers continued to use previously run newspaper strips, they adapted and illustrated the plots of numerous B Westerns then playing theaters, and they even raided the files of Big Little Books for material. Their wisest move, however, lay in hiring competent cartoonists and allowing them to create a host of new series that existed for comic books only.

These "All Original! All New!" comic books boasted many veteran cartoonists from the newspaper strips and **illustrators** from the **pulp magazines** that then flourished, individuals who had been granted free rein to use their imaginations in this upstart industry. One of the first comics in the genre, the aptly named *New Fun*, debuted in 1935. As it became established, its title changed to *More Fun*, but the content remained original material. Most of the artists' names were relatively unknown in the profession—Tom McNamara (1886–1964), Leo O'Mealia (1884–1960), Creig Flessel (b. 1912), Tom Hickey (b. 1910), and many others—but they did competent work and established a readership for *New Fun*. Their stories tended to run between four and eight pages, and, despite the title, most issues contained a mix of adventure and humor.

Close on the heels of *New Fun* came *New Comics* late in 1935, which then metamorphosed into *New Adventure Comics*, and finally into *Adventure Comics* in 1938. *Detective Comics* came along in 1937, reflecting in part the newspaper popularity of *Dick Tracy*. Filled with action and suspense, the stories read like illustrated versions of pulp fiction. Two young men, writer Jerry Siegel (1914–1996) and artist Joe Shuster (1914–1992), could be found on the roster of cartoonists contributing to these innovative comic books. Working as a team, their early creations only hinted at where they would eventually go in the industry, but they typified the eager newcomers moving into comic-book art.

In the early 1930s, Siegel and Shuster had created a character they called "Superman," but the concept languished and the two cartoonists took on other assignments to make ends meet. Finally, *Action Comics*, accurately sensing that readers liked larger-than-life heroes, decided to give **Superman** a chance in the June 1938 issue. The cover shows Superman single-handedly lifting a car, but his name remains conspicuously absent, and the publishers buried the story within the comic book. The issue sold reasonably well (an original copy has today become a priceless collectible), and in 1939 the first solo *Superman* comic rolled off the presses.

Soon after that pioneering issue of *Action Comics*, other oddly costumed crime fighters began appearing on the pages of the adventure comics. A comic book called *Funny Pages* featured the Arrow in the fall of 1938. Written and drawn by Paul Gustavson (1916–1977), the Arrow turned out to be a skillful archer who went around in a shapeless shroud in order to hide his identity.

At about the same time, *The Green Hornet*, a popular afternoon **radio** serial premiered in 1936 (it would run until 1952). This radio hero—based on the Lone Ranger of both radio and later comic fame—has a secret identity, wears a distinctive outfit, and has access to sophisticated weaponry. With *The Green Hornet* clearly in mind, artist Jim Chambers (active 1930s) drafted the Crimson Avenger for *Detective Comics* in 1938.

A twin to the radio serial, the Avenger also wears a mask and a flowing cape. Little did these artists realize they had initiated a new trend in comic books.

Not to be caught missing what appeared a sure bet, *Wonder Comics* introduced Wonder Man in May 1939, but his comic life proved short. The publishers of Superman claimed copyright infringement, and promptly quashed the new hero. But *Detective Comics*, already the owners of Superman, in 1939 felt free to introduce the Batman (the publishers soon dropped the "the") by cartoonist Bob Kane (1915–1998). Certainly a rival to Superman, Batman possessed no superhuman traits, relying instead on his superb physical skills. Soon, a small army of other characters with amazing attributes appeared: Captain Marvel, Captain America, Bulletman, Minute-Man, the Flame, the Blue Beetle, Spy Smasher, Wonder Woman, along with a number who remain justly forgotten. They began appearing in this burgeoning branch of the comic-book business in the late 1930s. Most would not achieve any real fame until the early 1940s, but their roots remain firmly planted in the 1930s.

Despite the rocketing popularity of this new breed of caped and masked superheroes, many publishers stayed with tradition, mixing reprints and original materials. The content taken from the **newspapers** covered the whole gamut of series, from the humorous *Smokey Stover*, *Smitty*, and *The Katzenjammer Kids*, to the **serials**, *Little Orphan Annie* and *Little Annie Rooney*, **the Gumps**, and *Winnie Winkle*, to the adventurous **Tarzan** (who appeared in several different comics), *Dick Tracy*, *Smilin' Jack*, and **Terry and the Pirates**.

Collectively, comic books, Big Little Books, and comic strips created a new national literature. Most comic books, particularly those featuring superheroes, treated the Depression as irrelevant. Legions of sociologists and critics have commented on the roles of such characters in American lives and fantasies, but most of their learned commentaries concern World War II and after, not the breadlines and unemployment of the earlier 1930s. As war engulfed Asia and the clouds of an almost certain new world war threatened Europe, the superheroes found a place battling the Axis and domestic spies. Comic books appealed to a broad audience; they played on basic American themes; and they proved enormously successful. Little Orphan Annie and Dagwood had made it through the Depression, and Superman and his super cohorts would see to it that the country made it through World War II.

See also *Blondie*; Western Films

SELECTED READING

Barrier, Michael, and Martin Williams, eds. *The Smithsonian Book of Comic-Book Comics.* Washington, DC: Smithsonian Institution Press, 1981.

Daniels, Les. *Comix: A History of Comic Books in America.* New York: Bonanza Books, 1971.

Goulart, Ron. *Over Fifty Years of American Comic Books.* Lincolnwood, IL: Mallard Press, 1991.

Jones, Gerard. *Men of Tomorrow: Geeks, Gangsters, and the Birth of the Comic Book.* New York: Basic Books, 2004.

COMIC STRIPS. Everyone, it seemed, read the daily newspaper comics during the 1930s. About two-thirds of all adults followed their favorite daily characters in the papers, and the number rose still higher for the colorful Sunday comics. The popularity of "the funnies" stood at an all-time high, and most American papers reserved at least a full page for the exploits of **Blondie, Dick Tracy, Flash Gordon, the Gumps**, *Krazy Kat*, **Apple Mary**, and innumerable others. Only in the last 60 years or so has the American comic strip received any critical acclaim, complete with museum retrospectives extolling the work of various cartoonists. This important visual art form enjoyed the attention of an audience of millions during its Depression-era heyday. Most members of that enthusiastic following usually viewed the comics as little more than daily doses of humor and adventure, a mindless respite from the grim realities of the time. As is the case with so much popular culture, only in hindsight do people appreciate the worth of an artist or a movement.

According to a *Fortune* magazine poll done in 1937, the 10 leading newspaper strips were ranked as follows, with no. 1 being the most popular:

1. *Little Orphan Annie* (created in 1924 by Harold Gray [1894–1968])
2. *Popeye* [correct title: *Thimble Theater*] (created in 1919 by Elzie Segar [1894–1938])
3. *Dick Tracy* (created in 1931 by Chester Gould [1900–1985])
4. *Bringing Up Father* (created in 1913 by George McManus [1884–1954])
5. *The Gumps* (created in 1917 by Sydney Smith [1877–1935]; carried on by Gus Edson [1901–1966] after Smith's death)
6. *Blondie* (created in 1930 by Chic Young [1901–1973])
7. *Moon Mullins* (created in 1923 by Frank Willard [1893–1958])
8. *Joe Palooka* (created in 1930 by Ham Fisher [1901–1955])
9. *Li'l Abner* (created in 1934 by Al Capp [1909–1979])
10. *Tillie the Toiler* (created in 1921 by Russ Westover [1886–1966])

Because a number of these strips had their beginnings some years earlier, readers had gained a familiarity with many of them by the onset of the Depression and doubtless felt comfortable following their favorite characters. In addition, audiences obviously liked to be amused: 8 of the 10 front-runners are humorous strips, thus supporting the old name of "funnies." Only *Little Orphan Annie* and *Dick Tracy* present more dramatic plots and, with their exaggerated villains and events, most readers knew better than to take them too seriously.

A fictional narrative in visual form, comic strips provide individual pictures, or frames, to create episodes. These episodes can occur daily, as in a gag-a-day series like *Blondie*, or they can take weeks or months, as in a serial adventure such as *Dick Tracy*. In many ways, a comic strip can be compared to a piece of motion picture film. A movie likewise contains individual photographs that take on meaning only when run through a projector at the proper speed. Walking into the middle of a movie and then exiting before it ends would hardly be a satisfactory way to watch films. Similarly, an individual episode of any comic might not be particularly funny or enlightening. But when read on a daily basis, the stories begin to cohere and the characters take on distinctive personalities. Most of the more successful strips of the 1930s did a good job of keeping the audience both entertained and satisfied.

Generally speaking, the decade's comic strips fall into three subject categories: (1) traditional daily humor series, (2) serial, or continued, stories, and (3) adventure comics. The old-fashioned humor comics do not overtly refer to the Depression, but instead provide daily laughs and simple solutions to any problems that might occur.

Growing out of the humorous strips of the 1920s, serial comics tend to retain much of the lightheartedness of that earlier genre, but the stories often become long and involved, focusing on people and relationships. Frequently designed to appeal to women, they also borrow from **radio soap operas**, a format then enjoying enormous popularity. The Depression gets reduced to a distant, external threat that the ordered person or group can defeat with relative ease.

The final category, adventure strips, stands as a product of the 1930s, and they demonstrate the clearest response to the times. With realistic drawing as their hallmark, the adventure comics describe a disordered world, but reiterate the ideas that all problems can be remedied, that no disturbance is interminable.

A sampling of the leading American newspaper comic strips of the 1930s would include the following (this annotated list omits the 10 favorites mentioned above; the identified cartoonists are those most associated with particular strips during the 1930s):

Representative Humorous Comic Strips of the 1930s

Title	Running Dates	Creators with Birth & Death Dates	Comments
Felix the Cat	1923–1967	Writing: Pat Sullivan (1885–1932); drawing: Otto Messmer (1892–1983)	Although Sullivan took much credit for *Felix*, Messmer did almost all the writing and drawing.
Fritzi Ritz	1922–1968	Ernie Bushmiller (1905–1982)	Given the popularity of Fritzi's niece, in 1938, this strip became known as *Fritzi Ritz and Nancy*. Soon thereafter the title shrank to *Nancy*.
The Inventions of Professor Lucifer G. Bitts	1907–1948	Rube Goldberg (1883–1970)	A single-panel cartoon, the zany devices portrayed in the series gave rise to the popular expression "a Rube Goldberg invention."
The Katzenjammer Kids	1897–present	Rudolph Dirks (1877–1968) & Harold H. Knerr (1882–1949)	This strip originated with cartoonist Rudolph Dirks, but ownership problems caused him to leave the successful series in 1914. Harold H. Knerr then took it over, a position he held throughout the 1930s.
The Captain and the Kids	1914–1979	Rudolph Dirks (1877–1968)	Dirks, after losing *The Katzenjammer Kids*, proceeded in 1914 to create *The Captain and the Kids*, a virtual twin to "the Katzies." From 1914 on, the two competing strips ran at the same time, with some papers carrying one, and others featuring its competitor. In retrospect, the two are almost indistinguishable.
Krazy Kat	1910–1944	George Herriman (1880–1944)	

Title	Running Dates	Creators with Birth & Death Dates	Comments
Mutt and Jeff	1907–1983	Bud Fisher (1884–1954)	
Polly and Her Pals	1912–1958	Cliff Sterrett (1883–1964)	
Reg'lar Fellers	1917–1949	Gene Byrnes (1889–1974)	
Skippy	1925–1945	Percy Crosby (1891–1964)	
Smitty	1922–1974	Walter Berndt (1899–1979)	

Representative Serial (or Continuity) Comic Strips of the 1930s

Title	Running Dates	Creators with Birth & Death Dates	Comments
Apple Mary	1934–1938	Martha Orr (1908–2001)	This series carried on, after 1938, as *Mary Worth* (1939–present) with different artists and writers.
Barney Google	1919–present	Billy DeBeck (1890–1942)	By the end of the 1930s, this strip had become *Barney Google and Snuffy Smith* because of the popularity of Snuffy. Today, it has evolved into a daily gag series known only as *Snuffy Smith*.
Betty	1920–1943	Charles Voight (1887–1947)	
Boots and Her Buddies	1924–1969	Edgar Martin (1898–1960)	
Dixie Dugan	1929–1966	Writing: J. P. McEvoy (1895–1958); drawing: J. H. Striebel (1892–1962)	
Freckles and His Friends	1915–1973	Merrill Blosser (1892–1983)	An early example of a teen-age strip that survived for several generations.
Gasoline Alley	1918–present	Frank King (1883–1969)	One of the few strips in which characters aged with the passage of time.
Little Annie Rooney	1929–1966	Writing: Brandon Walsh (1883–1955); drawing: Darrell McClure (1903–1987)	The melodramatic plot involving an orphan and her faithful dog comes primarily from the success of the rival strip *Little Orphan Annie*, but other precedents can be found. Both series enjoyed success during the Depression years.
Somebody's Stenog	1916–1941	A. E. Hayward (1885–1939)	
Winnie Winkle the Breadwinner	1920–present	Martin Branner (1888–1970)	

Representative Adventure Comic Strips of the 1930s

Title	Running Dates	Creators with Birth & Death Dates	Comments
Buck Rogers in the 25th Century	1929–1967	Writing: Phil Nowlin (1888–1940); drawing: Dick Calkins (1895–1962)	For most readers, this strip served as their introduction to **science fiction**.
Dan Dunn	1933–1943	Norman Marsh (b. 1910)	A virtual look-alike for the more popular *Dick Tracy*, the two detective strips ran concurrently during the 1930s.
Flash Gordon	1934–1993	Alex Raymond (1909–1956)	
Prince Valiant	1937–present	Hal Foster (1892–1982)	
Scorchy Smith	1930–1961	Noel Sickles (1910–1982)	
Secret Agent X-9	1934–present	Writing: Dashiell Hammett (1894–1961); drawing: Alex Raymond (1909–1956)	Hammett wrote the continuity for the strip only until 1935; Raymond ceased drawing it late that year and the series was taken on by others.
Smilin' Jack	1933–1973	Zack Moseley (1906–1993)	
Tarzan	1929–present	Hal Foster (1892–1982)	Foster drew *Tarzan* until 1931; he came back to do Sunday panels only until 1937. Rex Maxon (1892–1973) then drew the dailies. Burne Hogarth (1911–1996) picked up Sundays in 1937.
Terry and the Pirates	1934–1973	Milton Caniff (1907–1988)	
Wash Tubbs	1924–1988	Roy Crane (1901–1977)	

Generally speaking, comic strips reinforce American values and beliefs. One of the purest forms of popular culture, the comics had embarked on one of their most expansive and innovative periods during the 1930s. Visually, comic strips assist readers in their perceptions of the world. Abstraction in any academic sense is absent from the frames of a typical newspaper strip. The dark, threatening frames of *Little Orphan Annie* and *Dick Tracy* suggest that one cannot be too careful; danger lurks around every corner. But strips like *Blondie* and *Gasoline Alley* provide a brighter, cheerier vision. Within the family, safe in a home, there lies security. Tracy and Annie seldom enjoyed this kind of security; they had to operate in a cold, uncaring environment, separated from home and family. Clearly, the loner faces more risks in American society.

By using the mass medium of **newspapers**, comics relied on simple graphics to tell their stories. They proved inexpensive, they had wide distribution, and millions read them simultaneously. By aiming at the largest possible audience and practicing daily repetition, they created a familiarity and acceptance rarely found in any other mass medium.

See also Big Little Books; Comic Books; Hillbillies; *Life & Fortune*; Magazines; Movies; Serials; *Superman*

SELECTED READING

Goulart, Ron. *The Adventurous Decade: Comic Strips in the Thirties*. New Rochelle, NY: Arlington House, 1975.

———, ed. *The Encyclopedia of American Comics*. New York: Facts on File, 1990.

Horn, Maurice, ed. *100 Years of American Newspaper Comics*. New York: Gramercy Books, 1996.

———. *The World Encyclopedia of Comics*. New York: Chelsea House, 1976.

Walker, Brian. *The Comics before 1945*. New York: Harry N. Abrams, 2004.

CONTRACT BRIDGE. A card game that claims roots to the ancient game of whist, bridge has evolved from an early variant called auction bridge to its current contract format. By the mid-1920s, the auction concept had been successfully challenged by players who preferred what they saw as a more scientific approach to the entire game. Four players sit at a table and each is dealt 13 cards; the couples facing one another become partners, and they have to collaborate by "bidding" their hands, an attempt to inform one another of the relative value of individual cards they hold. One partnership outbids the other and thereby establishes a "contract" of how many tricks it expects to take. If this sounds confusing, it should. Bridge stands among the most difficult of all card **games**, and it requires a mastery of the rules, along with intense concentration, for teams to be consistently victorious.

Ely Culbertson (1891–1955), an expert player, tirelessly promoted contract bridge, writing what he called *The Contract Bridge Blue Book*, a best-selling primer that first came out in 1930. Starting in 1929, for many years he also edited *Bridge World*, a periodical devoted to the game. Culbertson encouraged players to follow his strategy of "honor tricks" for evaluating the strength of the dealt hands, and his advice took the nation by storm. In 1931, as a coup de grâce for the auction system, he teamed up with one of his supporters in a tournament conducted in New York City against two of the best auction players. Called "the Battle of the Century" among aficionados, Culbertson and his partner won decisively.

With that well-publicized victory, contract bridge took off in popularity, eclipsing all other card games. Elaborate scoring procedures, complete with extra points and penalties, became standard elements of the contest. The more arcane the rules and scoring, the better people seemed to like them. Tournaments, often involving numerous teams and countless contracts, added to the acclaim bridge already enjoyed. Even in the darkest days of the Depression, the sales of playing cards actually rose, with some 50 million decks a year being purchased during 1930–1932. By 1931, over 500,000 individuals had signed up to take bridge lessons at YMCAs, parks, and anywhere else that offered them. Conservative estimates said that 20 million people played the game. To serve this interest, over 1,000 **newspapers** carried syndicated articles on improving play, and manufacturers rushed to market various shuffling devices, along with scorepads, table covers, and anything else they thought might appeal to the bridge-playing crowd.

During this heady time, some of the more prominent bridge tournaments had the unique distinction of being broadcast, hand by hand, play by play, over **radio**. In hushed tones, experts explained rules and strategies, along with critical appraisals, to enthusiastic, unseen audiences. As bridge mania grew, Culbertson found himself accepted as the leading authority on the game, and eager players snatched up his how-to books. They sold steadily for years, and even received annual updates. He made several film shorts that explained the basics of the game, and these played in theaters across the land, an added feature that went along with newsreels, cartoons, and previews. The decade also saw Culbertson writing a daily syndicated column that ran in hundreds of newspapers. Complete with diagrams detailing the cards held by each player, it showed readers how to play sample hands, both offensively and defensively.

In the latter half of the 1930s, a rival bridge expert rose to challenge Culbertson's media dominance. Charles H. Goren (1901–1991), a lawyer by **education**, published *Winning Bridge Made Easy* in 1936. In this book, he touted his "point count system," a direct challenge to Culbertson's "honor tricks" approach. In short order Goren had legions of followers, and he would soon assume the title of "Mr. Bridge." By the end of the decade, and for many years thereafter, Goren ruled as the last word on strategy and play. Culbertson, never as competitive as Goren, retired from active tournament play in 1935, perhaps correctly sensing his reign was coming to an end. He did, however, continue to publish his books and columns, and many fans clung to the Culbertson system of play. In the meantime, Goren's syndicated newspaper columns, at the expense of those penned by Culbertson, drew an avid readership, and another of his books, *Contract Bridge Complete*, emerged as the authoritative bible for most players. Regardless of which system one followed, by the end of the 1930s, contract bridge stood unchallenged, the nation's most popular card game.

See also Best Sellers; Fads; Leisure & Recreation

SELECTED READING
Olsen, Jack. *The Mad World of Bridge.* New York: Holt, Rinehart and Winston, 1960.
Parlett, David. *The Oxford Guide to Card Games.* New York: Oxford University Press, 1990.

CRIME. Throughout the first third of the twentieth century, statistics tracking crime in the United States show a gradual rise. An increase in violent acts, in particular homicide, caught both public and media attention, and many became convinced the nation was engulfed in a wave of lawlessness. In 1900, the death rate by murder had been 1.2 persons per 100,000 population. By 1930, it had climbed to 8.8 per 100,000, and then jumped to 9.7 per 100,000 in 1933, the statistical high point. After that, a sharp decline ensued, so that 1940 witnessed a rate of 6.3 per 100,000. (As a point of reference, in 2005 the rate stood at 5.5 per 100,000.) Certainly the public's concern was justified. Although the perceptions of a runaway "crime wave" contain a measure of exaggeration, perceptions often exceed reality.

Many of the crime-related problems of the 1930s saw their origins in the preceding decade, especially with the 1920 ratification of the Eighteenth Amendment to the U.S. Constitution and the passage of the Volstead Act that same year. Together, these measures forbade the manufacture or sale of **alcoholic beverages** and became the law of the land—Prohibition—a law doomed to failure almost from the start. Citizens found many ways to purchase and consume alcohol, assisted by countless people eager to supply their needs. With much of the population defying Prohibition, illicit bars and speakeasies flourished, and importers and distributors operated outside the law, often with the assistance of professional criminals. The unintended result was that liquor-connected crime spread across the nation, reaching a crescendo of sorts in the late 1920s and early 1930s.

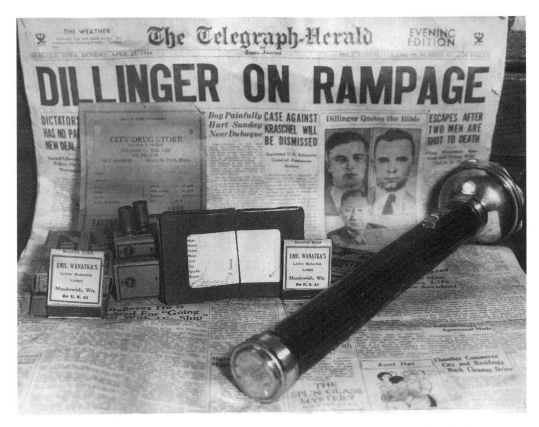

A newspaper headline of the era underscores public interest in crime. (Courtesy of Photofest)

Although much of this illegal activity involved battles between rival criminal organizations, innocent citizens occasionally got caught in the crossfire, which both alarmed people and aroused curiosity about lawbreakers and their ways.

Mired in what seemed an endless economic crisis, people looked for diversions from their problems. Many escapes presented themselves: **fads, jigsaw puzzles, games**, sports, **radio, movies**, newspapers, **magazines**, mysteries—harmless pastimes all. But underlying the Depression there existed a worry that American institutions like hard work, thrift, and respect for the law were being eroded. This concern manifested itself in a morbid curiosity about the actions of those gangsters who so dominated the news media in the early 1930s. No longer just robbers or kidnappers or murderers, people dubbed the publicized lawbreakers of the early 1930s "public enemies," individuals out to destroy the traditional values of society.

Fanned by an endless series of sensational news accounts provided by an occasionally fawning, and other times frenzied, press, the actions of a handful of criminals-gangsters-racketeers took on a near-legendary quality. Basking in virtual celebrity status and capturing the nation's imagination, these outlaws with romanticized names became Robin Hoods for some and for others murderers who toted Tommy guns and shot down innocent citizens. Almost daily, it seemed, bank robberies, shootouts, and other illegal acts filled the front pages of the nation's **newspapers**. The criminal numbers, however, shrank, thanks to tireless pursuit by law enforcement agencies.

Between 1933 and 1935, the following high-profile cases were resolved, usually by death: "Machine Gun" Kelly (1900–1954), captured in 1933; John Dillinger, "the Mad Dog of the Midwest" (1903–1934), shot and killed in 1934; "Baby Face" Nelson (1908–1934), shot and killed in 1934; "Pretty Boy" Floyd (1904–1934), shot and killed in 1934; Bonnie and Clyde (Bonnie Parker, 1910–1934; Clyde Barrow, 1909–1934), shot and killed in 1934; and "Ma" Barker (1880–1935), shot and killed in 1935. By late 1934, the crime wave had crested; it quickly ebbed, dropping 50 percent between 1933 and 1940. Any admiration for colorful criminals virtually disappeared in those years, replaced by a new respect for those agencies that had brought the crime wave under control.

As they awaited the restoration of order, individual citizens, powerless to stop such outrages, might see parallels in crime and the seeming inability of the nation's institutions to do much in the face of an economic collapse. In the darkest days of the Depression, public perceptions could easily equate law and lawlessness with order and anarchy. These disparate elements, in the eyes of many, swung back and forth, and the outcome remained in doubt. Or so much popular culture of the time would have it.

Movies of the era often celebrate the rise of criminals, disciplined, tough, self-made men who overcome obstacles and achieve success. *Little Caesar* (1930), *The Public Enemy* (1931), and *Scarface: The Shame of a Nation* (1932) constitute a trilogy of successful gangsters who "made it" in the underworld. They might die in the final reel, but until then they dominate the action, pictures of cocksure success, strutting across the screen. These swaggering characters and the public's continuing interest in them fostered **gangster films**, a new genre of motion pictures. These and many other movies vilify bankers and businessmen, greedy exploiters who steal from the poor and make the rich richer. Usually the law, such as it is, appears bumbling and often corrupt; officers capture the bad guys almost by chance.

These films lack staunch defenders of tradition, men who respect and represent American ideals. Without such heroes, the gangsters usurp these roles, becoming by default distorted models of success. Novels and **pulp magazines**, on the other hand, provided the detective character—unafraid, knowledgeable, ready to match wits or bullets with any and all villains. Often portrayed as a virtual vigilante, one who sometimes acts outside the confines of legal niceties because he cannot depend on standard law enforcement, this fictional figure flourished in much contemporary literature. In the guise of **Dick Tracy** and his ilk in the **comic strips** and innumerable private investigators in mystery stories, such a character lacked a real-life counterpart. Then, in the mid-1930s, life imitated art and provided someone who could fill the role.

Franklin D. Roosevelt's (1882–1945) 1933 inauguration signaled a time of profound change in American life: Prohibition, the source of income for so many gangsters, had been repealed; the **New Deal** promised to return the country to prosperity and full employment; and J. Edgar Hoover (1895–1972), the director since 1924 of the little-known **Federal Bureau of Investigation (FBI)**, would rise to be the crime fighter around whom the nation could rally. But Hoover reached that lofty position because of the campaign against crime launched by Roosevelt's newly appointed attorney general, Homer Stille Cummings (1870–1956).

Cummings orchestrated a series of actions that changed the face of federal law enforcement in the United States. With his blessing, Congress in 1933 greatly expanded the powers of the FBI with the Lindbergh law, so named because of the tragic kidnapping and murder of aviator Charles Lindbergh's (1902–1974) infant son. In 1934, several bills collectively called the crime control laws broadened the Lindbergh provisions, made bank robberies and kidnapping federal crimes, and granted federal agents the right to carry arms. As a concrete symbol of the government's intent to confront and punish criminals, Cummings oversaw the construction of Alcatraz Prison, a forbidding, maximum security fortress erected in 1933–1934 on a rocky island in San Francisco Bay. From a distance, citizens could take comfort that the worst of the worst would be confined there. Al Capone (1899–1947) had the distinction of being among the first residents of "the Rock."

Thanks to Cummings's efforts, Hoover and his cadre of men began to replace the outlaws that had so fascinated and frightened the nation. Their implacable hostility toward all criminals led many to believe that crime cannot pay, that gangsters deserve their fates, a significant turnaround in national attitudes in a brief span of time. The stern federal agent, well-trained, incorruptible, and ready to do battle, gradually replaced the arrogant thug. The best possible representation of this new law officer showed up on the nation's movie screens in 1935 with the film *G-Men*. A Warner Brothers effort, the picture stars James Cagney (1899–1986), the same actor who just four years earlier had given life to *The Public Enemy* as a murderous criminal. Cagney remains murderous, but he now serves the law, so his killer instincts can be forgiven. A mix of vigilante, *Dick Tracy*, pulp detective, and disciplined federal officer, the movie G-man fights on the front lines in the war on crime.

The purveyors of mass entertainment, always alert to commercial success and shifts in popular attitudes, from the mid-1930s onward shifted their focus away from the criminal. They featured instead the government agent, along with the honest cop on the beat and the upright lawyer who bests his sleazy rivals in previously crooked courts. Titles like *Public Hero #1* (1935), *Show Them No Mercy!* (1935), *Let 'em Have It* (1935), and *Public Enemy's Wife* (1936) blazed on marquees, the lure being action, but the theme revolved around a crime-fighting government agent. Sometimes presented in a breathless documentary style that took pains to show the inner workings of law enforcement agencies, these films, along with similar radio shows, eased around any objections about gratuitous violence by using mayhem in the service of melodrama. Such an approach appeased critics, and the image of the "lawless thirties" evolved into an era that respected justice and playing by the rules, even if guns occasionally still had to be drawn. In addition, the FBI and its leader, J. Edgar Hoover, received recognition—either by name or by association—as the architects of this successful war on crime.

By the conclusion of the decade, law enforcement emphases had moved away from the native criminal element and turned toward the threats of subversion by dissidents and foreign nationals. Axis spies, evil Nazis, and barbaric Japanese replaced the romanticized Capones, Dillingers, and Kellys that had preoccupied so many just a few years earlier. In the space of a decade, public unease about a perceived crime wave had been replaced by a confident attitude that the government, in the form of Hoover and the FBI, had crime under control and now guarded the country from both within and without.

See also Alcoholic Beverages; Hollywood Production Code; Lindbergh Kidnapping; *Little Caesar*; Mysteries & Hard-Boiled Detectives; Prohibition & Repeal

SELECTED READING
Moquin, Wayne, ed. *The American Way of Crime: A Documentary History*. New York: Praeger, 1976.
Powers, Richard Gid. *G-Men: Hoover's FBI in American Popular Culture*. Carbondale: Southern Illinois University Press, 1983.
Silberman, Charles E. *Criminal Violence, Criminal Justice*. New York: Random House, 1978.

CROSBY, BING. A native of Tacoma, Washington, Harry Lillis Crosby (1903–1977) would eventually emerge as the most popular male vocalist of the decade. Childhood friends bestowed on the young Crosby the lasting nickname of "Bing," and soon his proper names had been forgotten. In 1920, he enrolled in Gonzaga University, a Jesuit school in Spokane, and began to play the drums (or "traps") in a local band, the Musicaladers, led by Al Rinker (b. Alton, 1907–1982). In addition to performing, Crosby listened almost ceaselessly to **music**, spending countless hours with every **radio** broadcast he could find, as well as hanging out at record stores spinning and memorizing the latest discs.

After a handful of paying jobs with the Musicaladers, Crosby found the lure of show business irresistible and dropped out of college his senior year to join forces with Rinker. During the group's performances, Crosby would frequently sing, usually through a megaphone, as did numerous vocalists then. Electronic amplification and quality microphones still lay in the future, but his singing nonetheless provided a hint about the direction his career would take.

Dwindling engagements led to the breakup of the Musicaladers in 1925. Working primarily in local theaters, Crosby and Rinker polished a new act that featured the hits of the day, along with a healthy mix of **jazz** and blues. Later that same year, the pair set off for Los Angeles and fame and fortune. Once situated, they dusted off their routine and secured a succession of vaudeville jobs in the lively show business scene that characterized southern California.

Good luck came their way when the enormously popular bandleader Paul Whiteman (1890–1967), a man always on the lookout for talent, heard about them. A meeting was arranged, and in 1926 Rinker and Crosby found themselves part of Whiteman's extensive organization, a giant step in their careers. Late in that year, they made their recording debut in Chicago with the orchestra and then went on tour with Whiteman and wound up in New York City. In the process, Crosby met or knew the work of many important musicians, such as Louis Armstrong (1901–1971), **Duke Ellington** (1899–1974), and Bix Beiderbecke (1903–1931), individuals who would have a significant influence on his artistic growth as a vocalist. He also associated with movie and radio stars and in the process built a network of friends that would also contribute to his flowering as a show business personality.

Later in 1926, Crosby and Rinker met another young musician, Harry Barris (1905–1962), who happened to be a good pop songwriter. The three formed an instant rapport, and out of that came the Rhythm Boys, the name a variation on the Happiness Boys, a popular radio duo noted for mixing music with patter. Whiteman immediately took notice, installed the trio in his orchestra, and even landed them several recording contracts. In time, Crosby took more and more solos, becoming the lead voice in the threesome. Barris contributed a number of original compositions to the group, including the popular "Mississippi Mud," a trifle he penned in 1927. As the 1920s drew to a close, and with the Great Depression just beginning to be felt, Crosby, the Rhythm Boys, and Whiteman continued their relationship, but economic realities would soon change everything.

By the early 1930s, Crosby had secured a place for himself as a popular vocalist, albeit in the context of the Rhythm Boys. The advent of electric amplification and improved condenser microphones allowed him to sing softly—instead of belting out a number, as many singers did at the time—and intimately caress the lyrics. Utilized by Crosby and several of his contemporaries, especially **Rudy Vallee** (1901–1986), this singing style was dubbed "crooning," and the name stuck. Throughout the remainder of the decade, Bing Crosby would stand out as the greatest crooner of them all. In the meantime, Whiteman gave the Rhythm Boys remarkable freedom; they could record and perform independently when not tied to commitments with the orchestra.

Whiteman's long-anticipated film, *King of Jazz*, opened in the spring of 1930. Innumerable production delays had postponed its release, but it served to introduce Bing Crosby to a national moviegoing audience. Influential in the long run for its visual artistry, in the short view of things, *King of Jazz* did poorly at the box office, a victim of the public rejection of the film musical, a rejection that would not change until 1933 and the release of ***42nd Street***. When Universal Studios rereleased the picture in the footsteps of *42nd Street*'s success, it did much better and Crosby enjoyed top billing, a reflection of his growing fame. An anthology-type movie that showcases individual songs and performers, *King of Jazz* proved an important steppingstone for Crosby.

Shortly after the movie's 1930 premiere, the Rhythm Boys amicably split with Whiteman. Poised to go out on their own, they appeared in some forgettable films and played equally forgettable venues. The trio signed with popular bandleader Gus Arnheim (1887–1955), cut a number of **recordings**, appeared on his radio show, and received featured billing with the aggregation. Crosby's voice dominates these performances, and marks his inevitable emergence as a soloist. One of Arnheim's musicians listened to Crosby attentively; **Russ Columbo** (1908–1934), destined to become another of the decade's leading crooners, appreciated Crosby's efforts and incorporated much of his style into his own performances. In early 1931, Crosby scored the first big hit of his own with "I Surrender, Dear" (music by Harry Barris, lyrics by Gordon Clifford [1903–1968]). That success led Crosby to break with the group in 1931 and become a solo performer; he would never look back.

Most male vocalists in the popular field at that time tended to be tenors, but Crosby possessed a warm baritone. In addition, he displayed skill with many different kinds of lyrics and rhythms. After breaking up with the Rhythm Boys, Crosby signed with Brunswick Records, the true beginning of his career. Jack Kapp (1901–1949) led the label, and he encouraged Crosby at every turn, serving as mentor and friend. One of the first tunes Crosby cut for his new employer, "Just One More Chance" (music by Arthur Johnston [1898–1954], lyrics by Sam Coslow [1902–1982]), quickly became a hit, the first of dozens he would record throughout the decade. No other singer came close to him, not then nor in the 1940s. At 28 years of age, he had no equals among male vocalists.

By 1932, Bing Crosby had emerged as a force in popular music. He performed in every genre, from Western songs, such as "The Last Round-Up" (1933; words and music by Billy Hill [1899–1940]), to Christmas carols like "Silent Night" (1935; traditional), and everything in between. Since much of his background with Whiteman and the Rhythm Boys involved jazz and blues, he had come to know numerous black performers. Racial segregation ruled the day on radio and in the recording studio, so almost never did white performers work alongside their black counterparts. Crosby, however, changed this imbalance somewhat when in 1931 he recorded "Dinah" (written 1924; music by Harry Akst [1894–1963], lyrics by Sam M. Lewis [1885–1959] and Joe Young [1889–1939]) with the Mills Brothers, a black vocal quartet that had long been popular, but never in conjunction with white artists. An instant hit, "Dinah" demonstrated how silly such restrictions were, but its success had little impact on industry practices. Undeterred, Crosby cut a couple of sides with Duke Ellington and his orchestra early the following year, along with another session with the Mills Brothers.

With songs like "I Found a Million-Dollar Baby in the Five and Ten-Cent Store" (1931; music by Harry Warren [1893–1981], lyrics by Billy Rose [1899–1966] and Mort Dixon [1892–1956]), "Try a Little Tenderness" (1933; music and lyrics by Harry Woods [1896–1970], James Campbell [active 1930s], and Reg Connelly [1896–1963]), and the poignant **"Brother, Can You Spare a Dime?"** (1932; music by Jay Gorney [1896–1990], lyrics by E. Y. Harburg [1896–1981]), Crosby made direct references to the Depression. The last song has emerged as a symbol of the economic calamity, a credit to Crosby's rendition. Most of his output, however, remained more romantic than topical, including such best sellers as "It's Easy to Remember" (1935; music by **Richard Rodgers** [1902–1979], lyrics by **Lorenz Hart** [1895–1943]), "Sweet Leilani" (1937; music and lyrics by Harry Owens [1902–1986]; an Academy Award winner for the year, from the movie *Waikiki Wedding*), and "What's New?" (1939; music by Bob Haggart [1914–1998], lyrics by Johnny Burke [1908–1964]).

In 1934, in a convoluted transaction, Jack Kapp left Brunswick and formed a new label called Decca, a name associated with an established English recording company. Kapp brought Crosby, and a number of other Brunswick stars, with him, and proceeded to make American Decca a force in the industry. Other artists flocked to the fledgling company and by decade's end, one-third of all the singles sold in the United States boasted the Decca label. During the 1930s, Crosby alone recorded more than 2,600 titles, and his name consistently topped any lists of hits.

In his later recordings, Crosby lowered his pitch slightly, dropped some of the vibrato, and branched out into other genres. He gradually moved away from straight crooning and even injected some humor into the style with "Learn to Croon" (1933; music by Arthur Johnston, lyrics by Sam Coslow), a tune that almost denies that style of singing. By the mid- to later 1930s, people might still refer to Bing Crosby as a crooner, a singer of sad or saccharine ballads, but his easygoing manner took those things in stride, and his banter, always a part of his personality, laughed off his troubles.

With his growing success in recordings, the Columbia Broadcasting System (CBS radio) offered Crosby his own show in 1931. At first called *Fifteen Minutes with Bing Crosby*, the series went through name and sponsor changes, but he stayed with the network through 1935. While there, he took "Where the Blue of the Night (Meets the Gold of the Day)" (1931; music by Fred E. Ahlert [1892–1953], lyrics by Roy Turk [1892–1934]) as his theme song. For the next 40 years, the tune would be associated with him and few other singers would even attempt it.

At the beginning of 1936, Crosby made a switch to the rival National Broadcasting Company (NBC radio), where he took over *The Kraft Music Hall* from Al Jolson (1886–1950). Already a successful show during Jolson's tenure, it soon became a Thursday night ritual for millions of radio listeners, and Crosby would remain with it until 1946. He had moved from radio crooner to radio star.

In a bow to the stupendous impact of radio, Paramount Pictures in 1932 released a film titled *The Big Broadcast*. Rather than fighting the networks, Hollywood decided to borrow some of the medium's biggest names and capitalize on their popularity. The picture features numerous radio stars—**Kate Smith** (1907–1986), George Burns (1896–1996) and Gracie Allen (1895–1964), bandleaders Vincent Lopez (1895–1975) and Cab Calloway (1907–1994), and many others—but Bing Crosby shares top billing with actor Stu Erwin (1903–1967), a significant breakthrough. During the early 1930s, Crosby had already worked in a succession of Mack Sennett (1880–1960) two-reelers, short films that usually mixed music and comedy. Along with his radio work and recordings, these **movies** allowed people to recognize his face as well as his voice. *The Big Broadcast* proved a box office success at a time when most **musicals** did not do well and ensured that Crosby would soon land more roles and become a top-flight movie star, eventually appearing in over 25 full-length features by the end of 1940.

Crosby's movie work includes a handful of first-rate vehicles—*College Humor* (1933), *We're Not Dressing* (1934), *Mississippi* (1935), *Sing, You Sinners* (1938)—but most stand as amiable mediocrities, pleasant time wasters that capitalize on his casual crooning style. Probably only the most die-hard Crosby fans can recall *Too Much Harmony* (1933), *Two for Tonight* (1935), *Double or Nothing* (1937), or *Paris Honeymoon* (1939), typical products of his popularity. Sustained by wafer-thin plots, the movies give Crosby ample opportunity to sing and do some acting. The pictures fared reasonably well, and demonstrated how different media—radio, recordings, and film—can interconnect.

In the process of becoming a multimedia star, Crosby and the people around him created a persona, that of the easygoing, likable guy, someone of inherent modesty and enduring optimism. For the Depression years and the war years following, this image appealed to millions. He represented fair play, and his audience trusted him. Something of a playboy in his earlier years, he changed with the times, serving as a beacon of decency for many. Crosby, an astute businessman, in reality had to practice his air of casualness, and few people realized how powerfully he influenced show business and the fortunes of many in the industry.

See also Race Relations & Stereotyping; Radio Networks; Songwriters & Lyricists

SELECTED READING

Crosby, Bing. *Bing Crosby: It's Easy to Remember*. 4 CDs. Proper Records, 2001.

Giddins, Gary. *Bing Crosby: A Pocketful of Dreams*. Vol. 1, *The Early Years, 1903–1940*. Boston: Little, Brown, 2001.

Whitcomb, Ian. "The First Crooners, Volume One: The Twenties." http://www.picklehead.com/ian/ian_txt_first crooners1.html

———. "The First Crooners, Volume Two: 1930–1934." http://www.picklehead.com/ian/ian_txt_first crooners2.html

———. "The First Crooners, Volume Three: 1935–1940." http://www.picklehead.com/ian/ian_txt_first crooners3.html

D

DESIGN. The outward appearance—mass, shape, finish—of a wide range of products underwent significant change during the 1930s. The decade opened with the angularity and applied ornamentation of **Art Deco** serving as the last word in modernism; it closed with the sinuous curves and sleek surfaces of **Streamlining** leading the way. Between 1929 and 1940, momentous shifts occurred in American design, from humble home appliances to airliners, from pencil sharpeners to complex machines.

On a symbolic level, the public witnessed these ongoing changes through popular culture. Since millions of Americans went to the **movies** weekly, art directors and set designers made them visually aware of the very latest ideas in **architecture** and interior decoration. **Fred Astaire** (1899–1987) **and Ginger Rogers** (1911–1995) would dance their way through nine movie **musicals** during the 1930s, but what a difference between the quaintly old-fashioned look of *Flying Down to Rio* (1933), the first of the series, and the later sleek modernity of *Carefree* (1938).

The set designs for Hollywood **movies** reappeared in swank cocktail lounges and elegant nightclubs in many of the nation's larger cities. A white lacquered piano, its traditional curves amplified by the absence of any applied decoration, might be the centerpiece, and the bar could be polished black Bakelite (a popular plastic of the day) with chrome highlights. Even the crystal stemware would reflect the latest in avant-garde design. It all represented modernism, the new instead of the old, and it had its place in fantasy and glittering **restaurants** and night spots. Despite this celluloid and occasional commercial reinforcement, the American home remained a bastion of tradition, and it would be many years before these expressions of modernity found wide acceptance in most people's domestic lives.

A case in point: chromed tubular steel, shiny plastics, glass curtain walls, and luxurious accessories characterize the bathrooms—when seen at all—in many films. Given **Hollywood Production Code** restrictions, these sumptuous pleasure palaces always lack visible toilets, and they exist mainly in the imagination, a far cry from the cramped, utilitarian spaces that served the same purposes in most homes.

For most people, especially during a time of economic unrest, a typical middle-class home mixed the old with the new (but not too new), a sprinkling of colonial, Victorian, utilitarian, and maybe an occasional Art Deco or Streamlining accent. Maroon, mauve, cream, tan, and Depression green, a medium gray green particularly favored for kitchens, led the way for interior colors, with blues and peach popular for accents. Flowered draperies and wallpapers could be found in most rooms, along with patterned linoleum or rugs. In a bow to the movies, a daring homeowner might have an end table constructed of chromed tubing and black lacquered surfaces, but most of the furniture would be bulky and traditional. A large easy chair or two dominated the living room, and occasionally bore the name "Bumstead." Dagwood Bumstead, the main character in Chic Young's (1901–1973) newspaper comic strip *Blondie*, enjoyed lounging in such a chair, and furniture makers capitalized on the series' popularity. As an economy measure, thrifty owners placed slip covers, frequently in bold flower prints, over these pieces.

Knickknacks abounded: mantel clocks, decorative lamps, and smoking accessories allowed for some innovation in design. The room itself might be traditional, but the added touches could incorporate Art Deco and Streamlining motifs. Stylized nude figurines, along with tropical fish and jungle birds, and maybe greyhounds and whippets, provided some leeway in expressing one's modernism. And, since Prohibition ended in 1933, cocktail sets in chrome and Bakelite could also be found in some homes.

In a reaction against the boxy, angular appliances of the late 1920s and early 1930s, both General Electric and Sears, Roebuck offered Streamlined refrigerators by the middle of the decade. To accompany them, combined hutch and work areas made of enameled steel, along with similar eating tables, became the vogue. A big cookie jar also emerged as a design item in the American kitchen. Their shapes ranged from replicas of Aunt Jemima to stylized clowns and penguins; no matter what form it took, homemakers deemed the cookie jar an important component of the well-furnished kitchen.

"Depression glass," so desired by contemporary collectors, signified cheap, mass-produced glass kitchenware carried by every dime store in the country. An entire service of four place settings could then be had for about $2 (roughly $30 in contemporary dollars), and extra tumblers cost just pennies. Depression glass (also called "tank glass") came in many colors, but pink, burgundy, amber, and several distinctive greens proved the most popular. Frequently offered as a premium at numerous events because of its low cost, "dish night" at a neighborhood theater meant Depression glass would be the prize.

Fiesta Dinnerware, a line of table settings that has never gone out of production, first appeared in 1936. It then came in five colors and could be mixed or matched. Not as cheap as Depression glass, Fiesta became a staple of better department stores. The parent company, however, also made cheaper versions for variety stores.

In the larger world of industrial design, many individual designers rose to some fame during the decade. The firms for which they worked publicized their efforts, and gradually the names of a small coterie of industrial designers became familiar to the public. The following alphabetical list, while hardly conclusive, identifies a number of the more prominent designers active during the 1930s:

Norman Bel Geddes (1893–1958). His highly influential book *Horizons* (1932) articulates many of the precepts that underlie Streamlining during the 1930s. His fertile imagination foresaw Streamlined ocean liners, futuristic aircraft, multilane highways, and vast airports. Bel Geddes also worked as a Broadway set designer, creating inventive backdrops for a number of plays. On the consumer side, he conceived memorable cocktail sets, furniture and accessories, appliances and **radio** cabinets, including several Philco models and the 1940 Emerson Patriot. A number of his bolder ideas appeared in the Futurama exhibit he designed for the **New York World's Fair** in 1939.

Donald Deskey (1894–1989). Best known for the lavish interiors he designed for New York's **Rockefeller Center (Radio City)** in 1932, Deskey also worked with carpeting, furniture, and exhibited widely in the nation's top museums.

Henry Dreyfuss (1904–1972). Once employed by Norman Bel Geddes for theatrical work, Dreyfuss also designed numerous useful objects. His 1937 Thermos bottle has become a classic, instantly recognizable. In 1938, he created the iconic Big Ben alarm clock for Westclox, but his talents also went into such areas as utensils, toasters, and even the china and stationary for the New York Central's 20th Century Limited (1938), a Streamlined train of the day.

Paul Frankl (1887–1958). European by birth, Frankl brought a continental sensibility to design that relied less on mass production and machine aesthetics than did the work of his American counterparts. His primary fame rests with his Skyscraper furniture, first introduced in 1927. These pieces reflect, in miniature, a modern tall building. Complete with setbacks and a strong verticality, they emphasize the connections that often exist between the monumental and the mundane.

Raymond Loewy (1893–1986). Probably the best known of the decade's bumper crop of industrial designers, Loewy first came to public attention in 1929 with his sleek, somewhat Streamlined duplicating machine for the Gestetner Duplicating Company. Several Westinghouse radio cabinets followed, and in 1934 he displayed a complete office suite at the Metropolitan Museum's industrial design show that helped transform thinking about the modern office. Highly productive, no assignment was too big or too small. Loewy designed the Hupmobile automobile in 1934; several **buses** for Greyhound followed, and his appliances, especially the Sears, Roebuck Coldspot refrigerator, remain classics of the era. He pioneered Streamlining in several ships, and his S-1 locomotive (1937) for the Pennsylvania Railroad became a prototype for sleek, fast **trains**.

Eliel Saarinen (1873–1950). Best remembered as an architect, the Finnish-born Saarinen first pursued his profession in Europe. He moved to the United States in 1923 and broadened his interests to include furniture and associated accessories. He displayed an influential dining room at the Metropolitan Museum's 1929 show on architecture and industrial arts. In 1934, he constructed what he called "a lady's room" for another Metropolitan Museum exhibition. In both shows, he displayed such items as furniture, glassware, serving combinations, and silver services.

Walter Dorwin Teague (1883–1960). Teague initially attracted attention in 1930 with his Baby Brownie camera housing for Eastman Kodak; he also designed the Bantam Special camera for the company in 1936. A versatile designer, for several years he created the distinctive housings for Bluebird radios manufactured by the Sparton Radio Company (1933–1936). Glassware and textiles also bore his mark, as did several modernistic Texaco **gas stations**. He ended the decade with credit for both the Ford Motor Company and the National Cash Register buildings at the New York World's Fair (1939–1940).

Russel Wright (1904–1976). A colleague of Norman Bel Geddes in theater design, Wright moved into metal household items, such as spun aluminum, at the onset of the 1930s. He designed serving sets and flatware, but ceramics and earthenware captured his attention several years later. He introduced American Modern dinnerware in 1937, and it went into mass production in 1939; its pleasing, minimally Streamlined shapes caused American Modern to remain a consistent seller until 1957 when the company discontinued it. Wright also created the popular Modern Living line of casual furniture; a break with the tradition of heavy, formal furniture pieces, the line brought him considerable renown.

See also Automobiles; Aviation; Century of Progress Exposition; China Clippers; Chrysler Building; Douglas DC-3; Empire State Building; Fairs & Expositions; Food; International Style; Photography; Prohibition & Repeal; Stage Productions; Frank Lloyd Wright

SELECTED READING
Hanks, David A., & Anne H. Hoy. *American Streamlined Design: The World of Tomorrow*. Paris: Flammarion, 2005.
Horsham, Michael. *20s & 30s Style*. Secaucus, NJ: Chartwell Books, 1989.
Johnson, J. Stewart. *American Modern, 1925–1940: Design for a New Age*. New York: Harry N. Abrams, 2000.
Meikle, Jeffrey L. *Twentieth Century Limited: Industrial Design in America, 1925–1939*. Philadelphia: Temple University Press, 1979.
Wilson, Kristina. *Livable Modernism: Interior Decorating and Design during the Great Depression*. New Haven, CT: Yale University Press, 2004.
Wilson, Richard Guy, Dianne H. Pilgrim, and Dickran Tashjian. *The Machine Age in America: 1918–1941*. New York: Harry N. Abrams, 1986.
Woodham, Jonathan M. *Twentieth-Century Design*. New York: Oxford University Press, 1997.

DESSERTS. Americans enjoy desserts, and not just **ice cream** and apple pie. During the 1930s, foods containing sugar, a cheap commodity, flourished. But cakes, always popular in the United States, proved a challenge to make because milk and eggs were costly commodities. The Depression cake, unique to this decade, addressed this dilemma. Depression cakes consist mainly of sugar—lots of sugar, given its low price—flour, spices, and water or coffee, but no eggs or milk. Remarkably, the cakes actually taste good.

Fried cakes—today, people call them doughnuts (or donuts)—have been around for centuries. They achieved notoriety during World War I when Salvation Army women served American soldiers dough that had been cut into strips, twisted into crullers and fried. The soldiers, already referred to as "doughboys," cheered the arrival of these doughnuts and, by playing on words, soon called these women "doughnut girls" or "doughgirls." The war ended in 1918, but not the popularity of doughnuts. When he served as assistant secretary of the navy, **Franklin D. Roosevelt** (1882–1945), later to become the nation's president during the Depression, reputedly ate six doughnuts at one sitting while at a naval air station in France.

New York City has the distinction of being the home of the first doughnut company, the Doughnut Corporation of America, founded in 1921. The firm's first retail outlet, the Mayflower Shop, opened on Times Square in 1931 and flourished. People attending the 1933–1934 **Century of Progress Exposition** could see doughnuts produced by machine. Declared the most popular **food** at the event, a doughnut, sugared or glazed, cost less than a nickel (about 75 cents in contemporary money). That same year, in the hugely successful film *It Happened One Night*, rugged newspaperman Clark Gable (1901–1960)

Two typical recipes from the 1930s; these "Depression cakes" call for sugar but use no expensive ingredients such as eggs or milk. (Photograph by Nancy Blackwell Marion)

teaches runaway heiress Claudette Colbert (1903–1996) how to dunk a doughnut in coffee. Two additional **movies** from the 1930s employ doughnuts in their story lines. *Broadway Melody of 1936* (1935) contains a number of scenes with actors eating and dunking doughnuts, and *Doughnuts and Society* (1936) revolves around two women who share a partnership in a doughnut shop.

In 1937, Vernon Rudolph (1915–1973) started a doughnut enterprise by selling a yeast-raised doughnut to grocery stores in Old Salem, a part of Winston-Salem, North Carolina. Given his location, people stopped by his factory, wanting to buy hot, fresh doughnuts. Rudolph quickly changed his wholesale business, which he called Krispy Kreme, to include direct sales to customers. In time his little Krispy Kreme enterprise would become one of the leading doughnut chains in America.

Toll House cookies, another 1930s creation, came from the kitchen of Ruth Wakefield (c. 1903–1977), a dietitian and lecturer on food. Along with her husband, she opened the Toll House Inn located in a facility halfway between Boston and New Bedford, Massachusetts, a place where passengers had once paid tolls and changed horses as they traveled between the two cities. Mrs. Wakefield baked for guests staying at her Toll House Inn and her creations met with considerable approval.

In a 1937 experiment, Wakefield chopped a chuck of semisweet chocolate into pieces and stirred them into the dough of a Butter Drop Do cookie mix. Her efforts resulted in a sweet cookie she named for the inn, the Toll House cookie. Today, most people call Wakefield's invention a chocolate chip cookie. Betty Crocker in 1939 featured this new treat in her **radio** series *Famous Foods from Famous Eating Places*. Success led to an immediate agreement between Wakefield and food giant Nestlé to print the recipe on the wrapper of the Nestlé Semi-Sweet Chocolate Bar. Capitalizing on good sales, Nestlé also began offering chocolate morsels in convenient, ready-to-use packages.

The famous Girl Scout cookies had their earliest beginnings with some Scouts who in 1917 sold cookies as a way to finance their activities. By 1922, a publication from national Girl Scout headquarters provided a cookie recipe that, if used by troops across the country, would standardize this fund-raising project. For the remainder of the 1920s and on into the early 1930s, Girl Scouts in different parts of the country baked and sold this simple cookie. In the mid-1930s, the Greater Philadelphia Girl Scout Council and the Girl Scout Federation of Greater New York introduced commercially baked sugar cookies. Shortly thereafter, the national headquarters began a process that licensed commercial bakers to manufacture sugar cookies that could be sold by Girl Scouts across the country. By 1937, some 125 Scout councils participated in this national effort.

Baking at home satisfied both the American sweet tooth and the Depression pocketbook. Old favorites took on fresh looks and new products appeared on the market, many retaining their popularity well beyond the Depression.

See also Candy; Coffee & Tea; Grocery Stores & Supermarkets

SELECTED READING
Cookies. http://www.whatscookingamerica.net/History/CookieHistory.htm
Girl Scout Cookies. http://www.girlscouts.org/program/gs_cookies/cookie_history
Lovegren, Sylvia. *Fashionable Food*. New York: Macmillan, 1995.
Steinberg, Sally Levitt. *The Donut Book*. New York: Alfred A. Knopf, 1987.
Taylor, David A. "Ring King." *Smithsonian Magazine*. March 1998, 20, 22, 24.

DICK TRACY. The creation of cartoonist Chester Gould (1900–1985), *Dick Tracy* has the honor of being the first realistic detective comic strip, debuting in 1931. The 1930s witnessed an upsurge in violent **crime**, and various popular media, from **movies** to **radio**, reflected this rise. Newspaper comics, until this time a place for humor, romance, and fantasy, soon followed suit. Gould's innovative series—originally called *Plainclothes Tracy* by the artist—had attracted the eye of Captain Joseph Medill Patterson (1879–1946), the colorful head of the *Chicago Tribune–New York News* syndicate. The *Tribune-News* group led the way with action and adventure **comic strips** throughout the decade, and Patterson himself suggested using the gangland term "Dick" (meaning a detective), and dropping the more prosaic "Plainclothes."

Gould, who had struggled for years to come up with a salable series, decided he would create an adventure series that depicted police procedures with some measure of accuracy. Hardly the greatest cartoonist in terms of artistic skills, he nonetheless drew action-packed frames that attracted the reader's eye. His square-jawed hero represents a stern, unforgiving approach to law enforcement, a character not the least reluctant to employ lethal violence if he thinks the situation calls for it. In many of the breathless stories that Gould would spin for the next 46 years, Tracy has to kill his adversaries, usually in an explicit shoot-out. Readers loved this new approach to the "comics," reflecting as it did the sensational tabloid headlines of the era. Since Chicago had the unfortunate reputation of being the center of organized crime in America, it seemed only appropriate that the nation's first comic strip that focused on the police and their endless battles with an array of villains should have the support of the influential *Tribune*.

Employing a unique visual style that combines humorous caricatures with hard-edged realism, *Dick Tracy* soon emerged a 1930s favorite. The rat-a-tat-tat of machine guns, high-speed car chases, and cliff-hanging suspense became hallmarks of this new breed of comic art, and hundreds of **newspapers** carried the series. Gould's villains often tend toward the grotesque, although one of his first, "Big Boy," was clearly modeled on Chicago's own Al Capone. More characteristic, however, would be "The Blank," an apparently faceless man who almost kills Tracy several times in a 1937 episode. When finally subdued, "The Blank" turns out to be a criminal by the name of Redrum ("murder" spelled backward) and his disguise involves cheesecloth stretched over his face. Villains such as Flattop, Flyface, Measles, Rhodent, and a host of other miscreants would later populate the strip, but during the 1930s Gould, still exploring this new territory, satisfied himself and his readers with less bizarre types.

Sprinkled amid all the action is Tracy's on again-off again romance with Tess True-heart and his relationship with Junior, his ward and protégé. No woman ever exhibited more patience than Tess, but Tracy, the action-oriented male, seems to find fighting crime his primary interest, relegating Tess to a background role. Junior, introduced in 1932, often takes up a disproportionate amount of the detective's time. An orphan, Junior epitomizes the mischievous "kid" (also Tracy's frequent name for him) so popular in movies then, a well-meaning adolescent who gets into predicaments that usually require Tracy's aid if they are to survive. The inclusion of the soap opera–like romance, along with Junior's antics and the exaggerated villains, gave *Dick Tracy* an appeal to a broad-based audience.

From 1934 on, **radio networks** began carrying a serial featuring the stalwart detective. It remained on the air until 1947 and the demise of virtually all dramatic programming. Further testimony to the popularity of Gould's creation occurred when Hollywood produced several cheaply made *Dick Tracy* **serials** during the later 1930s. In 1932, Tracy had the honor of being the first comic character to appear in a Big Little Book. Taken from his newspaper strip exploits, this pioneering publication did well enough that over 20 subsequent Tracy adventures were added to the growing list of titles, including one consisting of stills taken from a 1937 movie serial and another based on a radio script. The success of the **Big Little Books** led, in the late 1930s, to the issuance of a number of **comic books** that also featured the hawk-nosed character.

Although the narrative in *Dick Tracy* occasionally becomes a soapbox for Chester Gould's strict law-and-order sermonizing, most of the time the artist allows the stories themselves, coupled with his stylized black-and-white graphics, to satisfy any ideological points he might want to make. With Hollywood turning out **gangster films** by the dozen, network radio producing dramas and serials celebrating law enforcement, and hard-boiled detective novels selling briskly, the 1930s provided fertile soil for cartoonists who wanted to move in that direction. As the decade progressed, a number of other detective strips, including *Dan Dunn* (1933–1943; a blatant Tracy imitation in all ways), *Red Barry* (1934–1938), *Secret Agent X-9* (1934–1996), *Radio Patrol* (1933–1950), *Don Winslow of the Navy* (1934–1955), and *Charlie Chan* (1938–1942), appeared in newspapers around the country. None, however, ever equaled the success of *Dick Tracy*.

See also Federal Bureau of Investigation; Mysteries & Hard-Boiled Detectives; Soap Operas

SELECTED READING

Gould, Chester. *The Celebrated Cases of Dick Tracy, 1931–1951.* Secaucus, NJ: Wellfleet Press, 1990.

———. *Dick Tracy, the Thirties: Tommy Guns and Hard Times.* New York: Chelsea House, 1978.

Marschall, Richard. *America's Great Comic-Strip Artists.* New York: Stewart, Tabori & Chang, 1997.

Roberts, Garyn G. *Dick Tracy and American Culture: Morality and Mythology, Text and Context.* Jefferson, NC: McFarland & Co., 1993.

DIONNE QUINTUPLETS. On May 28, 1934, a remarkable multiple birth took place in remote northern Ontario, one destined to make overnight celebrities of the Dionne quintuplets. Oliva (1904–1979) and Elzire Dionne (1909–1986), the parents, lived in Corbeil, Ontario, Canada, a tiny hamlet near Lake Nipissing and the town of North Bay. A poor, French-speaking farm family, they had not anticipated quintuplets when the five girls—Emilie, Marie, Yvonne, Annette, and Cecile—were born two months prematurely. Each baby averaged just under two pounds at birth, and many thought they would not survive. But survive they did, much to the relief of a world increasingly aware of them.

Almost from the time of their birth, the "quints," as the press immediately dubbed them, became front-page news. For a Depression-weary populace, they served as a ray of sunshine amid mostly gloomy reports about the world in general. In fact, they ignited a media frenzy for pictures, feeding schedules, health updates, clothing choices, and any other tidbits to satisfy a public hungry to know everything about them. The only other happening of the time that equaled this kind of press fervor would be the **Lindbergh kidnapping**, a tragic episode that began with the **crime** in 1932 and culminated with the 1935 trial and subsequent execution. Both stories covered years—the intense coverage of the quints would last until the 1940s—and both, in their own ways, achieved a level of popular attention that most news events can never hope to equal.

Until that time, no quintuplets had lived beyond infancy, so the five Dionnes made medical history. Delivered by two local midwives, the care of the quints soon became the responsibility of Allan Roy Dafoe (1883–1943), an Ontario physician who made the girls his special cause.

Dafoe told provincial officials that, given their poverty and the burdens of raising so many infants of the same age, the elder Dionnes made unfit parents. The Ontario

The Dionne quintuplets at a swimming pool. (Courtesy of the Library of Congress)

government agreed and placed Dr. Dafoe in charge of their well-being. This situation would endure until 1944, when the Dionnes regained custody of their daughters. In the meantime, Dafoe received funding to build the Dafoe Hospital and Nursery, or "Quintland" or "Dionneville" as some called it. Located next door to the Dionne home, it developed into a state-run viewing area that exploited the novelty of living quintuplets.

Terrified that the infants would contract infectious diseases, Dafoe kept them visible but in virtually sterile isolation. Until they were nine, they spent most of their waking hours separated from the curious crowds that flocked to "Quintland" to catch a glimpse of these young celebrities. In a large viewing area the doctor had designed, the girls could play, and the public viewed them from behind gauze curtains. Through much of their early development, they therefore could see shadowy movement and hear muffled voices through the veils, but their exposure to the real world remained incomplete. The artificiality of this arrangement and the absence of any normal upbringing carried a heavy cost in emotional scars suffered by all five throughout their lives.

Because of ceaseless press coverage of every activity the quintuplets engaged in, the public took them to its heart, but at the cost of making them specimens in a glass jar. In the mid-1930s, the peak years of their popularity, upward of 6,000 people a day trekked up to Corbeil for a glimpse of this phenomenon. Before their childhoods had ended, over 3 million visitors had been to their remote home.

A shrewd businessman, Dafoe quickly sensed the money to be made from such a marketable property as five identical sisters. With the support of provincial officials, he struck deals with major manufacturers for product endorsements. The money would go into government coffers. Since the girls were too young to endorse anything themselves, it fell to Dafoe and the Ontario bureaucracy to work out the financial arrangements. Large corporations, many from the United States, where the quints enjoyed as much popularity as they did in Canada, rushed to have their blessing. The Colgate-Palmolive-Peet Company (today Colgate-Palmolive), a large producer of toiletries, ran innumerable advertisements showing the fivesome, all smiles, with an accompanying text that breathlessly told how much they liked Colgate Dental Crème (the older term for toothpaste) and Palmolive Soap. Other firms dutifully lined up: Carnation Milk, Quaker Oats, Karo Syrup, Body by Fisher, Lysol disinfectant, along with doll makers, **candy** makers, silversmiths, photographers, tourist agencies, and countless others.

The "Quintuplets' Lullaby," featuring words and **music** by Canadian composer Gordon V. Thompson (1888–1965), enjoyed brief popularity during the mid-1930s, as did just about anything else associated with the five. But their fame was fleeting; by the time they reached adolescence, the girls no longer received much press coverage and a new generation had found other personalities to admire. In 1954, Emilie died of an apparent epileptic seizure. Marie suffered a blood clot to the brain and died in 1970; her sister Yvonne followed in 2001 after a bout with cancer. Today, Annette and Cecile reside quietly in Canada, but from 1934 until the early 1940s, they lived under a government-sanctioned microscope, and lost irrevocably any chance at experiencing a normal childhood.

As a footnote to the Dionne story, the provincial government of Ontario in 1998 paid the surviving quintuplets some $4 million (Canadian) as compensation for their treatment under official auspices when young.

See also Advertising; Fads; Newspapers; Toys; Youth

SELECTED READING
Dionne Quintuplets. http://www.city.north-bay.on.ca/quints/digitize/dqdpe.htm
Pierre, Berton. *The Dionne Years: A Thirties Melodrama*. New York: Penguin, 1977.
Tesher, Elle. *The Dionnes*. New York: Doubleday, 1999.

DISNEY, WALT. Born in Chicago, Illinois, as Walter Elias Disney (1901–1966), his family moved first to a farm in Missouri in 1906, and then to Kansas City, Missouri, in 1910. While still a teenager, Disney joined the Red Cross and drove ambulances in Europe during 1917–1918. He left the ambulance service in 1919 and, because of some prior schooling in art, dreamed of a career as a commercial artist. In 1920, Disney formed a partnership with another young man, artist Ub Iwerks (1901–1971), the first of several important collaborators in realizing his dreams.

The two set up a business venture that failed. From there, Disney, Iwerks, and another promising artist, Fritz Freleng (1906–1995), created Laugh-o-Grams, a company specializing in short cartoons. It created some imaginative animations, but a lack of business left the fledgling concern bankrupt.

In 1923, at the behest of his older brother, Roy Disney (1893–1971), Walt moved to Burbank, California, and, working out of the proverbial garage, established Disney Brothers Studios. Although he could not draw well, Disney possessed a fertile visual imagination. He would sketch out his unending ideas, and staff artists, particularly Iwerks in these early years, brought them to cartoon fruition.

The team created *Oswald the Lucky Rabbit* in 1927; Oswald bore many resemblances to the later Mickey Mouse, and enjoyed some early popularity. Unfortunately, Universal Studios owned the rights to Oswald and held on to them when a falling out among the principals occurred. Unable to draw Oswald anymore, Disney and Iwerks created a new animal character, an intelligent mouse that would make cartoon history. That mouse bore the name Mickey. He made his debut in early 1928 in a short called *Plane Crazy*, a silent cartoon. Disney saw the possibilities of adding sound to his productions and followed *Plane Crazy* with the sound-enhanced *Steamboat Willie* that same year.

Disney himself provided the voice of Mickey, a job he continued to perform until 1947. An instant success, *Steamboat Willie* launched the newly named Walter Disney Productions into a remarkable number of short animated features. Mickey, however, would remain the all-time favorite, and between 1928 and 1940, the amiable rodent starred in 110 cartoons.

With Mickey Mouse riding high, Disney created *Silly Symphonies* in 1929, a series of creative cartoons that explored the limits of the animated medium. The first effort, titled *Skeleton Dance*, captivated audiences. Initially, Disney produced these films in black and white, but in 1932, intrigued by the new Technicolor processes being developed, he began releasing them in color, starting with *Flowers and Trees*. The move vastly improved their public appeal, and in time 75 *Silly Symphonies* reached the screen before being discontinued in 1938. Virtually everyone in Hollywood admired their artistry, and Disney collected an unprecedented seven Academy Awards in the Best Short Subject (Cartoons) category during the 1930s.

Most of Disney's cartoon work, both print and animated, remained resolutely nontopical throughout the Depression era, although that neutrality would change radically with World War II. Well-known faces might occasionally be caricatured or familiar landmarks might appear, but his work espoused escapism, humor, and whimsy; little or nothing about the Depression and its effects appears. One of his *Silly Symphonies*, however, struck a nerve during those troubled days. In May 1933, just a few months after **Franklin D. Roosevelt**'s (1882–1945) inauguration as President, the Disney studios released *Three Little Pigs*.

On the surface, this 10-minute cartoon tells the story of Fifer Pig, Fiddler Pig, and Practical Pig. Threatened by (Big Bad) Wolf, the pigs scurry home. The wolf blows down Fifer's straw house, as he does Fiddler's flimsy stick one. But Practical Pig's sturdy brick house resists the wolf's attacks. The song "Who's Afraid of the Big Bad Wolf," with music and lyrics by Frank Churchill (1901–1942) and Ann Ronell (1905–1993), shortly became a big hit, and many attribute its success to the message they saw as implicit throughout both the cartoon and the **music**: with a mix of hard work and practicality, people can beat the Depression; even with the "wolf" at your door, if you're prepared, he can't get in. It may not be what Disney and his staff had intended, but many took its imagery that way. In the darkest days of the Depression, *Three Little Pigs* and its accompanying song seemed just the tonic the nation needed.

Although the studio concentrated most of its efforts on movie cartoons, it did not ignore other media. When the 1930s began, Disney and Iwerks went their separate ways, although the artist would rejoin Disney in 1940. In the meantime, Disney had hired Floyd Gottfredson (1905–1986) in 1929. In Iwerks' absence, Gottfredson took over a new Mickey Mouse newspaper comic strip that debuted in 1930, a job he would hold until 1975. In time, Gottfredson created Mickey's print persona, one that millions of readers would come to know through the popular strip.

While Mickey Mouse became identified with Disney enterprises, one of the *Silly Symphonies*, a short called *The Little Wise Hen* (1934), introduced a new character, Donald Duck. A popular addition, he reappeared in a later 1934 Mickey Mouse cartoon, *The Orphan's Benefit*. He soon showed up in several more, and finally in 1937 came *Don Donald*, the irascible duck's first solo effort. A year later, Donald's nephews, Huey, Dewey, and Louie, made their debuts. Over 50 Donald Duck cartoons played theaters by 1941, and he sometimes eclipsed Mickey in popularity.

Beginning in 1935, Donald occasionally had bit parts with Mickey in the latter's well-established comic strip. Just as had occurred with other animated cartoons, Donald got a syndicated daily strip of his own three years later. From then until 1969, it would be drawn by Al Taliaferro (1905–1969). Although a comic book featuring Donald Duck appeared in England in 1937, none would be published in the United States until 1942. Carl Barks (1901–2000), a cartoonist often associated with Donald Duck, joined Disney in 1935, and he worked on many of the animated cartoons of the mid-1930s and later. His greatest fame, however, would come in the 1940s and the enduring popularity of Donald Duck **comic books**.

As his cartoons and **comic strips** grew ever more polished, and with Mickey Mouse and Donald Duck achieving tremendous popularity, Disney began envisioning a full-length animated feature. Working with all his staff, he planned a retelling of the legend of Snow White, a Grimm brothers fairy tale. During the Christmas holidays of 1937, he unveiled the fruit of that planning: **Snow White and the Seven Dwarfs**, an instant hit.

Emboldened by the positive reception given *Snow White*, Disney soon had other **movies** on the drawing boards. *Pinocchio* and *Fantasia* both came out in 1940, and *Dumbo* in 1941. Preliminary work had also commenced on another classic, *Bambi*, destined to reach theaters in 1942. Although he continued to churn out short cartoons and comic strips, Disney recognized, at the end of the 1930s, that his company's future rested with full-length feature films.

In any discussion of Walt Disney and his life, it becomes necessary to note many of the people who aided him on his path to success. But their contributions would be worth little without his genius for storytelling, his eye for character, and his shrewd business sense. He might not draw or plot as well as his many artists and writers, but Walt Disney parlayed the skills of others into the greatest popularity that cartooning has even seen.

See also Newspapers

SELECTED READING
Finch, Christopher. *The Art of Walt Disney: From Mickey Mouse to the Magic Kingdoms*. New York: Harry N. Abrams, 1975.
Schickel, Richard. *The Disney Version*. Rev. ed. Chicago: Ivan R. Dee, 1997.
Thomas, Bob. *Walt Disney: An American Original*. New York: Disney Editions, 1994.

DOUGLAS DC-3. For the decade, no airplane better summarizes the changeover from wood and canvas, struts and wires, than the Douglas DC-3. First introduced by the Douglas Aircraft Company in a slightly different version as the DC-1 in 1933, this all-metal, Streamlined craft heralded the arrival of modern aerodynamics and technology to the field of **aviation**.

First manufactured in 1936, the DC-3 dominated commercial aviation throughout the decade. (Courtesy of the Library of Congress)

This transformation in aircraft design commenced when a competitor, the Boeing Airplane Company, introduced a somewhat similar passenger airplane a few months before its rival unveiled the DC-1. The Boeing 247 came off the assembly lines in February 1933. A Streamlined, two-motor, all-metal monoplane, the 247 possessed impressive statistics: it could fly at about 160 miles per hour for 800 miles, and it carried 10 passengers, although a cramped interior proved a drawback. Just four months later, the Douglas Aircraft Company unveiled a new airliner of its own, the DC-1.

Douglas manufactured only one prototype. Satisfied with its safety and performance, engineers rushed into production its successor, the DC-2, an airplane that exceeded the Boeing 247 in virtually all specifications. In the meantime, United Airlines, a carrier with corporate connections to Boeing and anxious to obtain a modern passenger plane, ordered all of the company's initial production run. Since that meant Boeing could not guarantee prompt delivery of 247s to other airlines, the commercial carriers looked elsewhere, turning their attention to Douglas.

The DC-2 featured a completely enclosed fuselage built as a single shell, or monocoque, and passengers and crew rode in a quiet, spacious cabin at speeds undreamed of until then. The DC-2 could cruise at almost 200 miles per hour—faster than most

133

military planes of the day—and stay aloft for some 2,000 miles, much farther than other commercial craft. Most telling, perhaps, the DC-2 carried 28 passengers, 18 more than Boeing's 247 model. Almost from the start, orders flooded into the Douglas offices, with the result that approximately 200 DC-2s would be built between 1933 and 1936. Boeing could never approach that level of success, manufacturing only 75 of their 247s.

By late 1935, executives from American Airlines began talking to Douglas designers about a modified version of the DC-2, an airplane capable of flying nonstop from New York City to Chicago. For longer flights, especially at night, they wanted to provide onboard sleeping arrangements for their customers. The idea of berths grew out of passenger train **travel**, where accommodations for sleeping had long been offered. The company developed the Douglas Sleeper Transport (DST) or "Skysleeper," as promoters called it, a dual-purpose airplane. By day, the DST would carry, as before, 28 passengers; at night, it boasted specially designed seats that folded together to make horizontal, bed-like arrangements for 14 patrons. At the rear of the cabin separate men's and women's dressing rooms, with toilets, allowed privacy. In order to accomplish all this, Douglas created a larger DC-2, calling the new model a DC-3.

DST or DC-3, Douglas's improved transport plane, made its debut in the summer of 1936 and outshone any and all competition. Within a short time, the DC-3 had become the mainstay of American commercial aviation. That dominance also extended to many foreign carriers; they found, as did their American counterparts, that the DC-3 offered a standard of mechanical reliability unequalled by any other plane. Economical to fly, it seldom required repairs other than normal maintenance. In production from 1936 until 1946, Douglas built well over 10,000 DC-3s, making the two-engine monoplane the most successful airliner of all time. It also proved profitable; by 1938, DC-3s were carrying over 90 percent of all commercial air passengers in the United States. Experts estimate that at the beginning of the twenty-first century, hundreds of DC-3s remain in active service around the world, a testament to the plane's ruggedness and durability.

See also Advertising; Buses; China Clippers; Design; Streamlining; Trains; Transportation

SELECTED READING

The American Heritage History of Flight. New York: Simon & Schuster, 1962.
Corn, Joseph J. *The Winged Gospel: America's Romance with Aviation, 1900–1950.* New York: Oxford University Press, 1983.
Douglas DC-3. http://www.douglasdc3.com
Hudson, Kenneth. *Air Travel: A Social History.* Totowa, NJ: Rowman & Littlefield, 1972.

DRACULA. The title of a Victorian-era novel, *Dracula* achieved its greatest popularity as a 1931 movie. Written in 1897 by Bram Stoker (1847–1912), he claimed his book was based on legends about a fiendish Count Dracula, or Vlad the Impaler. Capitalizing on popular beliefs about vampires, the "undead," and other widespread superstitions, Stoker's novel caught the public's imagination and became a best seller. In 1927, a stage version enjoyed modest success, but not until 1931 did Hollywood belatedly discover Stoker's tale. That year Universal Studios released *Dracula*, based more on the play than the book; it would become a classic film.

Bela Lugosi (1882–1956) (*right*), as the evil count, threatens Edward Van Sloan (1881–1964) in 1931's *Dracula*. (Courtesy of Photofest)

Only one in a long succession of pictures about the legend of Count Dracula, director Tod Browning's (1882–1962) retelling of the Dracula legend has influenced generations of moviegoers, set and costume designers, and performers. German director F. W. Murnau (1888–1931) had overseen an expressionistic silent movie interpretation of the vampire story titled *Nosferatu* in 1922. According to Murnau, the word "Nosferatu" means a "living corpse" or "vampire," but his film bears little resemblance to its later American sound counterpart and ultimately had little effect on how audiences perceived this kind of horror.

Browning, on the other hand, had the good fortune to land Romanian-born actor Bela Lugosi (1882–1956) for the title role. Previously unknown to the general public, Lugosi had created a distinctive persona for the evil count during the 1927 stage production. Although he had played a variety of roles prior to Dracula, his performance attracted attention and created an enduring image of Dracula, one that even contemporary performers still acknowledge.

Speaking with a peculiar accent that no linguists can trace, but one that people love to imitate, and swathed in a black cape that now serves as a standard for children dressed up as the count for Halloween, his stage and later screen performances catapulted him to stardom. For the remainder of his professional life, Lugosi found himself typecast for roles in **horror and fantasy films**, and audiences expected him to speak with his odd accent, look malevolent, and generally reprise the character of Dracula, no matter what the movie or the plot. As a result, for the next quarter century he acted in a few of the best (*The Black Cat*, 1934; *Mark of the Vampire*, 1935)—and many of the worst (*Night of Terror*, 1933; *Murder by Television*, 1935, *Shadow of Chinatown*, 1936)—scary **movies** ever produced by Hollywood. Often reduced to playing an embarrassing caricature of himself in later years, Lugosi's depiction of Dracula stands as the actor's outstanding achievement in a decidedly uneven career.

The flimsy plot—by now almost a cliché—offers a villain doomed to darkness and gloom, since vampires cannot survive the bright rays of the sun. Living his lonely life in a castle perched atop a crag, Dracula lures the unwary to his lair so he can drink their blood, the source of his immortality. Screenwriters saw to it that Dracula's destruction always hinged on uncertainty: seemingly dead as the end credits scroll on screen, the vampire may or may not really be dead—he might just resurface in a subsequent horror film. Audiences accepted this uncertainty, and a succession of movies played to this expectation.

For the turbulent 1930s, the success of *Dracula* helped escalate horror and fantasy films into a popular genre whose very escapism served as an antidote to the grim economic realities awaiting audiences outside the theater. Inside, the creepy play of light and shadow on the screen, accompanied by exaggerated acting on the part of virtually everyone involved, created a mood of melodramatic suspense, and people willingly suspended any disbelief as plots and action unfold. For a couple of thrilling hours, **movies** like *Dracula*, **Frankenstein** (1931), *The Bride of Frankenstein* (1935), *Freaks* (1932), *The Mummy* (1932), and **King Kong** (1933) alternately thrilled and frightened millions, giving them a temporary respite from the Depression. For many, the 1930s will be remembered as the golden years of the Hollywood horror film, and *Dracula* will rank among the best.

See also Best Sellers; Stage Productions

SELECTED READING

Beck, Calvin Thomas. *Heroes of the Horrors.* New York: Macmillan, 1975.

Brunas, Michael, John Brunas and Tom Weaver. *Universal Horrors: The Studio's Classic Films, 1931–1946.* Jefferson, NC: McFarland & Co., 1990.

Clarens, Carlos. *An Illustrated History of the Horror Film.* New York: Capricorn Books, 1967.

E

EARHART, AMELIA. With a combination of boyish good looks, a jaunty attitude toward taking risks, and heaps of publicity provided by a celebrity-obsessed media, Amelia Earhart (1897–1937) rose to fame quickly. The American public, still fascinated with the exploits of Charles Lindbergh (1902–1974) and his 1927 solo transatlantic flight, transferred a measure of its adulation to this young aviatrix, the term then used to identify a woman pilot. In return, she established new records for speed and distance, not just for women, but for the larger field of **aviation**.

Earhart had first been bitten by the flying bug in 1920 when, as a passenger, she climbed into the open cockpit of a flimsy biplane and found herself above Los Angeles for about 20 minutes. That experience led her to seek out Anita "Leta" Snook (1896–1991), another pioneering woman aviator, who taught her to pilot an airplane.

In 1922, Earhart gained attention when she set a women's altitude mark by climbing to 14,000 feet. She continued her exploits and in June 1928 received an invitation to be the sole passenger on a flight across the Atlantic. Until then, no woman had crossed the ocean by airplane. Wilmer Stultz (active 1930s) piloted a Fokker trimotor, and Louis "Slim" Gordon (active 1930s) served as flight mechanic. The three flew from Newfoundland to Wales, and the press nicknamed Earhart "Lady Lindy," an allusion to Charles Lindbergh's nickname of "Lucky Lindy." She, however, displayed little patience playing the role of passenger, even a record-breaking one.

Just a year later, Earhart herself took the controls and completed an east-to-west solo flight across the continental United States, another first for women. Her growing fame allowed her to join Transcontinental Air Transport (TAT, later to be TransWorld Airlines, or TWA) as a spokesperson encouraging other women to fly commercially. She also helped organize the Ninety-Nines, a group of 99 women pilots who likewise promoted aviation.

In her ceaseless efforts to popularize flying, Earhart pushed for the creation of a women's Los Angeles to Cleveland, Ohio, air race, or derby. In 1929, with comedian Will Rogers (1879–1935) in attendance, the first such derby took place. Given the absence of males, Rogers quipped it should be called a "Powder-Puff Derby," and the name stuck. By whatever term, these air races further heightened public awareness of women in aviation.

The 1930s proved Amelia Earhart's banner decade. Piloting a Lockheed Vega, a streamlined craft for the era, she established several women's speed records in 1930.

Aviatrix Amelia Earhart (1897–1937). (Courtesy of the Library of Congress)

Well aware that no one, man or woman, had flown solo across the Atlantic since Lindbergh, she undertook the challenge in 1932. Taking off from Newfoundland in May, almost five years to the day after Lindbergh, she successfully landed in Ireland. The feat earned her a tickertape parade in New York City and additional celebrity.

She wrote for *Cosmopolitan* magazine and dabbled in **fashion** design. Her 1932 flying suit, created for the members of Ninety-Nine, featured loose trousers, a zippered top, and large pockets. It found favor outside aviation circles, and *Vogue* magazine advertised it. An "Amelia Earhart" label helped sell women's sportswear in stores like Macy's and Marshall Field's.

More importantly, however, Earhart continued to fly and break records. In 1935, she became the first person to challenge the Pacific Ocean, piloting a plane from Hawaii to Oakland, California. She went on the lecture circuit, flying herself from Los Angeles to Mexico City (a first), and then from Mexico City to Newark, New Jersey (another first). But all the speeches and the **travel** served only as a rehearsal for her dream: a flight around the world.

It came as no surprise when she announced such plans in 1936. Plotting an equatorial route of some 27,000 miles, a feat no one else had yet tried, she planned to make the journey in a Lockheed L-10 Electra, one of the most modern planes of the day. Earhart selected Frederick Noonan (1893–1937) as her navigator; he possessed both marine and flight navigational expertise, needed skills since much of the journey would be over water.

After a delay in California, Earhart and Noonan regrouped in Miami, Florida, and embarked on June 1, 1937. Following the equator, they flew to Puerto Rico, then to South America, Africa, across the subcontinent of Asia, on to southeast Asia, and then to New Guinea. They had completed 20,000 miles and had only 7,000 to go. On July 2, the two departed Lae, New Guinea, bound for Howland Island, a sliver of land in the vast Pacific. Somewhere over open water, the plane disappeared. In news stories that rivaled in emotion any event of the decade, reporters chronicled Earhart's lost flight and the efforts to locate it.

The U.S. government instituted extensive searches, ultimately spending over $4 million (roughly $56 million in contemporary dollars) in attempts to find traces of the fliers or their aircraft. The disappearance of Amelia Earhart has entered American popular folklore. **Movies** have been produced, books written, new searches attempted, and conspiracy theories of every kind advanced, but she, Noonan, and the Lockheed Electra remain missing, a tantalizing, unsolved mystery of the 1930s.

See also Advertising; Magazines; Newspapers; Radio; Eleanor Roosevelt; Streamlining; Shirley Temple

SELECTED READING
Earhart, Amelia. http://ellensplace.net/eae_intr.html
Long, Elgen M., and Marie K. Long. *Amelia Earhart: The Mystery Solved.* New York: Simon & Schuster, 1999.
Rich, Doris L. *Amelia Earhart: A Biography.* Washington, DC: Smithsonian Institution Press, 1989.

EDUCATION. In 1929–1930, slightly over 28 million children and adolescents attended either public or private schools. During the first two years of the economic crisis, most schools operated about as usual, but by the fall of 1931 they began experiencing serious financial strains. Unemployment and lower incomes meant lower tax revenues and less money for the schools. In real numbers and on a percentage basis, more white students went to school than did the children of minority groups.

Some business leaders argued that the country could no longer afford universal public education, with the most extreme proponents wanting to close the schools altogether. Others felt schools should remain open but that instruction be restricted to trade skills and job training. The majority of Americans, however, wanted to maintain high standards and expose children and adolescents to a solid educational experience.

To solve the unbalanced budgets of the early 1930s, many communities shortened their school year from a national average of eight months to six months. Across the country, the duration of a school year varied; children in rural areas usually spent less time in classes than their urban counterparts. Administrators also abolished numerous programs, especially extracurricular activities that went beyond the basics of reading, writing, and arithmetic. School districts issued used textbooks, halted construction projects, and reduced the size of staff and salaries. Some of the worst cuts occurred in rural districts and in the South where by 1934 an estimated 20,000 public schools had closed their doors to about 300,000 children. These cuts hit black students the hardest. Southern states segregated schools by race, and those for black children historically received less money and resources than those attended by white children.

Teachers and other educators strove to preserve both their jobs and the quality of education. In Illinois, the Chicago system served as an example of schools staying open simply because dedicated teachers continued to work even knowing they would not be paid. In an attempt to gain some political clout, the National Education Association (NEA) created the Joint Committee on Emergency Education to raise awareness of the problem and lobby for solutions.

After the election of **Franklin D. Roosevelt** (1882–1945) in 1933, the federal government assumed a greater share of the financial aspects of economic relief, which in turn released local and state money for other uses; 32 states had increased aid to education by the mid-1930s. Closed schools reopened, most for eight or nine months, and the majority offered a curriculum focused on basic academic subjects—along with courses that prepared young women to manage their future homes efficiently and raise their children intelligently, while giving young men instruction on how to provide a reliable family income. Programs in art and **music** became available through the **Federal Art Project**

A one-room school in rural Alabama. (Courtesy of the Library of Congress)

(FAP, 1935–1943), and the **Federal Music Project** (FMP, 1935–1943). These initiatives also offered work for many unemployed teachers, artists, and musicians.

Adult-supervised organizations, such as the Boy Scouts, Girl Scouts, Young Men's or Women's Christian or Hebrew Associations, helped the struggling schools by offering after-school activities including athletics, drama, and crafts. These efforts became an important part of the educational system and frequently utilized school facilities. Community organizations also offered adult education and vocational training courses at local schools in the evenings.

Along with a decrease in tax revenues, other conditions during the 1930s affected the educational system. Financial hardships forced people to postpone marriage and having children, which resulted in a decline in the birth rate. That in turn, altered elementary school enrollment. At the same time, the number of students in high school skyrocketed; many young people who could not find jobs extended their educational careers. Thus, despite a decrease in the national public school enrollment, a higher percentage of the school-age population actually attended school, an additional strain on financially strapped school systems.

Even with the growing desire for an education and the sharp increase in the number graduating from high school, enrollment in colleges and universities dropped about 10 percent between 1932 and 1934, but then increased during the second half of the decade. The number of women pursuing a college education rose slightly during the 1930s, but their percentage of total college enrollment decreased because of the growing number of men attending four-year institutions. Many college-educated women opted for marriage over a career, but some entered professional careers, and an estimated one-fourth of all women attempted to combine both matrimony and a full-time job.

As the country recovered from the Depression, the number of college and university faculty increased, as did the number and variety of courses. Traditional arts and science schools added programs in the fields of business, engineering, anthropology, political science, and sociology. Some colleges and universities also offered courses related to everyday life. Indiana University's course on marriage, begun in 1938 by zoology professor Alfred Kinsey (1894–1956), stands as perhaps the most striking example. Also, college life took on an increasingly serious aspect as more students showed an interest in history and became actively involved in political discussions.

For many of the students enrolled in college during the worst of the Depression, it took ingenuity to remain in school. Some managed to find work; many cooked meals in their rooms; and others had their own cows and chickens for milk and eggs. The colleges, despite their own dwindling resources, attempted to grant financial concessions to gifted and promising students with little or no money.

Beginning in 1934, the federal government provided financial aid through the Federal Emergency Relief Act (FERA; 1933–1935) and assisted 75,000 college students during the second half of the 1933–1934 academic year. They worked as teacher and library assistants or did clerical tasks. In return, the federal government paid these student workers, selected by their colleges or universities, a maximum of $20 a month (over $275 in today's dollars) during the school term. In 1935, administration of this aid program moved to the National Youth Administration (NYA; 1935–1943) and expanded aid to include graduate students under the age of 25, along with a special fund created for black graduate students.

The NYA also provided financial relief and job training to unemployed young people who did not attend school. By 1938, NYA educational programs had enrolled over 480,000 individuals, almost half of them women. Other **New Deal** initiatives also served as alternatives to schools and offered educational opportunities. For example, the **Civilian Conservation Corps** (CCC, 1933–1942) primarily provided work for unemployed, single male youths. It too embraced educational components. The Works Progress Administration (WPA, 1935–1943; name changed to Work Projects Administration in 1939) provided financial assistance to states in five areas: general adult education, literary classes for adults, vocational education, vocational rehabilitation, and nursery schools for preschool children from underprivileged homes.

Lack of tax dollars for adequate funding may have been the primary issue for schools during the 1930s, but concern by parents and others often centered on what constituted the best learning conditions. In response, two notable education events took place during the 1930s: literacy programs and testing. The educational publisher Scott-Foresman and Company introduced its *Elson-Gray Basic Readers* in 1930. Created and written by William S. Gray (1885–1960), Zerna Sharp (1889–1981), and William H. Elson (active 1930s), these texts are better known as "Dick and Jane" or "See Spot Run." The series contains stories featuring the same set of siblings, Dick, Jane, and Sally, along with their dog, Spot. Heavily illustrated, the pictures intend to help new readers associate a word with its meaning and teach reading through a whole word (or look-say) method, rather than using rote exercises with phonics. Scott, Foresman retired the Elson-Gray books in 1940, but retained the characters and the look-say method in its successors.

In October 1930, the Progressive Education Association established the Commission on the Relation of School to College. It had as its mission the study of the relevance of high school curriculum to college admissions and success. The Eight-Year Study, as it came to be called, tracked two groups of students from their first year in high school until college. Periodic tests of two groups, one taught in high school by the so-called progressive method and the other by a more traditional approach, attempted to determine if one group or the other scored better. The results favored progressive education, but perhaps the Eight-Year Study's most significant contribution involved the incorporation of periodic testing into the school year, a practice that has continued into the present.

By the end of the 1930s, the nation's total public school budget equaled the pre-Depression figures and public and private schools accommodated 95.5 percent of 5- to 17-year-olds nationally. Enrollment in colleges and universities had increased markedly. Through New Deal programs, young people and adults seeking a vocational education could receive basic shop training, skills that allowed them to secure jobs in the country's industrial base.

See also Federal Theatre Project; Federal Writers' Project; Leisure & Recreation; Race Relations & Stereotyping; Youth

SELECTED READING

Kyvig, David E. *Daily Life In the United States, 1920–1940*. Chicago: Ivan R. Dee, 2004.
Moreo, Dominic W. *Schools in the Great Depression*. New York: Garland Publishing, 1996.
Rollin, Lucy. *Twentieth-Century Teen Culture by the Decades: A Reference Guide*. Westport, CT: Greenwood Press, 1999.
Shannon, David A., ed. *The Great Depression*. Englewood Cliffs, NJ: Prentice-Hall, 1960.
Ware, Susan. *Holding Their Own: American Women in the 1930s*. Boston: Twayne, 1982.

ELLINGTON, DUKE. Born Edward Kennedy Ellington (1899–1974) in Washington, D.C., this versatile composer-arranger-pianist-bandleader gained the nickname "Duke" at an early age because of his suave elegance. By the onset of the 1930s, critics and colleagues recognized Ellington as one of the most important musical luminaries of the day, a reputation he would burnish for the rest of his life. Comfortable in the realms of **jazz**, blues, **swing**, show tunes, and popular songs, he created an enormous body of work that continues to be performed and recorded. His sheer output—thousands of compositions—helped define American **music** for the twentieth century.

While still in his late teens, Ellington had become established in the local Washington music scene and had organized a number of pickup bands to play for various social functions. Within a few years, he went to New York City, assumed leadership of a band, and began composing in earnest. Such early classics as "East St. Louis Toodle-oo" (1926), "Birmingham Breakdown" (1926), "Creole Love Call" (1927) and "Black and Tan Fantasy" (1927) came from these formative years; fortunately, numerous older **recordings** exist that capture the promise of both his writing and his orchestra at this stage of his career.

But Ellington also had to cater to preconceptions about jazz and black musicians. Many people, fans and critics alike, characterized (and marketed) his work as "jungle music," the old stereotype of African origins and primitive tom-toms. He did indeed make use of growling brasses, sensuous reeds, and exotic rhythms, and some of his recordings from the 1920s echo this conceit. That he could both create so-called jungle music and transcend it at the same time serves as a testament to Ellington's genius. Despite the obvious racial connotations in this phrase, it also describes the innovative compositions and sound the young composer and arranger was developing at the time.

In 1927, the Ellington aggregation moved to Harlem's famed Cotton Club, an engagement that would endure until 1932. During this time, his genius blossomed. He wrote an early extended work, "The Mooche," in 1928, and the band's first real hit, "Mood Indigo" (originally titled "Dreamy Blues"), in 1930. That year also counted the up-tempo "Rockin' in Rhythm" and "Ring Dem Bells." Following the extended stay at the Cotton Club, the Ellington band found itself in demand. Concerts, clubs, and tours came along in profusion, but the hectic schedule did little to slow down Ellington's composing. A sampler of highlights from the 1930s:

1931: "Creole Rhapsody" (another extended work)
1932: "Sophisticated Lady" (lyrics added by Mitchell Parish [1900–1993] in 1933) and "It Don't Mean a Thing (If It Ain't Got That Swing)" (one of the first mentions of "swing" in the context of music)
1933: "Drop Me Off in Harlem," "Merry-Go-Round," and "Daybreak Express"
1934: "Solitude" and "Stompy Jones"
1935: "In a Sentimental Mood" and "Reminiscing in Tempo" (an extended work)
1936: "Echoes of Harlem" and "Caravan" (cowritten with Juan Tizol [1900–1984])
1937: "Azure" and "Diminuendo and Crescendo in Blue" (another extended work)
1938: "Prelude to a Kiss" and "I Let a Song Go Out of My Heart"
1939: "Ko-Ko" and "Something to Live For" (cowritten with Billy Strayhorn [1915–1967])
1940: "Don't Get Around Much Anymore" (originally titled "Never No Lament"), "Cotton Tail," "In a Mellotone," and "Day Dream" (cowritten with Strayhorn)

The 1940s would see no lessening of Ellington's talent; the hits—most would eventually become standards—continued unabated, and the orchestra remained distinctive. His flair for texture and tonality placed him on a unique plane; no one else duplicated his orchestra's sound, and his always-innovative compositions and arrangements put him far ahead of his contemporaries.

The Ellington orchestras, often described as extensions of the man himself, employed some of the most talented sidemen of the day. During the 1930s, his brass players included people like Rex Stewart (1907–1967), Cootie Williams (1910–1985), "Tricky Sam" Nanton (1904–1948), and Lawrence Brown (1907–1988), while artists such as Barney Bigard (1906–1980), Johnny Hodges (1906–1970), Ben Webster (1909–1973), and Harry Carney (1910–1974) anchored the reeds. His rhythm sections featured Sonny Greer (1895–1982), Billy Taylor (1906–1986), Jimmy Blanton (1918–1942), and, of course, Ellington himself on piano. Ivie Anderson (1905–1949) handled the bulk of the vocal chores for the decade.

As an acknowledgment of the band's success, Ellington and his sidemen appeared in several **movies**, a rare accomplishment for black entertainers in those racially segregated days. Three band shorts, *Black and Tan* (1929), *A Bundle of Blues* (1933), and *Symphony in Black* (1935), introduced many white audiences to the novelty of an all-black orchestra. They also appeared on screen in *Check and Double Check* (1930), a full-length feature that capitalized on the remarkable popularity of the **Amos 'n' Andy radio** show.

Not much of a motion picture, but it does present the Cotton Club Orchestra in its prime and even boasts **Bing Crosby** (1903–1977) vocalizing with the band.

The 1930s saw Duke Ellington's composing become increasingly urbane and refined; the "jungle music" phase of his career was relegated to the past. His compositions and performances can hardly be categorized as either white or black, but instead live on as part of the canon of American music.

See also Race Relations & Stereotyping; Songwriters & Lyricists

SELECTED READING
Dance, Stanley. *The World of Duke Ellington.* New York: DaCapo Press, 1970.
Jewell, Derek. *Duke: A Portrait of Duke Ellington.* New York: W. W. Norton, 1977.
Tucker, Mark, ed. *The Duke Ellington Reader.* New York: Oxford University Press, 1993.
Yanow, Scott. *Swing.* San Francisco: Miller Freeman Books, 2000.

EMPIRE STATE BUILDING, THE. An icon of New York City, a symbol of hope in the darkest days of the Great Depression, no other skyscraper in the world better epitomizes the concept of the tall building than does the Empire State Building (1931). When it opened its doors on Fifth Avenue between West 33rd and 34th Streets, this archetype towered 1,252 feet into the skies above Manhattan, making it far and away the tallest building—as well as the tallest man-made structure—in the world. Its 102 stories allowed it to retain first place among skyscrapers for the next 41 years, when it would be displaced by 1972's ill-fated World Trade Center.

Designed by the firm of Shreve, Lamb & Harmon, the Empire State Building's sleek, restrained **Art Deco** styling signaled the decline of the heavily decorated skyscraper; the gargoyles and other applied ornament of the nearby **Chrysler Building** (1930; 77 stories and 1,040 feet) spoke to an earlier era. William Lamb (1883–1952) functioned as the chief designer of the tower, and he favored the stripped-down minimalism that serves as the hallmark of the famous skyscraper. Primarily a means to save on expenses, it also signals in its unadorned verticality how the stark **International Style** would gradually encroach on new buildings.

The Empire State Building not only achieved status as the world's tallest skyscraper but also broke other records. From conceptual **design** to the opening ceremonies took only 27 months (1928–1931). The actual construction phase ran from March 1930 until May 1931, or just a little over 13 months. Some 3,000 workmen employed assembly-line methods, and frequently erected more than one story a day. Curious crowds would gather at the building's base and gawk as riveters and other crews perched themselves on the rising steel frame and went about their dangerous business. This furious pace allowed the tower to come in under cost estimates, a remarkable achievement in any age.

Clad in granite and Indiana limestone, with nickel-steel and aluminum trim from the sixth floor upward, it features flush windows that give the exterior a smooth, uninterrupted quality. In fact, the building exudes a stately air, unlike some of its more boisterous neighbors built during the 1920s. For the times, it suggests probity and strength, needed qualities in the dismal period that followed the exuberant Jazz Age. It also soars upward, confidence in the face of pessimism. Despite these optimistic readings, a more dubious side to the Empire State Building involved finding paying tenants for the huge office tower. Skeptics dubbed it "the Empty State Building," since the owners managed to recruit only half as many tenants as hoped for. Not until after the Depression did it achieve full occupancy, and not until 1950 did it finally turn a profit on its many leases.

Documentary photographer Lewis Hine (1874–1940) captured the construction of the Empire State Building in a lengthy series of extraordinary pictures that have become the definitive record of that momentous event. He assembled those photographs, along with a number of others dealing with physical labor, into a book titled *Men at Work: Photographic Studies of Modern Men and Machines* (1932). The Empire State Building sections have since been separated into a volume on that structure alone, *Lewis W. Hine: The Empire State Building* (1998). These iconic views of workers, or "skyboys," going about their tasks while high above the city fail to show Hines himself, sometimes suspended in a special basket 1,000 feet over Fifth Avenue, composing and taking his shots.

In order to reach its great height, the structure boasts a spire atop its crown that had originally been designed as a mooring mast for dirigibles. Lighter-than-air craft had captured the public's imagination in the late 1920s, and

The Empire State Building at night. (Courtesy of the Library of Congress)

many people envisioned a time when silent, comfortable airship **travel** would become commonplace. Cities raced to have mooring facilities for the great hydrogen-filled Zeppelins. In theory—at least for the Empire State Building—the ponderous craft would glide up to the skyscraper and attach, nose-first, to the mast. Countless passengers would then alight from the gondola of the airship and descend, via a gangplank, to the building itself. In retrospect, such a departure would have been harrowing in the best of circumstances and probably impossible under windy conditions.

In 1931, in an experiment, a small, privately owned airship did connect with the mast, but uncertain, buffeting winds caused the crew to sever the connection, marking an end to the dream of dirigible travel into the heart of New York City. The mast stood unused until, after some modifications, it became the city's primary **radio** and **television** antenna, a function it continues to fulfill.

King Kong (1933), one of the great fantasy **movies** of the decade, employs the building's spire in a more imaginative way. Kong, the giant ape of the title, clambers to the top of the Empire State Building in a memorable sequence. With a screaming Fay Wray (1907–2004) clutched in his huge paw, he defies the "civilized" world that has put him in this predicament. Army Air Force planes, like pesky gnats, buzz around him, their machine guns chattering. Kong eventually falls to his death, but not before the Empire State Building, a symbol of triumphant modern technology, briefly stars in this classic movie.

See also Airships; Architecture; Photography; Rockefeller Center; Streamlining

SELECTED READING

Hine, Lewis W. *Men at Work: Photographic Studies of Modern Men and Machines*. New York: Dover Publications, 1977.

Pacelle, Mitchell. *Empire: A Tale of Obsession, Betrayal, and the Battle for an American Icon*. New York: John Wiley & Sons, 2001.

Robinson, Cervin, and Rosemarie Haag Bletter. *Skyscraper Style: Art Deco New York*. New York: Oxford University Press, 1975.

Tauranac, John. *Empire State Building: The Making of a Landmark*. New York: St. Martin's Press, 1997.

F

FADS. Usually consisting of trivial interests enthusiastically pursued by many people for a short period of time, fads require leisure time, a commodity available to many during the 1930s. Shorter work weeks or outright unemployment caused many Americans to seek low-cost diversions for their free time, and the 1930s provided them in abundance. In the area of **music**, **swing** and boogie-woogie attracted legions of fans, and dancers strove to master the **jitterbug**. **Contract bridge**, **Monopoly**, **miniature golf**, pinball machines, yo-yos, and bingo also had their moments during the decade. After the initial excitement died down, some activities that originated as fads became a part of ongoing popular culture.

The 1930s did not lack for off-beat crazes. People tried to drink prodigious quantities of coffee or set records for sustained gum chewing. Eating contests challenged participants to swallow more pies, eggs, clams, oysters, spaghetti, hot dogs, and the like in the shortest possible time. Rock-a-thons urged entrants to rock continuously in old-fashioned rocking chairs. To win this event, a contestant had to stay both in motion and awake longer than anyone else, and that meant not being lulled to sleep by the gentle movement of the rocking chair.

Many fads focused on endurance, and winners could claim money, **food**, or other prizes that offered some concrete relief during the era's economic difficulties. For example, with **marathon dancing**, all dancers benefited during the contest by being provided free meals and a cot for sleeping. The couple that danced the longest total time won a prize, usually a paltry sum of money. The marathon concept extended beyond dancing and included walking and talking, nonstop piano playing, seesaw riding, and kissathons, the last involving lip-to-lip adherence for hours or days.

Tree and flagpole sitters, a test of endurance carried over from the 1920s, involved climbing to the highest branches of a tree or to the top of a pole and attempting to remain there for weeks, even months. The sitters, most of them young, established a fee prior to ascending to their perches or had a partner collect money on the ground throughout the course of the event. The longer sitters stayed aloft, the more money they received and the more entertainment they provided the gawkers below.

Other physical feats also gained popularity. Entrepreneurs established individual and team bicycle contests designed to set records for the longest continuous time on a bike. Organized races, usually called six-day bicycle races, also took place. Riding on small makeshift wooden tracks, two-person teams, usually a man and woman, circled the track for six entire days, taking turns and fighting exhaustion. Joe E. Brown (1892–1973), a well-known comedian, appeared in 6 *Day Bike Rider* (1934), a movie that reflected this fad's popularity. The 4,000-mile **roller skating** derby, modeled after the six-day bicycle race, emerged as yet another physical endurance challenge and brought a new kind of cheap entertainment to audiences. Abandoned warehouses and other indoor spaces became rinks to accommodate the growing interest and participation in this sport.

On a less strenuous but potentially riskier level, the chain letter seemed to guarantee easy money. It all began in the spring of 1935 in Denver, Colorado, and shortly thereafter had swept the country. A person receives a letter with a set number of names and addresses, say five or six. The recipient scratches off the first name, and replaces it with his or her name at the bottom of the list. But there's a catch: the recipient must also send a dime (about $1.50 in contemporary money) to the person whose name got scratched and mail five copies of the letter with the new list to five additional people. In five progressions—and assuming the chain remains unbroken—the sender's name rises to the top and he or she makes a small fortune in dimes. Seldom, however, does the chain remain intact, and even less frequently does anyone make money. For a few months in 1935, such letters nonetheless swamped post offices across the country; even the White House and celebrities received them. Almost as fast as the fad developed, interest waned and by July 1935 it had passed into oblivion.

During the 1930s, language served as the source of a fun fad, the knock-knock joke. It goes like this:

[Set Up]: Knock. Knock.
[Response]: Who's there?
[Teaser]: Ivan
[Response]: Ivan who?
[Punch line]: Ivan workin' on the railroad.

Or Dwayne ("Dwayne the bathtub, I'm drowning!"), or Snow ("Snowbody but me."), and so on. The possibilities were endless, and people loved them. This fad peaked in 1936, but like chain letters, knock-knock jokes have cropped up perennially ever since. That same year it even served as the source of a minor hit, "The Knock-Knock Song" (words and music by Bill Davies, Vincent Lopez, Johnny Morris, and Jimmy Tyson [all active 1930s]), for the Vincent Lopez Orchestra. Band members cried out, "Knock, knock," and a vocalist responded with "Who's there?" And so it would go through yet another corny punch line.

In the early years of the decade, language also contributed to a fad with the spread of "Hooverisms." They all referred to President **Herbert Hoover** (1874–1964) and his apparent inability to deal effectively with the Depression. A collection of tents, cardboard boxes, tarpaper shacks, and the like became known as "Hoovervilles." Usually located close to railroad tracks, they sufficed as housing for the homeless and unemployed, especially in large cities. In these temporary villages, many slept under layers of **newspapers** known as "Hoover blankets." Turned inside out, the white lining of jacket or pants pockets showed the owner had no money and people dubbed them "Hoover flags." Dinner might consist of rabbits—"Hoover hogs"—cooked over an open fire. Well-worn shoes, usually with visible holes, were "Hoover shoes," and "Hoover leather" described the cardboard used to resole them.

"Hoovercart" and "Hooverwagon" rodeos, which first appeared in North Carolina in 1933, involved hitching teams of mules to the back halves of broken down Model-T Fords for a race over an obstacle course. The event quickly became the rage across the country. Finally, a "Hoovercrat" described someone who still voiced faith in the beleaguered president.

Perhaps one of the most surprising fads of the decade had its origin in 1935 at Harvard University. A freshman swallowed a live goldfish, apparently on a dare. Boston reporters had been informed of the upcoming event, and from their coverage other college students repeated the stunt on their campuses within days. Quickly established as a full-fledged fad on American campuses, the intent shifted from gulping down just one goldfish to swallowing the greatest number. New records were set daily—28 fish at the University of Michigan, 29 at Boston College, and 33 at Albright College. In 1938, an MIT student set the unofficial record by swallowing 42 goldfish in succession. There might have been a Depression, there might be a war looming, but in the time-honored tradition of American students, there was always time for silliness.

See also Automobiles; Coffee & Tea; Education; Games; Fashions; Hobbies; Leisure & Recreation; Youth

SELECTED READING

Hoffmann, Frank W., and William G. Bailey. *Sports and Recreation Fads*. New York: Haworth Press, 1991.

Marum, Andrew, and Frank Parise. *Follies and Foibles: A View of 20th-Century Fads*. New York: Facts on File, 1984.

Panati, Charles. *Panati's Parade of Fads, Follies, and Manias*. New York: HarperCollins, 1991.

Sann, Paul. *Fads, Follies, and Delusions of the American People*. New York: Crown Publishers, 1967.

FAIRS & EXPOSITIONS. Since time immemorial, people have flocked to fairs. They provide amusement, information, celebration, and a respite from the day-to-day world. Despite the economic challenges of the time, the 1930s proved no exception. Citizens attended an untold number of agricultural fairs as well as larger expositions that attempted to show how life becomes better as a result of hard work, technological advancement, and healthy living.

The 1933–1934 **Century of Progress Exposition (Chicago World's Fair)** and the 1939–1940 **New York World's Fair** stand as the decade's most important. Two other large celebrations qualified as World Fairs: the California Pacific International Exposition (San Diego, California, 1935–1936) and the Golden Gate International Exposition (San Francisco, California, 1939–1940). Smaller events during the 1930s included the Yorktown Sesquicentennial (Yorktown, Virginia, 1931), the Texas Centennial Central Exposition (Dallas, Texas, 1936), the Greater Texas and Pan American Exposition (Dallas, Texas, 1937), and the Great Lakes Exposition (Cleveland, Ohio, 1936–1937).

The Yorktown Sesquicentennial opened on October 16, 1931, as a four-day celebration of the surrender of the British and the 1781 conclusion to the Revolutionary War. The post office issued a 2-cent commemorative stamp, and speeches, fireworks, band concerts, reenactment of the final battle, military displays, and remarks by President **Herbert Hoover** (1874–1964) marked the event.

Texas observed 100 years of independence from Mexico by staging the 1936 Texas Centennial Central Exposition in Dallas. The state coupled the Dallas exhibition with regional fairs, and the events complemented a dual theme of history and progress. The Hall of Negro Life marked a milestone, the first recognition of black American culture at an important, widely publicized fair, although black Americans encountered considerable hostility and segregated facilities throughout the fairgrounds.

On June 12, 1937, The Greater Texas and Pan American Exposition opened in Dallas on the heels of the Texas Centennial Central Exposition that had closed the previous fall. Twenty-one independent nations located in the New World organized commercial and governmental exhibits to celebrate their development and to promote international goodwill. The Pan American Casino, an amusement center, presented stars of stage, screen, and **radio** in an air-conditioned setting, and a symphony shell featured **music** and light and comic operas. The exhibition ended October 31, 1937, after several million fairgoers had passed through the turnstiles during its brief run.

Before the Dallas festivals had closed, the Great Lakes Exposition, with Streamlined **architecture** the dominant building style, opened in the summer of 1936, marking the centennial of Cleveland's incorporation as a city. Many workers received compensation from the Works Progress Administration (WPA; 1935–1943; name changed to Work Projects Administration in 1939), and selected exhibits from Chicago's Century of Progress Exposition made the move to Cleveland. More than 7 million people viewed the midway shows and toured the commercial and government displays. In a spirit of sharing, some of these exhibits later reappeared in New York's World's Fair.

The Aquacade, a marine theater featuring a stage that floated in Lake Erie, served as the centerpiece of the Cleveland celebration. Producer Billy Rose (1899–1966) provided a show starring Johnny Weissmuller (1904–1984), who played **Tarzan** in the **movies**, and Olympic swimmer Eleanor Holm (1913–2004). During the summer of 1937, Bob Crosby (1913–1993) and his Bobcats orchestra joined the show, adding a taste of **jazz** to the event.

Much greater prestige accrued to those festivals that gained the designation World's Fair. In 1934, business leaders in San Diego, encouraged by the financial success of the Century of Progress Exposition and the opportunity to reuse some of those exhibits, finalized plans for the California Pacific International Exposition, and succeeded in gaining the coveted title.

Employing the newest Hollywood lighting techniques, it opened on May 29, 1935, and incorporated into its architectural plan the Spanish-Colonial Revival buildings in Balboa Park that had distinguished an earlier fair, the 1915–1916 Panama California International Exposition. In addition, it drew on a number of more contemporary **Art Deco** designs for some of the new buildings and towers.

The exposition offered entertainment and displays of consumer goods and mechanical inventions intended to encourage a hope for a "golden tomorrow." True to this theme, exhibit structures (called palaces) included the Palace of Better Housing, the Palace of **Food** and Beverages, Palace of **Education**, Palace of Science, Palace of Water and **Transportation**, and the Palace of Pacific Relations. Entertainment ranged from bizarre sideshows to a performance of Felix Mendelssohn's (1809–1847) *Elijah*. The Columbia Broadcasting System (CBS radio) broadcast some of the orchestral and musical group performances. Many Hollywood and sports celebrities, politicians, and government officials, including President **Franklin D. Roosevelt** (1882–1945) and First Lady **Eleanor Roosevelt** (1884–1962), attended as spectators or participated in special events.

The San Diego fair closed on September 9, 1936, with a small surplus of money, although the 6.75 million visitors fell short of original expectations. It had nonetheless brought countless tourists to San Diego and created many jobs, with 65 percent of the workers receiving their wages from the federal government.

Community leaders in San Francisco likewise had gained the World's Fair classification for the upcoming Golden Gate International Exposition, a festival that commenced in February 1939. It highlighted Pacific unity and honored the construction of the world's two longest suspension bridges, the San Francisco–Oakland Bay Bridge (1936) and the Golden Gate Bridge (1937), both of which spanned portions of San Francisco Bay. The WPA had supported these projects and also contributed to the building of Treasure Island, the largest man-made island of its time. It served as the fair's site with 400 acres of usable space, and people could arrive via a 900-foot-long causeway or at docks and ferry slips for boats.

With the theme "Pageant of the Pacific," the grounds housed exhibit and administration buildings, towers, gardens, elaborate pools, statues, and two aircraft hangars of steel and concrete, since the site was slated to become the city's new municipal airport. An eclectic mixture of architecture allowed the commercial and agricultural displays to show the wares of more than 40 countries and the 48 states. Billy Rose's Aquacade showcased future movie star Esther Williams (b. 1922) and other synchronized swimmers in breathtaking high dives and spectacular group formations. Also, the Cavalcade of the Golden West, with 300 actors and 200 animals, presented the history of the West regularly during the run of the exposition.

The Gayway, the exposition's amusement center, provided, together with the exhibit areas, a dazzling example of technological advancement by generating light visible for 100 miles. The fair closed on September 29, 1940, and despite an attendance of a little over 17 million, incurred a debt of half a million dollars. Treasure Island never served as San Francisco's airport; instead it became a primary naval base and embarkation point for U.S. forces heading to the Pacific during World War II.

With the financial challenges of the decade, the cities sponsoring these fairs had to justify spending millions of dollars to present what might be viewed as frivolous events. In some instances, actual attendance fell below projections and the festivals lost money, but the sponsors claimed both short and long-term benefits. For the short term, they brought visitors that added to the income and revival of many local businesses. These fairgoers spent hours or days being amused, instructed, and diverted by the exhibits and special shows that allowed manufacturers and organizations to display products and services. Fairs also boosted the regional and national images of their sites, and they created jobs.

Long-term benefits included new buildings, parks, and planned urban centers that often contributed examples of contemporary architecture for future generations to enjoy. The exhibits developed new markets for sponsors and exhibitors alike, plus they showcased the best in fine arts and **design**. Through displays of ethnic foods and customs, millions of American citizens learned about other nations. As an important sociological benefit, particularly in troubled times, fairs and expositions always showed the positive side of things; they uplifted and cheered everyone in attendance, restored hope in national progress, and created a vision of future prosperity.

See also Buses; Design; Race Relations & Stereotyping; Radio Networks; Songwriters & Lyricists; Stamp Collecting; Streamlining; Swimming; Swing; Travel

SELECTED READING

Dickinson, Leon A. "Ways to Yorktown," *New York Times*, 11 October 1931. *Historic New York Times*. Proquest, Lynchburg College Library, Lynchburg, VA.

Findling, John E., and Kimberly D. Pelle, eds. *Historical Dictionary of World's Fairs and Expositions, 1851–1988*. Westport, CT: Greenwood Press, 1990.

Rydell, Robert W., John E. Findling, and Kimberly D. Pelle. *Fair America: World's Fairs in the United States*. Washington, DC: Smithsonian Institution Press, 2000.

FASHION. Throughout the 1930s, millions of Americans went to the **movies** to briefly escape the hard times; while there they learned about the latest hairstyles and fashions. Most people liked what they saw on the screen, and a select few could afford the extravagant clothing that the stars wore, such as furs and the latest evening dresses that echoed the verticality of a skyscraper. But most moviegoers could only hope to copy the new styles in as economical a way as possible. Established fashion houses and traditional elite fashion **magazines** found their authority greatly diminished as more and more of the general population turned to popular culture as their arbiter of taste. Generally speaking, the October stock market crash of 1929 marked a turn in fashion **design** from the flat, angular, boyish lines of the 1920s to one of softness, curves, and simplicity.

Women's Clothing. In a noticeable change from the previous decade, curves, slimness, smoothness, and ready-to-wear describe women's fashions of the 1930s. Along with belts, women wore more form-fitting undergarments and dresses, so the waist, hips, and bust reappeared, while longer skirts covered the knees. In both summer and formal gowns, the back, once hidden, could again be seen, daring and sexy, but within the confines of the **Hollywood Production Code**.

New assembly line technology developed for the clothing industry allowed the greatest range of styles and prices ever seen. Most American women became enamored of mass-produced clothes made from affordable materials like cotton, linen, and rayon. The simple print dress, cut to fit the average figure, outsold other dresses. It also offered the advantage of not readily showing spots or stains, thereby keeping cleaning costs to a minimum.

For those watching expenses during the Great Depression, Sears, Roebuck offered cheap "Sears-Ettes"; the name quickly changed to "Hooverettes" to make a humorous association with President **Herbert Hoover** (1874–1964) and the nation's economic woes. These reversible, wraparound dresses tied at the side, could fit almost anyone, and offered another way to cut cleaning costs.

In addition to using cheaper materials, some manufacturers reduced their expenses by selling a garment that could be finished at home; the buyer stitched up the seams and hem. Many women preferred doing more than just the simple finish details; they wanted to update or create their own and their children's wardrobes. For this growing market, publishers like McCall's and Butterick provided an extensive line of pattern books; piece goods stores stocked a variety of fabrics and materials; and Sears catalog and retail stores sold sewing, knitting, and crocheting supplies.

American women in the 1930s consulted advertisements, mail-order catalogs, and articles in popular magazines for fashion suggestions. They might read *Vogue*'s spread on the look for the season, but they also went to the movies and found, for example, useful information for planning a wardrobe through careful study of Joan Crawford's (1905–1977) clothes in her latest film. Hollywood leading ladies cooperated: dozens of stars, such as Claudette Colbert (1903–1996), Loretta Young (1913–2000), and Ann Sothern (1909–2001), lent their endorsements for "Autograph Fashions" found in Sears, Roebuck catalogs. Manufacturers likewise responded to the Hollywood influence; soon after a film's release, copies of the fashions seen in it appeared on store racks at moderate prices. In addition, articles about current fashions abounded in *Hollywood, Modern Screen, Movie Mirror, Photoplay, Screenland,* and similar fan magazines.

Obeying the dictates of style, padded shoulders grew in popularity and sleeves became puffier. Because more women wore daytime suits, dressy blouses held an important spot in most wardrobes. The material manufacturers used for skirts and dresses was often cut on the bias. This meant the fabric clung to the contours of the body, giving a fluid drape to an article of clothing. Companies like Maidenform and Warners introduced

Typical women's fashion from the 1930s. (Courtesy of Photofest)

sized-bras, and in 1931 the development of Lastex by the United States Rubber Company turned the heavy girdles of the past into lighter, more comfortable garments with stretch. Finally, nylon stockings experienced immediate success with their introduction in 1939.

An increasing awareness of the importance of exercise influenced more women to look to sports for good health and enjoyment. Sportswear therefore became lighter, less burdensome, and specific to the activity. For example, women tennis players appeared on the courts wearing socks, along with a pleated skirt and sweater, but bare legged. By 1933, some dressed in conservative shorts or culottes, which meant shedding several pounds of unneeded garments, such as corsets.

Likewise, **swimming** attire lost much of its extraneous bulk and appeared more form-fitting and Streamlined. Two-piece bathing suits, especially those made of light materials, gained popularity by mid-decade. Stretchable Lastex added to the comfort of the bathing cap that covered most or all of a woman's hair when in the water.

Trousers, like the loose ones worn by Katharine Hepburn (1907–2003), appeared as an important wardrobe item not only for golf or bicycling but also for casual lounging at home, and even for formal evening wear. Thanks to Barbara Stanwyck (1907–1990) and other stars appearing in **Western films**, a few women dared to wear jeans, especially when horseback riding.

Again, looking to the stars for leads, and much to the joy of Max Factor, Elizabeth Arden, Revlon, and Maybelline, nail polish, especially dark colors, along with matching lipstick, pencil-lined eyebrows, false eyelashes, powder, rouge, and mascara, enjoyed widespread use. Fan magazines frequently published features showing a popular actress in the process of applying makeup and giving advice about techniques.

Since the majority of women could not afford expensive jewelry, many purchased costume items such as necklaces, hatpins, clips, bangle bracelets, and a variety of earrings. Bold unusual buttons also added excitement to an outfit. Favorite jewelry designs made of enamel as well as stamped metal and molded plastic included the zigzags, chevrons, and other geometric shapes that tended to characterize the **Art Deco** style.

Hats continued to be a fashion necessity, and the cloche from the 1920s retained a degree of popularity. Smaller hats worn tilted over the right eye and requiring an elastic strap to secure the hat to the back of the head achieved favor after 1932. Actress Greta Garbo (1905–1990) added to the popularity of two hat styles, the Empress Eugenie, made of soft felt and often featuring a feather, such as what she wore in *Romance* (1930), and the pillbox, a simple, round design she sported in *As You Desire Me* (1932). Several variants on Tyrolean models, including the trilby, also sold well, as did tams, turbans, babushkas, berets, and sailor hats. The fashion industry boosted consumption by encouraging the color coordination of hat, handbag, gloves, and shoes.

The small hats of the 1930s complemented the longer tresses that style dictated. Technology also added new possibilities for hair fashions, including improved electric curling irons and permanent-wave machines. They supported the popularity of the sculpted look, as did marcelled waves, a substitute for permanent waving. Electric hair dryers had been around since the 1920s, but refined temperature settings and multiple speeds marked an improvement on earlier models.

As with clothing, the movies influenced hair styles. In the early 1930s, Jean Harlow (1911–1937), "the Blonde Bombshell" of the movies, popularized platinum blonde hair. Not everyone was born a natural blonde, but dyes, henna rinses, and bleaches enjoyed a vogue as women tried to improve on nature.

In 1933, John Breck (active 1900s–1930s), a New England shampoo manufacturer, deviated from the usual generic shampoo mix that washed most hair and offered his product in three types—dry, normal, and oily. His son, Edward Breck (active 1930s–1940s), became head of the company in 1936 and hired commercial artist Charles Sheldon (1889–1960) to paint portraits of glamorous women with beautiful hair. These illustrations would come to be known as the Breck Girls. This continuing series will be remembered as one of America's longest running and most successful **advertising** campaigns.

Men's Clothing. Fashion shifts for men were less pronounced than those for women, and with the exception of the zipper fly, which replaced buttons and became standard by mid-decade, a suit purchased in 1939 closely resembled one bought in 1930. Wide neckties, accompanied by equally wide lapels, continued to be worn. Most business suits consisted of three pieces: pants, jacket, and vest. Virtually all men wore hats or caps, with the fedora the favorite. As the decade progressed, a trend toward less formal dress for males emerged, a trend that included sports jackets worn with slacks of a contrasting color and the disappearance of the vest. A wider variety of headgear became available, with soft felt snap-brims and panamas the most popular models.

Perhaps the most noticeable change in men's fashions came with padded and broader shoulders. The lounge suit, less formal than the traditional business suit, featured a tapered waist and sometimes a belted back, along with a single-breasted jacket. The lightweight seersucker suit became available in 1936 and allowed more comfortable warm-weather wear. Palm beach cotton and the mohair suit also sold well.

Wide trousers, initially popularized in the 1920s, became somewhat narrower. By the mid-thirties, however, young men's trouser styles favored high, exaggerated waistbands and a return to extremely wide cuffed bottoms. But well before the decade ended, pants again became slimmer and straighter. Through all of this, older and more conservative males tended to avoid any changes whatsoever.

In 1936, the Bass Shoe Company produced its Weejun, a comfortable slip-on shoe that gained popularity, particularly with college students. This shoe promoted a more casual mode of dress and helped popularize the term "loafer." Many began inserting a shiny penny in the piece of leather that went across the instep, giving birth to the "penny loafer."

Jockey introduced its now-famous soft cotton brief in 1934, a comfortable change from "long johns" (underwear that covered arms, legs, and torso) or other cuts made of coarse lisle, muslin, or scratchy wool. Swimming apparel continued toward the conservative look with dark, heavy knit wool trunks and sleeveless shirts still the rule. A daring variation occurred early in the decade when a few men appeared without tops at New York beaches. This break with tradition caught on with young men across the nation and by 1934 the Sears catalog featured swimming trunks with no tops.

In 1939, Johnny Weissmuller (1904–1984), a champion swimmer at the 1924 and 1928 **Olympic Games** and the star of a number of *Tarzan* movies, modeled one-piece, topless swimsuits containing Lastex for BVD advertisements. Lastex, important to women's undergarments as well as men's swimsuits, also benefited male fashions in the manufacture of hosiery. Elasticized socks reinforced with Lastex made garters a dispensable accessory.

Although most men's clothing styles saw little change, their personal grooming habits underwent some significant shifts. Dry shaving—no razor, no soap—became possible with Schick Corporation's 1931 introduction of the electric razor, an instant success. By the end of the decade, numerous companies had sold 1.5 million models a year at the relatively high cost of $15 to $25 each (roughly $215–$360 in contemporary dollars). The popularity of the electric shaver caused **hotels**, ocean liners, **trains**, and passenger airplanes to provide power sources in convenient areas, such as bathrooms.

Until the 1930s, antiperspirants and deodorants had been used primarily by women. This situation changed dramatically when advertisers began to target men. Lifebuoy Soap ads, spoken over **radio** stations in a foghornlike voice, warned about BO (body odor) in endless commercials, and sales shot up. For hair styling, most men still preferred the pompadour style, which required hair creams or greases to achieve the "slicked down" look. But some movies showed male actors with their hair natural and tousled by the wind. Once again, films made a significant impression and the pomaded look slowly faded. By the end of the decade lotions and the like continued to be widely used but only to maintain a part and some slight control. Many men relied on just a comb and water.

Children's Clothing. Children's wear also experienced change. During the 1930s, two influences determined the direction of styles for little girls: first, the outfits worn by the two youngest members of the British royal family, Princesses Elizabeth (b. 1926) and Margaret (1930–2002), and second, anything worn by child movie star **Shirley Temple** (b. 1928). During these years, little girls dressed like children, not small adults. At the beginning of the decade, they looked about the same as they did during the 1920s, wearing short dresses with matching bloomers that showed. By the mid-1930s, girls everywhere adopted the Shirley Temple look of a high-waisted or straight-cut dress and a large ribbon for the hair, especially after the young star began modeling her own line of clothes in the Sears catalog. The decade ended with dresses having a more natural waistline with fuller skirts and puffed sleeves, although pinafores, sunsuits, and playsuits also held great appeal.

Boys often wore scaled-down versions of men's suits, but with short pants instead of regular trousers. Some youngsters might be seen in sailor suits complete with scarves, insignia, and bell-bottoms. Those 8 to 12 years old preferred knickers, elasticized pants that ended just below the knee and tucked into high argyle socks. Virtually all boys, just like their older brothers and fathers, owned several hats. Two popular models were the traditional white canvas sailor's cap and a leather aviator's helmet like that worn by Charles Lindbergh (1902–1974) and other well-known pilots.

Adolescents' Clothing. By their teens, both girls and boys moved to adult clothing, conventional dresses for the girls and long pants for the boys. Of course, by virtue of being teenagers, they were exposed to most clothing **fads**, but the severity of the Depression at the beginning of the decade and the recession toward the end prevented most adolescents from indulging in passing fashions.

For all ages, casual dress became more acceptable. As the 1930s progressed, industries and businesses increasingly provided employees paid vacations, usually a few days or one week. The resulting increase in individual and family **travel** influenced acceptance of less formal attire during the day and in the evening when dining at a restaurant or hotel. By the middle of the decade, many younger women appeared in public wearing shorts instead of slacks or dresses. Also, with the increased emphasis on people being outdoors for leisure, not just work, a suntan became not only acceptable but also a status symbol. To aid in the process, General Electric manufactured ultraviolet lamps for inexpensive home tanning sessions, and Coppertone made a fortune selling various lotions that enhanced tanning.

The 1930s represented a time of conservative fashions with a majority of people favoring simplicity and practicality. Femininity made a comeback; men practiced more intensive personal grooming; and the leading fashion authorities for Americans moved from Paris to the movies and other popular culture venues.

See also Aviation; Amelia Earhart; Illustrators; Jerome Kern; Leisure & Recreation; Restaurants; Youth

SELECTED READING

Batterberry, Michael, and Ariane Batterberry. *Fashion: The Mirror of History.* New York: Greenwich House, 1977.

Blum, Stella, ed. *Everyday Fashions of the Thirties: As Pictured in Sears Catalogs.* New York: Dover Publications, 1986.

Laubner, Ellie. *Collectible Fashions of the Turbulent Thirties.* Atglen, PA: Schiffer Publishing, 2000.

FEDERAL ART PROJECT (FAP). At a time when unemployment claimed almost 25 percent of the nation's workforce, **Franklin D. Roosevelt** (1882–1945) took office as president of the United States. At his 1933 inauguration, he offered the promise of a **New Deal** designed to alleviate this and related problems. His administration soon thereafter recommended relief for those hit hardest by the Great Depression through a multitude of programs. One of the first, the Public Works of Art Project (PWAP; 1933–1934), received funding from the newly created Civil Works Administration (CWA; 1933–1934). Managed by the U.S. Treasury Department, the PWAP served as a pioneering art program, providing emergency assistance with minimum qualifications for enrollment. It strove to employ artists who would create works that fell under the general theme of the "American scene."

The Treasury Department assigned Edward Bruce (1879–1943), a successful lawyer, banker, and painter, to organize and direct the PWAP. The agency divided the country into 16 regions, each headed by a local art authority, and the program operated for six months with remarkable accomplishments. In that brief time, about 3,750 artists produced over 15,000 pieces of art, many of outstanding merit. A large exhibition of paintings at the Corcoran Gallery in Washington, D.C., marked the successful end of the PWAP, and most of the creations from this program went around the country to adorn schools, hospitals, public libraries, and museums.

Throughout the life of the PWAP, the Roosevelt administration steadily advocated the idea of artists as productive members of society, just like laborers and factory employees. On a similar plane, the Artists' Union, formed in New York City in 1934, advanced and protected the rights of their members; its magazine, *Art Front* (1934–1937), likewise supported the needs of artists.

By 1935, the government had devised an umbrella agency called the Works Progress Administration (WPA; 1935–1943; the name changed to Work Projects Administration in 1939). Headed by Harry Hopkins (1890–1946), the WPA oversaw various New Deal programs. In one of its first moves, the WPA founded Federal Project Number One; it housed four bureaus that emphasized cultural concerns: art, **music**, theater, and writing. The Federal Art Project (FAP: 1935–1943), one of the four programs, had Holger Cahill (1887–1960) at its helm, and it supplanted the previous Public Works of Art Project. The FAP employed painters, sculptors, graphic designers, and photographers who met professional standards as well as the relief requirements set by their respective states. It became the largest art project ever undertaken by the federal government.

Although meaningful work for unemployed artists served as the principal function of this project, Director Cahill also placed a strong emphasis on the promotion and dispersion of art throughout the United States. The FAP had branches in all 48 states, with the majority of participants found in New York City. In light of the city's importance, in December 1935, a Federal Art Project Gallery opened there, and received considerable attention from the media, which sometimes denounced the "bad art" that emerged from federally subsidized programs. During the second half of the decade, some government officials began to question enrollees with possible leftist leanings. New York City police arrested 219 artists in 1936 when they protested a proposed 19 percent cut in the number of workers active in the four federal arts programs in the city.

The various FAP offices across the country operated somewhat autonomously. Collectively, they offered three types of activities: art production, art **education**, and art

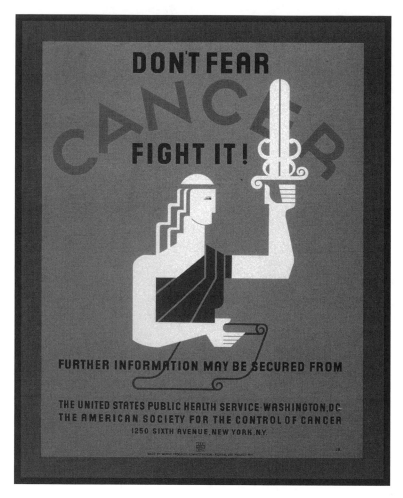

A poster, commissioned by the Federal Art Project, promotes health awareness. (Courtesy of the Library of Congress)

research. This approach allowed some painters and sculptors to continue in their studios. However they worked, their output can only be called phenomenal. Public institutions, such as schools in rural settings, received on permanent loan 85,000 of about 100,000 easel paintings done during the program's existence. Over 250,000 prints of various subjects from 12,581 original designs significantly raised the production totals. Sculptors alone created over 13,000 pieces, ranging from small ceramic figures for public schools and libraries, to monuments for parks, housing developments, and historic battlefields.

Artists, along with art teachers, participated in the education division and lent their talents to settlement houses and 100 community art centers in 22 states, each week providing instruction in techniques, along with classes in appreciation. "Art caravans," cars and panel trucks equipped with supplies, traveled the countryside, making instruction available to all. Art education for children evolved as a strong outreach program, and the FAP staff regularly organized exhibitions of their work, as well as that of adult students.

The primary output of art research, and one of the most impressive projects undertaken by the FAP, involved the *Index of American Design*, a wide-ranging attempt to find, identify, and provide precise reproductions of distinctive American artifacts. From 1935 to 1942, painters working in centers in 32 states combed museums and private collections to compile a 22,000-plate index of selected objects, such as glassware, ceramics, costumes, textiles, quilts, weather vanes, farm implements, metalwork, **toys**, furniture, and other items characteristic of the varied lifestyles of Americans across the country. The National Gallery of Art in Washington, D.C., now houses portfolios of this seminal work.

Other FAP accomplishments included over 2,250 murals completed for hospitals, schools, and other public places. Approximately 500,000 photographs, as well as two educational films, one on the painting of a fresco and the other on how to make a mosaic, document both FAP and WPA work. The Arts Services section furnished illustrations and posters to the other Federal One divisions—music, theater, and writing. Today, the Prints & Photographs Division of the Library of Congress in Washington holds 908 boldly colored and graphically diverse original posters from the FAP. A scenic **design** division rendered models of historic stage sets and architectural models for planning and educational use; it even boasted a stained glass unit that worked out of New York City.

At the time of the formation of the Federal Art Project, the Treasury Department directed two parallel programs. One, assigned to Edward Bruce, called the Treasury Department Section of Painting and Sculpture (1934–1938), evolved into the Treasury Department Section of Fine Arts (1938–1939) and then into the Section of Fine Arts (1939–1943), usually shortened to "the Section" or just Section. At the time of this last name change, officials transferred the project from the Treasury Department to the Federal Works Agency (FWA), an agency created in 1939 at the time the Public Works Administration (PWA; 1933–1939) was abolished. The FWA consolidated those groups of the federal government dealing with public works. Officials designed the Section and another Treasury Department program, the Treasury Relief Art Project (TRAP; 1935–1939), to expedite the decorating of new public buildings. Employing works of the highest quality, these programs undertook the job of making art accessible to all people.

To implement these goals, Louis A. Simon (1867–1958), already the supervising architect for a huge building program for post offices and courthouses all over the United States, in 1934 began working under Bruce and had direct jurisdiction over the Treasury Department Section throughout its several name changes. Funding came from an administrative order authorizing the expenditure of one percent of the total cost of each public building for decoration, provided funds were still available on completion.

The Treasury Relief Art Project, funded by the WPA, functioned more directly as a relief program. Initially, 90 percent, and six months later, 75 percent, of the artists working with TRAP came straight from relief rolls. Like the other Treasury Department projects, TRAP used its budget for the decoration of federal buildings. Artist Olin Dows (1904–1981) served as its national director.

Many of the TRAP jobs, like those of the Section, centered on both old and new post offices. Whatever the type of building, a selected structure tended to be located in an area with available, qualified artists who could carry out the job. Frequently, a master artist had primary responsibility, with one or more assistants helping with the execution. Under this arrangement, TRAP produced 89 murals and 65 pieces of sculpture,

A 1934 mural painted by Scaisbrooke Langhorne Abbot (1908–1985). It originally hung in the entrance to the Lynchburg, Virginia, city hall. (Photograph by Nancy Blackwell Marion)

some of which can be found at six Public Works Administration housing projects. TRAP also employed over 100 painters to create easel pictures and prints. Miscellaneous jobs involved drafting, **photography**, and framing.

The placement of murals depicting images of the "American scene" in at least one new post office in each state stands as perhaps the best-known Depression art project. Guidelines urged that the works reflect scenes and events of local interest. Often mistaken as WPA/FAP art, credit for these murals actually rests with artists hired by the Treasury Department. Open, anonymous competitions determined who would be granted contracts, as in any other government job.

Once awarded a commission, the muralist had to negotiate and work with Post Office Department personnel, the community, and the Treasury Department staff as to the final content. Genre themes of Americans at work or leisure repeatedly appeared. **Social Realism**, though popular at the time, rarely provided subject matter for these murals; Americans standing in breadlines cannot be found on the walls of post offices from the era. Instead, the viewer sees, in addition to local scenes, the celebration of daring and heroic historic events. For those murals still in place today, localities possess a colorful record of some of their heritage, as well as a glimpse of the public's taste at an earlier time.

During the nine years of its artistic involvement with the arts, the Treasury Department held 193 competitions; the first large one, for decorations to the new Department of Justice and Post Office Department Buildings in Washington, awarded contracts to 11 painters. Several gained lasting reputations, including George Biddle (1879–1943), John Steuart Curry (1897–1946), Rockwell Kent (1882–1971), and **Reginald Marsh** (1898–1954). The competition also selected **Thomas Hart Benton** (1889–1975) and **Grant Wood** (1892–1942), but they had to withdraw because of other commitments. Over the course of these competitions, a total of 1,205 artists received contracts for 1,124 murals and 289 pieces of sculpture.

National and world conditions toward the end of the decade led to concerns about budgets and funding reductions, which, in turn, signaled the beginning of the end of government assistance to the arts. From 1941 until the closing of most New Deal programs, money dwindled and the number of artists working with these programs steadily declined. Those remaining with the FAP did work for the military and the Office of Civilian Defense, until they, too, were phased out. These artists produced camouflage patterns and illustrations for guidebooks for U.S. soldiers going abroad, made visual training aids for the War Department and Air Force, and turned out armbands and posters.

Some of the thousands of painters, printmakers, and sculptors who participated in one or more of the federal art programs gained only momentary recognition, while others advanced as representatives of high quality contemporary American art. But whatever the artist's reputation, both the FAP and the Treasury Department projects produced a wealth of work that can still be enjoyed. In the heartland of America, a piece by Grant Wood executed under the PWAP auspices hangs at the Iowa State College Library in Ames. In New York City, a visitor to the New York Public Library can view four large panels executed for the FAP by Edward Laning (1906–1981) or see paintings done by Reginald Marsh in 1937 at the U.S. Custom House. On the opposite side of the country, the Coit Tower in San Francisco contains murals furnished by 25 painters under the direction of Victor Arnautoff (1896–1979), the influential muralist. Elsewhere, museums, post offices, customs buildings, and other sites boast pieces by New Deal artists such as Arshile Gorky (1904–1948), Marsden Hartley (1877–1943), Jackson Pollock (1912–1956), and Philip Guston (1913–1980).

The New Deal art projects clearly advanced the idea of artists as workers and art as a cultural labor worthy of government support. The **New York World's Fair** of 1939–1940 showcased both FAP and Section work, giving one last hurrah to these programs' contributions to the art world and society in general.

See also Architecture; Federal Music Project; Federal Theatre Project; Federal Writers' Project; Illustrators; Leisure & Recreation; Magazines; Regionalism

SELECTED READING

Marling, Karal Ann. *Wall-to-Wall America: A Cultural History of Post Office Murals in the Great Depression.* Minneapolis: University of Minnesota Press, 1982.

O'Connor, Francis V., ed., *Art for the Millions: Essays from the 1930s by Artists and Administrators of the WPA Federal Art Project.* Greenwich, CT: New York Graphic Society, 1973.

———. *The New Deal Art Projects: An Anthology of Memoirs.* Washington, DC: Smithsonian Institution Press, 1972.

Park, Marlene, and Gerald E. Markowitz. *Democratic Vistas, Post Offices, and Public Art in the New Deal.* Philadelphia: Temple University Press, 1984.

FEDERAL BUREAU OF INVESTIGATION (FBI). A government agency, part of the Department of Justice, the FBI can trace its roots to the presidency of Theodore Roosevelt (1858–1919). He founded a group originally called the Bureau of Investigation with the intent that it could provide him favorable public relations and "research" (investigative) assistance about political enemies. Limited in the scope of its activities, the bureau attracted little attention until 1932 and the infamous kidnapping of aviator Charles A. Lindbergh's (1902–1974) infant son. Both Presidents **Herbert Hoover** (1874–1964) and **Franklin D. Roosevelt** (1882–1945) granted the agency significantly increased powers in the aftermath of that case. Congress in 1933 passed the Lindbergh law, strong antikidnapping legislation that allowed the FBI to immediately step into investigations provided state lines had been crossed or postal services had been employed in the commission of the **crime**. Throughout the remainder of the 1930s, the once-anonymous agency made headlines and gained the reputation of an elite law enforcement unit.

Much of the FBI's success can be attributed to its energetic director, J. Edgar Hoover (1895–1972). During World War I, Hoover, a young civil servant, had joined the Intelligence Division of the Justice Department; in this job he developed passionate anticrime, anticriminal attitudes. In 1921, Hoover moved to Justice's Bureau of Investigation (officials added the word "Federal" in 1935) as its deputy director. After three years, he became the full-fledged leader of the bureau, a post he would hold until his death almost half a century later. Wise in the ways of bureaucracies and media imagery, especially after the sensational news coverage accompanying the **Lindbergh kidnapping**, Hoover made sure the FBI became widely known and remained in the public eye.

In 1935, Warner Brothers released an action-packed James Cagney (1899–1986) movie titled *"G" Men*. A box office success, "G-men" (government men) became part of everyday speech. Hoover welcomed the term to identify his agents, although it could just as accurately apply to any law officer in the employ of the federal government. A similar film that year, one that revolved around kidnapping and G-men, was *Show Them No Mercy!* It also highlighted the resourcefulness of federal agents.

With an astute program of public relations, the bureau cultivated the image of an organization made up of clean-cut, crusading young men, ready to fight crime under any circumstances. Three women entered the bureau's ranks in the 1920s, but all had resigned by 1928. No women served as agents at any time during the 1930s. Despite this inequity, the agency thrived, providing stories about arrests and captures to eager media outlets. Capitalizing on the success of the movie *"G" Men*, a popular, long-running **radio** show called *Gang Busters* (1935–1957) initially used materials culled from actual cases supplied by Hoover and his staff. For its first few broadcasts, it carried the title *G-Men*. The show also featured details about most-wanted criminals and attempted to sound as authoritative and official as possible.

Newspaper comics picked up on the rising fame of the FBI with series like *War on Crime* (1936–1938), a strip that also claimed to be based on bureau files. Other **comic strips**, lacking access to the agency, nonetheless freely used the term G-men for their heroes; they took it for granted readers would link their characters to the FBI. **Pulp magazines**, such as *The Feds* and *G-Men*, found an audience, as did **Big Little Books**. The latter, usually targeted at younger readers, occasionally bore titles like *Junior G-Men* and *Ace of the G-Men*. "Junior G-Men Clubs" also flourished during the later 1930s, an acknowledgment of the sweeping popularity enjoyed by the FBI.

In addition to favorable media coverage, a series of spectacular shootouts and arrests in the mid-1930s heightened the agency's prestige. Mayhem and gore aside, the end of any criminal careers met with public acclaim. Although the FBI did not always directly participate in these encounters, Hoover saw to it that reporters understood the agency's connections to most newsworthy cases. He himself participated in several well-publicized arrests, although local law enforcement officials did not always welcome the heavy-handed presence of the FBI and its director.

Basking in favorable publicity, Hoover and the agency emerged as the iconic symbols of law enforcement; as long as villains threatened the public safety, Hoover and his agents would be there to thwart them. A stern, all-knowing father, he brooked no rivals. Amid considerable press coverage, Hoover opened an FBI National Academy in 1935; it assured that agents would receive the latest scientific training and equipment. The bureau assiduously blocked publicity about individual agents; they did their jobs quietly, behind the scenes, and their professionalism encouraged teamwork, not individual heroics.

An example of Hoover's disdain for publicity-seeking agents occurred in July 1934. Acting on tips as well as a lengthy investigation, FBI personnel set up an ambush outside a Chicago movie theater for "Public Enemy No. 1" John Dillinger (1903–1934). When he came into sight, a bloody shootout ensued, and Dillinger died on the street. The press identified Melvin Purvis (1903–1960), the agent in command of the ambush, as "the man who got Dillinger." Purvis became an overnight celebrity, an honor he freely accepted, although no evidence exists to indicate that he actually fired the fatal shots. Suddenly an individual agent overshadowed the director himself, a situation Hoover did not relish.

In the meantime, Purvis found himself in the fortunate position of being on the scene when the FBI cornered "Pretty Boy" Floyd (1904–1934) in October. In fact, he mortally wounded the gangster. From there, Purvis, happily riding on a crest of publicity, publicly vowed to hunt down "Baby Face" Nelson (1908–1934), another criminal still on the loose. But Hoover denied Purvis a third spectacular capture. He pulled him from the Nelson case before its resolution and without a shot being fired. Then, using writers and reporters friendly to the FBI, Hoover set out to create new versions of the Dillinger and Floyd incidents, versions that in effect erased Purvis's name.

In subsequent retellings, the agency emphasized the importance of an investigation conducted by many agents, along with the irrational fears that criminals harbored about the FBI. Conspicuous by his absence in these stories, Purvis came to be seen as just another player on a team. Lacking any assignments, and out of favor with the director, Purvis resigned from the FBI in the summer of 1935, his star already fading. The legions of Hoover supporters continued to discount the work of what they saw as a publicity-seeking individual. In 1960, forgotten by the public, Purvis committed suicide. Hoover, on the other hand, flourished, the one person in the FBI allowed personal publicity, and by extension the most respected crime fighter in the nation.

As these events transpired, the motion picture industry, which had in the early 1930s been presenting lawbreakers almost as heroes in **gangster films**, did an about-face and dutifully followed Hays Office, or **Hollywood Production Code**, restrictions on the depiction of criminals. Following the release of *"G" Men*, Hollywood churned out dozens of pictures that celebrated law enforcement, the FBI in particular. One aspect of the rash of "G-men" features emanating from Hollywood ran counter to Hoover's attempts to downplay individual heroics. Without exception—and this exception also held true in all manner of popular media—these productions featured identifiable heroes. They might be members of a team, but they had names, from the prosaic "Dan Fowler" and "Jimmy Crawford" to the more exotic-sounding "Agent X-9" and "Operator 5," and their fans idolized them.

The new anticrime movies emphasized a repeated message: crime does not pay. Metro-Goldwyn-Mayer, one of the biggest and most powerful studios, in 1935 launched a series of movie shorts under that umbrella title and often used FBI personnel in the productions. The series, which eventually numbered 24 features, lasted until 1939. Never before had a single federal agency enjoyed such sustained public and media acclaim.

With World War II in the offing, the focus of the FBI underwent a shift. From gangsters and racketeers, the emphasis moved to spies and other subversives. J. Edgar Hoover remained in the forefront, exhorting citizens to beware of any suspicious behavior, and the agency geared up for war. The love affair between the bureau and its public would continue for many years to come.

See also *Little Caesar*; Movies; Newspapers; Prohibition & Repeal

SELECTED READING
Powers, Richard Gid. *G-Men: Hoover's FBI in American Popular Culture*. Carbondale: Southern Illinois University Press, 1983.
Turner, William W. *Hoover's FBI: The Men and the Myth*. Los Angeles: Sherbourne Press, 1970.

FEDERAL MUSIC PROJECT (FMP). Following the election of **Franklin D. Roosevelt** (1882–1945) to the presidency in 1932, his administration created a number of new government agencies, and in 1935 launched the Works Progress Administration (WPA; 1935–1943; name changed to Work Projects Administration in 1939), a massive relief program for the unemployed. Under the leadership of Harry Hopkins (1890–1946), the arts received special attention. Federal Project Number One fostered programs for art, **music**, theatre, and writing. The music component, called the Federal Music Project (1935–1943), provided employment for musicians unable to find jobs in their field. It also promoted music as an enjoyable leisure activity and integral part of community life. Organized into educational and performing units, the program focused on musical production, composition, and performance, but also stressed music **education** and appreciation, plus the preservation of local musical traditions.

The FMP offered free or low-cost concerts in schools, community centers, churches, orphanages, prisons, hospitals, public parks, and rental halls, and also provided vocal and instrumental lessons for poor adults and children, music appreciation programs, and training for music teachers. In addition, the project financially assisted community band, choral, symphonic, opera, and chamber group performances. During its four-year history, the FMP sponsored approximately 250,000 public concerts attended by some 150 million people in 43 states and Washington, D.C. In 1939 alone, an estimated 132,000 children and adults in 27 states received music instruction every week through the auspices of the FMP.

As with all sectors of American life, the Great Depression had hit musicians hard, as it had other areas of employment. Even before the 1929 stock market crash, the competition from **radio**, **recordings**, **jukeboxes**, and **movies** challenged anyone attempting to pursue a career in music. Thousands lost their jobs when symphonies and opera companies canceled seasons, **hotels** and **restaurants** eliminated musical entertainment, music students dropped classes, and school boards either slashed or completely cut funds for music programs and activities. Despite these bleak reminders of the Depression, at its peak the FMP employed 16,000 musicians, composers, conductors, and teachers.

Hopkins appointed Nikolai Sokoloff (1886–1965), former conductor of the Cleveland Symphony Orchestra from 1918 to 1933, as director of the Federal Music Project. Sokoloff, a Russian-born, Yale-educated violinist, attempted to promote what he believed to be an acceptable form of American music, that is, "cultivated" music over any "vernacular" formats. Under Sokoloff's leadership, the FMP urged the mass dissemination of

Many Americans received their first exposure to opera and other classical music through the Federal Music Project. (Courtesy of the Library of Congress)

highbrow music and programs that utilized symphonies, concert bands, and orchestras in preference to **swing** bands, gospel choirs, blues singers, and the like. To help achieve this goal, the FMP received $9.6 million out of an initial allocation of $27 million for the four art projects.

Sokoloff recognized the potential of radio and hoped to strengthen the possibility that classical music could rise to the forefront of programming. If successful, radio would then transmit "good" music to cities and rural areas where producing live shows faced difficulties. As a step in this direction, the project began recording snippets of symphonies and other music in 1936, eventually creating 315 one-minute musical vignettes taken from a large repertoire to send to any station that requested them. But Sokoloff was not alone in seeking to familiarize people with classical music. Prior to the birth of the FMP, both the National Broadcasting Company (NBC radio) and the Columbia Broadcasting

System (CBS radio) had been airing programs compatible with his aspirations. Examples of the networks' efforts included Walter Damrosch's (1862–1950) widely popular *Music Appreciation Hour* (NBC, 1928–1942), *The Metropolitan Opera* (NBC, 1931–1958; CBS, 1958–1960; consortium, 1960–present), *The Radio City Music Hall of the Air* (NBC, 1932–1942), and coverage of numerous symphony orchestras from cities as diverse as Rochester, New York, and Minneapolis, Minnesota.

The Composers Forum Laboratory, a 1935 FMP program introduced in New York City, afforded composers the opportunity to submit their work for review by a committee of musicians and project leaders. It favored new works with distinctive American themes; the compositions the committee accepted underwent rehearsal and public presentation with complete instrumentation. Branches of the laboratory also opened in Boston, Chicago, Philadelphia, Detroit, Cleveland, Milwaukee, Minneapolis, Los Angeles, and San Francisco.

Before the creation of the Federal Music Project, the United States had 11 recognized symphony orchestras; the FMP staff tried to increase this number by assisting interested cities in creating or reviving new or previously existing orchestras. Their efforts commenced in 1936, with a strong response from cities like Tulsa, Oklahoma, Philadelphia, Pennsylvania, and the state of Illinois. New groups, such as the Arkansas Symphony Orchestra, founded in 1938, and the San Antonio Symphony Orchestra, founded in 1939, received assistance. Within a short time, the FMP could boast 34 more American orchestras, along with thousands of radio broadcasts that reached millions of listeners across the country.

As it did with the Composers Forum Laboratory, the FMP favored musical initiatives that involved distinctly American themes. In 1938, it underwrote the first and only American Music Festival, one of the FMP's most ambitious undertakings. This three-day gala helped celebrate George Washington's (1732–1799) birthday and showcased FMP units performing favorites such as "When Johnny Comes Marching Home," "Yankee Doodle," the music of Stephen Foster (1826–1864), and the marches of John Philip Sousa (1854–1932). The American Music Festival ran in over 100 cities and employed more than 6,000 musicians. Encouraged by its popularity, planning for a repeat festival in 1939 immediately got under way. Unfortunately, the WPA budget cuts of that year precluded that event.

Also in 1938, the production of an opera titled *Gettysburg*, written by inexperienced composer Morris Ruger (1902–1974), with a libretto by Arthur Robinson (active 1930s), coincided with the 75th anniversary of Abraham Lincoln's (1809–1865) original 1863 Gettysburg Address. The planners of this offering hoped that an opera based on a beloved American president would bring the FMP positive publicity and increased support. After three presentations, one being on the Fourth of July over NBC's Blue Network, critics and FMP administrators agreed that the opera did not contain sufficient quality material and would not be performed again.

Sokoloff's emphasis on the promotion of classical music displayed favoritism toward European-derived "white" music and minimized the contributions of Native American, black, Mexican, or Asian composers. But this bias went only so far. At an Easter morning service in Miami, in 1936, an FMP-supported black choir of 100 voices sang for a sizable gathering of churchgoers. Additionally, the American Folk Singers, a Massachusetts group made up of black performers, sang both spirituals and classical choral works before large crowds in that state. On the West Coast, blacks participated in a 1938 concert conducted by composer William Grant Still (1895–1978), and it drew the highest attendance for an FMP event in Los Angeles for that season.

Classical music notwithstanding, the FMP subsidized efforts to collect and record indigenous American folk music, especially in the southeast and south central regions of the country. In 1937, as a part of its intent to perpetuate local musical traditions, the FMP published *Spanish American Folk Songs*. The next year, folklorist Charles Seeger (1886–1979), who had earlier worked with the father-son team of John (1867–1948) and Alan (1915–2002) Lomax in collecting folk materials, joined the agency as head of the Folk and Social Music Division. Seeger promoted the preservation of folk expression, along with musical education, but his efforts to save ethnic music came late in the agency's life and never reached fruition.

Budget cutting and the threat of war marked the beginning of the end of the FMP. First, in 1939, came a name change from the Federal Music Project to the WPA Music Program, followed by the actual shutdown of the agency in 1943. The final reports for the FMP, the largest single employer in Federal Project Number One, underscored its successes. Many felt that America had grown culturally richer as a result of the FMP, which had advanced interest in and consciousness of music in many parts of the country.

See also Federal Art Project; Federal Theatre Project; Federal Writers' Project; Leisure & Recreation; New Deal; Race Relations & Stereotyping; Radio Networks

SELECTED READING

Bindas, Kenneth J. *All of This Music Belongs to the Nation*. Knoxville: University of Tennessee Press, 1995.

Crawford, Richard. *America's Musical Life*. New York: W. W. Norton, 2001.

Young, William H., and Nancy K. Young. *Music of the Great Depression: American History through Music*. Westport, CT: Greenwood Press, 2005.

FEDERAL THEATRE PROJECT (FTP). The **New Deal**'s Works Progress Administration (WPA, 1935–1943; name changed to Work Projects Administration in 1939) established many initiatives, including the Federal Project Number One, a wide-ranging program focusing on the arts. One facet, the Federal Theatre Project (1935–1939), employed, on average, 10,000 people a year, with more than 12,000 people at its peak in 31 states and New York City. The FTP offered dance and acting classes at many of its sites and performed plays, not only in professional theaters, but in churches, convents, circus tents, university halls, showboats, community centers, and the **Civilian Conservation Corps** (CCC, 1933–1942) camps–in short, any place willing to sponsor its shows. Despite accumulating an impressive record of successes, the FTP became one of the most controversial of the Federal One projects, accused of supporting subversive Communist ideas and wasting money, even though all these projects together spent less than 3/4 of 1 percent of the total WPA budget.

Well before the stock market crash of 1929, live theater experienced competition from **movies** and **radio**. Recorded **music** in talking pictures replaced the silent film orchestra; large numbers of stagehands and technicians found themselves without jobs; and Hollywood's star system overshadowed most stage performers. For its part, radio satisfied changes in public taste by airing a variety of entertainment, all of which could be received in the comfort of the home.

W.P.A. FEDERAL THEATRE PROJECT LIVING NEWSPAPER PRESENTS

POWER

BY ARTHUR ARENT

RITZ THEATRE 48th STREET West of Broadway

The Federal Art Project created this poster for its sister organization, the Federal Theatre Project. (Courtesy of the Library of Congress)

The Depression amplified these problems by putting an additional 20,000 theatrical workers out of work when attendance dropped sharply and playhouses closed. Harry Hopkins (1890–1946), a key architect of many New Deal programs, became head of the Federal Emergency Relief Administration (FERA, 1933–1935), and later served as the administrator of WPA. Hopkins believed that society had a responsibility to save the talents of the men and women in the arts, as well as those laboring in America's factories.

He appointed Hallie Flanagan (1889–1969), a professor from Vassar College, as director of the Federal Theatre Project. She led the organization in establishing two major goals: (1) hiring experienced actors, directors, playwrights, designers, vaudeville artists, and stage technicians then on relief rolls, and (2) making theater a vital part of community life so it could continue to function when the federal program ended. Flanagan's plan stressed administrative decentralization; it identified five regions of the country, and each area had to decide on theatrical projects that would offer plays of social and political relevance for local audiences. Her emphasis on this kind of experimental theater discomfited many politicians, a situation that steadily escalated and contributed to the program's eventual demise.

During the course of its existence, however, the FTP presented over a thousand productions, with most performed free. New York City, the home for most live theater in the U.S., served as the center for the bulk of the program's activities. Playwright Elmer Rice (1892–1967) had responsibility for a wide range of the city's FTP happenings—classical plays, along with new and experimental productions, children's theater, puppet shows, a Yiddish vaudeville unit, the Anglo-Jewish Theater, the Negro Theatre Project, and a German theatrical group.

In an effort to make drama germane and engaging, Flanagan and Rice oversaw the creation of "the Living Newspaper," one of the project's more controversial endeavors. It served as a theatrical documentary and applied techniques developed for radio and screen by the **March of Time** (radio: 1928–1945; film: 1934–1951). The Living Newspaper format used a common man as a unifying character and included a mix of news, drama, fact, fiction, editorializing, and satire, all of which informed the audience of the aspects of a problem and then called for specific actions to solve it. This component of the FTP had a rough start. Outside censorship prohibited the opening of its first production, *Ethiopia*. Politicians feared that this dramatization of dictator Benito Mussolini's (1883–1945) ongoing invasion of Ethiopia would offend Italians.

Bowing to the edict of not depicting heads of state, the playwrights turned to contemporary headlines about social issues as starting points. The Living Newspaper commented on topics such as flawed government bureaucracy in *Triple-A Plowed Under* (1936) and deplorable housing conditions in America's largest city with *One-Third of a Nation* (1938). The last, an exceptionally busy play, provided employment for many, casting 67 actors who took on 195 roles. In New York, 60,000 bought tickets for *Power* (1937), a Living Newspaper on the Tennessee Valley Authority (TVA), clearly a sign of public interest in these topical plays.

By 1936, some congressmen who originally supported the New Deal became active critics of the program. Among them, Martin Dies Jr. (1900–1972) served as chairman of the newly created House Un-American Activities Committee (HUAC), nicknamed the Dies Committee. Charged with identifying disloyal and subversive organizations, the committee began investigating, among other things, the appropriateness of government-financed theater.

Flanagan responded to this pressure by moving from a focus on the accomplishments of each region to a national exchange of plays, directors, and ideas. For example, the Negro Theatre Project put on Shakespeare's (1564–1616) *Macbeth*. Directed by **Orson Welles** (1915–1985) and produced by John Houseman (1902–1988), the group moved the setting of the 1606 tragedy to contemporary Haiti and it toured Federal Theatre houses all over the country. On October 27, 1936, the FTP tried an even more daring venture by simultaneously presenting in 21 theaters in 17 states a dramatic version of Sinclair Lewis's (1885–1951) *It Can't Happen Here*. This adaptation of his 1935 novel emphasized its antifascist themes and enjoyed great audience appeal; over 500,000 people saw the show during its run of 260 weeks.

Even with these successes, the FTP's 1937 productions took place amid rumors of impending cuts in funding. *The Cradle Will Rock*, a musical written by Marc Blitzstein (1905–1964), and another Orson Welles and John Houseman production, opened after a couple of false starts in June of that year. The clearly leftist leanings in this production's protest songs prompted conservative congressional groups, such as the Dies Committee and the House Committee on Appropriations, to block its opening at its originally intended theater. The cast and crew, however, secured the small Venice Theatre in New York City to stage the production. But they encountered a new obstacle: the musician's union forbade its members to perform because of a disagreement about pay. Displaying great ingenuity, the show finally opened with Blitzstein playing a piano on stage and the actors scattered about in the theater seats speaking their lines as a single spot searched them out. *The Cradle Will Rock* played at the Venice for two weeks, moved to the larger Windsor Theatre in early 1938, and ended its run after 108 performances.

Another controversial musical, *Pins and Needles*, followed *The Cradle Will Rock*. Sponsored by the International Ladies Garment Workers' Union (ILGWU), the plot revolves around labor unions versus "the Bosses" and contains what surely must be the most noteworthy song title of the Depression—"Sing Me a Song with Social Significance" (1937; words and music by Harold J. Rome [1905–1993]). Premiering in November 1937, its overwhelming success forced a move from its initial small home, the Labor Stage, to the larger Windsor Theatre, the same house that had earlier presented *The Cradle Will Rock*. *Pins and Needles* continued its run into 1940 and set a record for 1930s **musicals** with 1,108 performances.

Not all the FTP offerings dealt with controversy. In 1937, in an attempt to reach out to more diverse audiences, Paul Green's (1894–1981) historical drama *The Lost Colony* opened in a WPA-built outdoor theater on Roanoke Island, off the coast of North Carolina. A success then, this story of Sir Walter Raleigh's (c. 1552–1618) doomed colony has continued to play each summer in its island setting. Earlier that spring, Irish playwright George Bernard Shaw (1856–1950), along with his American counterpart Eugene O'Neill (1888–1953), had released their plays, 9 from Shaw and 14 from O'Neill, to the FTP for nationwide production at a low rental rate.

In another daring move, the FTP in 1938 crossed racial barriers by producing *The Swing Mikado* in Chicago. Seen by 250,000 in that city alone, this jazzy interpretation of Gilbert and Sullivan's 1885 operetta featured an all-black cast. After a five-month Chicago run, it traveled to New York City for 86 performances on Broadway. The opening night in New York saw First Lady **Eleanor Roosevelt** (1884–1962), a long-time supporter of the Federal Theatre Project, as well as Harry Hopkins and Mayor Fiorello LaGuardia (1882–1947), in attendance. Its success inspired impresario Mike Todd (1909–1958) to mount a similar production, *The Hot Mikado*, which contained even more **jazz**, **swing**, and blues. Dancer Bill "Bojangles" Robinson (1878–1949) headed its black cast, and timely jokes about the political situation of 1939 abounded. Eventually, *The Hot Mikado* ended up at the **New York World's Fair** (1939–1940), where individual tickets cost under a dollar (about $14.50 in contemporary dollars).

As the decade drew to an end, the Federal Theatre Project, encouraged by its successes, planned to expand its offerings, but controversies and politics had created powerful critics. Some objected to the idea of subsidized theater; others challenged what they considered radical messages in many of the plays. With pressure from several sides, and the strongest objections revolving around political issues, the WPA withdrew federal funding and America's first great attempt at endowing the dramatic arts and developing a federation of theaters across the country came to an end. For a brief moment, despite myriad problems, American theater boasted a strong supporter in the federal government, and the FTP certainly reached out to people who had not normally participated in any way with dramatic activities. On June 30, 1939, the curtain fell for the last time, not only on *Sing for Your Supper*, a topical revue, but also on the Federal Theatre Project.

See also Design; Federal Art Project; Federal Music Project; Federal Writers' Project; Political Parties; Race Relations & Stereotyping; Franklin D. Roosevelt; Stage Productions

SELECTED READING

Brown, Lorraine. *Federal Theatre, Melodrama, Social Protest, and Genius*. http://memory.loc.gov/ammem/fedtp/ftbrwn00.html

Craig, E. Quita. *Black Drama of the Federal Theatre Era*. Amherst: University of Massachusetts Press, 1980.

Flanagan, Hallie. *Arena: The History of the Federal Theatre*. New York: Benjamin Blom, 1940.

Mathews, Jane DeHart. *The Federal Theatre, 1935–1939: Plays, Relief, and Politics*. Princeton, NJ: Princeton University Press, 1967.

FEDERAL WRITERS' PROJECT (FWP). After winning a landslide victory against Republican incumbent **Herbert Hoover** (1874–1964), **Franklin D. Roosevelt** (1882–1945) took office on March 4, 1933, as the 32nd president of the United States. Throughout Roosevelt's first term, his administration rushed into existence a number of new government agencies. The Works Progress Administration (WPA, 1935–1943; name changed to Work Projects Administration in 1939), not least among them, came into being in 1935. This group, an umbrella for many other ambitious programs, had the responsibility of putting unemployed citizens back to work in jobs that utilized their skills and simultaneously served the public good. Federal Project Number One, a WPA division that focused on creative activities, oversaw the Federal Writers' Project (1935–1943) along with corresponding programs for art, **music**, and theater.

Harry Hopkins (1890–1946), director of the WPA, appointed Henry Alsberg (1881–1970) as chief administrator of the Federal Writers' Project. Each of the 48 states, as well as New York City and Washington, D.C., had branches of the FWP. Alsberg served until 1939, followed by John D. Newsom (1893–1954), who headed the program until its dissolution in 1943.

The FWP provided work relief for beginning and experienced authors, newspapermen, researchers, and historians, who carried out writing and research projects approved by the WPA. Most importantly, the program allowed them to continue to exercise their talents and practice their craft. The FWP also offered employment to lawyers, teachers, librarians, ministers, architects, draftsmen, and other white collar workers. Enrollees in another federally supported agency, the National Youth Administration (NYA, 1935–1943), also provided research assistance.

From 1935 to 1943, the FWP systematically published the American Guide Series, an easily readable and informative collection of narratives about each state and Alaska. The Guides stand as the best known of the agency's projects. The majority of these books contain three parts: the first section consists of essays on the state's geology, industry, history, agriculture, literature, **architecture**, economy, racial and ethnic groups, arts, and **leisure and recreation** opportunities; next come descriptions of the state's major cities and towns, along with maps indicating points of interest; the last and largest section provides guided tours with a detailed mile-by-mile trip across the state on its principal roads, north to south and east to west.

As more and more people traveled throughout the nation in **automobiles**, it soon became apparent that earlier, nongovernment publications had not kept abreast of the nation's growth and expansion. The American Guide Series filled this gap with its books about the states and pamphlets covering many cities across the country such as New York; Washington, D.C.; New Orleans; Los Angeles; Philadelphia; Milford, Connecticut; Charlotte, North Carolina; and Lincoln, Nebraska, to name but a few. Regional guides for areas such as the Oregon Trail and U.S. Route One, and local guides for sites like Death Valley and Mount Hood, were also produced by the Federal Writers' Project.

In January 1937, the *Idaho Guide*, the first published volume in the American Guide Series, arrived just in time for the convening of the 75th session of the U.S. Congress. An intense prepublication publicity campaign announced the availability and importance of this and the other forthcoming guides. **Newspapers** ran articles and filler pieces based on material in the books; **radio** stations broadcast information; and exhibits at public libraries, the Smithsonian Institution, public schools, and **fairs and expositions**, all of which contributed to strong interest and initial high sales.

The work of the FWP required many people and careful coordination. For example, to create the American Guide Series, teams of writers and researchers, themselves residents of the subject state, toured every corner of their assigned area interviewing people, gathering information, and recording extensive notes. They then sent written reports based on their findings to the FWP staff in Washington, who edited copy, approved the materials for publication, and secured publishers. Encyclopedic in their thoroughness, the American Guides gave no authorial credits; the writers labored in anonymity. This series not only served automobile tourism but also represented one of the few FWP projects that received almost unanimous praise.

Information gathered for the series led to other projects, among them the publication of books, articles, pamphlets, and monographs on all aspects of American life: history, architecture, folklore, nature studies, **photography**, and artwork, along with children's educational materials and essays about local customs. As they worked, FWP researchers recorded the life stories of more than 10,000 men and women from all parts of the United States, people who represented various occupations and national and racial groups. This allowed for significant contributions in the areas of folklore and ethnic studies, the first such materials to reach the general public.

Starting in 1932, John Lomax (1867–1948) and other members of his family established an affiliation with the Music Division of the Library of Congress. The Lomaxes traveled the country during this time recording songs to add to the Library's Archive of American Folk Song. Then, during 1936 and 1937, Lomax added to his titles first folklore editor for the Federal Writers' Project and consultant to the Historical Records Survey (HRS). For these two agencies, he directed folklore research and the gathering of narratives by former slaves. He also assisted with the development of an interview questionnaire to be used by project researchers.

Benjamin Botkin (1901–1975) followed Lomax as consultant and folklore editor in 1938. Botkin oversaw workers who interviewed former slaves in more than a dozen states and, in 1944, after the FWP had been dissolved, assembled a selection of these interviews in *Lay My Burden Down; A Folk History of Slavery*. Other ethnic studies publications from the FWP include *The Armenians in Massachusetts* (1937), *The Hopi* and *The Navaho* (1937 and 1938), *The Italians of New York* (1938), and *Jewish Families and Family Circles of New York* (1939). *Sodbusters: Tales of Southeastern South Dakota* (1938) and *South Carolina Folk Tales; Stories of Animals and Supernatural Beings* (1941) represent both the folklore and folk music contributions of the project.

In addition to the myriad FWP writing and research projects, Alsberg attempted to present the most talented authors with additional outlets for creative work. Through his efforts, the nationally popular *Story Magazine* in 1938 sponsored a writing contest for FWP employees. The judges included novelist Sinclair Lewis (1885–1951), newspaper columnist Lewis Gannett (1891–1966), and Harry Scherman (1887–1969), then president of the Book-of-the-Month Club. Out of 600 entrants, the judges declared Richard Wright (1908–1960) the winner. Wright's collection of four short stories, *Uncle Tom's Children*, dealt with the cruel prejudices of whites and the unyielding resentment of blacks. By winning the contest and being published, Wright won the attention of a wide audience for the first time. The prize money of $500 (about $7,300 in contemporary dollars) permitted him to finish a novel, *Native Son*, which came out in 1940. Also, while working with the FWP, Wright gathered material for another book, *Twelve Million Black Voices* (1941), a nonfiction work produced in collaboration with Farm Security Administration (FSA) photographer Edwin Rosskam (1903–1985).

A number of other writers who worked for the FWP during the turbulent 1930s went on to establish lasting reputations. They include: Conrad Aiken (1889–1973), Nelson Algren (1909–1981), Saul Bellow (1915–2005), John Cheever (1912–1982), Willard Motley (1909–1965), Studs Terkel (b. 1912), Margaret Walker (1915–1998), and Frank Yerby (1916–1991). Some authors drew on their work with the project for future publications, such as Arna Bontemps (1902–1973) and Jack Conroy (1898–1990), who cowrote *They Seek a City*, an important study of black migration published in 1945. Ralph Ellison (1914–1968) used material from FWP interviews with Harlem residents when writing his 1952 novel, *Invisible Man*.

Luther Evans (1902–1981) led researchers on a project to evaluate resources in the area of history and genealogy. Initially begun with the FWP, this vast work came to be called the Historical Records Survey (HRS). Personality and management conflicts between Evans and Alsberg led to the HRS becoming an independent section of Federal Project Number One in November 1936. It drew on unemployed clerks, teachers, writers, librarians, and archivists who cataloged, analyzed, and compiled inventories of state and county records. Their work included a historic and legal description of counties and the value of their records, while state materials stressed manuscript collections and church archives.

In addition to the records survey, the HRS carried out other projects, such as providing supplements to the union list of newspapers, surveying portraits in public buildings, collating the collections of presidential papers and messages, developing bibliographies of American history and literature, indexing American musicians, historically listing and indexing unnumbered executive orders, and creating an atlas of congressional roll-call votes. The HRS employed, on average, 2,500 employees a month, with a high of 6,000 in 1938. After it became a part of the government's Community Service Program in 1939, however, the HRS could claim only 12 central office employees.

After the Pearl Harbor attack in December 1941, the Federal Writers' Project became known as the Writers' Unit of the War Services Division of WPA and produced recreational guides for servicemen. But at its 1936 peak, the Federal Writers' Project required the expertise of some 6,500 men and women; by the time of its closing, this agency had produced, including the American Guide Series, more than 276 books, 701 pamphlets covering many cities across the country, and 340 articles, leaflets, and radio scripts, altogether totaling 3.5 million copies. It also left for future students of American civilization an enormous amount of valuable unpublished materials. Perhaps the largest publishing project in U.S. government history, it cost about $27 million (roughly $393 million in contemporary dollars). Both literary and historical in nature, the accomplishments of the Federal Writers' Project equal any of the WPA's more construction-oriented projects.

See also Book Clubs; Education; Federal Art Project; Federal Music Project; Federal Theatre Project; Magazines; Race Relations & Stereotyping; Travel; Youth

SELECTED READING
Hobson, Archie, ed. *Remembering America: A Sampler of the WPA American Guide Series.* New York: Columbia University Press, 1985.

Penkower, Monty Noam. *The Federal Writers' Project: A Study in Government Patronage of the Arts.* Chicago: University of Illinois Press, 1977.

Weisberger, Bernard, A., ed. *The WPA Guide to America: The Best of 1930s America as Seen by the Federal Writers' Project.* New York: Pantheon Books, 1985.

FIELDS, DOROTHY. In a profession long dominated by men, Dorothy Fields (1905–1974) challenged tradition and rose to become an outstanding songwriter and lyricist. In the twentieth century—particularly in its first half—only a small number of women approached success in the competitive field of songwriting. For the 1930s, examples would include Bernice Petkere (1901–2000), composer of such hits as "Close Your Eyes" (1932) and "Lullaby of the Leaves" (1932); Ann Ronell (1906–1993), who enjoyed success with "Willow Weep for Me" (1932) and the immensely popular "Who's Afraid of the Big Bad Wolf?" (1933); and Kay Swift (1897–1993), who penned "Can't We Be Friends?" and cowrote, with lyricist **Ira Gershwin** (1896–1983), "Dawn of a New Day" (1939), the official theme song of the 1939–1940 **New York World's Fair**. But by all measures of songwriting success—hits, number of compositions, variety, longevity—Fields towered above all her female counterparts.

Born into a show business family, Dorothy Fields's father, Lew Fields (1867–1941), made up half of the successful vaudeville team called Weber and Fields, the other half being Joe Weber (1867–1942). Despite her background, Fields did not find it easy breaking into the theatrical and musical world. But she brought organization and discipline into her quest, and her career flourished, eventually covering some 50 years and producing more than 300 songs. A clever, engaging lyricist, she started out in Tin Pan Alley in the 1920s, teaming in 1926 with composer Jimmy McHugh (1894–1969) for a number of good tunes. Together they created such standards as "On the Sunny Side of the Street" (*Lew Leslie's International Revue*, 1930), "Don't Blame Me" (*Clowns in Clover*, 1933), and "I'm in the Mood for Love" (*Every Night at Eight*, 1935). Their collaboration would last until 1935.

In the early 1930s, she, McHugh, and many others joined the exodus to Hollywood hoping to find lucrative work in **musicals**. Once there, she continued her association with McHugh, but began collaborating with other composers as well, such as Arthur Schwartz (1900–1984) and Oscar Levant (1906–1972). Her work with **Jerome Kern** (1885–1945), however, merits particular attention.

Beginning with *I Dream Too Much* in 1935, they joined forces on six **movies**, and her career moved constantly upward. Two of the pictures star **Fred Astaire** (1899–1987) **and Ginger Rogers** (1911–1995), the era's phenomenally popular dancing team. *Roberta* (1935) features such gems as "I'll Be Hard to Handle," "I Won't Dance," and "Lovely to Look At." For their second Astaire-Rogers film score, Kern and Fields created the **music** for *Swing Time* (1936). Many fans maintain that *Swing Time* ranks as one of the best musicals of the 1930s. That judgment comes in no small measure because of the superlative score that graces the movie. "The Way You Look Tonight," the Academy Award winner for Best Song in 1936, highlights the picture. But *Swing Time* contains almost nothing but highlights: "A Fine Romance," "Pick Yourself Up," and "Never Gonna Dance." All these timeless songs became popular hits and embellished the careers of everyone involved.

Another product of the Kern-Fields working relationship, *When You're in Love* (1937), stars Grace Moore (1898–1947), a prominent opera star. The movie resembles their earlier *I Dream Too Much* (1935), which served as a showpiece for contralto Lily Pons (1898–1976). Neither is particularly memorable, the best number, "Our Song," coming from *When You're in Love*.

Their fifth pairing, *Joy of Living* (1938), boasts both a story and lyrics by Fields. A combination of screwball comedy and musical, the film stars the capable Irene Dunne (1898–1990). The jump from musicals to comedy should not be thought a great one, since many film comedies utilize music as part of their plots, and vice versa. The term "musical comedy" in fact effectively bridges any gap between the two genres. Several standards, like "You Couldn't Be Cuter" and "Just Let Me Look at You," highlight the screenplay, a bright, cheery entry among the movies of the day.

One Night in the Tropics (1940), the final Kern-Fields concoction, stars the rising comedy team of Bud Abbott (1895–1974) and Lou Costello (1906–1959). This bit of fluff features "You and Your Kiss," "Back in My Shell," and "Simple Philosophy." Fields clearly made her living as a popular, commercial songwriter. In retrospect, it is remarkable how much of her music, often written for decidedly inferior movies, lives on, while the films themselves have been mercifully forgotten.

Dorothy Fields returned to New York around 1941 to resume writing for the Broadway theater, her first love. She remained productive and successful until her death in 1974.

See also Screwball Comedies; Songwriters & Lyricists

SELECTED READING

Block, Geoffrey. *Enchanted Evenings: The Broadway Musical from* Show Boat *to Sondheim*. New York: Oxford University Press, 1997.

Fields, Dorothy. http://www.dorothyfields.co.uk/home.htm

Winer, Deborah Grace. *On the Sunny Side of the Street: The Life and Lyrics of Dorothy Fields*. New York: Schirmer Books, 1997.

Zinsser, William. *Easy to Remember: The Great American Songwriters and Their Songs*. Jaffrey, NH: David R. Godine, 2000.

FLASH GORDON. Science fiction and fantasy enjoyed multimedia popularity during the 1930s, and perhaps the most successful manifestation of the future appeared on Sundays in hundreds of newspaper comic supplements: *Flash Gordon*. The creation of cartoonist Alex Raymond (1909–1956), the strip first appeared in January 1934.

Other science fiction tales also appealed to audiences at this time, chief among them *Buck Rogers in the 25th Century*, a rival comic strip that had debuted in 1929, the creation of Phil Nowlin (1888–1940) and Dick Calkins (1895–1962). For sheer artistry and imagination, however, nothing quite equaled *Flash Gordon*.

An instant hit among readers, the series chronicles the adventures of Gordon, a handsome space swashbuckler who, accompanied by the beautiful Dale Arden and the brilliant Dr. Zarkov, explores the mysteries and dangers of an alien planet named Mongo. The trio encounters a worthy adversary in Ming the Merciless, an evil emperor bent on destroying them in insidious ways. It may sound like the stuff of **pulp magazines**, but in Raymond's hands these plot devices coalesce into a continuing tale of good versus evil that works, thanks to the exciting graphics.

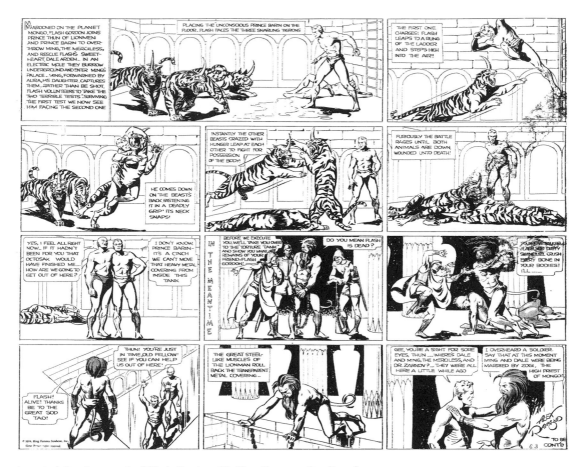

A typical Sunday panel of *Flash Gordon*. (© King Features Syndicate)

Raymond's equally vigorous *Jungle Jim* also premiered in 1934, serving as a "top" to *Flash Gordon*. Many Sunday series had such tops—usually about one-quarter the size of the primary strip—done by the same artist but featuring different characters. A rival to the popular **Tarzan** comic strip and **movies**, *Jungle Jim* depicts the exploits of a fabled "great white hunter" in Africa. A prolific artist, Raymond also briefly drew *Secret Agent X-9*, a daily based on the hard-boiled detective stories of Dashiell Hammett (1894–1961).

A master of clear, concise drawing, along with a good eye for color, Raymond possessed a fluidity of penmanship unmatched by most other cartoonists. He did not feel constrained to follow the traditional linear series of boxes (or frames) that characterized newspaper comics to tell his stories; instead, his drawings swell vertically and horizontally as the art and story demand. A Sunday page might consist of several small pictures to advance the plot and culminate in a large drawing encompassing a quarter of a newspaper page that brings events to a thrilling climax. In addition, Raymond treated his readers to a distinctive mix of the contemporary and the romantic.

Instead of the clunky, awkward spaceships that had defined most science-fiction illustration until then, Raymond indulged his drafting skills with a vision of Streamlined modernism when picturing anything mechanical or technological, such as weapons, rockets, or

architecture. Sleek spacecraft cruise by towering cities of chrome and glass, but his characters may be on horseback, wearing flowing capes and robes that hark back to the days of knights and maidens. Flash must often defend Dale's honor in a grueling sword fight, and no ray guns enter the picture. It proved a curious mix of styles and eras, but it worked well for the series.

Although Raymond often receives credit for writing the continuity of *Flash Gordon* in its formative years, the scripting chores actually fell to Don Moore (1901–1986), an author who continued in that capacity for the remainder of the decade. In light of Raymond's crushing artistic load with *Jungle Jim* and *Secret Agent X-9*, small wonder he required help. Raymond's artistic assistant, Austin Briggs (1908–1973), began drawing a daily version of *Flash Gordon* in 1940. Bound for the Marine Corps, Raymond left the Sunday strip in 1944 and relinquished the series to Briggs. It never again reached its former greatness, but *Flash Gordon* carried on in the **newspapers** with a succession of new writers and **illustrators** until the mid-1990s.

For the 1930s, the popularity of the strip spawned something of a small *Flash Gordon* fad. In 1936, a Universal movie serial titled simply *Flash Gordon* played for 13 thrilling episodes at Saturday matinees everywhere. The episodes made a minor star of former Olympic swimmer Larry "Buster" Crabbe (1908–1983) as the intrepid hero. The serial's success brought about two sequels, *Flash Gordon's Trip to Mars* (1938) and *Flash Gordon Conquers the Universe* (1940), both again featuring Crabbe. The actor also played Buck Rogers in a movie of the same name (1939), a look-alike film that differed little from the Flash Gordon sagas except for its title.

King Comics, one of innumerable comic book titles on the market in the later 1930s, reprinted in color Flash Gordon's Sunday episodes in their entirety. A number of independent **radio** stations attempted a serial beginning in 1935, but the aural effects could never equal the screen's visual ones, and it disappeared in 1936. A novel, *Flash Gordon in the Caverns of Mongo* (1936), attributed to Raymond but probably ghostwritten, likewise attracted some attention, but not as much as the movie **serials** and comic-strip incarnations.

No other series better foretold a Streamlined, smooth-functioning future than *Flash Gordon*. The strip outlived its creator, Alex Raymond, but the 1930s marked its heyday. With the economic system in a shambles and unemployment at record levels, with dictators challenging democracy and armies massing along European and Asian frontiers, the simultaneous escapism and realism of this fictional world attracted a wide range of readers and made it a perennial favorite.

See also Comic Books; Comic Strips; Mysteries & Hard-Boiled Detectives; Streamlining; Swimming

SELECTED READING

Goulart, Ron, ed. *The Encyclopedia of American Comics*. New York: Facts on File, 1990.
Horn, Maurice, ed. *100 Years of American Newspaper Comics*. New York: Gramercy Books, 1996.
Marschall, Richard. *America's Great Comic-Strip Artists*. New York: Stewart, Tabori & Chang, 1997.
Raymond, Alex. *Flash Gordon: "Mongo, the Planet of Doom."* Princeton, WI: Kitchen Sink Press, 1990.

FOOD. For many, the Great Depression conjures up gloomy images of breadlines, soup kitchens, apple selling, and hoboes at the backdoor asking for food. Certainly, some people suffered hunger, primarily in the poorest rural areas of the country, and government agencies and nonprofit organizations tried to provide relief. But overall the Depression had little effect on people's food consumption or physical well-being. Consequently, the food sections of general **magazines** and **newspapers** devoted little space to the population's struggles to make ends meet, despite official reports citing malnutrition among the unemployed and chronically poor. Likewise, the **advertising** and promotional activities of food producers ignored some of the realities of the Depression.

Yet those same food producers, along with women's magazines and appliance manufacturers, regularly supplied the public with millions of free recipes to assist with home cooking. These publications, presented in the form of articles or pamphlets, told housewives how to prepare a variety of dishes from a limited pantry. They also stressed the benefits—increased efficiency and lower costs—of using recipes and owning new appliances for successful food preparation and entertainment.

Taking advantage of **radio**'s widespread popularity and impact, food manufacturers and processors created attractive over-the-air spokespersons for their products. The fictitious Betty Crocker represented General Mills, a huge milling company; she dispensed recipes and kitchen tips on many stations beginning in the mid-1920s. *The Betty Crocker Show* quickly became a radio institution, running on either the National Broadcasting Company (NBC radio) or Columbia Broadcasting System (CBS radio) networks continuously until 1947 and then on the American Broadcasting Company (ABC radio) network until 1953.

Not surprisingly, from the early to mid-1930s, other food companies imitated General Mills, hiring magazine home economists to appear on radio. In their daytime shows, these economists offered advice and food preparation hints that required the use of products from the companies they represented. On-air cooking personalities of the 1930s included Ida Bailey Allen (1885–1973) and John MacPherson (1877–1962). Allen's show, *The Radio Homemakers Club*, ran on CBS radio from 1928 to 1935 and on NBC radio from 1935 to 1936. Allen also authored a popular booklet, *When You Entertain: What to Do and How* (c. 1932). In it, she mentions Coca-Cola by name several times; in a clever promotion and advertising strategy, the giant soft drink company in turn gave away millions of copies of *When You Entertain*.

MacPherson, billed as *The Mystery Chef* on NBC, CBS, and ABC radio from 1930 to 1948, claimed that his hobby of cooking and hosting a radio show embarrassed his mother, thus explaining the effective show business ruse of a mystery man. Playing on this theme, his program focused on how to take the "mystery" and trouble out of preparing meals. Thousands of listeners made MacPherson and his program one of the top-ranked offerings. To answer the demands of these listeners, a cookbook, *The Mystery Chef's Own Cook Book: Presenting Marvelous Meals at Lower Cost* (1934), appeared on the bookstands and went through several editions.

Even the U.S. Department of Agriculture employed radio to get its message to homemakers, sponsoring *Aunt Sammy* (1926–1935), a show briefly heard as *Housekeeper's Half-Hour* in 1926. Broadcast to isolated rural audiences, Aunt Sammy represented the domestic side of Uncle Sam, or so the government agency claimed. These programs used different women at various small, local stations all reading the same scripts on such subjects as food preparation, laundry, floor care, and other household hints. The Department of Agriculture encouraged listeners to send in for booklets emphasizing healthy, economical eating habits.

Cookbooks provided another source of help for the struggling cook, offering ways to make food preparation more understandable and easier. *Better Homes and Gardens Cookbook*, first published in 1930, became a mainstay for the decade. It emphasized the importance of serving simple meals, a theme repeated in other cookbooks.

Irma Rombauer (1877–1962) faced a bleak future after the death of her husband in 1931. He had left little money for supporting a family. At her own expense, Rombauer had the A. C. Clayton Printing Company, a St. Louis firm, publish 3,000 copies of her personal collection of recipes and cooking techniques. She called the anthology *The Joy of Cooking: A Compilation of Recipes* (1931), and it covered all the basics of cooking, even including a chapter on leftovers. Its encyclopedic approach of providing recipes, tips, and explanations for everything culinary guaranteed both the inexperienced and experienced cook success. Her venture attracted the attention of Bobbs-Merrill, which published the first revision of *The Joy of Cooking* in 1936; since then it has undergone several revisions and remains a basic reference in many American kitchens.

In 1939, Rombauer and her daughter, Marion Rombauer Becker (1903–1976), wrote *Streamlined Cooking*, a book aimed at the late 1930s "career girl" with the title playing on the popular **design** style of the times. *Streamlined Cooking* advocated the utility of the pressure cooker, a newly introduced small appliance. It also emphasized, for cooks pressed for time, how to use frozen fruit. This attempt to capitalize on the success of *The Joy of Cooking* had few takers, and soon disappeared from bookstores.

Even **Eleanor Roosevelt** (1884–1962), the president's wife, wrote a book dealing with food during the Depression. In *It's Up to the Women* (1933), she urged women who had less money for food to study all the latest suggestions about the efficient preparation of inexpensive yet nourishing meals. She said that thrifty cooking and housekeeping could greatly contribute to keeping the American family financially solvent in those most difficult times.

These various personalities, along with many authors of numerous other cookbooks and recipe pamphlets, promoted an increasing homogenization of American foodways. Life in most homes had changed from earlier times. During the 1930s, simpler meals for the wealthier had become the norm, especially since kitchen help had almost disappeared by the late 1920s. At the same time, meals had improved for less affluent households. These two convergent situations brought about a standardization of the American diet. From urban centers to isolated farmhouses, cooks learned the same techniques, received advice about the same products and appliances, and shared the same recipes. Their success meant that national tastes were replacing regional and ethnic ones.

For example, by the 1930s a typical American breakfast consisted of citrus fruit, dried cereal, and milk or eggs and toast. Many cereal manufacturers, through advertisements on radio, offered premiums with the purchase of their product—Ralston Purina on *Tom Mix Ralston Straightshooters* (1933–1951), Wheaties on *The Jack Armstrong Show* (1933–1951), and Cheerios on *The Lone Ranger* (1939–1956). Children across the country regularly mailed cereal box tops to the sponsoring companies awaiting the return of a Tom Mix (1880–1940) decoder button or a Jack Armstrong pedometer. This successful marketing strategy kept families tuned to these shows, promoted sales, and provided premiums for the children.

At lunchtime, Americans consumed a combination of a sandwich, salad, or soup. A popular 1930s comic strip called **Blondie** featured Dagwood Bumstead as its main character. Drawn by cartoonist Chic Young (1901–1973), the series regularly featured Dagwood raiding the refrigerator to create his favorite late evening snack: a mountainous pile of dissimilar leftovers placed between two slices of bread. This concoction promptly gained the name Dagwood sandwich and the creation continues in today's hoagies, grinders, and submarines.

Following long-established tradition, the evening meal continued to be the largest one of the day. Dinner typically consisted of a roast or broiled meat, potatoes, vegetables, and a light **dessert**, but with smaller portions than what people ate in previous years. The condition of excess weight received attention in both print media and radio. Home economists and nutritionists suggested reducing the quantity of food and eating healthier foods. Others advocated reducing diets such as the Hay's Diet, the Hollywood Eighteen-Day Diet sponsored by California citrus growers, and various two-food diets—such as tomatoes and hard-boiled eggs, or baked potatoes and buttermilk. Reflecting these trends, *Better Homes and Gardens* magazine published its first diet article in 1932. Americans, especially women in the middle and upper classes, responded favorably to their recommendations.

Lighter, simpler meals not only addressed weight and health, but helped Depression-era families deal with the reality of having less money to spend on food. Throughout the crisis, most food prices remained low, which pleased everyone except those in the food industry. Well aware of the financial hardships, but also wanting a profitable business, grocery store operators focused on how to attract customers into their stores. In a few cities, some entrepreneurs converted abandoned buildings into "warehouse food stores" and advertised "cut-rate" prices. In contrast to the corner grocery store where the clerk handed the customer items from behind a counter, shoppers at these "warehouse" arrangements engaged in self-service by choosing the food products to be purchased from displays on tables. Many consider these establishments the precursors of the first supermarkets.

The Depression did change the way Americans ate, changed where and how they shopped for food, determined if they entertained at home or if they dined out, and at what kind of **restaurants**. In order to live within the limits of a tight budget, some families baked their own bread; they grew fruits and vegetables, canning them instead of purchasing comparable products. Sure-Jell, a powdered pectin introduced by General Foods Corporation in 1935, benefited these homemakers by ensuring home-canned jams and jellies set properly.

The subject of vitamins also entered the picture during the 1930s. Stirred by information from home economists and nutritionists on the importance of nutrients in the diet, the American public wanted to know about vitamins. How do they work in body chemistry? How does one incorporate them into a modern lifestyle? At this time, enriched food provided the primary way to get extra vitamins. The trend of self-service at the supermarket allowed consumers for the first time to read labels and compare packaging, assuring themselves that a product contained the ingredients they wanted. With increased awareness of the value of nutrients and vitamins and the possible inferiority of canned and prepackaged foods, efforts began in the early 1930s to update the Food and Drug Act of 1906. Proponents immediately met opposition from food and drug conglomerates. A concern about profit margins and an attempt to maintain the status quo contributed to a five-year political battle.

Healthier food emerged as a popular "cause" during the 1930s and public awareness about the dangers of additives and processed food grew. In 1933, Arthur Kallet (1902–1972) and F. J. Schlink's (active 1930s) best-selling *100,000 Guinea Pigs*, an indictment of the food industry, contributed to even more intensified discussions. Public discontent focused both on the presence of impure foods in the marketplace and the failure of the Food and Drug Administration (FDA) to act against them.

Some food manufacturers sided with aroused citizens and urged legislation that would assure the nutrition and safety of canned, prepackaged, and **frozen foods**. It took a disaster—100 deaths in 1937 as the result of the distribution of an untested sulfa drug containing a toxic chemical—to bring about the 1938 passage of a revised and expanded Pure Food and Drug Act. The new law called for more extensive labeling and testing of food products, and even evaluated cosmetics. The FDA introduced standards that also required new drugs to be demonstrably safe before marketing.

That same year, the laboratory synthesis of vitamins permitted their incorporation in pills. Although some state legislatures declared vitamins to be drugs and only available at pharmacies, they ranked second only to laxatives in direct sales at the drugstore. Seeing a marketing opportunity, Kroger and Independent Grocers' Alliance (IGA) grocery stores in 1939 challenged the druggists and state legislatures by stocking their stores with vitamins and allowing them to be sold over the counter (i.e. without a prescription), a move supported by the wording of the new Food and Drug Act. After that, vitamins could be found in most **grocery stores and supermarkets**.

Despite the economic hardships and growing concerns about food and health, Americans continued to use a wide variety of foods in social situations. Entertaining during the 1930s frequently occurred in the home and centered on snacks and dining. The afternoon tea party, a carryover from the 1920s, continued to be a popular gathering, especially for women. The menu consisted of **coffee and tea**, along with sandwiches, small cakes, and cookies. The array of sandwich fillings such as celery and olive, chicken and pineapple, open-faced jelly and cream cheese, curried carrot, and apricot horseradish, encouraged creativity by the hostesses. The final preparatory step involved removing the crusts and cutting the sandwiches into small, dainty shapes.

Club luncheons (sometimes breakfasts or suppers) brought women together for the stated intention of charitable activities, gardening, **contract bridge**, study, or sewing groups. By serving food, this form of entertainment again provided the hostess the opportunity to present her full scope of culinary talents. Sandwich loaves covered with a cream cheese frosting had the appearance of cake and fooled the guests until cut. The "surprise sandwich loaf" consisted of bread spread with various fillings and stacked. A variation, the "ribbon sandwich," simply alternated slices of white and wheat bread. The "checkerboard sandwich loaves" placed a spread on alternating dark and light strips of bread assembled into a loaf with a checkerboard appearance.

Coupling entertainment with food did not limit itself to women. The Sunday night supper, a popular social format for couples or entire families, used a chafing dish or the newest electric toaster or electric waffle iron for serving the meal. This allowed the hostess, who doubled as the cook, to be with her guests and show off her new appliances.

Favorite dishes might include Welsh rarebit, grilled cheese sandwiches known as "cheese dreams," and waffles with anything that could be poured or spooned on them.

Firms that marketed appliances capitalized on the themes of ease and simplification of food preparation and how that left homemakers and parents more time for family activities. They stressed that many small appliances could be used for both cooking and home entertainment. Most fundamental innovations in domestic refrigeration design, except for automatic defrosting, had been made by the mid-1930s, and typical refrigerator ads promoted advance preparation of food dishes. The housewife could then store them in the refrigerator until meal time and final cooking.

Many new food items made their debuts during the 1930s, with the most popular requiring little or no preparation. Wonder Bread began selling loaves of sliced bread in 1930, a breakthrough that revolutionized sandwich making, including those served at club luncheons. Bisquick (1931) allowed biscuits to be baked in one simple step. Easy cake mixes followed Bisquick's success, and Miracle Whip Salad Dressing appeared in 1933. A year later, Campbell's Chicken Noodle and Cream of Mushroom soups along with a virtual blitz of other prepared foods—precooked hams, canned gravies, bottled salad dressings, prepared appetizers, and variety items—could be purchased. Heat 'n' eat Ragu spaghetti sauce and Kraft macaroni and cheese dinners showed up on grocers' shelves in 1937. Hormel & Company's Spam (1937; the name derives from the marriage of "spicy" and "ham") traveled directly from its familiar rectangular can to the table. Composed of a processed, pork-based, spiced luncheon meat, it provided many with the only protein they could afford.

Babies benefited from the innovations of the 1930s. Gerber introduced the first commercial line of baby food in 1931. Tradition has it that, in the late 1920s, Daniel Gerber (1898–1974) and his wife, Dorothy (d. 1988), at the suggestion of their pediatrician, experimented with making strained baby food for their daughter, as opposed to using the standard liquid diet then recommended for infants. They liked the result and Gerber decided to take their kitchen experiment to his firm, the Fremont Canning Company. At this time, new food products seldom received national distribution. Also, baby food until the 1930s could usually be found only at drugstores, since distributors categorized it as a specialty item that required a prescription. In an attempt to make strained baby food an "everyday item," the Fremont Canning Company embarked on several ingenious advertising campaigns to promote Gerber products. Salesmen drove distinctive **automobiles**, and print ads urged consumers to send in coupons that identified favorite grocery stores; in return they received six cans of baby food for a dollar and Fremont learned about stores possibly willing to stock their label.

The company's logo featured the famous Gerber baby, an original work drawn in 1928 by Dorothy Hope Smith (1895–1955). Shortly after Gerber introduced its commercial line of strained baby food, rival Beech-Nut plunged into the fray, offering 13 varieties of baby food in glass jars instead of cans.

Snacks appearing for the first time on the market included Frito Corn Chips (1932), Nabisco's Ritz Crackers (1934), and Lay's Potato Chips (1939). Banana-filled Hostess Twinkies (1931) doubled their usefulness by serving as either snacks or **desserts**. Some old standbys took on new appearances and gained additional popularity. J. Wellington Wimpy, a character introduced in 1931 by cartoonist E. C. Segar (1894–1938) in his *Thimble Theater*, loves to eat hamburgers. Wimpy's fame rests on his remarkable consumption of this food, and he played a significant role in popularizing this American favorite.

In Denver, Colorado, Louis Ballast (1910–1975) operated the Humpty Dumpty Barrel Drive-In, which featured hamburgers on the menu. In order to add variety to the fare, one day he placed a slice of cheese on a raw hamburger, heated both, and thus gave birth to the cheeseburger. Ballast even applied for a trademark on the term "cheeseburger" in March 1935, although his success remains in dispute.

The lowly hot dog also enjoyed a moment of fame during the 1930s. England's George VI (1895–1952) visited the United States in 1939 and President **Franklin D. Roosevelt** (1882–1945) and Mrs. Roosevelt served as his hosts. The first family decided to introduce something truly American to the royal family, and on June 11, 1939, they served Nathan's hot dogs at a picnic given at the Roosevelts' Hyde Park estate. The press provided the affair extensive coverage, and the menu appeared on the front page of the *New York Times*.

Prohibition, from its institution in 1920, affected entertainment and eating in America. With Repeal in 1933, liquor again became legal and cocktail parties reappeared as another means of home entertainment. As a rule, the hosts served both nonalcoholic and **alcoholic beverages** along with light snacks. The cocktail party allowed for the use and display of new gadgets—the electric snack server and hot plate, and percolators.

Fine, expensive dining at plush establishments declined with Prohibition. But not being able to buy an alcoholic drink or the fact that eating at home saved money did not entirely stop people from frequenting restaurants, especially for lunch. Diners, greasy spoons, hamburger stands, drive-ins, coffee shops, delicatessens, automats, lunch counters, beaneries, taverns, and tearooms offered inexpensive meals and served a certain portion of the population, usually those who chose not to cook, those who worked too far from home to get back for a meal, and those on the road.

Another form of eating out—church suppers, political barbecues, civic holiday picnics and festivals—provided an inexpensive way for families and communities to eat and socialize outside the home. Even though regional foods had decreased in popularity, the menus for these gatherings showed considerable latitude in the preferred foods and methods of cooking: fried and smoked pork and chicken in the South, with seafood added along the coast; freshly butchered pork and chicken in the Midwest; barbecued beef and chili in Texas and other parts of the Southwest; salmon barbecues and fish fries in California; and clam bakes or clam chowder, along with the New England boiled dinner of meat and vegetables, in the Northeast.

The food consumed by Americans during the 1930s did not differ greatly from preceding decades. Radio programs, advertising, **comic strips**, recipe pamphlets, and other popular culture outlets emphasized using widely known brands and foods, a move that led to a decline in ethnic eating and general acceptance of the "American diet." In a few regions, however, some ethnic cooking survived and various festivals allowed people to sample these tasty dishes. For example, Cajun delicacies in Louisiana, Scandinavian dishes in the north central states, and Mexican foods in the Southwest continued to be prepared in traditional ways, but most of the general population knew little about them. Overall, ethnic cooking went through a sharp decline with the acceptance of a national menu, especially in restaurants. One exception proved to be Italian cooking, particularly spaghetti and meatballs cooked in a mild tomato sauce; this dish enjoyed a wide base of popularity and remained on menus everywhere.

Throughout the decade, the sale of food moved from the corner grocery store to the supermarket while production of foodstuffs shifted from small producers to large corporations. New appliances guaranteed more efficient food preparation. Despite massive government transformations, changing employment patterns, and economic hardships, Americans noticed only slight changes in their basic diet, while at the same time experiencing an increase in available food items and accessories to purchase.

See also Candy; Ice Cream; Prohibition & Repeal; Radio Networks; Soft Drinks

SELECTED READING
Baby Foods. http://www.gerber.com/gerberbaby
Becker, Ethan. Personal interview, 20 May 2005.
Bundy, Beverly. *The Century in Food: America's Fads and Favorites*. Portland, OR: Collectors Press, 2002.
Hooker, Richard J. *Food and Drink in America: A History*. New York: Bobbs-Merrill, 1981.
Levenstein, Harvey A. *Revolution at the Table: The Transformation of the American Diet*. New York: Oxford University Press, 1988.
Lovegren, Sylvia. *Fashionable Food: Seven Decades of Food Fads*. New York: Macmillan, 1995.

FOOTBALL. The Depression had negative effects on all sports. Even college football suffered. After years of soaring attendance during the 1920s, the numbers plummeted with the onset of the economic downfall. And for the average fan, professional games remained virtually invisible, played before sparse crowds in open fields, city lots, or small stadiums. Lack of spectators, for both college and professional play, meant negligible receipts for teams. The vexing issue of finances during the 1930s forced everyone involved with football to search for ways to generate income.

Colleges and universities reduced coaching staffs, cut back on practices, and even threatened to drop football as a varsity sport. As they tightened their belts, they also worked diligently to stir enthusiasm for the game. In short order, the following events spurred public interest in collegiate football:

1934: first College All-Star Game organized
1935: first Heisman Trophy awarded (to Jay Berwanger [1914–2002], University of Chicago)
1935: creation of the Orange Bowl
1936: creation of the Sun Bowl
1937: the Sugar Bowl and the Cotton Bowl join the elite bowl roster
1938: first Blue-Gray game played

In the mid-1930s, several colleges considered granting contracts to **radio** stations for commercial broadcasts of their games, despite cries from traditionalists that such steps would destroy live stadium attendance. Yale University in 1936 allowed a Connecticut station to carry a play-by-play of one of its games, with Atlantic Refining, as the sponsor, paying Yale the princely sum of $20,000 (about $290,000 in contemporary dollars).

These measures brought much-needed financial help to schools fortunate enough to have sponsored broadcasts; attendance had bottomed out in mid-decade, although it began a long, slow climb for the remainder of the 1930s. But other problems also beset the game during the 1930s. Accusations of racial and ethnic prejudice influenced the public's perceptions of football, and they came from many directions. Some felt the sport encouraged brawn over brain; others saw it as an exercise in mayhem; still others lamented its lack of "gentlemanly qualities."

A rash of serious player injuries raised concerns about the safety of the game. American colleges responded by instituting various rule changes that quickened play as well as cutting down on injuries. A smaller, easier-to-grasp ball led to increased passing and a faster, more visual game. A clause introduced in 1932 ruled that the football itself became dead when any part of the player (except feet and hands) touched the ground. School officials also required some padding, although not until 1939 did they mandate helmets.

In light of these modifications, a new breed of player began to gain headlines, replacing some of the brute characteristics associated with earlier years of the game. For example, quarterback Sammy Baugh (1914–2005) graduated from Texas Christian University in 1937 and joined the Washington Redskins. His superlative passing, a deadly accurate sidearm style, earned him the name "Slingin' Sammy."

Although football would not achieve the popular success it gained in the postwar years, its visual qualities of rapid movement, crashing linemen, and jarring tackles attracted the attention of many in the entertainment field. Over 40 **movies** featured football during the 1930s, far more than any other athletic activity. In 1931 alone, theaters showed *Mickey's Stampede* and *The Spirit of Notre Dame*, the latter dedicated to Knute Rockne (1888–1931), the fabled Notre Dame coach. On a more realistic level, *Touchdown* took a harsh look at the pressures placed on players, and two 1931 documentaries, *Football Thrills* and *Pro Football*, detailed the game. The latter picture fell under the category that theaters and booking agents labeled a Pete Smith "oddity." Smith (1892–1979) built a successful career producing and narrating humorous films that purported to "tell all" about various sports and other activities.

The following year, *70,000 Witnesses*, *Hold 'em Jail*, *That's My Boy*, *The All-American*, and *Rackety Rax* entertained audiences. Even the popular **Marx Brothers** got into the action with *Horse Feathers* (1932), a spoof on college football. Groucho (1890–1977) plays the president of a small college determined to win the big game, and the resultant high jinks rollicked audiences. *College Coach* (1933) pairs Dick Powell (1904–1963) and Pat O'Brien (1899–1983) in a collegiate mix of **music** and comedy, and **Bing Crosby** (1903–1977) sings and acts in *College Humor* (1933). After a pause, three more titles joined the cinematic football ranks in 1936: *Pigskin Parade*, *Rose Bowl*, and *The Big Game*; the last includes a host of real collegiate stars. *Pigskin Parade* also offered a young **Judy Garland** (1922–1969) her first major role. *Two Minutes to Play* and *Life Begins in College*, the latter featuring the Ritz Brothers, a comedy act similar to the Marx Brothers, brightened marquees in 1937, as did *Pigskin Skill*, another Pete Smith film, this one a "specialty." The forgettable *Cowboy Quarterback*, along with *$1000 a Touchdown* and *Hero for a Day* closed out the decade. These movies set no attendance records, but they proved modestly profitable for the studios producing them.

Mass-circulation **magazines** such as the ***Saturday Evening Post*** and *Collier's* offered seasonal fiction and articles, often accompanied by four-color covers featuring football motifs done by leading **illustrators**. Several **pulp magazines**, bearing titles like *All-American Football Magazine*, *Sport Story Magazine*, and *Football Action*, likewise ran stories about the sport, although their readership could not approach that achieved by the *Post* and *Collier's*. Even a few novels depicted the game, but none reached **best seller** status. Not until after the end of World War II and the subsequent rise of **television** would football begin its relentless march toward dominance among American sports.

See also Education; Race Relations & Stereotyping

SELECTED READING

Oriad, Michael. *King Football: Sport and Spectacle in the Golden Age of Radio and Newsreels, Movies and Magazines, the Weekly and the Daily Press.* Chapel Hill: University of North Carolina Press, 2001.

Watterson, John Sayle. *College Football: History, Spectacle, Controversy.* Baltimore: Johns Hopkins University Press, 2000.

Whittingham, Richard. *Saturday Afternoon: College Football and the Men Who Made the Day.* New York: Workman Publishing, 1985.

42ND STREET. Possibly the best-known movie musical to come out during the grimmest Depression years, *42nd Street* (1933) breathed new life into a faltering film genre. In 1927, the introduction of sound to motion pictures held out great promise for integrating **music** into a production. In 1930, the first sound movie to win the Academy Award for Best Picture went to a musical, MGM's *Broadway Melody* (released in 1929). The future looked bright, and then the bottom fell out. By 1931, no studios wanted to risk much on **musicals**; too many had been made, audiences were sick of them, and the Depression had caused movie attendance to plummet.

Warner Brothers, one of Hollywood's legendary studios, entered the 1930s flush with success. But in 1931 the company lost $8 million (about $107 million in contemporary dollars), followed by a $14 million loss in 1932 (about $207 million). Things could not get much worse, and so Warner Brothers took a calculated gamble. Earlier musical films, of the few attempted, included such titles as *Lilies of the Field* (1930), *Song of the Flame* (1930), and *Kiss Me Again* (1931). None did well at the all-important box office, so Warner Brothers turned to a wholly original format as a way to attract audiences.

The gamble paid off. With little to lose, the almost-bankrupt company in 1933 released *42nd Street*. Categorized as a "backstage musical" because it supposedly gives the audience an insider's view of the doings of the cast, it helped create the myth of the gutsy chorine, a young woman who fights overwhelming odds for her big chance in an upcoming show. Making her movie debut, Ruby Keeler (1909–1993) takes over at the last minute for the ailing lead, played by Bebe Daniels (1901–1971). She of course wows the audience and stardom beckons. As a result of *42nd Street*, Keeler did indeed tap her talented feet to fame and many more major roles.

Featuring a memorable score by veteran songsmiths Harry Warren (1893–1981) and Al Dubin (1891–1945), *42nd Street* soon had people lined up at their local theaters, recapturing the audience that a short time earlier had seemingly abandoned movie musicals. With numbers like "Shuffle Off to Buffalo," "Young and Healthy," the romantic "You're Getting to Be a Habit with Me," and the title song, it would be difficult not to enjoy the music. Director Lloyd Bacon's (1889–1955) tight direction keeps everything

The finale from the groundbreaking 1933 musical *42nd Street*. (Courtesy of Photofest)

moving at a crisp pace, and the picture runs under 90 minutes. The dancing, and lots of it, displays the unique choreography of Busby Berkeley (1895–1976), and *42nd Street* launched his film career in spectacular fashion.

Whereas most musicals produced prior to *42nd Street* lack realism or any awareness of the passing scene, this low-budget, black-and-white entry possesses a grittiness, a knowledge of adversity. Set in the ongoing Depression, it is of and about the Depression. Jokes alluding to the harsh times abound, and the all-American quality of gumption, the ability to see a difficult situation through to a successful conclusion, helps give the picture its tone.

The successful release of *42nd Street* signaled the rebirth of the musical, and its tough, but not hard, characters allow for some social commentary not often found in popular films. From the opening scenes of tryouts for the chorus line and the knowledge that not everyone will make it, to the team effort to put together a superlative show, *42nd Street* supports President **Franklin D. Roosevelt**'s (1882–1945) statement that the only thing the nation need fear is fear itself. The show goes on, the team spirit triumphs—an ideal message for a nation still mired in economic problems.

The worsening crisis had shaken the country's faith in hard work and deferred gratification, a situation that allowed directors and screenwriters an unusual forum. *42nd Street* affirms the old American belief in labor and its resultant rewards, that singing and dancing your heart out will bring about good things.

See also Fred Astaire & Ginger Rogers; Movies; Songwriters & Lyricists

SELECTED READING
Altman, Rick, ed. *Genre: The Musical*. Boston: Routledge & Kegan Paul, 1981.
Hirschhorn, Clive. *The Warner Brothers Story*. New York: Crown Publishers, 1979.
Springer, John. *All Talking! All Singing! All Dancing! A Pictorial History of the Movie Musical*. Secaucus, NJ: Citadel Press, 1966.

FRANKENSTEIN. One of the most acclaimed horror pictures of the 1930s, *Frankenstein* typified the escapism that dominated much Hollywood production during that troubled decade. Universal Pictures, a Hollywood studio that enjoyed considerable success with the 1931 release of **Dracula**, also entertained the idea of producing a movie version of Mary Shelley's (1797–1851) classic *Frankenstein, or, The Modern Prometheus*, written in 1818. A 1930 stage dramatization, written by Peggy Webling (active 1930s), had aroused some attention and the studio planned to base the movie on that version. Bela Lugosi (1882–1956), the star of *Dracula*, had been considered for the role of the fabled creature, but he balked because the envisioned makeup would render him unrecognizable. As a result, James Whale (1889–1957), the designated director for *Frankenstein*, chose an acquaintance, William Henry Pratt, a veteran British character actor who used the stage name of Boris Karloff (1887–1969) to play the monster. It proved the perfect match.

Through the magic of cosmetics, Karloff underwent a transformation, one that fixed in the popular mind for decades to come just how Dr. Frankenstein's creature should look. The squared head, massive brow, and sunken eyes, along with the lumbering gait and mumbled attempts at speech, have been repeated again and again in subsequent films dealing with the Frankenstein legend, and Karloff's interpretation has remained the standard.

Movie producers early on sensed the visual qualities inherent in Shelley's novel; in 1910, and again in 1915, silent films attempted to retell the story of mechanically created life. In Germany, director Paul Wegener's (1874–1948) *Golem* (1914; remade 1920; the title translates as "a body lacking a soul") exerted a strong influence on director Whale. Wegener's inspiration, however, came more from Jewish legend than Mary Shelley. But the dark, shadowy imagery employed in *The Golem* reappears in Whale's *Frankenstein*, and this exaggerated use of chiaroscuro would dominate the cinematography in American **horror and fantasy films** throughout the 1930s.

Universal's *Frankenstein* casts Colin Clive (1900–1937) as Dr. Victor Frankenstein, the unfortunate inventor whose name would always be associated with his man-made monster. The set depicts a lonely laboratory, jammed with pseudoscientific instruments, located somewhere in central Europe. Amid stylized lightning and storm, the doctor brings life to his creation. In a memorable sequence, Karloff's character evolves from a bandage-swathed corpse into a living, breathing being cursed with the mind of a madman.

The remainder of the film chronicles Dr. Frankenstein's helplessness in controlling his monster, and the simultaneous growth and frustration contained in Karloff's nuanced performance as the doomed mutation. A mix of melodrama and occasional pathos,

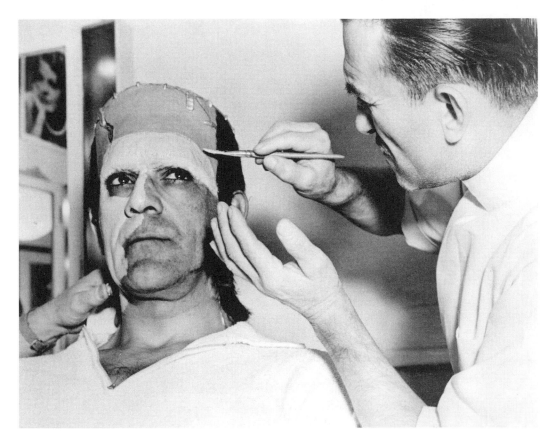

Boris Karloff (1887–1969) being transformed into Frankenstein's monster by makeup artist Jack Pierce (1889–1968). (Courtesy of Photofest)

Frankenstein emerged a box office success beyond anyone's expectations. Its escapism brought in audiences eager for a respite from the grim realities of the Depression, and also spurred other studios to hop onto the profitable cycle of churning out horror movies. Karloff reprised his Frankenstein monster role twice during the 1930s, with *The Bride of Frankenstein* (1935) and *Son of Frankenstein* (1939).

The actor became so associated with the horror genre that he seemed to be almost on call for roles requiring a frightening character. *The Mummy* (1932), *The Mask of Fu Manchu* (1932), *The Ghoul* (1933), *The Black Room* (1935, with the actor in a dual role), and *The Walking Dead* (1936) served as variations on the singular role he had created for *Frankenstein*. Audiences loved his malevolence—with or without makeup—and previews and theater posters need say only "Karloff" in order to draw a crowd. The busy actor appeared in over 50 pictures during the 1930s, and his career continued at an active pace until his death in 1969.

In the meantime, the image of the Frankensteinian monster, as created by James Whale and Boris Karloff, established itself as an icon in American popular culture. Uncounted "Frankenstein" **movies** have come out since 1931, but none has ever achieved the success or the recognition bestowed on this Depression-era version. Most have had to imitate, either slavishly or through allusion, their debt to Whale's and Karloff's accomplishment, an accomplishment that at the time people probably saw as just another picture in a continuing string of low-budget horror films.

See also Stage Productions

SELECTED READING

Beck, Calvin Thomas. *Heroes of the Horrors*. New York: Macmillan, 1975.

Bojarski, Richard, and Kenneth Beale. *The Films of Boris Karloff*. Secaucus, NJ: Citadel Press, 1974.

Brunas, Michael, John Brunas, and Tom Weaver. *Universal Horrors: The Studio's Classic Films, 1931–1946*. Jefferson, NC: McFarland & Co., 1990.

FROZEN FOODS. Since the late nineteenth century, foods, especially fish, poultry, and meat, had been frozen and shipped for wholesale distribution. In the early 1900s, fruit joined this list when West Coast growers began freezing fruits and berries. The processes varied but all had the intent to prevent further deterioration of foods already going bad. This approach fostered the opinion that frozen food meant poor quality; complaints centered on damaged texture and inferior flavor.

In an attempt to overcome these deficiencies, Clarence Birdseye (1886–1956), a **food** manufacturer, in 1923 received a patent for a method to quick-freeze his products. He had developed a twofold system of packing fresh foods and then flash-freezing them under high pressure in consumer-size, waxed cardboard boxes. His invention stands as a significant technical development that preserves texture and flavor.

Birdseye founded the General Seafoods Company in 1924. General Mills later owned it, and then sold the enterprise in 1929 to Frosted Foods Company, a corporation formed by Postum Company and Goldman-Sachs Trading Corporation. In this process, General Seafoods became the General Foods Corporation and converted its Birdseye brand name to Birds Eye. According to Clarence Birdseye, this change returned the family name to its original form. Supposedly, an early ancestor saved the life of an English queen by shooting an attacking hawk squarely through its eye.

Birds Eye frosted foods first appeared on March 6, 1930, in a test market of 18 stores in Springfield, Massachusetts. The company featured 27 kinds of frozen fruits, vegetables, fish, and meats and intentionally named these products "frosted" food as a way of lessening resistance from consumers associating "frozen" with damaged texture and poor flavor. Product development activities intensified and a second round of test markets occurred in 1934. Held in Syracuse and Rochester, New York, the results showed moderate consumer interest in frozen products, enough to continue work toward wider distribution.

Throughout most of the 1930s, the iceboxes and electric refrigerators manufactured for food storage contained a very small space, if any, for frozen food. Such items had to be eaten on the day of purchase, so the individual consumer gained little advantage by regularly purchasing "frosted" food. Refrigerator manufacturers addressed the home storage issue as the decade progressed; by the late 1930s, the latest models displayed significantly larger freezer compartments and home freezers also began to attract buyers. With these improvements, frozen foods could be purchased in larger quantities and safely stored.

Resistance to frozen food came not only from the retail consumer. Grocery stores also made their products inaccessible; many had large, glass-fronted white freezer cabinets, closed to the customer, which held the boxes of frozen foodstuffs. An assistant on the other side retrieved the buyer's selection. Many stores, however, simply did not have cases for frozen food, citing expense for their absence. Butchers complained that individual frozen cuts of meat would take away their livelihood and refused to stock them. In addition, **restaurants** and other eating establishments, fearing patron opposition, either refused to use frozen products or sold frozen food as fresh.

To lure shoppers and to promote an increase in sales, Birds Eye distributed recipe pamphlets such as "20 Minute Meals" (1932), which they hoped would make clear the convenience and time-saving component of purchasing and preparing frozen foods. To broaden the base and number of **grocery stores and supermarkets** selling their products, around 1934 the company developed a customer-friendly, less expensive freezer case and leased it to stores for a modest sum.

Restaurants found that customers usually could not tell the difference between frozen and fresh foods. In fact, frequently diners, upon learning the truth, congratulated the establishment on its progressive thinking. The restaurant business therefore began to see a marketing advantage for using this new product. Throughout the decade, General Foods allotted significant resources for continuous technological improvements and inventive promotional strategies. Inspirational pamphlets on the art of "telling and selling" hung in grocery store employees' washrooms. For two weeks each year, all new Birds Eye dealers had the services of a dietitian to educate their clerks and customers. The company mailed postcards showing the frozen food "special of the week" to lists of distributors' 100 best customers. With these ploys, public interest in Birds Eye frosted foods gradually grew.

General Foods officials agreed with Clarence Birdseye's vision of success for his product and they invested heavily in the endeavor. His system ensured his reputation as "father" of the frozen food industry in the United States. In recognition of his accomplishment, at the 1939 **New York World's Fair**, General Foods had the only frozen food exhibit. With the close of the decade, Birds Eye could announce larger sales, project continued growth, and face competition as other frozen food companies appeared, such as Honor Brand, Stokely–Van Camp, and Pratt Frozen Foods. Du Pont Cellophane, a leader in frozen food packaging, placed the first full-color frozen food advertisement on the inside back cover of a December 1939 issue of the *Saturday Evening Post*. After many years of experimentation and innovation, frozen food proved to be a stable commodity, not a passing fad.

See also Advertising; Magazines

SELECTED READING

Birds Eye Foods. http://www.birdseyefoods.com/corp/about/clarenceBirdseye.asp

Frozen Foods Industry. "The Formative Years: 1930–1941." *Frozen Food Age* 46 (August 1997): 34–40.

———. "How It Began." *Frozen Food Digest* 8 (April–May 1993): 74–99.

Levenstein, Harvey A. *Paradox of Plenty: A Social History of Eating in Modern America*. New York: Oxford University Press, 1993.

G

GAMES. During the years of the Great Depression, at-home diversions included visiting, listening to the **radio**, and engaging in **hobbies** such as **stamp collecting**, reading, and putting together **jigsaw puzzles**. Games of many kinds also provided an economical way for Americans to occupy their **leisure and recreation** time. For those wanting entertainment outside the home, community centers, churches, and recreational facilities offered opportunities for meeting and enjoying inexpensive games and other leisure pursuits.

Card games, especially **contract bridge**, increased rapidly in popularity during the 1930s. The sale of cards rose and many people enrolled with various organizations to take lessons. Conservatively speaking, 20 million people played the game by 1931, some as a social engagement within the home and some on a competitive basis in tournaments. Throughout the decade, **newspapers** published columns on how to improve play and prominent bridge matches could at times be followed on radio.

Games of chance likewise had their fans. One such game, bingo, had been played under the names lotto or beano at carnivals and fairs for many years before the Depression. Edwin S. Lowe (active 1920s–1930s), a toy salesman, stopped off at a carnival in Georgia in December 1929 and played beano for the first time. Participants had to purchase printed cards and then a pitchman called out numbers while players tried to match up beans on their cards in order to complete a row diagonally, horizontally, or vertically. Successful completion of a row titled the lucky cardholder to call out "beano" and win a prize.

The large, boisterous crowd playing beano fascinated Lowe; he went home to New York City, developed a small version of the game, and invited friends to his apartment to play. The same enthusiasm felt in the Georgia carnival tent soon engulfed his apartment and he decided to develop the game for mass production. Supposedly, Lowe had observed a woman playing the game who, when she realized she had a winning combination, got tongue-tied and yelled out "bingo!" instead of "beano." He liked the name and applied it to his company's first 12-card and 24-card versions, and the bingo craze began. But problems soon arose. Large groups of players reported that several cards sometimes produced several simultaneous winners, an uncomfortable situation immediately addressed by Lowe. He hired a Columbia University math professor, Carl Leffler (active 1920s–1930s), to solve the problem. With Leffler's help, Lowe's company in 1930 manufactured over 6,000 numerically different cards, thus eliminating multiple winners. Lowe went on

People playing bingo at a state fair in Louisiana. (Courtesy of the Library of Congress)

to publish bingo instruction manuals, as well as pamphlets that described how to use the game for fund-raising activities.

In the early 1930s, church halls and community centers across the country, along with special occasions such as firemen's carnivals and county fairs, sponsored some 10,000 bingo games a week. Since it was inexpensive to play, many patrons patiently stayed with the game all evening, hoping to win a ham, a box of groceries, a tin of coffee, or actual cash. Some disgruntled citizens occasionally complained that bingo constituted gambling and made attempts to ban it, but public enthusiasm for the cards and the markers won out. Throughout the decade, the game's popularity remained high and millions still carried the hope of winning something for nothing.

Lowe never obtained trademark protection for his new game, which meant that competitors soon had their own versions of bingo. In time, the word entered the language, both as a noun identifying the game and as an interjection. "Bingo!" came to mean "that does it!" or "I've got it!" Despite the competition, Lowe made a fortune by selling the cards and markers to various civic groups, churches, and charitable organizations.

Any game that promised prizes or rewards received a warm Depression-era welcome from people anxious to give it a try. Advertisers used newspapers, **magazines**, and radio spots to urge listeners, in return for prizes, to complete a limerick praising a certain product or to find the name of an item hidden in a cartoon. Social critics in 1938 estimated that a 1,000 percent increase in all kinds of prize contests had taken place since the beginning of the Depression; 25 million people participated on an average of twice a year in the quest for something for nothing.

Punchboard, another game of chance, blossomed in the 1930s. This game, granted a patent in 1905, required a small block of cardboard containing hundreds or even thousands of holes. Each hole held a slip of paper called a "ticket" and a buyer could purchase as many holes as he or she wanted at about a nickel per hole (roughly 76 cents in contemporary money). Only one of those concealed slips of paper awarded cash; the rest were worthless. But which one? Usually, a winning slip paid $2.50 (about $38), but with so many holes, the odds favored the house. Punchboards offered a momentary thrill and little else to the consumer, and big profits to the vendor. By 1939, manufacturers stamped out an estimated 150,000 punchboards daily, or some 50 million each year.

Other devices favored by Americans to win something effortlessly included slot and pinball machines. One such game, bagatelle, a forerunner to pinball, could be found in penny arcades both before and after the Depression. It used a cue, small balls, and a board with holes at one end. During the 1930s, a nickel bought you 10 shots and players who sank all or most of their shots received prizes, usually cameras, clocks, fountain pens, or similar items.

As technology advanced, bagatelle increased in complexity but still offered prizes. First, an arrangement of pins blocked direct shots to a hole and the name became "pin games." Next, eliminating the cue stick changed the name again, this time to "pinball." Three such pinball machines, the Whoopie Game, the Baffle Ball, and the Bally-Hoo, that came out in the early 1930s, featured a mechanical plunger that propelled the ball through the difficult course. In 1933, Harry Williams (active 1930s) of the Pacific Amusement Company of California designed Contact, a game with dry-cell batteries that powered colored lights and rang a bell.

The easily accessible slot machines and pinball games could be found in cigar stores, filling stations, cafes, drugstores, game parlors, and at lunch counters. The establishments offering this entertainment successfully evaded existing gambling laws for many years by claiming they provided "games of skill," not "games of chance." By 1933, manufacturers offered 62 different pinball games that sold about 250,000 units annually.

Pick-up-sticks, introduced in 1936 by New York's Gimbel Brothers Department Store, quickly caught on and Macy's and Woolworth stores soon joined in and offered the game too. Together, the three stores sold nearly 3 million sets during the first year of availability. Neither new nor unique, pick-up-sticks resembled a game once enjoyed by American Indians with straws of wheat. The game can be played alone or with a group and may have gotten its name from the children's nursery rhyme "five, six, pick up sticks." It requires physical dexterity since the object revolves removing, one by one, the sticks from a random pile without disturbing those remaining. Eugene Leavy (active 1920s–1930s), a toy buyer for Gimbels, orchestrated the American production of the game by borrowing from a Hungarian version known as Marokko. Initially considered by some to be too frivolous to excite the American public, at the height of the 1930s craze, the pick-up-sticks manufacturer was turning out almost 30,000 boxed sets a day.

Ping-Pong, a more physically demanding game, had its introduction in the 1880s in England. Played indoors on a flat table divided into two equal courts by a low net, it resembles a miniature tennis court. Both singles and doubles could be played, and it required small paddles to propel an almost weightless celluloid ball back and forth across the net. "Ping-Pong" supposedly echoed the sound of the ball hitting the paddles. Cyclically popular in the United States, the game emerged as a fad during the 1920s when Parker Brothers set out to exploit Ping-Pong through heavy **advertising**. The company had earlier bought the American rights to the name from an English game manufacturer.

In turn, it trademarked Ping-Pong for its complete line of equipment and formed the American Ping-Pong Association to conduct national tournaments.

The number of Ping-Pong enthusiasts grew rapidly and Parker Brothers lost its monopoly on manufacturing the equipment. In 1931, the New York Table Tennis Association came into being, sponsoring national tournaments in competition with those sponsored by Parker Brothers. Recognizing the game's growing popularity and the resultant confusion of two groups hosting similar matches, the two associations merged in 1934 as the United States Table Tennis Association (USTTA) and introduced international competition. During the 1930s, Ping-Pong reportedly ranked as the most popular intramural sport in large American universities; the United States alone accounted for over 10 million players with some 5 million tables in private homes.

With high unemployment and more available leisure time, the Depression years also witnessed a rise in the popularity of board games. Since the early 1900s, dozens of companies had produced board games for both entertainment and educational purposes. **Monopoly**, the most famous and continuously popular of all, traces its origin back to a 1904 game called the Landlord's Game. Charles Darrow (1889–1967), an unemployed resident of Philadelphia, copyrighted a variation of the Landlord's Game in 1933 and two years later reached an agreement with Parker Brothers to take over its production and distribution.

Many game designers of the 1930s developed themes that echoed the times. The Sunday **comic strips** had their spin-offs with the **Dick Tracy** Detective Game and *Oh, Blondie* from the Whitman Publishing Company. Parker Brothers' Hi Yo Silver! reflected the popularity of the radio **serial** *The Lone Ranger*, while Whitman Publishing Company recognized the sports world with the Kentucky Derby **Horse Racing** game. The South Pole Game and the Lindy Flying Game, inspired by Admiral Richard E. Byrd (1888–1957) and Charles Lindbergh (1902–1974), respectively, serve as examples of popular educational games that employed actual events as their foundations.

The manufacture of games rose to new heights during the 1930s. A National Recreation Association survey in 1934 showed that, in order to save money, many Americans engaged in sedentary and solitary activities at home such as playing games. Employers occasionally provided entertainment opportunities in the form of family picnics that featured games and sports. At these affairs some staged contests with small cash prizes. Games of chance remained popular throughout the decade, with a 1939 poll showing that one-third of the population admitted to occasionally betting a nickel or so. The life of many of the popular games of the 1930s consisted of a brief, enthusiastic obsession, while a few, like Monopoly, have enjoyed an uninterrupted and enthusiastic following.

See also Education; Serials

SELECTED READING

Dulles, Foster Rhea. *A History of Recreation: America Learns to Play*. Englewood Cliffs, NJ: Prentice-Hall, 1965.

Hoffman, Frank W., and William G. Bailey. *Sports and Recreation Fads*. New York: Haworth Press, 1991.

Johnson, Bruce E. "Board Games: Affordable and Abundant, Boxed Amusements from the 1930s and 1940s Recall the Cultural Climate of an Era," *Country Living* 20:12 (December 1997): 50–54.

GANGSTER FILMS. A controversial movie genre that attracted an enthusiastic following in the early 1930s, most of the pictures focused on colorful criminals and their ongoing wars with the forces of law and order. The success of gangster films reflected the popular fascination with lawbreakers and their resultant celebrity in all forms of media.

The movie industry quickly recognized the dramatic potential inherent in unfolding current events. Throughout the 1920s, Hollywood studios had cranked out a small but steady stream of stories about criminals and their milieu, climaxing in the silent classic *Underworld* (1927), directed by Josef von Sternberg (1894–1969). This film, most critics agree, established the standards for the genre, especially for the flood of gangster pictures that poured forth during the early 1930s. Unremittingly dark and shadowy, with bursts of violence, *Underworld* remains a classic of its type.

The advent of sound in the late 1920s changed few of the conventions established by that pioneering movie, except that now the characters could talk aloud in the colorful language screenwriters presented as the "true" argot of the underworld. Early talkies like *Broadway* (1929) and *The Doorway to Hell* (1930) laid the groundwork for a succession of pictures depicting the lives of criminals. Leading the list would be **Little Caesar** (1930), the first important sound film in the gangster genre.

Close on the heels of *Little Caesar* came *The Public Enemy* (1931), another significant **crime** movie. Directed by William A. Wellman (1896–1975), *The Public Enemy* elevated actor James Cagney (1899–1986) to stardom in his role as Tom Powers, a petty crook who graduates to being a ruthless murderer. As with *Little Caesar*, the plot focuses almost exclusively on the rise of a gangster, a person with few redeeming qualities, who completely dominates the screen with his cocky presence. Gangster movies of the 1930s present a distorted view of the American myth of success, one which downgrades respect for the law and **education**. Many viewed the latter as a waste of time for the man of action. These pictures tend to portray those who play by the rules and acquire formal learning as weak and powerless.

Scarface: Shame of a Nation (1932), another seminal film, created a kind of gangster trilogy with *Little Caesar* and *The Public Enemy*. Directed by Howard Hawks (1896–1977) and produced by Howard Hughes (1905–1976), it stars Paul Muni (1895–1967) in a career-defining role. Playing Tony Camonte, a character loosely based on Al "Scarface" Capone (1899–1947), a real-life gangster who dominated the headlines about crime, Muni imbues his character with a psychotic drive for success in the bootlegging rackets. With its explicit violence and incessant focus on Camonte, the picture, like its predecessors, celebrates lawlessness, even when it leads to death. With law enforcement often portrayed as inept and corrupt, the success of these latter-day outlaws, both real and on screen, fed into a national resentment toward authority and its failures. Small wonder, then, that crime films found a receptive audience.

Male-dominated, the gangster genre usually portrays a young man who rises in the world of crime, achieves power, and then suffers a violent downfall. Occasionally the 1930s saw a woman take on some variation of this role, such as in *Madame Racketeer* (1932), *Blondie Johnson* (1933), and *Ladies They Talk About* (1933), but these films proved the exception.

Gangster films also provided steady employment for a number of actors who became typecast as hoodlums, recurring "heavies" in the cinema underworld. For example, actors

George Raft (1895–1980), Barton MacLane (1902–1969), Jack La Rue (1902–1984), Bruce Cabot (1904–1972), and George Bancroft (1882–1956) repeatedly menaced anyone who challenged them in film after film. Humphrey Bogart (1899–1957) parlayed this style of acting into stardom, particularly as the chilling Duke Mantee in *The Petrified Forest* (1936).

With so much emphasis on the exploits of criminals, a backlash eventually occurred. By the mid-1930s, critics both within and without the industry clamored for **movies** that glorified the good guys instead of just the bad ones. In response, Hollywood pulled from general release some of its more controversial gangster films, including *Little Caesar* and *Scarface: Shame of a Nation*. It promptly shifted gears and began producing a number of films that depicted various law officers apprehending the very villains so recently celebrated on screen. James Cagney, reversing his screen persona, led this transition, starring in 1935's "G" Men, a fast-paced tale of government agents battling crime. The once-bad guy had metamorphosed into an upstanding citizen, although his methods might be questionable. In reality, although these new heroes wore badges, little else distinguished them from their criminal adversaries.

In short order, *Show Them No Mercy!* had federal agents battling kidnappers; *Little Caesar*'s Edward G. Robinson (1893–1973) appeared in *Bullets or Ballots* (1936) as Johnny Blake, a crusading detective; and Humphrey Bogart recast himself in *Crime School* (1938) as a reformer of wayward boys. Innumerable other films followed—*Manhattan Melodrama* (1934), *Special Agent* (1935), *Racket Busters* (1938), *Smashing the Money Ring* (1939); the day of the idolized gangster had come to an end.

With all the attention given to crime on the streets, inevitably a number of films also attempted to explain the causes of antisocial behavior. Easy answers, all related to ignorance and poverty, presented themselves with the Depression. For the movies, the city and its widespread unemployment and despair created a breeding ground for crime and juvenile delinquency. This environment repeatedly appears in pictures like *City Streets* (1931), *Dead End* (1937), *Boy of the Streets* (1937), *Angels with Dirty Faces* (1938), and *They Made Me a Criminal* (1939). Solve the economic dilemma, they argue, and the related social ills will disappear, although most end rather bleakly, the root problems still in place.

By the end of the decade, gangsters and lawmen still appeared in movies, but they constituted a minor part of Hollywood's overall production. The crisis of the Depression had lessened, and the threat of war and the calls to patriotism had created new themes for the motion picture industry.

See also Federal Bureau of Investigation; Hollywood Production Code; Mysteries & Hard-Boiled Detectives; Prohibition & Repeal; Teenage & Juvenile Delinquency Films

SELECTED READING

Clarens, Carlos. *Crime Movies: From Griffith to the Godfather and Beyond*. New York: W. W. Norton, 1980.

Parish, James Robert, and Michael R. Pitts. *The Great Gangster Pictures*. Metuchen, NJ: Scarecrow Press, 1976.

Rosow, Eugene. *Born to Lose: The Gangster Film in America*. New York: Oxford University Press, 1978.

Yaquinto, Marilyn. *Pump 'em Full of Lead: A Look at Gangsters on Film*. New York: Twayne, 1998.

GARDNER, ERLE STANLEY. For leisure reading, mystery stories ranked high among people's choices in the 1930s, carrying over from a surge of popularity that occurred during the 1920s. And few mystery writers ranked higher than Erle Stanley Gardner (1889–1970). One of the most prolific writers of all time, Gardner wrote hundreds of short stories, 122 novels, along with **travel** books and other miscellaneous works.

Born in Massachusetts, family moves took him west, first to Alaska and finally to California, the state he would call home for the rest of his life. After a brief fling at college, he worked in local law offices and gradually became interested in the entire judicial process. An apt student, he read and studied, passing the California bar in 1911. He began to practice law shortly thereafter, but did not prosper as an attorney, although he won most of his cases and often defended underdogs. Gardner's legal experiences would later figure importantly in his fiction.

In order to make ends meet, and to satisfy an urge to try something creative, Gardner began writing short fiction at night, churning out thousands of words at the end of each day. His new avocation got off to a slow start, however, accompanied by many rejection slips. But Gardner persevered, and finally sold his first stories in 1923. Before he ever attempted a novel, Gardner became an important presence in the then-flourishing pulp magazine industry.

Erle Stanley Gardner (1889–1970), creator of Perry Mason. (Courtesy of the Library of Congress)

Periodicals like *Argosy*, *Black Mask*, *Detective Action Stories*, *Detective Story*, *Dime Detective*, and *Double Detective* bought his work, and he quickly turned to writing full time. As his output increased, Gardner created ongoing characters, such as Black Barr, a western detective and gunslinger, Ed Jenkins, the "Phantom Crook" and con artist, and Lester Leith, another memorable confidence man. He sometimes injected a humorous note into his characters' names, with the likes of Paul Pry (an investigator) and Ed Migraine (a headache for those who encountered him). By the beginning of the 1930s, Gardner reigned as "king of the pulps," with new stories coming out at a furious rate from his seemingly boundless imagination, and causing some to dub him a "one-man fiction factory."

In the early 1930s, Gardner decreased but did not abandon his output in the hectic world of the pulps in order to turn to longer fiction. His stories continued to appear on the pages of numerous **magazines** throughout the decade. He even created a crusading attorney named Ken Corning, something of a model for Perry Mason, his most famous creation. Corning took the lead in six short tales written for *Black Mask* during the early 1930s. In 1933, Gardner published *The Case of the Velvet Claws*, his first novel, and it introduced Perry Mason, a lawyer who practiced detection on the side. That year also saw *The Case of the Sulky Girl*, the second in what would be a long line of Perry Mason stories. Thereafter, at least two new novels, and sometimes more, came out each year, a pace Gardner sustained throughout the 1930s, 1940s, 1950s, and most of the 1960s. Not until 1968 did he drop back to just one novel a year, with *The Case of the Careless Cupid*. Despite this apparent slowdown, Gardner continued to write until his death in 1970, and seven novels came out between 1969 and 1973, his publisher rationing out the final posthumous manuscripts for three years.

In the 1930s alone, Gardner published 22 novels:

15 Perry Mason novels
The Case of the Velvet Claws (1933; the first Perry Mason novel, made into a movie in 1936)
The Case of the Sulky Girl (1933)
The Case of the Lucky Legs (1934; movie in 1935)
The Case of the Howling Dog (1934; a movie in that year)
The Case of the Curious Bride (1934; movie in 1935)
The Case of the Counterfeit Eye (1935)
The Case of the Caretaker's Cat (1935; movie in 1936, but titled *The Case of the Black Cat*)
The Case of the Sleepwalker's Niece (1936)
The Case of the Stuttering Bishop (1936; movie in 1937)
The Case of the Dangerous Dowager (1937)
The Case of the Lame Canary (1937)
The Case of the Substitute Face (1938)
The Case of the Shoplifter's Shoe (1938)
The Case of the Perjured Parrot (1939)
The Case of the Rolling Bones (1939)
3 Doug Selby novels (a crusading district attorney)
The DA Calls It Murder (1937)
The DA Holds a Candle (1938)
The DA Draws a Circle (1939)
1 Terry Clane novel (a former diplomat who befriends and assists California's Asian community)
Murder Up My Sleeve (1937)
3 novels written under pseudonyms
The Clue of the Forgotten Murder (1935; written as Carleton Kendrake)
This Is Murder (1935; written as Charles J. Kenny)
The Bigger They Come (1939; written as A. A. Fair, the first of the Bertha Cool/Donald Lam series that would continue for many years thereafter)

The stir that Gardner's Perry Mason character caused led directly to Hollywood and a string of six **movies** in four years. Hardly top-rank films, these low-budget offerings nonetheless attracted audiences, people probably already familiar with Gardner and his fictional character. In *The Case of the Howling Dog* (1934), Warren William (1894–1948) portrays Perry Mason, as he does in *The Case of the Curious Bride* (1935), *The Case of the Lucky Legs* (1935), and *The Case of the Velvet Claws* (1936). Warner Brothers replaced William with Ricardo Cortez (1899–1977) in *The Case of the Black Cat* (1936; based on *The Case of the Caretaker's Cat*), whom they then dropped, giving the Mason role to Donald Woods (1906–1998) for *The Case of the Stuttering Bishop* (1937). **Radio** and **television** later discovered Perry Mason in the 1940s and 1950s, respectively.

More important for his legions of readers, perhaps, involved the serialization of his stories. *Liberty*, a popular mass-circulation magazine of the era, initially took three of his works and spread each out over several weeks. The mighty ***Saturday Evening Post***, far and away the country's leading general magazine, in 1937 succeeded in obtaining serial rights to Gardner's forthcoming novels, an arrangement that substantially increased his income. Finally, in 1940, the mass marketing of cheap paperback books became a reality, led by Pocket Books. No writer proved more popular for the new publisher, and Gardner won a guaranteed $100,000 annual contract for the paperback rights to his fiction (roughly $1.5 million a year in contemporary dollars). After all the years of struggle with **pulp magazines** and sometimes less-than-robust hardcover sales, he found the financial security he had long sought.

Gardner freely admitted that he wrote for the money, and he wrote fast, leaving character development to other authors, instead stressing speed and maintaining reader interest. He did, however, take considerable care when constructing plots, filling small notebooks with longhand details about his latest story. These he arranged and edited until everything could stand on its own. To maintain his pace as a writer, Gardner forsook a typewriter and bought a dictating machine. He would then organize and compose his notes and read them into the instrument, often at the rate of 15,000 words per day. He hired several secretaries skilled in dictation who would transcribe the results. With his own handwritten corrections on these typed copies, he sent the manuscripts off to his publishers, eliminating the laborious and time-consuming chore of typing his own material.

Never a great stylist, although not above occasional alliteration in his titles, such as "Lucky Legs," Caretaker's Cat," "Dangerous Dowager," "Shoplifter's Shoe," and "Perjured Parrot," Gardner proved unusually adept at plotting. He eschewed sociological and psychological commentaries; he favored spinning a good whodunit and letting others make the learned literary insights into motivation and background. His straightforward approach appealed to millions, especially during the Depression when escapism found favor in virtually every medium.

Over his long career, Gardner wrote 86 Perry Mason tales, or over 70 percent of his total novel output. Twenty-eight A. A. Fair stories, or 22 percent, starred Bertha Cool and Donald Lam as a pair of sleuths who also enjoyed great popularity among readers. The remaining novels, countless short fiction pieces, and collections make for a substantial bibliography. Although no accurate figures about his total book sales are available, most estimates place them in the hundreds of millions. Widely translated, Erle Stanley Gardner certainly stands near the head of any list of best-selling American writers, past or present.

See also Best Sellers; Crime; Gangster Films; Leisure & Recreation; Mysteries & Hard-Boiled Detectives

SELECTED READING
Gardner, Erle Stanley. http://www.erlestanleygardner.com
———. http://hometown.aol.com/mg4273/Gardner.htm
Hughes, Dorothy B. *Earle Stanley Gardner: The Case of the Real Perry Mason*. New York: Morrow, 1978.
Reilly, John M. *Twentieth-Century Crime and Mystery Writers*. New York: St. Martin's Press, 1991.

GARLAND, JUDY. A famous performer in a variety of media, Judy Garland (1922–1969), born in Grand Rapids, Minnesota, as Frances Ethel Gumm, made her singing debut at age three. Billed as "Baby Gumm," Frances appeared on stage in the Gumm Sisters Kiddie Act with her two older siblings, Mary Jane (1915–1964) and Virginia (1917–1977). The three continued to appear in local vaudeville and benefits, as well

Judy Garland (1922–1969) singing "Dear Mr. Gable (You Made Me Love You)" in *Broadway Melody of 1938* (1937). (Courtesy of Photofest)

as performing on **radio**, all the while honing their skills. In 1927, the family moved to California, and the trio, now calling themselves the Gumm Sisters, took their act throughout the Los Angeles area and even appeared in some short musical films. Her Hollywood career commenced at age seven with the brief *Starlet Revue* in 1929. A number of other short pictures followed, and in 1934, the three sisters received an invitation to perform at the 1933–1934 **Century of Progress Exposition** (Chicago World's Fair).

While appearing there, Frances Gumm decided that show business was in her blood and became, with some professional advice, Judy Garland. The Gumm Sisters' act broke up in 1935, and Frances/Judy set her sights on a career in the **movies**. Between the mid-1930s and 1940, she would make 12 feature films and several more shorts. Among the latter, Garland shares the bill with Deanna Durbin (b. 1921), another promising performer, in *Every Sunday* (1936), an 11-minute musical. Much of the picture's interest lies in watching two young women on the thresholds of their professional careers.

Garland followed that effort with her first full-length picture, 20th Century Fox's *Pigskin Parade* (1936), an unlikely comedy about **football** and radical politics that depends on confusion for its laughs. Amid the touchdowns, the 14-year-old sings "It's Love I'm After" (music by Sidney D. Mitchell [1888–1942], lyrics by Lew Pollack [1895–1946]), and her innocent poise plus her voice made an impression on both Hollywood and the recording industry.

In recognition of her vocal talent, Decca Records signed her to a contract in 1936, and Garland immediately began to issue a steady stream of **recordings** with big-name orchestras. She would, during the remainder of the 1930s, cut dozens of sides for the label. Shortly thereafter, Metro-Goldwyn-Mayer, the leading producer of movie **musicals**, cast her in *Broadway Melody of 1938* (released in 1937). Part of a series of MGM "Broadway Melodies" (1935, 1937, 1940), the films allowed the studio to publicize its roster of stars, both established and new. This particular version boasted, among others, Robert Taylor (1911–1969), Eleanor Powell (1912–1982), and George Murphy (1902–1992), some of the brightest names of the day.

Against this intimidating competition, Garland holds her own during her time on screen. In a show-stopping sequence, she croons, while looking wistfully at a photograph of actor Clark Gable (1901–1960), "Dear Mr. Gable: You Made Me Love You" (1913; music by James V. Monaco [1885–1945], lyrics by Joseph McCarthy [1885–1943]; "Dear Mr. Gable" segment scripted by Roger Edens [1905–1970]). A defining moment for Garland, the song opened many doors for the young star, and her career continued to flourish.

That same year, MGM brought out a second full-length feature with their new property; she did not enjoy top billing yet, but she edged closer to it. *Thoroughbreds Don't Cry* teamed her with another rising star, Mickey Rooney (b. 1920), prompting eight more pairings for the two young actors. During the 1930s alone, they appear on screen together in four additional pictures—*Love Finds Andy Hardy* (1938), *Babes in Arms* (1939), *Andy Hardy Meets Debutante* (1940), and *Strike Up the Band* (1940)—and the studio kept finding scripts that they could share, if only for brief moments, finally ending in 1948 with *Words and Music*.

The teenage chemistry between Garland and Rooney appealed to audiences, and their innocence and good spirits contrasted sharply with the dark side of adolescence depicted in so many **teenage and juvenile delinquency films** that rose to some prominence at that time. The plots about "putting on a show" and then-current dating rituals may seem hackneyed today, but Garland and Rooney brought an air of naiveté to the screen that doubtless reassured many a worried parent.

In the movie *Listen, Darling* (1938), MGM costarred her with Freddie Bartholomew (1924–1992), another in the studio's stable of popular youthful actors. Their scenes together, not as lively as those she shares with Mickey Rooney in other pictures, nevertheless play reasonably well as the two humorously plot and scheme over parental suitors. Best of all, Garland delivers a splendid rendition of "Zing! Went the Strings of My Heart" (1935; words and music by James F. Hanley [1892–1942]), reinforcing her growing reputation as both a star and an outstanding singer.

Her combination of innocence and effervescence led Garland to the role of Dorothy in the much-acclaimed **Wizard of Oz** in 1939. Almost 17 when filming began, Garland knew how to perform in front of a camera by then, and how to hold her own with other performers. By giving her top billing in this big-budget picture, MGM formally acknowledged her rise to stardom. The Academy of Motion Picture Arts and Sciences obviously agreed; it awarded Garland a special Academy Award for a performance by a juvenile.

A production that boasts one highlight after another, perhaps nothing else in the movie musically equals her wistful vocal on "Over the Rainbow" (music by Harold Arlen [1905–1986], lyrics by E. Y Harburg [1896–1981]). Although *The Wizard of Oz* received immediate acclaim, and "Over the Rainbow" won an Academy Award as Best Song, two popular bands, Glenn Miller (1904–1944) and His Orchestra and Bob Crosby (1913–1993) and His Bobcats, first made radio's **Your Hit Parade** with recorded versions of the tune, overshadowing Garland's vocal rendition. But 1939 marked the peak of the big band era, and only over time would Judy Garland's soundtrack version become the standard. She eventually so consolidated her considerable hold on the song that most people now associate "Over the Rainbow" with Judy Garland alone.

Her fame assured, the actress/singer went on to make more movies and increased her concert, nightclub, and radio appearances. The future, in the form of marital problems, bad career choices, and health issues, would not be kind, and she followed a bumpy road until her untimely death at 47. Despite many setbacks as an adult, Judy Garland has endured as one of the great show business personalities of the twentieth century.

See also Children's Films; Jazz; Swing; Toys

SELECTED READING
Clarke, Gerald. *Get Happy: The Life of Judy Garland.* New York: Random House, 2000.
Coleman, Emily R. *The Complete Judy Garland: The Ultimate Guide to Her Career in Films, Records, Concerts, Radio, and Television, 1935–1969.* New York: Harper & Row, 1990.
Frank, Gerold. *Judy.* New York: DaCapo Press, 1999.

GAS STATIONS. Also called "filling stations" and "service stations," these highly visible roadside businesses expanded significantly just prior to and during the Depression years. Propelled by the need for gasoline to operate cars, along with a safe and efficient way to dispense it, gas stations paralleled the growth of the automotive industry and became an important service to motorists in the 1920s and 1930s.

Automobiles that used gasoline instead of electricity or steam as a power source had been developed as early as 1893. In 1902, the Olds Motor Works assembled 2,500 gasoline-driven cars, but at a price that could be managed only by wealthy hobbyists. Not until the founding of General Motors and the introduction of the Model T Ford in 1908 did assembly line production of gasoline-driven automobiles create vehicles at more affordable prices, with the result that new outlets for petroleum products flourished.

Prior to the widespread availability of gas stations, people went to general stores, blacksmith shops, or repair shops to purchase gasoline. They filled open buckets, pails, and jars and used funnels to pour it into the car's tank, a messy and dangerous process. The gasoline itself, sometimes of questionable quality, could evaporate slightly, become polluted, or both, not to mention its susceptibility to spilling and fire. Recognizing these difficulties, many inventors and oil companies investigated better ways for access and delivery, while simultaneously working on providing a more trustworthy fuel.

No particular individual or company can be cited as the inventor of the gasoline pump and no specific building can be acknowledged as the first bona fide gas station. Several entrepreneurs conceived the basic ideas, but only a handful pursued and obtained patents. For example, John J. Tokheim (1871–1941) received a patent in 1901 for a device he called the "visible measuring pump." Initially to be used for kerosene, he continued to improve his invention, and by 1906 it could draw gasoline from an underground storage tank and dispense it through a hand-operated pump. Tokheim's invention stood out from the competition because of its ability to accurately measure the quantity of gasoline delivered and thereby fairly calculate the cost to the customer.

The Automobile Gasoline Company in St. Louis, Missouri, developed a quick and efficient process in 1905 that involved a garden hose transferring gasoline from a gravity-fed storage tank directly to the automobile. An attendant provided assistance by sticking the end of the hose into the automobile tank's filler neck. At about this same time, a Standard Oil of California (Socal) employee mounted an upright 30-gallon tank on wooden posts adjacent to a curb in Seattle, Washington. He used the "hose with a valve and gravity" technique to fill gas tanks. Others emulated these simple systems, and the term "filling station" became associated with curbside pumps and various storage containers.

A typical suburban gas station of the mid-1930s. (Courtesy of the Library of Congress)

Regardless of how they took on fuel, automobiles proliferated and the petroleum industry experienced rapid growth. By the early 1930s, 20 large oil companies with familiar names like Standard Oil of New Jersey (and also California, Indiana, and Ohio), Atlantic, Gulf, Phillips, Pure, Shell, Sinclair, and Texas (Texaco) accounted for three-quarters of the nation's refinery capacity. Distribution included both company-owned-and-operated outlets and retail operations run by independent dealers, with most of the larger oil companies developing chains that utilized both types.

Automobiles require drivers, gasoline, and roads. No shortage of drivers existed, and the petroleum companies supplied the gasoline. But roads posed a problem. Local governments reluctantly assumed some responsibility for their immediate needs, but paid little, if any, attention to intercity highways. Thus, improved roads for long-distance **travel** lagged behind the other necessities. Oregon in 1919 adopted the first state gasoline tax, 1 cent (about 12 cents in contemporary money) on each gallon sold, and led the way in building highways financed by automotive usage.

Not until 1932 did the federal government levy the first national gasoline tax: 1 cent per gallon (about 15 cents in contemporary money). Officials allocated the revenue to restore declining highway funds, with most of the spending focused on secondary roads that complemented the two-lane highway system connecting major cities. Both state and federal taxes on gas increased throughout the 1930s, and in 1938 the Federal Aid Highway Act called for the construction of four-lane superhighways. The project stalled, however, because of insufficient funds and the growing threat of war.

The 1920s had seen the petroleum industry move rapidly to serve the growing numbers of automobiles on the road, but the Depression downturn meant that gasoline production and capacity exceeded demand. In 1933, one gallon of gasoline cost, on average, 19.64 cents as compared to 23.26 cents in 1926 (roughly $2.96 and $2.63, respectively, in contemporary dollars). The lowest price, 13 cents ($1.96), occurred in 1934; it moved up to 14 cents ($2.07) in 1935 and continued upward with economic recovery. At the same time, registered motor vehicles declined from 26.5 million in 1930 to 24 million in 1933. The number of miles traveled, 206 billion in 1930, dropped to 201 billion in 1933. Undeterred, gasoline stations continued to proliferate, from almost 124,000 in 1930 to 170,000 in 1933. As they multiplied, their architectural designs progressed from curbside pumps to sheds, to houses, and then to houses with canopies. Each change acknowledged the importance of operating efficiently and maintaining high visibility along the roadside.

Decreased driving in the Depression created fierce competition among distributors, and the "gas" station, as a recognizable structure and critical marketing link, had replaced the more primitive "filling" station. Architect C. A. Petersen (active 1920s and 1930s), a popular designer of gas stations, in 1927 created a prefabricated house concept for the Pure Oil Company that he called an "English cottage." It serves as a good historical example of a standardized gas station **design** that became a successful marketing tool for the company. Motorists recognized the distinctive, steep-roofed structures, and business increased.

The concept of using houselike designs promoted the placement of gas stations in residential neighborhoods during the 1920s and 1930s. A station that resembled a house proved more acceptable, especially to middle- and upper middle-class families, than did a more commercial-looking building. It blended in with the surroundings and conveyed a homelike environment where customers could be comfortable. Of course, these stations also had to provide certain services. Some, but not all, even offered rest rooms. The addition of a canopy to protect attendants and customers from weather conditions or a bay to increase the space for repairs became commonplace, but all in all they remained low-key, unobtrusive structures.

The residential gas station, however, possessed certain inherent limitations, the primary one being size. To counter decreasing gasoline sales, many oil companies wanted to increase the number and kind of auxiliary products they offered and place greater emphasis on auto repair. To accomplish these goals, the companies needed to build larger stations to accommodate such changes. With increased size came a fundamental architectural shift, and the more contemporary models superseded the homey residential stations.

In 1934, the Texaco Corporation hired industrial designer Walter Dorwin Teague (1883–1960) to create a new look for the company, a building that would promote maximum sales appeal. He submitted a white, Streamlined box that gave the impression of speed, modernity, and progress. It allowed for larger display areas for the tires, batteries, and other products now offered, as well as larger and more efficient bays for repairs. Other companies quickly adopted variations on his trim, rectangular design, often employing terra cotta, porcelain, and generous amounts of plate glass in the construction process. Frequently competitors modified Teague's flat roof or added some other feature to facilitate customer recognition. With a larger building and additional products and services to offer, the "gas" station had evolved to a "service" station. Many moved from residential neighborhoods to more heavily traveled locations, usually ones providing easy highway access.

Despite the design changes, highway visibility remained a major concern. Some companies incorporated specific, tasteful colors into their stations. In the case of the aforementioned Pure Oil Company, the use of white for the building and bright blue for the roof made the stations easily identifiable to the passing motorist, allowing the facility to be seen as an extension of a particular oil company that provided both dependable service and products.

The 1930s also witnessed the increased use of large, highly visible corporate logos and mascots. For example, in 1934, the Magnolia Petroleum Company, a predecessor to Mobil Oil, erected a large oil derrick on the roof of a downtown Dallas, Texas, building. The derrick supported two 35-by-50-foot red neon signs that formed the image of Pegasus, a great flying horse of mythology. Magnolia's instantly recognizable flying red horse became the company's logo. No matter the neighborhood or city, an oil company and its products could be known by the **architecture** and other corporate symbols that suggested a positive experience for customers.

Stiff competition, however, did not allow a company the luxury of depending entirely upon architecture and location. Methods to undercut the other stations included giveaway promotions such as glassware or dinnerware, and free services, like checking tire pressure and cleaning the windshield. Free road maps enticed travelers. In fact, these maps encouraged competitors to outdo one another with eye-catching colors and attractiveness. Peter Helck (1893–1988), a prominent automotive illustrator, created maps for the Sinclair Oil Company with pictures of lush gas station scenes, a place where everyone would want to buy gas. As part of the campaign, artists depicted well-dressed, happy women in a service station setting, making the maps a promotional tool to show that the gas station offered a clean, safe, and friendly haven for women needing to buy gas.

Advertising imagery frequently included smiling, uniformed attendants, ready to do the customer's bidding. In reality, these cheerful men often did wear company uniforms, and cleaning the windshield and checking the tires and fluids—as well as pumping the gas—became a ritual at most well-run stations. Phillips Petroleum added drama to its advertising. They underwrote famed aviator Wiley Post (1899–1935) as he sought to achieve new altitude records, and stunt flyer Colonel Art Goebel (1895–1973) flew for the company writing Phillips 66 in huge letters in the sky while an associate stayed in **radio** contact and sold Phillips products on the ground.

Several petroleum companies used radio as a means of promoting their products. The Mobil Corporation sponsored *Mobiloil Concerts* from 1929 through 1932 on the National Broadcasting Company (NBC radio) network. The show featured Erno Rapee (1891–1945) as the conductor. Cities Service used NBC to carry *The Cities Service Concerts* from 1925 to 1956, and the series fostered many musical careers, especially that of Jessica Dragonette (1900–1980), one of the more memorable voices of early radio. On the West Coast, Standard Oil underwrote *The Standard Hour*, another musical offering on NBC. It ran successfully from 1926 until the mid-1950s, and represented the company's interest in media-based **education**. Not all shows involved music; some oil firms, like Sinclair, sponsored news broadcasts and public affairs programming.

The Texas Oil Company in 1932 premiered *The Texaco Fire Chief* series on NBC. A popular variety show, it starred Ed Wynn (1886–1966), a former vaudeville headliner who found a new home on radio. When ratings slipped, comedian Jimmy Durante (1893–1980) replaced Wynn in 1935, but the show ceased airing in 1936. Texaco, however, maintained a presence on radio with *The Texaco Star Theater*, a variety series that ran from 1938 to 1946 on the Columbia Broadcasting System (CBS radio). Not to be outdone, Shell Oil had singer Al Jolson (1886–1950) competing with *Shell Chateau*, another variety program that ran from 1935 until 1937, as did Gulf Oil with *Gulf Headliners* (1933–1935), starring Will Rogers (1879–1935) in a mix of comedy and **music**.

From its lowly beginnings in sheds with crude pumps along a curb, the American gas station had, by the 1930s, evolved into a roadside icon. It promised more than fuel; it functioned as an important link in the country's growing love affair with the automobile. The customer bought an image, an understanding that the business guaranteed the best in products and service; that needs, both automotive and personal, would be attended to; and that pleasant, trouble-free driving had become a part of the American way of life.

See also Aviation; Illustrators; Musicals; Streamlining; Transportation

SELECTED READING

Dunning, John. *On the Air: The Encyclopedia of Old-Time Radio*. New York: Oxford University Press, 1998.

Jakle, John A., and Keith A. Sculle. *The Gas Station in America*. Baltimore: Johns Hopkins University Press, 1994.

Witzel, Michael Karl. *The American Gas Station*. New York: Barnes & Noble Books, 1999.

GERSHWIN, GEORGE, & IRA GERSHWIN. These two talented brothers helped bring American popular **music** to new levels. George (1898–1937) composed in ways previously untried; Ira (1896–1983) wrote some of the most unforgettable lyrics ever set to song.

Both entered the field of music at early ages. George started playing the piano as a child. By 1912, his skills earned him pocket money and soon thereafter he had become what the trade called a song plugger. The job originated on New York's Tin Pan Alley, a section of Manhattan's 28th Street between Fifth Avenue and Broadway, where **songwriters and lyricists**, arrangers, and pluggers congregated and interacted with various music publishers; it came to mean the popular music business in general. Song plugging involved taking new tunes to different music publishers in hopes of getting them printed and distributed as **sheet music**. Most pluggers did not write the music they pushed, but they tried hard to convince reluctant publishing firms that their songs and lyrics stood the best chances of commercial success. George soon realized he should be plugging his own music, not someone else's.

In 1919, after writing the melodies for over 30 tunes, George finally met with success; his song "Swanee" became a hit. With lyrics by Irving Caesar (1895–1996), "Swanee" was recorded by Al Jolson (1886–1950), a commanding star of stage, vaudeville, **recordings**, and, later, **movies**. His rendition captivated listeners and it soon became a popular favorite.

While George's star rose, Ira tentatively sought recognition in the competitive field of journalism. He had been an English major at college, and developed some skills as a prose writer; a few reviews and magazine articles came from his pen in 1916–1917, but nothing earthshaking. He finally sensed that perhaps his genius also rested with music.

The two brothers in 1918 worked together for the first time, creating "The Real American Folk Song (Is a Rag)," their contribution to *Ladies First*, a Broadway trifle of the day.

They also joined forces for "Waiting for the Sun to Come Out," a number featured in the 1920 musical *The Sweetheart Shop*. Using the pseudonym "Arthur Francis," Ira continued to labor, on his own, as a lyricist. Success did not come overnight. *Two Little Girls*, a musical produced during the summer of 1921, featured his lyrics, along with music by Vincent Youmans (1898–1946). But he and his brother also had many fresh ideas that would soon come to fruition.

A string of popular Broadway **musicals** at last put the Gershwin name in lights, plays like *Lady, Be Good!* (1924), *Oh, Kay!* (1926), *Funny Face* (1927), and *Show Girl* (1929). Not only did their collaborative efforts do well, but George gained the added reputation of being a "serious" composer. In 1924, he had premiered *Rhapsody in Blue*, a concert piece commissioned by bandleader Paul Whiteman (1890–1967) that received considerable acclaim. A number of preludes and other varied compositions followed, solidifying his position as a significant figure in American music.

Composer George Gershwin (1898–1937). (Courtesy of the Library of Congress)

In 1930, the brothers premiered *Strike Up the Band*, the rewrite of a 1927 play that never got to Broadway. The musical included such gems as "Soon" and "I've Got a Crush on You," as well as the title song. Although *Strike Up the Band* contains nothing topical, it delighted Depression-weary audiences. Immediately on the heels of *Strike Up the Band* came another production featuring Gershwin music. Called *Girl Crazy*, the musical cast two players who became stars during the 1930s, Ethel Merman (1908–1984) and Ginger Rogers (1911–1995). It also featured a score that would become a star in its own right, including "Bidin' My Time," "Embraceable You," "But Not for Me," and the inimitable "I Got Rhythm," particularly as sung by Merman. Her rendition, certainly one of the most energetic performances of any song in any musical, overnight made her one of the biggest sensations on the Broadway stage.

As economic conditions worsened around the country, the Gershwins, emboldened by the success of *Girl Crazy*, collaborated on *Of Thee I Sing* in December 1931. The show's book was written by George S. Kaufman (1889–1961) and Morrie Ryskind (1895–1985), two important theatrical figures. Much of the plot revolves around presidents, politics, and the foibles of governments. The resulting story, satirical and topical, features music to match. Out of that mix came "Love Is Sweeping the Country," "Of Thee I Sing (Baby)," and "Who Cares?" Audiences responded enthusiastically. The play ran for 441 performances, the longest ever for a Gershwin show, and won a Pulitzer Prize for Drama in the libretto and lyrics category.

Along with their Broadway success, the brothers contributed the music to *Delicious* (1931), a musical film notable for another of George's forays into more serious composing. For *Delicious*, he wrote a piece variously called *Manhattan Rhapsody*, *New York Rhapsody*, and *Rhapsody in Rivets*. The first two titles refer to the movie's locale, the last to a section that suggests a riveter working on a construction project. These themes

Lyricist Ira Gershwin (1896–1983). (Courtesy of the Library of Congress)

later coalesced into the *Second Rhapsody for Piano and Orchestra* (1932), an expanded version of the music heard in the film. Not as well-known as his *Rhapsody in Blue*, the work nonetheless shows his continuing interest in blending popular themes with classical writing.

The following year, 1932, Hollywood bought the rights to *Girl Crazy* and brought it to the screen. A lackluster adaptation, the musical had to wait until 1943, when it resurfaced as a sparkling Mickey Rooney (b. 1920)–**Judy Garland** (1922–1969) vehicle. After being retitled, *Girl Crazy* came around yet again in 1962 as *When the Boys Meet the Girls*, a testament to the original play's staying power.

The Gershwins returned to Broadway in early 1933 with *Pardon My English*. It failed to arouse much interest, despite having a melodious score, and closed after a disappointing 46 performances. It contained such standards as "Lorelei" and "Isn't It a Pity?" and might have been expected to do better. Audiences clearly thought otherwise.

Despite the commercial failure of *Pardon My English*, the brothers opened *Let 'em Eat Cake* in the fall of 1933. Working once more with writers Kaufman and Ryskind, they proceeded to mount another topical play, one filled with Depression-era references in their lyrics. Numbers like "Down with Ev'rything That's Up," "Union Square," and the title song made for a sequel to *Of Thee I Sing*, even to the point of bringing in characters from the earlier production to the new one. Musically, however, about the only number of any real distinction in *Let 'em Eat Cake* was the romantic "Mine," and one good song could not save the day. After 90 performances, it closed.

George and Ira's music, as bright and original as ever, could not always overcome the plays, but the brothers never looked back and continued to innovate. For example, George wrote the intriguing *Variations on "I Got Rhythm"* in 1934; he had always held a special interest in the show-stopping number from *Girl Crazy*, and this extended exposition reflected that interest. Even bigger projects, however, awaited development.

After an out-of-town run in Boston, they unveiled **Porgy and Bess** at New York's Alvin Theater in 1935. Their final Broadway production, critics have debated whether or not *Porgy and Bess* should be seen as musical theater posing as opera, or opera that contains elements of musical theater. Whatever its classification, this unique team clearly envisioned *Porgy and Bess* as an attempt to challenge an environment more used to frothy musical comedies, a play that straddles the difficult line between high art and popular entertainment.

In the summer of 1936, the brothers left New York and headed to Hollywood. Already established in the film capital with their previous movies, they proceeded to amaze everyone with their inventiveness in a trio of new pictures. First came *Shall We Dance*, the seventh in a remarkable group of musicals starring **Fred Astaire** (1899–1987) **and Ginger Rogers**. This movie served as the only Gershwin contribution to the series, but the songs range from the lovely "They Can't Take That Away from Me" to the happy "Slap That Bass," and in between come "Let's Call the Whole Thing Off" and "They All Laughed." Music of this caliber shows off Astaire and Rogers at their best, and virtually the entire score has entered the realm of standards, those familiar chestnuts known by all.

RKO Pictures, the studio that had released *Shall We Dance*, doubtless wanted to cash in on the ongoing popularity of Astaire, Rogers, and the Gershwins, but an additional collaboration could not be arranged at that moment. Instead, RKO concocted a second picture, *A Damsel in Distress* (1937), a look-alike that stars Fred Astaire and substitutes Joan Fontaine (b. 1917). Thanks to another bright score, plus the comedy of **radio** stars George Burns (1896–1996) and Gracie Allen (1895–1964), the film passes muster, but Joan Fontaine can never equal Ginger Rogers on the dance floor. Memorable songs like "A Foggy Day," "Nice Work If You Can Get It," and "Things Are Looking Up" lift *A Damsel in Distress* above the general run of movie musicals and reinforce the shared genius of the Gershwins.

The final film in the trio, *The Goldwyn Follies* (1938), brings a number of celebrities together, but not always successfully. It also sports another fine Gershwin medley. George died in 1937, but *The Goldwyn Follies* had already gone into production. Thus the numbers heard in the movie stand among his last works. "Love Walked In," "I Was Doing All Right," and the poignant—in light of his death—"Love Is Here to Stay" easily survive the silly plot and make a fine legacy. In order to complete the project, Ira worked with composer Vernon Duke (1903–1969) on "Spring Again."

Strike Up the Band (1940) served as the final film of the era to claim a joint Gershwin score. Ostensibly a remake of the 1930 Broadway show of the same name, the movie version mysteriously drops virtually all the original music—"Soon," "I've Got a Crush on You"—for a rather flavorless score done by others.

Over the years, the Gershwins produced a timeless body of work, the kind of music that never goes out of date. The melodies of "Beginner's Luck" (*Shall We Dance*, 1937), "I Can't Be Bothered Now" (*A Damsel in Distress*, 1937), and "Our Love Is Here to Stay" (*The Goldwyn Follies*, 1938) certainly linger in the mind, but the words bring the music to life, the recalled snippets of a line or two that allow the song to live on in memory. After George's untimely death, Ira continued to write for many years, working with a number of different composers.

See also Magazines; Political Parties; Stage Productions

SELECTED READING

Hyland, William G. *George Gershwin: A New Biography*. New York: Praeger, 2003.

Jablonski, Edward. *Gershwin*. New York: Doubleday, 1987.

Rosenberg, Deena. *Fascinating Rhythm: The Collaboration of George and Ira Gershwin*. New York: Penguin Books [Plume], 1991.

Zinsser, William. *Easy to Remember: The Great American Songwriters and Their Songs*. Jaffrey, NH: David R. Godine, 2000

GOLF. At the time of the Great Depression, golf suffered the onus of being a "rich man's sport." The game had grown sharply in suburban popularity during the 1920s, especially among those able to afford memberships in exclusive country clubs. With the crash, however, few could pay the dues any longer, memberships dwindled, many

Spectators watch a round of golf. (Courtesy of the Library of Congress)

clubs had to close their doors, and golf momentarily fell into the doldrums. Then, in an ironic turn of events, the Depression provided a beneficial side effect for everyday golfers. As enrollments fell off in once-exclusive clubs and private courses, the directors had to democratize them and open their links to public play. In addition, the Works Progress Administration (WPA; 1935–1943, name changed to Work Projects Administration in 1939) built many city-owned municipal courses projects during the Depression years, doubling their number from 10 years earlier. By the end of the decade, more people played golf than in 1930, and most of these new enthusiasts lacked any formal club affiliations.

Another spur to the game in the early 1930s involved a young man named Bobby Jones (1902–1971). An amateur player from Georgia, Jones rose to fame during the 1920s by winning many national and international tournaments, making him the world's ranking golfer. In 1930, however, he achieved in the sport what many thought to be unattainable: the "grand slam." In that year, Jones won the British Amateur and the British Open, and for a moment his exploits captured the public imagination. When he got back to the States, he even received a ticker-tape parade from the city of New York. But those two victories provided only half the story. Jones then proceeded to win both the 1930 U.S. Open and the U.S. Amateur championships, giving him all four major championships in a single year, a feat that allowed him to bask in reams of media-generated celebrity in those dark early days of the Depression.

In the popular mind, Bobby Jones represented the little guy beating the pros. The public took him to its heart, and golf had its first real superstar, an inspiration to weekend players everywhere. Following his Grand Slam, he retired from the game at the age of 28, but remained in the limelight throughout the decade. He went on **radio** with a weekly show that re-created high points of his illustrious career, made several golf instruction films for Warner Brothers, lent his name to Spalding for a new line of clubs, and was instrumental in designing and setting up a new course in Augusta, Georgia, that would become home to the prestigious Master's Golf Tournament.

Apparently Hollywood maintained reservations about golfing **movies**, and only a few pictures other than the Bobby Jones instructional films came out during the decade. In

1930, Fox Films released *Part-Time Wife*, with Leila Hyams (1905–1977), a romantic drama about a woman who loves golf. Eight years later, *Change of Heart*, a remake of *Part-Time Wife*, played in theaters, this time around with the little-known Gloria Stuart (b. 1910) as the woman golfer. A musical, *Follow Thru* (1930), and another romantic picture, *Love in the Rough* (1930), along with a handful of comedy shorts, round out the bill for the 1930s, a dismal decade in the realm of films about golf.

See also Advertising; Leisure & Recreation; Musicals

SELECTED READING
Grimsley, Will. *Golf: Its History, People, and Events*. Englewood Cliffs, NJ: Prentice-Hall, 1966.
————, ed. *A Century of Sports by the Associated Press Sports Staff*. New York: Associated Press, 1971.

GONE WITH THE WIND (NOVEL & MOVIE). This best-selling 1936 novel was written by Margaret Mitchell (1900–1949); its 1939 movie adaptation went on to become one of the most successful motion pictures in the history of Hollywood. Mitchell, a reporter for the *Atlanta Journal* and a native of that city, began writing *Gone with the Wind* in 1926, ostensibly for her own amusement, if the subsequent mountains of publicity for the novel and its author can be believed. The book recounts the life of Scarlett O'Hara, one of the more memorable heroines of fiction, and much of the story has entered the national memory. By the end of the decade, the book had gone through innumerable reprintings, could be found in a variety of translations, and continued to sell briskly. The movie version electrified audiences and rekindled sales of the book, although it would be difficult to call the end result a faithful adaptation of the novel.

The remarkable acceptance of *Gone with the Wind* perplexed—and angered—many of those in the literary establishment of the time; they charged that the novel, and later the movie, consisted of little more than Southern soap opera and possessed little merit. Their complaints, however, fell on deaf ears. Commercial success—it had sold more than 1 million copies by the end of 1936, and would go on to sell millions more—does not automatically equate with mediocrity, however, and a sufficient number of critics saw enough good qualities in the novel that it won the Pulitzer Prize for Literature in 1937. The perfect story for a nation that had just struggled through an economic depression, it attracted readers and viewers everywhere. Mitchell herself commented that the book's basic theme revolved around survival, certainly a fitting subject for the times. The novel's closing words, spoken by the indomitable Scarlett, seemed a prescription for the ills that continued to beset the country: "I'll think of it all tomorrow.... After all, tomorrow is another day."

Mitchell began writing *Gone with the Wind* while recuperating from an accident. She knew both Civil War and Atlanta history intimately and made that knowledge the foundation of her novel. Literary sleuths have been tempted, over the years, to read much of Mitchell's own personal history into the work, but that kind of analysis, even if partially factual, runs the risk of distorting the creative process. Autobiographical or purely fictional, *Gone with the Wind* cloaks itself in a romantic story and resists contemporary references. A denial of the present can be a form of response to it, but Scarlett, along with

Rhett Butler, Ashley Wilkes, Melanie Hamilton, and Tara, Scarlett's idealized planta-tion home, so enamored its audiences that few probably approached the story in such terms.

Almost from the time that Macmillan, the book's publishers, circulated prepublica-tion copies, the possibilities of a movie version began to be discussed. Mitchell herself took no interest and wanted no part in these conversations, leaving it all in the hands of intermediaries. In 1936, David O. Selznick (1902–1965), a brilliant producer and studio executive at Metro-Goldwyn-Mayer, succeeded in procuring the motion picture rights, but it would take him and an army of screenwriters, editors, and production personnel almost three years to bring it to the screen.

To pique public interest in the picture, MGM waged a nationwide talent search, commencing in 1937, to select the actress who would play Scarlett. Finally, after reams of studio-generated paper had been expended discussing possible choices, Vivien Leigh (1913–1967), a little-known British actress, won the part, although how genuine the media contest had been remains open to question. Given his popularity, looks, and screen persona, everyone correctly assumed Clark Gable (1901–1960) had secured the role of Rhett Butler. In the meantime, fan **magazines**, such an important part of movie publicity in the 1930s, breathlessly reported on anything even remotely associated with the project. As the December 1939 opening night approached, MGM went so far as to replicate the portico of Tara for a gala celebration at Loew's Grand Theater in Atlanta. All the hoopla paid off: *Gone with the Wind* immediately rocketed to the top of any and all movie listings, and it has continued to be an enduring motion picture classic.

Although very much Selznick's pet project, the movie of course required a director. George Cukor (1899–1983; *Little Women* [1933], *Camille* [1936], others) initially took the helm of the picture, but after nine weeks of hectic shooting, Victor Fleming (1889–1949; *Treasure Island* [1934], *The Good Earth* [1937], others) replaced him. Not even Fleming, fresh from his success with **The Wizard of Oz** (1939), could handle such a mam-moth production; he collapsed on the set, and MGM finally had to have the help of vet-eran Sam Wood (1883–1949; *A Night at the Opera* [1935], *Madame X* [1937], others), to bring it to completion, although Fleming usually gets listed as the sole director in the screen credits. Some 15 screenwriters, including Sidney Howard (1891–1939), F. Scott Fitzgerald (1896–1940), and Ben Hecht (1894–1964), labored to create a workable script while trying to remain true to Mitchell's prose, and no one seems absolutely sure who should get recognition for what.

The Academy of Motion Picture Arts and Sciences harbored no such doubts. It awarded *Gone with the Wind* an Oscar for Best Picture of 1939, declared Victor Fleming Best Director, Vivien Leigh Best Actress, and Hattie McDaniel (1895–1952) Best Sup-porting Actress. Sidney Howard took the award for Best Screenplay, and three more Academy Awards went to others connected with the production.

The negotiations over the *Gone with the Wind* script have become the stuff of Hollywood legend; for weeks the producers and people representing the **Hollywood Production Code** went back and forth over innumerable details, most of which would be seen today as mere nitpicking. When the two sides had agreed upon just about everything, there remained one problem word in the script: "damn." In a climactic scene, Gable's Rhett Butler utters the famous sentence, "Frankly, my dear, I don't give a damn," almost the same words that Mitchell had penned (in the book, the line lacks the lead-off "Frankly"). Either way, the discussion seems innocuous by today's standards, but vitally important both to the novel and the movie. In that period of strict code adherence, much often rode on little, and the code explicitly forbade profanity. The discussion went back and forth. Finally, Robert Breen (1890–1965), the stern man in charge of enforcing code regulations and the last word in any troublesome interpretations, reluctantly gave in, a rare concession. The forbidden "damn" remained in the script and the picture went on to become one of the fabled successes in the history of Hollywood.

Variously called "the greatest movie ever made," "a woman's picture," "a potboiler," and "an expensive soap opera," *Gone with the Wind* certainly wrapped up the 1930s in grand style. An expensive exercise in historical escapism, it taps into the country's continuing fascination with its own past. Perhaps the story's recurring theme of overcoming adversity, of moving from victim to survivor, is about as "timely" as the cinematic *Gone with the Wind* ever gets. But for sheer entertainment, the real reason people attend **movies**, it stands as the champion of the decade.

See also Best Sellers; Soap Operas; Spectacle & Costume Drama Films

SELECTED READING

Flamini, Roland. *Scarlett, Rhett, and a Cast of Thousands: The Filming of* Gone with the Wind. New York: Macmillan, 1975.
Howard, Sidney. GWTW: *The Screenplay*. Ed. Richard Harwell. New York: Macmillan, 1980.
Mitchell, Margaret. *Gone with the Wind*. New York: Macmillan, 1936.
Pyron, Darden Asbury. *Southern Daughter: The Life of Margaret Mitchell*. New York: Oxford University Press, 1991.
Vertrees, Alan David. *Selznick's Vision:* Gone with the Wind *and Hollywood Filmmaking*. Austin: University of Texas Press, 1997.

GOODMAN, BENNY. A native of Chicago, Benny Goodman (1909–1986) enjoyed the distinction of being crowned the "King of **Swing**." During his long tenure as a popular bandleader, he fronted some of the most important and influential swing orchestras and groups of the 1930s. He began studying the clarinet at age 10; he first played professionally in the 1920s. Like so many musicians at that time, Goodman worked with various groups, including a stint with the Ben Pollack (1903–1971) orchestra in the latter years of the decade. In addition to playing with Pollack, he did considerable freelancing and recording and knew many of the major instrumentalists of the era.

Goodman met **music** critic and entrepreneur John Hammond (1910–1987) in 1931, and from that association he came to know, and play with, Teddy Wilson (1912–1986), a black pianist. In the later 1930s, Goodman and Wilson collaborated in creating some memorable trio and quartet **recordings**, one of the first instances of an openly interracial musical partnership in what then existed as a mostly segregated profession.

In 1932, Goodman formed his first group, a small orchestra whose main claim to fame was that it accompanied **Russ Columbo** (1908–1934), a crooner who blazed a brief but intense career. Two years later, Goodman organized his own swing-oriented orchestra, a 12-piece aggregation that quickly gained some notice. Because of the growing popularity of dance music at this time, the National Broadcasting Company (NBC **radio**) contracted the Goodman orchestra to play on the network's *Let's Dance* program, a Saturday night show that premiered in December 1934 and aired from 10:30 P.M. until

Clarinetist and band leader Benny Goodman (1909–1986). (Courtesy of the Library of Congress)

1:30 A.M. in the East (three hours earlier on the West Coast). Most listeners had to stay up late to catch the band, plus Goodman's group shared the spotlight with the Latin sounds of Xavier Cugat (1900–1990) and the blander melodies of Kel Murray (active 1930s). Despite the time slot, the broadcasts gave him national exposure, and he even titled the band's theme song "Let's Dance" (1935; music by Joseph Bonime, Gregory Stone, and Fanny Baldridge [all active in 1930s]).

The money earned on *Let's Dance* gave Goodman the freedom to pay some of the country's top arrangers to add quality music to the band's repertoire. On the advice of Hammond, he secured the services of **Fletcher Henderson** (1897–1952), one of the best in the business, and a fine bandleader in his own right. Henderson contributed charts for such classics as "Blue Skies" (composed in 1927), "Sometimes I'm Happy" (composed 1927), "King Porter Stomp" (composed 1925), and many others; the orchestra subsequently recorded them and Goodman felt decidedly optimistic about the future. With his contract with NBC expiring in the spring of 1935, promoters urged Goodman to take the band on the road.

That summer the musicians embarked on an east-to-west tour, but much of the cross-country audience sat unprepared for the jazzy rhythms and solos—what would come to be called swing—that characterized the aggregation. Management and dancers wanted current hits or old standards, and some even requested that he play "more slowly" or skip the up-tempo numbers. Contrary to some of the stories that have been told about the trip, however, it cannot be called an unmitigated disaster. People had been listening to their radios, and so Goodman and his band had some prior fame. Locations like Pittsburgh and Salt Lake City gave the group reasonably warm welcomes. An even greater change occurred when the band played Oakland, California. Since people on the West Coast heard *Let's Dance* at a more reasonable time, they knew what to expect and they liked what they heard. From Oakland, the orchestra moved to Los Angeles' Palomar Ballroom. Many credit that particular 1935 concert with sparking the Swing Era. A rousing success, it alerted young people everywhere that a new musical form had arrived.

Heading back east, the band played to another warm welcome in Chicago's Congress Hotel. The Windy City pinned the label "swing" on Goodman's music, and the name stuck—along with the band: the Congress Hotel booking stretched out for eight months. While ensconced there, Goodman, with no particular fanfare, introduced Teddy Wilson as a member of his trio, with Gene Krupa (1909–1973) on drums. No one openly objected, everything went smoothly, and their playing marked one of the first instances of public racial integration in popular music. A number of mixed-raced recordings had been made before this event, but in the confines of a studio, never before a live audience. Goodman's trio format would grow to a quartet when Lionel Hampton (1908–2002), a black vibraharpist, joined their ranks. Both Wilson and

Hampton became permanent additions to the band, which led a few other orchestras to begin integrating their ranks as the decade moved on.

After his eventual return to New York City in 1936, Goodman continued to play dances, but to much more appreciative audiences. Other offers followed: in the summer, the band landed a new radio contract. *The Camel Caravan*, a show that had originally debuted over the Columbia Broadcasting System (CBS radio) in 1933, hired the aggregation, and used *Benny Goodman's Swing School* as part of a new title. Broadcast on Tuesday evenings, the refurbished show would last for three years on CBS and then move to rival NBC for an additional year.

Ballrooms and dancehalls bid for open dates; the band toured New England and played the Steel Pier in Atlantic City. Hollywood beckoned, and the Benny Goodman Orchestra had bit parts in two motion pictures, *The Big Broadcast of 1937* (1936) and *Hollywood Hotel* (1937). Always busy, they also cut studio recordings for several labels at this time.

While all these offers were coming in, the Madhattan Room, a posh ballroom located in New York's Hotel Pennsylvania, signed the clarinetist and his orchestra to a long-term contract that commenced at the end of 1936. Since his work at the Madhattan Room involved evenings only, Goodman agreed to play a matinee at the Paramount Theater on Times Square. The orchestra arrived early at the theater for rehearsal on March 3, 1937, a cold, wintry morning. But people had already been waiting outside the theater since before dawn; the youthful crowd grew as opening time approached, the line snaking around the theater. Worried police ordered the management to open the Paramount's doors at 8:00 A.M., and over 3,000 fans piled inside, while another 2,000 disappointed ones milled around on the street.

After a brief rehearsal in the theater's basement, the band assembled on an ascending stage and rose to the cheers of thousands of enthusiasts. As the orchestra went into its numbers, the fans, warmed by the music, got up and began to **jitterbug** in the aisles. Ushers had no luck in getting them back into their seats, and the impromptu dance and concert continued, with happy teens surging down to the band itself; a few of the more daring got on the stage and jitterbugged next to the musicians. Everyone seemed to take it all in stride, and the orchestra played five shows that day. Estimates place overall attendance at 21,000 people, far more than would ever hear the band in a hotel setting. Goodman even made a return visit to the Paramount in 1938, and history repeated itself—the audience out in the aisles, the dancing—giving birth to a swing tradition.

In January 1938, Benny Goodman and His Orchestra stormed Carnegie Hall, one of the citadels of high culture. Impresario Sol Hurok (1888–1974), a man usually connected to the classical world of symphony orchestras and chamber groups, arranged the event. The remarkable attention Goodman had been receiving in concerts, hotel appearances, and on radio had convinced many that he deserved a more "respectable" hearing, that perhaps swing had qualities unappreciated by the musical elite.

Carnegie Hall billed his appearance as a "**jazz** concert," although "swing concert" would probably serve as a more accurate description. Swing or jazz, Goodman and his entourage legitimized contemporary popular music for the broadest possible audience. Replete in cutaway and tails and clearly the main attraction, Goodman led his big band, along with his trio and quartet, and all the players came properly attired in tuxedos. A number of black musicians made guest appearances, performing side by side with their white counterparts, demonstrating how, in a segregated society, swing could act as a bridge, bringing races and cultures together. No one danced in the aisles, but the black-tie audience clearly tapped its feet and relished the exposure to this new phenomenon. Fortunately, sound engineers recorded the concert, preserving the moment.

Following Carnegie Hall, Goodman went on to other successes. Some of the best instrumentalists and vocalists in the land performed with his various bands, and many a career had its beginnings in the orchestra's ranks. By the time of the concert, swing had become the dominant musical form in the United States. Thanks largely to records and radio, but also because of live shows, dance appearances, disc jockeys, **jukeboxes**, and the **movies**, swing amassed the largest, most diverse audience any musical form had ever enjoyed. And much credit must go to "the King of Swing." Goodman proved an innovator on many levels, both musical and social. Because of his enormous popularity and commercial success, he probably did more to make swing a national trend during the 1930s than any other musician.

See also Count Basie; Duke Ellington; Hotels; Glenn Miller; Race Relations & Stereotyping; Radio Networks; Youth

SELECTED READING
Collier, James Lincoln. *Benny Goodman and the Swing Era.* New York: Oxford University Press, 1989.
Firestone, Ross. *Swing, Swing, Swing: The Life and Times of Benny Goodman.* New York: W. W. Norton, 1993.
Simon, George T. *The Big Bands.* New York: Macmillan, 1967.
Yanow, Scott. *Swing.* San Francisco: Miller Freeman Books, 2000.

GRAND OLE OPRY. The most successful country music **radio** show ever, *Grand Ole Opry* first came on the air in the fall of 1925 as the *WSM Barn Dance*. That initial title reflected the success of another, similar show, **The National Barn Dance**. Both broadcasts had sprung from the fertile brain of George Dewey Hay (1895–1968), a radio programming pioneer. He had developed the idea of a live country music show in 1924 while working with WLS, a Chicago station. Success took him the following year to Nashville, Tennessee, and WSM. There he created the *WSM Barn Dance*, a show almost identical to his previous Chicago effort. To prevent confusion, the WSM program in 1927 changed its name to *Grand Ole Opry*, hardly "Grand Opera" but a humorous play on words.

A strong signal, coupled with the rising popularity of country music, helped *Grand Ole Opry* attract a wide audience on Saturday nights, its regular time. The National Broadcasting Company (NBC radio), already leading the country field with *The National Barn Dance*, picked up the show for network audiences in 1939 and kept it in the schedule until 1957. From the end of the 1930s onward, listeners could therefore hear both *The National Barn Dance* and *Grand Ole Opry* in back-to-back time slots on network radio. With the demise of most network programming in the 1950s, WSM kept *Grand Ole Opry* when NBC dropped it, and it has continued on the air, a Nashville institution, into the present.

Often called a "hillbilly show," *Grand Ole Opry* made no effort to alter that perception. Listeners heard a broadcast of a stage show that relied on rustic humor, costumes, and numerous amateur musicians, many from the surrounding Tennessee hills. Eager audiences traveled for miles to be entertained by Dr. Humphrey Bate (1875–1936) and His Possum Hunters, harmonica player Deford Bailey (1899–1982), banjoist Uncle Dave Macon (1870–1952) and his guitarist son Dorris (active 1930s), George Wilkerson (active 1930s) and the Fruit Jar Drinkers, the Crook Brothers (Herman and Lewis; active 1930s), and singer Roy Acuff (1903–1992) and His Smoky Mountain Boys. George D. Hay even created a continuing role for himself in the skits, performing as "the Solemn Ole Judge."

In time, the production grew more polished, but it never forsook its rural roots. Like its Chicago counterpart, *Grand Ole Opry* quickly outgrew the WSM studios and began to perform in a series of ever-larger Nashville theaters and auditoriums. It added new entertainers and attracted new fans. Hollywood eventually took note of this phenomenon, and in 1939 Republic Pictures released *Grand Ole Opry*, a low-budget musical starring many of the Nashville regulars. From the time of its humble radio beginnings, this hillbilly-oriented show introduced millions of listeners to a hitherto undiscovered niche area of American popular culture.

See also Hillbillies; Movies; Musicals; Radio Networks

SELECTED READING
Dunning, John. *On the Air: The Encyclopedia of Old-Time Radio*. New York: Oxford University Press, 1998.
Wolfe, Charles K. *A Good-Natured Riot: The Birth of the Grand Ole Opry*. Nashville, TN: Country Music Foundation Press, 1999.

GRAPES OF WRATH, THE (NOVEL & MOVIE). John Steinbeck (1902–1968) made his literary debut in 1929 with *Cup of Gold*, a novel that received several good notices but did not sell well with the general public. Undaunted, he wrote two more works of fiction, but they also had little impact. With the publication of *Tortilla Flat* in 1935, he finally began to establish a following. The next year saw *In Dubious Battle*, a tale of migrant fruit pickers in California. At about the same time, Steinbeck wrote a series of newspaper articles dealing with the seasonal farm laborers who worked in the fertile California valleys. *In Dubious Battle* and the journalism served in many ways as the direct predecessors of *The Grapes of Wrath* (1939). He next published *Of Mice and Men* (1937), the story of two itinerants, Lennie and George. It caught everyone's attention, and at age 35, John Steinbeck had arrived.

With *Of Mice and Men*'s success assured, Steinbeck turned to a pet project, a novel that incorporated his interest in the effects of the Dust Bowl in the Midwest, the plight of migratory workers, and shifts he had observed in American culture during the worst of the Great Depression. These were large themes by any estimation, and Steinbeck worked diligently for almost two years. *The Grapes of Wrath* appeared in bookstores in the spring of 1939.

An overnight sensation, the novel won acclaim from critics and public alike. It also generated considerable controversy; newspaper editors, librarians, and politicians from the southwestern tier of states, but especially Oklahoma and even a few farther afield, condemned the book for language, vulgarity, questionable situations, and what many felt constituted an un-American (i.e., unflattering) view of their localities. Numerous schools and libraries banned it, and some would-be censors wanted the publisher, the Viking Press, to suppress any further printings, but their appeals fell on deaf ears. Steinbeck's work was enjoying extensive publicity, and that equaled escalating sales. Shortly after its release, and wisely sensing the excitement generated by the book, movie producer Darryl F. Zanuck (1902–1979) purchased the film rights to *The Grapes of Wrath* for the then-princely sum of $75,000 (slightly over $1 million in contemporary dollars). The book won that year's Pulitzer Prize, and it remained entrenched on best-seller lists throughout 1939 and well into 1940.

When he started writing *The Grapes of Wrath*, Steinbeck envisioned alternating chapters, one of exposition (Route 66, roadside diners, migrant camps, etc.), followed by one more narrative in nature, the continuing story of the trials besetting the Joad family. Although he did not stick unwaveringly to this pattern, he came close, and the alternations give *The Grapes of Wrath* a unique structure. Employing cadences reminiscent of the King James Version of the Bible, along with earthy humor and hillbilly stereotypes, the Joads' story retells in contemporary terms the flight of the Jews out of Egypt as told in Exodus. Steinbeck freely inserts a mix of religious imagery and realistic detail in his story to give it universality. The expository sections, in particular, use varying styles, from a flat, reportorial tone to soaring rhetorical passages to create a portrait of the southwestern United States in the early 1930s, a time when the plight of dispossessed farmers had reached its height. These slices of life, sometimes funny, sometimes heartbreaking, show Steinbeck's sharp perceptive powers. The narrative parts, on the other hand, showcase a gifted storyteller, and the Joads emerge as a memorable family of survivors.

With the book still fresh in everyone's minds, 20th Century Fox in 1940 released a film adaptation, an unusually quick media turnaround. The studio had wisely assigned the picture to director John Ford (1894–1973). A veteran of countless productions dating back to 1917 and the completely forgotten *Red Saunders Plays Cupid*, Ford had, during the 1930s, established a reputation as a sensitive director capable of adapting varied material into memorable **movies** like *The Informer* (1935), *Stagecoach* (1939), and *Drums along the Mohawk* (1939). In addition, the studio brought on board the gifted Nunnally Johnson (1897–1977) as screenwriter. Johnson had previously worked with Ford on *The Prisoner of Shark Island* (1936), another historical picture, so the two knew one another and shared some interests.

By the end of the decade, when both the book and the movie had aroused the public, the country had weathered most of the rigors of the Great Depression and indeed enjoyed something of an economic upswing. Whereas the novel displays strong liberal sympathies (even—some of his more upset critics would claim—leftist, Communist, or socialist tendencies), the movie avoids direct criticism of the big targets of the book: banks and corporate agriculture. Chase Manhattan Bank may have played a silent role in that decision, since it owned considerable stock in 20th Century Fox. At any rate, the villains in the film become nameless "theys" rather than being identified as greedy financial institutions as Steinbeck does in his writing.

Johnson also reordered the sequences found in the novel, so that the movie's upbeat conclusion has the Joads arriving at a pleasant government camp, an episode taken from much earlier in the original story. The desperate ending that appears in the published *Grapes of Wrath* has the Joads living miserably in a boxcar. Daughter Rose of Sharon, who recently delivered a stillborn child, in a final act of charity offers her breast to a starving man, a faint note of hope that life will go on. With the restrictions presented by the **Hollywood Production Code**, such a scene obviously could not be included in any major movie of the 1930s or 1940s, making Johnson's repositioning of chapters understandable. In acknowledgment of the excellence of both book and movie, the two variations work. The happier ending to the film hardly mitigates its overall power, and Steinbeck loses little in the transition, although those devoted to the novel have argued strongly against the change.

Because of the calm sincerity he projected on screen, Henry Fonda (1905–1982), a popular actor and one whom John Ford had used previously, plays Tom Joad, the central figure in the story. A stellar supporting cast complements Fonda. Shot as a stark black-and-white slice of realism, the movie resembles some of the documentary **photography** commissioned by the Farm Security Administration (FSA; 1937–1943), a **New Deal** government agency that wanted Americans to witness the living conditions many endured.

The Grapes of Wrath received a total of seven Academy Award nominations (Best Picture, Best Director, Best Screenplay, Best Actor, Best Supporting Actress, Best Sound Recording, and Best Film Editing), and won two of them. It lost for Best Picture of 1940 to *Rebecca*, another outstanding film. John Ford won as Best Director. In the supporting actress category, Jane Darwell (1879–1967) captured the award for her strong portrait of Ma Joad, the person who holds the clan together.

An unblinking portrait of Depression-era America, both in print and on film, *The Grapes of Wrath* has emerged as an American classic. In 1962, Steinbeck received the ultimate accolade for an author when the Swedish academy awarded him the Nobel Prize in Literature. In their comments, the judges mentioned *The Grapes of Wrath* by name.

See also Auto Camps; Automobiles; Woody Guthrie; Hillbillies; Newspapers; Political Parties; Regionalism; Religion; Restaurants; Social Consciousness Films; Travel

SELECTED READING
Bergman, Andrew. *We're in the Money: Depression America and Its Films*. New York: Harper & Row [Colophon], 1971.
French, Warren G. *John Steinbeck*. New York: Twayne, 1985.
Parini, Jay. *John Steinbeck: A Biography*. New York: Henry Holt, 1995.
Sklar, Robert. *Movie-Made America: A Cultural History of American Cinema*. New York: Vintage Books, 1994.

GROCERY STORES & SUPERMARKETS. Prior to the 1930s, a loose collection of small, independent grocery stores, both urban and rural, dotted the United States. These establishments primarily served neighborhoods and offered their customers full, personalized service—fresh vegetables and dairy products from local farmers, orders placed by telephone, monthly credit accounts, and home delivery of purchases. If shoppers came to the store, they would ask a clerk behind the counter for specific items that employees boxed or bagged. The customer then took them home or had them delivered.

The late 1800s and early 1900s witnessed the appearance of a series of shopping innovations, including cash-and-carry and self-service, which led to the evolution of a new

An old-fashioned neighborhood grocery store in Newark, Ohio. (Courtesy of the Library of Congress)

concept of grocery retailing. By the 1930s, this enterprise came to be called a "supermarket," a spacious business with large inventories of **food** products and nonfood items.

During the earlier reign of small mom-and-pop grocery stores, several variables necessitated daily shopping. At home, refrigerators and iceboxes, some without any freezer components, kept only small amounts of food fresh and edible. In many communities, each grocery store specialized in specific products requiring stops at several—the butcher, the baker, and the produce dealer. In rural areas, enterprising village grocers sent huckster wagons out into the countryside to sell a wide variety of small items, making customers dependent upon when the wagons arrived. Frequently the staples, canned goods, and prepared foods they carried would be bartered or exchanged for fresh dairy products, vegetables, eggs, meats—items that would then be sold in the grocers' stores.

The Great Atlantic and Pacific Tea Company (commonly known as A&P), founded in 1859, serves as one example of a specialized food business evolving into a chain grocery store. Located in New York City, the A&P sold spices, **coffee,** and **tea.** In light of its early success, the company opened more stores and in 1880 began manufacturing baking powder, its first branded food product designed to sell in its own retail outlets. By the end of the nineteenth century, A&P inventories included a wide range of grocery items. Continuing to be innovative in its operation, A&P instituted a cash-and-carry policy in 1912, opened its 10,000th store in 1923, and featured unadorned furnishings and fixtures in its 1927 "no frills" A&P Economy Store in Jersey City, New Jersey.

In another part of the country, Clarence Saunders (1881–1953) in 1916 founded a grocery store in Memphis, Tennessee. Over the succeeding years, his Piggly Wiggly Corporation offered to hundreds of independently owned outlets the opportunity to be franchised under the Piggly Wiggly name, giving birth to a successful grocery chain. Mr. Saunders felt that the traditional transactions between customers and clerks resulted in wasted time and man hours, and he introduced self-service in Piggly Wiggly markets. Unlike a small, independent grocery store where shoppers received continuous, personal assistance, this concept allowed the shopper to select both prepackaged and loose food products directly from shelves and containers. Most customers carried baskets, made their choices, and took their selections to a cash register for purchase.

On the West Coast, Safeway Stores opened for business in Los Angeles, California, just before World War I as the Sam Seelig Company. The enterprise quickly grew, and a 1926 merger of the now-600 Seelig stores with the 673 Skaggs' Cash Stores created a new chain and the Seelig's Safeway name became official in 1927. Throughout the country, the new chain stores of the 1920s and 1930s boasted of their large number of locations. The space of each individual store, however, remained limited and carried a small inventory.

Despite the success of cash-and-carry and self-service in the chains, most small operators did not explore these retailing methods until the early 1930s. With the Depression, merchants, well aware that people had less money to spend for food, began to focus on how to attract customers to their stores and some followed the A&P, Piggly Wiggly, or Safeway examples. Entrepreneurs converted abandoned buildings into "warehouse grocery stores" and advertised cut-rate food prices. Shoppers at these warehouse arrangements engaged in self-service by strolling along aisles and choosing their purchases from displays stacked high on large, easily accessible tables. As a rule, customers, food manufacturers, and distributors liked such an innovative approach.

In 1930, Michael Cullen (1884–1936), with several years experience as a clerk with A&P, and sales manager for two other chains, Mutual Grocery and Kroger Stores, leased an abandoned garage close to a busy shopping district in Jamaica, New York. There he opened the King Kullen Market, the business usually credited with being the first of this new kind of "cafeteria" grocery store. Ten times the size of most stores of that time, King Kullen Market carried fresh meat and groceries, and promised to keep prices low. The stores enjoyed considerable early success, and 17 King Kullen markets served customers throughout the Northeast by the end of 1936.

Big Bear market in Elizabeth, New Jersey, followed suit in 1932. Cincinnati, Ohio, boasted Albers Super Markets, which had the honor in 1933 of being the first to formally use the term "supermarket." Food Fair in Harrisburg, Pennsylvania, advertised itself as a 10,000-square-foot giant, quality food, price-cutter store. That same year, Kroger Grocery & Bakery Company in Cincinnati constructed the first parking lot to surround a grocery store, offering spaces for 75 vehicles; the company had learned from surveys that 80 percent of their customers used **automobiles** for shopping.

Safeway converted many of its smaller stores into larger operations; it reached its peak as a chain in 1936 with 3,370 stores. At the same time, the first Giant Food Store opened in Washington, D.C., which gave the United States more than 1,200 chain-connected supermarkets operating under many different names in 84 cities. Throughout the 1930s, the opening of these stores resulted in the closing of many small, independent operations.

The successful development of the modern American supermarket had been driven by the marketing principle of meeting consumers' needs. According to the Super Market Institute, a national trade association for supermarket owners and operators organized in 1937, such an enterprise arranges its products in departments, deals in food and other merchandise, does a minimum of $250,000 annually, and operates on a self-service basis. According to the institute, efficiency can be increased by self-service; visibility and variety will promote sales; and profit comes from large inventories that move quickly. New products advertised on the **radio** soon became available to almost everyone; even nonprescription drugs and other nonfood items could be purchased at one's local supermarket.

Certain advantages occurred with the shift from the small grocery store to the self-service supermarket. The careful shopper who wished to compare the differing prices of a product offered by more than one company could save money and accomplish it in a leisurely manner without any assistance from a clerk. Larger, departmentalized stores meant greater inventory and, as food manufacturers vied for the best display areas, they created an atmosphere for competitive pricing.

Innovation and competition went hand in hand. In 1933, the "ready-to-heat-and-eat" section, or "pantry shelf," made its first appearance. Here the shopper could find one-step-preparation foods such as soups, baked beans, beef stew, corned beef hash, prepared spaghetti, and pudding. Sylvan Goldman (1898–1984), owner of Standard Food Markets and Humpty Dumpty Stores in Oklahoma City, Oklahoma, invented the shopping cart in 1937. This device on wheels could be pushed through the store aisles allowing customers to carry more items comfortably during a single shopping trip, thereby boosting sales.

Drawbacks to the supermarket, of course, existed. Many Americans still preferred the old ways of grocery shopping, especially receiving credit and placing an order by telephone for home delivery. The size and anonymity of the larger stores precluded any kind of close customer relationship, and to keep prices as low as possible, most stores refused to grant credit to their patrons or to offer free deliveries.

Although the atmosphere of the 1930s supermarket can hardly be compared to the bright, shiny emporiums of today, these early predecessors, often housed in abandoned garages and warehouses, nevertheless met with success. They had created a way to address changing consumer needs through a novel method of merchandising.

See also Advertising; Candy; Desserts; Frozen Foods; Ice Cream; Soft Drinks

SELECTED READING

Gwynn, David. Grocery Stores. http://www.groceteria.com/about/host.html

Mariani, John F. *The Dictionary of American Food and Drink*. New Haven, CT: Ticknor & Fields, 1983.

Mathews, Ryan. "1926–1936, Entrepreneurs and Enterprise: A Look at Industry Pioneers Like King Kullen and J. Frank Grimes, and the Institution They Created." *Progressive Grocer* 75:12 (December 1996): 39.

———. "1926–1936, the Mass Market Comes of Age: How the Great Depression, the Rise of Mass Media and World War II Helped Create a Mass Consumer Market." *Progressive Grocer*, 75:12 (December 1996), 47.

GUMPS, THE. A newspaper comic strip drawn by Sidney Smith (1877–1935), *The Gumps* first appeared in 1917, survived until 1959, and rose to its greatest popularity during the 1920s and 1930s. *The Gumps* might be considered the prototypical domestic series, tracing as it does the lives of a lower middle-class family through social changes, wars, economic upheavals, and the vagaries of everyday living.

Born in Illinois, Sidney Smith held a variety of jobs in his youth and appeared to be heading nowhere in the field of art. In 1908, he created *Buck Nix*, an anthropomorphic goat that appeared first in the *Chicago Examiner*. Hardly a memorable strip, and crudely drawn, *Buck Nix* gave Smith the idea of a serial format that would entice readers to follow the adventures of a recurring set of characters.

The *Chicago Tribune* took on Smith in 1912 to do sports drawings, and *Buck Nix* became *Old Doc Yak*. In time, it caught the attention of Captain Joseph Medill Patterson (1879–1946), the copublisher of the *Tribune* and founder of New York's *Daily News*. A legend in the world of comic-strip marketing, Patterson shepherded such classics as *Gasoline Alley* (1918–present), *Winnie Winkle* (1920–present), *Moon Mullins* (1923–1993), **Little Orphan Annie** (1924–present), **Dick Tracy** (1931–present), and many others to fame and success. Possessed of an unerring sense regarding popular taste, Patterson had no reservations about suggesting story and character ideas to his growing stable of cartoonists. When he saw Smith's *Old Doc Yak*, he discerned a potential for greater things and determined to expand the scope of the cartoonist's work.

Under Patterson's tutelage, Sidney Smith in 1917 developed a concept that Patterson would christen *The Gumps*. A long-forgotten word from early nineteenth-century slang, "gump" means a foolish, stupid person. Patterson liked to use the term when referring to common, ordinary people, that is, the typical reader of his **newspapers**. In the strip he envisioned, the main characters would fit this definition and, he hoped, readers would identify with them. His guess paid off, and from its 1917 debut onward, *The Gumps* enjoyed a growing audience. *Old Doc Yak* soon disappeared from the paper's pages. The talking goat briefly—1930–1934—resurfaced as a "topper" for *The Gumps* on Sunday, appearing as a short strip above the regular, full-size series below it.

The Gumps focused on a handful of characters: Andy Gump, "inventor of the flower pot," the family patriarch, a cigar-chomping man with no visible chin; his long-suffering wife, Min (short for Minerva), who must put up with Andy's endless schemes and half-baked ideas; Chester, their precocious son; Uncle Bim Gump, a gullible billionaire who also lacks a lower jaw; Tilda, the repulsive, wisecracking maid who shows no respect for anyone; and Hope, the family cat, who usually lazes about in the sun. By any standard, one of the most execrably drawn American **comic strips** of any era, some theorists maintain that its very lack of artistic merit made it more appealing to its audience because it harbored no pretensions about its drawings or its characters. People apparently felt a kinship with the realism and folksiness portrayed in *The Gumps*, and its soap opera pace and melodramatic plotting kept readership high.

A number of marketing tie-ins between the strip and selected products followed. Two popular songs came out during the early years of the strip, "Oh! Min" (1918; words by Ole Olsen [1892–1963], music by Isham Jones [1894–1956]) and "Andy Gump" (1923; words and music by Harold Dixon [active 1920s]), and a *Gumps* board game materialized in 1924. Several movie cartoons featured the characters, and the family appeared in **Big Little Books** reprints. In 1931 a **radio** program could be heard, the first comic strip to be adapted to the new medium. *The Gumps* ran from 1931 to 1937 on the Columbia Broadcasting System (CBS radio) network. A succession of **toys** and other collectibles also testified to the popularity of the series.

That popularity spelled financial success for Smith; in 1922, he signed a $1 million contract (roughly $12 million in contemporary dollars) with the *Tribune-News* syndicate. It guaranteed him $100,000 a year ($1.2 million) for 10 years, plus a Rolls-Royce automobile for signing, making Sidney Smith the first million-dollar cartoonist. By the 1930s, *The Gumps* ranked at the top of the comics pantheon and in the fall of 1935 the syndicate offered him a new contract: $150,000 a year for three years (roughly $2.2 million a year), another new record. He agreed to the terms, but late that same night, while driving home, his car ran off the road, killing him instantly.

Given the success enjoyed by *The Gumps*, Patterson and *Tribune-News* officials wasted no time in finding a successor to Smith. Fellow cartoonist Stanley Link (1874–1957), who had ghosted some of drawing in the early 1930s, initially received the nod, but no contractual agreement could be worked out. As a result, Gus Edson (1901–1966) took over the series in late 1935, a job he would retain until the syndicate canceled *The Gumps* in 1959 because of poor circulation numbers. Edson, unfortunately, proved even less of a draftsman than Smith, plus he lacked the storytelling skills on which his predecessor had capitalized. *The Gumps* suffered, and once-loyal readers deserted the strip, along with the newspapers carrying it.

During the 1920s and until Sidney Smith's tragic death, however, *The Gumps* had no equal. It addressed the concerns of its readers—money, health, family—in straightforward terms. In the grim days of the Great Depression, it stood almost alone among comic strips when it came to talking directly about the economy. Andy Gump invested in the stock market and lost, making no secret of his dimmed hopes. People got sick; family squabbles—serious ones—came out in the stories. The Gumps' less than luxurious standard of living, right down to Andy's comic but rattletrap car, became part of the strip's lore. Smith said these characters were not unlike the audience reading about them. Employing a form of comic naturalism, he established a rapport with his readers unusual for the make-believe world of cartooning. For the Depression years, the underdogs found a voice in *The Gumps*.

See also Automobiles; Comic Books; Games; Serials; Soap Operas

SELECTED READING
Goulart, Ron, ed. *The Encyclopedia of American Comics*. New York: Facts on File, 1990.
Smith, Sidney. *The Gumps*. New York: Charles Scribner's Sons, 1974.
Walker, Brian. *The Comics before 1945*. New York: Harry N. Abrams, 2004.

GUTHRIE, WOODY. A native of Oklahoma and named for President Woodrow Wilson (1856–1924), Woody Guthrie (1912–1967) learned to play the guitar and the harmonica at an early age. A youthful veteran of hard times, Guthrie wandered throughout Texas and Oklahoma, absorbing the flavor of the region and compiling knowledge about various kinds of regional **music**. Eventually he would write more than a thousand songs, many of which relied on the compositions of others for their melodies.

Guthrie has come down to the present as a major voice in the protest movements of the 1930s. In reality, he enjoyed at best a limited following during the decade; not until the 1940s and after did he come into his own as a significant voice in American music. An early composition, "So Long, It's Been Good to Know Ya" (1935; originally titled "Dusty Old Dust"), became a minor hit. Its music derived from a traditional work by Carson

Robison (1890–1957) called "Ballad of Billy the Kid" that had been written in 1930; Guthrie reworked the material and added his own words. Among his better-known songs, the tune represents his style well. A "Dust Bowl ballad," it reflects the hard times of the Depression, especially the harsh weather and drought conditions experienced by farmers in the western half of the nation. Ironically, the song gained its greatest popularity not in 1935, but in 1951 when a folk group called the Weavers recorded it in a time far removed from depressions and Dust Bowls.

After the limited success of "Dusty Old Dust," Guthrie in 1936 left behind a wife and three children and journeyed westward. A free-wheeling spirit, he cared little about respectability. He would have a series of romances, two more marriages, and several additional children, including contemporary folksinger Arlo Guthrie (b. 1947). He joined the steady stream of migrants, or "Okies," heading for the "promised land" of California. His trek, and that of thousands of others, would be chronicled by author John Steinbeck in his epic *The Grapes of Wrath* (1939), one of the enduring literary works from the decade. From that experience, Guthrie developed a deep-seated sympathy for the downtrodden, and it became a dominant theme in his work.

Folk singer Woody Guthrie (1912–1967). (Courtesy of the Library of Congress)

He eventually reached Los Angeles and in 1937 managed to land a slot on KFVD, a local **radio** station, playing a mix of hillbilly and traditional folk music **recordings**. Maxine Crissman (active 1930s), who received billing as "Lefty Lou," shared microphone duties with him, and their show, *Woody and Lefty Lou*, lasted for two years. During their tenure, they talked and sang over the air, developing a dedicated audience in the process.

A tireless songwriter, Guthrie continued to compose while on the West Coast. He celebrated the poor ("If You Ain't Got the Do Re Mi," 1937), the dispossessed ("I Ain't Got No Home," "Dust Bowl Refugees," both 1938), the region ("Talking Dust Bowl Blues," mid-1930s), and even some outlaws ("Pretty Boy Floyd," 1939). As the 1930s wound down, much of his music took on more of a political edge, and by the 1940s he had moved to compositions about the labor movement and social inequities and injustices. But, contrary to popular belief, that segment of Guthrie's career took place after the 1930s.

The *People's World*, a Communist periodical based in Los Angeles, in 1938 hired Guthrie to write a newspaper column that went by the name of "Woody Sez." In it, he presented himself as something of a homespun, populist philosopher, and he espoused the causes of working people and farmers, a thread he would amplify in his music. Since the *People's World* had Communist Party connections, his association with the paper tainted his reputation in the eyes of many and would haunt him during the 1940s and 1950s, a time of rabid anti-Communism.

Encouraged by his modest successes, and tired of the regimen of broadcasting and writing, Guthrie left Los Angeles in early 1940 and traveled to New York City. Once there, he met many people, including musicians, intellectuals, political activists, and labor supporters. Friends also introduced him to some of the leaders in commercial music circles, an introduction that led to a contract with RCA Victor Records to organize and record some of his music. He cut 14 sides for the label, and his efforts came out as an album, *Dust Bowl Ballads* (1940; reissued, with additional music, in 1964). The collection enjoyed modest success and that same year the Columbia Broadcasting System (CBS radio) hired him to host a network show called *Pipe Smoking Time*, the title a nod to the sponsor, Model Tobacco. Although short-lived, it further broadened his audience and led to other radio appearances.

Woody Guthrie today remains as perhaps the best-known musical spokesperson for the dispossessed. Historically, those in the nation's lower economic echelons, such as laborers and farmers, have often been ignored in popular culture. Because they occasionally found a small voice through music, albeit to limited audiences, protest music flowered during the 1930s as people tried to articulate their woes and anger through song. Pro-labor and anti-business, Guthrie's songs endeared him to workers and angered, in his words, "the bosses," "the fat cats," "the Big Crooks," and "the Greedy Rich Folks"—anyone he saw manipulating and controlling the fate of ordinary working-class people. Guthrie's was not a solitary voice; many singers protested on the side of labor throughout the 1930s. If recorded at all, their music usually could only be heard on obscure labels, and their names have largely been lost, as have the majority of their songs.

Were it not for John Lomax (1867–1948) and his son Alan (1915–2002), knowledge of this rich musical heritage of working-class America, especially that of the southern half of the country, would be limited today. In 1932, the Macmillan Publishing Company accepted John Lomax's proposal for a wide-ranging anthology of American folksongs and ballads. The Library of Congress, through its Archive of American Folk Song, provided recording equipment so he could capture this music in the field instead of at a studio.

Eventually, Alan Lomax met Woody Guthrie. In March 1940, he recorded several hours of music and conversation with the singer for the Library of Congress, finally released as a multidisc album in 1964. In addition, Guthrie, Lomax, and folksinger Pete Seeger (b. 1919) in 1940 compiled a book of labor-oriented protest songs. Given the times, many considered the collected lyrics too radical, and no publisher could be found. Eventually, however, attitudes mellowed and *Hard Hitting Songs for Hard-Hit People* came out in 1967, a time of renewed interest in folk and protest music.

During his 1940 New York City sojourn, Guthrie heard, over and over, **Irving Berlin**'s (1888–1889) patriotic tribute to the nation, "God Bless America" (1918), a composition that had found new popularity in a 1939 recording by **Kate Smith** (1907–1986). Guthrie felt that "God Bless America," rousing and sincere as it may be, inaccurately portrayed the country. In response, he wrote "This Land Is Your Land," arguably his best-known composition. The melody came from a country blues called "Rock of Ages" by Blind Willie Davis (active 1930s). The **Carter Family**, pioneers in popularizing country and blues-influenced music, had recorded this song as "When the World's on Fire," and their version features Maybelle Carter (1909–1978) employing her distinctive guitar style. Guthrie, who had few qualms about "borrowing" the music of others, incorporated the Carter version into his own composition.

He did not record "This Land Is Your Land" until 1944 when Moses "Moe" Asch (1905–1985), the founder of Folkways Records, encouraged him to do so. Initially, his recording had little public impact. Not until the song reached huge audiences through the versions recorded by such popular artists as Bob Dylan (b. 1941) in 1961, Pete Seeger in 1962, and Peter, Paul, and Mary (Peter Yarrow, b. 1938; Paul Stookey, b. 1937; Mary Travers, b. 1936) in 1962 did "This Land Is Your Land" achieve its iconic status. The song displays Guthrie's yearning for social equality among all Americans and serves as a fitting summation of the career of this "Dust Bowl Balladeer."

See also Best Sellers; Hillbillies; Newspapers; Political Parties; Radio Networks; Songwriters & Lyricists

SELECTED READING
Guthrie, Woody. *Bound for Glory*. New York: Penguin Books [Plume], 1943.
———. http://www.geocities.com/nashville/3448/dbball.html#bg
Guthrie, Woody, & the Carter Family. http://xroads.virginia.edu/1930s/radio/c_w/cw-front.html
Lomax, Alan, ed. *Hard Hitting Songs for Hard-Hit People*. New York: Oak Publications, 1967.
Santelli, Robert, and Emily Davidson, eds. *Hard Travelin': The Life and Legacy of Woody Guthrie*.
  Hanover, NH: Wesleyan University Press, 1999.

H

HENDERSON, FLETCHER. The career of bandleader and arranger Fletcher Henderson (1898–1952) illustrates many of the problems faced by black musicians in the 1930s. His orchestra could reasonably be called the hottest band in the land at the beginning of the decade, but the rampant racism of the time kept his genius concealed from a potentially huge audience.

Born in the small town of Cuthbert, Georgia, Henderson studied classical **music** with his mother, but received his formal **education** as a chemist. In 1920, he moved to New York City, ostensibly to work in the chemical industry, but his race caused most doors to be closed to him. Henderson therefore began plugging songs for Black Swan, an important black music publishing group. He put together his first band in 1924; that same year he landed a contract with New York's Roseland Ballroom, a job that would last for 10 years and give him a measure of financial security during that time.

During its stay at Roseland, the Fletcher Henderson Orchestra saw many important black musicians pass through its ranks, including trumpeters Louis Armstrong (1901–1971) and Rex Stewart (1907–1967), saxophonists Benny Carter (1907–2003) and Coleman Hawkins (1904–1969), clarinetist Buster Bailey (1902–1967), and arranger Don Redman (1900–1964). Despite the high caliber of musicianship exhibited by the aggregation and the long stay at the ballroom, commercial success eluded Henderson. The band cut a number of **recordings**, but most of them came out on minor labels, or what the industry called "race records," a term indicating that distribution would be directed at a minority black audience.

The Henderson band finally recorded for RCA Victor in 1932, but the company failed to promote it effectively and sales languished. Victor, like its predecessors, limited its distribution of his recordings, focusing on what it perceived as centers of black trade, a practice that kept his music from spreading to a larger (i.e., white) audience. After the contract with Roseland expired, Henderson, never a good manager, found his finances shaky. He met with John Hammond (1910–1987), an important music critic who seemingly knew everyone in the business, and a man who admired Henderson's work. Hammond set up a meeting between Henderson and clarinetist **Benny Goodman** (1909–1986), leader of an up-and-coming **swing** orchestra. As a result, Henderson began selling some of his best arrangements to Goodman in 1934. Among swing enthusiasts, this transaction brought Henderson a measure of recognition, but it arrived in terms of a successful white band.

Although they involved such gems as "Blue Skies" (composed in 1927), "Sometimes I'm Happy" (composed 1927), "King Porter Stomp" (composed 1925), and many others, Goodman's celebrated performances did little to increase Henderson's public name recognition. Within musical circles, however, Henderson's expertise caused other bandleaders to avail themselves of his skills. Examples would include the Isham Jones (1894–1956) orchestra and the Tommy (1905–1956) and Jimmy (1904–1957) Dorsey bands. This kind of work gave Henderson the financial security to continue fronting groups of his own throughout the 1930s, but his bands lacked commercial success. He played piano for Goodman in 1939, a position that accorded him greater visibility with the public than most of his stints as the leader of his own band.

In spite of the commercial frustrations he faced, Fletcher Henderson did as much, if not more, than anyone to define swing. Beginning in the 1920s and continuing through the 1930s, his use of riffs, or repeated musical phrases, along with a skillful interplay between the brasses and reeds, emerged as hallmarks of the new popular style. His use of both freewheeling **jazz** improvisation and tight, formal arranging gave Henderson's numbers a distinctive quality that other orchestras moved to emulate. For the 1930s, white bands like Benny Goodman, the Dorseys, Harry James (1916–1983), and **Glenn Miller** (1904–1944) perhaps represented elements of the Henderson approach most faithfully.

As has been the case numerous times in American life, a seemingly invisible black artist helped immeasurably to lay the groundwork for what would later become a dominant part of the majority, or white, culture. Lacking attractive, strongly promoted recording contracts with major companies, and often forced to play in less than ideal conditions, Fletcher Henderson soldiered on, with little expectation of the profits and celebrity that frequently accrued to his white counterparts.

See also Race Relations & Stereotyping

SELECTED READING
Magee, Jeffrey. *The Uncrowned King of Swing: Fletcher Henderson and Big Band Jazz.* New York: Oxford University Press, 2004.
Yanow, Scott. *Swing.* San Francisco: Miller Freeman Books, 2000.

HILLBILLIES. With the economy struggling and millions out of work, the image of the hillbilly—sly, independent, resilient, able to survive despite the lack of any apparent job—held a certain appeal. The customs and culture of mountain folk, people who live in remote areas on the fringes of society, have long been a part of American humor and folklore. With literary and musical roots dating back to the early days of the republic, the concept of a subculture that has somehow developed on its own has always attracted popular attention.

In the turbulent 1930s, that attention grew into a minor cultural phenomenon, and the term "hillbilly," a word coined in the late nineteenth century and used pejoratively, shifted in its meanings and gained wide circulation in various media. The hillbilly stereotype that emerged has only a slight basis in reality; instead, it arose primarily out of the collective forces of mass media bent on popularizing a figure that would be commercially viable.

During the 1930s, popular hillbilly manifestations occurred in the following ways:

Comic Strips & Cartoons. In 1934, Paul Webb (1902–1985) began drawing single-panel cartoons featuring stereotypical hillbillies that he called "mountain boys" for the newly published *Esquire* magazine. His characters populate a timeless Appalachian–Ozark–Blue Ridge hinterland cut off from civilization, and his sketches epitomize the down-and-out, but never conquered, mountain characters of the public imagination.

That same year, the booming newspaper comic strips welcomed two new additions, Al Capp's **Li'l Abner** and Billy De Beck's *Snuffy Smith*. *Li'l Abner* focused on the creation of an entire hillbilly community, Dogpatch, U.S.A. *Snuffy Smith*, on the other hand, grew out of a recurring figure in the long-running series *Barney Google* (1919–1940s), a sports-oriented strip. De Beck (1890–1942) had casually introduced Snuffy, a Kentucky hillbilly, into one of Barney's adventures; in a short time, he replaced Google, and today the series continues under different artists as *Snuffy Smith*.

Snuffy, a diminutive caricature of the "typical" hillbilly and completely unlike Webb's lean, lanky mountain boys or Capp's Abner, became popular. A moonshine-makin' rascal, he steals chickens, gambles, and lords it over Maw, his long-suffering wife. But he also survives, often by his wits, in a world he never made, one for which he takes no responsibility.

Radio. The countrified comedy dialects of two actors, Chester Lauck (1902–1980) and Norris Goff (1906–1978), led to a long-running radio series called *Lum and Abner* (1931–1954), a show that brought hillbilly humor into American living rooms. Set in the mythic town of Peabody Ridge, Arkansas, the two characters run the old-timey Jot 'em Down Store, and the scripts chronicle their low-key conversations with other members of the community and the occasional visitor. Somewhat in the mold of **Amos 'n' Andy**, another successful offering then running on network radio that employed dialect, *Lum and Abner*, attracted a devoted listenership. With success came several **movies**, the first of which, *Dreaming Out Loud* (1940), played theaters at the end of the decade.

Music & Recordings. Country music began to make its first appearances on radio stations in the mid- to late 1920s. By the 1930s, this musical format could be heard on many stations, both urban and rural. WLS, a Chicago-based station, broadcast **The National Barn Dance** throughout the decade, whereas WSM, a Nashville, Tennessee, station, carried **Grand Ole Opry**. Thanks to their strong signals and central locations, the two shows attracted large audiences, estimated at anywhere from 5 to 10 million listeners on Saturday nights in back-to-back time slots.

Both programs, along with a handful of others, helped raise public consciousness about country music. As evidence of the growing popularity of such music, mail-order giants Sears, Roebuck and Montgomery Ward soon offered country and hillbilly records in their catalogs.

Movies. Always alert to popular trends, the movie industry wasted little time in releasing hillbilly-oriented pictures. Around the country, theaters advertised both cartoons and feature films with titles like *Kentucky Kernals* (1934), *Mountain Music* (1937), *Down in Arkansaw* (1938), *A Feud There Was* (1938), *Kentucky Moonshine* (1938), and *Musical Mountaineers* (1939). One such film, *Spitfire* (1934), stars the usually sleek, sophisticated Katharine Hepburn (1907–2003) as a grubby, uncouth mountain woman. A monument to miscasting, the picture nevertheless suggests how popular images of hillbillies had found a niche in American mass media.

See also Carter Family; *The Grapes of Wrath*; Woody Guthrie; Magazines; Newspapers; Radio Networks

SELECTED READING

Dunning, John. *On the Air: The Encyclopedia of Old-Time Radio*. New York: Oxford University Press, 1998.

Horn, Maurice, ed. *100 Years of American Newspaper Comics*. New York: Gramercy Books, 1996.

Peterson, Richard A. *Creating Country Music: Fabricating Authenticity*. Chicago: University of Chicago Press, 1997.

Williamson, J. W. *Hillbillyland: What the Movies Did to the Mountains and What the Mountains Did to the Movies*. Chapel Hill: University of North Carolina Press, 1995.

HOBBIES. Wanted or not, the Depression brought much more free time into many people's lives. As a result, hobbies, specific activities pursued voluntarily in nonwork hours for pleasure, soared in popularity during these difficult years. Social critics saw hobbies as an acceptable way to use new **leisure and recreation** hours, and they encouraged all Americans, especially the unemployed, to acquire at least one hobby as a productive activity to fill idle time. Educators and other professionals advocated the positive benefits of an avocation during stressful times, and businesses sponsored hobby shows and hobby clubs for both employees and the general public. Throughout the decade, the mass media—**newspapers**, **magazines**, and **radio**—ran columns, feature articles, and programs describing the leisure pursuits of celebrities and local citizens, and community organizations often featured hobbyists as guests at their meetings.

Hobbies consumed energy in a healthy way, reinforced the work ethic, increased productivity, taught new skills that could be transferred to jobs, and brought about a sense of fulfillment. For young people, a hobby held both immediate and long term benefits: it occupied free time constructively, which meant staying out of mischief; it rewarded hard work; it dispensed information; and it promoted activities good for a lifetime. Some enthusiasts went so far as to advocate hobbies as a means of preventing juvenile delinquency.

Many government and private organizations actively supported hobbies as a part of daily life. School systems provided hobby **education** in the regular curriculum through a variety of instructional programs; they added free, how-to-do evening classes for adults and joined others in the sponsorship of hobby clubs. Municipalities and recreation centers opened their doors for handicraft guild meetings and work sessions providing supplies, tools, and machinery that many individuals and families otherwise could not afford. Organizations for children and adolescents, such as the Boy Scouts, Girl Scouts, and Camp Fire Girls, expanded their programs to include hobby activities and clubs, and places of worship scheduled opportunities for members to participate in sewing circles and quilting bees.

Hobbies magazine, consolidated from several periodicals, debuted in 1931 and billed itself as a publication for collectors. It sponsored shows in major cities across the country during its heyday. Newspapers likewise created or enlarged hobby sections and Macy's department store in New York City displayed the work of hobbyists regularly.

On radio, *Hobby Lobby*, a human interest program, began broadcasting in October 1937 on the Columbia Broadcasting System (CBS radio). The host, Dave Elman (active 1930s), interviewed people with unusual hobbies, such things as building lifelike sculptures from burnt toast or collecting elephant hairs. *Hobby Lobby* doubled its audience each year for three seasons and at its peak received 3,000 letters a week from hobbyists who wanted to appear on the program. The rival National Broadcasting Company (NBC radio) put *Hobbies for the Larger Leisure* in its schedule. The show featured experts discussing unique pursuits, both their own and those of others.

Across the country, people engaged in handicrafts such as leather work, woodworking and furniture building, metalwork, basket weaving, and knitting. Gardening provided multiple benefits—the mental activity of learning and decision making, physical activity, a sense of accomplishment, and **food** for the table. More than one survey of leisure activities in the 1930s placed gardening in the top tier. Garden clubs, once the domain of well-to-do society women, experienced a growth in both numbers and diversity of membership. Ceramics, collectibles, coins, model railroads and layouts, watercolors and oils, **photography**, reading—the list of hobbies pursued during the 1930s goes on and on.

Model building, especially model airplanes of various kinds, emerged as one of the more popular pastimes. Media outlets covered this activity and related events almost as eagerly as they did the growing **aviation** industry. Newspapers and radio stations started model clubs, and in 1934 the largest, Junior Birdmen of America, could boast publishing magnate William Randolph Hearst (1863–1951) as its founder. The Sunday Hearst newspapers carried the "Junior Birdmen Feature Page," which contained information about aviation in general and model building techniques in particular. Municipalities and department stores offered classes in model construction and even established clubs similar to the Junior Birdmen. They published instruction manuals geared to young hobbyists, and held meets that allowed modelers to show off their skills. NBC's *Model Airplane Club of the Air* reached rural listeners who lacked access to clubs such as those available in larger cities.

The Jimmie Allen Club, an aviation adventure serial, first aired on radio in 1933. Immediately popular, Jimmie Allen, a boy pilot, solves mysteries, hunts for treasure, and races in air shows. Listeners could join the Jimmie Allen Flying Club and receive premiums, such as a set of wings, a membership emblem, or a Jimmie Allen picture jigsaw puzzle. A weekly club newsletter that went out to some 600,000 youngsters included information about flying lessons and model airplane plans.

In the mid-1930s, the Hollywood branch of the Jimmie Allen Club included child stars Mickey Rooney (b. 1920) and **Shirley Temple** (b. 1928). Their membership reflected the coeducational possibilities for both model building and the aviation industry. Interest in the radio show prompted Paramount Studios to shoot a Jimmie Allen movie, *Sky Parade* (1936); the film failed at the box office. Enthusiasm for the radio broadcasts also waned, and the show went off the air in 1937.

With so much emphasis on the benefits of hobbies and learning new skills, some people argued that hobbies like **jigsaw puzzles** or collecting in general lacked productivity, taught few, if any skills, and therefore did not qualify as hobbies. Nonetheless, jigsaw puzzle sales reached into the millions during 1932 and 1933 and remained high throughout the decade. Puzzles became a favorite time killer, and for many, the most popular hobby of the Depression.

Stamp collecting, another passive activity, but one that provided knowledge about places and people, emerged as one of the best-known hobbies of the 1930s. Dating back to the nineteenth century, philately (its official name) gained publicity from an ardent collector, President **Franklin D. Roosevelt** (1882–1945). Not only did he collect, he designed a number of U.S. commemorative stamps during his terms in office. Roosevelt endorsed the hobby as a worthwhile endeavor, and its overwhelming popularity probably grew from the president's celebrity status. The decade saw countless new American commemorative stamps issued by Roosevelt's close friend and postmaster general of the United States, James A. Farley (1888–1976).

Hobbies of every description played a significant role in daily life by easing some of the stress of the uncertain times. Jobs might have been scarce, but the work of a hobby could go on forever; some even led to employment as illustrated by contemporary magazine articles featuring profiles of people who had turned their hobbies into vocations.

See also Fads; Games; Movies; New Deal; Radio Networks; Serials; Teenage & Juvenile Delinquency Films; Toys; Youth

SELECTED READING
Corn, Joseph J. *The Winged Gospel: America's Romance with Aviation, 1900–1950.* New York: Oxford University Press, 1983.
Dunning, John. *On the Air: The Encyclopedia of Old-Time Radio.* New York: Oxford University Press, 1998.
Gelber, Steven M. "A Job You Can't Lose: Work and Hobbies in the Great Depression." *Journal of Social History* 24:4 (Summer 1991): 741–766.

HOLLYWOOD PRODUCTION CODE. This term refers to a written set of standards governing the language and content of motion pictures. By the early 1920s, many people found objectionable material in **movies**, a popular medium that attracted large audiences. Scripts and costumes, attitudes and beliefs—both implied and inferred—served as grist for the critics' mills, and Hollywood became fearful that attempts at censorship might be imposed on filmmakers by groups outside the industry. In a move to defuse any concerted efforts to create a form of national review (i.e., censorship), the Motion Picture Producers and Distributors Association (MPPDA) in 1922 created the "production code" to assuage those attacking the freewheeling medium. The code addressed nudity, obscenity, profanity, and a host of other topics, and the MPPDA intended that the studios and producers would handle these issues as a form of self-regulation. To represent both the code and the industry, the MPPDA chose former postmaster general, Presbyterian elder, and Republican Party chair Will H. Hays (1879–1954) to enforce its rulings. He became so associated with the production code and its provisions that his sphere of activity soon came to be called the Hays Office.

Thinking they had blunted, or deflected, most attacks on commercial filmmaking, the MPPDA relaxed, and throughout the 1920s the code did little more than act as a high-sounding shield against any criticism mounted at Hollywood and its practices. Everything functioned on a quasi honor system, with studios agreeing to the terms of the code, but more abstractly than concretely. Interpretative violations occurred with considerable frequency, especially in the areas of overt violence and sex, with few serious attempts to alter movie content. Filmmakers did more or less as they pleased, with scant fear of punishment.

With the advent of sound in 1927, the movies talked, at times outraging various groups with what they said. In a disorganized way, those upset with the morality and tone of films threatened boycotts and censorship, causing some renewed alarm within the industry. In February 1930, the MPPDA adopted a revised production code and established a Studio Relations Committee (SRC) to monitor compliance. The SRC followed a set of guidelines drawn up in 1927 that contained a list of 38 "don'ts" and "be carefuls" for most aspects of filmmaking. Hays hired Joseph Breen (1890–1965), a former reporter and public relations expert, as a spokesperson for this revision, and the studios again agreed to follow its rules. In practice, however, most restrictions remained lax and the code continued to be ineffectual.

During the period 1930 to 1933, the Depression caused movie revenues to drop, a situation that convinced the studios that only with the inclusion of more sex, violence, and profanity would people return to theaters. So, despite the existence of the code and Hays' attempts to bolster its influence, film content tended to ignore its proscriptions and instead grew even more controversial, a situation that brought about renewed criticism. Until that time, any film produced, distributed, or exhibited in violation of code standards faced a $25,000 fine (roughly $370,000 in contemporary dollars). So slight a penalty, since a movie might easily make in excess of $100,000 in profits ($1.5 million), meant producers could accept the fine and continue to distribute their films. More stringent rules were needed and the impetus came from outside the industry.

Religious groups of all denominations voiced increasing concerns about the questionable content they perceived in movies. As a result, a group of disgruntled Episcopal and Catholic bishops met in 1933 to address their disappointment with the industry. Out of that grew the Catholic Legion of Decency, a series of nationwide citizens' review boards made up of nonmovie people. They watched films prior to their general release and assigned them ratings. If these reviewers found anything objectionable (usually revolving around sex, **crime**, violence, nudity, and religion) in a picture, they could recommend changes or elisions; if no alterations were forthcoming, they might issue a rating of C for "condemned." The Legion of Decency recommended boycotting any condemned film, an economic action tantamount to outright censorship. Talk also spread in Washington and Hollywood about possible legislation and government controls on movie content being exercised, a very real threat at a time when several states and cities already had their own review boards, and when federal, state, and local agencies of all kinds were rapidly growing and expanding their powers.

Faced with the necessity of doing something to fend off boycotts, censorship, or government intervention, and to quell the growing call for change in the industry, Hays and Breen finally initiated strict enforcement of the code's provisions. Hays made Breen chair of the Production Code Administration (PCA); all scripts had to pass his office's scrutiny. In 1934, any film lacking Breen's and the PCA's seal of approval would be denied theatrical distribution, a draconian measure endorsed by the major studios. Since those same studios controlled most movie theaters, failure to receive PCA sanction became the kiss of death in a medium dependent on box office receipts for survival. Faced with this kind of threat, producers did their utmost not to violate the code for the remainder of the 1930s, and on into the 1940s. Their surrender signaled significant changes in the content of post-1933–1934 American movies, particularly any episodes containing elements of graphic sex, crime, or violence.

The "don'ts" and "be carefuls," so blithely ignored in the past, took on fresh meaning, and new films coming into theaters reflected this change. Rather than negotiate or compromise, Warner Brothers and United Artists in 1934 withdrew the previously released **Little Caesar** (1930) and *Scarface: Shame of a Nation* (1932) from further theatrical distribution ("too much violence," "celebration of gangsters"), and the two movies languished, unseen, for some 50 years before once more going into theaters. By then, discussion of the code no longer concerned anyone, the Legion of Decency had lost its clout, and people could see virtually anything.

In theory, code restrictions were applied equally across the board; that is, no single type or genre of movie merited special treatment. In actuality, after 1934 comedies and cartoons tended to receive milder criticism from the PCA than did dramas and crime pictures. Violence occurring in a cartoon might be accepted by Breen's office, whereas similar acts in a dramatic production would not. Thus the **screwball comedies** and other adult-oriented comedies of the era often escaped the censor's blue pencil, even though their double entendres and sight gags contained material deemed inappropriate by any close reading of the code. On the other hand, a comedy star like Mae West (1892–1980), noted for her risqué dialogue, had to tone down her act to gain code approval, so not all comedy got by easily. Even a blockbuster picture like **Gone with the Wind** (1939) had its moments with the Hays Office, a process that took weeks and illustrates how seriously the code was taken during the later 1930s.

See also Federal Bureau of Investigation; Gangster Films; Propaganda & Anti-Axis Films; Teenage and Juvenile Delinquency Films

SELECTED READING

Bernstein, Matthew, ed. *Controlling Hollywood: Censorship and Regulation in the Studio Era.* New Brunswick, NJ: Rutgers University Press, 1999.

Leff, Leonard J., and Jerold L. Simmons. *The Dame in the Kimono: Hollywood, Censorship, and the Production Code from the 1920s to the 1960s.* New York: Grove Wiedenfeld, 1990.

HOOVER, HERBERT. Born of Quaker parents in West Branch, Iowa, and called Bert as a boy, Herbert Clark Hoover (1874–1964) served the United States as its 31st president from 1929 to 1933. Orphaned at age 10, Bert moved to Oregon to live with relatives in 1885. Shy and withdrawn, he attended the Friends Pacific Academy in Newberg. He then went to Stanford, a new California university, enrolling in 1891. Four years later he graduated with a degree in geology and obtained employment in the mining industry. He learned all aspects of the business, and landed several assignments abroad.

Returning to the United States in 1899, he married Lou Henry (1874–1944), whom he had met at Stanford, and the couple set sail for China for work with the Chinese government. With his considerable foreign experience, Hoover rose rapidly in the mining field, and in 1908 started his own engineering firm. At the same time, he wrote for professional journals, lectured, and published a manual for engineers and managers, all of which burnished his reputation as a progressive and enlightened businessman.

By 1914, Hoover had amassed a private fortune of some $4 million ($81 million in contemporary dollars) and retired from active business. When World War I broke out in Europe that year, the Hoovers resided in London; they immediately assisted stranded

Herbert Hoover (1874–1964), the 31st president of the United States, and his wife, Lou Henry Hoover (1874–1944). (Courtesy of the Library of Congress)

American travelers attempting to return home. Driven by his Quaker upbringing toward good works, he next established the Commission for Relief of Belgium, an organization that provided millions of tons of **food** to starving people in war-torn Belgium and France.

After the United States entered the conflict in 1917, President Woodrow Wilson (1856–1924) appointed Hoover U.S. food administrator. He had the responsibility of overseeing the overseas distribution of foodstuffs needed by the American and Allied soldiers, as well as maintaining adequate supplies for Allied civilians and people in the United States. Hoover called his program of meatless Mondays and wheatless Wednesdays "food conservation," but many Americans called it Hooverizing. Despite people's carping, the measures proved successful. When the war ended, Hoover accompanied Wilson to Paris as his personal adviser and received considerable credit for reorganizing the shattered European economy. These accomplishments caused the press to laud him as a leading American humanitarian.

Once back in the United States, the Hoovers built a home overlooking the Stanford campus, and he opened mining offices in San Francisco and New York City. Hoover served as secretary of commerce under both Warren G. Harding (1865–1923; president, 1921–1923) and Calvin Coolidge (1872–1933; president, 1923–1929). He reorganized the Commerce Department; from a minor agency it grew into an important and complex organization. Regulation of **radio** and the airways came under his jurisdiction, and as the **aviation** industry developed, he strongly promoted codes and regulations that led to the Air Commerce Act. In a short time, Herbert Hoover had become one of the most visible men in the country.

Coolidge declined to run again for president in the 1928 election, and Hoover immediately became the Republican favorite to oppose the Democratic candidate, Alfred E. Smith (1873–1944). With a campaign slogan of "A chicken in every pot and a car in every garage," Hoover achieved an overwhelming victory, gaining 58 percent of the popular vote and 444 of the 531 electoral college votes. Because of his private wealth, he donated his presidential salary to charitable organizations.

At the time of the election, the final years of the Roaring Twenties, the stock market had been experiencing a frenzy of activity, reaching unparalleled heights in September 1929. Investors bought stocks on borrowed money, or on margin, by putting only a portion of the needed money down, expecting the rest to come from profits. With no laws to stop them, banks also invested in the stock market, using their depositors' money. Hoover understood the risks involved with this kind of gambling and tried to stop it. He asked for an examination of banking procedures and the passage of laws to reform and strengthen the system, and suggested to the nation's more influential bankers that they cease market speculation, but to no avail. On October 29, Black Tuesday, just seven months after Hoover's inauguration, the stock market crashed.

In the face of the financial panic, Hoover believed that the country suffered from a crisis of confidence and he worked to restore faith in the economic vigor of the nation. He announced that he would keep the federal budget balanced, but would at the same time cut taxes and expand public works spending. He urged business, industry, labor, financial, and agricultural leaders to retain workers' purchasing power through the maintenance of wages.

Speaking as a conservative, he stressed the importance of minimal federal intervention in economic affairs. He believed it important that recovery arise from the willing cooperation of private businesses working with state and local governments and volunteers, not federal handouts. For some time he had strongly supported public-private cooperation, fearing that too much meddling weakened two important American values, individuality and self-reliance. Despite his remonstrances, few listened. His stance on nonintervention led to a public perception that he functioned as a "do-nothing" president and the blame for much of what was going wrong fell on his shoulders.

During 1930 and 1931, the recovery from the Depression swung like a pendulum. By the spring of 1930, the economy started to show some signs of an upswing, but in August a prolonged drought in the Plains states had worsened. Rain had not fallen in any quantity for several years; the once-verdant earth cracked open; parched crops died under a blazing sun. Hoover saw drought relief emanating from state and local municipalities, but people clamored for the president to offer direct federal aid.

Seemingly powerless in the face of calamitous events, Hoover soon found his surname the butt of many jokes. A Hooverville consisted of a collection of tents, cardboard boxes, tarpaper shacks, and the like that served as housing for the homeless. Usually located close to railroad tracks, Hoovervilles multiplied during the early 1930s. "Hoover blankets," accumulated **newspapers** under which the jobless and homeless often slept, provided a different kind of shelter. Scarcity of food forced some to eat small game, all of which got called "Hoover hogs." Rundown shoes, usually with visible holes in the soles, became "Hoover shoes," and "Hoover leather" meant the cardboard inserted to resole them. "Hoover flags" referred to empty pockets; when destitute people turned their pockets inside out to indicate that they were broke, the exposed white linings somewhat resembled flags. "Hoovercart" and "Hooverwagon" rodeos began in 1933 and swept the country. The events involved hitching mules to the sawn-off back halves of decrepit Model T Fords and racing them through obstacles, the bumpy course a symbol of the equally bumpy economy. Not all Americans opposed Hoover and his programs, however, and those who had faith in the beleaguered president gained the name Hoovercrats.

In 1931, **Grant Wood** (1891–1942), a popular Regionalist painter from Iowa, depicted Hoover's early rural home in a canvas titled "The Birthplace of Herbert Hoover." Hoover held the honor of being Iowa's first citizen to reside in the White House and clearly stood as its most famous resident, although, given the times, not necessarily its favorite son.

In the spring of 1931, Europe sank further into an ongoing economic crisis, an event that negatively affected the American banking system. Hoover presented many proposals to Congress: programs to reform the banking program, to expand public works across the country, and to create the Reconstruction Finance Corporation (RFC), an agency that could grant government loans to save banks, farms, railways, and businesses from bankruptcy. Congress passed several public works bills as well as the RFC but rejected the banking reforms. Many of the nation's banks therefore continued to teeter on the brink of insolvency.

The successful establishment of the RFC, however, put the federal government into the role of regulating business, something Hoover philosophically opposed, but he believed it had to be done to counter the current economic dangers. He also allowed direct aid to drought-stricken farmers in the form of foodstuffs and cotton cloth.

Searching for solutions, Hoover signed acts that raised tariffs on a large number of imported items and hiked various taxes and fees, including postage rates. Many saw these moves as betrayals of promises made earlier and felt that they deepened the crisis significantly. By the summer of 1932, an election year, the Great Depression saw 12 million workers unemployed, and 18 million more seeking assistance. Sensing defeat, but stuck in a bind, the Republican convention nominated Hoover to run against the Democrat candidate, **Franklin D. Roosevelt** (1882–1945). Despite Hoover's ceaseless efforts and limited successes, the public blamed him for the country's problems and Roosevelt won by a landslide, gaining 57 percent of the popular vote and 472 of the 531 electoral college votes.

After this crushing defeat, the Hoovers returned to their California home. For the first 18 months following Roosevelt's inauguration, Hoover remained publicly silent. He devoted his energies to the Boys' Clubs of America and to the Hoover Institute on War, Revolution, and Peace at Stanford, a public policy research center founded by him in 1919. Over time, it has amassed a huge archive of documentation related to both Hoover and World Wars I and II.

Starting in the fall of 1934, through both publications and speeches, Hoover became a major critic of the **New Deal**. He simultaneously pursued his own reentry into politics, unsuccessfully seeking the 1936 and 1940 Republican presidential nominations. When war broke out in Europe in 1939, Hoover, as a private citizen, established the

Polish Relief Commission, which for two years fed 300,000 children in the German-occupied territory of Poland.

Following the war, President Harry Truman (1884–1972) sent Hoover on a worldwide mission to assess the needs of the hungry and the capabilities of food-producing countries. For the rest of his long life, Hoover readily accepted periodic assignments from the country's leaders, published extensively, and continued to devote himself to the institute and to Boys' Club of America activities. He partially reclaimed his tattered reputation and lived long enough to receive acknowledgment as both an elder statesman and world humanitarian.

See also Book Clubs; Political Parties; Regionalism

SELECTED READING

Burner, David. *Herbert Hoover: A Public Life.* New York: Alfred A. Knopf, 1979.

Fausold, Martin L, ed. *The Hoover Presidency: A Reappraisal.* Albany: State University of New York Press, 1974.

Lyons, Eugene. *Herbert Hoover: A Biography.* Garden City, NY: Doubleday, 1964.

HOPPER, EDWARD. Born in Nyack, New York, just a few miles north of New York City, painter Edward Hopper (1882–1967) became, in time, a masterful interpreter of urban America. Interested in art from childhood, he studied illustration at the New York School of Art after graduating from high school. Robert Henri (1865–1929), an important American painter from the early twentieth century, served as one of his teachers. The informal leader of the so-called Ashcan School (c. 1908–1918), Henri and a group of young artists broke away from many of the academic restraints of the era, striving for greater freedom and modernism in American art. The Ashcan School emphasized painting realistically, especially unadorned scenes of city life, a theme that often characterizes Hopper's work, although he himself never became a part of the movement.

In 1906, following about five years of study with Henri, Hopper embarked for Europe. Although he pursued no formal study, he painted constantly, refining his own techniques and ideas. He traveled again to Europe in 1909 and 1910, and then returned to the United States and never crossed the Atlantic again.

Hopper supported himself during these formative years through illustration and commercial work. He apparently disliked the assignments, and the work stiffened his desire to be self-supportive through his own art. To achieve this goal, he mastered printmaking and etching. By the mid-1920s, Hopper exhibited his prints with some frequency, and many of the themes found in his mature painting began to appear in this medium.

By the end of the 1920s, Hopper had decided on his primary subject, the nation's cities and towns. American **architecture**, with all its varied styles, fascinated him, and he delighted in looking at buildings from unusual perspectives, as in *City Roofs* (1932). Commonplace architectural details took on importance in his work, causing observers to look at structures anew. With the close of the decade, recognition finally came; galleries and museums regularly showed his watercolors and oils, they slowly started to sell, and he could give up the commercial assignments.

In 1930, Hopper purchased land on Cape Cod. He and his wife would summer on the Cape and spend the remaining months at their apartment in New York's Greenwich

Village. Firmly ensconced as an artist, Hopper commenced to produce a remarkable succession of paintings, many of which have become American classics.

He saw in the city an opportunity to exercise his pictorial skills to their fullest. Texture—concrete, steel, marble, wood, stone—and myriad combinations of forms allowed him to experiment with light and shadow. Few American painters have ever captured those fleeting moments of early morning light (*Early Sunday Morning*, 1930), or the last rays of evening (*Gas*, 1940) as effectively as Hopper. His urban night scenes, interior and exterior, illuminated by murky street lights, dim lamps, and neon, likewise stand as unique, as in *Room in New York* (1932). He chose not to portray the usually brightly lit skyscrapers silhouetted against the sky or the gaudy electric signs that proliferate along a main thoroughfare; his city at night conveys a more intimate quality, and he painted it as if the usual boisterous activities of horns and traffic and crowded sidewalks have come to a halt. Just a few people populate these pictures, "nighthawks" as he called them (*Nighthawks*, 1942). In this regard, he can be contrasted with another important urban painter of the 1930s, **Reginald Marsh** (1898–1954), who features an endless, loud parade of city folk who seem never to slow down amid the bright, garish lights of downtown.

The people in Hopper's canvases usually appear alienated from their environment, as in *Room in Brooklyn* (1932) or *Hotel Room* (1931). An almost eerie quiet pervades his canvases, and no one seems to be communicating with anyone else. His pictures reveal a sense of loneliness, suggesting that his people cannot speak, which gives a forlorn, desolate air to much of his work (*Barber Shop*, 1931). Anything hopeful has gotten away. His paintings project a sense of detachment, and he carefully places the viewer outside the scene. In Hopper's cityscapes, he removes the urban hustle and bustle, replacing it with a visual inertia that stifles all activity (*The Circle Theatre*, 1936).

Edward Hopper resists easy labeling. Since he had been painting well before the onset of the Great Depression, he had mastered an identifiable style years earlier. Some might try to claim Hopper as a Regionalist; like **Thomas Hart Benton** (1889–1975), **Grant Wood** (1891–1942), and other fellow artists, he painted the American scene, and he certainly captured a sense of place in his work. But, despite the loneliness suggested in many of his paintings, he tended—with the exception of some of his New England scenes, especially the watercolors—to avoid the rural emphases found in so many Regionalist works. Even when depicting the countryside, he showed no particular celebration of the richness, the fecundity, found in the land, and he created no heroic images of yeoman farmers harvesting the crops. Neither did he paint nature at her most furious; the howling storms and threatening clouds have no real place in his work. Hopper's rural landscapes instead focus on light and the textures of the land, not on its symbolic qualities (*The Camel's Hump*, 1931). Like the city in his urban paintings, the countryside appears motionless, the only dynamic element being the play of light upon the scene.

Because he depicts the urban environment as essentially cheerless (*New York Movie*, 1939), a place of alienation, the Social Realists tried at times to claim him. But political or social commentary seldom if ever appears in his compositions. The urban emphasis seems to be the only common denominator between him and them, a tenuous connection at best. The Great Depression does not become a part of his urban compositions, and to suggest economic parallels between his paintings and the world outside them would be stretching a point.

Hopper remained active and productive well beyond the 1930s. In a remarkably steady career that lasted until his death in 1967, he created a body of work that belongs to him alone, a splendid painter who avoided the artistic passions of the day. He gave the world a portrait of twentieth-century America, one that showed a growing urbanism, a gradual assimilation of the past into the present, but done without any sensationalism.

See also Advertising; Illustrators; Regionalism; Charles Sheeler; Social Realism

SELECTED READING
Goodrich, Lloyd. *Edward Hopper*. New York: Harry N. Abrams, 1971.
Levin, Gail. *Edward Hopper as Illustrator*. New York: W. W. Norton, 1979.
———. *Edward Hopper: The Art and the Artist*. New York: W. W. Norton, 1980.

HORROR & FANTASY FILMS. It can be argued that "horror" and "fantasy" stand apart as genres of popular film, each possessing its own characteristics. But they also share many traits, especially imagination and the creative use of special effects. Both rely on the viewer's willing suspension of disbelief, and both appeal to predictable emotional responses. For example, most horror pictures attempt to frighten; most fantasy films hope to enthrall. Both do so with cinematic devices that fool the eye and transport spectators to new and unimagined realms. Often, these characteristics get intermixed, making differences in the two genres impossible to define. Does 1934's *Black Cat* stand as a film adaptation—neither horror nor fantasy—of a nineteenth-century short story by Edgar Allan Poe (1809–1849)? Or does it exist as a fantasy film about the remarkable "sixth sense" residing in a cat? Or does it function as a horror movie designed to frighten audiences with the realization that ordinary, seemingly harmless, things possess monstrous capabilities? Many of the horror and fantasy productions coming from Hollywood in the 1930s blurred such lines, but these quibbles did not deter patrons eager for the latest motion pictures. Especially in the early years of the decade, new fantasy and new horror awaited audiences on an almost weekly basis.

With the Depression a reality that could be forgotten in the confines of a theater, Hollywood rose to the occasion with a series of **movies** that took horror and fantasy, but especially horror, to new heights. These films had absolutely nothing to do with economics, although many of them made handsome profits for their makers. Watching features like **Dracula** (1931), **Frankenstein** (1931), *The Mummy* (1932), *White Zombie* (1932), *The Ghoul* (1933), **King Kong** (1933), *The Vampire Bat* (1933), *The Invisible Man* (1933), *The Raven* (1935), and *The Walking Dead* (1936), audiences could sit back and, instead of relaxing, be scared out of their wits, or merely entertained, depending on their mood and the story unfolding on the screen. Escapism at its best, these pictures quickly spawned a nearly endless parade of sequels and imitators, such as *Son of Kong* (1933), *The Bride of Frankenstein* (1935), *The Black Room* (1935), *Mark of the Vampire* (1935), *The Werewolf of London* (1935), *The Invisible Ray* (1936), *Dracula's Daughter* (1936), *Revolt of the Zombies* (1936), *Son of Frankenstein* (1939), and *Tower of London* (1939), to name just a few.

The success of the horror and fantasy genres launched countless careers. The following charts list some of the actors and directors who achieved fame working in these areas.

Outstanding Actors in the Horror and Fantasy Genre

Name (birth and death dates)	Representative Motion Pictures (in chronological order)
Lionel Atwill (1885–1946)	*Dr. X* (1932), *The Vampire Bat* (1933), *Mystery of the Wax Museum* (1933), *Murders in the Zoo* (1933), *Secret of the Blue Room* (1933), *Solitaire Man* (1933), *Mark of the Vampire* (1935), *The Son of Frankenstein* (1939)
Colin Clive (1900–1937)	*Frankenstein* (1931), *The Bride of Frankenstein* (1935), *Mad Love* (1935)
Boris Karloff (1887–1969)	*Frankenstein* (1931), *The Old Dark House* (1932), *The Mask of Fu Manchu* (1932), *The Mummy* (1932), *The Ghoul* (1933), *The Black Cat* (1934), *Bride of Frankenstein* (1935), *The Raven* (1935), *The Black Room* (1935), *The Walking Dead* (1936), *The Invisible Ray* (1936), *Son of Frankenstein* (1939), *Black Friday* (1940), *Before I Hang* (1940)
Peter Lorre (1904–1964)	*M* (1931), *Mad Love* (1935), *Crime and Punishment* (1935), *Stranger on the Third Floor* (1940), *You'll Find Out* (1940)
Bela Lugosi (1882–1956)	*Dracula* (1931), *Murders in the Rue Morgue* (1932), *White Zombie* (1932), *Island of Lost Souls* (1933), *Night of Terror* (1933), *The Black Cat* (1934), *Mark of the Vampire* (1935), *The Raven* (1935), *Murder by Television* (1935), *The Invisible Ray* (1936), *Son of Frankenstein* (1939), *The Human Monster* (1940), *Black Friday* (1940); Lugosi also made a number of **serials**, including *The Whispering Shadow* (1933), *The Return of Chandu* (1934), and *The Phantom Creeps* (1939), *Black Friday* (1940)
Claude Rains (1889–1967)	*The Invisible Man* (1933), *Crime without Passion* (1934), *The Clairvoyant* (1934)
Basil Rathbone (1892–1967)	*Kind Lady* (1935), *Love from a Stranger* (1937), *Son of Frankenstein* (1939), *Tower of London* (1939)
Fay Wray (1907–2004)	*The Most Dangerous Game* (1932), *The Vampire Bat* (1933), *Mystery of the Wax Museum* (1933), *King Kong* (1933), *Black Moon* (1934)

Outstanding Directors in the Horror and Fantasy Genre

Name (and Dates)	Representative Motion Pictures (in chronological order)
Tod Browning (1882–1962)	*Dracula* (1931), *Freaks* (1932), *Mark of the Vampire* (1935), *The Devil-Doll* (1936), *Miracles for Sale* (1939)
Merian C. Cooper (1893–1973)	*King Kong* (1933), *The Monkey's Paw* (1933), *Son of Kong* (1933), *She* (1935)
Michael Curtiz (1886–1962)	*Doctor X* (1932), *Mystery of the Wax Museum* (1933), *The Walking Dead* (1936)
Rowland V. Lee (1891–1975)	*Love from a Stranger* (1937), *Son of Frankenstein* (1939), *Tower of London* (1939)
Ernest B. Schoedsack (1893–1979)	*Rango* (1931), *The Most Dangerous Game* (1932), *King Kong* (1933), *The Monkey's Paw* (1933), *Son of Kong* (1933), *Dr. Cyclops* (1940)
James Whale (1889–1957)	*Frankenstein* (1931), *The Old Dark House* (1932), *The Invisible Man* (1933), *Bride of Frankenstein* (1935)

The people listed in the charts above virtually defined the horror and fantasy genres during the 1930s. Once audiences identified them with such movies, these actors and directors found it hard to do anything else, especially the actors. For example, Boris Karloff had moved from stock company roles to film acting in 1916 as an extra. By 1919, he had graduated to small parts and found his métier. Some 80 or so movies later, Universal cast him in 1931's *Frankenstein*, and his grim performance as the monster made him a star. After that, most of his assignments consisted of similar parts, ranging from the title role in *The Mask of Fu Manchu* (1932) to a mad doctor in *The Man They Could Not Hang* (1939). Many a marquee dropped his first name; just "Karloff" in lights or on a poster guaranteed a crowd.

Similarly, Bela Lugosi labored in obscurity from 1917 until 1931, working in dozens of forgettable pictures; then he appeared in Tod Browning's *Dracula* and shot to stardom. Hungarian-born, Lugosi affected a peculiar accent when speaking English; if a film called for a strange, menacing character, Lugosi often got the part. *Dracula*, however, proved his defining role, just as *Frankenstein* did for Boris Karloff.

Given the popularity enjoyed by horror films during the 1930s, it took little time for enterprising producers to team Karloff and Lugosi. Their first joint appearance occurred with *The Black Cat* (1934), a retelling of the classic Poe short story. Shortly thereafter, the two made cameo appearances in 1934's *Gift of Gab*, a musical with many guest stars. Success brought about *The Raven* (1935), another Poe adaptation, followed by *The Invisible Ray* (1936), *Son of Frankenstein* (1939), and two mediocre efforts in 1940, *Black Friday* and *You'll Find Out*. Their last pairing occurred in 1945 with *The Body Snatcher*.

Other actors also profited from the vogue for horror movies. Lon Chaney Sr. (1883–1930), "the man of a thousand faces" and a master of makeup, had made a major name for himself playing monsters in the silent era. He did one sound film, *The Unholy Three* (1930), a remake of his previous (1925) hit of the same name, and it predicted great things for his career, but he died in 1930. His son, Lon Chaney, Jr. (1906–1973), carried on his father's traditions, first in a fantasy film titled *One Million B.C.* (1940) in which he plays a prehistoric caveman. The younger Chaney, however, would not make his mark in horror features until later in the 1940s.

Another popular hit, *Werewolf of London* (1935), stars the little-known Henry Hull (1890–1977) and deserves some attention as the first in a long cycle of werewolf films. The popular novelist H. G. Wells (1866–1946) had penned a frightening story called *The Island of Dr. Moreau* (1896) that deals with a mad scientist and his cruel experiments with animals and human beings, or "beast men." In the first of several motion picture adaptations, director Erle C. Kenton (1896–1980) created what many feel stands as the best of the lot. Called *The Island of Lost Souls* (1933), and starring Charles Laughton (1899–1962) as the evil doctor, it bears comparison with *King Kong*, another picture with dark undertones released that same year.

During the 1930s, fantasy motion pictures never captured the public imagination on a scale to equal that of horror movies. On the other hand, many horror pictures, such as *The Island of Lost Souls*, spilled over into fantasy. Likewise, the various tales of man-made monsters (e.g., *Frankenstein*) and vampire tales (e.g., *Dracula*) depend on strong fantasy elements to convey their stories. For the decade as a whole, *King Kong* stands as the definitive model for this kind of blending.

A fair number of fantasy films nonetheless played theaters, and several attracted wide audiences. Two full-length cartoon features, both created by the genius of **Walt Disney**

(1901–1966), enthralled both young and old in the latter years of the decade: *Snow White and the Seven Dwarfs* (1937) and *Fantasia* (1940). Regular features also explored the realm of fantasy. Lewis Carroll's (1832–1898) *Alice in Wonderland*, a novel written in 1865, has, over the years, received well over a dozen movie treatments; two of them were produced during the 1930s, the first in 1931 and the second in 1933. The 1933 version boasts a roster of Hollywood stars—including such luminaries as Gary Cooper (1901–1961) as the White Knight, W. C. Fields (1880–1946) as Humpty Dumpty, and Cary Grant (1904–1986) as the Mock Turtle—but the end result comes across as a plodding tale. Burdened by a decision to have the actors wear masks purporting to represent their characters, and shot in black and white (quality color prints would not come along until the later 1930s), this *Alice in Wonderland* hardly qualifies as the stuff of fantasy.

A more exciting fantastic vision emerged with the various **Tarzan** adaptations of the 1930s. The many stories of a man "raised among the apes" captured an enthusiastic audience, and eight different adventures played in theaters between 1932 and 1940.

Two final fantasies from the 1930s merit mention: *Lost Horizon* (1937) and **The Wizard of Oz** (1939). Both represent Hollywood moviemaking at its best and have become screen classics. Together, horror films and fantasy films constitute an important part of celluloid history. During the 1930s, they jointly stood as a Depression-era genre that provided audiences a welcome bit of escapism far removed from the everyday stresses of modern life.

See also Hollywood Production Code; Musicals; Science Fiction

SELECTED READING
Beck, Calvin Thomas. *Heroes of the Horrors*. New York: Macmillan, 1975.
Brunas, Michael, John Brunas, and Tom Weaver. *Universal Horrors: The Studio's Classic Films, 1931–1946*. Jefferson, NC: McFarland & Co., 1990.
Soister, John T. *Of Gods and Monsters: A Critical Guide to Universal Studios' Science Fiction, Horror, and Mystery Films, 1929–1939*. Jefferson, NC: McFarland & Co., 1999.
Vieira, Mark A. *Hollywood Horror: from Gothic to Cosmic*. New York: Harry N. Abrams, 2003.

HORSE RACING. A true spectator sport, horse racing attracted significant crowds throughout the bleak years of the Depression, although the numbers were admittedly below what the track normally drew. Not until 1936 did attendance again climb toward the totals enjoyed before the crash. The widespread legalization of betting brought with it the lure of easy money, certainly a tempting consideration in those straitened times. Both pari-mutuel and oral betting through bookies flourished, and the track purses reflected a continuing level of public interest.

Several outstanding racehorses made their mark during the 1930s. First came Gallant Fox, "the Bear from Belair," galloping to victories in the Preakness, the Belmont Stakes, and the Kentucky Derby during the 1930 season. Each a race for three-year-olds, winning all three in one season earned the title Triple Crown. Only the second time it had occurred in American racing (Sir Barton had done it for the first time in 1916), it signified the highest honor the sport could bestow and the most ballyhooed accomplishment in racing. Keeping it all in the family, Gallant Fox's son Omaha repeated the feat in 1935. Then, in 1937, War Admiral managed it yet again, making the 1930s an extraordinary decade in terms of Triple Crown winners.

Despite the hard times, people still managed to get to the local track and place a bet or two. "The sport of kings" retained its popularity throughout the 1930s as this crowded grandstand shows. (Courtesy of the Library of Congress)

Equipoise (1928–1938), nicknamed "the People's Horse" and "the Chocolate Soldier," dominated the sport during the early Depression years, winning Horse of the Year honors in 1932–1933. But another horse displaced Equipoise in the fans' affection later in the decade. **Seabiscuit** (1934–1947), all the rage everywhere, achieved celebrity status and guaranteed large crowds wherever he appeared. Probably the best-known of the countless race horses of the era, he faded from popular memory after his 1940 retirement. The 2001 publication of Laura Hillenbrand's (b. 1967) best-selling *Seabiscuit: An American Legend* rekindled public interest and allowed a new generation to learn about him and his impact on American horse racing.

Along with outstanding horses, the 1930s also saw jockey Eddie Arcaro (1916–1997) embark on a career that would eventually make him one of the greatest riders of all time. He posted his first victory in 1932; from then on, there was no stopping him, and owners vied for his services. Arcaro retired at the end of 1961 with 4,779 wins.

On the technical side, the photo finish became a part of racing in 1935. Until then, judges, relying on their eyes, named the victors, no matter how close the call. Although only a handful of dead heats ever emerged with this system each year, it clearly was subject to human error. After the installation of cameras at tracks, the number of ties ballooned, suggesting that miscalls had frequently occurred in the past. Not everyone liked the new technology, but it removed doubts in tight finishes.

Radio and public address systems also became a part of horse racing at this time. Clem McCarthy (1882–1962), with his distinctive gravelly voice, along with a machine-gun delivery, served as the primary network announcer for the sport during the 1930s and 1940s. In 1928, he had the honor of being the first sportscaster to cover the Kentucky Derby on radio; he would continue to do so for the next 22 years, as well as giving avid listeners a running commentary on most other major races of the day.

Because of horse racing's strong visual qualities, Hollywood quickly realized its potential for exciting movie sequences. Just a few of the racing pictures of the 1930s include *At the Races* (1934), a comedy featuring Edgar Bergen (1903–1978) and his dummy, Charlie McCarthy; and another comedy, *David Harum* (1934), starring the popular Will Rogers (1879–1935). Rogers also appeared in *In Old Kentucky* (1935), which was not released until after his death. Early in his career, Clark Gable (1901–1960) did *Sporting Blood* (1931); after becoming a major star, he topped the billing in MGM's *Saratoga* (1937). Director Frank Capra (1897–1991) led stars Warner Baxter (1889–1951) and Myrna Loy (1905–1993) through the sentimentality of *Broadway Bill* (1934), while *Kentucky* (1938) earned Walter Brennan (1894–1974) an Academy Award for Best Supporting Actor.

Shirley Temple (b. 1928), the sensationally popular child star, made *Little Miss Marker* in 1934, based on a Damon Runyon (1880–1946) racing story; it led to three eventual remakes, along with innumerable variations. **Judy Garland** (1922–1969) and Mickey Rooney (b. 1920), two other youthful performers who enjoyed a big following, would eventually do five pictures together during the decade; their first outing as a team, *Thoroughbreds Don't Cry* (1937), revolves around horse racing. Two contemporary actresses, Ginger Rogers (1911–1995) in *Wine, Women, and Horses* (1937) and Betty Grable (1916–1973) in *The Day the Bookies Wept* (1939), brought a woman's perspective to the sport. Probably the best-known equestrian picture of the decade, however, remains the **Marx Brothers'** *Day at the Races* (1937). The zany trio pretty much takes away any mystique the sport of kings might possess. The Ritz Brothers, sometime cinema and comedy rivals of the Marx Brothers, tried to compete with *Straight, Place, and Show*, an anemic offering that came out in 1938.

Long associated with wealth, horse racing found a popular following throughout the 1930s. It afforded spectators excitement and escape, and the allure of a big win and monetary rewards tempted fans, rich and poor. A chimera perhaps, but the tracks did a good business despite the Depression, and a succession of celebrity horses kept interest at a high pitch.

See also Fred Astaire & Ginger Rogers; Movies; Photography; Polo

SELECTED READING
Robertson, William H. P. *The History of Thoroughbred Racing in America.* Englewood Cliffs, NJ: Prentice-Hall, 1964.
Simon, Mary. *Racing through the Century: The Story of Thoroughbred Racing in America.* Irvine, CA: Bowtie Press, 2002.

HOTELS. The hotel business prospered during the 1920s and then went into a sharp decline in the 1930s. For the twenties, occupancy rate stood at a healthy 85 percent and construction reached an all-time peak as both large cities and small towns subsidized the building of hotels to accommodate visitors and bolster civic pride. In many communities, the most prominent building—and frequently the fanciest and most elaborate—was the local hotel (or hotels, since larger cities usually had more than one). They often outshone the local courthouse and city hall. Among the outstanding hotels built during this boom period, the Los Angeles Biltmore (1923), Chicago's Knickerbocker (1927), St. Petersburg Beach's Don CeSar (Florida, 1928), New York's Waldorf-Astoria (1931), and Washington, D.C.'s Mayflower (1925) and Hay Adams (1927) would have to be included in any listing. Many other first-class hotels also went up in this period of unbridled optimism.

The 1931 Waldorf-Astoria was not the first one in New York City bearing that prestigious name; the original, which opened it doors in the late 1800s, closed them in 1929 in order to sell the valuable Manhattan real estate on which it stood. Shortly thereafter, the **Empire State Building** (1931) arose on the site of the grand old hotel. But work soon commenced on the hostelry's successor, an even more sumptuous version of the original.

The onset of national Prohibition in 1920 temporarily impacted the hotel business. Those hotels with bars, cocktail lounges, and dining rooms depended on liquor sales for a significant percentage of their income. Many establishments chose to close their bars and lounges, and some converted their restaurant facilities to sandwich or coffee shops. Since wines fall into the category of **alcoholic beverages**, some predicted that Prohibition would bring about the end of fine dining. Certainly Prohibition had an effect on **restaurants** and any kind of beverage service, but most hotel dining rooms managed to survive the Depression years, albeit with more limited menus and often a reduction in service.

Financial difficulties directly related to the Depression and declining occupancy proved more damaging than Prohibition. By 1932, 80 percent of all hotel mortgages were in default; 32 percent could not cover property taxes from revenues; and 15 percent could not meet payrolls. In the meantime, the occupancy rate for the decade dropped to 65 percent.

Other factors contributed to the decline as well. Prior to the 1930s, hotels located in the downtown sections of cities dominated the lodging industry. Often built near railroad stations, they proved inconvenient for those traveling by car. Once constructed, such hotels catered to salesmen and others arriving by rail, a practice that continued into the 1930s. Locations in the midst or at the edge of congested business districts made it difficult for **automobiles** to load or unload, and parking presented another set of problems, especially during the evening rush hour.

Since they had been built on expensive land, hotels of necessity charged high prices—a typical room averaged $5.60 (roughly $85 in contemporary dollars) as compared to $2.50 ($36 in modern terms) for a motel room, and the motel did not suffer traffic woes. With the economic crisis, budget-minded businesses cut employee **travel** allowances, an action that sent once-steady hotel trade to **motels**; vacationers, in the past a potential source of income, likewise sought ways to decrease their traveling costs and opted for **auto camps**, tourist courts, or motels.

Hoteliers recognized the necessity of adapting to motorists' needs and some added more parking spaces. A few even had special automobile entrances constructed.

Roney Plaza Hotel, Miami Beach, Florida, 1925. (Courtesy of the Library of Congress)

Perception, however, was another problem. Much of the public, particularly people unfamiliar with the routines followed in such establishments, found hotels intimidating. Anyone who went to the **movies** regularly saw **Fred Astaire** (1899–1987) in a tuxedo, or even white tie and tails, and **Ginger Rogers** (1911–1995) in a floor-length gown enjoying cocktails and dinner at a posh hotel, before whirling around the nearby dance floor. This image of dressiness got reinforced in hundreds of films, and not just **musicals**. Gangsters and their molls also frequented these places, as did wealthy professionals, celebrities, and a host of other types from the "upper classes." Although these images might be distortions, or at least exaggerations, popular thinking, erroneous or not, made the larger, more formal big-city hotels off-limits for a considerable part of the population.

In response, many hotels abolished the dress codes that in fact they had long maintained, especially for dining. In particular, the requirement for formal evening attire in the dining room virtually disappeared. But some establishments, again in larger cities, failed to relax dress codes enough to accommodate the casual dress worn for automobile travel or provide free parking and special automobile entrances. Instead, they redecorated rooms, reducing their formality in quest of a more homelike atmosphere, and they tried little things like redesigning menus to appeal to women's and children's special tastes and hiring more female staff to add to the comfort of women guests. Some even deigned to advertise on highway billboards. But this did not suffice; business continued to decline. The glory days of the American hotel had come to a close.

Another kind of accommodation, the resort hotel, usually located in the mountains or at the sea or lakeside, originally targeted wealthy families that arrived by train. Husbands worked year-round in the city so their wives and children could spend the summer months in pleasant surroundings away from urban congestion and heat. As automobiles overtook passenger **trains** in popularity, many of these resorts began to cater to less affluent vacationers who arrived by car. The hotels constructed parking lots and strove to get their names listed in guidebooks that would make people aware of them. For example, in 1917 Triple A (the American Automobile Association, or AAA) began publishing a widely distributed guide for its members that recommended destinations, as well as lodging for overnight or longer. By the 1930s, many considered it a reliable source of information, and it included resort hotels.

The repeal of Prohibition in 1933 provided a slight boost to the hotel business, especially in cities. With alcoholic beverages again legal, some hotel dining rooms reopened. Slight improvements in the nation's economy also encouraged modest hotel construction. Plans that had been on hold moved forward; for example, the Statler Hotel chain, which already had properties in Boston, Buffalo, and New York City, built a large new hotel in Pittsburgh, Pennsylvania, in 1937. Conrad Hilton (1887–1979), whose holdings in the hotel business began with the 1919 purchase of the Mobley Hotel in Cisco, Texas, prospered during the 1920s. A native of New Mexico, Hilton had by 1939 built the state's tallest building, the 10-story Hilton Hotel in Albuquerque. The Albert Pick Company boasted 16 hotels in eight states by 1937, and Sheraton had four by 1939. The chains hoped to attract customers through a strong corporate identity that guaranteed satisfaction with all their facilities.

These efforts, though impressive, accomplished little more than to keep the hotel industry alive. The American Automobile Association estimated that in 1929 approximately 75 percent of all travelers lodged in hotels, a number that dropped to 61 percent by 1937 and to only 46 percent in 1939. In an attempt to turn the industry around, the American Hotel Association (AHA) launched an **advertising** campaign in 1938–1939 that highlighted hotel advantages: prestige, service, comfort, central location, and professionalism. But the lodging figures indicate that both vacation and business travelers continued to search for convenience and economy over prestige and service.

See also Fashion; Food; Gangster Films; Leisure & Recreation; Prohibition and Repeal

SELECTED READING
Belasco, Warren James. *Americans on the Road: From Autocamp to Motel, 1910–1945.* Cambridge, MA: MIT Press, 1979.
Jakle, John A., Keith A. Sculle, and Jefferson S. Rogers. *The Motel in America.* Baltimore: Johns Hopkins University Press, 1996.
Liebs, Chester H. *Main Street to Miracle Mile.* Baltimore: Johns Hopkins University Press, 1995.

I

ICE CREAM. Many tales and myths surround the origin and development of ice cream, including stories that connect this treat with the likes of Marco Polo (1254–1324) and Charles I of England (1600–1649). Whatever the true history of ice cream, the treat probably had its American introduction as early as the mid-1700s.

Some facts about ice cream in the United States include the following: Dolly Madison (1768–1849), wife of President James Madison (1751–1836), served it at the 1813 inaugural ball. A hand-cranked freezer had been invented and patented in 1843. In 1926, the continuous freezer, which yielded a high-quality product, appeared. Since the mid-1800s, ice cream parlors have existed, especially in larger cities, and the dining cars on **trains** once carried ice cream as a standard menu item. Dry ice (solid carbon dioxide) became available in 1930 for, among other things, keeping ice cream cold.

Prohibition, or the Eighteenth Amendment to the U.S. Constitution, made it unlawful to manufacture, sell, or transport intoxicating liquors. It became law in January 1920, and saloons throughout the country closed. As a result, soda fountains and pool halls experienced a significant increase in business. Breweries such as Anheuser-Busch switched part of their product line to ice cream, a momentous change. During the 1920s, the annual national consumption of ice cream increased significantly, from 260 million gallons to 365 million gallons.

With the onset of the Great Depression, annual ice cream production dropped and did not rebound until 1934. In order to survive during this difficult period, ice cream wholesalers searched for markets beyond the traditional ice cream stands and parlors. This led them to **grocery stores and supermarkets**. A major obstacle for expansion into this lucrative market involved the absence of refrigerated cases for **frozen foods** within the stores. In addition, homes lacked refrigerators or ice boxes with freezer space. At best they could accommodate only one or two frozen food packages. But all that quickly changed when grocery stores acquired freezer cases, and the first dual-compartment, dual-temperature home refrigerator appeared on the market in 1939.

As far as grocery stores went, the New York Eskimo Pie Corporation in 1930 temporarily solved the cold storage problem for both stores and homes by providing insulated containers. The company manufactured its ice cream in cylindrical molds that would fit inside refrigerated Thermos vacuum jars. It supplied the grocery store with a large vacuum container for storing the ice cream and smaller ones for customers to take home with their purchases. Hefty deposits on the take-home containers ensured their return to the grocery store for reuse. When placed in a refrigerator at home they would keep ice cream in a frozen state for 24 hours, or about 7 hours without refrigeration.

In 1931, the Great Atlantic and Pacific Tea Company (A&P), a successful grocery chain, started offering hardened ice cream in pint cartons in its northern New Jersey stores. The following year they added this product to their stores in New York City and surrounding areas while also providing shoppers insulated bags for carrying the ice cream home.

In addition to ice cream in pint cartons and vacuum containers for home consumption, ice cream parlors and soda fountains had long sold individual scoops in cones or dishes. With their easy portability, cones had become popular wherever people walked—city streets, **fairs and expositions**, beaches, and amusement parks. Some researchers credit the 1904 World's Fair in St. Louis as the original home for the cone, but no reliable documentation has been found to identify the inventor of this handy edible container. After the St. Louis exposition, however, the manufacture and sale of cones proliferated and continued throughout the 1930s.

Creating novel shapes for ice cream and other frozen treats represents another industry focus during both the 1920s and 1930s. Harry B. Burt Sr. (active early 1920s—d. 1926) of Youngstown, Ohio, in 1923 had been granted patents for what he called the Good Humor Sucker, a chocolate-covered ice cream bar. To promote his new product, Burt painted a delivery truck white, equipped it with bells, dressed drivers in white uniforms, and sent them into local neighborhoods to sell directly to the consumer. After Burt's death, the Good Humor Corporation of America began granting franchise arrangements nationally. During the 1930s, Burt's inspired scheme of the Good Humor Man ringing bells and selling ice cream from a truck became a familiar scene in communities across the United States.

Frank Epperson (b. 1894–active in 1920s) in 1924 received a patent for the Popsicle, frozen ices on a stick that came in seven fruit flavors. Shortly thereafter, he sold his rights to the Joe Lowe Company of New York City, a firm that offered a double-stick version of the Popsicle during the Depression. The sticks kept the eater's hands clean, and two sticks allowed a budget-minded family to purchase one treat that could be broken apart and shared by children.

Christian Nelson (1893–1992) owned a small Iowa ice cream shop in the 1920s and created a candy he named the "Temptation I-Scream Bar." In 1934, Nelson followed the example of Popsicle by placing his chocolate-covered ice cream bar on a stick and calling it an Eskimo Pie. Within a short time, Eskimo Pies had national distribution.

In 1929, Clarence Vogt (active 1920s) of Louisville, Kentucky, applied for a patent for a continuous freezer, a device that cooled the ice cream mix. The machine pumped the cooled ice cream into a reservoir, and then forced the mixture through a vacuum pipe into a freezer where the mix quickly reached the desired consistency. Before receiving the patent, Vogt sold his rights to the Cherry-Burrell Corporation. By 1932, Cherry-Burrell had advanced the process, so that their machines could harden ice cream in about five minutes. Almost half the ice cream manufactured in the United States came from their continuous freezers by the end of the decade.

The ice cream companies founded in the 1930s displayed various growth patterns—some remained local or regional, some closed after a period of time, and some eventually spanned most of the country. Howard Johnson's, Friendly's, and Dairy Queen are representative of those operations that attained national recognition.

Howard Johnson (1896–1972), a New England businessman, in 1925 used his mother's ice cream recipe to manufacture three classic flavors—vanilla, chocolate, and strawberry. He enjoyed success with a soda fountain in his drugstore in the Wollaston section of Quincy, Massachusetts, and that encouraged him to open beachfront ice cream stands along the coast. By the 1930s, his enterprises had expanded to include family-style **restaurants** serving full meals, as well as hot dogs and what in time would become his trademark, 28 flavors of ice cream. By the end of the decade there were 107 Howard Johnson's in the eastern United States.

In Springfield, Massachusetts, two brothers, S. Prestley Blake (b. 1915) and Curtis L. Blake (b. 1917) in 1935 sold ice cream at a business they called the Friendly Ice Cream Company. Their 5-cent double-dip cones (about 75 cents in contemporary money) attracted lots of customers and five years later they opened a second Friendly shop in West Springfield where they added **food** to the menu. Within a decade the Blakes had locations throughout Massachusetts and Connecticut. In 1979, Friendly became a part of Hershey Foods Corporation, and in 1988 the business, now part of an investor group, changed its name to Friendly's.

J. F. McCullough, along with his son Alex (both active 1930s), Iowa-based ice cream manufacturerers, owned the Homemade Ice Cream Company in Davenport. The father and son shared a belief that ice cream tasted better in the soft creamy form that it takes before going into the freezer step of the continuous freezer process. The two worked on creating a recipe and a machine for producing a commercially viable soft-frozen dairy product, and on August 4, 1938, they held an introductory sale at a friend's ice cream store in Kankakee, Illinois. Within two hours they had sold over 1,600 portions of soft ice cream at 10 cents each (about $1.45 in contemporary money), a rather high price at the time. The McCulloughs continued to improve the process and the dispensing machines. By 1940, they had opened their first soft ice cream store in Joliet, Illinois. At one point during the development of this product, the McCulloughs admired a herd of cows and J. F. commented, "Cows, the queen of the dairy." Shortly thereafter, their business carried the name Dairy Queen.

The manufacture of ice cream by the end of the 1930s had moved from labor-intensive factories to a production process using continuous freezers. The consumer could purchase ice cream in several different forms, choose from a nearly endless variety of flavors, and shop at innumerable outlets. Ice cream appeared on menus in restaurants, in the dining cars of trains, and at White House events. It had become as American as apple pie.

See also Candy; Design; Desserts; Leisure & Recreation; Prohibition & Repeal

SELECTED READING

Dairy Queen. http://www.davidsdairyqueen.com/history.html
Funderburg, Anne Cooper. *Chocolate, Strawberry, and Vanilla: A History of American Ice Cream.* Bowling Green, OH: Bowling Green State University Popular Press, 1995.
Good Humor Ice Cream. http://www.icecreamusa.com/goodhumor/know.asp

ICE SKATING & HOCKEY. Ancient ice skates, with bones serving as the blades and leather thongs for tying them to the feet, have been found in a glacial valley in Switzerland, suggesting the sport had been developed some 3,000 years ago. Over that span of time, little has changed other than the evolution and sophistication of the skate itself.

Throughout the eighteenth and nineteenth centuries, skating found enthusiastic participants. By the early twentieth century, standards for freestyle and figure techniques had been put in place, and ice skating had become both a participatory and a spectator sport. Sanctioned competitions replaced the older, more informal, displays of skill.

During the 1930s, people enjoyed skating when the weather permitted, but the sport lacked a broad base of official support. Even ice hockey remained essentially undiscovered in much of the United States; an activity far more popular in neighboring Canada. Figure skating, on the other hand, achieved visibility in the 1930s thanks to one person in particular. Sonja Henie (1912–1969), a native of Norway, emerged as ice skating's first truly big star. Until her rise to fame, earlier skaters—Jackson Haines (1840–1875), Irving Brokaw (1870–1939), Charlotte Oelschlagel (aka Charlotte Hayward; active early twentieth century), Maribel Vinson Owen (d. 1961)—had enchanted onlookers with their skills, but places to witness exhibitions of skating prowess existed only in the larger cities, and so skating had relatively few fans in the United States. Before Sonja Henie, "the Norwegian Doll," and without **television** to bring this visual sport into the nation's living rooms, most people knew little about it.

Henie had won, among other titles, the world's figure skating championship in 1927; she would successfully defend it for a decade. The title, however, carried little prestige across the Atlantic in the United States, where people viewed it more as a European victory. But Henie also earned gold medals for figure skating in the 1928, 1932, and 1936 **Olympic Games**, and the resultant publicity fanned her celebrity throughout the Western world. After her victories in 1936, she retired from competition and joined a professional American skating revue. Then she tried the **movies**—American movies. Eleven motion pictures would follow, with six of them produced during the 1930s.

Henie proved an instant hit with audiences. Possessed of limited acting ability, she relied on her skills as a skater, plus the talents of a host of set designers and choreographers, and a big budget for her staged production numbers. Screenwriters cannily placed her movies in a winter wonderland that allowed lengthy displays of her expertise on ice, with the result that films like *One in a Million* (1936), *Thin Ice* (1937), *Happy Landing* (1938), and *Second Fiddle* (1939) garnered few critical raves, but they drew in the curious, and they convinced millions of people to go out and buy a pair of skates. During Henie's years of stardom, the number of skating rinks in the United States increased dramatically, and she doubtless inspired untold numbers of would-be Olympians to try some jumps and spins on frozen ponds and lakes. She also freed women of the constricting outfits propriety had demanded. In her competitions and her movies she wore short skirts, and women skaters everywhere began to imitate her. A new era in skating attire had begun.

Ice hockey likewise struggled to gain popular acceptance. Although the sport probably dates back to some time in the seventeenth century, most scholars agree that the modern variant came into being around the mid-nineteenth century. With acceptance came rules and organization. The Stanley Cup, hockey's most prized trophy, had its inception in 1892, and several Canadian leagues competed for it. Professionals replaced amateurs as enthusiasm for the game grew, and 1917 saw the birth of the National Hockey League (NHL). Although it consisted almost entirely of Canadian players and teams (Winnipeg,

Ottawa, Toronto, Montreal, Halifax, etc.), the NHL nonetheless stirred interest in the United States.

Amateur hockey flourished in American schools and colleges in the years following World War I, laying the groundwork for a solid base of players and fans. In the northern tier of states, hockey actually outdrew **basketball**, and a haphazard network of teams played throughout the 1920s. In 1924, the Boston Bruins gained admittance to the NHL, opening the doors to American money and additional teams. The league continued its growth and split into Canadian and American divisions, with the New York Rangers successfully winning the coveted Stanley Cup in 1933 and 1940. The Chicago Blackhawks accomplished it in 1934 and 1938, and the Detroit Red Wings emerged victorious in 1936 and 1937. These American teams might have had mainly Canadian players on their rosters, but U.S. fans took pride in hometown franchises beating their once-mighty northern neighbors. Not until after World War II would American-born hockey players begin to make their influence and numbers felt.

Hollywood, attracted by the growing popularity of the game, the relatively small size of a hockey rink, and the sometimes explosive encounters between players, attempted several low-budget pictures about the sport during the 1930s. *King of Hockey* (1936), *The Game That Kills* (1937), *Idol of the Crowds* (1937), and *The Duke of West Point* (1938) typify the hockey films of the era. *Idol of the Crowds* features John Wayne (1907–1979) in a completely uncharacteristic role as a chicken farmer turned hockey player.

See also Design; Education; Fashion

SELECTED READING

Brown, Nigel. *Ice-Skating: A History*. New York: A. S. Barnes and Co., 1959.
Copley-Graves, Lynn. *Figure Skating History: The Evolution of Dance on Ice*. Columbus, OH: Plataro Press, 1992.
Stewart, Mark. *Hockey: A History of the Fastest Game on Ice*. New York: Franklin Watts, 1998.
Whedon, Julia. *The Fine Art of Ice Skating*. New York: Harry N. Abrams, 1988.

ILLUSTRATORS. During the 1930s, American illustrators created a collective body of work that merits attention. They carried on a tradition begun in the nineteenth century, one that celebrated the illustration as a form of visual art that could stand beside those works produced by their more "serious" counterparts. In **magazines**, books, posters, and seemingly endless **advertising**, these frankly commercial artists turned out thousands of pictures, often polished, sophisticated compositions that could be displayed in almost any museum. Generally realistic in their treatment of subjects, they reflected changes and trends in American culture, but they also offered their vast audiences a high level of consistent aesthetic excellence. Although most Americans were not aware of the movements and leaders in the rarified world of high art, they did not lack exposure to significant paintings and drawings.

Critics through the years have shunted aside most American illustrators, calling their work too narrative or too commercial, maintaining that it lacks any serious purpose other than telling a story or promoting a product. This kind of derisive attitude has long been the bane of much popular culture; elitist critics find it difficult to accept work aimed at a mass audience. The situation worsens if the illustration finds a large, receptive audience. If so many people like it, can it possibly be any good?

Throughout the nineteenth century, and on into the twentieth, illustrations—as opposed to photographs—dominated both publishing and advertising. Oils, watercolors, wood block prints, etchings, pen and ink, and many other techniques remained the preferred media for many artists, even after printing technology allowed the economical reproduction of photographs. Not until the late 1920s did the photographic illustration (or no illustrations at all) begin to replace more traditional forms of artistic expression, a trend that continued through the 1930s. What began slowly grew steadily during the early years of the economic collapse; by the mid-1930s, **photography** ruled advertising, displacing many illustrators and changing the face of the medium. For their part, book and magazine publishers, suffering dwindling profits, often stopped including illustrations in the pages of their products. Illustrators faced a shrinking market.

The following events occurred in the magazine world between 1929 and 1939: in 1929, *Youth's Companion*, long a user of illustrations in its content, ceased publication; in 1930, *The Century* went out of business. The original *Life* magazine closed up shop in 1936, bought by the owners of *Time* magazine in order to begin the "new" *Life*, a weekly journal that utilized photographs almost exclusively. Finally, in 1939, *Scribner's Magazine*, one of the last survivors from the nineteenth century, stopped publishing, another victim of the times and changing tastes. For illustrators, about the only bright spots in this dismal chronology occurred when two new magazines, bucking the trends, made their debuts. In 1925 the *New Yorker* came on the scene, a periodical that used drawings freely and featured illustrated covers. Several years later, in the depths of the Depression, *Fortune* magazine had its 1932 premiere, a sophisticated business journal that likewise boasted illustrated covers and articles. Both enjoyed success during the decade, exceptions in an industry beset with falling profits and difficult decisions.

Not all was lost; old stalwarts like the ***Saturday Evening Post***, *Collier's*, *McCall's*, *Cosmopolitan*, and others continued to employ illustrators, as did many advertisers. But the encroachment of photography, along with economic belt-tightening, pointed the way to the future. By the end of the 1930s, far fewer traditional illustrations graced books, magazines, and advertising.

Without a doubt, the most successful illustrator—financially and in terms of public recognition—for the 1930s was **Norman Rockwell** (1894–1978); his closest competitor, probably **N. C. Wyeth** (1882–1945). Neither Rockwell nor Wyeth, however, completely dominated the field of illustration. Numerous other artists also found lucrative assignments and turned out high-quality paintings and drawings. Most, however, have been forgotten, although many of their works, especially in the wide-ranging area of advertising, linger in the memory. Those familiar with advertising art of the 1930s certainly can recall examples like the beautiful Breck girls for Breck Shampoos, a series initiated by Charles Sheldon (1889–1960). The handsome men modeling Arrow collars and shirts came mainly from J. C. Leyendecker (1974–1951), whereas more feminine beauty appeared in endless, but anonymous, Coca-Cola ads. Otis Shepard (1893–1969) initiated the modernistic, airbrushed Wrigley twins for Wrigley chewing gum.

The following list, hardly inclusive, names just some of the important illustrators active during the 1930s. Notable or distinctive achievements accompany the mention of the artists; all these artists found steady employment during the Depression years and their work continues to draw praise.

Some Significant American Illustrators of the 1930s

McClelland Barclay (1891–1943): his sophisticated Body by Fisher illustrations helped form perceptions about automotive art.

Howard Chandler Christy (1873–1952): a fine portrait painter, his "Christy girls" raised the standards of feminine beauty in illustrations.

T. M. Cleland (1880–1964): noted for his striking architectural compositions.

Dean Cornwell (1892–1960): an artist who gained fame as a muralist.

Albert Dorne (1904–1965): a prolific contributor of illustrations for stories in the *Saturday Evening Post*.

Anton Otto Fischer (1882–1962): a popular artist, his marine paintings appeared frequently in both books and magazines.

James Montgomery Flagg (1877–1960): best remembered for his patriotic depictions of Uncle Sam during World War I, Flagg became a favorite of sophisticates and celebrities in the postwar years.

Peter Helck (1893–1988): a master of automotive art, as well as depicting almost anything else mechanical.

John Held Jr. (1899–1958): most famous for his humorous beaux and flappers during the 1920s, Held moved on to more serious themes in the 1930s.

Dorothy Hood (1902–1970): one of a handful of women active in illustration, Hood created distinguished **fashion**-oriented ads.

Rockwell Kent (1882–1971): often thought a "serious" American artist, but capable of carefully rendered and stylized drawings extolling expensive consumer goods for clients like Rolls-Royce **automobiles** and Steinway pianos.

Neysa McMein (1888–1949): another woman who made a name for herself, McMein created many covers for *McCall's* magazine and also did celebrity portraiture.

Maxfield Parrish (1870–1966): a popular artist, his paintings accompanying ads for Mazda lamps (GE light bulbs) appealed to a large public, and his Brown & Bigelow calendars circulated in the millions.

George Petty (1894–1975): his ads for Jantzen bathing suits celebrated the female form and led to the famous "Petty girl" pinups of World War II.

Willy Pogany (1882–1955): especially skilled in pen-and-ink illustration.

Norman Price (1877–1951): a strong historical sense informed many of his book illustrations.

Henry Raleigh (1880–1944): an illustrator for some of the most famous names in American literature whenever their stories appeared in the *Saturday Evening Post*.

Robert Riggs (1896–1974): particularly adept at portraying **circuses** and prizefights.

Mead Schaeffer (1898–1980): a favorite for creating illustrations for boys' adventure stories.

Jessie Willcox Smith (1893–1935): she focused on illustrations for children, but also did over 200 *Good Housekeeping* covers.

Two final illustrators deserve mention: Leslie Thrasher (1889–1936) and Haddon Sundblom (1899–1976). Both made unique contributions to the field. Thrasher, not a well-known name today, ranked among the leading illustrators of the 1920s and the first half of the 1930s. An accomplished painter, he earned his first significant commission in 1912 when he sold a cover to the esteemed *Saturday Evening Post*. Only 23 at the time, this contract placed him in the big leagues. After that breakthrough, Thrasher found himself in demand. A dream assignment came his way in 1926 when the editors at *Liberty* magazine, a rival to the *Saturday Evening Post*, offered him the chance to do a new cover each week for $1,000 per cover (roughly $11,000 in contemporary dollars). In a remarkable streak of creativity, he produced 360 cover illustrations for *Liberty*. The relationship came to an end in 1932, when shrinking revenues forced the publishers to cancel the contract.

Although not up to Rockwell's standards, Thrasher's work nonetheless represents good old-fashioned realism. Narrative in its approach, many of his *Liberty* covers depict the life and times of "Lil," a typical middle-class woman who also happens to be very attractive. Lil works as a stenographer, has a boyfriend whom she eventually marries, and ultimately gives birth to a baby boy. The storyline, one that would be echoed in Chic Young's (1901–1973) enormously popular comic strip *Blondie* then just beginning to run in many **newspapers**, attracted a wide audience for each successive cover. Readers liked Lil, contributing plot and picture ideas of their own in a contest that *Liberty* sponsored. A forgettable movie, *For the Love o' Lil* (1930), with Sally Starr (1909–1996) in the title role, capitalized on Lil's fame, as did a weekly **radio** show. These crossovers demonstrate how popular culture themes, when successful, seldom remain limited to a single medium.

Sundblom contributed an advertising image that has demonstrated, over the years, the power of effective illustration. An illustrator for the Coca-Cola Company, Sundblom in 1931 produced the first of a yearly Christmas painting for the firm featuring his version of Santa Claus. For the next 30 years, he depicted Santa Claus making his merry rounds, a frosty bottle of Coca-Cola in hand and enjoying "the Pause That Refreshes." His interpretation of jolly old Saint Nicholas created the modern-day Santa that now dominates Yuletide imagery and has been so accepted by the public.

An instant success—rotund, ruddy complexion, big smile, twinkling eyes, and all the rest—Sundblom's image was soon imitated by every other illustrator in the country. Not that Santa did not already exist in his red suit prior to 1931, but he tended to be more of an elfin figure, at times almost a gnome. And earlier Santas did not display much cheer; they could in fact appear somewhat frightening. N. C. Wyeth did several interpretations of Santa Claus before Sundblom came on the scene, but his man behind the beard seems sinister, hardly someone parents would want associating with little girls and boys. Norman Rockwell, who had himself painted some less-than-merry Saint Nicks earlier in his career, wisely adopted Sundblom's version of Santa in the 1930s, divorcing his new efforts from his previous work. Today, the 1931 Santa Claus of Haddon Sundblom has become a virtual generic model, imitated, reproduced, with little tinkering allowed.

The 1930s, following the standards established in preceding decades, proved a rich period for American illustration, but on a reduced scale. Unfortunately, too many skilled practitioners of the craft from the 1930s have been forgotten or labored in obscurity and remained anonymous.

See also Comic Strips; Gas Stations; *Life* & *Fortune*; Movies; Soft Drinks

SELECTED READING

Ermoyan, Arpi. *Famous American Illustrators*. New York: Society of Illustrators, 1997.

Holme, Bryan. *The Art of Advertising*. London: Peerage Books, 1982.

Meyer, Susan E. *America's Great Illustrators*. New York: Galahad Books, 1978.

Pitz, Henry. *200 Years of American Illustration*. New York: Random House, 1977.

Reed, Walt, and Roger Reed. *The Illustrator in America, 1880–1980*. New York: Society of Illustrators, 1984.

Roettger, Dorye. *Rivals of Rockwell*. New York: Crescent Books, 1992.

INTERNATIONAL STYLE. A term that identifies an architectural style that grew in importance and popularity throughout the 1930s. New York's Museum of Modern Art mounted an important show in 1932 that it called, simply Modern Architecture. Organized by architectural historian Henry-Russell Hitchcock (1903–1987) and architect Philip Johnson (1906–2005), this seminal exhibition displayed the work of a number of contemporary architects, most of them European, and employed the phrase "International Style" to describe their work. It traveled for almost two years and visited many American cities. In conjunction with the show, Hitchcock and Johnson coauthored *The International Style: Architecture since 1922* (1932), a book that introduced many people to both the term and these new **design** trends.

Hitchcock and Johnson argued for the rejection of classical detailing and ornamentation, stating that a building should be "honest"; it should be a reflection of itself and its underlying structure, not disguised to fit an arbitrary style. To them, the modernism of the 1930s celebrated a marriage of art and industrial design, and in saying this, they rejected most applied ornamentation. Their repudiation of decorative elements opened the way for the unadorned skyscraper that would characterize so much American **architecture** for the remainder of the century and became the hallmark of the International Style . The hubcaps and hood ornaments of the **Chrysler Building**, so beloved by generations of onlookers, were declared passé even as the skyscraper rose and the 1930s emerged as a transitional decade.

Only a few years earlier the Neoclassical Revival and Beaux-Arts Classicism had been the rage for larger commercial and public buildings in the United States. In 1934, John Russell Pope (1874–1937), an architect steeped in tradition, received the commission to design the Jefferson Memorial in Washington, D.C.; three years later he returned to do the National Gallery of Art, and most people found his traditional, classical designs entirely appropriate. Yet many American architects knew that such construction lagged behind ongoing international trends.

The threat of a new war in Europe prompted the steady emigration of architects to the United States. They introduced fresh, modern concepts to the nation, and their American counterparts realized a new, more austere and linear approach to design would eventually rule the day. Austrian-born Richard Neutra (1892–1970) arrived in 1923, one of the first of many émigrés. He settled on the West Coast, and his Lovell House (1929; Los Angeles) received considerable acclaim, an early signal that change blew in the wind. The construction of the Lovell House consisted of a light metal frame, white panels, and wide expanses of glass, resembled nothing previously seen. He followed that groundbreaking design with several more residences, including the Von Sternberg House (1935; also in the Los Angeles area), solidifying his reputation as a pioneering architect.

Rudolf Schindler (1887–1953), another Austrian, moved to the U.S. in 1914 in an effort to meet **Frank Lloyd Wright** (1869–1959), one of the leading American architects of that time. Not only did he connect with Wright, he also worked with fellow country-man Richard Neutra. Schindler's work with reinforced concrete and plain, unadorned facades placed him in the International Style school and furthered the cause of modern architecture in the United States.

While Neutra and Schindler went about creating distinctive buildings on the West Coast, several other Europeans settled in New England. Walter Gropius (1883–1969), an architect who in the 1920s founded the famous German Bauhaus (it loosely trans-lates as "house for building"), fled his native land in 1934 with the rise of Nazism. He made his way to Harvard University's Graduate School of Design, a welcoming refuge that also took in his compatriot Marcel Breuer (1902–1981), a Hungarian designer.

In 1937, Gropius built his own house in Lincoln, Massachusetts, and it serves as a good example of the new International Style. Its flat roof, smooth, taut facades, rectilinear shapes, and use of pale colors effectively sum up this approach to architecture. On the interior, the house features an open floor plan and functional, but not particularly deco-rative, furniture. For American designers, the influence of these foreign architects had immeasurable impacts, and the insularity of the profession in the United States received a stiff challenge.

Not everything in the International Style revolved around residential designs. One of the earliest major commercial structures to reflect such changes went up in the City of Brotherly Love in 1932, the Philadelphia Savings Fund Society (PSFS) building. Jointly designed by an American, George Howe (1886–1955), and a Swiss émigré, William Lescaze (1896–1969), the PSFS skyscraper shed existing traditions and boldly proclaimed itself a part of the International Style. Howe broke with his own past and embraced the more advanced thinking espoused by Lescaze. By so doing, the pair created the first major American office structure clearly inspired by European modernism.

Located in the heart of downtown Philadelphia, the lower portion boasts highly pol-ished granite that leads to a distinctive rounded corner. Shops occupy the ground level, and banking business is transacted on the second floor. The main shaft, built of limestone with gray brick spandrels, rises smoothly from the base with flush windows and minimal decorative elements. At the top, the letters "PSFS" are integrated into the tower. The final result represents a sharp break from anything that went before it.

Aware of these modern currents flowing across the Atlantic, American architects wasted no time in articulating their own interpretations of the International Style. Raymond Hood (1881–1934), along with John Mead Howells (1868–1959), employed elements of this new vision with their Daily News Building (1930) in New York City. Another important departure from tradition, and located in the shadow of the **Art Deco** Chrysler Building, the Daily News Building similarly possesses an ornate Art Deco facade at its base, but there the resemblance ends. The brick-covered steel frame of the building shaft remains unadorned, a soaring tower devoid of the decorative touches usu-ally applied to skyscrapers. And at its top, the building simply ends—no ornamented cornice, no classical pyramid, nothing—making it something of a prototype for the sleek, modern towers that typified the International Style.

Hood followed the Daily News Building with the McGraw-Hill Building (1930–1931), a revolutionary structure clad in glass and blue green terra cotta over a steel frame. From one angle it appears to be an Art Deco skyscraper, complete with setbacks, but from another it resembles a smooth slab that reaches into the New York sky. Clearly, the International Style had begun to make inroads on traditional design, and Hitchcock and Johnson chose it, in their eponymous book, as an example of the new style.

Rockefeller Center (1930–1940), one of the great construction projects of the Depression—or any other era, for that matter—also reflects Hood's influence. From its beginnings until the architect's untimely death in 1934, Hood actively participated in the development of this mammoth complex. His RCA Building (1934), the centerpiece of the development, echoes the earlier Daily News Building, but stands on its own as a splendid example of his modernist sensibilities.

Hood also contributed to the 1933–1934 **Century of Progress Exposition** (Chicago World's Fair). Although much of the architecture displayed at that modernistic fair reflects the prevailing influence of Art Deco and **Streamlining**, Hood's work on the Electrical Building displays elements of emergent styles, among them European modernism, or the International Style.

Another New York firm, Shreve, Lamb & Harmon, further transformed the urban skyline by designing a building reflective of these new trends. The **Empire State Building** (1931), possibly the most famous skyscraper of them all, soared into the air, a structure that had Art Deco roots, but one that in its sleek, smooth facade also looked to the future. The Empire State Building cannot be considered an International Style tower, but it possesses traits that later structures would emulate.

Not everyone embraced the International Style. Art Deco and the newer Streamlining enjoyed adherents who appreciated at least some applied ornamentation. For much of the decade, these two approaches actually overshadowed the stark austerity of the International Style, and not until after World War II would this form of modernism emerge as dominant, particularly when applied to high-rise office towers.

See also Fairs & Expositions; New York World's Fair

SELECTED READING

Hitchcock, Henry-Russell, and Philip Johnson. *The International Style.* New York: W. W. Norton, 1932.

Jordy, William H. *American Buildings and Their Architects: The Impact of European Modernism in the Mid-Twentieth Century.* Garden City, NY: Doubleday [Anchor Press], 1976.

Nash, Eric P. *Manhattan Skyscrapers.* Princeton, NJ: Princeton Architectural Press, 1999.

IT HAPPENED ONE NIGHT. In American cinema, looniness got transferred to a type of comedy entirely new to the screen. Aptly named **screwball comedies**, these popular pictures set up ridiculous plot situations that then are resolved in equally ridiculous ways. One of the first movies to articulate the genre, and still a favorite, *It Happened One Night* (1934) offers a laugh-filled story that defies reason, but reason has little to do with screwball comedies. Directed by Frank Capra (1897–1991), it stars Clark Gable (1901–1960) and Claudette Colbert (1903–1996). At the time, studio publicists touted Gable as an action hero, a ladies' man with muscles, and Colbert had just played a very feminine romantic lead in *Cleopatra* (1934), a Cecil B. DeMille (1881–1959) costume epic. No one thought of either actor as a comedian.

Clark Gable (1901–1960) and Claudette Colbert (1903–1996) in a scene from *It Happened One Night* (1934). (Courtesy of Photofest)

In this landmark picture, Gable and Colbert enthusiastically trade wisecracks and engage in physical comedy, revealing themselves to be skillful comic artists. The movie revolves on a simple premise, one that drives most screwball comedies: when will the two antagonists realize they are in love? Director Capra keeps the waters roiled as the would-be lovers work their way up the East Coast by Greyhound bus, by decrepit car, and, in a classic bit of visual comedy, by hitchhiking. Closed **gas stations** and mechanical breakdowns compound their woes. Of course, love wins out in the closing frames, but not before lots of misunderstandings, coincidences, and turmoil have their time on screen. It hardly sounds funny, but funny it is, and the fast-moving script and tight direction keep it that way. Hollywood seemed to agree: in an unheard-of sweep, *It Happened One Night* took Best Picture, Best Actor, Best Actress, Best Director, and Best Screenplay at the 1934 Academy Awards, a feat not equaled again until 1975 with *One Flew over the Cuckoo's Nest*.

Colbert portrays a flighty, but wealthy, young woman, a stock figure in numerous screwball comedies, who has rejected her fortune in a quest for independence. Gable portrays a sturdy, cynical but sensible, reporter who winds up in Colbert's company. The mid-1930s marked a period when the **Hollywood Production Code** rigidly controlled film content, especially anything having to do with sex. Screenwriters had to work overtime to sneak anything by the censors, but a review of Hollywood movies from the era would show that they frequently succeeded. Not that *It Happened One Night* contains anything off-color—far from it—but it gleefully displays a liberal sprinkling of suggestiveness, all in good taste. The subtext of sex that drives most screwball comedies took on an unrivaled sophistication during the decade, resulting in a series of adult films in all the best senses of the term.

In a classic scene, Gable and Colbert have stopped for the night at an auto camp, the 1930s term for a crude cross between a motel and a roadside cabin. They have to share a tiny room, and so he rigs a clothesline and hangs a blanket, "the wall of Jericho," as a barrier between the twin beds. Colbert borrows a set of Gable's pajamas because she has none of her own with her. Popular mythology says that millions of women, after seeing the movie, demanded man-styled pajamas of their own. Myth or not, the whole episode carries a wealth of sexual innuendo that culminates with the two having breakfast the next morning, just like a married couple. Fortunately for audiences, code officials allowed the scene to be kept in the movie, even with its rather obvious implications. And, much later, the wall would come tumbling down.

Screwball comedies marked a shift in movie content. Although they rely on stereotypes to a degree, they do so by turning them around. For example, *It Happened One Night* does not concern itself with sophisticated lovers living in a luxurious **Art Deco** world; its milieu remains very much 1930s Depression America. Crowded **buses** full of working-class passengers, decrepit **auto camps** run by suspicious proprietors, and the grim reality of being broke provide the background for this picture. The theme of the movie, however, derives from tradition, the idea of reconciliation, of letting love eventually resolve any conflicts. But the success of this and other screwball comedies also demanded that every conceivable obstacle be placed in the lovers' way and that resolution come about in a zany, comedic way.

See also Automobiles; Fashion; Motels; Movies; Social Consciousness Films; Spectacle & Costume Drama Films

SELECTED READING
Capra, Frank. *The Name above the Title: An Autobiography*. New York: Macmillan, 1971.
Kendall, Elizabeth. *The Runaway Bride: Hollywood Romantic Comedy of the 1930s*. New York: Alfred A. Knopf, 1990.
Poague, Leland A. *The Cinema of Frank Capra: An Approach to Film Comedy*. New York: A. S. Barnes and Co., 1975.
Sikov, Ed. *Screwball: Hollywood's Madcap Romantic Comedies*. New York: Crown Publishers, 1985.

J

JAZZ. Throughout the twentieth century, jazz, possibly the country's most original art form, dwelt on the musical margins, a format created in the late nineteenth century principally by black Americans. The **music** grew out of a heritage of oppression and segregation, which in its earliest forms traced some of its roots back to Africa and the Caribbean. Jazz served as a form of artistic expression for black musicians unable to play in the more popular white bands. Negligible white audiences existed for this new music, and thus it matured in obscurity. Not until after World War I, as the nation lurched into the Roaring Twenties, the so-called Jazz Age, did it begin to attract a broader, more diverse audience. For the general public, any music lively and loud constituted jazz. For many young white musicians, the syncopated rhythms of jazz proved irresistible; soon white bands began trying to reproduce this raucous, often improvised, music, much to the dismay of their elders.

For the later 1920s and on into the 1930s, the greatest advances in jazz occurred in Harlem, the sprawling center of black population and culture in New York City. Throughout the 1920s, musicians flocked there, leaving behind the older New Orleans sounds, in order to hone their skills and find sympathetic colleagues. Ironically, many of the black cultural and moral leaders of the day turned deaf ears to jazz, striving instead to promote more "acceptable" white formats. Thus little about jazz will be found in writings about the much-vaunted Harlem Renaissance of the 1920s and 1930s. Despite this lack of community support, jazz nonetheless flourished, a sub-rosa expression of art and music, one that would lead to experimentation and eventually the advent of so-called modern jazz.

Innovators like **Duke Ellington** (1899–1974), James P. Johnson (1891–1955), Willie "the Lion" Smith (1987–1973), Art Tatum (1909–1956), and Fats Waller (1904–1943) cut their artistic teeth in Harlem clubs and at "rent parties," gatherings where the hat would be passed in order to pay the rent, and some of the best jazz of the day served as entertainment. The hard times of the early 1930s saw a continuation of the musical ferment in Harlem, much of which occurred unnoticed by white critics or listeners living just a few segregated blocks away.

Despite the musical advances transpiring in Harlem, along with Chicago, Kansas City, and the Southwest, the band that in the late 1920s garnered the most popular attention performed under the baton of white bandleader Paul Whiteman (1890–1967), the self-styled "King of Jazz." Although many would argue the highly arranged selections that

Whiteman played hardly constituted jazz, he nonetheless introduced white audiences to a kind of popular music that employed a rhythmic base and ensemble playing that scores of later bands would emulate. In addition, Whiteman had a decided flair for recognizing talent. Bix Beiderbecke (1903–1931), a cornetist hired by Whiteman, showed immense promise as a lyrical player. **Bing Crosby** (1903–1977), one of the premier vocalists of the twentieth century, joined the band in the later 1920s and would subsequently influence legions of singers; he early on displayed an ability to incorporate jazz phrasing into his renditions of even the most mediocre pop songs. Many other musicians who would attain stature among jazz instrumentalists passed through the Whiteman orchestras. He went far in introducing jazz elements to audiences everywhere, although it would be difficult to argue that his arrangements rivaled anything then being done by the relatively anonymous Harlem groups.

By the end of the 1920s, jazz—New Orleans style, riverboat, Chicago, Harlem, ragtime, Dixieland, dance band, instrumental, and vocal—had earned a proper place in any catalog of musical styles. Purists might insist on including only those groups that played the original music of New Orleans, but others wanted the hottest licks by a new generation of musicians who had assimilated popular music, dance tunes, and jazz. With the onset of the 1930s, jazz had become a complex amalgam of styles and approaches, now played by blacks and whites alike, but still perceived by many as "Negro music" dwelling on the margins of artistic legitimacy. Associations with jazz and drinking, drugs, **crime**, and other assorted vices continued to plague it, and the racial connotations also blocked its full-scale acceptance by the purveyors of popular culture.

For most Americans during the early 1930s, innocuous pop music dominated. Growing out of the European tradition of written scores and careful arrangements, the format placed little emphasis on improvised solos or unusual rhythmic patterns. Society dance orchestras took few chances; even the most up-tempo arrangements always suggested tight control; innovation and emotional expression had no place in such music. "Sweet bands" led by the likes of Eddy Duchin (1909–1951), Wayne King (1901–1985), Guy Lombardo (1902–1977), and Anson Weeks (1896–1969) pleased patrons with genteel, superficial fox trots. Many boasted **radio** shows, and their bland arrangements held few surprises. Beneath this languid surface, however, new currents churned the musical waters.

As the 1930s progressed, in a number of places in the Midwest and Southwest, as well as New York's Harlem, **recordings**, radio remotes, and appearances by bands led by **Count Basie** (1904–1984), **Fletcher Henderson** (1898–1952), Chick Webb (1902–1939), and others offered pleasant surprises to those willing to listen. Soloists, such as trumpeters Louis Armstrong (1901–1971) and Roy Eldridge (1911–1989), pianists Earl Hines (1903–1983) and Mary Lou Williams (1910–1981), and saxists Coleman Hawkins (1904–1969), Johnny Hodges (1906–1970), and Lester Young (1909–1959), expanded the vocabulary of both their instruments and the music they played. These aggregations and musicians, primarily black at first, paved the way for the most popular music of the period, **swing**.

Jazz came the closest it has ever come to truly widespread popularity during the brief period called the swing era, roughly the mid-1930s to the mid-1940s. Although jazz played an all-important role in the evolution of the swing phenomenon, it seldom breached the barricades of mass popular culture. Instead, jazz directed its appeal to innumerable subgroups, avid followers of particular forms of the music, fans who often disdained other styles and performers. Much of the swing so associated with the 1930s certainly grew out of jazz, just as much jazz of the time likewise borrowed from swing, but those who embraced swing might genuinely profess an ignorance about the larger subject of jazz itself (and vice versa).

Swing cannot be defined as jazz, at least not jazz in any academic definition of the term. It exists as an amalgam, a mix of dance music, popular songs, standards, and jazz that receives a rhythmic emphasis that causes the music to "swing," to be danceable, music to snap the fingers in time. Since its inception, jazz has always "swung," that is, it has always relied on rhythm as a pulsating force to carry a composition forward. The time assigned a song, such as 2/4 or 4/4, has little to do with the jazz feeling, or lack thereof, imposed on a tune—even a 3/4 waltz can be made to swing when performed by the right musicians. Hoagy Carmichael's (1899–1981) "Stardust" (originally composed in 1927), for example, may be a soulful, jazz-inflected ballad when played by a tenor saxophonist or a romantic pop tune when sung by a popular singer. For jazz, the right musicians, the right arrangements, the right improvisations, can impart a quality to a performance different from anything in the purely popular idiom.

Jazz had started the decade still in its relative infancy. Forward-looking musicians and performers, like Basie, Benny Carter (1907–2003), Hawkins, Henderson, and Tatum, remained in the minority. In the public mind, jazz and Dixieland (i.e., traditional, jazz-inflected music) remained virtually interchangeable terms. As the 1930s progressed, however, more complex compositions and arrangements, along with more of a break with the past, began to change people's perceptions about the music. Small combos that emphasized disciplined musicianship and soloists willing to work with a song's chord structure as well as its melody, signaled change in the wind. Big bands, such as Ellington's, played compositions that demanded concentration on the listener's part. The easy, toe-tapping music that once said "jazz" had been replaced by a more serious approach; it might still be rhythmic and danceable, but it no longer sounded like the jazz of the 1920s.

With swing in the ascendancy in the later 1930s, the lines separating jazz and swing grew increasingly blurred, and most people probably did not care. The **Benny Goodman** (1909–1986) band, one of the most popular of the day, could perform "I'm Always Chasing Rainbows" (originally written in 1918 for a Broadway musical) with a vocal by Helen Forrest (1917–1999), and a flag-waving instrumental arrangement of "Stompin' at the Savoy" (written in 1936 as an up-tempo dance number) in the same evening. Worlds apart, the rendition of "I'm Always Chasing Rainbows" might be categorized as swing or simply a sweet pop number, whereas "Stompin' at the Savoy" would more likely be identified as jazz. Same band, two songs, but with confusion reigning over definitions and categories. By the end of the decade, a band like the one led by **Glenn Miller** (1904–1944), arguably the most popular swing aggregation of them all, seldom had any jazz labels attached to it. Miller's band, with a number of respected jazz musicians in its ranks, played swing and popular music and little else.

The discussion might best end as a purely academic one. Jazz and swing remained inextricably linked during the 1930s and both had their ardent defenders. Jazz, more intellectual—more cerebral, perhaps—than swing, evolved into more categories than its close relative. Swing, more commercial, more oriented to popular music than jazz, had much the larger following for awhile, but faded more quickly. Jazz went on to other formats, reinventing itself as it did so. It has changed, but even today it is still jazz.

See also Alcoholic Beverages; Jitterbug; Musicals; Race Relations & Stereotyping

SELECTED READING
Gioia, Ted. *The History of Jazz*. New York: Oxford University Press, 1997.
Kirchner, Bill, ed. *The Oxford Companion to Jazz*. New York: Oxford University Press, 2000.
Stearns, Marshall. *The Story of Jazz*. New York: Oxford University Press, 1958.

JIGSAW PUZZLES. Whether intricately hand-cut from wood or mechanically stamped from cardboard, jigsaw puzzles emerged as one of the most popular diversions available to people during the Depression. This kind of puzzle can be traced back to England and the mid-1700s, and has enjoyed varying levels of favor ever since. Once considered an activity for children, the jigsaw puzzle began to attract adults around 1900 and erupted into a full-fledged fad in the 1930s.

Prior to the Depression, most puzzles consisted of pictures glued to thin wooden boards which were then meticulously cut, using a jigsaw, into various shaped pieces. The interlocking puzzle, although it did exist, proved rare. As a rule, the pieces merely matched up and could be easily disturbed. A slight breeze, a jarred table, could undo hours of patient work. For the times, they also carried a high price tag, given all the hand cutting. Priced at anywhere from a penny to 2 cents per piece (roughly 15 to 30 cents in contemporary money), a 500-piece puzzle could cost up to $10 (or $150 in the present), a small fortune for the Depression era. Bookstores and other outlets often rented puzzles for just a few cents a day, putting them within reach of a growing legion of fans.

Following the 1929 stock market crash, sales of puzzles began a perceptible climb. By the beginning of 1932, over 2 million of them sold weekly, and both retailers and manufacturers took notice. That same year, the die-cut cardboard puzzle had its introduction. Heavy die-cutting machines stamped the pieces from cheap fiber boards. Capable of endless reproduction, these new variations on an old diversion could be mass-produced so cheaply that almost anyone could then afford them. From newsstands to Woolworth's to up-scale department stores, the new cardboard puzzles flooded the marketplace. At first, they cost about 69 or 79 cents (roughly $10 or $12 in contemporary money), although merchants often gave them away as premiums for buying other items in the store. Some clever marketers even used puzzles as a form of **advertising**; the pieces formed a picture of a particular product and served as giveaways along with a purchase.

By late 1932 and early 1933, their peak years, the cardboard puzzles sold at the rate of 10 million units a week. To entice still more sales, dealers featured brand-new "picture puzzle weekly," "weekly jig saw," "jiggety jig," "jig of jigs," and "jig of the week" and patrons lined up, usually on Wednesdays, to buy the latest offerings, often on sale for only a quarter (about $4 today).

Jigsaw puzzle clubs sprang up everywhere, and members swapped favorites with friends, another means of keeping costs down. The rapid upswing of jigsaw popularity gave rise to some cottage industries. Many individuals earned a bit of extra money by laboriously hand-cutting plywood boards into puzzles. Despite the success of die-cut products, the wooden variety continued to have its fans, and many how-to **magazines** touted turning home workshops into small puzzle factories for profit. Patience, a good eye, along with sharp blades for a small, powered jigsaw meant that a few of these entrepreneurs could make a reasonable living turning out intricate puzzles.

During the height of the craze, over 200 professional firms entered the die-cut side of the business, while some 3,000 home craftsmen labored over their jigsaws. Puzzle contests and races (who could assemble one the fastest) proliferated, and several songs—"My Jig Saw Puzzle of Love," "You Made a Jig-Saw Puzzle Out of My Heart"—played on the **radio**. A periodical, *Jigsaw Puzzles*, could even be found on newsstands.

In their heyday, the puzzle fad exerted a beneficial effect on portions of the moribund economy. For example, the Upson Company, located in Lockport, New York, had been a leader in the manufacture of wallboard during the 1920s. The Depression, however, all but ended the construction business. But employees at Upson found that the fiber board used in making wallboard could also serve as the backing for a die-cut jigsaw puzzle. Out of that discovery grew one of the most popular puzzle brands of the 1930s: Tuco. Tuco, a play on the *Upson Co.*, featured a wide variety of colorful mounted pictures. They came in bright, identifiable boxes and, because they used inexpensive materials, cost little. The company, along with a handful of other manufacturers, did well in the darkest years of the Depression, shipping up to 50,000 new puzzles a day at their peak.

Tuco's success also illustrates the nature of **fads**. After the puzzle mania had passed in the 1940s, Upson attempted to continue its Tuco line. A fickle public, however, gradually turned away from the one-time industry leader, and in 1980, despite diversification, the Upson Company declared bankruptcy. Ironically, the expensive, hand-cut wooden puzzles that cardboard virtually replaced have retained a small, but loyal following. Now commanding true premium prices, craftsmen still meticulously cut hundreds, sometimes thousands, of small pieces for dedicated aficionados.

Psychologically, puzzles may have attracted people during the Depression because of certain positive qualities. For someone out of work and with little to look forward to, the jigsaw puzzle provided not just temporary entertainment. It also gave the person who had the patience to complete it a sense of accomplishment, a small success in a time that needed any little victories one might achieve. Of course, a really difficult puzzle also consumed considerable idle time, an important consideration for anyone with little to do.

All crazes must eventually cool down, and puzzles proved no exception. For the first half of the 1930s, jigsaw puzzles constituted a fad of unusually large proportions. As the Depression waned, so did enthusiasm for jigsaw puzzles, but sales remained high throughout the decade, and the austerity of the war years helped them retain a measure of popularity.

See also Leisure & Recreation

SELECTED READING
Hanna, Linda. *The Jigsaw Book*. New York: Dial Press, 1981.
Jigsaw Puzzles. http://www.puzzlehistory.com
Williams, Anne D. *The Jigsaw Puzzle: Piecing Together a History*. New York: Berkley Penguin, 2004.

JITTERBUG. Throughout the latter half of the 1930s, millions of Americans attended **swing** concerts; millions more listened on their radios and purchased **recordings** by their favorite bands and soloists. Swing thrives on rhythm—infectious, snap-your-fingers, toe-tapping rhythm—although it also can usually be hummed, whistled, and even sung. But for a whole generation of devotees, swing meant dancing. The 1920s may have had the Black Bottom, the Charleston, and the Varsity Drag, but

With the wide acceptance of swing, the jitterbug became one of the decade's most popular dance styles. (Courtesy of the Library of Congress)

these veterans evolved into new steps, and the 1930s boasted the Big Apple, the Lindy Hop, the Little Peach, the Shag, the Suzy Q, and Truckin'—an entirely new and contemporary collection that could easily be summed up in one word: jitterbug. Fast and furious, improvised or practiced, the jitterbug and its countless variants had people dancing as never before.

Before swing inundated everything, most popular **music** of the early 1930s could be danced to, and for a majority of people this translated as the fox trot, a relatively staid combination of medium-tempo steps. But dance crazes come and go in all decades, and the Depression years awaited something new and different. As had long been the case with much American musical culture, innovation often took place, as it did with blues and **jazz**, in the segregated black community. In this instance, change manifested itself in a body of music associated with big bands and swinging arrangements, and the energetic dancing that accompanied them.

Popular anecdote has it that this new style of dancing initially received the name Lindy, or Lindy Hop. A direct precursor of the better-known jitterbug, the name derived from Charles Lindbergh (1902–1974), or "Lindy," as many fondly dubbed him. The man who in 1927 had "hopped" the Atlantic Ocean, the first person to fly solo across that body of water, had become a national hero. In this somewhat acrobatic dance, partners "took off" and "landed," executing steps that suggested flight. If nothing else, the Lindy caused a couple to put on a performance, or, as the slang of the day would have it, "to cut a rug" (i.e., the couple's dance steps are so good—so "sharp"—that they destroy the rug or carpeting beneath their feet). The always-debonair **Duke Ellington** would compose, in 1937, a little ditty he called "I've Got to Be a Rug Cutter."

The inclusive term "jitterbug" arose to collectively identify a number of distinctive exhibition-style dances, several of which provided onlookers as much pleasure as the dancers themselves. Those who excelled in their efforts were known as "shiners," presumably because of their ability to shine on the dance floor. "Jitterbug" itself functioned as a verb or a noun: to jitterbug meant to dance, usually frenetically, and usually to swing-style music. The term itself probably derives from the jerky, or "jittery" motions that occur in the dance, and in nonmusical slang a "jitterbug" defined a person—possibly inebriated or similarly impaired—who had the "shakes," the "jitters." The dance received the same name, and when referring to people, a jitterbug could either be a dancer or, more broadly, any devoted swing fan.

In some circles, instead of the longer word, people preferred the simpler "bug," In 1934, the popular bandleader Cab Calloway (1907–1994), a colorful individual in his own right and someone who always stood in the forefront as a source of catchy terms to describe the latest popular culture trends, had released a recording bearing the simple title "Jitterbug." An up-tempo dance number composed by trumpeter Edwin Swayzee (1905–1935), this tune introduced the word to a wide public. Although momentum for the jitterbug had been growing, it now had quasi-official sanction as a song title, and it quickly grew into a full-fledged fad.

Calloway followed his recording by publishing a slim volume titled *Cab Calloway's Hepster's Dictionary: The Language of Jive* in 1936. It served as an insider's guide to the argot of jazz and swing then growing among fans and underwent several printings and revisions. "Jive" meant, at the time, either the language of swing music or the music itself, although those limited interpretations quickly broadened. For example, "frisking the whiskers" means what musicians (i.e., "cats") do in rehearsal; "knock" suggests obtaining something, as "I'll knock me some bread," when "bread" means money; and "cat," "hepcat," and "hepster" all designate knowledgeable friends, companions, musicians—those "in the know."

The **movies** and the recording industry quickly picked up on the growing popularity of the jitterbug. Hollywood released a number of short musical features, such as *Jitterbug Party* (1935), *Jittering Jitterbugs* (1938), *Public Jitterbug Number One* (1939), along with several animated cartoons. Even the classy **Fred Astaire** (1899–1987) **and Ginger Rogers** (1911–1995) performed "The Waltz in Swing Time" (music by Robert Russell Bennett [1894–1981]) for the 1936 movie musical *Swing Time*. Some of the many recordings that flooded the market included titles like "Got the Jitters" (1934), "Rug Cutter's Swing" (1934), "Call of the Jitter" (1934), "They Call Us Jitterbugs" (1935), "*Life* Spears a Jitterbug" (1938; a parody on a popular feature in *Life* magazine called "*Life* Goes to a Party"), "Jitters" (1939), and "Jitterbugs on Parade" (1939), to name only a few of the releases.

The mecca for devoted jitterbugs soon became the Savoy Ballroom. A huge uptown nightclub in New York's Harlem, it opened its doors in 1926 and called itself "the Home of Happy Feet." Throughout the heyday of the jitterbug, the Savoy's management had to replace the hardwood dance floor every three years. "Stompin' at the Savoy" (1936) served as an appropriate anthem of the era. Jointly written by **Benny Goodman**

(1909–1986), Edgar Sampson (1907–1973), and Chick Webb (1902–1939), with lyrics by Andy Razaf (1895–1973), this up-tempo dance classic shares its lineage with both Goodman's orchestra and Webb's Savoy house band.

Other dances associated with the jitterbug craze, but hardly jitterbugs in and of themselves, included the Shag, Truckin', and the Lambeth Walk, all popular in the later years of the decade. In the first, small hops and kicks served as the order of the day. Truckin' involved shrugging the shoulders rhythmically, plus raising an arm and pointing a forefinger upward. The Lambeth Walk, an import from England, had couples walking forward and then backward with their arms linked. At the proper moment, they would thrust their thumbs into the air and say "Oy!" Each enjoyed its moment of fame, and the Shag, with variations, lives on today.

Nothing, however, equaled the classic jitterbug itself. Danced to medium or up-tempo numbers, the faster the better for most fans, it calls for many steps and constant motion. In all its manifestations, the jitterbug generally met with disapproval from dance teachers, schools of dance, and others connected with more traditional forms of expression. Most predicted its imminent demise from the mid-1930s onward, although the predicted death never arrived; if anything, the patient got better and better with time, so that by 1940 many a former naysayer had attempted a step or two. The jitterbug represented a form of sexual equality and freedom for couples. It also helped signal the emergence of a mass **youth** culture, a culture that even hinted at racial harmony, although that would be a long time coming. Perhaps the jitterbug's main appeal lay in the title of a 1939 hit tune penned by Sy Oliver (1910–1988) and Trummy Young (1912–1984), and generally associated with the Jimmy Lunceford (1902–1947) band: "'Tain't Wha'cha Do (It's the Way That You Do It)."

See also Aviation; Count Basie; Fads; Fletcher Henderson; Jukeboxes; *Life & Fortune*; Magazines; Marathon Dancing; Glenn Miller; Musicals; Race Relations & Stereotyping; Radio; *Your Hit Parade*

SELECTED READING

Hazzard-Gordon, Katrina. *Jookin': The Rise of Social Dance Formations in African-American Culture*. Philadelphia: Temple University Press, 1992.

Stearns, Marshall, and Jean Stearns. *Jazz Dance: The Story of American Vernacular Dance*. New York: Macmillan, 1992.

JUKEBOXES. Music served as one of the most pervasive forms of popular culture in the 1930s, and the lowly jukebox emerged as an effective carrier of all the latest hit songs. For a nickel, and often six or seven plays for a quarter (or about 75 cents and $3.65, respectively, in contemporary money), a listener could select from dozens of single records, and the ubiquitous machines catered to every taste.

The roots of the term "jukebox" remain murky, but probably can be traced to the American South. A "juke" meant a house of prostitution in West Africa, and the word made its way to the United States during the days of slavery. Like most transitions, it took on new meanings in the slave states. Cheap dance halls in the South sometimes came to be called "jukes"—with an alternative spelling of "jook"—and occasionally even the dances themselves took on the term. Small bands and combos had traditionally played in these juke joints, but in the late 1920s coin-operated record machines began to replace the live music. In a matter of time, "juke" shifted in meaning from locale and dance to the machine supplying the music, from a nameless "record machine" to a "jukebox." From those shady beginnings, jukebox has evolved into an innocent term with no connections to its past, although manufacturers persisted in calling them "multiselector phonographs," "automatic coin-operated phonographs," and the like.

The forerunners of the contemporary jukebox can be traced to the late nineteenth century, but not until 1921 did anything resembling the modern record changer arrive on the scene. In 1927, a coin-operated model had been perfected by the Automatic Instrument Company (AMI). Shortly thereafter, J. P. Seeburg, Rudolph Wurlitzer, and the Rockola (later Rock-Ola) companies entered the business.

The reopening of lounges, bars, and nightclubs following the repeal of Prohibition in 1933 signaled a need for music. Cheaper than any band, jukeboxes became standard fixtures, springing up everywhere. Their popularity, coupled with their appeal to a youthful, nondrinking, audience, meant that jukeboxes also appeared in **ice cream** parlors, soda fountains, and **restaurants**—anywhere music might boost business. Customers enjoyed the cheap entertainment jukeboxes provided, and proprietors saw them as a lure for more customers.

By the end of 1933, about 25,000 jukeboxes could be found scattered across the country. The total skyrocketed to over 100,000 by the mid-1930s, 225,000 by 1937, and it just kept climbing. Wurlitzer, the leading manufacturer of coin-operated machines, was turning out 45,000 a year by 1939, and its competitors boasted equally impressive numbers. At the close of the decade, more than 400,000 coin-operated jukeboxes played the latest hits, and millions of listeners and dancers supplied them with endless nickels and quarters.

Jukeboxes represented a godsend for the record industry, which was beset with problems throughout the Depression years. Toward the end of the 1930s, these insatiable machines consumed 720,000 records a week, 30 million a year, or almost half of all phonograph **recordings** sold in the country. A successful record got endlessly repeated, both in its original version and by imitators. In order to appease their public, musicians sometimes found themselves in stylistic ruts. Managers and record companies felt musical artists had to keep sounding like their most recent hit, an approach that stifled creativity. On the other hand, colorblind jukeboxes provided black musicians the best possible outlet for a mass audience. Although they replaced live musicians who might otherwise be performing at a dance hall or club, in its mechanical way, the jukebox served as an equalizer in a segregated music world.

Despite the widespread exposure, **songwriters and lyricists**, along with many musicians, objected to the use of recordings for both jukebox and **radio** play. They felt that coin-operated devices and radio stations deprived both composers and performers of income, since most of them received no royalties when a patron's nickel keyed a song or a disc jockey spun a record. Belatedly, ASCAP (the American Society of Composers, Arrangers, and Producers), an organization dedicated to protecting the performing rights of musicians and songwriters, stepped into this debate. In late 1939, broadcasters and jukebox owners retaliated by forming BMI (Broadcast Music Incorporated). A long, bitter fight over musicians' rights erupted, one that would not be resolved until the mid-1940s. The dispute illustrated the increasing impact the jukebox had on the recording industry and on popular music.

Another form of technologically enhanced music also emerged in the 1930s. Muzak, a service that piped recorded music directly to restaurants, dancehalls, factories, and offices, made its debut in Cleveland, Ohio, in 1934. Armed with a catalog of soothing background melodies, Muzak made no attempt to play or promote the latest hits or dance numbers. Instead, the company packaged programmatic music that required no concentration, a subliminal sound massage that had no impact on the popular music business.

With their sinuous curves, shimmering plastic and shiny chrome, neon tubes and flashing lights, the jukeboxes of the 1930s reflected the popular **Streamlining** of the era. They represented modern urban **architecture**, skyscrapers in miniature. More importantly, jukeboxes made money, both for the establishments housing them and for the music business. During the **swing** era, jukeboxes helped encourage **fads** and styles in music, and because of their ubiquity, they went a long way in determining a record's popularity.

See also Design; Jitterbug; Prohibition & Repeal; Race Relations & Stereotyping; *Your Hit Parade*

SELECTED READING
Jukeboxes. http://www.tomszone.com
———. http://www.nationaljukebox.com/history.html
Lynch, Vincent, and Bill Henkin. *Jukebox: The Golden Age*. Berkeley, CA: Lancaster-Miller, 1981.

K

KERN, JEROME. Born into a middle-class family in New York City, Jerome Kern (1885–1945) studied **music** first with his mother, received more formal instruction in city schools and colleges, and completed his formal **education** in Germany. Like many of his contemporaries, at the beginning of his professional musical career, Kern worked as a song plugger on Tin Pan Alley, that section of 28th Street in Manhattan between Fifth Avenue and Broadway where **songwriters and lyricists**, arrangers, and pluggers congregated and interacted with music publishers; it eventually came to mean the popular music business in general. A song plugger's job involved taking new tunes to different publishing houses in hopes of getting them printed and distributed as **sheet music**. They had to convince reluctant firms that the songs and lyrics they plugged stood the best chances of commercial success.

Kern finally realized that he should be writing and plugging his own music, and in 1903 enjoyed some good fortune with a piece called "Mister Chamberlain." It featured lyrics by P. G. Wodehouse (1881–1975), a popular writer who would become a frequent collaborator in the early days of Kern's career. The following year, along with several others, Kern's name appeared on the playbill of a short-lived Broadway musical, Mr. Wix of Wickham. Buoyed, he determined to make his mark as a composer in musical theater and to collaborate with the best lyricists in the business.

He persevered, and eventually saw major stage hits like Sally (1920), with lyrics by Clifford Grey (1887–1941) and Buddy DeSylva (1895–1950); Sunny (1925), lyrics by Otto Harbach (1873–1963) and Oscar Hammerstein II (1895–1960); and Show Boat (1927), lyrics by Oscar Hammerstein II. As he established his name, Kern also built up a priceless network of musical associates on whom he could call, so that by the end of the 1920s he had established his name on Broadway. For audiences hungry for some old-fashioned romanticism, Kern's theater work provided it, making him a commercial and artistic success.

Always in demand, he completed the music for five shows from 1929 to 1939, starting with Sweet Adeline, a production that again featured the lyrics of Oscar Hammerstein II. It opened in September 1929, just prior to the stock market collapse. A deliberate exercise in nostalgia—the original "Sweet Adeline" had been composed in 1903 by Harry Armstrong (1879–1951)—the play focused on the Gay Nineties and tried to re-create a sense of innocence. Reality intruded with the crash, however, and the show closed.

Composer Jerome Kern (1885–1945). (Courtesy of the Library of Congress)

Although few remember *Sweet Adeline*, they may recall one of Kern's tunes from the show, "Why Was I Born?" Essentially unchanged, the play reappeared as a film, starring Irene Dunne (1898–1990) in 1935.

A versatile composer, and one with an eye for financial success, Kern saw great potential in the world of movie music with the coming of sound in the late 1920s. His association with Hollywood began early and lasted throughout his life. Universal Studios in 1929 had rushed out a sound-and-silent mix of Kern's 1927 stage classic *Show Boat*. Billed as a "Super Talking Picture," the production left much to be desired. The studio abbreviated portions of the original, substituting new, non-Kern material. With improving sound technology, *Show Boat* saw a second, more faithful movie adaptation in 1936, one that played on screens with much better results.

Sally, a film version of the 1920 play of the same name, premiered on screen in 1929. The producers unfortunately altered the score, bringing in new numbers, but at least the Kern-Hammerstein classic "Look for the Silver Lining" survived studio meddling. *Sunny*, another Kern production, was adapted for film in 1930; it had first played on Broadway in 1925. Although both the play and the film have long since been forgotten, "Who?" and "Sunny" live on from the score.

In 1931, Jerome Kern returned to Broadway. With the reliable Otto Harbach as his lyricist, Kern wrote the music for *The Cat and the Fiddle*. Subtitled "A Musical Love Story," two romantic standards, "She Didn't Say 'Yes'" and "The Night Was Made for Love," came from the play. The following year, Kern reunited with Hammerstein for *Music in the Air*. This work produced two more classics, "I've Told Ev'ry Little Star" and "The Song Is You," and despite the severity of the Depression, played for over 300 performances.

But all the foregoing productions may have seemed like dress rehearsals for 1933's *Roberta*, one of the true masterpieces among American stage **musicals**. Working again with Harbach, Kern created some of his loveliest melodies. "Smoke Gets in Your Eyes" and "Yesterdays" both come from *Roberta*, followed by "Let's Begin" and "The Touch of Your Hand." With such a splendid score, the plot becomes almost secondary. Produced in the worst days of the Great Depression, the story concerns the glamorous world of high **fashion**, hardly the most popular topic of the period. But Kern had mastered serving up escapism in his music, and such a romantic diversion probably functioned as a tonic for many in the audience. *Roberta* played for a respectable 295 performances and enjoyed a film adaptation soon thereafter.

With the success of *Roberta* still fresh in everyone's minds, Kern returned to Hollywood. Not until 1939 would he again compose for the theater, when he and Oscar Hammerstein II joined forces for *Very Warm for May*. A box-office failure, it closed out Kern's Broadway career, although he would continue to write for the movies. Despite its lack of commercial success, *Very Warm for May* did yield "All the Things You Are," another standard that has stood the test of time.

Once ensconced in the film capital again, Kern worked on converting his theatrical scores for the **movies**. With few changes, 1931's *The Cat and the Fiddle* adapted well to the screen in 1934, giving singing star Jeanette MacDonald (1903–1965) a good vehicle for her vocal skills. It was promptly followed by *Music in the Air* (1934), a show that had entertained Broadway audiences in 1932. It now appeared on movie screens across the land in a 20th Century Fox production with the esteemed Gloria Swanson (1897–1983) in the lead.

Not all of Kern's Hollywood work revolved around revisions of his Broadway successes; he also scored original movies. In 1935, *I Dream Too Much* came out; it features the then-rising opera star Lily Pons (1898–1976), which helps to explain the film's somewhat stilted, operatic presentation. The movie, designed around contralto Pons' singing, demonstrates that Kern doubtless felt more at home writing popular melodies than trying to fit his style to a particular singer. *I Dream Too Much* does mark, however, the first picture in which Kern teamed up with lyricist **Dorothy Fields** (1905–1974), a collaboration that would blossom in time.

Roberta, such a big hit on the Broadway stage in 1933, received the movie treatment in 1935. The third musical to feature **Fred Astaire** (1899–1987) **and Ginger Rogers** (1911–1995), it served as the first, but not the last, matchup of Jerome Kern with the two stars. This popular picture employs the original score Kern had put together with Otto Harbach, plus two new numbers with lyrics by Dorothy Fields and Jimmy McHugh (1894–1969). The resultant soundtrack, one of the best ever for any Hollywood musical, offers all the stage originals, plus a couple of new standards by Fields and McHugh, "Lovely to Look At" and "I Won't Dance."

On the heels of *Roberta* came ***Swing* Time** (1936), the third Kern-Fields outing and their second picture with Astaire and Rogers. Many people would hold that *Swing Time* ranks as the best of the nine movies the dancers made together during the 1930s. That judgment comes in no small measure because of the superlative score that graces the movie. "The Way You Look Tonight," the Academy Award winner for Best Song in 1936, highlights the picture. But *Swing Time* contains almost nothing but highlights: "A Fine Romance," "Pick Yourself Up," and the lilting "Waltz in Swing Time." All of these timeless songs became popular hits and embellished the careers of everyone involved.

Show Boat, which had been attempted as a silent-plus-sound movie in 1929, came to the screen a second time in 1936 (it would be remade yet again in 1951). The all-star production features Irene Dunne, **Paul Robeson** (1898–1976), Helen Morgan (1900–1941), and a host of others. The original music, such as "Ol' Man River," "Make Believe," and "Can't Help Lovin' Dat Man," sparkles. In addition, this adaptation adds several new numbers—"Ah Still Suits Me," "I Have the Room above Her," and "Gallivantin' Around"—and they take nothing away from the original.

Never resting on his laurels, Kern continued to create film scores. Paramount Pictures came out with *High, Wide, and Handsome* in 1937, yet another production featuring lyrics by Oscar Hammerstein II. A mix of history picture and musical, it purports to tell the story about the quest for petroleum in nineteenth-century Pennsylvania. The fact that Paramount felt impelled to couch a historical event in musical terms perhaps suggests some timidity on the studio's part to focus on a little-known page from America's past. Although few recall the movie, "The Folks Who Live on the Hill," a romantic song that never refers to oil or American history, has become a standard, one beloved by generations of vocalists.

When You're in Love (1937), cowritten with Dorothy Fields, stars Grace Moore (1898–1947), a prominent Metropolitan Opera star, and resembles the earlier Lily Pons showpiece *I Dream Too Much* (1935). Not particularly memorable, *When You're in Love* allows Moore to take a stab at bandleader Cab Calloway's (1907–1994) signature "Minnie the Moocher," a 1931 novelty number that had become a hit for him. By 1937, with everyone climbing onto the swing bandwagon, it may not have seemed too outlandish an idea for an opera star to tackle Cab Calloway and an up-tempo tune, although later generations might disagree.

The capable Irene Dunne takes the lead in *Joy of Living* (1938), a combination of screwball comedy and musical. It boasts both a story and lyrics by Dorothy Fields. Little separates the jump from traditional musicals to offbeat comedy, and in fact the term "musical comedy" effectively bridges any gap between the two genres. The bright and cheery *Joy of Living* boasts several standards like "You Couldn't Be Cuter" and "Just Let Me Look at You."

For his final film score of the decade, Kern worked yet again with Fields, and the two created the music for *One Night in the Tropics* (1940). This bit of fluff stars the rising comedy team of (Bud) Abbott (1895–1974) and (Lou) Costello (1906–1959) and features "You and Your Kiss," "Back in My Shell," and "Simple Philosophy." Abbott and Costello might seem a far cry from the majesty of *Show Boat*, but Kern functioned as a popular—and commercial—composer. In retrospect, he wrote much of his music for decidedly inferior movies, yet much of it lives on, while the films themselves have been mercifully forgotten.

As the 1940s progressed, Jerome Kern continued to write for the movie medium. Only his untimely death in 1945 stopped his prolific pen, but he had been responsible for the scores of some 24 movie musicals. Of that total, 10 consisted of reworkings of his previous stage plays, and these often included new music. His compositions could also be heard incidentally, and often uncredited, in a number of other pictures. His lyricist collaborators—Dorothy Fields, Oscar Hammerstein II, Otto Harbach—have to be counted among the best of the best, and collectively they made a lasting impact on American popular song.

See also Screwball Comedies

SELECTED READING
Block, Geoffrey. *Enchanted Evenings: The Broadway Musical from* Show Boat *to Sondheim*. New York: Oxford University Press, 1997.
Bordman, Gerald. *Jerome Kern: His Life and Music*. New York: Oxford University Press, 1980.
Zinsser, William. *Easy to Remember: The Great American Songwriters and Their Songs*. Jaffrey, NH: David R. Godine, 2000.

KING KONG. An immensely popular 1933 movie, it established new standards for special effects. Released by RKO Radio Pictures in 1933, *King Kong* stands in many ways as the decade's definitive fantasy film. It tells the story of Kong, a mythic "king of the great apes," and his forcible abduction from a primitive milieu to the skyscrapers of New York City. A variation on the Beauty and the Beast tale, its simple, touching plot resonated with Depression-era audiences who longed to escape the ongoing economic crisis just outside the theater door.

Codirected and coproduced by Merian C. Cooper (1893–1973) and Ernest B. Schoedsack (1893–1979), the picture saved the struggling studio from bankruptcy and has remained a popular favorite for years. Credit for the movie's memorable special effects goes to Willis O'Brien (1886–1962), a master technician who had made his mark with *The Lost World* (1925), a similar cinema fantasy that deeply influenced the design of *King Kong*. O'Brien employed every device then known to filmmakers, but contrary to popular belief, no men in ape suits parade before the cameras. Kong, a composite of models, both full-scale (the massive head, in particular) and miniature (most of the action scenes), lumbers through his role, tiny arms and legs manipulated by studio craftsmen. Still photographers captured these movements on film and editors arranged the frames into coherent sequences, while carefully constructed sets create an illusion of reality.

Although acting and characterization become secondary elements in *King Kong*, its story of an unspoiled creature thrust into an urban nightmare plays on recurring concepts of the "simple life" and the evils of the big city, in this case New York. Forgoing the special-effects route, contemporary **gangster films** like ***Little Caesar*** (1931) and **musicals** such as ***42nd Street*** often employed similar imagery, where the vast, impersonal city threatens the weak and innocent. Certainly Kong carries a primeval innocence with him, and he meets his end while atop the brand-new **Empire State Building**. This classic finale, army biplanes buzzing around an impotent Kong, a tiny, screaming Fay Wray (1907–2004) grasped in his furry paw, has become an iconic moment in American **movies**. All the frustrations, all the fears, of the public, powerless against the faceless, relentless forces of modern life, find expression in those closing frames. Kong falls; he cannot defeat these things he does not understand, a fitting fable for the depths of the Depression.

The overwhelming commercial success of *King Kong* led RKO to rush out *Son of Kong* later that same year. Again displaying the talents of Cooper and Schoedsack, the sequel proves that a movie needs more than just special effects or a unique character to sustain it. "Baby Kong" possesses none of the nobility of his illustrious father. The mystery and the grandeur are gone, and *Son of Kong* soon languished at the all-important box office.

The famous climax to *King Kong* (1933) with the giant ape atop the Empire State Building. (Courtesy of Photofest)

Other studios learned that special effects–centered movies like *King Kong* could make money, and the 1930s witnessed a succession of pictures that relied more on technology than they did narrative strengths.

See also Architecture; Horror & Fantasy Films

SELECTED READING
Bergman, Andrew. *We're in the Money: Depression America and Its Films*. New York: Harper & Row [Colophon], 1971.
Brosnan, John. *Movie Magic*. New York: St. Martin's Press, 1974.
Vieira, Mark A. *Hollywood Horror: From Gothic to Cosmic*. New York: Harry N. Abrams, 2003.

L

LEISURE & RECREATION. Leisure, the condition of having free, unhurried time, and recreation, the pursuit of enjoyable activities to occupy leisure time, became challenging realities for many Americans during the 1930s. In the midst of an economic crisis, people faced the need to fill nonwork hours with meaningful diversions.

Widespread layoffs during the Great Depression had caused a disproportionate segment of the adult population—a peak of 24 percent in 1933—to experience what could be called "imposed leisure." Efficient new technology contributed to unemployment; while some people retained their jobs they worked reduced hours with the imposition of the five-day workweek. In addition, the National Recovery Administration (NRA; 1933–1936), a **New Deal** program, exacerbated the situation by requiring decreased overtime for those covered by NRA codes. By 1935, two-thirds of employed Americans worked fewer than 40 hours a week, down from as high as 48 hours just a few years earlier.

A number of factors precipitated these changes in the national work experience. Prior to the Depression, Americans had begun experiencing a transition from a rural, agrarian society to an urban, industrial one. Recreational activities had become increasingly affordable and available to ordinary Americans. Attitudes and behaviors around leisure and recreation shifted, moving from a society of spectators to one of active participants. Also, vacations, once a perquisite reserved for the very few, entered the spectrum of daily life, as did expanded holiday observances. This new leisure emerged as a permanent feature of modern, industrial America, a right for all citizens. Its imposition led to a better quality of life, as municipal, county, state, and federal governments began spending money to promote recreation.

Immediately following the stock market crash of 1929, the majority of citizens continued to work. As unemployment began to grow, however, more and more people struggled financially. As a means of controlling family expenditures, recreational activities took place in or near one's home. A survey of 5,000 people commissioned by the National Recreation Association in 1934 on the use of leisure hours reported reading as the most common activity, followed by listening to the **radio**, conversation, gardening, and visiting. Results also indicated that, although they were engaged in these activities, a majority of respondents wanted to be doing something else, such as participating in sports, attending a play, or taking automobile excursions.

Poster advertising free band concerts. (Courtesy of the Library of Congress)

Many Americans during the 1930s engaged in recreational pursuits other than those covered in the survey. **Games** like **Monopoly** and activities like knitting and **jigsaw puzzles** also occupied increasing amounts of people's time. Card playing, a popular pastime, ranged from poker and blackjack among blue-collar workers to **contract bridge** for white-collar groups. Others enjoyed **bowling**, billiards, pool, penny-a-card bingo, and punch cards, especially city dwellers. For individuals uncertain about how to fill their free hours, in November 1933 the first issue of *Leisure, the Magazine of 1000 Diversions* came off the presses. Filled with suggestions for family entertainment, *Leisure* merged in 1938 with another popular magazine, *Yankee*, and continued to address the question of spare-time activities.

The widespread availability of personal **automobiles** and mass transit systems, especially **buses**, allowed for some diversions away from home, such as taking a Sunday drive to visit friends or relatives; traveling to a picnic site or park; fishing; and hunting. Attendance at spectator sports, however, decreased, as did some other leisure pursuits, because of costs. The chart at the top of the facing page illustrates the changes in participation in paid commercial recreation as the nation moved into the Great Depression and the subsequent resumption of activities that began in 1934 with recovery. A recession toward the end of the decade created a second decrease in business for the motion picture industry.

The lower chart on the facing page shows expenditures for leisure activities and reveals similar information that begins with an initial drop occurring in 1930, followed by decreases in all areas for 1931–1933. An especially significant change (−48%) took place from 1930 to 1931 in the purchase of radios, records, and musical instruments. Again, a turnaround in spending starts with the recovery in 1934 and then slows in 1938 because of the recession. In only one category, "Wheel Goods, Durable Toys, Sport Equipment, Including Boats & Pleasure Aircraft," do the expenditures for 1939 exceed those of 1929.

Not everyone viewed increases in leisure time as a positive development. Some sociologists, along with psychologists, scientists, educators, and politicians, saw increased leisure and accompanying recreational activities as a problem. Through numerous articles and books on the subject, they voiced a collective fear that passive recreation could lead to physical and psychological problems, a fear that energy not expended through work would be released in unhealthy, immoral, or illegal ways. They also worried that adults, mostly men, suddenly out of work and with time on their hands, might experience psychological problems related to feelings of diminished self-esteem.

Participation in Selected Recreational Activities

Year	Number of Bowlers	Motion Picture Average Weekly Attendance (in millions)	Hunting Licenses (in millions)	Fishing Licenses (in millions)
1929	147,000	80	6.429	n/a
1930	219,000	90	6.901	n/a
1931	224,000	75	6.368	n/a
1932	197,000	60	5.777	n/a
1933	148,000	60	5.742	4.858
1934	168,000	70	5.918	4.856
1935	216,000	80	5.988	5.121
1936	267,000	88	6.658	5.832
1937	329,000	88	6.86	6.902
1938	482,000	85	6.903	7,436
1939	535,000	85	7.511	7,858

Source: Historical Statistics of the United States, Colonial Times to 1970

Personal Consumption Expenditures

Year	Radios, Recordings, and Musical Instruments (in millions)	Toys, Sport Supplies, Nondurable (in millions)	Wheel Goods, Durable Toys, Sport Equipment, Including Boats & Pleasure Aircraft (in millions)	Books, Maps, Magazines, Newspapers, and Sheet Music (in millions)
1929	$1,012	$336	$219	$847
1930	$921	$281	$172	$776
1931	$478	$266	$159	$732
1932	$268	$207	$110	$581
1933	$195	$181	$ 93	$571
1934	$229	$200	$118	$606
1935	$248	$216	$136	$639
1936	$333	$242	$171	$698
1937	$385	$269	$210	$761
1938	$339	$268	$210	$735
1939	$420	$285	$228	$780

Source: Historical Statistics of the United States, Colonial Times to 1970

Many concerned parties promoted government intervention in the area of leisure as the answer to potential problems. President **Franklin D. Roosevelt** (1882–1945), during the first one hundred days of his administration, saw to it that leisure and recreation received attention. The construction of recreational facilities in both cities and rural communities became a major priority.

One piece of New Deal legislation, the Works Progress Administration (WPA, 1933–1943; name changed to Work Projects Administration in 1939), received money from the Federal Emergency Relief Administration (FERA; 1933–1935), the first federal allocations given for recreation. Charged with encouraging the unemployed to make use of their free time by improving physical, artistic, and intellectual capabilities, director Harry L. Hopkins (1890–1946) designated at least 30 percent of the WPA budget over its lifetime toward the most extensive recreation projects ever seen in the United States. The program went in two directions: to repair or build recreational facilities and to provide leadership training programs to ensure that these sites would receive proper use and supervision. Every state participated, and the program completed 12,700 playgrounds, 8,500 gymnasiums and recreation centers, 750 swimming pools, 1,000 ice skating rinks, and 64 ski jumps, and employed almost 49,000 individuals.

In 1935, Federal One, a program established under the auspices of the WPA, organized the arts into four major areas: **Federal Art Project** (FAP; 1935–1943), **Federal Music Project** (FMP; 1935–1943), **Federal Theatre Project** (FTP; 1935–1939), and **Federal Writers' Project** (FWP; 1935–1943). In addition to providing meaningful work relief for many unemployed artists, this effort made paintings, sculpture, writing, **music**, and plays available to people, thereby enhancing the leisure options of the general population.

Another government initiative, the **Civilian Conservation Corps** (CCC; 1933–1942), directed its efforts primarily to renewing the nation's forests. Along with this work, the participants also contributed to an increase of recreational and **travel** possibilities by constructing campgrounds complete with picnic shelters, **swimming** pools, fireplaces, and restrooms. Two scenic highways started by the CCC, the Blue Ridge Parkway (begun in 1935, completed in 1987) and the Natchez Trace Parkway (begun in 1937, completed in 2005), continue to offer pleasurable touring experiences.

Those who encouraged government intervention in helping Americans cope with their increasing spare time also advocated the need to involve the participants in constructive leisure pursuits. Many CCC work camps included instruction and activities in arts and crafts, such as work in leather, wood, and metal, as well as music, dramatics, reading and discussion groups, sports, nature walks, and hiking. Another program under the auspices of the WPA, the National Youth Administration (NYA; 1935–1943), enabled young people to remain in school; for those not attending an educational institution, the NYA provided training for future employment. Some of the NYA projects enhanced the nation's recreational options. For example, NYA participants helped in the development of New York City's public parks, renovated a boys' club building in Rhode Island, and built a community center in Oklahoma to be used by Boy Scouts, Girl Scouts, and 4-H clubs.

The federal government may have led the way in promoting improved and increased recreational opportunities, but local governments, businesses, and industries also participated, a step that many thought would mean continuation of the programs after federal assistance ended. Cities and towns, for instance, built enduring facilities such as **golf** courses. Local YMCAs and YWCAs provided important resources with indoor tracks, swimming pools, gyms, and game rooms. With new playing fields available, employers established **softball** teams for their employees and organized summer leagues hoping to promote physical fitness and provide a constructive use of leisure.

Then, as now, not all recreational activities involved the government or some outside group or program. Individuals often look for activities that simply amuse or fill an empty hour. Thus, in 1930, countless people enthusiastically embraced a fad called **miniature golf**, one that sprang up without any assistance from official agencies of any kind. Hobby clubs of every description likewise appeared, and some municipalities, along with schools and businesses, joined the WPA in sponsoring them. **Stamp collecting** proved particularly popular. Civic clubs, such as Rotary and Kiwanis, and fraternal associations like the Masons, Moose, and Elks, also offered members opportunities to share interests and group experiences.

Robert and Helen Lynd (1892–1970; 1896–1982), authors of *Middletown*, an influential 1931 study of everyday American life in Muncie, Indiana, returned to that community in 1935. Their visit produced *Middletown in Transition* (1937), and it reported findings similar to those made by the National Recreation Association—a gain in the popularity of gardening, listening to the radio, and adult reading. The authors found that **movies** remained a widely enjoyed entertainment. Recreational facilities and the events they sponsored, such as supervised playgrounds and parks, swimming pools, sports grounds, play centers, public square dances, concerts, and open-air theatrical performances, also increased in number and usage.

The following chart shows the growth in recreational facilities nationally between 1929 and 1939 in municipal and county parks only. New Deal programs acquired land for increasing the number of state and national parks, with 400,000 acres being added between 1933 and 1935; they oversaw the construction of facilities of the types listed at these sites. These figures clearly reflect the trends of the decade. While membership in private golf courses and country clubs decreased, municipal golf courses and **tennis** courts remained crowded. Beaches and swimming pools likewise saw heavy use. Some park personnel might lose jobs because of a lack of funds, but lifeguards continued to be employed. **Baseball** (or hardball) declined in popularity as did the number of baseball diamonds between 1929 and 1939. Softball, however, bloomed as the nation moved out of the Depression, and it displaced the national pastime as evidenced by the lack of statistics prior to 1934 and its significant growth thereafter. All other listed facilities ended the decade with a number greater than in 1929.

Municipal and County Park and Recreation Areas

Year	Baseball Diamonds	Softball Diamonds	Tennis Courts	Bathing Beaches	Swimming Pools	Golf Courses	Playgrounds under Leadership
1929	4,024	n/a	7,960	409	1,010	299	7,681
1930	4,322	n/a	8,422	457	1,042	312	7,677
1931	4,396	n/a	8,804	470	1,093	323	7,685
1932	4,161	n/a	9,267	472	1,094	374	6,990
1933	5,572	n/a	9,921	530	1,148	370	7,434
1934	3,838	5,313	9,420	496	1,016	343	8,384

Municipal and County Park and Recreation Areas (*Continued*)

Year	Baseball Diamonds	Softball Diamonds	Tennis Courts	Bathing Beaches	Swimming Pools	Golf Courses	Playgrounds under Leadership
1935	3,669	6,896	9,313	488	1,038	332	8,062
1936	3,568	7,369	10,029	516	1,142	354	9,490
1937	3,923	8,384	11,031	569	1,063	378	9,618
1938	3,902	8,833	11,310	564	1,162	354	9,712
1939	3,846	8,995	11,617	548	1,181	358	9,749

Source: Historical Statistics of the United States, Colonial Times to 1970

American popular culture, by its very nature a form of leisure, offered up countless movies, endless radio programming, and books and **magazines** of every description. Seldom, however, did these vehicles of popular culture make the subject of leisure—what is it? what do you do with it? how is it best spent?—a part of their content. **Youth** with too much free time became the focus of several movies, such as anything featuring the Dead End Kids, a popular series. Juvenile delinquency also received attention in pictures like *Wild Boys of the Road* (1933) and *Reformatory* (1938). On the other side of the coin, a handful of films, such as the well-received Andy Hardy movies, "discovered" adolescence, but they seldom explored the ramifications of leisure other than depicting teenagers and their activities.

Radio likewise steered clear of any discussions of the changing relationship between work and leisure, and followers of dramatic shows, **soap operas**, or **serials** learned little about the debates over the uses of free time. Popular fiction followed similar patterns, relying on an audience with time to read novels and stories and avoiding reminders for those very readers that abundant leisure concerned a number of social critics.

In all, the 1930s witnessed growth in a variety of recreational activities as Americans learned to cope with unemployment, reduced work hours, scarce resources, and additional free time. Those voicing concerns about increased nonwork hours claimed any accompanying problems could be solved through funded programs and, indeed, the federal government, as well as municipal, county, and state governments, responded, advancing America's recreational opportunities and facilities by at least a decade. Reviews of the work of various New Deal agencies indicate success also with **education** about the uses of leisure time and its acceptance as a part of daily life.

See also Best Sellers; Book Clubs; Comic Books; Fads; Hobbies; Marathon Dancing; Pulp Magazines; Teenage & Juvenile Delinquency Films

SELECTED READING

Currell, Susan. *The March of Spare Time: The Problem and Promise of Leisure in the Great Depression*. Philadelphia: University of Pennsylvania Press, 2005.

Historical Statistics of the United States, Colonial Times to 1970. Washington, DC: Bureau of the Census, U.S. Department of Commerce, 1975.

Kyvig, David E. *Daily Life in the United States, 1920–1940*. Chicago: Ivan R. Dee, 2004.

Steiner, Jesse F. *Research Memorandum on Recreation in the Depression*. New York: Arno Press, 1972 (reprint of the 1937 edition, published by the Social Science Research Council).

LIFE & FORTUNE. Two significant **magazines**, products of the same publisher, made their debut in the 1930s: *Life* and *Fortune*. Although *Life* came along in 1936, six years after *Fortune*, it shortly became one of the most widely read (or looked at) magazines in the history of American publishing, and soon overshadowed, at least in terms of readership and advertising volume, its older sibling. Both periodicals reflect the genius of Henry R. Luce (1898–1967), destined to become one of the most important figures in the history of American journalism.

Along with Briton Haddon (1898–1929), Luce in 1923 founded *Time*, the nation's first weekly newsmagazine. The two men, friends and classmates at Hotchkiss and Yale, saw a need for a periodical that would summarize the preceding week's events. An overnight success, *Time* served as the foundation of a publishing empire that would grow significantly during the 1930s. Haddon's untimely death in 1929 put Luce in charge of the entire operation, and he

Cover of *Fortune* magazine. (Courtesy of the Library of Congress)

energetically pursued their once-shared dreams for the next several decades.

In January 1930, just as the Great Depression began to make its enormous impacts felt, Luce introduced *Fortune*, a slick, thick monthly publication devoted to commerce. *Fortune* evolved from the business section of *Time*, and despite the steep economic downturn then being experienced by the nation, the magazine promised to focus its editorial content on corporate America, a risky choice in the eyes of many. Plus, when *Fortune* first appeared on newsstands, it carried a cover price of $1 per issue, unheard of then for a magazine. In equivalent contemporary money, a single copy would cost over $12.00, or almost $150 for a one-year subscription. Nevertheless, the upstart journal quickly snared an enthusiastic, albeit selective, audience.

Oversize and eye-catching, *Fortune* delivered a curious mix of business reporting with a liberal editorial stance. Articles about the right to strike, business ethics, exposés about shoddy manufacturers, and the need for government oversight in some industries belied *Fortune*'s assumed procapitalist position. Luce wrote that his new magazine would strive to reflect "industrial life" through reporting and pictures, and it succeeded admirably, as it continues to do today. An outstanding editorial staff hired the best writers and **illustrators** to be found. The pictures of photojournalist Margaret Bourke-White (1906–1971) graced the inaugural 1930 issue, just as they would, six years later, the premier edition of *Life*. Distinguished authors like James Agee (1909–1955), Dwight

Macdonald (1906–1982), and Archibald MacLeish (1892–1982), writers seldom associated with the world of business, brought their talents to bear on a variety of issues, contributing incisive critiques of social problems and analyses of cultural changes. Somehow, the innate conservatism of Henry R. Luce coexisted with the avowed liberalism of many of his staffers.

After the recession of 1937–1938, *Fortune* retrenched a bit editorially. Many of the young, progressive writers associated with the magazine's founding departed, replaced by staffers more comfortable with a less investigative, less confrontational approach to American enterprise. And, as World War II loomed at the end of the decade, covering the business implications of an international conflict took center stage.

One aspect of *Fortune* that will be long remembered involves its distinctive cover art. Featuring the work of the nation's top illustrators, and printed on quality heavy stock, each month's issue carried work by such creative individuals as Constantin Alajalov (1900–1987), Ernest Hamlin Baker (1889–1975), Miguel Covarrubias (1902–1957), Peter Helck (1893–1988), Diego Rivera (1886–1957), and **Charles Sheeler** (1883–1965). Antonio Petruccelli (1907–1994) enjoyed the distinction of creating the greatest number of entries, 21 between 1933 and 1939. Ernest Hamlin Baker's 14 efforts put him in second place. These artists, seldom bound by breaking current events, enjoyed great latitude in choices of, and approaches to, subject matter, setting the magazine apart from all other American periodicals of the day.

Despite the business orientation found in much of the magazine's editorial content, the journal's illustrators obviously enjoyed free rein in the realm of stylistics. Many *Fortune* covers display a forward-looking sense of modernism, and a few even border on avant-garde abstraction. The illustrative matter possesses an aesthetic quality of its own. Paintings and drawings could depict farmers or fishermen, a high-flying airplane or a trailer truck in heavy snows, a roller coaster or a battleship. The associations with "business" might be more conjectural than apparent, but the publication's devotion to art established a tradition of excellence that readers soon associated with *Fortune* as a whole.

The gathering clouds of World War II brought about—not unexpectedly—a heightened focus on that conflict, and the covers lost some of the eclecticism they had expressed during the 1930s. At the conclusion of the war, *Fortune* never regained the expressionistic freedom of the Depression years. Although a number of the illustrations from the 1930s reflect the **Regionalism** and **Social Realism** then in vogue, they seldom follow artistic fashion for its own sake. Instead, they show an independence of spirit that led to some of the most enduring illustrations in the annals of American magazine publishing.

After the successful premiere of *Fortune*, Luce introduced **The March of Time** on network **radio** in 1931, a weekly dramatization of the news that also served as a promotion for *Time*. It later went to a film version for theaters in 1934. Rapidly emerging as a media tycoon, Luce envisioned yet another new publication, something that could complement both *Time* and *Fortune*. Many of his ideas for this venture came from Clare Boothe Brokaw (1903–1987), an accomplished editor and playwright; the two married in 1935, and Clare Boothe Luce exerted considerable influence in the direction the pioneering magazine would take. Both believed that the weekly news summaries that defined *Time*, along with some of the visual qualities that so enhanced *Fortune*, could be incorporated in a true pictorial journal. Their vision coalesced with the November 1936 publication of *Life*.

The title comes from a humor weekly that had first appeared in 1883. This namesake had fallen on hard times in the 1930s, forcing its owners to put the venerable journal up for sale. Luce happened to be toying with the name *Look*, but a bargain price for the humor magazine changed his mind. He bought the struggling *Life* to acquire rights to the name, but his new venture held little else in common with the original publication.

When the slim first edition of *Life* arrived at newsstands, it cost a dime (about $1.50 in contemporary money) and offered more photographs than text. But it intrigued people, and it sold out wherever it could be found. Subsequent issues also did well, making *Life* one of the most successful magazine startups ever. Within four months, it boasted newsstand sales in excess of 1 million copies a week. Its early success almost spelled disaster; Luce had predicted sales in the neighborhood of 250,000 copies a week, and he predicated **advertising** rates on that figure. The lower the circulation, the lower the ad rates, and so Luce had to make up the per copy costs from corporate coffers, since the dime paid for the magazine did not cover production costs. The company lost several million dollars with those early issues, although it would recoup its losses manyfold once it could boost advertising rates to a figure that more closely matched actual circulation.

Luce took no chances with his new publication. He employed the best photographers available, with the result that the pictorial quality of *Life* remains unequalled. Margaret Bourke-White had the honor of providing the first cover, a stark black-and-white study of the then-incomplete Fort Peck dam in Montana; her work also serves as the basis of a visual essay on the lives of workers at this **New Deal** project, a joint venture of the Public Works Administration (PWA; 1933–1939) and the Army Corps of Engineers.

The arts of painting and **sculpture** always played a significant role in *Life*'s content, usually with photographic reproductions. Thus editors might run an article titled "New Deal Decorates the Old Deal's Buildings" (January 1937) covering the efforts of muralists in federal Washington, D.C. Or they might commission a famous artist like Rockwell Kent (1882–1971) to create accompanying illustrations for a piece. In the fall of 1937, Kent contributed futuristic pictures depicting possible scenarios detailing the eventual end of the earth; they ran with a feature about a show at the Hayden Planetarium.

Numerous continuing sections also piqued reader interest. Each week the magazine ran "Speaking of Pictures," a collection of photographs about the odd or unusual. "Life Goes to a Party" sent photographers to various social events around the country; "Movie of the Week" reviewed a new Hollywood release, accompanied with shots taken from the film in question and often with other studio publicity as well; and the self-explanatory "People" showcased the famous and not-so-famous. By September 1939, with war breaking out in Europe and already raging in Asia, *Life* began a series titled "The War in Pictures," an editorial admission of the conflict's certainty. In keeping with the magazine's title, the focus of both the **photography** and the print content continued to be on items of human interest, that is life.

Throughout the 1930s, a veritable who's who of artists and photographers displayed their work on *Fortune*'s and *Life*'s covers. Inside, the two magazines maintained the highest standards, *Fortune* with brilliant essays on commerce and associated topics and *Life* with picture spreads that came to define photojournalism.

See also Federal Art Project; Political Parties; Radio Networks

SELECTED READING

Augspurger, Michael. *An Economy of Abundant Beauty:* Fortune *Magazine and Depression America.* Ithaca, NY: Cornell University Press, 2004.

Okrent, Daniel. Fortune: *The Art of Covering Business.* Salt Lake City, UT: Gibbs-Smith, 1999.

Swanberg, W. A. *Luce and His Empire.* New York: Charles Scribner's Sons, 1972.

Wainwright, Loudon. *The Great American Magazine: An Inside History of* Life. New York: Alfred A. Knopf, 1986.

LI'L ABNER. In August 1934, *Li'l Abner,* a comic strip about hillbilly life, made its first newspaper appearance; it would ultimately become one of the most successful new series of the 1930s. Its creator, Al Capp (1909–1979), occupies a unique position among cartoonists: he, along with a handful of the hundreds of artists who have written and drawn American **comic strips,** is revered a poet of his profession. That select group includes such names as Richard Felton Outcault (1863–1928; *The Yellow Kid*), George Herriman (1880–1944; *Krazy Kat*), Walt Kelly (1913–1973; *Pogo*), and Charles Schulz (1922–2000; *Peanuts*), innovators who raised the lowly comic strip from newspaper entertainment to an art form.

Capp (née Alfred Gerald Caplin) brought to his hillbilly satire a lyricism and innocence that stand in sharp contrast to the darker sides of human nature he also explored. Together, these seeming opposites combined to make one of the most enduring—and endearing—strips in the history of the medium.

Like most of his counterparts, Capp struggled to create a series that would appeal to a broad public. While ghosting much of the drawing and writing for Ham Fisher's (1901–1955) popular boxing strip *Joe Palooka* in the early 1930s, he introduced a character called Big Leviticus. This loud, rowdy hillbilly brawler caught on, and Capp knew he needed to pursue this concept. He left Fisher in 1934, although Fisher wisely continued using Big Leviticus in *Joe Palooka.* After his departure, Capp began marketing a strip of his own. Eventually, he found a taker with United Features Syndicate.

Abner Yokum, along with Daisy Mae, Mammy, Pappy, and the other denizens of Dogpatch, U.S.A., a collection of dilapidated shacks located somewhere in the Ozarks, delighted readers. His sprawling cast of bizarre, often grotesque, characters brings a new meaning to the word "stupidity"; unschooled, unclean, and uncouth, they embark on adventures that defy description. The city slickers who occasionally appear in Dogpatch also give humanity a bad name. But despite all their failings, a kind of innocence pervades their actions. And Capp, always in control, displays a fondness for his players, even as he humiliates them. Abner, in particular, remains optimistic, a kind of latter-day Appalachian Pangloss, ever the naïf in a world he will never comprehend. Social satire at its best, *Li'l Abner* punctured pompousness; these people may not be the salt of the earth, but they are no worse than their "betters." The comic strip challenged the established social order of the real world, a bracing commentary on the threatened or changing norms of Depression America.

The figure of the hillbilly has long been a part of American humor. In 1931, *Lum and Abner,* two apparent country bumpkins, began a long (1931–1953) run on **radio. The National Barn Dance** went on network radio in 1933, as did **Grand Ole Opry** in 1939 (both had begun earlier, but broadcast to limited audiences). Novelist **Erskine Caldwell** amused readers with the shenanigans of Jeeter Lester in *Tobacco Road* (1932) and followed that with another big seller, *God's Little Acre*, in 1933. Clearly, the hillbilly's day had arrived. Veteran cartoonist Billy DeBeck (1890–1942) had created a popular strip called *Barney Google* in 1919. It enjoyed a large circulation, but for insurance he introduced a hillbilly figure in 1934, the same year as *Li'l Abner*'s debut. Snuffy Smith, pretty much a moonshining ne'er-do-well, quickly bypassed the regulars of *Barney Google* in appeal, causing the strip to be renamed *Barney Google and Snuffy Smith* in the late 1930s. DeBeck's series employs almost no satire; it depends instead on simple rustic humor and familiar mountain stereotypes.

Not so *Li'l Abner*. The dialect of Dogpatch consists of Capp's phonetic mispronunciations of much of the English language. Double exclamation points demand emphasis and heavy inking catches the eye. It matters not how Capp's characters speak but what they say. Loaded with puns and parody—plus a running commentary on the sad state of humankind—the strip attacks government, organized **religion**, marriage, do-gooders, and any other sacred cows that come within range. Readers loved it.

Because poetry relies on a unique voice, *Li'l Abner* transcends jokes, envisioning a world of its own that no one else can imitate. The syndicates that owned the rights to *Krazy Kat* and *Peanuts* knew better than to try to carry on the strips when their creators died, and so it was with *Li'l Abner*. Capp died in 1979, but his series had ended with his retirement in 1977. No longer the favorite it had been in its early years, it quietly expired; the once fresh and bright satire of 40 years earlier had grown coarse and brittle and Capp knew the time to quit had arrived. Ironically, *Snuffy Smith* has continued on into the present, dependable and predictable; although Billy DeBeck died in 1942, the series has been penned by replacement cartoonists.

For about a year, 1939–1940, the National Broadcasting Company (NBC radio) attempted a broadcast version of *Li'l Abner*, but it lacked listeners, sponsors, or both and quickly disappeared. An earnest attempt to replicate the strip on screen, but one that relies on real actors and not cartoon figures, came about in 1940. Largely forgotten today, *Li' Abner* the movie enjoys a certain resemblance to *Li'l Abner* the comic strip. It revolves around Sadie Hawkins Day, Capp's 1937 invention whereby women can openly pursue males and ask them to social events, a special day that caught on in high schools and colleges across the country. Some merchandising of Abner and Dogpatch items, such as buttons, cards, and the like, occurred during the decade, but not on any grand scale. The glory days for *Li'l Abner* tie-ins lay in the future. For most of the 1930s, attention remained focused on the strip itself.

See also Hillbillies; Movies; Newspapers; Radio Networks

SELECTED READING

Capp, Al. *The Best of* Li'l Abner. New York: Holt, Rinehart & Winston, 1978.
Horn, Maurice, ed. *100 Years of American Newspaper* Comics. New York: Gramercy Books, 1996.
Marschall, Richard. *America's Great Comic-Strip Artists*. New York: Stewart, Tabori & Chang, 1997.

LINDBERGH KIDNAPPING. On the evening of March 1, 1932, the infant son of famed aviator Charles A. Lindbergh (1902–1974) disappeared from his New Jersey home. Authorities immediately suspected kidnapping and soon thereafter received a convoluted series of ransom notes. A frenzied search ensued, and in April the

Charles A. Lindbergh (1902–1974) and his wife, Anne Morrow Lindbergh (1906–2001). (Courtesy of the Library of Congress)

Lindberghs paid $50,000 (roughly $740,000 in contemporary dollars) to the mysterious party or parties involved in the abduction. The ransom proved futile, and on May 12, 1932, workers found the child's partially decomposed body not far from his home.

In the meantime, the entire country followed the investigation into the kidnapping. Leads, most of them false, kept popping up, and police, state, and federal officers pursued them all. With the death of the child, outrage supplanted curiosity. With the grisly discovery of the body, President **Herbert Hoover** (1874–1964) sensed the temper of the nation and made the **Federal Bureau of Investigation** (FBI) the clearinghouse for the case; henceforth, all information pertinent to the kidnapping would go through that agency. The U.S. Congress, likewise reacting to the tragic cycle of events, enacted the so-called Lindbergh law. This 1933 statute made kidnapping a federal felony and provided the death penalty for anyone so convicted. In addition, if state lines had been crossed in execution of the kidnapping, or if threats or ransom notes depended on the U.S. Mail for delivery, federal agents (i.e., the FBI) took precedence over all other law enforcement officers and controlled the investigation.

The Lindbergh case dragged on into the fall of 1933. President **Franklin D. Roosevelt** (1882–1945) increased the FBI's powers, giving it exclusive jurisdiction over all aspects of the investigation, but a solution still eluded everyone. Clues, most of them useless, accumulated as the search proceeded. Finally, in August 1934—over two years after the abduction—authorities began to match some of the gold certificates used in the ransom payment to a narrow geographic area where these suspect bills appeared. Several alert individuals linked the certificates to Bruno Richard Hauptmann (1899–1936), a carpenter of German descent. In September, investigators found other incriminating evidence at Hauptmann's residence, enough that prosecutors indicted him for murder in October.

For five weeks, starting in January 1935, Hauptmann stood trial in Flemington, New Jersey. A small, out-of-the-way community, Flemington hosted what pundits called "the trial of the century." The proceedings generated a carnival-like atmosphere, as reporters and **radio** announcers from all parts of the country flocked to the tiny county courthouse. Readers and listeners hung on every word emanating from the packed courtroom. Ultimately, a jury found Hauptmann guilty of first-degree murder. Unsuccessful appeals followed, and on April 3, 1936, the state of New Jersey electrocuted Bruno Richard Hauptmann.

Considerable controversy has dogged the aftermath of the Lindbergh trial, with some saying officials anxious to close an embarrassing case railroaded Hauptmann and allowed the guilty parties to go free. Others maintain that the evidence clearly convicted him and the verdict stands as a just one. Certainly a heinous **crime** had been committed; Charles Lindbergh represented American idealism and heroism, and many associated an attack on him and his family as tantamount to an assault on American values. The resolution of the case reflected favorably on the FBI, and the agency emerged stronger, with greatly increased powers and jurisdiction. The publicity surrounding the proceedings demonstrated the powerful influence of contemporary mass media. **Newspapers** and radio could sway and inflame public opinion, and thanks to technology they could reach a far larger audience than ever before.

See also Aviation

SELECTED READING
Kennedy, Ludovic. *The Airman and the Carpenter*. New York: Viking Penguin, 1985.
Waller, George. *Kidnap: The Story of the Lindbergh Case*. New York: Dial Press, 1961.

LITTLE CAESAR. One of the first (1930) and most successful and memorable of a rash of **gangster films**, its release ushered in a new genre of **movies**. Motion pictures often follow cycles of popularity, and public taste tends to embrace one kind of film, then another, and then another after that. Those movies fortunate enough to be both produced in, and reflective of, any particular cycle, usually do well. Those that fall outside the cycle are as a rule doomed to oblivion, at least as far as the fickle public goes. For the early sound era, gangster pictures constituted one such cycle.

The majority of Hollywood films about criminals follow a predictable pattern: a small-time mobster (juvenile delinquent, sociopath, thief, etc.) rises in his "profession." He covets wealth and power, but ultimately he must pay. Following a lengthy and celebrated period of good fortune, he suffers an abrupt downfall. In many ways, this pattern acknowledges—with the exception of the downfall—the American myth of success, the story of the self-made man who goes from rags to riches. For many onlookers, especially in the Depression 1930s, legitimate pathways to this goal had closed. For the movie gangster, other avenues beckon. He basks in a certain mystique, a glamorous figure who happens to live life on the wrong side of the law.

Edward G. Robinson (1893–1973), the titular star of *Little Caesar* (1931). (Courtesy of Photofest)

Little Caesar introduces audiences to Cesare Enrico "Rico" Bandello, a violent criminal. Rico never drinks; he has nothing to do with women, loose or otherwise; and he remains doggedly focused on his climb to the top. Except for his nasty habit of killing people, he fits the American model of upward mobility well. Edward G. Robinson (1893–1973), already a Hollywood veteran by the time of *Little Caesar*, brilliantly portrays Rico on the screen. As he must, Rico dies at the conclusion of the picture, but the role functioned as a breakthrough that led to a long and successful career for Robinson. He would go from being typecast as a mobster in early films like *Night Ride* (1930) and *Outside the Law* (1930) to varied character parts, including police officers (*Bullets or Ballots*, 1936) and G-men (*Confessions of a Nazi Spy*, 1939). *Little Caesar*, however, remains Robinson's most memorable characterization.

Directed by Mervyn Leroy (1900–1987), the film soon became the prototype for virtually all subsequent gangster movies for years to come. As an early sound film, the dialogue, clichéd and almost corny to modern ears, established in the popular mind how criminals talk. For example, "the boys," "gorillas," and "mugs" represent fellow gang members; a "torpedo" carries a gun and shoots people; "dicks" and "flatfoot" refer to the police; "molls" and "skirts" are terms for women; and "the goods" (as in "I've got the goods on you") suggests incriminating information. As a result, throughout the 1930s, most movie gangsters speak in an underworld argot that comes more from the imaginations of screenwriters than it does from reality.

In addition to talking in a stylized way, the characters in *Little Caesar* evince a topsy-turvy code of behavior. Women serve as mere background, props, to the male leads. Feminine traits, like gentleness and sensitivity, should be avoided by men, even the good guys. Rico, devoid of love and caring, struts and snarls his way across the screen, intimidating everyone, intent only on attaining power over others. This kind of characterization forces almost the entire cast to react in a similarly two-dimensional way, and the movie creates a dark, sleazy universe of evil with few bright spots showing normal, decent human behavior. Even the violence, more imagined than visual, seems unrelenting, to the point that the **Hollywood Production Code**, in effect since 1930 but not actively enforced until 1934, insisted the movie be taken out of circulation. The code prohibited explicit violence and plots that rewarded criminal acts, and certainly *Little Caesar* has more than its share of both, imagined or otherwise. After its 1934 disappearance, the film did not go back into general circulation until 1953, when Code restrictions began to be relaxed.

Many people think the character of Rico Bandello has been adapted from the sordid career of Al Capone (1899–1947), probably the best-known of a host of gangsters who rose to notoriety during the early 1930s. But a number of historians and movie scholars suggest that the real model for Rico was "Sam" Cardinella, a minor but violence-prone

Chicago gangster, and that only a few elements of Capone's life fit the movie. Whether based on Capone or Cardinella, Rico's sensational rise to and fall from power parallel events then taking place in the country's large cities, especially Chicago and New York. Movies reflect their times, and the United States did suffer a wave of lawlessness in the last years of Prohibition.

The success of *Little Caesar* assured imitation. In short order, marquees promised action and thrills with titles like *The Public Enemy* (1931), starring James Cagney (1899–1986) as another seemingly tragic gangster; *Scarface; The Shame of the Nation* (1932), with Paul Muni (1895–1967) creating a Capone-like figure (Capone's nickname was Scarface, the result of a 1918 bar fight); and a host of lesser-known movies focusing on crimes and criminals.

See also Crime; *Dick Tracy*; Federal Bureau of Investigation; Prohibition & Repeal; Teenage & Juvenile Delinquency Films

SELECTED READING
Parish, James Robert, and Michael R. Pitts. *The Great Gangster Pictures*. Metuchen, NJ: Scarecrow Press, 1976.
Rosow, Eugene. *Born to Lose: The Gangster Film in America*. New York: Oxford University Press, 1978.
Yaquinto, Marilyn. *Pump 'em Full of Lead: A Look at Gangsters on Film*. New York: Twayne, 1998.

LITTLE ORPHAN ANNIE. One of the most conservative and topical **comic strips** ever to grace the pages of American **newspapers**, *Little Orphan Annie* represents the personal vision of its creator, Harold Gray (1894–1968). A product of the *Chicago Tribune/New York News* syndicate, *Little Orphan Annie* first began running in the summer of 1924. The title comes from an 1885 poem by James Whitcomb Riley (1849–1916), an immensely popular versifier of the late nineteenth century, whose work many Americans would have known at that time. Gray changed the dialect "Orphant" of the poem to the more correct "Orphan," but much of Riley's homespun philosophy about hard work, respect for elders, and a cheerful outlook on life appear in the comic strip.

Although Gray cannot be considered a realistic artist, he does succeed as an expressionistic one. Annie lives in a dark world of shadows, with threats around every corner. Like his fellow cartoonist Chester Gould, who created **Dick Tracy** in 1931, Gray shows a mastery of the use of solid areas of black; in both cases, it heightens mood and focuses attention. From the beginning, Gray's somber frames suggest the **movies** of the day, with Annie the star, always in the foreground, acting out a kind of continuing morality play. Since he did not do faces well, few close-ups appear in the strip; instead, Gray gives the reader a kind of film set, or tableau, with a series of medium- and long-shot depictions of his main character.

Annie herself is of indeterminate age, perhaps 10 or so at the beginning, and a few years older as time goes by. During the 1930s, possibly the most successful period for this long-running series, Annie appears to be about 12 or 13, but a remarkably mature 12 or 13, ready to take on any challenge. Accompanied by her faithful and ageless dog, Sandy, Annie moves through an America beset by many problems. But hard work and self-reliance, or "grit," a popular word for the times, provide the keys to happiness. A supporting cast, especially "Daddy" Warbucks, who serves as her surrogate father and occasional benefactor, moves in and out of the series, but usually the stories revolve around Annie, alone, and acting on her own. At a time of great unemployment and economic uncertainty, Annie's continuing homilies about looking out for oneself, while at the same time helping those in need, carried considerable significance.

Speech balloons crowded with dialog vie for space within each frame in *Little Orphan Annie*, one of the wordiest comic strips in the history of the genre. Annie herself has something to say about each and every ongoing event. This reliance on constant chatter gives Gray the chance to inject his own ideas into the balloons, and he seldom misses an opportunity to voice his opinions. In so doing, he makes Annie and himself kindred spirits, sermonizers on the virtues of private enterprise, small government, and the need for law and order, with "Daddy" Warbucks in the background as an oracle, reinforcing his ward's beliefs.

Despite her faith in capitalism and its rewards, Annie lives in constant tension. Her security can be swept away in a moment, and she regularly encounters poverty and turmoil. But her pluck, along with occasional luck, carries her through this world, and she never loses her inherent optimism. Like the characters in a modern-day *Pilgrim's Progress* (1678), those whom she meets personify human attributes. The villains have names like Ward Heeley, Bill McBribe, Mr. Chizzler, and Claude Claptrap, so there can be no doubt about their activities or intent. But the insecurity manifested in the comic strip reflects 1930s America. For millions of devoted readers, *Little Orphan Annie* represented a level of realism unmatched by others.

This devotion resulted in considerable merchandising of the little redhead in the red dress. Two movie adaptations, one in 1932 with Mitzi Green (1920–1969), the other in 1938 with Ann Gillis (b. 1927), played the nation's theaters. In 1930, *Little Orphan Annie* debuted on **radio**, earning the distinction of being the first of many late afternoon **serials** aimed at a juvenile audience. It would remain on the air until 1942, and most of that time Ovaltine, a powdered chocolate drink mix, sponsored it. The serial also pioneered in the promotion of premiums. Decoder rings, complete with top-secret user manuals, and Ovaltine shaker mugs have become collector's items, along with Annie rings, **toys, games, Big Little Books**, watches, and a host of other items. Grit, spunk, pluck, gumption—for a country mired in an economic depression, *Little Orphan Annie* personified those peculiarly American traits, and she demonstrated that anyone possessing them could overcome anything.

See also Advertising; Coffee & Tea; Youth

SELECTED READING

Gray, Harold. *Arf! The Life and Hard Times of Little Orphan Annie, 1935–1945*. New Rochelle, NY: Arlington House, 1970.
———. *Little Orphan Annie in the Great Depression*. New York: Dover Publications, 1979.
Marschall, Richard. *America's Great Comic-Strip Artists*. New York: Stewart, Tabori & Chang, 1997.
Young, William H. "That Indomitable Redhead: Little Orphan Annie." *Journal of Popular Culture* (Fall 1974): 309–316.

M

MAGAZINES. From the early nineteenth century on, magazines have occupied an important place in American cultural life. By the beginning of the 1930s, some 4,500 different periodicals circulated throughout the nation; at the end of the decade, despite the economic upheaval of the Great Depression, that figure had grown to over 6,000 titles. The vast majority of these magazines consisted of small-circulation publications catering to individual professions, businesses, and activities. Only a handful—50 to 100 at the most—could be called "general interest" magazines. But this small percentage distributed millions of copies to a diverse population, whereas the more specialized periodicals claimed select niche audiences and had far fewer readers per title. Any discussion of popular American magazines must therefore focus on this limited sample of large-circulation publications, not the larger world of specialty periodicals.

The technology that permitted the fast, widespread distribution of general-interest magazines was already well established by 1930. Linotype machines and web presses could print thousands of copies in almost no time; folding machines could put the final product together; and an efficient postal system could deliver mail virtually anywhere. When the Depression decade commenced, the circulation of magazines with large, diverse readerships stood at approximately 80 million; by 1940, it had grown close to 100 million. Clearly, the industry had more than weathered the crisis. Just a few titles—about 25 in all—led the way, such as the *American, Collier's, Good Housekeeping, Ladies' Home Journal, Liberty, McCall's*, **Reader's Digest**, and the **Saturday Evening Post**.

Just as important, **advertising** revenues, the lifeblood of a mass magazine, had stood at an all-time high in 1929; they made a significant rebound during the 1930s after suffering a sharp decline in the first years of the crisis. By 1939, although still not as high as a decade earlier, they nevertheless had recouped sufficiently that the future looked bright. Only a few titles went under during this period, and enough new publications came on the marketplace to offset those losses.

Some notable American magazines, often old friends in thousands of homes, did disappear. Without adequate readership and advertising revenue, sentiment alone could not sustain them. Mainstream titles like the *Literary Digest* (1890–1938), *Scribner's* (later called the *Century*; 1870–1930), the *Smart Set* (1900–1930), *Vanity Fair* (1913–1936), and the oldest of them all, the *North American Review* (1815–1939), ceased publication during the 1930s. Several new ventures—such as *Advertising Age* (1930), *Fortune* (1930), *Broadcasting* (1931), *Family Circle* (1932), *Esquire* (1933), *Newsweek* (1933), *U.S. News & World Report* (1933), *Bride's Magazine* (1934), *Mademoiselle* (1935), *Yankee* (1935), *Consumer Reports* (1936), *Life* (1936; ceased regular publication in 1972), *Look* (1937; ceased publication in 1971), *Popular Photography* (1937), *Woman's Day* (1937), *U.S. Camera* (1938), and *Glamour* (1939)—attracted millions of readers.

In addition, older well-known journals such as the *American* (founded 1911; ceased publication in 1956), *Better Homes & Gardens* (1922), *Collier's* (1888; ceased publication in 1957), *Cosmopolitan* (1886), *Good Housekeeping* (1885), *House Beautiful* (1896), *Ladies' Home Journal* (1883), *Liberty* (1924; ceased publication in 1951), *Reader's Digest* (1922), *Redbook* (1903), *Saturday Evening Post* (1821; ceased publication in 1969), *Time* (1923), and *Vogue* (1892) remained firmly ensconced in the magazine marketplace throughout the decade. During that time, a number of monthlies achieved the vaunted circulation level of approximately 1 million copies per issue, including the *American*, *Cosmopolitan*, *Good Housekeeping*, *Ladies' Home Journal*, and *Reader's Digest*. Of all the weekly general-interest magazines, only three could boast a steady circulation that exceeded 1 million or more copies: *Collier's*, *Liberty*, and the *Saturday Evening Post*.

First appearing on newsstands in 1924, the now-forgotten *Liberty* came into being as the shared child of two metropolitan **newspapers**, the *Chicago Tribune* and the *New York Daily News*. It featured some of the tabloid sensationalism of its parent *Daily News* but never could develop a solid advertising base. It consistently lost money—even as it built a large circulation—and Bernarr Macfadden (1868–1955), a colorful multimillionaire made rich from other publishing ventures, bought the struggling weekly in 1931.

A colorful, self-proclaimed "physical culturist," Macfadden had burst upon the magazine scene in 1899 with *Physical Culture*, a journal promising long life and good health through diet and exercise. *Physical Culture* proved wildly successful, and an emboldened Macfadden in 1919 introduced *True Story*, the first of an extensive line of confessional magazines he would put out. It, too, did extremely well, giving him the financial clout to try whatever he wanted in the publishing field.

Macfadden also reigned over 10 newspapers, among them the notorious *New York Evening Graphic*, or the "PornoGraphic" as those who detested its sensationalism called it. This tabloid journal gained a reputation for tampering with photographs—what the editors called a "composograph"—to capture certain effects. Readers, however, eventually tired of its menu of sex and scandal and the *Evening Graphic* died in 1932. That setback proved only temporary; in 1935 the combined monthly circulation of all the other Macfadden magazines totaled over 7 million copies.

He, and others, capitalized on a public fascination with inexpensive, exciting fiction and nonfiction by publishing a new line of titles called "**pulp magazines.**" Descendants of the dime novels of an earlier era and similarly printed on cheap paper and featuring low cover prices, they quickly captured an enthusiastic share of the market during the 1920s and 1930s. A host of look-alikes fought for precious newsstand space: *True Detective Mysteries*, *True Lovers,* and *True Romances* seldom told the truth, whereas *Modern Screen*, *Motion Picture*, *Silver Screen*, and countless other movie pulps exploited gossip in the film industry. *Amazing Stories*, *Astounding Stories*, *Dime Detective*, *Dime Mystery*, *Thrilling Detective*, *Thrilling Mystery*, and *Thrilling Wonder* provided the thrills, although *Spicy Adventure*, *Spicy Detective*, and *Spicy Western Stories* probably promised more than they could deliver. The perfect distraction for people with time on their hands, the pulps gave a momentary escape from the harsh realities of the Depression and proliferated throughout the period between the World Wars.

By purchasing *Liberty*, Macfadden acquired a title different from most other general magazines. For example, it attached a "reading time" note to each article, a small block that guaranteed a particular piece would take no more than "5 minutes, 30 seconds" to read (the numbers of course varied). A gimmick, to be sure, but it reflected the American obsession with doing things quickly and efficiently. The articles themselves tended toward the tawdry and sensational, with breathless prose on Al Capone, Huey Long, and other celebrities perhaps more notorious than illustrious. Macfadden employed *Liberty* as his personal soapbox, urging voters to reelect **Franklin D. Roosevelt** (1882–1945) in 1936, a stand that placed him and his magazine poles apart from the more conservative *Saturday Evening Post* and *Reader's Digest*.

Under Macfadden's guidance, *Liberty* gained readers, but it bore the reputation of being directed at the working class, not the more affluent middle class. Advertisers, rightly or wrongly, stayed away, placing their precious ad dollars in other publications they saw as potentially more profitable to them. Despite circulating a million or more copies each week, *Liberty* remained starved for advertising revenues. After a lingering decline, it finally expired in 1951. With its demise, the nation lost one of its most popular and unusual magazines, one that made no pretensions about being elitist or intellectual.

Among the newcomers to the magazine ranks of the 1930s, *Esquire* attracted considerable attention following its 1933 introduction. One of the first American journals to employ target marketing, it attempted to identify exactly who read it and then approached potential advertisers with readership profiles created for just this purpose. Since *Esquire* claimed to be a "gentleman's magazine," it sold itself accordingly. As a result, clothiers, various liquors, automobile companies, and the like bought space in the magazine, and it soon showed a profit. Sophisticated but always tasteful, *Esquire* usually escaped the onus associated with more sexually oriented "men's magazines," a fact not lost on advertisers.

Following the success of *Esquire*'s foray into target marketing, *Fortune* (founded 1930) did likewise and became one of the most advertising-heavy monthly magazines in the country. *Fortune*'s sister publication, *Time*, followed suit and did well, especially in light of the competition from two 1933 news-oriented entries, *Newsweek* and *U.S. News & World Report*. In 1936, *Life*, a pictorial journal of the week's events, entered the marketplace, and it provides the best example of target marketing. Its immediate acceptance by middle-class readers and resultant huge circulation convinced advertisers that *Life* held a key to reaching large audiences. By 1939, just three years old, *Life* could charge more for ad space than any of its competitors and had no lack of takers.

The covers gracing American magazines also deserve mention. Throughout the first half of the twentieth century, most magazine covers consisted of full-color reproductions of original works—oils, watercolors, pastels, drawings, cartoons, woodcuts, and so on. Although photographs and striking typography occasionally made up a cover, they did not dominate the industry until well after World War II, when the economies of time and reproduction costs gave them a significant edge over the more expensive, hand-done alternatives.

Many artists and **illustrators** made good livings creating cover art. The best known of them would be **Norman Rockwell** (1894–1978), particularly because of his long association with the *Saturday Evening Post*, a magazine for which he created a remarkable 322 covers over a period spanning the years 1916 to 1963. The talented Leslie Thrasher (1889–1936) provided a simplified version of the nostalgia created by Rockwell. Beginning in 1926, Thrasher painted 360 covers for *Liberty*, a streak that came to an end in 1932 only because of Depression belt tightening.

Many other individuals likewise made frequent appearances with the *American Magazine*, *Collier's*, *Fortune*, *Good Housekeeping*, *Ladies' Home Journal*, *Liberty*, and a host of others. Artists like Constantin Alajalov (1900–1987), Joseph Binder (1898–1972), Miguel Covarrubias (1902–1957), Erte (1892–1990), Paolo Garretto (1903–1991), J. C. Leyendecker (1874–1951), Paul Rand (1914–1997), and Edgar F. Wittmack (1894–1956) stand out among the leaders for the period.

Covers serve as a reader's introduction to a magazine, so publishers lavished considerable attention and expense on that aspect of their periodicals; an unattractive cover might deter a possible newsstand sale. But the subjects and their depiction also perform an additional task: they offer a quick, visual essay on styles, manners, and mores. Any survey of magazine covers from the 1930s, or any other period, for that matter, would reveal a wealth of information on countless aspects of American culture. Many such covers did not relate directly to the inside content of the magazine; they instead reflected the season (Christmas, Easter, etc.), or evoked moods—happy, humorous, nostalgic, sad, youthful—and often presented self-explanatory vignettes that stood on their own merits.

Mass-circulation American magazines as a rule paid little heed to the Depression, instead filling their pages with fiction, a few facts, and lots of entertaining features, such as puzzles, jokes and cartoons, interviews, photo essays, reviews, and the like. Their wide, diverse readership suggests they offered a form of journalistic escapism for troubled times and successfully functioned in this role.

See also Automobiles; Crime; Fashion; *Life* & *Fortune*; Movies; Photography

SELECTED READING

Armour, Richard. *Give Me* Liberty. New York: World Publishing Co., 1969.

Ford, James L. C. *Magazines for Millions: The Story of Specialized Publications*. Carbondale: Southern Illinois University Press, 1969.

Heller, Steven, and Louise Fili. *Cover Story: The Art of American Magazine Covers, 1900–1950*. San Francisco: Chronicle Books, 1996.

Hunt, William R. *Body Love: The Amazing Career of Bernarr Macfadden*. Bowling Green, OH: Bowling Green State University Popular Press, 1989.

Janello, Amy, and Brennon Jones. *The American Magazine*. New York: Harry N. Abrams, 1991.

Peterson, Theodore. *Magazines in the Twentieth Century*. Urbana: University of Illinois Press, 1964.

MARATHON DANCING. A competitive form of dancing, it awarded the couple that stayed out on the floor for the longest total time a prize, usually cash. In addition, all the contestants received room, board, and some even a paltry salary for as long as they participated. This kind of contest first appeared around 1928, but the fad had run its course by the beginning of the 1930s. Given the hard times, however, dance marathons held a peculiar appeal and found a new lease on life with the Depression. In the early, dark days of the economic collapse, people flocked to them, either to observe others or to pick up a few dollars and try for the prizes.

The rules were simple: a couple had to dance, or at least keep moving, for an hour. When 60 minutes had passed, they got 15 minutes off, and then they had to be back on the floor for another hour. If one fell asleep while dancing, the other had the responsibility for keeping him or her upright and mobile. Together the two could make $20 to $30 a week (roughly $295 and $440 in contemporary money) just holding each other up and shuffling their feet, plus they got two cots and eight free meals a day. Dancing all day and long into the night consumed an enormous quantity of calories, so they usually received rich, filling meals.

June Havoc (b. 1916; then called June Hovick), later a Broadway and Hollywood star, holds the dance marathon record: 3,600 hours of continuous dancing. She and her partner, Elmer "Sparkplug" Dupree (active 1930s), remained upright and moving for over 21 weeks, or about five months, in 1934. For their efforts, the pair shared a prize of $40 (roughly $600 in contemporary money). In 1935, Horace McCoy (1897–1955) published a novel titled *They Shoot Horses, Don't They?* This harsh, unsparing story worked its way up the best-seller lists and its title says it all; the dance marathons could hardly be called fun, and entrants suffered mightily for meager prizes, a few dollars, and free **food**.

Despite the hardships and the slim chance of winning, hundreds danced, and hundreds of others watched. To finance the food and shelter, along with the prizes, dance marathons charged spectators admission. Day after day, and long into the night, these onlookers observed the number of dancers dwindle as exhaustion thinned the ranks of participants. At times, as with the Hovick-Dupree team, the audience had to come back for weeks on end, and the nickels and dimes taken as admission added up for the promoters.

Several Hollywood films, such as *The Lottery Bride* (1930), *Sailor's Luck* (1933), and *Hard to Handle* (1933), attempted to capture some of the grittiness of these degrading exhibitions, but only *Hard to Handle*, with James Cagney (1899–1986), came remotely close. In reality, the cheap dancehalls, the pall of smoke over everything, and the exhausted dancers exceeded anything the movie studios could stage.

By the mid-1930s, dance marathons had again lost their crowd appeal. The worst of the Depression appeared to be over, and a greater sense of optimism pervaded the country. The virtual despair that characterized the many marathons seemed out of place, and so most locations closed their doors and sought other entertainments for the public.

See also Best Sellers; Fads; Leisure & Recreation; Movies

SELECTED READING
McCoy, Horace. *They Shoot Horses, Don't They?* New York: Simon & Schuster, 1935.
Sann, Paul. *Fads, Follies, and Delusions of the American People.* New York: Crown Publishers, 1967.

MARCH OF TIME, THE (RADIO & FILM). A remarkable series of film and **radio** documentaries underwritten by *Time* magazine, *The March of Time*, set new standards for broadcast journalism. Editorial and production control resided with the newsmagazine's board of directors, a conservative group chaired by Henry R. Luce (1898–1967), the founder of *Time*, **Life**, and **Fortune magazines**. Given its unique status as the editorial arm of a popular periodical, *The March of Time* often forsook journalistic

Filming an episode of *The March of Time*, a long-running and popular documentary series. (Courtesy of the Library of Congress)

objectivity in order to present a point of view endorsed by its owners. The programs presented hundreds of vignettes about the news of the day, going beyond the headlines to present insightful interpretations of events.

Radio broadcasts began in 1928. The first transmissions, 10 minutes in length, emanated from Cincinnati, Ohio, and immediately found a receptive audience. That same year, *The March of Time* went into syndication, gaining national network status in 1931 with the Columbia Broadcasting System (CBS radio). In 1937, the show shifted to the National Broadcasting Company (NBC radio), where it would stay until 1944. It moved to the new American Broadcasting Company (ABC radio) in late 1944 and continued broadcasting new episodes until the summer of 1945 when it went off the air.

The radio show usually employed 30-minute productions that played weekly. During the 1935–1936 season, however, *The March of Time* tried a new approach; it could be heard nightly in 15-minute performances, but the experiment lasted only a year. In the fall of 1936, it went back to the half hour format, a move that allowed more preparation and greater depth with the featured stories. *The March of Time* series went off the air between 1939 and 1941, but returned in order to cover much of World War II. Over the years, various sponsors associated themselves with the show, but one of the most consistent advertisers turned out to be *Time* magazine itself. The weekly periodical enjoyed exclusive sponsorship through the final eight years of broadcasting.

During its lengthy radio life, *The March of Time* employed a number of leading announcers as narrators for the aural documentary. Among the best known can be counted Westbrook van Voorhis (1903–1968) and Harry Von Zell (1906–1981), two broadcasting personalities whose voices millions recognized. Van Voorhis, with a distinctive, at times mellifluous, style, took over most of the announcing chores in 1933.

In addition to narration, the show frequently staged dramatizations of newsworthy events. In time, many different actors impersonated Presidents **Franklin D. Roosevelt** (1882–1945) and **Herbert Hoover** (1874–1964), Benito Mussolini (1883–1945), Adolf Hitler (1889–1945), Winston Churchill (1874–1965), and an unending series of other public figures. In order to add to an air of authenticity, the producers employed elaborate sound effects, an important contribution since the radio version could of course not use film clips. Because breaking news does not wait for producers and directors, the staff had to be ready for last-minute changes in scripts, and a fresh but important story might supersede a scheduled one. It all made for a hectic atmosphere, but one that relied on professionalism and a readiness to adapt to any situation.

The movie version of *The March of Time* premiered in theaters in 1934 and would run until 1951, when the pressures of **television** news brought about its demise. Throughout its run, Westbrook van Voorhis ably narrated the show once more. The vision of filmmaker Louis de Rochemont (1899–1978), who served as chief producer, deeply influenced the look of *The March of Time*. This visual counterpart to the radio version gave birth to the contemporary docudrama, the blending of the factual documentary with dramatic additions. Combining actual newsreel footage with dramatized segments, the show smoothly mixed truth with fiction based on fact, thus enlivening history, but at the expense of total, complete accuracy. Viewers witnessed a heightened reality, one in which actors often assumed the roles of people, living and dead, for dramatic effect.

Unlike regular 10-minute theater newsreels that chronicled the week's events and usually included such noncontroversial ephemera as beauty contests, sporting events, and the latest gadgets in brief sequences, *The March of Time* film documentaries ran once a month for approximately 20 minutes. The producers tackled just a handful of important news stories during that brief time on screen, often controversial ones involving politics, economics, or military subjects, giving them far more attention than did competing forms of journalism. As a rule, one story in particular dominated each "issue" of the show, receiving up to 15 minutes of discussion and dramatization.

The series also had the editorial courage to discuss contemporary issues in frank, unequivocal language and images, and often took a partisan stance, much to the distress of its critics. Almost from its inception, the series dealt with fascism, neutrality, isolationism, and especially German National Socialism, or Nazism, and the rise of Adolph Hitler. Virtually alone among news organizations of the 1930s, *The March of Time* made no secret of the threat to democracy posed by the Axis powers, a threat that would ultimately require an Allied response.

Despite its in-depth stories, its skillful dramatizations, and its editorializing, the series still had to compete with other entertainment features in the theaters where it played. Usually consigned to the middle of a so-called double bill, it ran with previews, cartoons, and other short subjects. Thus its careful discussions of current events constituted a small part of the larger theatrical offering. In the eyes of most of the audience, *The March of Time* doubtless lacked the impact of two full-length **movies** featuring top Hollywood stars.

See also Advertising; Radio Networks

SELECTED READING
Dunning, John. *On the Air: The Encyclopedia of Old-Time Radio*. New York: Oxford University Press, 1998.
Fielding, Raymond. The March of Time, *1935–1951*. New York: Oxford University Press, 1978.
March of Time (radio show). http://xroads.virginia.edu/MA04/wood/mot/html

MARSH, REGINALD. Born into an affluent family, Reginald Marsh (1898–1954) showed an aptitude for drawing and painting at a young age. After graduating from Yale in 1920, he set his sights on becoming an illustrator, moved to New York City, filling sketchbooks with everything he saw around him, a habit he would continue throughout his life. In 1925, Marsh joined the newly founded *New Yorker* magazine as a staff cartoonist, and later took a position drawing for the tabloid *New York Daily News*. These jobs gave him the freedom to wander the city streets, from Harlem to the Bowery, observing and sketching. He especially liked Coney Island, with its sea of bathers, teeming boardwalk, and garish sideshows. These experiences appeared in the many paintings he produced during the 1930s that chronicle life in the American metropolis.

For Marsh, a city street has nothing in common with one of **Charles Sheeler's** (1883–1965) empty factory complexes any more than it does with **Grant Wood's** (1891–1942) immaculately planted Iowa hillsides. The city and its teeming streets, as *In Fourteenth Street* (1934), are raucous, honky-tonk places, full of gritty details he makes no attempt to hide. The cheap neighborhood theater in *Twenty Cent Movie* (1936) may not be a downtown palace, but it possesses plenty of hustle and bustle along with its double features, and he plunges the viewer into the midst of noisy chaos, a place of visual turbulence.

Many painters of urban America, particularly Sheeler and **Edward Hopper** (1882–1967), present their city scenes as eerily quiet, creating an overriding feeling of loneliness, as if people cannot connect with one another. There exists a sense of detachment—they often place viewers at a distance from the subject, making them look across considerable space at the scene. Perhaps in some ways this device reflected the Depression economy, frozen and silent, unable to move. But not Reginald Marsh: he takes the opposite tack. He examines, up close, the big, crowded milieu familiar to millions of Americans. For example, the title *Ten Shots, Ten Cents* (1939) refers to a penny arcade sign, but the parade of people passing under the marquee capture the viewer's attention, not the words above them. Sheeler's and Hopper's carefully wrought city scenes make the onlooker ponder, but Marsh's resemble a candid snapshot, a moment in time.

Like many artists of the day, Marsh participated in the **Federal Art Project** (FAP; 1935–1943), a **New Deal** program that provided employment for painters and others needing assistance. From this came several mural commissions, such as *Transfer of Mail from Liner to Tugboat* (1936) and *Atlantic Liner in Harbor with Tugs* (1937) in the New York Customs House. Thanks to these commissions, along with his own vibrant paintings, Reginald Marsh achieved a modest popular success.

Although he enjoyed satirizing the rich in many of his works, he made no attempt to ennoble the poor and downtrodden; both play their roles and exhibit a sense that they accept their lot and belong in this environment. Because he will not judge either the city or its denizens, many of the Social Realists of the 1930s saw Marsh as an outsider,

A drawing by Reginald Marsh (1898–1954) of a Depression-era breadline. (Courtesy of the Library of Congress)

an artist fearful of taking sides in a politically charged era. But Marsh's celebration of city life also put him out of step with the Regionalists, since his version of the American scene conflicted with the more bucolic, nostalgic one supported by many in that movement. In one picture after another, Marsh recorded the growing urbanism of the United States, and his candor in depicting the life of a large American city (in his case, almost always New York City) places him more in league with the Social Realists than with the Regionalists. To that end, he even contributed black-and-white illustrations to *Fortune* magazine during the depths of the Depression. His scenes, often featuring the unemployed and the destitute, might seem a surprising choice for a business-oriented periodical, but the editors had few qualms about addressing the economic calamity, and they often turned to art as a means of showing how widespread its effects had become.

Whatever Marsh's classification, a human comedy parades across the many canvases and drawings he produced in the 1930s. Rich and poor, blacks and whites, silly and stately, from burlesque to the Bowery—they all crowd into his vibrant scenes. A master at depicting the human figure, he often alluded to classical antecedents for poses. He even published a textbook, *Anatomy for Artists*, in 1935. Thus bathers on a Coney Island Beach may resemble, at times, Grecian athletes, as in *Lifeguards* (1933) or *Coney Island* (1936). But a sly humor, something missing from much of the decade's other art, also permeates these pictures; beside the splendidly muscled **youth** sprawls an older man, unkempt and fat. Bums loaf in the sunlight, sharp-eyed panhandlers size up the crowd. He satirizes the whole of humanity and plays no favorites, but neither does he create villains. A voluptuous, Rubenesque woman plies the oldest profession in *Hudson Bay Fur Company* (1932), and Marsh celebrates her obvious sexuality, just as he delights in portraying a gaggle of wide-eyed men gaping at a burlesque queen in *Star Burlesk* (1933).

For viewers of his art, Marsh provides choice front row seats, so they get to see it all. He invites celebration—plunge in; this is the city, this is the way it is, and there's no need to be cerebral about it.

See also Thomas Hart Benton; Illustrators; *Life* & *Fortune*; Magazines; Regionalism; Social Realism

SELECTED READING

Cohen, Marilyn. *Reginald Marsh's New York: Paintings, Drawings, Prints, and Photographs.* New York: Dover Publications, 1983.
Goodrich, Lloyd. *Reginald Marsh.* New York: Harry N. Abrams, 1972.

Laning, Edward. *The Sketchbooks of Reginald Marsh.* Greenwich, CT: New York Graphic Society, 1973.

Sasowsky, Norman. *The Prints of Reginald Marsh.* New York: Clarkson N. Potter, 1976.

MARX BROTHERS, THE. A spirit of anarchy has often been present in American movie comedy, and that spirit never came more fully to the fore than in the pictures made by the Marx Brothers during the Depression decade. The five brothers—Groucho (1890–1977; b. Julius), Chico (1887–1961; b. Leonard), Harpo (1888–1964; b. Adolph), Zeppo (1901–1979; b. Herbert), and Gummo (1892–1977; b. Milton)—learned their comedic craft in the rough and tumble of vaudeville during the 1920s. Gummo, the least known of the quintet, dropped out of performing in the late 1920s and turned to management, something he practiced successfully with his own siblings. The remaining brothers enjoyed one movie hit after another during the 1930s, although Zeppo, usually cast as the straight man, also retired from active performing after the 1933 release of *Duck Soup*. He turned to business, became a Hollywood agent, and worked with his brother Gummo.

Early on, the Marxes had found success on Broadway with *The Cocoanuts*, a 1925 musical by George F. Kaufman (1889–1961) that featured **music** by **Irving Berlin** (1888–1989). Although much of their humor involves visual slapstick, it also relies on verbal comedy. The machine-gun repartee of Groucho, enhanced by the pseudo-Italian dialect of Chico, requires audiences to listen, and listen carefully, lest they miss some of the steady string of jokes. In 1929, Paramount Pictures released a film version of *The Cocoanuts*, and audiences loved it, successfully launching the Marx Brothers into the new world of talking **movies**. Their nonstop dialogue could never have been adequately handled by silent films, since audiences would have spent most of their time reading cards. Thereafter, the Marx Brothers entertained Depression moviegoers with a new comedy almost yearly; between 1929 and 1940, they starred in 10 films, and most of them did well.

Following *The Cocoanuts* came *Animal Crackers* (1930), *Monkey Business* (1931), *Horse Feathers* (1932), *Duck Soup* (1933), *A Night at the Opera* (1935), *A Day at the Races* (1937), *Room Service* (1938), *At the Circus* (1939), and *Go West* (1940). Although crowds flocked to any new Marx Brothers offering, after *A Night at the Opera* their films display a gradually diminished zaniness, the anarchic humor no longer flows as effortlessly, and the frenetic pace that marked the first five pictures grows progressively slower. While the country remained mired in the Great Depression, the Marx Brothers provided a hilarious, devil-may-care antidote to the glum conditions outside the movie theater; with a gradual recovery of sorts in the second half of the decade, it seemed the nation no longer required their patented brand of madcap comedy, humor that held nothing sacred.

Despite the slowdown in their later films—and even then, the brothers come across as funnier than any other comedy teams of the era—they created a series of movie classics that continue to live into the present. Margaret Dumont (1882–1965), a fine actress given the thankless task of being the foil to Groucho's constant wisecracks and schemes, accompanies them in six of their films during the 1930s. Typecast as a rich, befuddled society lady, unsure of what is going on around her, she adds immeasurably to the antic fun of the convoluted plots. Her role as a person of wealth and social standing who lacks any common sense doubtless played well to Depression-era audiences.

For many, two films, *Duck Soup* and *A Night at the Opera*, represent the Marx Brothers' greatest achievements. In *Duck Soup*, the politics of aggression and war get stood on their ear; with war clouds already forming in Asia and Europe, the brothers' inspired insanity reveals how quickly events can get out of hand. Initially not terribly popular with audiences, the film acquired a cadre of devoted fans that slowly grew, and today most movie buffs consider *Duck Soup* a classic of American cinematic comedy.

A Night at the Opera, the film that immediately followed *Duck Soup*, also has its ardent supporters. In this movie, Groucho, Chico, and Harpo take on the bastions of elite culture, making a shambles of everything they encounter, especially the institution of opera. Many citizens, rightly or wrongly, thought high culture the exclusive, inviolable property of the wealthy guardians of taste. Such attitudes provide fertile ground for the brothers' relentless attacks. The have-nots emerge victorious over the haves, another chapter in the old story of low culture taking on high art, with buffoonery winning out over elitism. *A Night at the Opera* supplies the kind of rude comeuppance Americans so enjoy.

The Marx Brothers continued to make movies into the 1940s, but their efforts come across as dim reflections of their earlier zaniness. Between 1929 and 1937, however, they had no real rivals, and their patented brand of humor thumbed its nose at Old Man Depression, always with a joke at the ready.

See also Circuses; Football; Horse Racing; Hotels; Musicals; Screwball Comedies

SELECTED READING

Anobile, Richard J., ed. *Why a Duck? Verbal and Visual Gems from the Marx Brothers Movies.* New York: Darien House, 1971.

Durgnat, Raymond. *The Crazy Mirror: Hollywood Comedy and the American Image.* New York: Dell Publishing Co. [Delta], 1969.

MILLER, GLENN. A Midwesterner by birth, (Alton) Glenn Miller (1904–1944) played trombone in a number of regional bands that toured for dancing in the mid- to late 1920s. Never an exceptional instrumentalist, Miller began arranging, in addition to his playing, for such bandleaders as Red Nichols (1905–1965), the Dorsey Brothers (Tommy, 1905–1956; Jimmy, 1904–1957), and **Benny Goodman** (1909–1986). These experiences led to a position with the Ray Noble (1903–1978) orchestra in 1935, and this steady employment allowed Miller to polish his arranging skills.

In a decade crowded with different bands, Miller realized that success demanded a distinctive "sound" that people would recognize and like. He experimented with various instrumental voicings, and discovered that a clarinet playing the melody an octave over the other reeds created a light, danceable sound. Commercial success, however, did not immediately fall on the heels of his discovery.

In 1937, Miller broke from Noble and organized an aggregation of his own. This initial effort, although it hinted at things to come, went nowhere and he had to break it up. He continued to write arrangements and formed a second band in 1938. This time around, Miller hired excellent sidemen, and he had the good fortune to land Ray Eberle (1919–1979), Marion Hutton (1919–1987), and the Modernaires (a singing group; active 1930s & 1940s) as his vocalists.

The orchestra attracted some favorable attention, and cut a number of **recordings** for several labels. These early efforts did not sell extremely well nor did they produce quite the sound Miller had been looking for, but they nonetheless served notice that the new band possessed the ability to play outstanding dance **music**. At the same time, Miller himself had developed a personable, easygoing stage manner that listeners and dancers enjoyed.

Good fortune nodded in the group's direction in the fall of 1938 when RCA Victor, a leader in the recording field, signed a contract with the orchestra. For the first time, records captured the inimitable "Miller sound," and in the early months of 1939, several hits followed. The band's engaging theme, "Moonlight Serenade," composed by Miller, with lyrics by Mitchell Parish (1900–1993), listeners found especially captivating, and people soon associated it with the orchestra. A companion piece, "Sunrise Serenade," a 1939 composition by pianist Frankie Carle (1903–2001) and lyricist Jack Lawrence (b. 1912), likewise had its admirers. Soon, other popular favorites like "Tuxedo Junction" (1939; music by Erskine Hawkins [1914–1993], Julian Dash [1916–1974], and William Johnson [active 1930s]), "Little Brown Jug" (1939; traditional; arranged by Bill Finegan [1917–2005]), and "Pennsylvania 6-5000" (music by Jerry Gray [1915–1976], lyrics by Carl Sigman [active 1930s, 1940s]) came out on Victor's Bluebird label.

Success begets success, and Miller soon found himself playing casinos, **hotels**, ballrooms, and packing in the audiences. The **radio networks**, which could not seem to get enough **swing** orchestras on the air to satisfy fans, discovered Miller just as his career took off. At the end of 1939, the Columbia Broadcasting System (CBS radio) inaugurated *Chesterfield Time*, a 15-minute music show that broadcast three nights a week. As his fame spread, more radio shows would follow.

In a long stint at the Glen Island Casino, a combination restaurant and ballroom overlooking New York's Long Island Sound, Miller continued to do his **radio** shows, using a remote setup that allowed him to broadcast directly from his location. At the beginning of 1940, the band recorded its biggest hit, "In the Mood" (1939; music by Joe Garland [1903–1977], lyrics by Andy Razaf [1895–1973]). Over the years, this recording would establish itself as one of the top-selling songs of the swing era, and the Glenn Miller Orchestra would go on to become one of the most popular swing bands of all time.

Many swing and dance band fans associate the Glenn Miller Orchestra with the 1930s. In reality, however, the band enjoyed success only during the last year or so of the decade. Not until the onset of the 1940s would it dominate every popularity poll and produce a string of nonstop hits. But success would prove fleeting; with the war, Miller enlisted and formed an army air force orchestra to play for the troops in the European theater of operations. In 1944, a military airplane carrying Miller disappeared in a storm over the English Channel; searchers found no remains. The band carried on, but without its popular leader, the subsequent Glenn Miller bands always seemed but shadows of the original.

In its brief heyday, the Miller aggregation epitomized versatility. It could play the slow, syrupy ballads, often accompanied by a singer who made no attempt to swing the lyric. But the orchestra could also perform **jazz**-tinged arrangements of up-tempo tunes that any swing band could envy. Miller straddled both camps, and he pleased both.

See also Restaurants; Songwriters & Lyricists

SELECTED READING

Simon, George T. *The Big Bands*. New York: Macmillan, 1967.

———. *Glenn Miller and His Orchestra*. New York: Thomas Y. Crowell, 1974.

Yanow, Scott. *Swing*. San Francisco: Miller Freeman Books, 2000.

MINIATURE GOLF. A variation on traditional **golf**, this form of the game briefly eclipsed it, sweeping the nation in 1930. Miniaturized golf courses first appeared in the early years of the twentieth century, both in the United States and abroad. These pioneering courses, rather crude affairs, tended to be located on private property and did not open their gates to the public. The modern game of miniature golf, available to all, owes its existence to Garnet Carter (1883–1954), a real estate developer who owned a resort called Fairyland atop Lookout Mountain near Chattanooga, Tennessee.

In addition to a hotel, Carter had laid out a regular golf course on his mountain site, and he decided to add an extensive putting area to boost attendance. In 1927, he took out a patent for "Tom Thumb Golf," the immediate predecessor to the modern game of miniature golf. Carter envisioned a leveled grass lawn containing some simple obstacles, usually open tin pipes through which the ball had to pass, to make the putting interesting and challenging.

Fairyland boomed and visitors flocked to Carter's innovation, to the point that their sheer numbers wore out the grassy areas. He then improvised a new surface, cottonseed hulls, which withstood the heavy traffic volume but still provided a good putting surface. Erstwhile competitors took it upon themselves to set up courses of their own. At first limited primarily to the northeastern and southeastern states, along with trendsetting California, the game took off. By some estimates, 4 million Americans played miniature golf on any given day in 1930 at 40,000 different locations. In response to his unexpected success, Carter began marketing Tom Thumb components that could be assembled on any site. He also tried a National Tom Thumb Open Championship at Fairyland in 1930. The event attracted many players, but by this time miniature golf had already established itself and spread across the country; Carter's tournament was only one of many competitive events.

Miniature golf courses appeared on empty lots, rooftops, roadsides, and anywhere else level surfaces could be found. If available acreage proved scarce or too expensive, the game went indoors, utilizing warehouses and other spacious, enclosed areas. It took little capital to establish a bare bones layout, including lights for night play, although the more elaborate constructions could cost tens of thousands of dollars. In the meantime, the obstacles grew in size and imagination, and skill became secondary to complexity and challenge. Cheap and accessible for its fans, miniature golf seemed the perfect recreational escape in the cash-strapped Depression.

With no end seemingly in sight for the game, the bubble suddenly burst, a one-year phenomenon. Just in the nick of time, Hollywood managed to release a comedy short titled *Tom Thumbs Down* (1931), possibly the only movie about miniature golf ever made. By the spring of 1931, the fad had fizzled and empty, abandoned miniature golf courses littered the landscape. Not until after World War II would the game see a resurgence of interest.

See also Fads; Games; Hotels; Leisure & Recreation; Movies

SELECTED READING

Liebs, Chester H. *Main Street to Miracle Mile: American Roadside Architecture*. Baltimore: Johns Hopkins University Press, 1985.
Miniature Golf. http://www.mastersnationalchamps.com/history.html

MONOPOLY. With high unemployment and more leisure time, the Depression years witnessed a rise in the popularity of board **games**. Monopoly, the undisputed champion, made its commercial debut in 1935. Its origins date back to 1904 and an innovative diversion called the Landlord's Game, a little-known pastime created by Lizzie Magie (aka Elizabeth Magie Phillips; active 1900s). She focused on the ethics of rents and impoverished tenants, and her game showed how landlords became progressively richer as they acquired property. The more real estate one owned, the better the chances of winning. Magie patented the Landlord's Game in 1904, and the original board bears a striking resemblance to the one in use with the more familiar Monopoly today.

Over time, Magie's creation underwent rules revisions and even evolved into regional variations, one of which used street names from Atlantic City, New Jersey. Most of these games consisted of homemade boards, often oilcloth with crayon-colored spaces, and items like buttons and thimbles for markers. By the late 1920s, the name had informally changed to Monopoly, since players attempted to gain real estate monopolies as they worked their way around the board.

Charles B. Darrow (1889–1967), a struggling Philadelphia architect, had played the Atlantic City variant, and saw in it the potential for widespread sales. He borrowed freely from Magie's Landlord's Game, along with its many permutations, and made up some samples for friends. Contrary to popular belief, Darrow did not "invent" Monopoly, but the alterations he imposed on these earlier products, along with his persistence in marketing his own version, brought about the modern-day game that millions know and love.

Copyrighting his mix as "Monopoly" in 1933, he sold several thousand homemade copies through the mail before attempting to get Parker Brothers, a major toy and game manufacturer, to carry his creation. Corporate shortsightedness initially caused the company to ignore him. In their eyes, Monopoly was "too dull, too complex, and took too long to play," so Darrow privately made up some additional sets and in 1934 got Wanamaker's Department Store of Philadelphia and F. A. O. Schwarz of New York to stock them. Interested consumers cleaned the shelves and Parker Brothers took a second look and reached an agreement with the architect in 1935. Under the terms of their contract, Parker Brothers gained all rights to both Magie's old tenant's game and Darrow's revisions. Monopoly would prove to be the most successful board game in history, and Charles Darrow retired a wealthy man.

Many people believe that the capitalistic focus of the game—the acquisition of wealth and property—made Monopoly an American favorite during the Depression, a time of economic challenge. But the game's continuing popularity in strong economic times suggests that people like the game for its own merits, not its possible socioeconomic underpinnings. For kids and grown-ups alike, nothing quite equals the thrill of building a hotel on Boardwalk or the disappointment of losing everything and having to drop out of the play.

See also Fads; Leisure & Recreation; Toys

SELECTED READING

Monopoly. http://www.hasbro.com/monopoly

———. http://tt.tf/gamehist/mon-index.html

Walsh, Tim. *The Playmakers: Amazing Origins of Timeless Toys*. Sarasota, FL: Keys Publishing Co., 2003.

MOSES, ROBERT. One of the most powerful nonelected officials in the history of New York City, Robert Moses (1888–1981) oversaw the transformation of much of the city's **transportation** infrastructure. Lacking formal training in engineering or management, he worked diligently in the administration of Governor Al Smith (1873–1944; governor 1918–1920, 1922–1928). Moses moved into appointed positions of considerable authority that allowed him to influence—if not dictate—the direction road, bridge, and tunnel construction would take in the Empire State.

During the 1930s, Moses acquired considerable influence in several city and state agencies, eventually taking on the chairmanships of the New York City Public Works Commission and the Long Island Parks Commission. These appointments gave him great latitude in making decisions, actions that revolved around the construction of highways to facilitate the flow of people into and around New York City. No lover of mass transit or indeed public transport of any kind, Moses saw the city as the servant of the automobile, and he attempted to restructure existing urban spaces to accommodate cars.

As his influence grew, he took on the chairmanship of the Triborough Bridge and Tunnel Authority (TBTA), an appointive position that granted him control of all the toll money that daily poured into the TBTA offices from the group's bridges, parkways, and tunnels. Almost by default, Moses and the TBTA became virtually autonomous, bypassing mayors and other elected officials in a quest to redesign the city's sprawling transportation network. As he amassed power, Moses saw to it that the TBTA had its own headquarters, along with a fleet of cars, trucks, and boats, all of which bore the TBTA flag and emblem.

One of the authority's most famous accomplishments focused on the construction of the Triborough Bridge, a 1930–1936 undertaking. Almost simultaneously, the Henry Hudson Bridge saw its lower level become operational in 1936; the upper level followed suit in 1938. Then came the Bronx-Whitestone Bridge, a crossing that gave access to thousands of people intent on seeing the 1939–1940 **New York World's Fair** at Flushing Meadows.

Moses, however, did not content himself just with bridges. The West Side Highway, one of the city's first expressways, was constructed during 1927–1931. He ordered it to be built over the remains of an abandoned elevated train that once served the western side of Manhattan. The Belt Parkway (or Circumferential Parkway) opened in 1934. Toward the end of the decade, a flurry of projects marked Moses' dominance in the planning of roadways for the city: the Whitestone Expressway began to take shape in 1939, as did the Gowanus Parkway, another elevated route for **automobiles**. The Queens Midtown Tunnel opened in 1940, and building commenced on the Long Island Expressway that same year.

Three other projects that Moses supervised included, first, the completion of roads allowing access to Jones Beach in 1929 and 1930. Not open to mass transit, the Jones Beach construction nonetheless allowed millions of motorists to enjoy the pristine Atlantic beaches. Second, he oversaw much of the planning and building for the 1939–1940 World's Fair. One of the great expositions of the twentieth century, The World of Tomorrow promised a technological future in which everything functioned in a smooth, Streamlined way. Finally, Moses took leadership in the creation of New York City Municipal Airport, a major facility dedicated in October 1939. Most people today know

Robert Moses (1888–1981) with a model of proposed construction projects. (Courtesy of the Library of Congress)

the busy field as LaGuardia Airport, renamed in 1947 for New York's popular mayor, Fiorello LaGuardia (1882–1947; mayor from 1933–1945).

For better or worse, Robert Moses left a lasting imprint on New York City and how large metropolitan areas handle increasing volumes of vehicular traffic, especially automotive. His supporters argue he saved the city from gridlock by opening up fast, multi-lane highways that allowed drivers to move rapidly through crowded urban congestion. His detractors maintain he destroyed much of the fabric of the city by bulldozing down huge swaths of housing, replacing entire neighborhoods with concrete and macadam, and turning his back to alternative transport such as light rail and **buses**. For some, he represented the master builder, a man of his times; others saw him as insensitive to the human scale, believing that all he wanted to do was move cars rapidly over the face of the city and, in so doing, blitzing much of what he claimed to save. For the 1930s, however, Robert Moses represented a hopeful view, a man ready to tackle any large-scale transportation challenges.

See also Fairs & Expositions; Trains; Travel

SELECTED READING
Burns, Ric, James Sanders, and Lisa Ades. *New York: An Illustrated History.* New York: Alfred A. Knopf, 1999.
Caro, Robert A. *The Power Broker: Robert Moses and the Fall of New York City.* New York: Vintage Books, 1975.

MOTELS. The exact date and site of America's first motel remain unknown, although some time in the early twentieth century seems a safe guess for the date. Cabins and cottages located along the road preceded what would become the standard motel configuration: a row of connected rooms facing a public highway. In the 1920s, private and municipal **auto camps**, sometimes called tourist parks, offered, for a fee, tent sites in many communities across the country. By the 1930s, the ownership of most of these tourist facilities had shifted to individual entrepreneurs and primitive tent setups had been replaced by cabins or cottages. Their name changed from auto camp to auto court, motor court, motor village, or tourist court. Since the rooms in these units often interconnected with one another, they served as the forerunners of the modern motel. By whatever name, motels rapidly increased in number throughout the later 1920s and on into the 1930s—an estimated 3,000 in 1928 had jumped to almost 10,000 in 1935, and then rose to about 13,500 at the close of the decade.

In 1926, hotelier James Vail (active 1920s), along with architect Arthur Heineman (active 1920s), coined the term "mo-tel," a combination of motor and **hotel**. Based in San Luis Obispo, California, the two planned to build 18 motor inns, or mo-tels, along the West Coast from San Diego, California, to Seattle, Washington. Their first establishment, the Milestone Mo-Tel, opened in San Luis Obispo on December 12, 1925; its name later changed to the Motel Inn. Because of the 1929 crash and the onset of the Great Depression, their dreams of a pioneering chain of motels never materialized.

Despite disrupting many business plans, the economic collapse helped some individuals involved in the fledgling motel industry. Providing lodging along the roadside offered opportunities for small businesses and for people who wanted to turn unprofitable land into income. Nationwide demand for improved facilities fueled the growing motel business. Depression or not, middle-class Americans continued to take automobile vacations, albeit with some financial restraints. Budget-conscious businesses decreased **travel** allowances and urged salespeople to drive their cars instead of traveling by train; in addition, they encouraged employees to stay in motels rather than more expensive **hotels**.

For both the tourist and the business traveler, price, convenience, and amenities made motels attractive, and they appeared to be a good business venture for the owners of such enterprises. For those owning or having access to land adjacent to a highway, it took little to enter the motel business. Construction of these simple structures involved a small cash investment and presented few problems. How-to and builders' **magazines** cooperated by offering articles filled with advice, along with plans featuring specific dimensions and material lists. In some operations, the whole family participated, and dividing up the labor decreased the need for hired help.

Early motels tended to be one-story buildings with easily accessible rooms that usually offered one or two windows, plus a screen door for ventilation. This arrangement presented a sharp contrast to the traditionally small, cramped, and poorly ventilated hotel rooms that always seemed to be up several flights of narrow stairs. Features like these contributed to the growing popularity of motels. In addition, the absence of porters, bell captains, and other personnel to tip kept the price reasonable, and convenient parking meant the easy transport of bags from car to room.

By the mid-1930s, increasing competition caused many motel owners to upgrade their facilities and expand their amenities. Carpeting covered bare floors; brand-name mattresses lured sleepy motorists; and adjacent diners or **restaurants**—along with nearby **gas** stations—provided extra bonuses. In time, highly visible **swimming** pools and patios, and perhaps some playground equipment, became options for motels wanting to catch motorists' attention.

A few motel entrepreneurs went as far as to employ architectural gimmicks to attract travelers. For example, a Kentucky businessman named Frank Redford (active 1930s) built a series of concrete wigwams in Horse City, Kentucky, in 1933. He had first sold gas and **food** out of a tepee-shaped structure, and public curiosity caused him to add six separate "sleeping rooms." Their exteriors resembled wigwams, and he christened the venture Wigwam Village. Although Redford was not the first to employ this motif, he wisely patented his designs; he would go on to construct a total of seven such villages around the country. Another approach involved discarded railroad stock, such as cabooses and passenger cars. Kimmel's Pullman Cabins in Lyons, Colorado, took four cars from the C&S Railroad and placed them alongside the primary highway leading into the Rocky Mountains. Tourists could sleep in Pullman luxury before proceeding on their journey. Forts, castles, log cabins, ranches, historic sites—imaginative individuals tried many different treatments for their motel designs.

During the 1930s, two methods for operating motels emerged: the franchise chain and the referral chain. The franchise chain involved building a series of accommodations that used repetitive architectural designs and color schemes, along with identical names. Some even intentionally placed each facility a day's travel apart. In this arrangement, the company owned some of the motels but contracted others out to independent operators, who then enjoyed the advantage of a known name and reputation.

Edgar Lee Torrance (1894–1971), along with D. W. Bartlett (active 1930s), built the Alamo Plaza Tourist Apartments in Waco, Texas, in 1929. The use of the term "tourist apartments" attempted to convey the superiority of this facility over "tourist cabins," and apparently travelers liked the connotations. Torrance experienced immediate success and two years later constructed a second establishment in Tyler, Texas. These two groupings carry the honor of being America's first successful motel chain. He changed the name slightly in 1935 when he crossed state lines to build the Alamo Plaza Tourist Courts in Shreveport, Louisiana. By the end of the decade Torrance owned seven Alamo Plazas in five southern states.

His snow-white buildings featured a two-story facade that suggested the Alamo, and the **design** imparted a sense of history for the weary tourist. Inside, Torrance offered showers, brand-name mattresses, and hardwood floors. Starting in 1936, the Alamo Plazas installed some of the first guestroom telephones found in motels anywhere. As a chain, they promised familiarity, consistency, and comfort, conditions held in high esteem by the traveler away from home; the Alamo Plazas presented strong competition for smaller, independent motor courts and motels.

TraveLodge, another example of a successful chain, originated in 1935 when Scott King (active 1930s) opened King's Auto Court in San Diego, California. Over the next five years, King built 24 motels throughout Southern California. Rather than maintaining both ownership and management as Torrance had with his chain, King pioneered a co-ownership method of motel operation, and adopted the collective TraveLodge name in 1940. King's company and the owner-managers established contractual guidelines for payment of mortgages, management fees, and other expenses, along with the sharing of profits.

Despite the success of a small number of motel chains, individual mom-and-pop operations nevertheless predominated throughout the 1930s. Many of these participated in the second major motel business strategy, the referral chain—independent owners working together for their common good. Members of the group agreed to cooperate in upgrading properties and thereby created networks of quality motels through which referrals could be made. United Motor Courts (UMC), a referral chain whose original membership came mainly from California and Arizona, organized in 1933 and published an annual guidebook for tourists. UMC members guaranteed tourists clean rooms, quality beds, and good service. In 1937, the Tourist Cottage Owners' Association (TCOA) merged with UMC. TCOA had originally organized in the southeastern section of the country in 1932 as a trade association, a group of business competitors who voluntarily collected and disseminated information that would assist members with mutual business problems. The UMC-TCOA merger gave the two groups a combined membership that extended from the Pacific across the southern tier of states toward the Atlantic.

Another group, the National Tourist Lodge-Motor Court Trade Association (NTL-MCTA), came along in 1933, but it virtually disappeared within a year. Successful efforts to reinvigorate NTL-MCTA in 1937 included a new name, the International Motor Court Association (IMCA). Their publication of the first motel trade magazine, *Tourist Court Journal*, gave the industry a reference for standards. In 1939, the former Quality Inns initiated Quality Courts. This new organization consisted of seven southern motel operators who split off from United Motor Courts. To make themselves known, they immediately printed 10,000 copies of their own travel directory.

With motels becoming a permanent part of the American landscape by the late 1930s, a number of people outside the industry stepped in to assist travelers and promote this new addition to the tourist scene. In 1929, Emmons Walker (active 1920s and 1930s) of Dover, Massachusetts, produced annual guidebooks rating motels and hotels and listing lodgings primarily along the Atlantic seaboard from Quebec, Canada, to Florida. Likewise, Ray A. Walker (active 1920s and 1930s) of Haverhill, Massachusetts, published *Cabin Trails: A Dependable All-Year Service for Discriminating Motor-Vacationists* in 1939. The Travelers, located in New York City, sold a directory titled *Approved Travelers Motor Courts*. The 1938 copy of this publication listed 178 motels concentrated largely in the Northeast. During this same year, in addition to the guides the Travelers operated downtown and roadside information offices in some of the larger cities—New York, Washington, D.C., Miami, St. Petersburg, Los Angeles, and at the Georgia-Florida state line north of Jacksonville, Florida

The American Automobile Association (AAA) had published its first annual hotel directory in 1917. "Hotel," an inclusive term, referred to all types of lodging—hotels, cabins, cottages, auto courts, motels—that met the standards designated by visiting AAA representatives. In 1926, the automotive organization issued its first tour book, another annual publication that contained suggestions for lodging, restaurants, and noteworthy sites. About this time, the major oil companies also established travel bureaus to spread the word on better places to stay.

Duncan Hines (1880–1959), a traveling salesman with a flair for evaluating restaurants and lodging, in 1936 published his first guide, *Adventures in Good Eating*. By 1939, this slim volume had made the best-seller list. In between, he created *Lodging for a Night* (1938), a handbook for wary motorists looking for a reliable place to get a night's sleep.

With these two works, a "Recommended by Duncan Hines" sign hanging outside a business became a valuable marketing tool utilized by establishments around the country.

During the 1930s, travel had become increasingly widespread for black Americans, but most lacked good information on lodging and dining. Segregation and discrimination still made getting anywhere a difficult endeavor. In 1936, an annual publication geared specifically to blacks called the *Green-Book* became available. Along with lists of welcoming lodging facilities, the book contained recommendations for restaurants, gasoline stations, taverns, liquor stores, and barber and beauty shops that did not impose racial restrictions. Another specialized guide, the *Directory of Negro Hotels and Guest Houses in the United States*, published in 1939 by the U.S. Travel Bureau, likewise presented a listing, but a less comprehensive one.

Despite the sharp rise in the number of people staying at motels, some considered this economical form of lodging an undesirable choice. Not everyone stopping at a motel had the most honorable intentions, or so many thought. In an article written for *American Magazine* at the end of the decade, J. Edgar Hoover (1895–1972), the director of the **Federal Bureau of Investigation** (FBI), declared motels, tourist cabins, and anything in between to be immoral, a form of lodging that led to corruption. But these strong words, despite having been written by a well-known **crime**-fighting celebrity, had little effect on the growing motel industry. World War II, not Hoover, would slow the expansion of motels, but following the conflict the industry would enter into a period of unparalleled growth.

See also Architecture; Best Sellers; Race Relations & Stereotyping; Trains

SELECTED READING

Belasco, Warren James. *Americans on the Road: From Autocamp to Motel, 1910–1945.* Cambridge, MA: MIT Press, 1979.

Jakle, John A., Keith A. Sculle, Jefferson S. Rogers. *The Motel in America.* Baltimore: Johns Hopkins University Press, 1996.

Margolies, John. *Home Away from Home, Motels in America.* New York: Little, Brown, 1995.

MOTORSPORTS. By the onset of the Depression, American racing cars had gotten larger and faster, and the major domestic automakers displayed an interest in the sport. Public attention mounted as Buick, Chrysler, Ford, Hudson, Packard, and Studebaker all developed custom speedsters, and the Indianapolis 500 served as a kind of proving ground for automotive innovation. By 1936, the first Daytona 250 had been held, utilizing the beach, dunes, and track. Officials measured the winning speed as just over 70 mph.

For the 1930s, two drivers, Louis Meyer (1904–1995) and Wilbur Shaw (1902–1954), captured the attention of the public by winning races and blazing a number of records. They followed in the footsteps of racing pioneers like Barney Oldfield (1878–1946) and Ralph DePalma (1883–1956) and helped keep auto racing afloat during the difficult Depression years. Both Meyer and Shaw devoted much of their careers to winning the Indianapolis 500, auto racing's premier event at the time. Driving a variety of cars, some of which they had a hand in designing and building, the two doggedly pursued their goals throughout the decade, despite mishaps and injuries. Meyer succeeded in winning the coveted race in 1928, 1933, and 1936, and placed second in 1929; Shaw came out victorious in 1937, 1939, and 1940, and took second place in 1933, 1935, and 1938. For the 1930s, Louis Meyer and Wilbur Shaw clearly stood as the most dominant presences at the Indianapolis classic, overshadowed only by the increasing speeds their racing cars could achieve. When Meyer first won in 1928, he reached 99.48 mph; Shaw's speed in 1940 averaged 114.28 mph; as a point of contrast, officials calibrated the winning speed in 2006 at 157 mph.

The ongoing quest for ever-faster cars led drivers like Ab Jenkins (1883–1956) to concentrate their efforts on setting new land-speed records. Jenkins pushed to get the Bonneville Salt Flats in Utah recognized as a test track area. Consisting of smooth, dry lakebeds, its unobstructed expanses allowed drivers to push experimental cars to the utmost. Over the 1930s, Jenkins drove Pierce-Arrows, Duesenbergs, and a series of Mormon Meteors to new records, achieving a then-incredible 157 mph in 1937.

While Jenkins pursued speed on the desert salt flats, an Englishman, Sir Malcolm Campbell (1885–1948), came to Utah to do likewise. He electrified the world when he drove his Bluebird, one of a series of similarly named experimental vehicles, to an unheard of 301.13 mph in September 1935. Hardly a racing car, such as Ab Jenkins had been driving, the Bluebird resembled a Streamlined rocket ship, as well it might. Powered by a 2,500-hp Rolls-Royce airplane engine and weighing over five tons, the Bluebird existed only to break records. Campbell's 301 mph lasted briefly, and then other experimental speedsters went still faster, but Campbell's effort resonated with the public and gained the most headlines. For the lean Depression years, such efforts—coupled with success—provided a bit of good news amid all the gloom.

Hollywood reacted to **automobiles** and speed by churning out a spate of racetrack **movies**. A sampling: *Burning Up* (1930) features Richard Arlen (1898–1976) as a daredevil driver; James Cagney (1899–1986) takes the wheel in *The Crowd Roars* (1932); Wallace Reid (1917–1990) does likewise in *The Racing Strain* (1933); and Paul Kelly follows suit in *Speed Devils* (1935). No less a rising star than James Stewart (1908–1997) has the lead in *Speed* (1936), while Dennis O'Keefe (1908–1968) pilots still more racing cars in *Burn 'em Up O'Connor* (1939). Ann Sheridan (1915–1967) and Pat O'Brien (1899–1983) costar in *Indianapolis Speedway* (1939), and two Buck Jones (1885–1942) **Western films**, *High Speed* (1932) and *Ride 'em Cowboy!* (1936), mix horses and horsepower. None of these movies ever broke any box-office records; apparently only a limited, but enthusiastic, audience attended.

See also Design; Science Fiction; Streamlining

SELECTED READING

Libby, Bill. *Great American Race Drivers*. Chicago: Cowles Book Co., 1970.

Motorsports. http://beta.motorsportsforum.com/ris01/legends.htm

Olney, Ross R. *Great Moments in Speed*. Englewood Cliffs, NJ: Prentice-Hall, 1970.

MOVIES. Throughout the 1930s, motion pictures took their place as one of the most popular of the popular arts. The advent of sound in 1927 had captivated audiences, and movie attendance skyrocketed from a weekly average of 57 million tickets in 1927 to over 90 million by the end of the decade. Theaters struggled to convert their outmoded equipment to the new technology, and for a brief period the number of movie houses actually declined. As the 1930s began, however, movies seemed Depression-proof; despite the dire economic news, the attendance figures from 1929 held steady, but only briefly. Then the numbers began to drop: 80 million in 1931, 60 million in 1932, finally bottoming out at 50 million in 1933. More than one-third of the paying audience had disappeared, and over 5,000 theaters closed their doors. Not until mid-decade did the industry begin the long climb to normalcy and prosperity.

During this turbulent period, banks took financial control of many once-independent studios. Proud names like MGM, Paramount, RKO, Fox Films, and 20th Century Films (combined in 1935 as 20th Century Fox) felt the stress of mergers and declining profits, but they nonetheless continued to make hundreds of movies, and a remarkable number of their productions have come down to the present as memorable examples of motion picture art.

Like all forms of popular culture, commercial cinema goes through cycles, with certain themes, or styles—frequently called genres—predominating. These cycles of popularity may last only a few months, to be supplanted by something new or different that has tweaked the public's fickle imagination. As a rough generalization, all movie genres enjoyed some level of popularity during the decade, but the ones listed in the chart below led the others, at least in the time periods indicated. A few major genres, such as **gangster films**, **musicals**, and **screwball comedies**, account for many of the classic pictures of the decade. But their dominance could be displaced, and one genre might overlap another in terms of box office success.

Dominant Film Genres during the 1930s

Years of Greatest Popularity	Genre	Characteristics	Representative Examples (year of release)
1930–1932	Gangster Films	Dark and violent, often celebrating the rise of a self-made criminal.	*Little Caesar* (1930), *The Public Enemy* (1931), *Scarface: The Shame of the Nation* (1932)
1931–1935	**Horror & Fantasy Films**	Somber retellings of classic stories along with new ones created for the movies. All feature the use of special effects.	*Dracula* (1931), *Frankenstein* (1931), *King Kong* (1933)
1933–1935	Musicals	Filled with **music** and dance, they express a humorous cynicism toward wealth and respect for hard-won success through snappy dialogue.	*42nd Street* (1933), *Gold Diggers of 1933* (1933), *Flying Down to Rio* (1933)
1932–1935	**Social Consciousness Films**	Films that deal with contemporary social problems, including the Great Depression and its consequences.	*I Am a Fugitive from a Chain Gang* (1932), *Heroes for Sale* (1933), *Black Fury* (1935)
1934–1939	Screwball Comedies	As the name suggests, comedies that defy reason or logic but eventually manage to restore order to a slightly manic world.	*It Happened One Night* (1934), *Bringing Up Baby* (1938), *The Awful Truth* (1939)

Years of Greatest Popularity	Genre	Characteristics	Representative Examples (year of release)
1937–1940s	**Teenage & Juvenile Delin-quency Films**	The discovery of adolescence and the problems and joys connected with that age group.	Any of the *Andy Hardy* films (1937–1940s), *Angels with Dirty Faces* (1938), *Strike Up the Band* (1940)
1937–1939	**Spectacle & Costume Drama Films**	Lavish production qualities, often based on recent **best sellers**. These films purport to re-create historical events, but frequently sacri-fice accuracy for story and special effects.	**Gone with the Wind** (1939), **The Wizard of Oz** (1939), *Drums along the Mohawk* (1939)
1939–1940s	**Propaganda & Anti-Axis Films**	Movies that shed neutrality and acknowledge the likeli-hood of a new world war and eventual American involvement.	*Blockage* (1938), *Confessions of a Nazi Spy* (1939), *Idiot's Delight* (1939)

When interpreting any listing, it must be remembered that exceptions to both years and genres occurred. For example, a musical like *Carefree* did well in 1938, that is, after the peak years for musicals, but the presence of **Fred Astaire** (1899–1987) **and Ginger Rogers** (1911–1995) would probably ensure any picture's success, regardless of year. *Son of Frankenstein*, a 1939 horror movie, capitalized on the prior popularity of the earlier *Frankenstein* (1931) and again drew patrons to the box office. In 1935, "G" Men sup-posedly celebrated not criminals but law officers, as did *Bullets or Ballots* (1936), but the gunplay and stars like Jimmy Cagney (1899–1986) and Edward G. Robinson (1893–1973) made these films difficult to differentiate from their gangster antecedents.

Innumerable other exceptions to such groupings could be mentioned, but the chart nonetheless remains a reasonable guide to shifting audience tastes and Hollywood offer-ings from 1930 to 1940. Four genres—**children's films, operettas, serials,** and **Western films**—do not appear in the chart but receive discussion elsewhere in this encyclopedia. Although they never clearly dominated the movie market at any one time, these sec-ondary film styles constituted important components of the overall industry. As a rule, they went their quiet way, year after year, making modest profits for their producers and satisfying their devoted audiences.

See also Crime; Walt Disney; Leisure & Recreation; *Snow White and the Seven Dwarfs*

SELECTED READING

Balio, Tino. *Grand Design: Hollywood as a Modern Business Enterprise, 1930–1939*. Vol. 5 of *His-tory of the American Cinema*. Charles Harpole, gen. ed. 10 vols. New York: Charles Scribner's Sons, 1993.

Baxter, John. *Hollywood in the Thirties*. New York: A. S. Barnes & Co., 1968.

Bergman, Andrew. *We're in the Money: Depression America and Its Films*. New York: Harper & Row [Colophon], 1971.

Crafton, Donald. *The Talkies: American Cinema's Transition to Sound, 1926–1931*. Vol. 4 of *History of The American Cinema*. Charles Harpole, gen. ed. 10 vols. New York: Charles Scribner's Sons, 1997.

MUSIC. One of the most pervasive forms of popular culture during the 1930s, music provided Americans with a wide range of sounds, rich in composition, innovation, and variety. It embraced the "sweet" orchestras as well as the **Jazz** Age groups, and the rhythmic **swing** sounds of the big bands dominated as never before during the second half of the decade. Omnipresent **jukeboxes**, located in soda fountains, **restaurants**, and, especially after the repeal of Prohibition, bars and taverns, brought the latest hit sounds to everyone, as did *Your Hit Parade*, a popular **radio** program that informed audiences about the nation's top-ranked popular songs.

The increased ownership of phonographs in the 1920s, coupled with the subsequent purchase of **recordings**, had produced a decline in the sales of **sheet music**; people became accustomed to listening to their favorites instead of playing them on home instruments. By the 1930s, radio had gained a sizable audience and competed fiercely with the recording industry. Going from a luxury to a household necessity, radio broadcast more music then ever before, ranging from classical to country as it tried to accommodate all tastes. As a rule, the commercial success of a new song therefore depended upon both record sales and widespread airplay.

Movies, offering a momentary respite from Depression hard times, served as an unending source of music, from extravagant **musicals** to **Western films** with **singing cowboys**, from new songs to old standards. Likewise, Broadway productions as never before gave the nation timeless tunes. Only a small number of theatergoers actually saw Broadway's musicals, but thanks to records, radio, sheet music, and movie adaptations, people across the county became acquainted with the latest from the Great White Way.

Musicians, along with millions of other Americans, suffered from the effects of the Great Depression, and musicians were no exception. The government-sponsored **Federal Music Project** (FMP; 1935–1943), an innovative **New Deal** agency that functioned under the Works Progress Administration (WPA, 1935–1943; name changed to Work Projects Administration in 1939), at its peak employed some 16,000 musicians, **songwriters and lyricists**, composers, conductors, and teachers of music. The FMP commissioned new works, supported symphony orchestras, sought out unique musicians and music to feature in recordings, gave assistance to younger composers, and sometimes oversaw premiere performances of their work.

Labor & Protest Songs. With high unemployment, and one of the worst droughts in its history, music from this era might be expected to highlight these crises. The opposite, in fact, generally occurred. Few people listened to union and protest songs, despite unrelenting media publicity about labor disputes throughout the 1930s, With such a paltry audience, this music seldom got recorded, and the difficulties faced by miners, textile workers, and farmers, as expressed in song, often went unheard.

Sarah Ogan Gunning (1910–1983) and Florence Reese (1900–1986) nevertheless raised their voices in protest against the economic and social injustice they saw around them. Gunning, whose "Come All Ye Coal Miners" (1931) and 'Dreadful Memories" (1932) dealt with the fate of miners and their impoverished families in Harlan County,

Throughout the Depression, music of all kinds enjoyed great popularity. (Courtesy of the Library of Congress)

Kentucky, gained at best limited recognition. She moved to New York City in 1935 and during the later years of the decade cowrote labor songs with the more famous **Woody Guthrie** (1912–1967), performing at rallies alongside him as well. Reese, the wife of a union organizer, composed "Which Side Are You On?" during a 1931 strike by the United Mine Workers of America, a song that became an anthem for much of the labor movement, but remained unknown by the majority of the population.

In a similar vein, Aunt Molly Jackson (1880–1960), a half sister to Sarah Ogan Gunning and a songwriter since early childhood, in 1933 wrote "Miner's Hungry Ragged Blues" and "Poor Miner's Farewell," and both did reasonably well within labor circles. Jackson also recorded hundreds of titles in 1928 for the Archive of American Folk Song, a music collection housed at the Library of Congress. Some of her compositions appeared in the Industrial Workers of the World's (IWW) 1933 *The Red Book*. A pamphlet that fit into a worker's shirt or back pocket, it contained various labor songs and originated with the Workers Library, a left-wing, radical publisher affiliated with the IWW.

Not all protest music addressed coal mining. Dave McCarn (1905–1964), Bob Miller (1895–1955), and Dorsey Dixon (d. 1961) penned numerous songs telling of the dissatisfaction of southern textile workers and their attempts to organize. Singers like Tillman Cadle (1902–1994), Maurice Sugar (1891–1974), and a host of anonymous others protested on the side of labor throughout the 1930s.

At this same time, Earl Robinson (1910–1991), a composer who received an academic music **education**, chose to involve himself in various left-wing causes. His songs "Joe Hill" (1936) and "Abe Lincoln" (1938) did not enjoy commercial success, but they attracted a cult following. Robinson's patriotic "Ballad for Americans" (1938), with lyrics by John Latouche (1914–1956), cries out against racial discrimination and persecution of all kinds. It achieved considerable renown as the result of a Columbia Broadcasting System (CBS radio) performance by singer **Paul Robeson** (1898–1976) in November 1939. The live audience erupted with a thunderous 15-minute standing ovation at the end of the song and brought both the singer and the composer nationwide acclaim. Robeson continued to perform the ballad on radio as well as recording it for Victor Records. "Ballad for Americans" immediately soared to the top of the charts and both the national Republican Party and the Communist Party featured it at their respective 1940 conventions.

Folk Music. Folk music also developed a small but devoted following. This form of musical expression generally originates and evolves through the process of oral transmission by the common people (the "folk") of a particular region. Many of the numbers recorded by the famous **Carter Family** in the 1930s represent this genre. A. P. Carter (1891–1960) led the trio, a group made up of himself, his wife, Sara (1898–1979), and her cousin Maybelle (1909–1978). For years, A. P. had traveled throughout the mountains of the Southeast and gathered old Appalachian songs, hymns, and lyrics from the people living there. In addition, the trio included other formats in their repertoire, most of which could fall under the broad category of country music.

Not all folk music traces its beginnings to the past; songwriters and lyricists, both amateur and professional, also create new folk songs. Woody Guthrie turned out to be one of the most famous. One of his early compositions, "So Long, It's Been Good to Know Ya" (1935), originally titled "Dusty Old Dust" and considered a "Dust Bowl ballad," describes the harsh weather and drought conditions on the Great Plains during the 1930s. Most of his music, however, did not receive its just recognition until the 1940s and later, although many of his works remain associated with the Depression years.

Radio executives at this time felt a responsibility to include some educational shows in their programming, and CBS broadcast *The American School of the Air* for 18 years, from 1930 to 1948. On its Tuesday broadcasts, the show featured "Folk Music of America," giving a showcase for songs new and old. The network made the production available to schools as a teaching supplement.

In order to preserve a portion of the musical heritage of the country, John Lomax (1867–1948) and his son Alan (1915–2002) traveled the country's back roads, especially in the rural South, from 1932 to 1942. During that time, they recorded over 10,000 songs that included a wide variety of music, ranging from folk and blues to labor and protest songs. The Macmillan Publishing Company accepted a proposal from the Lomaxes for an anthology of these songs and the Archive of American Folk Song provided the recording equipment. Although World War II cut their project short, they produced one of the finest collections of American folk music available anywhere.

Ethnic Music. An offshoot of the folk idiom, ethnic music in the United States tended to be localized and seldom achieved much popularity. Cajun songs, for example, rarely went beyond the borders of Louisiana. If any Cajun groups, such as the Hackberry Ramblers, enjoyed commercial success, it usually meant they had added country music or currently popular songs to their programs. One ethnic song, Czech in its roots with a murky history, defied the rules. "Beer Barrel Polka" probably had its origins in the mid-nineteenth century. An American, Lew Brown (1983–1958), added

English lyrics in 1939, with assistance from Wladimir A. Timm (active 1930s). The tune, widely recorded, received extensive radio play, and became a popular hit. Generally, however, polkas or other Czech music did not achieve commercial success, nor did much of anything else possessing strong ethnic components.

Country Music. Hardly the mass-market force it would later become in American culture, country music also searched for a diverse audience during the 1930s. The economic reality that few club owners had much available cash during the Depression greatly reduced the number of country musicians hired to perform at clubs or dancehalls. It therefore became crucial for aspiring artists in all genres to have exposure on the national **radio networks** as well as recording contracts. To illustrate: country music had been played on rural radio stations as early as the mid- to late 1920s, but most Americans had little acquaintance with this musical format. The National Broadcasting System (NBC radio), however, sensed enough of a following to pick up a Chicago show on affiliate station WLS. Initially called *The Barn Dance*, NBC changed the name to **The National Barn Dance** and began broadcasting it in 1933. Alka-Seltzer, a pain relief medicine, provided continuous sponsorship during the Depression years. Aired on Saturday evenings, the show primarily performed country tunes along with some swing, pop numbers, and rural humor by what became a cadre of regular performers plus their weekly guests.

The **Grand Ole Opry**, a competing show, offered similar fare out of station WSM in Nashville, Tennessee. The Opry, often called a "hillbilly show," originated in 1925, and NBC gained network rights to it in 1939. It offered humor, costumes, and numerous local amateur musicians and immediately followed *The National Barn Dance* for those who could pick up both broadcasts. The Opry quickly outgrew the WSM studios and performed in several Nashville theaters and auditoriums. Because of the popularity of these two shows, other rural radio stations began scheduling country music programs, but none demonstrated success comparable to that achieved by *The National Barn Dance* and *Grand Ole Opry*.

Although most urban audiences heard country music only on radio, some of its performers managed to establish successful careers through recordings. Jimmie Rodgers (1897–1933), a guitarist and vocalist often called "the Father of Country Music," took the name "the Singing Brakeman" from his days of working on the railroad. He frequently appeared in railroader's gear, although his job had long since ended. This workingman status immediately connected him with his mostly blue-collar audience. Rodgers' musical trademark involved distinctive "blue yodels," a cross between a Swiss yodel and a blues moan. His varied compositions attracted many admirers and, during a brief recording period that ran from 1927 until his death six years later, Rodgers cut over 100 songs that rang up sales estimated at over 12 million records.

Western Swing. A blend of big band Dixieland, swing, and jazz, along with some blues, country music guitars and violins, usually called fiddles, and singing, Western swing evolved alongside the national swing craze during the closing years of the decade. This unique music, mainly performed and heard in the southern and western states, especially Oklahoma and Texas, originally bore the names "Hillbilly Swing," "Okie Jazz," "Country Swing," "Southwestern Swing," and "Texas Swing." Its practitioners included such colorfully named bands as the High Flyers, the Tune Wranglers, and the Oklahoma Playboys.

One group, Bob Wills (1905–1975) and His Texas Playboys, included drums and horns in its instrumentation, thereby linking it with the big bands then beginning to rule the musical roost. Wills had first performed with the Fort Worth, Texas, Light Crust Dough-boys, a name bestowed on them by their radio sponsor, the Burris Flour Company. Wills left the Doughboys in 1932 to form his own band, one that played primarily in Texas and neighboring states. In a short time, the Texas Playboys filled dancehalls and roadhouses whenever they went. Versatile, they could perform blues, rags, stomps, and syrupy bal-lads, as well as occasional jazz and swing numbers. The band landed a recording contract cutting sides like "Milk Cow Blues" (1934; words and music by Kokomo Arnold [1901–1968]). Their biggest hit, "San Antonio Rose" (1940; words and music by Bob Wills), made the national charts.

Prior to Wills, many string bands, playing variations of country music with guitars, fid-dles, and other instrumentation, as well as swing numbers, traveled constantly, going from one small town to another, playing endless one-night stands in dancehalls and bars. Often called "territory bands," they covered a small geographical area, a practice that limited their exposure and their attractiveness for record firms looking for national sales. On those rare occasions when such bands did land a record contract, the companies usu-ally promoted them only to narrow niche audiences, just as they did with "race records" for black performers and listeners. Western swing, with the possible exception of Bob Wills, seldom received national promotion or distribution.

Blues. A vocal and instrumental form, the blues originated in the United States in the late nineteenth century, having evolved from African chants, work songs, and black spirituals. In many ways, the blues presented a history of the black experience in America, and by the 1930s it had become firmly established as a part of the nation's musical tradition, especially jazz. The blues have flourished in urban centers such as Chicago and New York, as well as on rural back roads. Just a few of the nota-ble blues artists from this period include Huddie Ledbetter (1888–1946; better known as Leadbelly), Big Bill Broonzy (1893–1958), Lonnie Johnson (1894–1970), Robert Johnson (1911–1938), Memphis Minnie (1897–1973), Bessie Smith (1894–1937), and Josh White (1908–1969). They, along with countless others, some known, some anon-ymous, could be found performing in clubs, roadhouses, joints, and dives, creating a legacy unique to the United States.

Gospel. Sometimes referred to as good news music, gospel also gained in popularity during the 1930s. The Reverend Thomas A. Dorsey (1899–1993), the acknowledged father of modern gospel songs, initially distinguished himself as a blues pianist. He offered a new style that combined traditional blues with spirituals, Baptist hymns, and other formats found in black churches. It quickly gained acceptance and, by 1932, Dorsey headed a gospel publishing house. In that same year, after the deaths of his wife and daughter, he wrote "Precious Lord, Take My Hand," a number that has become perhaps the best-known gospel song of all time. Another Dorsey piece, "There Will Be Peace in the Valley" (1937), has achieved enduring fame.

Sister Rosetta Tharpe (1915–1973), a skilled guitarist, presented her gospel message in several Decca recordings. "Hide Me in Thy Bosom" (1938) became a hit for her and its success led to an invitation from entrepreneur John Hammond (1910–1987) to appear in his 1938 *From Spirituals to Swing* concert. Hammond, also a producer for Columbia Records, expressed concern about the continuing racial divide in jazz and swing, a situation that led him to organize this star-filled concert that integrated jazz, swing, blues, Dixieland, gospel, and even some folk music. Divided into seven sections, the program ranged from Sister Tharpe's gospel to big band swing by the **Count Basie** orchestra. Following her appearance in *From Spirituals to Swing*, Tharpe recorded another hit, "This Train," in 1939, and its wide sales helped put gospel permanently on the musical map.

Classical Music. On the "serious" side of music, American classical composers waged a constant struggle to attract attention to their work. Although critics might laud these talented people, orchestras tended to perform a "safe" repertoire of established composers from the eighteenth and nineteenth centuries, such as Bach (1685–1750), Beethoven (1770–1827), and Tchaikovsky (1840–1893). Aware of this ongoing struggle, composer Aaron Copland (1900–1990) experimented with writing original music that reflected American culture instead of European models, an approach he felt the American public would accept more readily. Although his greatest and most popular works lay ahead of him, he nonetheless became one of the decade's best-known composers with pieces like *Music for Radio (Prairie Journal)* in 1937, followed the next year by *Billy the Kid*. Copland also wrote a number of film scores, including 1939's *The City*, a film shown continuously at the **New York World's Fair**, and *Of Mice and Men* (1939), a popular adaptation of John Steinbeck's (1902–1968) novella of the same name that had come out in 1937 to considerable acclaim.

A handful of other composers also achieved some limited recognition during the decade, chief among them Ferde Grofe (1892–1972). Born Ferdinand Rudolf von Grofe, he stands among a tiny circle of composers who established a popular following during the 1930s. An arranger and orchestrator for the popular Paul Whiteman (1890–1967) orchestra, Grofe in 1931 created *The Grand Canyon Suite*, an impressionistic composition that attempts to picture the canyon through the medium of music. The public liked the suite, especially "On the Trail," a section that evokes the sounds of donkey hooves descending the canyon. Much played on radio, *The Grand Canyon Suite* gained Grofe conducting and arranging jobs, and he emerged as one of the more visible composers of the 1930s.

Not nearly as well-known, William Grant Still (1895–1978) made a living in the early days of his musical career arranging compositions by the famed blues writer W. C. Handy (1873–1958). He also worked as an arranger for bands and theatrical productions. Still found additional employment with small record labels oriented to black consumers, such as Black Swan. While working busily in the nonclassical field, he found time to study composition at Oberlin College in Ohio and in New York with Edgard Varese (1885–1965), the French-born composer. Still combined his studies and many experiences to produce symphonic works that included *African-American Symphony* (1931) and *Lenox Avenue* (1937), and the operas *Blue Steel* (1935) and *Troubled Island* (1938).

Any discussion of formal American composition must include George Gershwin (1898–1937). After writing his famous *Rhapsody in Blue* in 1924, he experimented with other formats, such as two 1932 pieces, *Second Rhapsody* and *Cuban Overture* (originally titled *Rhumba*). Although he will be remembered first and foremost for his enormous impact on American popular song, his classical side led the way for others to assimilate the traditional and the nontraditional, especially jazz and blues.

Other Figures in the Area of "Serious American Music" for the Era

Howard Hanson (1896–1985), director at the Eastman School of Music in Rochester, New York, premiered two symphonies in the 1930s.

Roy Harris (1898–1979) used American folk music, dance rhythms, and jazz in his writing and had three symphonies performed during the decade.

Walter Piston (1894–1976), Roger Sessions (1896–1985), and Virgil Thomson (1896–1989) also received public recognition, albeit limited, for their efforts.

Many people believed that the key to appreciating "academic" music lay with education. Individuals in broadcasting, the recording industry, and New Deal projects felt an obligation to provide the American public access to classical music and to increase the size of the listening audience. The Federal Music Project supported instruction in music and music appreciation and funded countless classes that allowed 14 million students to take lessons. The broadcasting industry supported programming that did not focus entirely on performances but also included educational shows about the music and how to appreciate it.

One of the most successful programs of this type came from the National Broadcasting Company. *The Music Appreciation Hour* ran from 1928 to 1942 and aired every Friday at 11:00 A.M. in order to be convenient for use by schoolteachers. The show's producer and erudite host, Walter Damrosch (1862–1950), became something of a celebrity. He spoke directly to his audience, composed mainly of schoolchildren, about good music and illustrated his talks with recorded and live examples, never patronizing them in any way. Some rural schools, lacking receivers, would gather students on Friday mornings around an automobile equipped with a radio to listen to *The Music Appreciation Hour*.

The two primary radio networks, NBC and CBS, in a competitive battle for prestige, boasted in-house symphony orchestras led by world-renowned conductors that performed regularly. In addition, they saw to it that their programming included broadcasts by important orchestras across the country. Thus they aired programs such as *The Cleveland Symphony Orchestra* (NBC, 1932–1936; CBS, 1935–1936; NBC, 1936–1938), *The New York Philharmonic Orchestra* (CBS, 1927–1963), and *The NBC Symphony Orchestra* (NBC, 1937–1954). Of course, both networks also had connections to the recording industry and hoped that hearing classical music on the radio would prompt people to buy similar recordings.

Prominent sponsors supported these efforts, both for their own prestige and because it boosted sales. *The Firestone Hour* (NBC, 1928–1954; ABC, 1954–1957) became one of the longest-running such shows on radio. *The Ford Sunday Evening Hour* (CBS, 1934–1942) and *General Motors Concerts* (NBC, 1929–1937) permitted the two companies to present their products in a dignified cultural setting. Several conductors gained considerable celebrity during the 1930s through this radio exposure. Arthur Fiedler (1894–1979), Andre Kostelanetz (1901–1980), Leopold Stokowski (1882–1977), and Arturo Toscanini (1867–1957) can be counted among this select group.

Money and jobs may have been scarce, but the 1930s possessed music in abundance. A dramatic increase in the number of recordings available for sale, the development of a close relationship between recordings and radio, the attempts by classical composers to appeal to a broader range of people, and the effects of swing on everyone and everything produced significant changes for musicians and music lovers alike. Listeners developed a wide range of preferences, making it possible for many different kinds of music to coexist. Despite the growth of alternative musical formats, however, popular songs and swing music easily dominated the decade.

See also Advertising; George & Ira Gershwin; Hillbillies; Jitterbug; Prohibition & Repeal; Race Relations & Stereotyping; Youth

SELECTED READING

Erenberg, Lewis A. *Swingin' the Dream: Big Band Jazz and the Rebirth of American Culture*. Chicago: University of Chicago Press, 1998.

Ewen, David. *All the Years of American Popular Music*. Englewood Cliffs, NJ: Prentice-Hall, 1977.

Shaw, Arnold. *Let's Dance: Popular Music in the 1930s*. New York: Oxford University Press, 1998.

Young, William H., and Nancy K. Young. *Music of the Great Depression: American History through Music*. Westport, CT: Greenwood Press, 2005.

MUSICALS (STAGE & SCREEN). In April 1930, the Academy of Motion Picture Arts and Sciences (AMPAS) met for only the second time—the group had first convened in 1929—to determine what **movies** and what performers would win Academy Awards. The winner for Best Picture went to *Broadway Melody*, a 1929 Metro-Goldwyn-Mayer (MGM) musical that employed a crude early version of Technicolor, but also capitalized on the wide availability of sound in most theaters by then.

Clichéd and wooden by contemporary standards, *Broadway Melody* nonetheless impressed critics and audiences alike. Both stage and film musicals generally come across to their audiences as bright and breezy; they momentarily take people's minds off unpleasant realities; and they usually have more success than something dramatic that may reinforce glum feelings. With all these requisites, and with an Academy Award to boot, *Broadway Melody* inspired a wealth of new productions. That same year, 1929, Hollywood studios released 32 musical films, and, since they made money, the total jumped to an astronomical 72 in 1930, an all-time record for the industry.

Given the cyclical nature of virtually all forms of popular culture, movie musicals fell into the doldrums at the all-important box office in 1931, with 16 releases. It can be argued that the Depression caused this downturn, but other kinds of movies continued to draw patrons, especially, at the time, **gangster films**. So, while some other genres made money, the first few years of the new decade saw only a handful of attempts at producing musicals—the total fell to a mere seven in 1932, and not until 1933 and the unexpected success of Warner Brothers' **42nd Street** did **music** and dancing reinstate themselves with studios and audiences.

Flush with *42nd Street*'s success, Warner Brothers promptly released *Gold Diggers of 1933*. It, too, did well, and Ginger Rogers (1911–1995), emerging as a star in her own right, sings a cheery number called "Gold Digger's Song (We're in the Money)," with music by Harry Warren (1893–1981) and lyrics by Al Dubin (1891–1945). Destined to become two of the leading Hollywood songsmiths of the day, their work runs counter to all the grim statistics then gaining headlines. "We're in the Money" epitomizes the spunky, "can-do" attitudes espoused by many of the era's musicals, and helps to explain their renewed popularity.

For the remainder of the 1930s, musicals filled an important niche in Hollywood's crowded production schedule, with over 400 going into national release. The Motion Picture Academy recognized this renascence with Best Picture awards for *The Great Ziegfeld* (1936) and, a few years later, *Going My Way* (1944). By and large, however, critical recognition for film musicals lagged behind their public acceptance.

While the film capital dithered about the future of the motion picture musical, Broadway, the traditional home of such shows, went its merry way, putting on one popular production after another, along with its fair share of flops. Despite the success of shows like *Girl Crazy* (1930), *The Band Wagon* (1931), *Of Thee I Sing* (1932), and *Anything Goes* (1933), and the longevity of the music connected with them, not even stage musicals could escape the Depression's impact. In pre-Depression 1928, some 37 such shows had opened to mostly packed houses; the next year, 32 new offerings enticed audiences. But in 1930, the number fell slightly to 28. Hardly a momentous drop, since most people thought the economic slump would be brief, and many of the new shows had been planned prior to the October crash. Then reality struck: 1931 listed only 20 musicals, then 18 in 1932, and 13 in 1933. The numbers stayed low—10 to a dozen new productions—for the remainder of the decade, and then World War II intervened. The numbers reached in the late 1920s and early 1930s would never again be attained.

During much of the decade, the cream of American popular **songwriters and lyricists** could be found close to Broadway on New York's Tin Pan Alley. This remarkable pool of talent pumped much-needed blood into the so-called legitimate theater, in many ways sustaining it during the long, trying economic times of the Great Depression. Although only a small percentage of the nation's population attended these shows, effective promotion and technology allowed many more people to experience this music. Most of the audience outside New York City knew about the latest theatrical hits through **radio** and **recordings**, although **sheet music** also remained a force, albeit a declining one. Of course, if a musical became a movie, then the potential audience size soared. But the real reason these songs gained popularity rests with the music itself. The Broadway songwriters of the 1930s turned out an amazing number of enduring tunes, songs that today are called standards. Naturally, not everything achieved this estimable rank, so corny, mawkish, and downright silly songs also assaulted the ears and sensibilities of listeners. Nonetheless, the decade remains a unique period when one realizes just how many standards—those lasting melodies, those memorable lyrics that continue to come to mind—came from the Great White Way.

In any reckoning of the Broadway musical during the 1930s, the talents of **Irving Berlin** (1888–1989), **George** (1898–1937) **and Ira Gershwin** (1896–1983), **Jerome Kern** (1885–1945), **Cole Porter** (1891–1964), and **Richard Rodgers** (1902–1979) **and Lorenz Hart** (1895–1943) must always be considered. Broadway mounted 194 musicals between 1929 and 1940; of that total, 39, or 20 percent, boasted scores by these exceptional talents. Their collective contributions to American popular and show music during the 1930s have no equal, generations after many of the plays themselves survive only in memory.

In the middle years of the decade, a number of composers and lyricists, unable to find steady employment on Broadway, fled to Hollywood. Their flight hardly signified a cessation of creativity, and many occasionally made forays back to New York when a new play beckoned. The film studios observed what attracted theater audiences and quickly bought the film rights to successful shows. In many cases, the dust had hardly settled on the stage before a movie adaptation went into motion picture production. By the close of the 1930s, Hollywood had churned out some 450 musicals. And almost any movie project that Messrs. Berlin, Gershwin, Kern, Porter, Rodgers, or Hart collaborated on stood a better-than-average chance of being profitable at the box office, which meant they exerted a significant impact on the movies of the period.

A Representative Sampling of American Musicals, Both Stage and Screen from 1929 to 1940

1929 Titles	Composers & Lyricists	Comments
Stage:		
Sweet Adeline	Jerome Kern (1885–1945), music; Oscar Hammerstein II (1895–1960), lyrics	An exercise in nostalgia, set in the 1890s. It featured Helen Morgan (1900–1941). A movie adaptation made in 1935 stars Irene Dunne (1898–1990).
Fifty Million Frenchmen	Cole Porter (1891–1964), music and lyrics	An early Porter effort, the show offered "You Do Something to Me"; it went to the screen in 1931 but without his songs.
Movies:		
The Broadway Melody	Arthur Freed (1894–1973), music; Nacio Herb Brown (1896–1964), lyrics	Veteran entertainer George M. Cohan (1878–1942) performs his "Give My Regards to Broadway" (written 1904).
The Cocoanuts	Irving Berlin (1888–1989), music and lyrics	The film version of Berlin's 1925 stage play, it introduced the **Marx Brothers** to a mass public.

1930 Titles	Composers & Lyricists	Comments
Stage:		
Blackbirds of 1930	Eubie Blake (1883–1983), music; Andy Razaf (1895–1973), lyrics	All-black revues constituted a continuing part of the New York City stage scene.
Strike Up the Band	George Gershwin (1898–1937), music; Ira Gershwin (1896–1983), lyrics	In addition to the title tune, the Gershwin brothers contributed "Soon" and "I've Got a Crush on You"; the 1940 film version stars **Judy Garland** (1922–1969) and Mickey Rooney (b. 1920).
Movies:		
Check and Double Check	**Duke Ellington** (1899–1974), music (also others)	A film that capitalized on the enormous popularity of the radio team of **Amos 'n' Andy**, it was more a situation comedy than a true musical.
King of Jazz	Milton Ager (1893–1979), music; Jack Yellen (1892–1991), lyrics	A showcase for the Paul Whiteman (1890–1967) Orchestra, it featured vocalist **Bing Crosby** (1904–1977).

A Representative Sampling of American Musicals, Both Stage and Screen from 1929 to 1940 (*Continued*)

1931 Titles	Composers & Lyricists	Comments
Stage:		
The Band Wagon	Arthur Schwartz (1900–1984), music; Howard Dietz (1896–1983), lyrics	This was the final appearance on stage together for siblings Fred (1899–1987) and Adele (1898–1981) Astaire, one of Broadway's premier dancing partnerships. Filmed in 1953.
Billy Rose's Crazy Quilt	Harry Warren (1893–1981), music; Billy Rose (1899–1966) & Mort Dixon (1892–1956), lyrics	A good Depression song came from this musical, "I Found a Million-Dollar Baby (in a Five-and-Ten-Cent Store)."
Movies:		
Cuban Love Song	Jimmy McHugh (1894–1969) & Herbert Stothart (1885–1949), music; **Dorothy Fields** (1905–1974), lyrics	Former vaudeville star Jimmy Durante (1893–1980) provides comic relief.
Delicious	George Gershwin (1898–1937), music; Ira Gershwin (1896–1983), lyrics	One of the few joint Gershwin ventures into the movies, the film introduces *Manhattan Rhapsody*, a composition that would become 1932's *Second Rhapsody for Piano and Orchestra*.

1932 Titles	Composers & Lyricists	Comments
Stage:		
Earl Carroll Vanities	Harold Arlen (1905–1986), music; Ted Koehler (1894–1973), lyrics	The show, a revue, introduced the standard "I Gotta Right to Sing the Blues."
Gay Divorce	Cole Porter (1891–1964), music and lyrics	One of the great Porter scores, including "Night and Day," was brought to the screen in 1934 as *The Gay Divorcee*, with **Fred Astaire** (1899–1987) **and Ginger Rogers** (1911–1995).
Movies:		
The Big Broadcast of 1932	Various	With radio gaining in popularity, the film industry took some of the new medium's biggest stars and put them in a movie. Includes Bing Crosby (1904–1977), **Kate Smith** (1907–1986), and Cab Calloway (1907–1994).
Crooner	Little Jack Little (1899–1956) & John Siras (active 1930s), music; Joe Young (active 1930s), lyrics	The title reflects the craze for crooning then in vogue.

1933 Titles	Composers & Lyricists	Comments
Stage:		
As Thousands Cheer	Irving Berlin (1888–1989), music and lyrics	A topical musical, done as a Living Newspaper. Mostly humorous, but it included Ethel Waters (1896–1977) performing a wrenching "Suppertime."
Roberta	Jerome Kern (1885–1945), music; Otto Harbach (1873–1963), lyrics	One of Kern's best; it included "Smoke Gets in Your Eyes" and "Yesterdays." Made into a movie in 1935 and for **television** in 1969.
Movies:		
Flying Down to Rio	Vincent Youmans (1898–1946), music; Gus Kahn (1886–1941) & Edward Eliscu (1902–1998), lyricists	The movie that introduced Fred Astaire (1899–1987) and Ginger Rogers (1911–1995) to an adoring moviegoing public, it features a rousing "Carioca."
Footlight Parade	Harry Warren (1893–1981), music; Al Dubin (1891–1945), lyrics	Ruby Keeler (1909–1993) and Dick Powell (1904–1963) sing and dance, cementing a popular partnership that endured for much of the decade.

1934 Titles	Composers & Lyricists	Comments
Stage:		
Anything Goes	Cole Porter (1891–1964), music and lyrics	One of the great Broadway musicals, it featured Ethel Merman (1908–1984) singing some of her best numbers, including "Blow, Gabriel, Blow." Adapted for film in 1936 and again in 1956.
Ziegfeld Follies of 1934	Vernon Duke (1893–1969), music; E. Y. Harburg (1896–1981), lyrics	In addition to an all-star cast, the show introduced a new standard, "What Is There to Say?"
Movies:		
Belle of the Nineties	Arthur Johnston (1898–1954), music; Sam Coslow (1902–1982), lyrics	Features the inimitable Mae West (1893–1980) singing "My Old Flame."
Bright Eyes	Richard Whiting (1891–1938), music; Sidney Clare (1892–1972), lyrics	Child star **Shirley Temple** (b. 1928) gets to sing her signature song, "On the Good Ship Lollipop."

1935 Titles	Composers & Lyricists	Comments
Stage:		
Jumbo	Richard Rodgers (1902–1979), music; Lorenz Hart (1895–1943), lyrics	Staged to resemble a circus, this extravaganza offered Rodgers and Hart's "Little Girl Blue" and "My Romance." Made into a movie in 1962.
May Wine	Sigmund Romberg (1887–1951), music; Oscar Hammerstein II (1895–1960), lyrics	A modernistic and offbeat offering from Romberg dealing with psychoanalysis that does not neatly fit the usual "operetta" definition; it contained "Once around the Clock."
Movies:		
Gold Diggers of 1935	Harry Warren (1893–1981), music; Al Dubin (1891–1945), lyrics	Dubin and Warren, by this time Hollywood veterans, contribute the memorable "Lullaby of Broadway."
Top Hat	Irving Berlin (1888–1989), music and lyrics	A dazzling Berlin score makes this fourth Astaire/Rogers outing one of their best, with tunes like "Cheek to Cheek," "Isn't This a Lovely Day?" and "Top Hat, White Tie, and Tails."

1936 Titles	Composers & Lyricists	Comments
Stage:		
On Your Toes	Richard Rodgers (1902–1979), music; Lorenz Hart (1895–1943), lyrics	An ambitious musical, it included Rodgers' ballet suite, "Slaughter on Tenth Avenue." Made as a movie in 1939.
Ziegfeld Follies of 1936	Vernon Duke (1903–1969), music; Ira Gershwin (1896–1983), lyrics	An edition of the Follies that introduced "I Can't Get Started (with You)," a topical number that Bob Hope (1903–2003) sang on stage to Eve Arden (1909–1990).
Movies:		
Big Broadcast of 1937	Ralph Rainger (1901–1942), music; Leo Robin (1900–1984), lyrics	A film that blends radio stars and their movie counterparts. **Benny Goodman** (1909–1986) and his band hint at the gradual dominance of **swing.**
Pennies from Heaven	Arthur Johnston (1898–1954), music; Johnny Burke (1908–1964), lyrics	This picture has Bing Crosby (1904–1977) crooning the title tune and includes **jazz** trumpeter Louis Armstrong (1901–1971).

1937 Titles	Composers & Lyricists	Comments
Stage:		
I'd Rather Be Right	Richard Rodgers (1902–1979), music; Lorenz Hart (1895–1943), lyrics	A musical with strong political overtones, George M. Cohan (1878–1942) played President **Franklin D. Roosevelt** (1882–1945).
Pins and Needles	Harold Rome (1908–1993), music and lyrics	An unusual off-Broadway show, produced by the International Ladies Garment Workers Union, it ran for a record-breaking 1,108 performances, and featured such numbers as "Sing Me a Song of Social Significance."
Movies:		
Gold Diggers of 1937	Harry Warren (1893–1981), music; Al Dubin (1891–1945), lyrics	Another snappy score from Warren and Dubin kept this series going, with numbers like "With Plenty of Money and You" and choreography by Busby Berkeley (1895–1976).
Ready, Willing, and Able	Richard Whiting (1893–1981), music; Johnny Mercer (1909–1976) lyrics	Thanks to elaborate sets, Ruby Keeler (1909–1993) can dance on the keys of a giant typewriter while she sings "Handy with Your Feet."

1938 Titles	Composers & Lyricists	Comments
Stage:		
The Cradle Will Rock	Marc Blitzstein (1905–1964), music and lyrics	In keeping with the success enjoyed by *Pins and Needles* (1937), this labor-oriented musical had its roots with the **Federal Theatre Project** (FTP) and soon became a cause célèbre, running for 108 performances.
Knickerbocker Holiday	Kurt Weill (1900–1950), music; Maxwell Anderson (1888–1959), lyrics	The highlight of this show occurred when actor Walter Huston (1884–1950) more or less spoke the words to "September Song" and made it a hit. It became a movie in 1944.
Movies:		
Sweethearts	Victor Herbert (1859–1924), music and lyrics (first performed in 1913)	The craze for **operettas** continued unabated, especially those with Jeanette MacDonald (1903–1965) and Nelson Eddy (1901–1967), even if it meant resurrecting older works, such as this 1913 Herbert chestnut.
Thanks for the Memory	Hoagy Carmichael (1899–1981), music; Frank Loesser (1910–1969), lyrics	A Bob Hope (1903–2003) vehicle, but the Carmichael/Loesser score provides plenty of good music such as "Two Sleepy People."

A Representative Sampling of American Musicals, Both Stage and Screen from 1929 to 1940 (*Continued*)

1939 Titles	Composers & Lyricists	Comments
Stage:		
Stars in Your Eyes	Arthur Schwartz (1900–1984), music; Dorothy Fields (1905–1974), lyrics	Ethel Merman (1908–1984) and Jimmy Durante (1898–1980) headed the cast singing Fields' sophisticated lyrics.
Very Warm for May	Jerome Kern (1885–1945), music; Oscar Hammerstein II (1895–1960), lyrics	Although it ran for only 59 performances, this Kern/Hammerstein collaboration offered the standard "All the Things You Are."
Movies:		
Babes in Arms	Richard Rodgers (1902–1979), music; Lorenz Hart (1895–1943), lyrics	Among Hollywood's most popular younger players, Judy Garland (1922–1969) and Mickey Rooney (b. 1920) exude innocence and charm, plus they do well together in musicals. Adapted from the 1937 stage version.
The Wizard of Oz	Harold Arlen (1905–1986), music; E. Y. Harburg (1896–1981), lyrics	A beloved musical for all ages, with a splendid score, it includes "Over the Rainbow," "We're Off to See the Wizard," and "The **Jitterbug**."

1940 Titles	Composers & Lyricists	Comments
Stage:		
Cabin in the Sky	Vernon Duke (1903–1969), music; John Latouche (1917–1956), lyrics	An all-black musical, it features Ethel Waters (1896–1977) doing "Taking a Chance on Love." Made as a movie in 1943.
Pal Joey	Richard Rodgers (1902–1979), music; Lorenz Hart (1895–1943), lyrics	This classic tale of a heel has Gene Kelly (1912–1996) in the title role; the enduring score includes "I Could Write a Book," "Bewitched, Bothered, and Bewildered," and "Zip." The show came to the screen in 1957, and **Frank Sinatra** (1915–1998) famously reprised the part of Joey.
Movies:		
Pinocchio	Leigh Harline (1907–1969), music; Ned Washington (1901–1976), lyrics	One of **Walt Disney**'s (1901–1966) animated gems, the film has some memorable music, especially "When You Wish upon a Star" and "Whistle While You Work."
You'll Find Out	Jimmy McHugh (1895–1969), music; Johnny Mercer (1909–1976), lyrics	Although it features horror stars Boris Karloff (1887–1969), Bela Lugosi (1882–1956), and Peter Lorre (1904–1964), this really exists as a vehicle for Kay Kyser (1905–1985) and his band. A swing era picture, music comes before the scares.

Broadway and Hollywood provided the nation with an ample supply of timeless music. Shows and movies like *Roberta*, *Girl Crazy*, and *On Your Toes* lit up marquees, creating more standards than anyone realized at the time. Radio, records, **jukeboxes**, and sheet music assured that millions everywhere got to know the tunes. Despite the bleakness of the Depression, musicals continued to attract backers, delighting their audiences everywhere.

See also Circuses; Leisure & Recreation; New Deal; Stage Productions

SELECTED READING

American Musical Theater. 6 LPs. Smithsonian Collection of Recordings. R 036, 1989.

Green, Stanley. *Ring Bells! Sing Songs! Broadway Musicals of the 1930s.* New Rochelle, NY: Arlington House, 1971.

Henderson, Amy, and Dwight Blocker Bowers. *Red, Hot, & Blue: A Smithsonian Salute to the American Musical.* Washington, DC: Smithsonian Institution Press, 1996.

Hischak, Thomas S. *Through the Screen Door: What Happened to the Broadway Musical When It Went to Hollywood.* Lanham, MD: Scarecrow Press, 2004.

Mordden, Ethan. *Sing for Your Supper: The Broadway Musical in the 1930s.* New York: Palgrave Macmillan, 2005.

Springer, John. *All Talking! All Singing! All Dancing! A Pictorial History of the Movie Musical.* Secaucus, NJ: Citadel Press, 1966.

MYSTERIES & HARD-BOILED DETECTIVES (PRINT & FILM). Many **best sellers** came and went throughout the 1930s—*The Good Earth*, *Anthony Adverse*, **Gone with the Wind**, **The Grapes of Wrath**, for example—but no category of fiction boasted more fans and sold more consistently than mysteries. Individual titles in this genre might not generate huge, headline-making sales, but the sheer volume of releases, coupled with millions of devoted readers, made for steady business and profits.

Writing about **crime**, criminals, and how they do what they do dates back to the earliest literature. The gothic tales of the eighteenth century, along with the nineteenth-century exploits of Edgar Allan Poe's (1809–1949) Inspector C. Auguste Dupin and Arthur Conan Doyle's (1859–1930) Sherlock Holmes, delighted audiences. The dime novels of the turn of the century promised thrills without end, and the rise of **pulp magazines**, with their lurid covers, continued the tradition. Throughout the years, the formula has almost always remained the same: a crime is committed, confusion reigns, a hero takes control of the situation, and justice is done. Getting to justice constitutes the fun—who committed the crime (or "whodunit?" a popular name given the entire genre), and how will the villain be caught?

Part of the pleasure readers experience with mysteries rests with the comfort provided by the formula of order–disorder–restoration of order. Within that loose definition, writers could let their imaginations run free, introducing nasty criminals, nastier crimes, and clever heroes who could unravel even the most sinister schemes. The Great Depression, with uncertainty at every turn, provided an ideal climate for the sureties contained within the pages of a good mystery.

The period between the two world wars—1920–1940, in round numbers—has been called the golden age of mystery fiction, at least a particular kind of mystery fiction. During these 20 years, a diverse collection of writers, many of them English—but authors who nonetheless enjoyed a wide following in the United States—penned an unusually large number of enduring novels about crime and detection. Most of these stories relied on brains, not brawn, and then often took place in stately drawing rooms instead of the "mean streets" of so much contemporary mystery writing. In many ways a last gasp of Victorian gentility, golden age novels frequently featured a talented amateur sleuth, sometimes referred to as a "great detective," who uses external clues and his (or her) intuition to solve the seemingly unsolvable. Gunplay and violence take a back seat to the challenge of the puzzle presented by the crime. These plots invite readers to participate in a literary game of matching wits with the hero, a game in which the unwritten rules decree that the reader have access to all clues (including red herrings, or misleading clues) and that no tricks, such as last-minute revelations, hidden information, and the like, can be played. This kind of mystery fiction, an intellectual exercise for the aficionado, flourished in the 1930s and continues to draw countless fans today.

The following writers enjoyed particular popularity as creators of sophisticated puzzles of crime and detection, especially during the Depression era:

John Dickson Carr (1906–1977). Born in Pennsylvania, Carr, who also employed the pseudonyms Carter Dickson and others for some of his writing, spent the years 1931 to 1948 in England, and many of his tales have either an English or European setting. Acknowledged as a master of the "locked room" puzzle—stories that present crimes that seem to defy any rational solution—Carr introduced Dr. Gideon Fell, a lexicographer, as his primary hero in *Hag's Nook* (1933), a story in which the portly, erudite gentleman astounds everyone by deducing what happened. A popular writer, Carr also featured Fell in *The Three Coffins* (1935), *The Crooked Hinge* (1938), and *The Problem of the Wire Cage* (1939), among others, and carried on the tradition of the mystery story as a proper and civil entertainment.

In contrast to most of his contemporaries, Carr did not have the pleasure, either personal or financial, of seeing his stories go to film in the 1930s. Not until the late 1940s did **movies**, **radio**, and later, **television**, begin to mine his trove of materials.

Leslie Charteris (1907–1993). The child of a Chinese father and an English mother, Leslie Charles Bowyer Yin changed his surname to Charteris in 1926. More than almost any other author of the era, Charteris exemplified the man of the world. A variety of colorful jobs and adventures led him to writing, and in 1928 he created Simon Templar in a novel titled *Meet the Tiger!* The stories involving Templar, better known as "the Saint," made some stir, since his debonair character exists as something of a rogue, operating on both sides of the law. In the end, however, Templar always comes down on the right side.

The prolific Charteris wrote a string of Saint adventures during the 1930s, such as *The Avenging Saint* (1931), *The Saint vs. Scotland Yard* (1932), and *Saint Overboard* (1936), plus several collections of short stories culled from various pulp **magazines** in which he had been published. Such was the series' popularity that *Meet the Tiger!* in 1945 became *The Saint Meets the Tiger* to capitalize on the hero's fame; most of his early work similarly received new titles with the word "Saint" included.

Hollywood liked the ambiguity of the hero-scoundrel and cast Louis Hayward (1909–1985) as Simon Templar in *The Saint in New York* (1938). Shortly thereafter, the always-suave George Sanders (1906–1972) took over the role for five pictures. His reign began with *The Saint Strikes Back* (1939; based on the 1932 novel *Angels of Doom*) and ended with *The Saint in Palm Springs* (1941), for which Charteris contributed the screenplay.

Other Saint movies would follow throughout the remainder of the century, along with a long-running television series.

Agatha Christie (1890–1976). This distinguished English mystery writer has become universally known as "the first lady of crime." One of the most popular authors of any time, her books have sold in the hundreds of millions, and most of them remain in print. Her first effort, *The Mysterious Affair at Styles* (1920), introduced the dapper Belgian detective Hercule Poirot, a character destined to appear in another 33 titles, along with a host of Poirot short stories. In 1930, with *The Murder at the Vicarage*, she created Miss Jane Marple, a delightful amateur sleuth who seemingly stumbles onto crimes but always manages to find the solution. A Christie mystery follows the rule of classic golden age detection—a background of sophistication and wealth, a puzzling crime, and nothing kept from the reader.

During the 1930s alone, Christie wrote some 24 novels, along with 3 plays, and 2 radio scripts. Ahead of her time, she also adapted "Wasp's Nest" (1937) and "Love from a Stranger" (1938) for television productions. Among her novels from that period, *Murder on the Orient Express* (1934), *The A.B.C. Murders* (1936), *Death on the Nile* (1937), and *And Then There Were None* (aka *Ten Little Indians*) (1939) have remained especially fresh for contemporary readers.

Frequently adapted for film, Christie's movies include *Alibi* (1931; taken from 1926's *The Murder of Roger Ackroyd*), *The Lacquered Box* (1932; taken from her 1930 play, *Black Coffee*), *Lord Edgware Dies* (1934; taken from the 1933 novel of the same name), and *A Night of Terror* (1937; aka *Love from a Stranger*; taken from a 1934 story, "Philomel Cottage"). Regardless of medium, her work exemplifies the best of the golden age writers.

Ellery Queen. Another best-selling author from the 1930s, Ellery Queen is the pen name of two cousins, Manfred B. Lee (1905–1971) and Frederic Dannay (1905–1982). The first Ellery Queen novel, *The Roman Hat Mystery*, appeared in 1929. In it, readers immediately discover that both the author and the main character are one and the same, a strategy employed in all subsequent Queen mysteries. An instant success, *The Roman Hat Mystery* prompted the two Brooklyn-born writers to continue their efforts. One of their best, *The Dutch Shoe Mystery*, came out in 1931. Three years later, they published *The Chinese Orange Mystery* and *The Adventures of Ellery Queen*, the latter a collection of short stories. They ultimately wrote 33 novels about their character. On the last pages, just before the solution, they frequently included a "challenge to the reader," a device to test observation and memory. Can the reader, possessing the same information as Ellery Queen, solve the puzzle? A gimmick, but one that proved popular.

Given the attraction of mysteries in any format, several Ellery Queen tales have been adapted to film. For the 1930s, Donald Cook (1901–1961) took the detective's role in *The Spanish Cape Mystery* (1935), followed by Eddie Quillan (1907–1990) in *The Mandarin Mystery* (1936), and Ralph Bellamy (1904–1991) in *Ellery Queen, Master Detective* (1940). Low-budget efforts, their clever plotting kept audiences entertained.

Dorothy L. Sayers (1893–1957). Another English writer, Sayers quickly developed an American following in the 1920s with a series of books featuring Lord Peter Wimsey, an eccentric aristocrat who dabbles in solving crimes. Sayers's detailing of the English upper classes, often laced with genteel humor, endeared her to many readers, and several of her novels written in the 1930s, such as *Strong Poison* (1930),

Murder Must Advertise (1933), and *The Nine Tailors* (1934), have become classics of the genre on both sides of the Atlantic.

With a lack of physical action characterizing Sayers's stories, they proved difficult to film, but two adaptations did play movie theaters in the 1930s. A slow-moving *Silent Passenger* (1935; screenplay by Sayers) marked Lord Wimsey's less-than-auspicious film debut; another effort, *Busman's Honeymoon* (based on her 1937 novel), came along in 1940. Despite the presence of Robert Montgomery (1904–1981) as Wimsey in the latter picture, the movie got lost among a welter of faster-moving, faster-paced mysteries on celluloid.

S. S. Van Dine. The pseudonym of Willard Huntington Wright (1887–1939), a Virginia-born scholar, journalist, art critic, and editor, he made his pen name famous when he introduced amateur detective Philo Vance. A literary alter ego, Vance first appeared in *The Benson Murder Case* in 1926. An imperious snob, the detective initially intrigued readers, but his popularity waned during the 1930s when his disdain for lesser mortals seemed out of place in the midst of a worldwide economic depression.

Vance's decline took some time, however, and titles like *The Scarab Murder Case* (1930) and *The Casino Murder Case* (1934) continued to attract a sizable public. The unusual *Gracie Allen Murder Case* (1938) features the popular real-life comedian, a star of both radio and movies. In addition, Van Dine's early novels found prompt conversion into movies, such as *The Canary Murder Case* (1929) and *The Benson Murder Case* (1930). Well ensconced in pictures, with 10 films during the 1930s alone, Philo Vance may have enjoyed more popularity on screen than he did in books; actors like Basil Rathbone (1892–1967; *The Bishop Murder Case*, 1930), William Powell (1892–1984; *The Kennel Murder Case*, 1933), Edmund Lowe (1890–1971; *The Garden Murder Case*, 1936), and Warren William (1894–1948; *The Gracie Allen Murder Case*, 1939) took on the role of the learned detective. Van Dine also wrote a series of stories in the early 1930s for Warner Brothers; the studio then converted at least some of them into short features.

In contrast to the rather subdued and genteel mysteries about crime and the fine art of detection, a darker side to mystery writing exploits violence, sex, and general disorder. Appropriately called the hard-boiled format, this approach to crime writing is America's greatest contribution to the overall mystery genre. As a rule, snappy dialogue, frequent gunplay, and a general disregard for legal niceties characterize much within this free-wheeling category. But, since both genteel mysteries and hard-boiled ones deal with crime and criminals, what might seem poles apart also have much in common.

Dashiell Hammett (1894–1961). Among the first writers to explore the limits of tough-guy prose and ultimately one of the most important writers in the hard-boiled genre, Hammett also brought the best credentials to the job. He worked, beginning in 1915, for the Pinkerton National Detective Agency as an operative, or "op" in the slang of the day. Out of this experience grew "the Continental Op," a nameless detective employed by the fictional Continental Agency, and the hero of a series of short stories Hammett wrote during the 1920s for the influential *Black Mask*, one of the leading pulp magazines.

Over three dozen short stories later, Hammett felt ready to tackle longer fiction. Two novels, *The Dain Curse* and *Red Harvest*, both published in 1929, announced the arrival of a new talent and the birth of a new genre of mystery writing, the hard-boiled detective novel. They featured his Continental Op again, but in longer, more complex adventures. The following year saw the release of *The Maltese Falcon*, Hammett's third novel, which introduced detective Sam Spade, a character much like the Op. Neither wealthy nor sophisticated in the manner of Lord Wimsey or Ellery Queen, this new breed of crime solver gets beaten up, drinks too much, and more or less staggers to a resolution. These bedraggled, tough-talking heroes presaged the decline of the great detective and the rise of a more commonplace, identifiable figure, one more appropriate to the despair many felt in the Depression.

Hammett followed *The Maltese Falcon* with *The Glass Key* (1931), an offbeat tale that would feature not Spade, but a sympathetic gangster, Ned Beaumont, as its primary character. He followed this departure with *The Thin Man*, his last novel, in 1934. This work introduced readers to Nick and Nora Charles, a wealthy, debonair couple who practice some amateur sleuthing. His writing career went downhill after *The Thin Man*, although Hammett would help script *Secret Agent X-9*, a popular detective comic strip drawn by Alex Raymond (1909–1956), for several years.

Although he wrote little after 1934, Hammett's efforts took on a life of their own in Hollywood and later on network radio. The initial movie adaptation of *Red Harvest*, played as *Roadhouse Nights* in 1930. The following year, *The Maltese Falcon* saw the first of several incarnations, with Ricardo Cortez (1899–1977) as Sam Spade. It came around again in 1936, bearing the title *Satan Met a Lady*. Warren William (1894–1948) plays Spade, but the script calls him "Ted Shayne." In 1941, Warner Brothers released what most critics call the definitive version, with Humphrey Bogart (1899–1857) at his best as Spade.

Little-known Hammett short stories, such as *City Streets* (1931), *Woman in the Dark* (1934), and *Mister Dynamite* (1935) also appeared in theaters, and the cinematic adaptation of *The Glass Key* (1935) remains a good interpretation of his novel bearing the same name. George Raft (1895–1980), noted for his gangster portrayals, handles the role of Ned Beaumont.

Hammett's biggest splash in the movies, however, did not occur with his tough-guy gangster tales, but in a long series of pictures, and comedies at that, all loosely taken from 1934's *The Thin Man*. That same year, MGM brought out *The Thin Man*, said to be an interpretation of Hammett's novel. Starring William Powell (1892–1984) and Myrna Loy (1905–1993) as Nick and Nora Charles, the movie owes more to screwball comedy than it does to mystery. With murder and mayhem replaced by witty banter, *The Thin Man* struck a chord with Depression-era audiences. In no time, MGM released *After the Thin Man* (1936), a picture even farther removed from Hammett's original creation. Marquees advertised *Another Thin Man* in 1939, and then *Shadow of the Thin Man* (1941), *The Thin Man Goes Home* (1944), and *Song of the Thin Man* (1947). All six star Powell and Loy, and somewhere along the line Dashiell Hammett had been completely forgotten.

Radio adaptations did not take place until the 1940s. Sam Spade, *The Thin Man*, and "the Fat Man" (loosely based on a character from *The Maltese Falcon*) all enjoyed runs on the networks. The hard-boiled detectives of the 1920s and 1930s had become part not just of crime fiction but of American popular culture.

Raymond Chandler (1888–1959). Chicago-born, Chandler spent his boyhood in England and on the Continent. While abroad, he wrote some desultory poetry and essays, eventually returning to the United States and settling in California. He served with the Canadian army in World War I; after the armistice, he studied accounting and became an executive with a California oil company. Alcoholism lost him his job, and he decided to write mysteries for the popular pulp magazines of the day. With "Blackmailers Don't Shoot," a story published by *Black Mask* in 1933, he felt encouraged to continue writing. Over the next several years, ten more stories appeared in *Black Mask*, seven in *Dime Detective*, and a handful of others in competing periodicals. Realizing he could not make a decent living with pulp fiction no matter how much he wrote, Chandler began working on his first novel, *The Big Sleep*, which came out in 1939. In it, he introduced Philip Marlowe, a wisecracking, down-at-the-heels detective, and one of the more enduring characters in American fiction.

His second novel, another Marlowe outing, bore the title *Farewell, My Lovely* (1940). This book and *The Big Sleep* firmly established Chandler as one of the most important mystery writers of the late 1930s and beyond. These two works also made him the logical inheritor of the mantle worn by Dashiell Hammett. Unlike the more mean-spirited Continental Op, however, Philip Marlowe acts on his own battered set of personal ethics, a kind of weary knight errant in a bleak, unethical world. Chandler's use of poetic devices, especially metaphor and simile, have given him a reputation as a master of style, and he brought a new dimension of literacy to hard-boiled crime fiction.

Both movie and radio adaptations of Raymond Chandler's work would prove successful, but not until the 1940s and later. His fame in the 1930s, such as it was, remained limited to short stories and *The Big Sleep*.

James M. Cain (1892–1977). A college graduate at age 18, Cain drifted in search of a career. He wrote for several **newspapers**, tried his hand as a playwright (*Crashing the Pearly Gates*, 1926), and finally moved to Hollywood as a scriptwriter in 1930. Cain failed at writing for the movies, but he became fascinated with lurid news reports about lust and murder, themes he employed with his first novel, *The Postman Always Rings Twice* (1934). An immediate success, the book brought offers for additional work, and he obliged.

Double Indemnity (1936) followed, and it too sold well. In the novel, he employs a favorite device, that of a femme fatale, and much of the plot comes from crime reports he read in tabloids. The writing, spare and direct, equaled anything that might be found in pulp magazines, making Cain a member of the hard-boiled school of fiction. Instead of world-weary private eyes investigating vicious crimes, he focused on ordinary people caught up in events they can no longer control. Led on by their desires, they get trapped and their world crashes down around them. Detection and intellect have little play in this universe, and Cain, hard-boiled as he is, leaves mystery behind in his dogged exploration of human frailty.

Rex Stout (1886–1975). A Midwesterner by birth, Stout engaged in countless menial jobs as a young man while he tried to find markets for his stories and poems. After travel to Europe, and several books, and some success as a novelist—*How Like a God* (1929) received good notices—Stout returned to the United States and tried his hand at mystery writing. The **Saturday Evening Post** serialized his first effort, a tale titled *Fer-de-Lance*, and it came out in book form in 1934. It did well, probably because of its improbable detective hero, Nero Wolfe.

Skirting a narrow line between the elegant golden age detectives and their more hard-boiled kin, Stout created in Nero Wolfe a massively overweight, agoraphobic, **food-** and orchid-loving aesthete who spends his time holed up in his Manhattan brownstone. He assigns the physical chores of detection to his feisty sidekick, Archie Goodwin, a man not above occasional violence. This unlikely duo caught the public fancy immediately, and with titles like *The League of Frightened Men* (1935), *Too Many Cooks* (1938), and *Some Buried Caesar* (1939), Stout had emerged as a leading mystery writer by the end of the decade.

The Nero Wolfe franchise remained popular until Stout's death and enjoyed a revival with three television series, the first in 1979, followed by a second in 1981, and yet another in 2001. During the 1930s, *Meet Nero Wolfe* (1936; a retitling of *Fer-de-Lance*) and *The League of Frightened Men* (1937; based on the novel of the same name) entertained moviegoers. Lionel Stander (1908–1994) plays Archie in each; Edward Arnold (1890–1956) plays Wolfe, followed by Walter Connolly (1887–1940) in the second film.

Nero Wolfe in many ways resembles the Philo Vances, Lord Wimseys, and Hercule Poirots of a more refined school of storytelling. His personal idiosyncrasies and sheer intellect bring to mind Gideon Fell and Ellery Queen. The acceptance of a harder, darker world outside the drawing rooms and parlors of these characters leads to a more modern, less romantic approach to crime.

Erle Stanley Gardner (1889–1970). Another writer who straddles the gulf between suave detectives and brawling gumshoes, Gardner began, as did so many other authors during the 1920s and 1930s, by writing for the pulps. In 1933, however, he published *The Case of the Velvet Claws*, his first novel. It introduced readers to Perry Mason, a brilliant attorney who often acts more like a private detective. In that initial work, Mason in fact seems closer to the tough private eyes of hard-boiled fiction than he does to the more sophisticated characters found in the likes of John Dickson Carr or Ellery Queen. Over time, however, the rough edges got smoothed out, and Perry Mason moved more and more in the direction of classic crime fiction and farther away from the rough-and-tumble worlds of Hammett and Chandler.

Earl Derr Biggers (1884–1933) and John P. Marquand (1893–1960). Brief mention must be made of a pair of writers who created a unique body of mystery fiction. Biggers stands behind the figure of Charlie Chan, a Chinese detective who made his debut in 1925; Marquand can boast Mr. Moto, a Japanese sleuth who first appeared in 1935. These distinctive Asian characters attracted considerable popular attention, initially in books, and later in successful movie series.

The Ohio-born Biggers created his "Oriental detective" following a vacation in Hawaii. He would write six Chan novels, four in the 1920s and two in the 1930s, *Charlie Chan Carries On* (1930) and *Keeper of the Keys* (1932). Almost as soon as Biggers completed one, Hollywood movie studios bought the rights to it. The Chan movies proved so successful that demand quickly outstripped supply, and so a string of original films, "based on a character created by Earl Derr Biggers," became the norm.

Basically undistinguished B movies, the many screen presentations of Charlie Chan ranged from *The Black Camel* (1931) to *Charlie Chan in Paris* (1935) to *The Sky Dragon* (1949). Warner Oland (1879–1938), a native Swede, starred in 16 such adventures; Missourian Sidney Toler (1874–1947) played the detective in 22 pictures; and Boston-born Roland Winters (1904–1989) completed the extended series with 6 appearances. Despite the availability of competent Chinese actors, the studios clearly felt compelled to hire white players to impersonate an Asian detective, a commentary on the racial attitudes of the times.

A nondescript comic strip based on Biggers's detective appeared in newspapers beginning in 1938; cartoonist Alfred Andriola (1912–1983) supplied the artwork. After the Japanese attack on Pearl Harbor in December 1941, some people deemed it unwise to have a strip featuring any Asian heroes, and its syndicate unceremoniously dropped it in 1942. In retrospect, the books, the movies, and the comics all failed to break any substantive ground for mysteries, finding their popularity instead with the continuing amiable character of Charlie Chan.

Marquand, a prize-winning American author best known for delicately drawn novels of social manners such as *The Late George Apley* (1938), also produced a popular series of tales that employed exotic settings. His stories involve Mr. Moto, an operative with the Japanese secret service. Capitalizing, no doubt, on the ongoing popularity of Charlie Chan, four Mr. Moto mysteries came out during the 1930s, beginning with *No Hero* in 1935. Based on a short story titled "Mr. Moto Takes a Hand" that the *Saturday Evening Post* serialized, its success led Marquand to continue the adventures of his fictional character. *Thank You, Mr. Moto* (1936), *Think Fast, Mr. Moto* (1936), and *Mr. Moto Is So Sorry* (1938) completed the series for the decade, although others would follow. In each case, the *Saturday Evening Post* ran them as **serials**, greatly broadening the audience.

Hollywood, always on the lookout for a marketable series, wasted no time in adapting the Japanese detective for film. Eight movies came out between 1937 (*Think Fast, Mr. Moto*) and 1939 (*Mr. Moto Takes a Vacation*) before international events and a growing distrust of Japan brought the series to a halt. Peter Lorre (1904–1964), an Austrian-born actor, played Moto in every one. Once again, the studios chose a non-Asian for the lead, and makeup and large glasses cannot hide the fact. Like the Charlie Chan movies they reflect the racism that continued to permeate the film capital. Despite their popularity, neither Charlie Chan nor Mr. Moto can be considered among the great detectives, nor do they fit comfortably into the hard-boiled genre that had gained so much popularity during the decade.

Mysteries in general enjoyed continuing good sales during the 1930s. Whether they involved a sophisticated drawing-room puzzle or quick fists and faster guns, tales of crime and detection were among the most successful of all literary types throughout the decade.

See also Comic Books; Comic Strips; Federal Bureau of Investigation; Gangster Films; Race Relations & Stereotyping; Radio Networks; Screwball Comedies

SELECTED READING

Ball, John, ed. *The Mystery Story*. San Diego: University of California, San Diego, 1976.
Collins, Max Allan. *The History of Mystery*. Portland, OR: Collectors Press, 2001.
Mystery Movies. http://www.mysterymovies.com/index.htm
Symons, Julian. *Bloody Murder: From the Detective Story to the Crime Novel*. New York: Viking-Penguin, 1985.